KINDRED SPIRITS

KINDRED SPIRITS

*The <u>Spirit</u> <u>Journal</u> Guide to
the World's Distilled Spirits
and Fortified Wines*

~

F. PAUL PACULT

NEW YORK

Library of Congress Cataloging-in-Publication Data

Pacult, F. Paul.
Kindred spirits : the Spirit journal guide to the
world's distilled spirits and fortified wines /
by F. Paul Pacult.—1st ed.
p.   cm.
Includes bibliographical references.
ISBN 0-7868-8172-0
1. Liquors.   2. Liqueurs.   3. Fortified wines.   I. Title.
TP597.P33   1997
641.2'5—dc21   96-39289
CIP

Designed by Jessica Shatan

FIRST EDITION
2 4 6 8 10 9 7 5 3 1

For my Sue

Contents

Wines—United States · Port—Australia · Fortified and Dessert
Wines—South Africa · Montilla—Spain

ACKNOWLEDGMENTS

This effort is the culmination of over eight years of near-constant work. Assistance along the way has been plentiful and generously given by hundreds of people from all parts of the globe. Their contributions, direct and indirect, kept feeding the hungry entity that grew into *Kindred Spirits*. Recognition of the following people is most fitting:

Helen Ann Daniels, for encouragement right from my first writing attempts.

Pamela Nystul and MMY, for showing me how to traverse beyond the boundaries.

Rodney D. Strong, a true friend who always told me I could write and should do so whatever the cost.

Susan Hall, who taught me through example how one-pointed dedication to work without sacrificing whimsy could make goals materialize.

Roberta Morrell and Peter Morrell, for helping me to get established in New York City. Sam Morrell, for so many pleasant lunches.

Rich Colandrea of *The New York Times*, the first person to ask me to write about spirits (for *The New York Times Magazine*).

Alexander Douglas, for creating the look of *F. Paul Pacult's Spirit Journal* and for many years of listening to my whining.

Ralph Pagan, Cynthia Gillick, and Richard Hinman, dear friends.

Lory Roston, for seeing life in a unique way.

Jack and Virginia Haas, for the many meals in the magical three years that I dwelled in the mountains of northeastern Pennsylvania.

Gary Regan and Mardee Haidin-Regan, kindred spirits of the truest variety.

Robert Dubin, Martin Slattery, Arthur Shapiro, Michael Luftglass, Suzanne Tobia, Howard Lasky, Jeff Blumenfeld, Peter Bordeaux, Larry

Shapiro, John Rector, Ansley Coale Jr., and Peter Angus, valued friends and supporters all.

Booker and Annis Noe, for the finest home cooking and hospitality in Kentucky.

Jimmy Russell, Elmer T. Lee, and Bill Samuels, for more insights into the Bourbon industry than I was probably ever supposed to receive. Rest assured, I am discreet.

Guillermo Romo, for enlightening me about authentic tequila.

Harriet Lembeck and John Poister, two special people who had the courage to write about distilled spirits before they were fashionable.

Josh Greene of *Wine & Spirits,* David Stevens of *Playboy,* Duncan Christy and Brian Cook of *Sky-Delta,* Nancy Nicholas of *Connoisseur,* Bob Keane and Richard Brandes of *Beverage & Food Dynamics* and *Cheers,* all longtime friends and editors.

Campbell Evans, Tony Tucker, Willie Phillips, Mark Lawson, Mike Gunn, Brian Morrison, James McEwan, Pip Hills, Jim Turle, Yvonne Scott, and countless others, for making my education of Scotch whisky and Scotland as much a delight as it's been an honor.

Claire Coates, Dominique Lherahoux, Alexandre Gabriel, Alfred Vanderbilt, and Chris Donlay, whose assistance with regard to cognac opened up that marvelous world to me.

Amélia Lourenço, for being my patient and efficient tutor in the Douro.

The kind people of The Wines of Spain office in New York, for making my various trips to Jérez de la Frontera productive and memorable.

Diane Kerner, Jeff Ort, Susan Tarrence, John Riggio, Tom Collins, Rick Marks, Bob Haidt, and Roger Schwoerer of *The New York Times,* for so many wonderful times and over twenty Sunday supplements.

The scores of generous people within the distilled-spirits, fortified-wine, and public relations industries who have proven to be reliable contacts over the years. Most notably, Jeff Pogash, Hilary Peck, Joanne Burston, Jay Poust, Chris Massie, Bernard La Borie, Steve McCarthy, Jennie Perdue, Nancy DeKalb, Keith Steer, Hugues de la Vergne, Harrison Jones, Shirley Alpert, Alain Royer, Aileen Robbins, Maria Colon, Alfredo Cruz, Laura Baddish, Bevin Gove, Karin Timpone, Pat Iocca, Jim Rossbach, Keith Steer, Ann Riives, and Ann Higgins.

Cheryl To, general manager of *Keens Steakhouse,* for allowing me to have such a remarkably friendly place in Manhattan to conduct spirits tastings.

Richard Pacult, for tirelessly proofreading hundreds, but what must have seemed like thousands, of manuscript pages.

Bob Lescher, my agent, Rick Kot, my editor at Hyperion, and Lauren Root, for making it all happen so swiftly and efficiently.

And last, but by no means least, the loyal and vocal subscribers and supporters of *F. Paul Pacult's Spirit Journal,* who, in truth, have, as much as anyone, kept the flame burning since February of 1991.

F. PAUL PACULT
Suffern, New York, January 1, 1997

INTRODUCTION

Answering the Bell

Everyone should believe in something.
I believe I'll have another drink.

The above quote has been attributed to several people, including Groucho Marx and W. C. Fields. It doesn't matter who said it. The humor, which is inherent in the message, is enough. For at least six thousand years, drinking beverages made of alcohol has been a source of amusement, reflection, and relaxation. From the Chinese of the eighth century B.C. to the Greeks of the fourth century B.C. to Americans at the close of the twentieth century A.D., having a drink of liquor at the end of a tough day has rounded the edges and smoothed the ruffles of life. Alcoholic beverages, most assuredly, are not a panacea. But neither are they a demon when consumed with a sense of balance, respect for oneself and others, and intelligence. Whiskies, brandies, rums, gins, tequilas, vodkas, ports, sherries, liqueurs, and madeiras are merely items on a long menu of pleasures that enhance the daily experience of responsible, fully functional people. These ancient drinks are embellishments, not necessities.

Despite the constant drumbeat of the evils of alcohol from the conservative extremists, spirits are at an unprecedented pinnacle of recognition in the U.S. Once the remarkably misguided experiment of Prohibition failed in the early 1930s, legal drinking rose dramatically until the world became wrapped up in World War II. During the postwar era people across the world celebrated their new prosperity with the popular whiskies, gins, and brandies of the day. The best hour of the day during this "What are you drinking" era (which lasted two and a half decades) was Happy Hour.

The people born after World War II, however, chose a different path once they reached legal drinking age in the late 1960s and early 1970s. By large measure, they rejected their parents' lifestyle of Scotch-on-the-rocks and canapés and instead selected, no doubt through peer pressure, the road either of abstinence or that of lighter, less aggressive alcoholic beverages, like wine coolers, beer, or fine wine. As a result, sales of distilled spirits—and in particular, the dark-colored types like whiskey and brandy—suffered severe drops in sales during the late 1970s and into the late 1980s.

Strange how life moves in cycles. As many of the postwar revolutionaries and radicals evolved into 1990s accountants, stockbrokers, and investment bankers, their tastes reflected the natural deepening of the adult palate. With the worlds of beer and wine amply traversed by the Baby Boomers, newer, more profound challenges were desired. Enter single-malt Scotch, vintage port, Grande Champagne cognac, single-barrel and small-batch bourbon, 100% blue agave *añejo* tequila, oak-aged rum, *almacenista* sherry, and boutique grappa and brandy.

Today, as we stand peering into the approaching face of a new millennium, distilled spirits, especially the upper-echelon products, are the darlings not only of the well-heeled, but likewise of increasing numbers of the wannabe well-heeleds. Even Generation X is going upscale. It's not so much a new era as much as it is something of a replay of the late 1930s and the late 1950s, decorated with different accessories.

I came to writing about distilled spirits and fortified wines with palpable reluctance. After spending a decade (1973–1982) working for a Sonoma County, California, winery, then known as Sonoma Vineyards, now as Rodney Strong Vineyards, my first few years in New York City were devoted to establishing myself as a wine journalist and educator. In the spring of 1983, only three months after dropping into the cauldron of Manhattan, I took a day job in a fabled, atmospheric wine and spirits shop, Morrell and Company. At night and on days off, I wrote articles about wine. Two years later I opened up *Wine Courses International* in the Tribeca loft in which I was living for the purpose of conducting wine appreciation classes and tastings. Since the loft was near Manhattan's financial district, the patrons were largely workers from the canyons of Wall Street. By 1988, regular classes and tastings were being held and, to my delight, fully attended.

One particular group in the fall of 1988 included three gentlemen—Rich Colandrea, Bob Haidt, and Roger Schwoerer—from *The New York Times*. They were attending one of my four-week classes to broaden their wine acumen, since they sold advertising space to metropolitan New York liquor retailers. This fortuitous connection eventually planted the seed of my being asked by the group manager, Rich Colandrea, to create and write a special advertising supplement devoted only to Scotch whisky for *The New York Times Magazine* to be published in the fourth quarter of 1989. Privately, I was horrified at the thought because, one, I knew very little about spirits, and, two, I fancied myself a wine maven. I was still of the mind that spirits were consumed only by people who were making arrangements for their retirement in communities with names like Whispering Pines or Sheltered Meadows.

When I bounced the *Times*'s offer by a couple of my wine-writing acquaintances, they scoffed at it, saying, "This is 1988. Nobody wants to know about whiskies, much less write about them." Their open disdain for distilled spirits made a tiny bell ring in the recesses of my gray matter that forced me to reexamine my reluctance. I called Rich and told him, quite as a lark, that I'd be delighted to write the Scotch whisky piece. With that call, my life took a sharp right turn onto a highway for which I had no map and on which I was ill-prepared to proceed. At the time, I didn't even know that when one refers to the whisky of Scotland the letter "e" is not employed in the word "whisky."

Fortunately, the deadline was months away, and I knew I had ample time to research my topic. With a stroke of luck, I was able to be included on a press trip to Scotland in May of 1989. Being in Scotland that first time convinced me that I would be smart to spend more time writing about spirits. The writers with whom I traveled in Speyside, Islay, and the Orkney Islands indicated frequently and candidly that while they were genuinely fascinated with Scotch whisky, their bread-and-butter writing focused almost exclusively on wine. I found that I was increasingly, if silently, jubilant to hear their views and preferences.

Upon returning home, inspired and enthusiastic, I carefully wrote the 10,000-word Scotch piece and helped put it together graphically. The four-color, 28-page section, mundanely titled "Scotch Whisky—A Consumer Guide," appeared on Sunday, December 3, 1989. This groundbreaking supplement was the first "advertorial" of its kind in the United States on any type of distilled-spirit category. The section was a major success and a certified coup for the *Times*. Word about it spread throughout the distilled-spirits industry, and before I knew it, I was contracted for two more *Times Magazine* advertising supplements, another on Scotch and one on cognac, armagnac, sherry, and port. Suddenly, my office was being inundated with every imaginable type of distilled spirit made on the planet for my review and comment.

On the strength of these first three *Times Magazine* supplements, editors for whom I had been writing about wine began asking me to prepare articles on spirits. Magazines that I had never written for started approaching me to submit articles on distilled spirits and fortified wines. Within the span of two years, I had gone from being a wine writer and educator in the big town, who previously had been just one of the pack, to one of the country's few writers who regularly addressed the joys and mysteries of distilled spirits.

In late 1990 the concept of a newsletter that would be committed to writing only about distilled spirits, fortified wines, and beers, kept surfacing in conversations with friends and associates, as no one in the U.S. was writing and lecturing about them on a continuous basis. My friend and business associate, Alexander Douglas, designed a newsletter format and I organized enough detailed tasting notes and ratings to fill sixteen pages. *F. Paul Pacult's Spirit Journal* was published for the first time in February 1991.

As founding editor, I established only two rules for the publication: first, that I wouldn't duplicate the efforts of others by featuring still and sparkling wines in *The Spirit Journal* (though I continued writing about wine in other publications) and, second, that Al and I would never accept advertising in any form and, thus, keep *The Spirit Journal* completely independent and unbiased.

The nonadvertising criterion has doubtless been paramount to the success of *The Spirit Journal*. Subscribers realized from the beginning that because there were no advertisers, I was not beholden to anyone. *The Spirit*

Journal offered straight talk, candid reviews, and honest ratings. Even when readers have disagreed with ratings, they, at least, have known that my views and conclusions have been impartial. Nothing has made me prouder than that aspect of *The Spirit Journal.*

Why is this important? With the competition so fierce within the alcoholic beverage industry, it regrettably has become commonplace for advertisers to lean on editors and writers for reviewing favors. The media, quite predictably, will publicly deny this allegation to their dying days, but I know it happens, because I've been approached both by advertisers, editors, and publishers to wax more poetical about products in magazines that live or die by advertising dollars. My mission for *The Spirit Journal* was to maintain total freedom from such influences, and I have kept to that goal for seven years. *The Spirit Journal* has never and will never accept advertising, period. I would stop publishing before breaking that vow.

Kindred Spirits is my official collection of tasting notes and ratings on over 1,200 beverages, taken mostly from the pages of *The Spirit Journal.* A good number of the reviews included herein have, however, never been published anywhere. Other reviews have been updated since their original publication, as some items have been retasted.

I do not claim that *Kindred Spirits* includes reviews and ratings for every single distilled spirit and fortified wine currently sold in the marketplace. With the number of items available totaling in the thousands and with tens of new products entering the arena every month, it couldn't. *Kindred Spirits* should, rather, be considered a work-in-progress. What this book does provide is the broadest, most comprehensive compilation of highly detailed evaluations and ratings on every distilled-spirit and fortified-wine category ever offered in any form. For the person wanting to learn more about these beverages, *Kindred Spirits* is the ideal introduction from which to launch his or her journey. Veteran spirits and fortified-wine imbibers will find in *Kindred Spirits* a worthy companion with which to expand and deepen their acumen by identifying the esoteric treasures of spirits. For people in the alcoholic beverage industry, who perhaps are familiar only with their own products, *Kindred Spirits* is the perfect vehicle with which to keep abreast of what the competition has been up to. For liquor retailers, bartenders, and restauranteurs who serve distilled spirits and fortified wines, the benefits of having in one volume the noted characteristics of hundreds of spirit items is obvious, since it's the only collection of its kind. Most of all, *Kindred Spirits* is a time-saving, money-saving guide for consumers planning forays into the sometimes overwhelming and confusing environs of liquor stores. I hope that *Kindred Spirits* will, in short, be used by all the kindred spirits who derive pleasure from the drinks born in the chambers of fermenters and the bellies of stills.

Here's looking at you.

THE NATURES OF
DISTILLED SPIRITS AND
FORTIFIED WINES

The term "distil" is derived from the Latin words *de stillare,* which mean "to drip down." Before we begin our journey, let's first understand in lay terms what distilled spirits and fortified wines are:

Distilled spirits, meaning brandies, whiskies, gins, rums, vodkas, tequilas, eaux-de-vie, and liqueurs, are liquids that contain varying degrees of alcohol. Alcohol levels can be as low as 15–20 percent, as in many liqueurs, or as lofty as 65–70 percent, as in the case of a handful of whiskies and rums.* The alcohol in these products is created by two separate processes, fermentation and distillation.

Fortified wines, meaning ports, sherries, madeiras, and aromatized wines, begin life as ordinary still wines. In other words, they are grape juice that has been fermented to make the beverage we know as wine. A still wine becomes a fortified wine when a spirit is added to it either during or after the fermentation process. Fortified wines range in the area of 15–22 percent alcohol.

Fermentation occurs when the innate sugars in a grain mash or fruit are

---

Proof is twice the measurable level of alcohol. For example, a 40 percent alcohol brandy is regarded as being 80 proof. The custom of declaring proof in alcoholic beverages began in England, two to three centuries ago. Distillers, anxious to measure the strength of their spirits, poured their libation onto black powder and struck a match. Whenever the spirit/powder combination went up in five-alarm fashion, the spirit was considered too strong. When the flame burned slowly and evenly in a shade of blue, the strength was considered desirable and the distiller would say, "That's gunpowder-proof." If the combination did not flame up at all, the distillers would conclude that there was too much water left in the spirit. The primary measuring stick was the mixture of half water and half alcohol, or 100 proof (50 percent alcohol), on which a flame would burn evenly.

transformed into alcohol by the dining habits of yeast cells. The yeast cells, which are living organisms, metabolize (some people use the term "devour") the sugar molecules, leaving behind equal amounts of ethyl alcohol and carbon dioxide (CO_2). Fermentation is a turbulent, even violent, process in which tremendous amounts of heat and gas are released into the immediate atmosphere. Fermentation stops either when all the sugars are converted to alcohol or when the alcohol level approaches 14 percent and the yeast cells cease their activity. In the case of some fortified wines, most prominently port, fermentation is halted by the addition of grape brandy. In the majority of cases, the alcohol level after fermentation runs from 5 percent on the low side of the scale up to 14 percent on the high side. Fermented grain mash is referred to as "beer," while fermented fruit juice is referred to as "wine."

(Fascinating asides: Fermentation can happen naturally, without interference from man. It's widely held that the first alcoholic beverages to be consumed by early man had probably developed on their own. Also, an ingredient doesn't necessarily have to contain natural sugar, as long as it has starch, which can be converted into sugar through a process known as malting.)

Distillation is not a natural sequence of biochemical events, like fermentation. It's more than safe to assume that it was most likely developed by alchemists in Asia and/or the Middle East as early as 1000 B.C. In its simplest form, distillation is the separation of alcohol from fermented mash (the beer or wine) through intense heat. Since alcohol has a lower boiling point (173.1 degrees Fahrenheit) than water (212 degrees Fahrenheit), distillation ends up being a surprisingly easy and logical process. Fermented grain mash or fermented fruit juice is placed into a still (either tall patent stills, which run continuously, or small pot stills, which operate in individual batches), and the still is heated. The boiling liquid within releases vapors (alcohol in cloud form) that rise into the top chambers of the still. When these vapors are cooled, they condense and return to liquid form. This colorless liquid, often called new spirit or distillate, is either distilled again to further raise the alcohol level or placed in storage, depending on what type of spirit is being produced.

(Interesting points: The lower the heat of distillation, the greater the flavor of the resulting distillate, while the higher the temperature, the more neutral the flavor. The distillation process is so basic that it's changed hardly at all over the centuries. Neither has the fundamental equipment of still and condenser been altered to any serious degree. The most revolutionary change in stills came with the introduction of the continuous still (a.k.a. column still, patent still, Coffey still) in the U.K. in the 1820s.)

WHEN THE SPIRITS
MOVE YOU

Tasting Distilled Spirits and Fortified Wines

There is nobody buts eats and drinks.
But they are few who can distinguish flavors.
—Tze-Sze, fifth century B.C.

Since I write about and evaluate beer, wine, and distilled spirits on a daily basis, I've come to realize that the three primary categories of alcoholic beverages must be approached independently for sampling purposes. Never in the same session will I mix beer tasting with wine tasting or spirits sampling with wine sampling. The natures of the beasts are as different as chalk is from cheese and, as a result, the beasts are best kept segregated.

Though I employ the same fundamental strategy in the judging of each, subtle variations characterize the individual experiences. As I noted earlier, my palate was trained first in the milieu of wine, where the alcohol content hovers in the comparatively narrow 10–14 percent range. When I began sampling distilled spirits, whose alcohol levels can reach into the stratospheric percentages of 50–60 percent, I made the unconscious error of applying the exact formula I used in wine tasting. The result was severe whiplash.

In wine or beer tasting, the proper procedure for smelling involves inhaling deeply with the nose inserted into the bowl of the sampling glass. During this comical-looking exercise, the lips are sealed in order to make the inhalation more forceful. In the first year that I was smelling whiskies (where the alcohol content begins at 40 percent), I was noticing severe irritation in my nasal cavity because of the elevated alcohol levels. While conducting a Bourbon tasting with Booker Noe, the Master Distiller Emeritus of Jim Beam, I offhandedly complained to him in a private moment about this uncomfortable situation, lamenting that perhaps I wasn't cut out for this type of evaluation.

"Mebee try leavin' your lips parted just a crack," suggested Noe in his patented down-home drawl. "Makes all the difference for some people."

After following his advice, I couldn't believe how much easier it was to sniff whiskey, or any distilled spirit, for that matter. By leaving the lips slightly open, you circumvent much of the alcohol harshness and are thereby able to focus on the pleasant, inherent virtues of the spirit. Other master distillers both in Scotland and France later confirmed Booker Noe's simple but effective recommendation. But nothing has sanctioned this practice more convincingly than years of nonstop spirits nosing.

THE NUTS AND BOLTS

Tasting is first a skill and then, after a decade or more, it develops into an art. The skill involves the mechanical ability to detect certain qualities in a spirit—most commonly, sweetness, bitterness, saltiness, and sourness. The art enters into the equation when one can, with agility and accuracy, store and then, later, recall those qualities in a split second.

I use four senses—sight, smell, taste, and touch—when I'm assessing any alcoholic beverage. Sight notes the color and purity of the spirit. Color is not as crucial as purity, and in most cases is simply window dressing. Purity is virtually always important. I say "virtually" because in some instances—say, vintage port—it's perfectly acceptable to detect sediment. Whiskies, brandies, eaux-de-vie, sherry, aromatized wines, and the white spirits of tequila, rum, gin, and vodka, on the other hand, should never have bits of material floating about, period. If they do, get a refund on that drink or that bottle.

Purity reflects the amount of care any beverage has received at the points of production, maturation, and bottling. All alcoholic beverages should be hygienically sound, no matter what they are, no matter where they come from. Cleanliness is imperative. Impurity is first noticed by the eye, but it is almost always confirmed by the nose. If a beverage smells unclean, musty, or foul, play it safe and either ask someone who's familiar with the specific beverage or its category if it's all right or, failing that, don't drink it at all.

Sight can also indicate age to me in certain types of fortified wines and spirits. If, say, a vintage port appears brown around the edges, then I know that it may be either at or past its prime. In the whiskey category, depth of color means nothing in terms of quality or age. With brandy, older cognacs and armagnacs normally are very dark, but in more pedestrian styles of brandy color means little.

While the appearance of a beverage is important, I consider its paramount sensory feature to be its aroma. Why? Because the membranes that make up the olfactory sense comprise more than 90 percent of the sense of taste. So chances are extremely high—though as I have learned over the years of professional tasting, not necessarily inevitable—that if you fancy the smell of something, you'll like its flavor.

The critical value of smell to the evaluation process is illustrated most pointedly whenever I have the infrequent cold or allergy. When this happens, my tasting operation closes down until my nasal passages and sinuses are clear. Take smell away, and taste goes with it. The other interesting thing about smell is that it is the most primal of the five senses. Smell was the preeminent sense eons ago when our species was still in the hunter-gatherer mode of existence. Searching for wild fruit or a kill in a hostile prehistoric environment automatically demanded a heightened level of smell, because often, when they couldn't see or hear danger lurking, our ancestors could smell its presence.

I'm convinced that smell is likewise the most subtle and nuanced of the senses and requires the most time to develop. In my evaluations, I spend more time sniffing a beverage than looking at it or tasting it. Smell is the bedrock of every evaluation I do.

Experts break smell down into two salient parts: aroma, which is the inherent, natural scent of the ingredients used to make the beverage, and bouquet, which is the smell that's influenced by human intervention during the production and maturation processes. To illustrate, take, for example, the fragrance of a single-malt Scotch whisky, such as the brilliant Macallan 18-Year-Old from Speyside. It's comprised of two very different aromatic factors that even the inexperienced person can detect: the keen, cereal-like intensity of the barley malt (the inherent aroma of the sole grain from which it is fermented and distilled), and the resiny sweetness of its aging vessel, an oak cask that once held sherry (the human influence). The beauty of this outstanding whisky is a function of the serene balance that has been achieved between its aroma and its bouquet, producing what I've judged to be a perfect nosing experience of five-star single-malt Scotch.

Every distilled spirit, every fortified wine must be judged thoroughly by nose on these two levels. In a multitude of beverages, one or the other will be missing or overshadowed by the other. Any awkward posture means that this highwire act will not succeed. Balance is everything when nosing any spirit or fortified wine, and balance is attained when no one aromatic aspect leaps out at you. The most elegant and classic aromas exhibit harmony and poise, power and finesse. As you will see by how few items have received five stars, my highest rating, achieving such ideal accord is rare.

I nose every item four times, usually taking about 10–12 minutes per item. Many beverages improve dramatically with aeration, so it's important to allow the libation some time to stretch its legs. The first pass right after the pour commonly gives you the biggest thrust. The really notable bouquets remain vital and firm throughout all four passes. Others are chameleons that keep changing from pass to pass. Still others never take flight. To help stimulate the meeker bouquets, I swirl the beverages vigorously in the glass, which will often rouse a spirit that's been asleep in its bottle for years.

I never warm distilled spirits, either while formally sampling or informally enjoying them. That's a hogwash concept undoubtedly served up by some moron in the advertising industry. Warmed whiskies, brandies, rums, and eaux-de-vie lose their aromatic properties too quickly.

The next stage, after sight and smell, is taste. Since I nose every beverage so exhaustively, the tasting part of the process, at least for me, serves more as a confirmation for the more crucial nosing stage than as an opportunity to discover crucial new territory. This, however, changes from item to item and sampling to sampling. Approximately one-third of the beverages I sample do reveal significant new dimensions in the mouth. The remaining two-thirds merely support and ratify the conclusions that I had already arrived at via nosing.

In the tasting process, I never take more than half an ounce into my mouth for the first of four samplings. I make sure that the tongue and side of my mouth are coated. The tip of the tongue detects sweetness, the sides of the tongue pick up saltiness and sourness, and the back of the tongue identifies bitterness or astringency, or both. After about twenty seconds of palate saturation, I spit the beverage out. (Spitting is key for self-evident reasons. When one is sampling distilled spirits or fortified wines or any alcoholic beverage, concentration diminishes rapidly when one doesn't spit the samples out.) I repeat this process three more times before jotting down my notes. A total of five minutes is normally allocated for tasting.

The two major checkpoints in tasting are the palate entry, that initial impression, and the midpalate stage, where the beverage is resting on the tongue. Very frequently, a whiskey, a brandy, or a sherry will evolve and develop astoundingly fast just from the entry to the midpalate. It's at this juncture that the fourth sense, touch, joins the action. While the beverage is in my mouth, I'm careful to note its texture (silky or raw), its weight (light, medium, or heavy), and its viscosity (thin or thick). The feel of a beverage is a very real impression, which has a bearing on the final score.

After spitting out the final tasting, I next gauge how the beverage reacts in the mouth and the throat by asking the following questions: Does it quickly disappear, or does the taste linger? Is it rough and fiery, or smooth and warm? Is it sweet or sour, bitter or supple? The aftertaste, or "finish," is highly significant in the bestowing of the final rating, because it's the last impression. The finish often snatches a star away from the final score if it bombs, or it can add a star if the aftertaste soars. The aftertaste is the summing up of the whole experience.

The Regimen

I devote approximately 15–20 minutes to each beverage, or sample three to four items over the course of an hour. My personal rules for formal tasting, in which detailed notes are taken and ratings are given, are simple and strictly adhered to:

- I try always to taste in the morning, normally from 8:00 A.M. to 12:00 noon. Being fresh and rested is the most important requirement.
- In order to have a clean palate, I never eat before tasting and I make certain to drink plenty of water between beverages.
- For all distilled-spirit categories, except for liqueurs, I sample a maximum of eight items on any given morning. Fortified wines, since they are lower in alcohol than the majority of spirits, are limited to no more than twelve per session.
- I always use the same glasses—stemmed wine glasses with a narrow bowl, which funnels the aroma—for distilled spirits and fortified wines. These glasses are always washed by hand in fresh water and

never with soap. I purposely do not employ snifters for brandies and whiskies because the broad, roomy bowl forces the aromatic properties to dissipate too quickly. All snifters in the world should be smashed and finely ground.

•I prefer sunny mornings when the daylight is sharp. I do not employ artificial light to evaluate the appearance of any product. My tasting table is bright white to ensure clear vision. The room is kept clean and orderly, and I never break my concentration by answering the phone or talking to anyone.

•When tasting in my facility, I include a "control" item from my library for the purpose of maintaining continuity in scoring for every session. These control products are always previously rated at a minimum of three stars.

•I never formally evaluate any product in the presence of a producer or a representative of a producer. I never discuss details of my findings until they are published.

TASTING RECOMMENDATIONS FOR CASUAL DRINKERS

To be sure, casual drinking and enjoyment shouldn't be saddled with as rigorous and structured a tasting system as I've just described. Yet, increasing numbers of people ask me how they can heighten their own direct sensory experience with distilled spirits and fortified wines. Many average consumers from all backgrounds and walks of life are becoming more serious both in their purchases and in their appreciation of fine libations. Someone who buys a more expensive item, like a VSOP cognac or a single-malt Scotch or a vintage port, understandably wants to derive as much pleasure and satisfaction as possible from that special beverage. Having the insight to appreciate the subtleties of more complex spirits and fortified wines helps to make that purchase a more fulfilling experience. Additionally, knowing what to look for and how to look opens up new worlds of awareness and enjoyment.

For casual drinkers who desire to expand and maximize their tasting abilities, I recommend a condensed version of a professional taster's regimen. For distilled spirits, including whiskies, brandies, white spirits, and liqueurs, begin by taking 10–15 seconds to gauge the color (if there is one) and purity of the libation. Spirits can be among the most fetching of beverages in terms of appearance, but go beyond the color and check to see if there exist any floating particles or sediment of any kind. With the exception of a handful of ludicrous liqueurs that have floating debris added by design, the overwhelming majority of distilled spirits should be free from any type of suspended bits or sediment.

Fortified wines, however, may be an entirely different story. Vintage port, in particular, may show some sediment near the bottom of an unshaken, undisturbed bottle. In this case, the sediment is completely proper. The way to avoid the bits is to slowly decant the bottle into another serving vessel. No sherry should display sediment. Only a few madeiras will.

Next, take a minute, at most two, to sniff the libation twice. When the beverage is a high-octane whiskey, brandy, liqueur, or white spirit with an alcohol level of 30 percent or higher, I strongly urge you to remember the "lips parted" trick when inhaling. Take in as much air through the lips as you do through the nostrils and you'll save yourself some pain. This method works for just about everybody, without lessening the aromatic impact that you want. Fortified wines should be nosed as you would a still wine, with the lips sealed in order to concentrate the aroma.

Inhale once. If the aroma is closed down or nonexistent, gently swirl the libation in the glass to help release the bouquet. Sniff a second time. Be patient. Remember that the spirit or fortified wine may have been trapped within the bottle for some years and may require a few moments to adjust to the new, open environment in which you've placed it. If after two minutes nothing is stirring aromatically, proceed right to tasting. You can always go back to smelling later.

Take a small amount into the mouth, maybe a half ounce to a full ounce, and allow the spirit or fortified wine to rest on the tongue for a few moments. First note what happened as the libation entered the mouth. Was it sharp? Was it sweet or dry? This first impression is often very different from the later intermouth impression of the midpalate. The midpalate impression comes after the beverage has had some time resting on the tongue. Is this taste different from that at the entry? If so, how is it different?

Next, swallow. Here's what to ask yourself: What's occurring in the throat and at the back of the tongue while I'm swallowing and immediately after I've swallowed? What are the primary characteristics of the aftertaste? Sweet? Dry? Harsh? Smooth? Bitter? And, how long does the taste linger? The mouth experience should be over within a minute. If the nose didn't develop in your initial pass, try sniffing it again.

The entire casual analysis should consume only three minutes, or four if you think you should return to the nose for another run-through. Within that very short timespan you should be able to ascertain an enormous amount of information about the selected libation. You might even want to jot down a few brief impressions regarding the appearance, smell, taste, and finish to keep as a reference for future tastings.

You'll find that the more items you sample in this easy analytical sequence, the more you build a storehouse of data to assist you in deepening your appreciation *and* your enjoyment of distilled spirits and fortified wines.

VIEWS ON REVIEWS AND RATINGS

One man's poison ivy is another man's spinach.
—George Ade, 1920

The opinions, reviews, and ratings found in *Kindred Spirits* and *The Spirit Journal*, as well as in my columns and other writings, are those of one individual. I believe, without reservation, that in the field of alcoholic beverage evaluation one voice is clearer and more precise over the long haul than the collective voice of a panel. I don't advocate group consensus because, having chaired tens of tasting panels for wine and spirits in years past, I've discovered that rarely is a true depiction of any product rendered within the framework of that format. Composite reviews of a panel usually end up reflecting the viewpoint of the person with the most chutzpah. However, for those critics who do choose to act on their own, the responsibility to sustain credibility is not to be cavalierly embraced.

But criticism, no matter how deeply steeped in expertise, is still at the end of the day mere personal opinion. Whatever your level of acumen, when it comes to taste you should never trust any palate more than the one you own. Critics, as I see it, exist to offer opinions that should be openly discussed. Their purpose is to offer information and experience, which together are meant to construct a platform only for further examination, not for the creation of dogma. One of the most delightful outcomes of my involvement with *The Spirit Journal* has been the debate it has spawned between myself and the subscribers. Some readers think my reviews are sound, others believe that I'm bordering on admittance to a rest home. That's the beauty of it. Debate. Talk. Connection. Exploration.

So while I, of course, want everyone to love and use this book, I'm fully aware that if, nothing else, *Kindred Spirits* rekindles interest in these frequently marvelous and oft' neglected libations, its mission will have been accomplished. I hope that the readers of *Kindred Spirits* go out and try these reviewed items and determine their worth through their own senses. If we agree, bravo. If we don't, bravo, as well.

My rating systems have changed once over the years. In the first two years of publishing *The Spirit Journal* I went with the crowd (= *The Wine Advocate, The Wine Spectator, The Wine Enthusiast, Wine & Spirits*) and employed the ubiquitous 100-point system. Regrettably, I was never quite certain what differentiated a port that was scored an 88 from one that was rated an 89. Most consumers don't care for such hairsplitting. I finally decided that it was a ridiculously picayune method of grading and opted to run with the straightforward one- to five-star format, which was warmly received by the subscribers.

The majority of items rated in the following sections fall within the two- to four-star range, because most are at least average, and some are truly excellent. The amount of one-star beverages is comparatively small. In order to qualify for that dismal rating, products must either be genuinely vile and disgusting or so far removed from the established standards of the category that they don't register in the world of reality. The five-star stratum is also thinly populated, and rightly so. These upper-echelon libations represent what I feel to be the prototypical products for their category. Just as in movies and literature, the classics are few, ageless, and treasured. But when they come along, it's heaven.

The star ratings mean the following:

★ **Disappointing:** A distilled spirit or fortified wine whose quality is either far below the established average standards for a certain category or is too far outside the category's long-standing criteria for quality. As a result of its blatant inferiority, it is NOT RECOMMENDED.

★★ **Average:** A distilled spirit or fortified wine of mediocre quality whose characteristics meet but do not exceed or enhance the established standards of quality for its category. Though this ordinary product may be perfectly acceptable to some consumers, it is NOT RECOMMENDED by the author.

★★★ **Above Average:** A well-made distilled spirit or fortified wine that is RECOMMENDED by the author. It's a product that displays better-than-average quality within the established standards of its category and, as such, has a very good chance of satisfying the tastes of most consumers.

★★★★ **Superb:** A HIGHLY RECOMMENDED distilled spirit or fortified wine whose attributes, in the opinion of the author, are of exemplary quality and character within the established standards of its category. An outstanding product that is worthy of a search.

★★★★★ **Classic:** HIGHEST RECOMMENDATION. That rare, highly distinguished, distinctive, and classical distilled spirit or fortified wine that represents a benchmark within its category. This product presents a standard against which its peers can be judged. A product of extraordinary quality, scope, and character that transcends price.

Half stars are not utilized in this scoring system.

Pricing: Included alongside the ratings are symbols that indicate the general suggested retail price of every item. Since price scales often differ dramatically from state to state, from city to city in the U.S., estimated price ranges are the best that any book distributed on a national basis can hope to do. Bottle sizes likewise differ, but the bottle size in most cases is 750 milliliters.

$:   **Under $20.00**

$$:   **$20.00–$50.00**

$$$:   **Over $50.00**

Finally, some of the ratings in the various categories begin with a special introductory section. These sections, standing apart or identified by the words "Author's note," underscore either producers whom I've visited or who, in my opinion, deserve supplementary attention because of their impact on certain categories.

THE PRACTICAL ENJOYMENT
OF DISTILLED SPIRITS
AND FORTIFIED WINES

If you drink, don't drive. Don't even putt.
—Dean Martin

The following are various random suggestions on the storage and service of distilled spirits and fortified wines.

In terms of storage, fortified wines should be stored in "cellar conditions," as you would keep fine still or sparkling wines. Keep your ports, sherries, and madeiras in a cool (48–55 degrees Fahrenheit), moderately humid (50–70 percent), and dark space. (Bright light is damaging to just about any kind of alcoholic beverage.) Lay the bottles on their sides to keep the cork moist. Dry corks crumble and shrink, allowing air to invade the bottle, thereby accelerating the aging process. Only vintage ports age further in the bottle. All other ports, plus sherries, are ready to be consumed upon purchase. Vintage madeiras likewise age in the bottle.

Once fortified wines are open, they should be consumed as soon as possible. Fino and manzanilla sherries are the ones that need the quickest consumption. Once you've opened a fino, manzanilla, or even an amontillado sherry, drink it within two days. Keep it refrigerated. With port, madeira, and stouter sherries, such as olorosos, palo cortados, and all creams, a period of one week to ten days is the absolute maximum that they should be allowed to remain open. Once the seal is broken, fortified wines become quite vulnerable.

As far as distilled spirits go, no bottle aging is required. You'd be amazed at how many times I've been asked the question, "How long should I age my bottles of single-malt Scotch and cognac?" Once a whiskey, brandy, white spirit, or liqueur is bottled, the maturing process ceases. All maturation occurs in the oak cask or holding tank. Distilled spirits are ready to be consumed immediately. Once you've opened a bottle of Scotch, bourbon, brandy, liqueur, or white spirits, it will remain drinkable for up to a year in most cases, but only if you keep it well sealed and out of heat and direct light. I personally don't leave bottles of spirits unconsumed for longer than two to three months at the very longest. I notice dramatic differences after a month or more.

As far as storage for distilled spirits goes, I prefer to keep my best spirits in the cellar until they are open. Excessive heat is not good for any type of alcoholic beverage, even if it remains unopened.

Glassware is always a controversial topic at tastings that I conduct, because I insist on using only one type of glass for spirits and fortified wines: a narrow-bowled wine glass or a Spanish *copita,* the traditional fino sherry glass used in Jérez de la Frontera, Spain. I have been urging readers and tasting participants to get away from using snifters for their brandies and whiskies because, aside from the fact that they're bloody ugly, they do nothing to enhance the aroma of spirits. As mentioned earlier, the shape of a fat snifter actually forces the smell of any spirit to dissipate too quickly, thereby robbing the drinker of one of the most important stages of enjoyment. A glass with a narrow, cylindrical bowl funnels the aroma straight up into the nasal cavity. Think narrow and cylindrical, not broad and open.

Also in the same vein and against custom, *do not* warm your brandies and whiskies with your hands or, worse, over a candle flame. Heat forces the aromatic properties to break up and vaporize too rapidly.

For liqueurs and superpremium tequilas and vodkas taken neat, I recommend very small one- or two-ounce cordial or shot glasses to concentrate the aromas and flavors. Small compartments heighten the intensity of liqueurs, tequilas, and vodkas. And, since only minute amounts of liqueurs and top-grade tequilas and vodkas should be served, cordial and shot glasses are perfect.

Serving temperatures for whiskies and brandies should be slightly warmer than cellar temperature. I suggest that fine whiskies and brandies be served at between 58 and 65 degrees Fahrenheit. Ports, oloroso and cream sherry, and madeiras should be served at cellar temperature, which is 48–55 degrees Fahrenheit. Fino and manzanilla sherry should be served cold at 40–45 degrees Fahrenheit, amontillado sherry at slightly below cellar temperature.

Vodkas, rums, gins, and tequilas should be served ice cold, except for when they are meant to be enjoyed neat. As a shot, tequila and vodka should be served at cellar temperature. Vodka should not be served ice cold—another myth—because severe cold takes away the aroma. Liqueurs are at their best anywhere from 58 to 65 degrees Fahrenheit, except for cream-based liqueurs, which should be served chilled (50–55 degrees) but not ice cold. Fruit brandies and eaux-de-vie should be served at cellar temperature.

In the matter of food accompaniment, of all distilled spirits and fortified wines, sherry makes the best companion for edibles. Indeed, the various types of sherry are frequently served throughout the course of a meal in Spain. Fino and manzanilla stimulate the appetite and complement light opening foods. Amontillado is a superb soup or salad course choice. Dry oloroso can go with lamb or stew main courses. And creams bring life to desserts.

Ports and madeiras are best kept to after dinner, except for white ports, which can be served as an aperitif. Some ports go well with chocolate.

Distilled spirits are usually best on their own. I should point out, however, that there is a growing movement in this country that espouses whiskey being paired with three or four courses of a meal. I've hosted several whiskey and food events in the last couple of years, and I've been surprised at how well small amounts of single-malt Scotch or bourbon can bring a new dimension to certain types of food. The evenings have typically begun with lighter whiskies being served as aperitifs or with light, usually salty hors d'oeuvres. Next, the soup course is accompanied by slightly deeper whiskies. The main course, normally a red-meat or game course, is washed down by a dry but complex whiskey, while the dessert course is joined by a sweeter, heavier style of whiskey. It works, but it's not for everyone. At this stage, I do not envision bourbon or single malts replacing wine as a dinner staple.

Most importantly, for all the expert suggestions and kibitzing, spirits and fortified wines should be enjoyed on our own terms, but always with the good sense of moderation.

In an age of so-called "political correctness," when personal freedoms are increasingly threatened, distilled spirits and all alcoholic beverages are under serious and steady attack both from a well-meaning constituency with legitimate concerns (Mothers Against Drunk Driving) and from an ill-informed, reactionary constituency with an agenda whose sole aim is the control of others' lifestyles and thoughts (the Christian right wing). Yet, freedom, by its very nature, doesn't tolerate intolerance, nor does it allow only a single voice to be heard in the heated debate of alcohol's place in society. This controversy, which at times has broken down into warfare, has colored the twentieth century. The 1990s have been yet another decade in which the sensory desires of the moderate many have been at direct odds with the conservative views of the belligerent few, who have yet to unyoke themselves from the unenlightened dogma of the seventeenth-century Puritans.

Certainly, you've heard it before, but I'll say it anyway because it's necessary and it bears repeating: It's plain stupid to drink, then drive. There is no excuse good enough for asinine behavior. Also, if you're pregnant, it's imperative to ask your doctor about whether or not you should refrain from imbibing during pregnancy. To my way of thinking, why take the chance?

It's amazing how far common sense can promote health and a long, productive future. If there's one thing I've learned about the alcoholic beverage community at large, it's that no one wants any consumer to get injured because of the misuse of alcohol. On the contrary: Every single person I know in the industry has spoken out on the importance of personal responsibility. When someone gets hurt, we all get hurt. Distilled spirits and fortified wines are some of the most delightful perks to living a good life, but only if they're perceived as ornaments to be handled with extreme care, not as essential equipment.

Drink well, drink wisely, and you may very well prosper.

BRANDY

Brandy is the beloved and ancient spirit that is distilled from the fermented juice of fruit. Just about any type of fruit can be and is turned into brandy. While fermented grape juice both from grapes and their byproducts are by far the most widely employed ingredients, equally luscious brandies are created out of the fermented juice of pears, peaches, plums, cherries, apples, and all kinds of berries, especially blackberries, strawberries, raspberries, and loganberries. Some of the world's more exotic brandies are even made from the pressed oils of flowers.

Brandies are distilled either in small copper-pot stills (commonly referred to as alembics) or in continuously running column stills, depending on the producer and the region's traditions. Maturing in oak casks deepens the color of grape and apple brandies, because of oxidation and contact with the wood, while softening the harshness brought about by the distillation process. The brandies born of most other fruits are rarely aged in wood and, as a result, are generally bottled young and while still crystal clear.

Grape brandies include the illustrious brandies of France, cognac and armagnac; Spain's meaty Brandy de Jérez and others; the high-volume brandies from the Central Valley of California and the small-batch, so-called boutique brandies from independent producers who dot the counties of northern California's wine-producing region; and assorted brandies from South America (the *piscos* of Peru and Chile), Greece, Germany, Italy, Israel, Australia, South Africa, and Mexico.

Other brandies—the frequently magnificent *eaux-de-vie* (pronounced, oh-duh-vee) and *grappas* (pronounced, grah-pah), to be precise—are normally as untinted as spring water, fragrant, and potent. Eaux-de-vie are the captured essences of the fruit and are customarily labeled with the name of the fruit. Grappa and *marc* (pronounced, mahr) are the fiery, unaged, and widely misunderstood (at least in the U.S.) distillates made from grape must or pomace, meaning the skins, seeds, stems, and pulp of grapes that have been pressed to obtain juice for the making of wine. Italy and France remain the flagship producers of grappa and marc, respectively, but in the last decade a handful of small California distillers have been making a name for themselves in the grape-must-spirit arena.

The word "brandy" is derived from the Dutch term *brandywijn,* which translates into "burnt wine." Brandy is indeed wine that has been boiled, or burnt, within the confines of a metal (most often, the highly workable copper) still. The Germans embraced *branntwein* as eagerly as the French did their *brandevin* and the Brits their *brandywine.* Brandy production in Europe came into full flight soon after the Moors were ejected from Spain in 1492 and the method of pot still distillation, which the Moors had prodigiously advanced, became an acquirable skill.

As you are about to discover, many of the most spellbinding distilled-spirits experiences occur within the boundaries of the greater brandy category. The depth and scope of flavors, aromas, textures, and appearances are unmatched in the realm of distilled spirits.

WHAT TO LOOK FOR IN A BRANDY

Purity. You should be able to see unobstructed through a brandy, even when it displays an amber-brownish tint. The best brandies have a warm glow about them when held up to a light or a window. Lesser brandies are dullish or lifeless. Sediment or suspended particles of any kind are a negative sign in brandy, an indication most likely of a problem in filtering or, worse, dirty barrels.

Aromatic and Flavor Properties. Grape-based brandies—the cognacs, armagnacs, and the like—should offer several layers of aroma and taste: the top layers are normally where the sweetness, nuttiness, or woodiness expose themselves, while the foundational layers are usually comprised of the fruity acid underpinning. Balance between acid, alcohol, fruit, and wood is what one looks for. No one element should dominate. When a brandy smells musty, moldy, or rancid, it signifies that the brandy has turned bad chemically, either because of oxidation (as a result of bad storage), old age, or unhygienic production practices. A bracingly sticky-sweet brandy normally means that lots of sugar or molasses was employed in its production in order to conceal a deficiency. In eaux-de-vie, the fruit source should be identifiable and true.

Finish. The most crucial question to ask is, How does the brandy feel in the throat? If it burns to the point of irritation or makes the throat feel raw, chances are it's a cheap brandy. The good to great brandies always go down the throat smoothly, and while they may make the throat feel warm, they won't burn.

Cognac—France

The town of Cognac in southwestern France is a rather mystical place. To tens of thousands of brandy aficionados, this energetic community of 23,000 people is a kind of shrine, a sacred place of pilgrimage where the spirit of cognac literally permeates the air. In and around Cognac the equivalent of millions of bottles of cognac are peacefully maturing in oak barrels at any given time. Since oak is porous, the evaporating brandy fills the air on the streets with what the Cognaçais poetically refer to as the "angel's share." The composed inhabitants are also quick to mention that they hold the benevolent angel's share to be responsible for the remarkable longevity of the area's citizens.

Situated on the banks of the Charente River about 200 miles southwest of Paris, Cognac is the rough geographic center and the unchallenged heart of the world's most illustrious brandy region. The town is encircled by a half-dozen officially designated vineyard districts, or *crus*, which fan out in roughly concentric circles. Approximately 235,000 acres are devoted to the grapes that make the acidic, tart, mouth-puckering wine that's later distilled and matured in oak.

Cognac made its commercial mark in the Middle Ages by being an important center for the distribution of salt for much of western Europe. These initial mercantile ties would be used later upon Cognac's emergence as a supplier of superior brandy in the seventeenth century. But it proved to be a royal marriage, the union of France's Eleanor of Aquitaine to Prince Henry of England in A.D. 1152, that would launch the region as a major wine source. Soon after, the Cognaçais were supplying both the thirst stimulator, salt, and the thirst slaker, wine, all across England.

However, a series of conflicts (including the Hundred Years War) damaged these links, and trade suffered. In 1515, Cognac's destiny took a turn for the better when one of their own citizens was crowned King of France. Francis I was, above all, a politician who remembered his roots. During his reign, he granted highly favorable tax advantages, loan exemptions, and even more beneficent privileges to the Cognaçais.

The eighteenth century, though rife with war and civil turmoil, witnessed the establishment of several major cognac players, most notably, Delamain, Hennessy, Rémy Martin, and Martell. With improvements in distillation technique, distribution, and viticulture, by the middle of the 1700s almost eight million liters of cognac were being produced annually. Shipments to Great Britain, via a third-party country to circumvent trade barriers, soared during this century, even though hostilities between France and England continued.

After Napoleon was expelled from France in 1815, the Cognaçais seized the chance to dramatically expand their markets throughout Europe and the New World. More influential producers, such as Hine, Monnet, Otard-Dupuy, and Courvoisier, opened for business during the nineteenth century. After France instituted free trade and England reduced custom tariffs in the 1860s, the Cognaçais could hardly produce enough cognac to satisfy the demand. By now, the Russians, the Dutch, and much of Latin America were also placing enormous orders for the brandy.

Then, in 1871, a voracious pest, the phylloxera vastatrix louse, began invading the vineyards of Europe. By 1880, the grapevines of the Charente lay devastated. Despair and chaos led many companies to ransack valued stocks to supply the continuing international demand. Other cognac houses simply closed down and sold their properties at as much as a 90 percent drop in value. But the Cognaçais aren't a people who quit easily. As the nineteenth century ended, the Charente region was rebounding, and a new era of viticulture dawned, a period that would make Cognac an even greater power in the world of distilled spirits. During the decades of Cognac's eclipse, a host of pretenders from Italy and Germany freely sold cheap swill under the name of "cognac." Some of these so-called brandies weren't even produced from grapes. Outraged, the Cognaçais vehemently fought to save their good name and that of their product. Legislation enacted both in 1905 and 1929 on their behalf issued safeguards against counterfeiters.

The subsequent tragedies of two world wars obviously caused grave injury to the Charente and its primary industry, but the 1950s and 1960s brought the resurgence of cognac around the world, as sales in the U.S., Great Britain, and the Orient skyrocketed. Today, the marketplace has never seen so many cognacs available to the global audience.

PRACTICAL INFORMATION

In the four centuries that brandy has been produced in the Charente, the recognition of the qualitative prowess of individual *crus*, in terms of viticulture, has led to a clear-cut pecking order. The pair of most highly regarded districts, Grande Champagne and Petite Champagne, inhabit the contoured landscape directly south of Cognac's town limits. The easy hillsides and chalky, calcareous soils in these *crus* combine to make the ideal environment for the cultivation of the holy trinity of cognac grapes: *ugni blanc,* the dominant variety; *colombard;* and *folle blanche.* Chalky soil produces acidic grapes, which, in turn, produce better brandies. These two *crus* provide distillers with the perfect wines with which to produce the most majestic, indeed profound, brandies of all.

Resting between Cognac and the village of Saintes is the third most important *cru,* the Borderies, whose brandies are celebrated for their appealing nutty perfume. The trio of remaining, lesser *crus,* which surround Cognac in wide bands, are Fins Bois, Bons Bois, and Bois Ordinaires. These immense areas offer a wide array of soil types and topographies, but basically their brandies, while perfectly palatable, are far less grand and imposing than those from the hallowed ground of the Champagnes and the Borderies.

Every cognac is the creation of the skill, insight, and intuition of each producer's cellar master, or *maître de chai.* These artisans combine as many as a hundred different brandies into the final blend that we enjoy after a meal. Virtually every cognac is a blend, and only in the rarest cases does a cognac come from a single cask. In my opinion, blending is actually preferable in the case of top-drawer brandy, because the blenders can take the best varieties from the many they have at their disposal and mix them together in the most complementary way.

Cognac is distilled twice in copper-pot stills that are heated over open flames. This system is commonly referred to as "the traditional Charentais method." The product of the first distillation, called *brouillis,* normally registers just under 30 percent alcohol. The second distillation, called *bonne chauffe,* ends up running at just over 70 percent alcohol, but never more than 72 percent. The duration of each distillation is around 12 hours. To produce the actual cognac, only the center part, or the "heart," of each distillation is collected. The spirit that comes out first, the "head," is extremely raw, while the last part, the "tail," is harsh as well. These portions are set aside for further distillation.

Other salient points concerning cognac involve the oak cask in which it is aged. The Cognaçais employ only French oak that comes either from the natural forest of Limousin or the manmade woodland at Tronçais. Cognacs aged in Limousin oak casks age more rapidly than those barreled in Tronçais oak, because Limousin is more porous and thus allows a faster rate of evaporation. The wood is split, never sawn, to fashion the staves. No nails or glue are employed to make the individual staves into barrels, which are held together by metal hoops. Barrels lose on average about 3 percent of the aging brandy a year to evaporation (the fabled share claimed by the angels). Oak is also a key contributor to the taste of cognac, the natural chemical components of tannin and lignin each imparting flavor to the aging brandy. The more pleasant of the two is lignin, which adds a hint of cinnamon or vanilla. Tannin, meanwhile, contributes to the deepening of the color of the brandy, which is clear when it's drawn off the still and placed into the cask.

Cognac rarely remains in cask past four decades. Every producer owns cherished stocks of ancient cognac, some of which are over a century old. These venerable brandies are stored in hermetically sealed large glass vessels, called demijohns. The demijohns are kept in the most sacred part of the cellar, the area referred to as the *paradis*. The *paradis* of every producer is its living library of the genealogy of the company.

One of the most common questions I receive at cognac tastings is, "What do the letters found on cognac labels stand for?" VS means Very Superior, VSOP means Very Superior Old Pale, and XO means Extra Old. While these three basic categories can incorporate several other names, they remain the primary designations. They also indicate a minimum age requirement as specified by law.

THE AGING REQUIREMENTS FOR COGNAC

Category	Legal Aging Minimum	Actual Aging in Most Cases
VS or Three-Star	2.5 years	4–7 years
VSOP, VO (Very Old), or Réserve	4.5 years	5–13 years
XO, Extra, Napoleon, Vieille Réserve, or Hors d'Age	6 years	7–40 years

Please be aware that the majority of cognacs are aged for much greater periods of time than the minimum, as indicated by the final column. When you find the terms "Fine Champagne" on a label, it signifies that the blend is made up only from cognacs that originated in Petite Champagne and Grande Champagne, with Grande Champagne accounting for at least 50 percent.

Another question I hear frequently is, "Are any additives put into cognac for flavoring?" Cane sugar syrup, in a maximum dose of 2 percent, can be legally added to take the harshness out of an unruly cognac. Caramel can also be added, not for flavoring, but to adjust the color. A more controversial practice is the early-stage addition of *le boise,* or the essence of oak chips, which imparts the flavor of greater age to a young cognac. Very few Cognaçais ever want to address this topic when it is raised, though it's been occurring for many years. It's difficult to gauge the overall impact of this questionable procedure, though some producers claim they do not utilize *le boise* at all.

The older the cognac, the better it will be served on its own, without ice or mixing. I prefer to drink a really exceptional cognac in a tall, slender wine glass. Simply serve cognac at room temperature, an experience that can be *Paradis* found.

A. DE FUSSIGNY

A. de Fussigny, headquartered in Cognac, is owned and operated by Alain and Anne Marie Royer. A. de Fussigny cognacs are regrettably minuscule lots of highly concentrated, very old cognacs, bought from finicky private producers who have stored away barrels for decades. Monsieur Royer, an energetically passionate promoter of his wares (he's told me several times that he travels half the year selling his cognacs) and cognac in general, purchases these lots and bottles them under the A. de Fussigny label. Currently carrying four cognacs, Monsieur Royer has even packaged them in unique style. His bottles are clear glass and are decorated with fascinating labels watercolor painted by Michel Bardin, a noted artist from Bordeaux. While the quality of these cognacs is truly remarkable, they are renegades, and, consequently, not for everyone. Because they are so different in their approach to cognac at the level of taste, more traditional cognac lovers may feel a bit threatened if they are accustomed to a more mainstream VSOP or XO every evening. For the more adventurous spirit, the de Fussignys are a brandy revelation of the first magnitude, and I can't recommend them strongly enough for lovers of brandy, port, or whiskey.

A. DE FUSSIGNY Très Vieille Grande Champagne Séries Rares Cognac 42% Alcohol

Gorgeous, orange/vermilion/red grapefruit color, immaculate purity; the rich, toasty, roasted-almond aroma leaps from the glass in tidal waves—the underpinning aroma of oaky spirit acting as the foundation for the more carefree nutty/fruity/roasted scents; on palate, vanilla overtones highlight the silky texture—complementary flavors of cream, banana, apricots, and faint spice combine to make this an admirably married Grande Champagne; this venerable cognac is over 50 years old, is unblended, and is in its natural barrel strength 42% alcohol; I can't think of too many more pleasing brandy experiences; this one ranks with the best that cognac has to offer.

RATING ★ ★ ★ ★ ★   *Highest Recommendation* $$$

A. DE FUSSIGNY Vieille Réserve Séries Rares Cognac Fine Champagne 40% Alcohol

The color is smashing, as medium amber/topaz hues capture the light; ideal clarity; the sensational, snappy bouquet features cinnamon, spiced apple, and hard cheese on the first two passes, then it turns grapy and concentrated on the final two nosings—a totally disarming bouquet; in the mouth, a dash of heat greets the palate as pronounced flavors of red berries, vanillin/oak, and tropical fruit meld beautifully at midpalate; I note medium heat at back of the throat as the finish begins; this hearty cognac packs a punch, but with a velvet hammer; a truly lovely combination of fineness and power; exquisitely dry in the slightly fiery finish; a blend of 60% Grande Champagne and 40% Petite Champagne.

RATING ★ ★ ★ ★   *Highly Recommended* $$$

A. DE FUSSIGNY XO Cognac 40% Alcohol

Amazingly rich-looking, limpid topaz/orange color, immaculate purity; the subtle, stately nose is judiciously peppered with spiced apples and ripe honeydew melon in the first and second passes—the last two nosings reveal the grapy/oaky side of this cognac and it's an exciting discovery; on palate, it's racy, razor-sharp, straightforward, and downright luscious, as bountiful flavors, including old oak cask, spirit, fabric, and coffee bean, enliven the taste buds; the texture is particularly silky; the flavor crescendo fades beautifully into a quietly potent finish; a brilliant blend of Grande Champagne, Fins Bois, and Petite Champagne cognacs; sincere kudos to proprietor Alain Royer.

RATING ★ ★ ★ ★   **Highly Recommended** $$$

A. DE FUSSIGNY Selection Cognac 40% Alcohol

Handsome, luminous, medium amber/vermilion color; ideal clarity; the highly spiced, extraordinarily intense, concentrated nose shows a distinct dried-flowers burst in the initial nosing—the bouquet is so complex that it can be endlessly sniffed, with new discoveries being made every other minute; the intensity continues in the mouth, as piquant flavors of minerals, flowers, and fruit entertain the palate; the moderately sweet aftertaste of sheer elegance and grace caps the experience; the quality of this cognac is top flight.

RATING ★ ★ ★ ★   **Highly Recommended** $$

A. E. DOR

Amédée-Edouard Dor founded his cognac house in 1858, several years prior to the phylloxera infestation of 1871. Today, the family has in its *paradis* some of the cognacs made from pre-phylloxera vines, making their reserve one of the most coveted in the entire world of brandy. It is these century-and-a-half-old cognacs that form the soul of A. E. Dor's contemporary cognacs. Upholding the tradition begun by Amédée-Edouard is Jacques Rivière, who currently directs the house.

A. E. DOR Hors d'Age No. 9 Cognac Grande Champagne 40% Alcohol

The lustrous, rich, dark amber/chestnut brown/cola color captures and enchants the eye, ideal clarity; the fabulous, off-dry, and perfumed nose offers voluptuous scents of egg cream, oak, vanilla, cake, and cocoa—the potency of the aroma remained strong through all four nosings; on palate, the serene richness is evident from entry to aftertaste—one of the classiest, densest, most spectacular cognacs I've ever evaluated—the handsome, behaved flavors of raisins and mild spice (clove and cinnamon, especially) are perfectly balanced and totally harmonious; the finish is polished and very extended and has an appley tail very much like the No. 8; this is a very old cognac, which was first aged in oak for five decades before being poured into demijohns; uncompromising quality all the way; a legend that deserves a spot in all great spirits collections.

RATING ★ ★ ★ ★ ★   **Highest Recommendation** $$$

A. E. DOR XO Cognac Fine Champagne 40% Alcohol

The luminous and lush, medium amber/clover honey color is enormously appealing, perfect purity; the nose is absolutely beguiling, heady, and multilayered with evolved aromas of orange blossom, ripe tropical fruit, and English toffee—the nose comes at you in forceful waves from the sampling glass—a stunner; the keen enjoyment of the agreeable nose is bested by the sexy mouthfeel and explosive flavor, which is highlighted by sweet oak, honey, overripe grapes, and vanilla cream; the sound, sturdy finish is medium long and completely satisfying, with a tail flavor of ripe peaches; this heavenly XO defines the word "bountiful"; the blending skill exhibited by this superlative cognac speaks volumes about the talent of Cognac's small-producer artisans.

RATING ★ ★ ★ ★   ***Highly Recommended*** $$$

A. E. DOR Hors d'Age No. 8 Cognac Grande Champagne 47% Alcohol

Extremely comely, lively, deep orange/vermilion hue, with sunshine-gold highlights; the melded, spirity nose offers coy, tempting glimpses of mildly sweet almonds, chocolate/cocoa, and coffee beans—the vibrant, clean, and compelling aroma is spectacular in its depth and richness; on palate, the opulence of the caramelly, warm, and sinfully decadent flavors wraps around the taste buds—the charred, oaky, and remarkable secondary flavor is in fact of bacon fat—this is one of the few instances when this quality has shown up in a cognac; it owns a slight appley quality in the long, lingering aftertaste, which brims with finesse; most certainly this is not a dainty or delicate cognac; there's one heck of a lot of punch (with the elevated alcohol level) and stuffing here; exquisite, meaty, and exceptional.

RATING ★ ★ ★ ★   ***Highly Recommended*** $$$

A. E. DOR VSOP Cognac 40% Alcohol

Pretty, corn gold/medium amber color, with some sediment showing; it's a full, rich, profoundly fragrant, and characterful nose for a VSOP—the aromas of cigar box, walnuts, and dried plums are magical and harmonious; texturally, A. E. Dor is one of the silkiest, slinkiest VSOPs I've sampled; in the mouth, the soft melon and banana flavors are beautifully accented by the right amounts of spice and spirit; the comforting aftertaste is medium long, off-dry, and exceedingly pleasant; a polite, well-mannered VSOP with all the markings of expert handling; my sole reservation on it is that, in my opinion, the flavor didn't totally fulfill the complexity that was promised in the aroma; other than that, bingo!—leaves the majority of other VSOPs in the dust.

RATING ★ ★ ★   ***Recommended*** $$

A. HARDY

In 1863, Antoine Hardy established Cognac A. Hardy after being employed as a taster and a broker in the Charente for only three years. Hardy's business was almost immediately successful, aided by the signing of the first commercial free-trade treaties between England and France. The firm survived the phylloxera pestilence, and even thrived, because of the large volume of wine Hardy stored away from the vigorous harvests of 1869, 1871, 1872, and 1875. Hardy later established lucrative commercial ties to Tsarist Russia, which in time became one of the firm's most important customers.

Eventually Hardy's son, Armand, assumed the mantle of responsibility and passed the business down to his children.

A. HARDY XO Cognac 40% Alcohol

Similar color to the Napoleon, but with a deeper touch of sunset orange/vermilion; the ripe-fruit element is more evident in this savory nose than in either of its younger siblings—a vastly elegant but solid bouquet; the ripe pear/apricot fruit and roasted-almond flavors shake hands with the classic rancio component, together forming a high-flying, mature, fruity, and cheese-like lush flavor/texture experience that approaches the upper echelon of the cognac category; it finishes firmly and long in the throat; this grand old brandy is an opulent, plump cognac that's as decadent as it is stylistic; I love this style of cognac because it's something of a throwback to a more generous era when master blenders weren't catering to the wimpy, trend-conscious drinking public that worships the word "light" (God help us).

RATING ★ ★ ★ ★   *Highly Recommended* $$$

A. HARDY VSOP Cognac 40% Alcohol

Burnished, luminous tawny/copper/orange color; the piquant, vivacious, very oaky, parchment-like nose sings all the high notes in the initial pass, then by the second pass it settles down into a smooth, slightly leathery, lemon/pineapple mellowness; hands down, an opulent, chewy, generously textured VSOP that's a joy to have on the palate—the happily married flavors of sweet oak, grapes, and vanilla go all out in the mouth, finally fading into a lovely round finish devoid of any heat/burn whatsoever; a well-structured, finely made VSOP that lands squarely in the company of the best VSOPs available.

RATING ★ ★ ★   *Recommended* $$$

A. HARDY Napoleon Cognac 40% Alcohol

Slightly deeper copper/russet/orange hue than the eye-catching VSOP; the individualistic, rich, intense, butterscotch, British hard-candy nose is the most aristocratic of the Hardys—as it aerates in the sampling glass subtle earthy, leafy, vinous components emerge to stand alongside the enchanting butterscotch quality; the depth detected in the nose is found in the taste as acres of sweet, chocolate-covered cherries and oak complement each other admirably well; the aftertaste contains too pronounced a measure of heat/bite in the throat as well as on the tongue, which took away one rating star—then it mellows out into a caramel/cherry taste that's delightful; overall a better-than-average, tony Napoleon that could have been even better.

RATING ★ ★ ★   *Recommended* $$$

ANSAC VS Cognac 40% Alcohol

Lustrous, bright amber/gold hue, perfect clarity; the piquant nose speaks of buttered popcorn, licorice, lead pencil, juniper, oxidation, truffles, and a hint of sage—an atypical nose that's strangely appealing; sweet to the taste and refreshingly simple and direct, the flavor begs for a twist of lemon; if you're looking for an affordable, straightforward, admittedly unspectacular cognac for mixed-drink purposes, here's one to seriously consider; Ansac puts to shame some of the big-name VS's (Hennessy, Courvoisier, and Salignac) that are selling for twice the price—on that basis alone I recommend it.

RATING ★ ★ ★   *Recommended* $

CHABANNEAU VS Cognac 40% Alcohol

Amber/brown color; the nose is standoffish and remote and requires too much time for aeration—I coaxed the bouquet out finally after nearly ten minutes of swirling and sniffing, which is just too long to expect most consumers to deal with—once it emerges, resiny, woody, mushroomy, musty qualities overshadow the fruit element—this aroma isn't worth all the sweat and patience; it's unabashedly sweet on the palate and falls uncomfortably close to being cloying; it doesn't have the agility of other inexpensive VS's, like Ansac; too syrupy and tutti-frutti sweet for my taste.

RATING ★ $

COURVOISIER

A fixture in the town of Jarnac since 1790, Courvoisier is one of the most recognized and widely distributed cognacs around the globe. (It is sold in over 160 countries.) The company was founded in the late eighteenth century by Emmanuel Courvoisier. An astute entrepreneur, Courvoisier was soon supplying brandy and wine to the Emperor Napoleon, and it has ever since been referred to as "Napoleon's cognac," even bearing his silhouette as its logo. Although some blends are predictably routine, overall the quality of the Courvoisier line is much better than average, considering the enormous amount of brandy they purchase, age, and bottle every year. Once you delve past the utilitarian VS and VSOP, you begin to sail in some deep waters. The Napoleon and Initiale Extra are standouts, as are the superlative VOC Extra, Cour Impériale, and Chateau Limoges Fine Champagne.

COURVOISIER Cour Impériale Cognac Grande Champagne 40% Alcohol

Seriously deep amber/topaz/rust color, with fetching copper highlights; the direct, creamy, and zesty nose emits lovely scents of vanilla, caramel, and hard candy—I very favorably responded to its piquant, vivacious presence in the nasal cavity on each of the four nosings; on palate, the absolutely scrumptious, sweet-sour, caramel/toffee flavors are wrapped in a weighty, velvety texture that firmly envelops the taste buds; it finishes full, clean, sweet, and mature; this winner is, along with the Succession "J. L.," Courvoisier's most seductive and flavorful cognac; Cour Impériale is a graceful and muscular Grande Champagne thoroughbred that's a treat for every sense from sight to smell to taste and touch; a chic, stylish elixir with very limited distribution—you may have to have it special-ordered by your liquor merchant; trust me, it's worth the trouble.

RATING ★ ★ ★ ★   **Highly Recommended** $$$

COURVOISIER Succession "J. L." Cognac Grande Champagne 41% Alcohol

Author's note: Succession "J. L." is an unblended Grande Champagne that has never been diluted. Over decades of aging in the same oak cask, it naturally reduced itself to a sublime 41% alcohol. Succession "J. L." was distilled near the turn of this century. So old is this cognac that some of the grapes used were of the now almost extinct folle blanche variety, which flourished as Cognac's staple grape prior to the phylloxera devastation. Successive generations of the "J. L." family tended to the venerable old brandy. Eventually, Jean-Marc Olivier, the Courvoisier cellar master, learned of the cognac. He asked the family if he could purchase it for the express purpose of offering it to the public, since such cognac treasures are rarely found. They agreed. Only 595 bottles of this spectacular cognac were made available worldwide (195 bottles for the U.S.). The bottle comes in a handblown bottle, which is sealed with an 18-carat-gold medallion.

Each bottle is numbered from 1 to 595; shockingly light-orange/amber/ sunshine-gold color that beautifully picks up the light; the immensely delicate and refined nose presents aromas of tropical fruit, coconut, and piquant spice in the first two passes, then in the third nosing it throws off just the barest hint of alcohol; the medium-bodied, satiny texture is sensationally agile and comforting; on palate, the elegant, perfectly married flavors of caraway seed, tangerine, and mandarine orange caress the taste buds in grand style; it carries moderate heat in the extended aftertaste; what surprised and pleased me most was this thoroughbred's drinkability and approachability.

RATING ★ ★ ★ ★   **Highly Recommended** $$$

COURVOISIER Chateau Limoges Extra Cognac Fine Champagne 40% Alcohol

Amber/topaz color, with orange/vermilion highlights; the keen aroma offers cola, cherries, and definite sweetness in an individualistic, snappy, and very disarming bouquet; the beautifully married flavor components of berries, grapes, spice, and mild tobacco come together in a harmonious mouth presence that shines brightest at midpalate—the ideal acid backbone lends balance to the supple fruitiness; the rather dry aftertaste is silky, smooth, and laden with berries and spice; I genuinely admired the quirky character of this lovely, offbeat cognac.

RATING ★ ★ ★ ★   **Highly Recommended** $$$

COURVOISIER VOC Extra Cognac 40% Alcohol

Lustrous deep amber/topaz color that borders on light brown; the instantly engaging and intensely fruity nose tenders fragrances of ripe oranges, pineapples, and pink grapefruit—I found it odd that there's so little evidence of wood in this citrusy tart bouquet; in the mouth it's exquisitely balanced and feels very old, as the developed, satiny, and rich, but not unctuous, texture cradles the palate; the smoky, oaky, substantial but quietly sweet flavors of citrus fruit are accented by an underpinning of caramel; the cultured aftertaste of fruit and nuts is confident and sublime, with no trace of heat or bite; along with the splendid Cour Impériale, my choice as the most alluring cognac from Courvoisier.

RATING ★ ★ ★ ★   ***Highly Recommended*** $$$

COURVOISIER Initiale Extra Cognac 40% Alcohol

Attractive, medium amber/topaz color, excellent purity; the stately, warm, inviting, and delicate yet firm nose offers succulent aromas of apples and almonds, but not much more; the deliciously sinewy, smooth, and feline feel at palate entry is bewitching and satisfying; the mature, melded flavors explode at midpalate into fine layers of tea, ripe tropical fruit, in particular, banana and guava; the aftertaste is regal, long, and decidedly toasty, with a judicious dash of roasted chestnuts; this is a very good cognac, no doubt, with an elegance and a warmth that are very appealing.

RATING ★ ★ ★   ***Recommended*** $$$

COURVOISIER Napoleon Cognac 40% Alcohol

Straight-on amber hue, with rust highlights; the lusty, full, round, assertive nose is hearty but not bullying—foundational aromas of caramel, vanilla cream, and red fruit underpin the aroma; the texture is chewy, fat, and generous, but slightly unglued; on palate, the lovely, fascinating, semisweet flavors are neatly layered—tastes of good English toffee, oak, cream, and vanilla shine at midpalate; the remarkably sensuous, sexy, low-key, sweet finish ends on an appealing note of cream; a captivating, well-made, if unspectacular, cognac.

RATING ★ ★ ★   ***Recommended*** $$$

COURVOISIER XO Cognac 40% Alcohol

Deep sunset-orange/amber, with copper-penny highlights; the curious nose at first is subdued, then with aeration it releases a robust, spirity rush that unfortunately obliterates any other existing aromas—the final pass is as banal and pedestrian as the first; the palate is the strong suit, as it displays handsome, virile, tightly wrapped, and moderately sweet flavors of butter, yellow grapefruit, and even roasted walnuts; this vastly disappointing cognac finishes meekly on an oddly neutral note, neither fruity nor sweet; this one perplexed me, since it doesn't have anywhere near the overall finesse or complexity of the more delectable Napoleon; on top of that the Napoleon is *half the price;* how any major cognac producer could allow their XO to be as off-track as this ill-conceived offering is beyond me.

RATING   ★ ★ $$$

COURVOISIER VSOP Cognac 40% Alcohol

Gold/amber color quite similar to that of the VS; the pungent, very aggressive nose gamely tweaks the olfactory sense into full waking consciousness, but delivers about as much depth of character and complexity as Kato Kaelin doing King Lear; as with the VS, it's admirably silky and smooth at entry—this one shows a smidgen more flavor and structural balance on palate than the lowly VS; it even displays a charming chocolate quality that slowly melts away into the slightly nutty, citrusy aftertaste; while hardly awe-inspiring, it does go down easily; reevaluated recently and upgraded.

RATING ★ ★ $$

COURVOISIER VS Cognac 40% Alcohol

Gold/amber color; the prickly, spirity, and austerely acidic nose possesses just the barest hint of fruit—this bleak, insipid aroma is something you'd expect from a lesser producer; it's startlingly but pleasingly mellow on palate after the unruly, forward nose—mild entry flavors of lemon and hard candy transform into a citrusy, sharp, and fiery finish; there's absolutely no question that this cognac's major flaw is that it leans way too heavily on acidity; with more fruit, this would potentially be an average VS; however, it ends up being only an earnest, simple, blue-collar cognac; perfectly fine for a mixer.

RATING ★ $$

DANIEL BOUJU Très Vieux Brut de Fut Cognac Grande Champagne 50% Alcohol

Mature, dark amber/orange color like a 20-year-old tawny port; the restrained, self-contained, and intense nose of licorice and Brazil nuts also shows nuances of ripe apple and apple cider in the background; one of the most richly textured cognacs I've tasted; in the mouth, dense, expansive, and spirity flavors of plums, prunes, oak, and dark caramel are perfectly married, with no one feature dominating; very warm at the back of the throat, the orangey aftertaste is curiously short, which almost lowered my score of five stars—almost, but not quite; nevertheless, this supple beauty provides one of cognac's most extraordinary, almost otherworldly experiences; one of the greatest distilled-spirit experiences that anyone could hope to have; I'd give it six stars if I wanted to break my own rules; aged a minimum of 32 years.

RATING ★ ★ ★ ★ ★   *Highest Recommendation* $$$

DANIEL BOUJU VSOP Cognac Grande Champagne 40% Alcohol

Dark amber/topaz color with a brilliant golden rim; the delicate, but direct nose of bittersweet chocolate is serene and sublime—the incredibly rich, toasty, roasted-nut, and marshmallow aromas in the endlessly fascinating nose evolved with every nosing pass—every time I'd sniff it another feature would emerge with aeration; in the mouth, the flavors of molasses, cane sugar, and honey are more like graceful hints than heavy-duty statements; the succulent mouth-feel is simultaneously commanding and refined; the cocoa/coffee finish is long, concentrated, and immensely satisfying; without question, the best VSOP cognac in existence; mortgage the house if you have to purchase this one; aged a minimum of seven years.

RATING ★ ★ ★ ★   *Highly Recommended* $$$

DANIEL BOUJU Extra Cognac Grande Champagne 40% Alcohol

Bedazzling, opulent, tawny/topaz hue, with orange/russet highlights; the soft, reticent aroma has scents of saddle leather, butter, and spirit, flecked with spice cake; the sexy, silky texture is dynamite; on palate, it's loaded with rich vanilla extract, dark caramel, and dark honey flavors that keep building in intensity as you move from sampling to sampling; it finishes very long, but serene; it reminds me of a maderized sweet wine, like Tokay; a revelation in cognac; this sinewy, atypical beauty has the guts and charisma of a vintage armagnac and the finesse and breeding of a top-flight cognac, all in one spectacular and unforgettable package; in a word, luscious; aged a minimum of 25 years.

RATING ★ ★ ★ ★   *Highly Recommended* $$$

DELAMAIN

Of the handful of cognac producers who deal only in truly outstanding cognacs from the best designated subregion, Grande Champagne, Delamain has been providing some of the best, limited-quantity cognacs (a minuscule 50,000 cases per year) since 1824 out of their Jarnac cellars. Today, they offer four different, very special, ultrapremium Grande Champagnes and nothing more. They don't even categorize them by the usual designations of VS, VSOP, XO, and so forth, but label them by their pedigree, by their inherent quality and age. Neither do they blend before aging in cask, which is the usual practice. Delamain uses no additives for flavoring or coloring. All brandies are matured in very old casks to avoid excessive tannin content. This fastidious producer rejects 80% of the samples submitted by independent growers/distillers and accepts no brandy younger than 15 years old. The Delamains themselves have been a multitalented and utterly fascinating family over the generations. Aside from being makers of superb cognac, various family members have been renowned generals, Irish Delft pottery makers, entomologists, archeologists, orthinologists, historians, authors, and publishers.

DELAMAIN Réserve de la Famille Cognac Grande Champagne 43% Alcohol

This single-cask Grande Champagne is unblended and is purchased from a distiller in Saint-Preuil, located in the finest area of Grande Champagne, when it is already 15 years old—it then is aged for another four decades at Delamain; this is an exquisite, one-of-a-kind Grande Champagne from top to bottom; I almost don't know where to begin; its deep topaz/cola/oloroso sherry color is gorgeous, penetrating, and fetching; the seductively fragrant, mature, self-possessed, roasted-nut/vanilla bouquet excites the olfactory sense as few cognacs can; its fathomless, fully melded flavors of gentle spice, citrus, dried fruit, oak, and herbs are unique, remarkably complex, yet sublime; this is an unusual and totally captivating distilled-spirit experience that should not be missed.

RATING ★ ★ ★ ★ ★   *Highest Recommendation* $$$

DELAMAIN Pale & Dry Très Belle Cognac Grande Champagne 40% Alcohol

When they say Pale, they're not kidding—this is one of the palest, yet one of the most golden/flaxen cognacs I've encountered; at the risk of sounding pathetically corny, I actually thought of sunlight when I looked at it—all right, so don't let me live it down; aside from its visual appeal, this incredible cognac is graced with an almond-like, crushed-violet bouquet that is nothing short of extraordinary; on palate, it's serenely focused on fruit, almost tropical in nature, reminiscent mostly of pineapple—the background flavors include black pepper, spirit, old oak, lead pencil, and red fruit—this mouth presence is so complex and dense that it's awe-inspiring; the medium-length finish provides the ideal sense of closure; an incredible cognac.

RATING ★★★★ *Highly Recommended* $$$

DELAMAIN Très Vénérable Cognac Grande Champagne 40% Alcohol

Sterling, warm, caramel/cola-brown color; the subdued, restrained, but vivacious aromas line up in multilayered rows of vanilla, spice, and barely discernable orange rind scents—the density and magnificence of this bouquet must be experienced to be believed; on palate, it's surprisingly buoyant, carefree, and on the lighter side; the velvety texture generously coats the mouth—intriguing herbal flavors, highlighted by a soft woodiness, survive well into the long, easy, satiny finish; this is one of Cognac's most stunningly elegant and delicious triumphs—glorious.

RATING ★★★★ *Highly Recommended* $$$

DELAMAIN Vesper Cognac Grande Champagne 40% Alcohol

If there is a disappointment with the Delamains, albeit only a mild one, it lies with this one; the autumnal amber/harvest gold color is truly lovely, the lilting aroma is a touch oaky, and the vanilla, slightly candied flavors are deeply concentrated and measured, yet compared to the more affordable Pale & Dry, it falls short, in my opinion, in the overall-impression category; this is not to say that I dislike it because that's hardly the case, but it fails to inspire in the end after giving such wonderful early signals; not a difficult one to score, because it's obviously better than average, but for Delamain better-than-average is average.

RATING ★★★ *Recommended* $$$

FRAPIN

Cognac Frapin is run by Geneviève Cointreau, a Frapin by birth, and Max Cointreau, the former Managing Director of Cointreau S.A., who retired from that position to develop an international market for Frapin. The Frapin family has resided in the Charentes since 1210 (or twenty generations) and today owns and controls a total of 300 hectares (740 acres) in Grande Champagne, more than any other single landholder. Grande Champagne's total size is approximately 12,000 hectares. The jewel property in the Frapin crown is the beautiful Chateau de Fontpinot, which is situated between the

Frapin distillery and the town of Segonzac. Of the 300 hectares lorded over by the Frapins, 200 are planted in *ugni blanc* grapevines, the preferred grape type for the making of cognac.

FRAPIN VIP XO Cognac Grande Champagne 40% Alcohol

Amber/gold/green color; the mature nose evokes scents of pungent oak casks and faint hints of rosemary and sage—I actually prefer the sensational aroma on the Chateau de Fontpinot; but once in the mouth, however, this ultrasexy XO throws its powerful yet elegant charms into overdrive—the succulent taste is so chiseled and textured that I almost can't believe it—crushed velvet, satin, silk, get the picture? decadent flavors of ripe plums, buttermilk biscuits, dark chocolate, and espresso come together in one of the best cognac experiences, in fact one of the finest distilled-spirit experiences I've had, period; the finish is every bit as classical as the flavor; a must-have item for anyone serious about cognac.

> *RATING* ★ ★ ★ ★ ★   *Highest Recommendation* $$$

FRAPIN Extra Réserve Patrimoniale Cognac Grande Champagne 40% Alcohol

By far, the deepest shade of amber/russet of the Frapins—it's almost more like an oloroso sherry hue than a cognac—it's absolutely stunning in appearance; this extremely limited bottling comes directly from the Frapin family's private reserve stock and is estimated to be between 20 and 30 years old; the subtle, slightly citrusy, smoky bouquet is deceptively potent and deserves at least 10 to 15 minutes of sniffing before you take the plunge into tasting; on the tongue this luxurious cognac sits there like a ball of satin as melony, woody, grapy, and altogether seductive flavors leisurely make their way down the throat; the finish is eternal; I found this to be one of the most profound, most complete cognac experiences in all four evaluation levels of appearance, smell, taste, and aftertaste; the sensory gratification is unmatched.

> *RATING* ★ ★ ★ ★ ★   *Highest Recommendation* $$$

FRAPIN Vieille Cognac Grande Champagne 40% Alcohol

Deep amber/harvest gold/copper ore color; age is 15–20 years; the floral, intensely woody bouquet makes me think that I may have to scoop out this luxurious cognac out of the bottle with a spoon—it's a seductive, semisweet, multidimensional bouquet; the taste is serene and balanced between a rich butteriness and a mellow, mature oakiness—the cognac generously coats the mouth in a sweet, ripe apple flavor that's an utter knockout; I detect an extended appley flavor in the aftertaste that's simultaneously delicate and potent; wow.

> *RATING* ★ ★ ★ ★   *Highly Recommended* $$$

FRAPIN Chateau de Fontpinot Très Vieille Réserve du Chateau Cognac Grande Champagne 41% Alcohol

Amber/mahogany color, perfect purity; distilled, aged, and bottled at the chateau; the rich, evolved, semisweet nose is so ideally crafted that no one attribute rushes out to take the lead—I initially picked up some cinnamon but that quickly faded—a third and fourth pass brought out fresh-cut cedar; not even a hint of heat or bite on the palate—sweet, ripe grapes, and a healthy dose of rancio delights the taste buds; the finish is very long, sure-footed, and fruity; a ripe, handsome, feminine cognac.

RATING ★ ★ ★ ★   *Highly Recommended* $$$

FRAPIN Cuves Rare Cognac Grande Champagne 40% Alcohol

Medium amber color; the age on this single vineyard cognac is roughly ten years old; the nose reminds me startlingly of marinated pears and apricots, with a trace of oak cask resin; on palate, the silky texture is divine and highly sophisticated—multilayered, sublimely sweet flavors of white-grape raisins, oak, and white chocolate meld beautifully into the concentrated but accessible aftertaste; on the third tasting pass, notes of light caramel candy and fresh key lime get added to the list of virtues; the only minor complaint I have is that it borders on being a tad too juicy and sweet; overall, however, I find this to be a very good cognac.

RATING ★ ★ ★   *Recommended* $$

GABRIEL & ANDREU Petite Champagne Cognac Lot 23, 42% Alcohol

Gorgeous honey/medium-amber color with bronze core highlights; the aroma is direct, off-dry, grapy, and very focused—this is not an expansive bouquet as much as it is concentrated and localized on the interplay of the grapes and the oak—I loved the serenity and the grace found in it, especially in the third and fourth passes; on palate, the flavor takes a slightly different tack than the bouquet in that it turns buttery and creamy sweet while spotlighting the sweeter side of oak—by midpalate, the vanilla taste from the oak is in high gear, dominating, but not bullying, the entire palate experience; the finish is honeyed, candied, and oaky in a round rather than angular way; what it comes down to is this, the mouth presence is so well defined and succulent that five stars is the only score that this cognac could get; restrained, balanced, and stately.

RATING ★ ★ ★ ★ ★   *Highest Recommendation* $$$

GABRIEL & ANDREU Borderies Cognac Lot 3, 40% Alcohol

Knockout medium amber/dirty orange/bronze color, perfect purity; the nose is hauntingly seductive and calmly sweet as the honeyed, gently spirited first pass goes a long way in charming the bejesus out of the sense of smell—subsequent nosings unfold like skins of an onion as deeper, nuttier (especially walnuts), and fruitier aromas evolve and mesh more with every pass; in the mouth, this is authentic cognac heaven, as beautifully balanced and sculpted flavors of ripe grapes, fine English toffee, and sweet oak are complemented by a classic smoldering warmth that comforts both the palate and the throat; the aftertaste is very extended, sweet without being juicy, and candied without being cloying; I marvel at the harmony exhibited by this top-rank thoroughbred.

RATING ★ ★ ★ ★ ★   *Highest Recommendation* $$

GABRIEL & ANDREU Grande Champagne Cognac Lot 18, 43% Alcohol

The prettiest and darkest of the G & A's—dark amber/topaz hue with copper/rust core features; the nose immediately gives away its place of origin—only a Grande Champagne could display this amount of layering and overall succulence—the bouquet settles down in a vanilla-wafer, sugar-biscuit, woody affair in the last two nosings—while complex, I didn't find it, to my surprise, as interesting a nose as either the G & A Borderies or Petite Champagne; by far, this is the most generous, buxom, and sweet G & A on the palate, as intense, almost syrupy, sherried flavors of toffee, nougat, and lanolin take the taste buds by force—this is not a nuanced cognac; the aftertaste is sweet, grapy, and more mannered than the entry and the mid-palate; round, lusty, and delicious.

RATING ★ ★ ★ ★   *Highly Recommended* $$$

GABRIEL & ANDREU Fins Bois Cognac Lot 8, 40% Alcohol

Pale amber/golden yellow color, excellent purity; the crisp, tart bouquet says sour apple, sour candy, and underripe grapes in the first two passes—moderately heady/spirity—in the third pass, a pleasantly mild, biscuity quality comes through the sour-fruit curtain—the fourth nosing seems tired, spent, and wan, as this cognac simply loses steam aromatically; in the mouth, it's mouth-puckeringly tart at entry, then it quickly turns bittersweet, finally going crisply sweet and intensely grapy at midpalate—the transformation from being a tart taste to a sweet taste is breathtakingly swift; the finish is unexpectedly sweet, ripe, and full, with a nuanced backnote of caramel; what it lacks in finesse and depth, it makes up for in flavor intrigue.

RATING ★ ★ ★   *Recommended* $$

GIBOIN Napoleon Réserve de Castex Cognac 40% Alcohol

Pretty brown/ocher/amber color, absolute purity; ripe mango, passion fruit leap from the glass in a sweet, concentrated fruit bouquet that turns nutty with swirling and time—a stately nose; the full, toasty, honey wheat, mature, sweet, toffee flavors come neatly wrapped in an exquisitely fine but muscular texture; it finishes as sleekly and quietly as a cat walking on velvet; outstanding quality; I was totally blown away by the superb balance and the ultrasexy feel.

RATING ★ ★ ★ ★   *Highly Recommended* $$

GIBOIN Sélection Borderies de l'Hermitage Cognac 40% Alcohol

The spitting image of the VSOP, the identical orange/medium amber hue; the nose emits sweet, ripe, scents of melon, spiced apple, and slate—a beguiling and concentrated bouquet that walks a fence with ripe fruit on one side and dry minerals on the other; the round, cushiony, and mellow flavor/texture combination is very impressive, but not quite in the league of the deft Napoleon; this one shows much more of the nut-meat quality one expects from a Borderies cognac; easy to drink, a complete delight.

RATING ★ ★ ★ ★   *Highly Recommended* $$

GIBOIN XO Royal Cognac Grande Champagne 40% Alcohol

By leagues, the darkest of the five Giboins—a chestnut-brown hue, with flecks of topaz in the core; the soft, ripe-banana, baked-caramel-custard, oaky, mature aromas tweak the nose cavity's olfactory machinery—the bouquet is nice, round, and warm; on palate, the caramel-custard quality is buttressed by a firm heat element—not a raging fire, but a quiet, reading-the-paper-and-petting-the-retriever, burning-embers warmth that is comforting and persistent; an altogether superb cognac with all its parts working in unison.

RATING ★★★★　　*Highly Recommended*　　$$$

GIBOIN VS Cognac 40% Alcohol

Standard-issue pale amber hue, good clarity; the heady, piquant, lemon-candy nose is touched with a smidgen of basil, pine, herbs—a forward, green-peppery delight—more zestier than most other VS's; this lovely cognac lies gracefully on the tongue, no heat or bite, offering well-crafted, chewy flavors of malted milk, overripe grapes, and cocoa; it ends in a focused swell of ripe fruit and toffee flavors that are delicious; this is a major discovery in VS cognac, which by and large is a study in mediocre, throwaway brandy.

RATING ★★★　　*Recommended*　　$$

GIBOIN VSOP Réserve de l'Hermitage Cognac 40% Alcohol

Medium amber/orange color; much more sedate and settled than the rollicking nose of the VS—owns a slightly minty, smoky, floral (juniper?) quality that's both elusive and intriguing—it noticeably gains in power with aeration time; it possesses a supple, sweet, candied splendor on the tongue—it's so full, mannered, and succulent that I automatically want to drink it rather than spit it out; there are few VSOPs that display such aplomb, character, and presence; another great find.

RATING ★★★　　*Recommended*　　$$

HENNESSY

Hennessy was founded by an Irish Catholic soldier named Richard Hennessy, who had volunteered to serve France's King Louis XV. While nursing battle wounds, Hennessy became acquainted with cognac, which was routinely given to recuperating soldiers during the eighteenth century. After a successful recovery, Hennessy decided to enter into the cognac trade. In 1765, he formally founded his company. Remarkably, within the span of only one year, Cognac Hennessy blossomed into the busiest cognac company of all, exporting the equivalent of 13,000 cases. Even more astoundingly, shipments increased ninefold within the subsequent 24 months. Hennessy had become so successful that by the start of the French Revolution in 1789, he was shipping roughly 240,000 cases annually. Along with other industry innovations, like inventing the "XO" category, Cognac Hennessy was the first producer to ship its cognac in bottles, which, of course, identified Hennessy as the producer. Over two and a quarter centuries after its founding, Cognac Hennessy is still guided by direct descendents of Richard Hennessy. Hennessy owns the most extensive cognac reserves in the world. Cognac Hennessey's blending responsibilities have been held within the same family, the Fillioux clan, for the remarkable span of seven generations. A huge 98% of production is exported.

HENNESSY Paradis Cognac 40% Alcohol

This legendary cognac is the amber/gold lookalike of the pretty VSOP Privilège, superb purity; the round nose is plump, unctuous, opulent but surprisingly agile—this is a nimble, classic bouquet, the Fred Astaire of the Big Four's top-of-the-line aromas—it shows saucy elements of pine needle, rancio, sweet oak, clover honey, and even spiced apple—it is, in a word, gorgeous; I think what makes Paradis so charming and irresistible is the cozy warmth that you feel when it's in your mouth—the ideally married, totally elegant flavors of old oak, fat rancio, soft cheese, wood smoke, white-cake batter, and bacon fat are really sublime, yet completely approachable; the aftertaste leans more to the wood component than fruitness or sweetness; this graceful, grand old dame is blended from over 100 eaux-de-vie, some of which are a century old; the pinnacle for Hennessy.

RATING ★ ★ ★ ★   *Highly Recommended* $$$

HENNESSY Sélection Davidoff Cognac 43% Alcohol

Very limited production; almost as deep as amber/dark wood brown as the splendid-looking XO—a lovely chestnut brown, with perfect clarity; this is the most vivacious (almost prickly) bouquet of the Hennessy lineup, as acidic but fully fruited waves jump from the sampling glass—it's the most spirity nose of the group, but not necessarily the most compelling—I still prefer the majestic fragrance of the Paradis; on the palate, the Davidoff is a savory mouthful that simultaneously satisfies and excites—the excitement is born of the mild alcohol bite at midpalate—but what I found most alluring was the creamy, rich palate entry that spoke of caramel and chocolate; a nationally available but hard-to-find beauty that's specially blended to complement cigars, hence the moniker reference to the fabled tobacconist.

RATING ★ ★ ★ ★   *Highly Recommended* $$$

HENNESSY XO Cognac 40% Alcohol

By considerable margin, this attractive cognac displays the darkest amber color of the Hennessys—indeed it borders on being a deep chestnut brown—to the eye, it's as dazzling a dark beauty as Ava Gardner in her prime; the nose is opulent, of a feminine lean, and elegant in its understatement—on the third nosing, to my delight I picked up the slightest hint of cheese-like, winey rancio as a delectable, if elusive, backnote fragrance; loads of rich, grapy flavors mingled with lean oak tannins in a very alluring and balanced mouth presence that doesn't inspire as much as it effortlessly pleases—the finish is clean, confident, very long, and shows sweet and none-too-subtle hints of dark caramel and English toffee; nicely orchestrated XO whose eaux-de-vie range in age from 10 to a whopping 70 years.

RATING ★ ★ ★   *Recommended* $$$

HENNESSY VSOP "Privilège" Cognac 40% Alcohol

Amber/harvest-gold tone, with pretty vermilion/rust highlights and excellent clarity; the agreeably fruity bouquet reminded me instantly of candied apples and pears, but it seemed reluctant (or incapable) to advance beyond speciousness into genuine aromatic complexity—this nose is carefree, easy, but ultimately shallow; the fruited quality continued on in the mouth as ripe apple and pear flavors nicely came across in a straightforward manner; the finish was unabashedly sweet (perhaps too saccharine-like for my taste) and uncomplicated; while this VSOP could never be accused of being an overachiever, its one-note, unpretentious fruit character might prove to be a welcome, accessible companion for cognac novices.

RATING ★★ $$

Hennessy VS Cognac 40% Alcohol

Medium amber/honey color, with orange highlights, superb clarity; the nose, which aerated for no less than 30 minutes, exhibited a pleasantly piquant marriage of citrus and dried herbs in the top layer—this rested upon a foundation aroma of nuts and grapes—on the fourth and last nosing, I noted a curious fabric-like aroma to which I didn't favorably respond; in the mouth, the anticipated mainstream simplicity dominated the flavor experience—don't misunderstand, this VS doesn't suffer from an unpleasant taste or aftertaste presence—this is more a matter of personality deficiency and the fear of not wanting to rock the boat with such an established brand; no surprises here, as it follows suit with the equally mundane VS efforts of both Rémy Martin and Courvoisier.

RATING ★ $$

Hine

Even though Hine is now owned by Moet-Hennessy Louis Vuitton (LVMH), the sixth generation of Hines, cousins Bernard and Jacques, still guide this outstanding producer, which was inherited by Thomas Hine from his father-in-law. Located on the banks of the Charente in Jarnac, Hine's elegant, straightline edifice mirrors the style of cognacs the family produces. The eaux-de-vie, or immature brandies, that are purchased are mostly Grande Champagne and Petite Champagne, with some Fins Bois. Only oak from the Limousin forest is used for aging. Easily one of the top ten cognac houses.

Hine 1953 Cognac Grande Champagne 42% Alcohol

A dark amber/orange blossom honey/amontillado sherry color with absolute clarity; the sublime nose is delicate, yet sure-footed, as semisweet scents of roasted nuts, new oak, and caramel come together in a totally complementary manner—this is a distinguished and highly compelling bouquet, one that shows flashes of rancio; on the palate, I find the flavors so ideally married that one characteristic doesn't dominate over the others— a rare and wonderful occurence—the supple flavors of nuts, oak, citrus (primarily tangerine), and sour hard candy impressed me; the aftertaste is long, sweet, warming, and elegant, with touches of spice; I prefer this beauty to the splendid Hine 1952 because it's markedly fuller and more substantial; an incredibly fine and satisfying Grande Champagne cognac; put this on your "must have" list.

RATING ★★★★   *Highest Recommendation* $$$

HINE 1952 Cognac Grande Champagne 42% Alcohol

Lustrous clover-honey/amber tone—perfect clarity; the direct, layered nose is dry to off-dry, melony, slightly woody, and even a tad herbal aromatically—its understatement and nuanced nature give testament to its overall harmony and brilliance; in the mouth, the round, firm texture is a delight and underpins the stately, courtly flavors of oak, spirit, and candied almonds; the finish is clean, warming, medium-long, and as beautifully balanced as the nose and the taste; while not a blockbuster in terms of sensory impact, this cognac's elegance, subtlety, and finesse catapults it near the top of the four-star rating category.

RATING ★ ★ ★ ★   ***Highly Recommended*** $$$

HINE Antique Très Rare Cognac Fine Champagne 40% Alcohol

Genuinely beautiful, medium amber/tawny/ocher hue, excellent purity; the bouquet offers highly perfumed, aromatic, piquant, sassy scents of roasted almonds and citrus fruit supported by an undercurrent of creaminess; the nuttiness and distinctively racy style continues on in beguiling, warm, and friendly palate that never overburdens the taste buds; the texture is opulent, supple, and sinewy; the fast, dry finish leaves the barest trace of caramel and departs quickly; superior quality; a cognac that doesn't adhere to the production restraints evidently placed on the more pedestrian VSOP; this cognac has been allowed to take a stylistic stand that amply comes across in fine fashion; would have been five stars but for the quick-exit aftertaste; aged 20–25 years.

RATING ★ ★ ★ ★   ***Highly Recommended*** $$$

HINE Triomphe Cognac Grande Champagne 40% Alcohol

The stately, medium amber/iced-tea color is a head-turner, ideal clarity; the nose is heady, potent, and concentrated with perfumey scents of tropical fruit (passion fruit or mango perhaps?), pears, apricots—the seductive, sexy bouquet ebbs and flows as it mixes with air—it's a challenging bouquet that keeps your attention—I loved it; the direct, dried fruit, slightly fiery flavors are beautifully balanced by the velvety texture; this winner is so polished it glides down the throat; the multilayered complexity packs a lambskin-gloved punch from start to finish; it's astringent yet round, it's elegant yet has a feral shadow following it; a truly compelling cognac; aged 45 years.

RATING ★ ★ ★ ★   ***Highly Recommended*** $$$

HINE Family Reserve Cognac Grande Champagne 40% Alcohol

Beautiful, deep topaz/ocher/rust color; the deceptively powerful aroma at first pass seems meek or, better described, bridled, then slowly and measuredly it builds with aeration into a sensory feast for the olfactory sense—after aeration, the nose brims with subtle fruit/nut/caramel layers, one never overshadowing the other; on palate, it has a tongue-tingling, acidy potency that is judiciously matched to the fruit and alcohol—obviously mature, clearly one heck of an ultrapremium cognac, the succulent product of highly competent, keenly adept producers who demand the best from their cognacs; positively enchanting; aged 60–70 years.

RATING ★★★★   **Highly Recommended** $$$

HINE VSOP Cognac Fine Champagne 40% Alcohol

Luminous golden color; the nose is spicy, mildly alcoholic, and medium sweet with mild aromas of English toffee and pepper; the texture is silky and medium-bodied, with a sleek, lean feel; on palate, it displays a distinct mandarin orange backbone, with barely discernable, underlying hints of hazelnuts—at midpalate, it's almost feminine in its pliant, supple posture; the lovely, round, understated finish borders on being timid; while enjoyable, it did not bowl me over, as it came off being too proper, too concerned with tradition and consumer perception of what VSOP "should" be rather than what it "could" be; it felt restrained, almost as though it wanted to be more daring but it wasn't allowed; aged 8–10 years.

RATING ★★ $$

JEAN DANFLOU

Jean Danflou was an artist descended from Bordeaux wine traders. In the 1920s, he started his own brandy house, which bottled fine eaux-de-vie, or fruit brandies. In time, Danflou expanded his line to include armagnac, cognac, and calvados, the splendid apple brandy from Normandy. He passed the reins of his company to his nephew (also named Jean Danflou) upon his retirement. Today, the company is operated by the nephew of the nephew of the founder, Pierre Glotin-Danflou. Danflou does not own its own vineyards, but rather, acting as a *négoçiant,* purchases from selected and highly trusted independent producers eaux-de-vie that it ages and blends. Jean Danflou's Fine Champagne is blended (65% Grande Champagne, 35% Petite Champagne) from eaux-de-vie that have been aged in oak 15–20 years, while the Grande Champagnes (100% Grande Champagne) have aged a minimum of 20 years, containing a foundational brandy that is over 50 years old.

JEAN DANFLOU Extra Cognac Grande Champagne 40% Alcohol

Marginally darker copper-penny/amber color than the Fine Champagne; more sedate, even restrained, than the gregarious Fine Champagne in the nose—this classy, very complex aroma offers hints of butter, toffee, tobacco, vanilla, baked pears, and oak; it's round, full-bodied, sweet, and smoky on the palate, with multiple layers of oaky flavors; it finishes beautifully and solidly in a toffee/buttery flourish that's extremely delectable and elegant; what it lacks in flash it makes up for in quiet strength and oodles of creamy, smoky drinking pleasure; this is one to wrap yourself around in the late evening.

RATING ★★★★   **Highly Recommended** $$$

JEAN DANFLOU Cognac Fine Champagne 40% Alcohol

Pretty copper-orange/amber color, superb purity; the engaging, acidic, raisiny, citrusy bouquet is assertive yet freewheeling—the second nosing pass introduces ripe apple and apricot aromas; it enters the palate as it smells, open, forward, and firm—the semidry flavors of baked apples, resin, and oak highlight the midpalate, then turn smoky and mildly citrusy in the extended finish; this is a buxom, direct, no-nonsense Fine Champagne that's sure to satisfy and stimulate even the most finicky of cognac drinkers.

RATING ★ ★ ★   *Recommended* $$

LEOPOLD GOURMEL

The zesty, spirited, and floral cognacs of Leopold Gourmel are excellent examples of what the Fins Bois contributes to the mural that is cognac. Brandies from these outer stretches of vineyard are typically shorter-lived, earlier maturing, and lighter than those from the Borderies, Petite Champagne, or Grande Champagne districts. For that reason alone, many brandy aficionados who prefer a more delicate, less ponderous cognac reach for cognacs from the Bois districts. The Fins Bois district neatly wraps around the smaller Champagnes and Borderies areas in a nearly complete, if somewhat irregular, circle. The prime vineyards of Fins Bois lie to the east and north of the town of Jarnac, where the earth turns chalky and crumbly. The Gourmel cognacs are born in these superior vineyards. Owner Pierre Voisin did not come into cognac by way of inheritance or family tradition. For years he was involved in the auto industry, working for Fiat as their quality control manager and later owning a Volvo dealership. His hobby of making cognac became a second career, and today his cognacs are among the finest that the Fins Bois has to offer. I urge you to try the L'Age des Fleurs and the Quintessence.

LEOPOLD GOURMEL L'Age des Fleurs Fins Bois Cognac 42% Alcohol
Much richer in color than the "du Fruit"—a comely orange/copper hue engages the eye; the nose is decidedly melony, evoking, in particular, cantaloupe—it also emits a candied-apple blast on the third pass that is immensely appealing; it's remarkably citrusy and clean on the palate, as tropical fruits, especially mango, headline the flavor marquee—the second tasting showcases a truly compelling creamy flavor, which has faint but seductive hints of mango, passion fruit, and honeydew melon—I found the flavor very satisfying and light years ahead of either the "du Fruit" or the "des Epices"; no heat or bite to be found in the succulent, fruity, and mildly spicy aftertaste; excitingly different and refreshing.

RATING ★ ★ ★ ★   *Highly Recommended* $$$

LEOPOLD GOURMEL Quintessence Fins Bois Cognac 44% Alcohol
The deepest orange/amber of the four, very good purity; the nose is rather closed on the first two passes, then on the third it begins to stretch its legs—the tart apple perfume, which seems to be the common thread among the Gourmels, gracefully emerges after 20 minutes of aeration— most consumers understandably would not want to wait that long; the most traditional of the four in terms of bearing, this fine Fins Bois offers deep flavors of toasty oak, vanilla extract, smoke, honey wheat, and toffee—indeed these notable flavor characteristics flex their muscles from palate entry

through to the luxurious and extended finish; while it's very nice and un-
failingly correct, I didn't find it as fresh and atypical as the "des Fleurs,"
which simply spoiled me rotten.

RATING ★ ★ ★   ***Recommended*** $$$

LEOPOLD GOURMEL L'Age des Epices Fins Bois Cognac 43% Alcohol

Considerably darker than the wheat-colored "du Fruit," this Fins Bois
is a light-to-medium gold/amber color; the sweetish nose possesses pro-
nounced fruit, especially ripe red apples and red plums in an attractive and
somewhat stylish bouquet; it carries much more flavor impact and profun-
dity than the limp "du Fruit" on the palate as straightforward and un-
abashedly sweet flavors of pineapple, vanilla biscuits, and coffee with milk
entertain the taste buds; the slight wave of heat detected at palate entry went
as quickly as it came, then reemerged at midpalate; the finish is long, but
very soft and even comforting; nowhere near as impressive as the superla-
tive "des Fleurs" but an altogether mannered cognac of modest but honest
proportions.

RATING ★ ★ $$$

LEOPOLD GOURMEL L'Age du Fruit Fins Bois Cognac 41% Alcohol

Gold/hay/autumnal hue; the vivacious, intensely grapy, and piquant nose
pricks the nose cavity sensors with an herbal/earthy quality that's different
and mildly pleasant—the third pass finds a mild chocolate/orange scent;
very grapy on the tongue at first, then comes a burst of unwelcome heat—
the alcoholic burn fades into a rather one-dimensional sweet flavor of grape
spirit, which is nice, but simple and totally unremarkable; this is by no
means a cognac to ponder with friends; I can see mixing applications that
would apply to many VS-level cognacs, but it's a subpar effort.

RATING ★ $$$

LEYRAT Napoleon Cognac 42% Alcohol

Gold/honey color; it possesses a mildly pleasant nose of bridled spirit,
semisweetness, and grapiness—it's the first Leyrat that actually resembles
cognac in terms of smell; it displays some mild gusto in the creamy flavor,
which goes slightly hot in the chocolatey aftertaste; this Napoleon is an ap-
preciable improvement over the disastrous Fine and VSOP, but inexplica-
bly it still has to fight for mediocrity; the entire line was retasted for *Kin-
dred Spirits,* with this cognac receiving an upgrade.

RATING ★ ★ $$

LEYRAT Fine Cognac 40% Alcohol

Very light gold/hay/flaxen color; terribly sedated, almost cereal-like nose
that projects next to nothing even after 30 minutes of aeration and repeated
swirling—delicate is one thing, stingy is another—finally, after three-quarters
of an hour, did a slight, semisweet aroma of paraffin emerge—what an or-
deal for just a fleeting scent of beeswax; it comes across nicely on the palate
entry, then rashly turns fierce at the back of the tongue as the spirit burns

the taste buds in an unfortunate display of heat and industrial-strength astringency; one of the least attractive cognac experiences I've had; avoid.

RATING ★ $$

LEYRAT VSOP Cognac 40% Alcohol

Medium gold color; the subdued nose gives off a tad more aroma than the inept and irretrievably awkward Fine Cognac—nevertheless, this aroma is still way too remote to bother with; acceptable on the palate, but still light years away from being pleasurable or compelling—a neutral-tasting, completely lackluster cognac whose lone charm is its finish, which is nice but hardly enough to salvage the inferior, insipid nose and taste; evaluating cognac is normally a fun and enriching activity—this bottom-feeding loser makes it tedious.

RATING ★ $$

LEYRAT Brut Absolu Cognac 44% Alcohol

Gold/honey color; the Leyrat sports a pleasing nose that is anything but offensive, but neither is it inspiring—it's mildly toasty, showing roasted nuts and a zesty push of manageable spirit, but second rate and lackluster on the whole; on the palate, this limp cognac shows decent balance and some alluring rancio creaminess on the tongue, then it rapidly fades in a measured, meek fashion in the humble finish; middle-of-the-road quality at best—timidity disguised as delicacy; don't be fooled.

RATING ★ $$

LEYRAT Brut de Futs Cognac 45% Alcohol

The darkest of the Leyrats—a medium honey/orange hue; Futs offers a more generous bouquet than its four siblings, as tropical fruit aromas come forth in an elegant manner; regrettably, the slack, astringent flavors don't fulfill the promise found in the nose; the aftertaste is wan and quick; the only recommendation I can offer is to the producer: Return to the drawing board after a serious study of the cognacs made by Delamain, Pierre Ferrand, Daniel Bouju, A. E. Dor, or A. de Fussigny; until then, these unforgivably limp, characterless cognacs that I recall being palatable 15 years ago are, today, an abomination.

RATING ★ $$$

LOUIS ROYER VSOP Cognac 40% Alcohol

Medium amber color; this VSOP has one of the oddest cognac bouquets I've encountered—it's almost more akin to a cordial in its herbaceously sweet demeanor—awkward truckloads of evergreen, cedar; the taste seems disembodied from the nose as overly sweet, caramelly, and unctuous flavors bludgeon the taste buds to death with bags of sugar; hardly what I'd call elegant or harmonious; it's too obvious, too "cognac by the numbers," and worst, too much of all the wrong things; one of the least attractive cognacs available.

RATING ★ $$

LOUIS ROYER XO Cognac 40% Alcohol

Deep amber color, with gold edges—pretty appearance; the nose to some people, I'm sure, could be identified as being "rich," while I find it clunky, heavy-handed, and too overtly reminiscent of caramel for my comfort level— I know that many cognac producers do add a minute amount of caramel for coloring, which is perfectly legal and totally nontoxic, but this syrupy cognac raises my suspicion; the pace picks up in a positive way in the mouth as broad-shouldered tastes of prunes, dark toffee, and old oak race to the rescue of the less-than-balanced nose; streamline the obese aroma and you may have something here; as it is, forget it.

RATING ★ $$$

MARCEL RAGNAUD

The cognacs of the Ragnaud-Sabourin house are labeled under the name Marcel Ragnaud in honor of the second-generation director of this small-production, high-quality producer. The soul of any cognac lies in the vineyard district that is predominant in the blend, and in this case, the soul is very rich indeed. Annie and Paul Sabourin, who now operate the estate, tend 50 hectares of vines located within the premium district of Grande Champagne. All Marcel Ragnaud cognacs are born in this single vineyard, assuring an intensity and grace that are utterly charming. (To avoid confusion when requesting these cognacs at your local spirit merchant, be aware that there is another Ragnaud label, Raymond Ragnaud. The family split decades ago, and one has no bearing on the other, except in name.)

MARCEL RAGNAUD Grande Réserve Fontvieille Cognac Grande Champagne 43% Alcohol

Deepest color of the entire Ragnaud line—it owns a topaz/dark-honey hue that's stately—some miniscule suspended particles; the rich, ripe apricot bouquet is inviting and warm, with just the slightest kick of spirit; "opulent" isn't quite strong enough a term to adequately describe the sinewy, sexy feel of this awesome brandy; the prominent sweet flavors on palate from entry to aftertaste are juniper, licorice, oloroso sherry, ripe grapes, and mint; it's totally different, much deeper, and older than its three siblings; it ends in a high-flying surge of mint and evergreen—its whistle-clean flavor reminds me of a Christmas tree odor; an unconventional, daring and utterly delicious Grande Champagne of the first rank; a bold, assertive cognac with lots to say.

RATING ★ ★ ★ ★   *Highly Recommended* $$$

MARCEL RAGNAUD VSEP Cognac Grande Champagne 41% Alcohol

Slightly deeper amber hue than the VE—this one has more of an orange tinge to it—also has a minor case of suspended particles; the low-key nose is quite spirity—so spirity in fact that initially it's difficult to get past the alcohol, then with aeration a rounded, toasty, biscuity quality emerges; it's remarkably sumptuous and plump on the tongue, loaded with unabashedly sweet, ripe-grape, coffee, and milk chocolate flavors; it finishes with pronounced pineapple and guava flavors that charmed me; not a chewy, husky blockbuster that has you pounding the table, but it nonetheless is a sassy, well-endowed cognac that's long on finesse.

RATING ★ ★ ★   ***Recommended*** $ $

MARCEL RAGNAUD Réserve Spéciale Cognac Grande Champagne 43% Alcohol

Clear, clean, no particles—gorgeous honey/amber color, with a gold/green rim; it's notably more generous in the nose than either the VE or VSEP—the aromas impart focused, but well-mannered off-dry scents of (curiously) maltiness, rice, and cereal, especially oats; the compelling laser-beam-like flavors of mandarin orange and pink grapefruit are kissed with a subtle touch of oak—this is a real mouthful that demands some attention; in the aftertaste the aggressiveness wanes as the flavor becomes sweet and raisiny in the throat—the tail of the finish seems almost timid after the pedal-to-the-metal assertiveness of the midpalate; Réserve Spéciale is a different, atypical animal altogether, right from the unique grain-like aroma—it might not turn everyone on who likes their Grande Champagne cognacs according to the prescribed formula, but I enjoyed and appreciated it.

RATING ★ ★ ★   ***Recommended*** $ $

MARCEL RAGNAUD VE Cognac Grande Champagne 41% Alcohol

Lovely amber color, with lemon yellow edges—I noticed some minute suspended particles from both sample bottles—problematic? I think not, but in appearance-influenced America it might cause some concern; the feinty, lightweight, citrusy, saddle-leather bouquet is too timorous for its own good; concentrated, heavily smoked flavors explode on the tongue like a racehorse leaping from the gate, then it turns mildly chocolatey and subdued on the tongue and sides of the mouth; it ends as quietly as the nose began, with soft, orangey, ripe-apple flavors; the sensory qualities run the gamut of being gentle one moment, feral the next—it's too uneven to be recommended.

RATING ★ ★ $ $

MARNIER VSOP Cognac Fine Champagne 40% Alcohol

Medium-deep amber/honey color, with orange highlights; offers up a decidedly fruity, direct, assertive bouquet of orange rind, licorice, cardamom—it's an astringent nose to which I didn't take; on palate, it's medium-weighted, but quite viscous—baked flavors of sweet oak, grapes, and pine dominate the palate from entry through to the fat, long aftertaste; I wanted to like it more than I did and almost ended up recommending it, but the over-the-top baked-pear quality was too effusive, therefore leaving no room for any other taste to emerge; middle-of-the-road.

RATING ★ ★ $ $

MARTELL

When one travels the world, one of the cognacs that seems to be everywhere from Singapore to London to Chicago to Buenos Aires is Martell Cordon Bleu. Luscious, ultrapremium Cordon Bleu, which was created in 1912, is one of cognac's most trusted and respected ambassadors. The history of Martell begins in 1715, when it was founded by Jean Martell of Jersey, making it the oldest of the Big Four cognac producers—Hennessy, Martell, Rémy Martin, and Courvoisier. By 1720, Jean Martell quite astoundingly was shipping 40,000 barrels annually through the ports of London, Liverpool, and Hamburg. After Jean's demise in 1753, his sons and widow took up the banner and led the company to further achievements. Today, the eighth generation of Martells operates the business, though the company itself was bought outright by Seagram in 1988.

One of the features that makes Martell unique among the major producers is its commitment to the brandies born in the Borderies, the smallest of the six Cognac districts. Martell receives over 60% of the annual total production from the Borderies area. Martell's Directeur Général, Jack Drounau, told me on my last visit that Martell prefers the Borderies eaux-de-vie because they are "nutty, sweet, and racy, with just a faint hint of violet scent." While Martell uses eaux-de-vie from the top four districts— Grande Champagne, Petite Champagne, Fins Bois, and the Borderies—the Martell style, he said, is defined the most by the Borderies floral, nutty virtues. Martell is the region's biggest landowner, controlling over 650 acres of vineyard. Production volume is so immense, however, that additionally Martell has contracts with 2,800 growers and distillers in the Cognac region, who supply 97% of the eaux-de-vie needed for yearly production. Martell operates three distilleries and controls more than ten others.

The company also owns its own cooperage. Only oak from the Tronçais forest is used, because it is tightly grained and imparts less tannins than other types of oak. In its huge inventory, Martell maintains a stock of more than 100 million bottles. All in all, I think the Martell cognacs are as good as any of the Big Four offerings. The feline, floral quality of each of their cognacs is absolutely captivating.

MARTELL XO Cordon Suprème Cognac 40% Alcohol

Attractive russet/amber color; similar in bearing to the friskier Cordon Bleu, but the XO pulls rank with its obvious maturity and grace—it emits very ripe, melony scents which are cushiony and voluptuous—this is a downright decadent bouquet; this beguiling blend of mature cognacs is a luscious example of how great the Borderies eaux-de-vie can be and proves that not all of cognac's heavy-hitters are the domain of the two Champagnes, though this beauty does include some Petite Champagne and Grande Champagne from Martell-owned estates; the fruit concentration is so perfectly balanced by a resiny, cheesy oakiness that you almost begin applauding with delight and affirmation; the aftertaste is stately and woody, indeed almost chunky in its final stages; I loved the touch of rancio in the aftertaste; this classic is an absolute must for any cognac lover; upgraded upon being recently reevaluated.

RATING ★ ★ ★ ★ ★   *Highest Recommendation* $$$

MARTELL Cordon Bleu Cognac 40% Alcohol

The deepest orange/ocher/amber hue of the five Martells and the only one that displayed cherry-red, burnished highlights when held up to the light—no question in my mind that this is one of the sexiest-looking cognacs of all; the nose is three or four levels deeper than the VSOP in terms of complexity and finesse, offering a semisweet perfume that features cantaloupe and honeydew melon in generous proportions—a first-rate bouquet that simply doesn't quit charming the bejesus out of you; right from its full-bodied entry onto the tongue, you know that this supple beauty is something very special—the firm, satiny, coffee, black-cherry, macadamia-nut flavors regale the taste buds to a round, thrilling flavor experience; the black-cherry taste dominates the sensuous, extended finish, backed by a luscious smokiness that's the icing on the cake; a superb cognac; aged 20–24 years.

RATING ★ ★ ★ ★   *Highly Recommended* $$$

MARTELL Extra Cognac 43% Alcohol

Closest in appearance to the fetching Cordon Bleu, but marginally less red, leaning more toward vermilion/orange; I think it has the loveliest, most elegant nose of the Martell quintet as rich, vibrant, and piquant scents of grapes and Brazil nuts are buttressed by subtler fragrances of cream and toffee; the 3% higher alcohol is barely noticeable so well crafted is it; chewy, slightly fiery, spicy flavors of vanilla, tapioca, and toffee disarm the taste buds; the aftertaste is dry to off-dry, candied, and very oaky; while not as luxurious in my opinion as the heavenly XO, it carries itself with great finesse and confidence; the perfume alone is worth the experience; it comes from the Martell "Paradis."

RATING ★ ★ ★ ★   *Highly Recommended* $$$

MARTELL VS Cognac 40% Alcohol

Very pretty ocher/amber color; the soft, grassy open-meadow aroma is easy, intensely floral but not directed or focused—pleasant but hardly ponderous as one would expect at this fundamental level; what it lacks in the blurred bouquet it more than makes up for in the tropical-fruit/banana taste that really impressed my palate—the flavor factor explodes on the tongue; the aftertaste is surprisingly long, but lean, as the full, mango/passion fruit/pineapple complement gives way eventually, almost begrudgingly, to a white-grape flavor at the tail end of the finish; doubtless the premier VS of the Big Four; aged five years.

RATING ★ ★ ★   *Recommended* $$

MARTELL VSOP Medaillon Cognac 40% Alcohol

Curiously, this cognac owns a slightly deeper amber color than either the much older XO or the Extra; the nose of the VSOP is more pointed than the marshmallowy VS—it offers an appealing, highly fruited array of scents including kiwi, lemon/lime, and nectarine, all supported by a lovely freshly cracked walnut backbone fragrance that's delightful; medium-bodied, silky texture; the charm of the nose gets betrayed by the austere, dry to off-dry, almost butterscotch-like flavor, which, while good and correct, doesn't inspire; I felt that this VSOP was too hard, almost brittle in its narrow flavor capacity; ditto, the finish; reach for the better-priced VS; aged ten years.

RATING ★ ★ $$

NICOLAS NAPOLEON VSOP Cognac 40% Alcohol

Like the attractive VS, the color is a high point—a rich amber/orange; the nose is all citrus—primarily tangerines and, all things considered, is not bad—there's even a backnote of pipe smoke; on the tongue, admittedly, it's quite sweet, but at least it's not cloying; the smoke steps in again as does some sweet oak—actually the sweetness does begin to wear the palate down as you get around to the finish; I've sampled worse and clumsier VSOPs than this one, but it's still miles from being recommendable.

RATING ★ ★ $$

NICOLAS NAPOLEON VS Cognac 40% Alcohol

Burnished, medium-deep amber/vermilion/orange hue—very pretty; the in-your-face bouquet touts a full-throttle resiny quality that's too synthetic and medicinal for my nose—it looks much sexier than it smells; in the mouth, this frightfully feeble, mouthwash-like cognac never gets off the ground—it's too everything in all the wrong things from entry through to the aftertaste—too oaky, too raw, and too candied; there's not the least hint of subtlety, finesse, or flavor development; not even a decent blue-light special; looks impressive, but once you open the bottle it's all downhill; good night, Irene.

RATING ★ $$

PIERRE CROIZET XO Cognac 40% Alcohol

Darkest orange/tangerine color of the three Croizets, but still by no means can it be termed dark in context to the category; the fruity, citrusy, tart nose needs some coaxing and patience before a final determination can be rendered—at last after 25 minutes in the glass it offers some rich wood/vanilla aromas; one of the more interesting herbal/mint tastes in the XO category—this is one luscious, toasty, almost yeasty/doughy XO that's kissed with underlying flavors of clover honey, mandarin orange, cake batter, and cocoa; the aftertaste is smoky, lush, orangey, and simply scrumptious; reflecting the house style, it's hardly a muscular, hearty, or fathomless XO, but it charms the drinker's socks off all the same.

RATING ★ ★ ★ ★   *Highly Recommended* $$$

PIERRE CROIZET Napoleon Cognac 40% Alcohol

Barely darker version of the VSOP—an orange/amber hue; this nose resembles that of the VSOP, pointing to the suave house style of Croizet, but it is more tart and citrusy, with a more apparent wood element; it feels good on the palate as a mild, mid-May warmth surrounds the taste buds; the flavor expectedly owns more maturity, more character than the VSOP, as two distinct taste levels entertain the palate—the dominant layer evokes tart green apple, while the secondary layer is an understated rancio/cheesiness that's the more beguiling factor of the two; it finishes very full and endowed, yet graceful; a well-crafted, velvet-glove-type of cognac whose best virtue is its understatement.

RATING ★ ★ ★   *Recommended* $$$

Pierre Croizet VSOP Cognac 40% Alcohol

Attractive, relatively pale orange/amber color; the delicate but stately bouquet of chocolate, unsweetened coconut, pears, and grapes begins in low gear and only shifts into second after a good 10–15 minutes in the sampling glass—a very appetizing nose indeed, but it's necessary to stick with it—one's patience is eventually rewarded; it tastes better on the second pass than the first—offers minor bite on the tongue, nothing serious—the sweet flavor consists mainly of milk chocolate and pears, with scant evidence of wood or vanilla (from wood); the aftertaste is correct; a simple, uncomplicated, unastonishing VSOP that provides a mildly pleasant, middle-of-the-road cognac experience.

RATING ★ ★ $$

PIERRE FERRAND

I was fortunate to have met with Pierre Ferrand in Segonzac the year before he retired in 1992, when investors Alexandre Gabriel and Jean Dominique Andreu obtained 80% of the interest in Cognac Ferrand (Monsieur Ferrand retains 20%). His energy and enthusiasm astonished me. The 75 acres of vineyards that supply the grapes for this small operation lie entirely within the elite Grande Champagne district. Cognac Ferrand produces a scant 8,000 cases a year, for the clearly defined mission of first Ferrand and now Gabriel and Andreu is not to mass-produce their cognacs. Rather, Cognac Ferrand creates cognacs that directly and eloquently address their Grande Champagne vineyards of *ugni blanc* grapes, without adding caramel or *boise*. As is the case with many of the smaller producers, the team at Cognac Ferrand goes far beyond the legal minimum aging requirements and makes its blends from decades-old cognacs. For example, Ferrand's youngest blend, Réserve de la Propriété, spends 15 to 25 years in cask before it is drawn off. The Sélection des Anges is made from cognacs that have been matured in cask from 25 to 35 years. And the unbelievably sexy Ancestrale comes mostly from cognacs produced from the 1923 harvest, which also happened to be Pierre Ferrand's father's first harvest. If someone held a gun to my head and demanded to know which cognac producer I thought was the best, I would tell them Ferrand.

Pierre Ferrand Réserve Ancestrale Cognac Grande Champagne 40% Alcohol

Sports a dazzling hot-pekoe-tea/brownish color that's absolutely pure; initially, the nose is temptingly coy, easily the subtlest of the Ferrands, but by the second pass that coyness erupts into a seriously potent bouquet that's a brandy aficionado's royal banquet of fruit, oak, and spice—doubtless one of Cognac's premier fragrances; on palate, piquant flavors of black pepper, dark caramel, cocoa, and strong black coffee take turns dominating the taste buds; the superbly satisfying aftertaste begins with a melange of spicy, nutty, and citrusy flavors, then settles down to an irresistible flavor of orange/chocolate; the fruit/alcohol/wood balance astounded me; clearly, the maturity of this exceptional cognac serves it and the drinker well; an extraordinary distilled-spirit experience; one that should not be missed; a scant 200 bottles are released yearly; do what you have to do to acquire one . . . including mayhem and murder.

RATING ★ ★ ★ ★ ★ **Highest Recommendation** $$$

PIERRE FERRAND Abel Cognac Grande Champagne 40% Alcohol

Pretty amber color, highlighted with russet/copper flecks, immaculate clarity; the sweet oak/vanilla aroma is just the start of the toasty, gentlemanly nose—what follows in polite but firm waves includes coconut, butter-cream candy, raisins, and that most fascinating and elusive of Grand Champagne cognac virtues, rancio—rancio is the creamy, cheese-like fragrance that is one of the most seductive aromas in all distilled spirits; the biscuity, lush, decadent flavor is so remarkably sensuous that it's almost gleefully sinful; this sinewy cat of a cognac finishes serenely, laced with subtle coffee-bean and spearmint flavors that go on and on at the back of the throat; easily one of the top ten cognacs that I've sampled; in one word—magnificent.

RATING ★ ★ ★ ★ ★ **Highest Recommendation** $$$

PIERRE FERRAND Réserve de la Propriété Cognac Grande Champagne 40% Alcohol

The tawny/amber color has golden core highlights, excellent purity; the sweeping nose is abundant, dry, but ambrosial—it's a plentiful, layered bouquet of ripe tropical fruit, sour hard candy, and roasted almonds—the final nosing was every bit as inviting and open as the first; medium-weighted and velvety; in the mouth, the totally gorgeous, vigorous, vital, broad grapy flavors mingle easily with citrus and wood notes; the mild heat noted in the middle aftertaste fades into a lovely orangey finish that gently but confidently lingers; one of the more multilayered finishes in the cognac category.

RATING ★ ★ ★ ★ **Highly Recommended** $$$

PIERRE FERRAND Sélection des Anges Cognac Grande Champagne 40% Alcohol

Medium amber/light brown color, superb clarity; the lusciously sweet, full-throttle, and outright aggressive nose spotlights aromas of roasted almonds, burnt toast, vanilla extract, and pine/resin—the third pass is the most boisterous and hearty—then it settles down with 20 minutes of aeration; it owns a broad-shouldered, husky texture; in the mouth, the power-packed, vanilla, creamy, mouthwatering flavors seize the taste buds—a laser-beam-like caramel flavor dominates between midpalate and the succulent finish; the curiously delicious, tart apple finish grows in mandarin orange/apple intensity and then ends incredibly smooth in an almost stately manner; what it doesn't possess in vigor, it has in round, focused, gentlemanly elegance; the finish is first rate and alone worth the price of the bottle.

RATING ★ ★ ★ ★   *Highly Recommended* $$$

REMY MARTIN

Rémy Martin has been one of this century's most extraordinary cognac success stories. Founded in 1724, the firm of Rémy Martin languished for 200 years as a second- or third-tier cognac producer until the dynamic André Renaud took command in 1924. The firm's previous owners never had direct access to old stocks and the best vineyards, which are the heart and soul of cognac quality. André Renaud's marriage to a member of the Frapin family, whose cache of old cognacs and vineyards in the prime Grande Champagne and Petite Champagne districts was among the finest of the period, began the modern era for Rémy Martin. Today, the company proudly emphasizes the fact that even their basic cognac, the Rémy Martin VS, is a Fine Champagne, meaning that it's a blend of the eaux-de-vie from the Champagnes, including by law at least 50% from Grande Champagne.

Yet, Renaud's stroke of genius proved to be more a marketing posture than a production decision. Realizing the potential of exporting cognac to the Far East, mainly Japan and China, Renaud hired a gentleman named Otto Quien, whose eventual accomplishments in salesmanship would place Rémy Martin in the same league as Courvoisier, Hennessy, and Martell, which controlled the majority of the cognac trade worldwide. Quien had the advantage of being very familiar with the Orient's penchant for quality and thus persuaded Renaud to allow him to push Rémy Martin's higher priced VSOP level of cognac. With the VSOP as its standard-bearer, Rémy Martin sales skyrocketed as Asians embraced this Fine Champagne cognac as their spirit of choice. As a result, to this day virtually all Rémy Martin stocks (96%) are sold outside of France, to over 160 countries.

In the 1990s influential and control-conscious Rémy Martin purchases eaux-de-vie from approximately 500 individual growers in addition to 20 distillers, who themselves buy from another 1,200 growers. Rémy Martin is also the owner of France's largest cooperage, Séguin-Moreau. The company was compelled to provide their own casks in order to guard against inferior barrels. They use Limousin oak, a practice that suits the stylistic philosophy of Rémy Martin, which leans more to freshness, approachability, and round, vanilla-like flavor rather than to extreme profundity, chewiness, or masses of depth.

REMY MARTIN XO Special Cognac Fine Champagne 40% Alcohol

Identical in appearance to the Napoleon—medium amber/pekoe tea/honey tone; a different, lustier animal, however, in the nose—the evidence of sweet old oak is much more prominent—further on down the line, this husky nose offers seductive biscuity aromas of cream, cake batter, and spice; a welcome, sensuous sweetness greets the palate and lingers all the way through the aftertaste—in the mouth it's as smooth as silk and multilayered—even flashes a glimpse of rancio in the finish; a well-endowed, chewy cognac of exceptional allure and richness; 80% Grande Champagne/20% Petite Champagne.

RATING ★ ★ ★ ★   ***Highly Recommended*** $$$

REMY MARTIN Extra Perfection Cognac Fine Champagne 40% Alcohol

The darkest of the Rémys—a dazzling medium amber, with brilliant orange/vermilion highlights; the toasty, creamy nose lazily wafts out of the sampling glass in luxurious waves of orange rind, coffee with cream, and candied nuts—it's a stunning, mature nose that gracefully balances potency and finesse; on palate, it's everything that one could ask for in an Extra—power, fathomless depth, oaky flavor, and a blockbuster finish that offers just the right amount of warmth and pizzaz; this is my favorite of the Rémys, mostly because of its vivacity and generosity; 90% Grande Champagne/10% Petite Champagne.

RATING ★ ★ ★ ★   ***Highly Recommended*** $$$

REMY MARTIN Louis XIII Cognac Grande Champagne 40% Alcohol

A slightly lighter amber/orange color than the Extra Perfection; Louis carries the classic and much coveted cheese-like quality, rancio, which is considered a hallmark virtue of outstanding Grande Champagne cognac—the sweet, oaky, mature aromas are totally harmonious, clearly having worked out all differences over the decades of aging; on palate, it's breathtakingly smooth, providing one of Cognac's most accessible top-shelf experiences; the aftertaste is so ethereal that it's like a ghost gliding through the night; there's no question that it's an absolutely luscious cognac, but I have to say that for overall satisfaction I preferred the Extra Perfection by the slimmest of margins; 100% Grande Champagne; the youngest cognac in this blend is 50 years old.

RATING ★ ★ ★ ★   ***Highly Recommended*** $$$

REMY MARTIN Napoleon Cognac Fine Champagne 40% Alcohol

Brilliant amber/orange blossom honey hue; the sweet, mellow nose is curiously reined-in at first, but is nevertheless very charming—as it aerates it emits more defined cocoa, coffee-bean, tropical-fruit, and butterscotch qualities; a quantum leap forward from the bargain basement VS and bland VSOP on the flavor and character scales, as delicious, beautifully balanced tastes of butter, toffee, and grapes gracefully come together into one flavor thrust that is genuinely lovely; soft, medium-long finish, touched with lanolin and sweet oak; composition breakdown—70% Grande Champagne/30% Petite Champagne grapes; this is more as it should be from such an esteemed producer.

RATING ★ ★ ★   ***Recommended*** $$$

REMY MARTIN VS Cognac Fine Champagne 40% Alcohol

Pale amber color; the zesty, spirity nose tweaks the olfactory sense, then sends off unattractive tart aromas of citrus and pineapple, all accentuated by a wispy hint of spice; on the palate, it is smooth, grapy, and slightly candied, but to my taste, surprisingly simplistic; the aftertaste throws moderate, barely acceptable heat in the throat; the only phase that I liked was the concentrated grapiness in the midpalate—other than that it's disappointingly ordinary, considering that it's a Fine Champagne.

RATING ★ $$

REMY MARTIN VSOP Cognac Fine Champagne 40% Alcohol

A marginally darker amber than the VS; it has a much rounder, more elegant nose than the feisty, astringent VS—this is a fresh, vegetal, vinous, nicely structured bouquet of bread dough, salad greens, and black pepper; no fire to address on the palate—it's so mellow at palate entry that it comes off as being dull and blunted—the limp, insipid flavor didn't at all fulfill the promise found in the expansive and inviting nose; the aftertaste is short, with a nip of heat; an undemanding beginner cognac, but not without its flaws; skip this and proceed directly to the VS of Martell.

RATING ★ $$

SALIGNAC

The firm of Cognac Salignac has a history that dates back to the beginning of the nineteenth century. Founded in 1802 by Antoine de Salignac, the company's ownership stayed within the family for over a century and a half before being assumed by Hiram Walker Gooderham & Worts in 1974. Then, 13 years later, Allied Lyons, the British conglomerate that devoured Hiram Walker, took the helm. The house style of Salignac accentuates delicacy and approachability rather than strength and fathomless depth. Clearly, the formula works. One of the recipe secrets that sets Salignac apart from virtually all of the other established houses of Jarnac and Cognac is that the Master Blender combines the eaux-de-vie prior to barrel aging. The reasoning behind the company's early blending procedure is to maintain a light, clean touch. Heavy, oaky, power-laden cognacs are not in line with the Salignac philosophy.

SALIGNAC Réserve Cognac Fine Champagne 43% Alcohol

By far the most attractive appearance of the Salignac line—a lustrous and opulent honey color; on the nose, it's seductively semisweet and properly concentrated, offering generous scents of oak, honey, lees, and leather; on palate, succulent chocolate and coffee-bean flavors are bolstered by a rich, velvety texture that envelops the palate; it finishes in a grand manner, with just a flash of heat in the tail; it's not stylish, but it is most certainly sound, balanced, and meaty; a bona fide mouthful of luscious old cognac.

RATING ★ ★ ★ ★   *Highly Recommended* $$$

SALIGNAC XO Cognac 40% Alcohol

The color is amber/cola-brown; the developed, melded, mature, very pleasant and welcoming aromas of smoke, old oak, and paraffin, with barely discernable hints of ripe grapes and rancio mildly impressed me; in the mouth, it's round, fat, sugarcane sweet, friendly, and delicious—on palate, the vanilla extract flavor rules the roost; the fatness continues in the extended, charming aftertaste; not a great XO by any stretch, but nevertheless its comfortable demeanor is like a favorite old jacket right from the start.

RATING ★ ★ ★   ***Recommended*** $$$

SALIGNAC VS Cognac 40% Alcohol

Bright, light orange/amber color; this VS starts with an engagingly fruity, citrusy and smoky, though not very deep, nose that shows just the slightest spirity twang to it; the appealing sweetness at palate entry flows through all the way to the mildly candied and simplistic aftertaste; no rocket scientist cognac here, but an easy, barely approachable mixer VS.

RATING ★ $

SALIGNAC VSOP Cognac 40% Alcohol

Marginally deeper orange/amber color than the VS; it offers more kick, more sass in the bouquet as assertive, no, amend that to aggressive, waves of alcohol, pine needle, and ethyl acetate (nail polish) pinch the olfactory sense—get my nose out of here; the combativeness of the nose tones down in the flavor, as this VSOP goes too sweet on the palate; regrettably, it has an astringent, harsh, and fleet out-the-door finish that does nothing to enhance or frame the nose or the taste; I actually thought the VS displayed more grip and more overall drinking gratification; basic, bare-bones cognac; steer clear.

RATING ★ $$

SALIGNAC Napoleon Cognac 40% Alcohol

Standard-issue amber color; the sedate, mature, moderately sweet nose comes at you with layers of oak, tobacco, and toffee; it exhibits a nice, if unrefined, presence in the mouth, where the headlining flavor is bittersweet cocoa from beginning to end—not much room is left for any other flavor element; it finishes inoffensively but, again, it invests its entire wad in a one-dimensional flavor that's more like a Solera Reserva Brandy de Jérez than a cognac; this one mystified me, as it doesn't drink at all like a cognac; with serious reservations I liked it, but not for the reasons that I normally like cognac.

RATING ★ $$

STAUB Napoleon Cognac 40% Alcohol

Beautiful, opulent, russet/copper/amber color; the nose is slightly burnt, grapy, and raisiny, but shows ample acidity so as not to let the fruit intensity go all sappy sweet; this Napoleon, while certainly not in the league of those from A. Hardy, Rémy Martin, Courvoisier, or Pierre Croizet, possesses a simple, rudimentary charm—it actually shows more character as it aerates; the taste offers a mildly pleasant cheesiness and an oaky twang that make it better than the other Staubs, but clearly this is not a cognac to be recommended.

RATING ★ ★ $$$

Staub VS Cognac 40% Alcohol

Light-to-medium amber/orange color; I can't say that the astringent aroma thrills the cockles of my taste buds—it's almost seed-like and pomace-like in its bearing; this hapless, lower-echelon VS has only a marginally better presence on the palate than the flat Nicolas Napoleon—a rudimentary cognac that's more akin to brandies from California than from the Cognac region of France, at least the Cognac region that I'm aware of—the flavor is modestly grapy and round, but the harsh, heavily candied aftertaste is too manufactured for my taste; could possibly be utilized as a mixer like a lesser Brandy de Jérez or a California brandy, but the problem is that it bears a cognac price tag, whereas a decent mixing brandy from California costs half as much.

RATING ★ $$

Staub VSOP Cognac 40% Alcohol

Lightish gold/honey/amber color; workman, blue-collar cognac nose that spotlights a raisiny sweetness and that's about all the way too one-dimensional in its aromatic scope—there's absolutely no sense of layering or complexity; in the mouth, it's as sweet as Pepsi and, indeed, comes off rather strikingly as a soda pop or a grape drink; anyone that would plunk down their cash for this brandy would have to be labeled a victim when there are other brandies available for half the price that don't carry the word "Cognac" on the label; no excuses—this simply doesn't cut it as a VSOP cognac, period.

RATING ★ $$

ARMAGNAC—FRANCE

What a feisty Jack Russell is to a huge, unconcerned Saint Bernard, armagnac is to cognac in terms of size and demeanor. The Armagnaçais are forever looking to outmaneuver their intramural rivals, the Cognaçais, but often to little avail. The Armagnaçais stress their vintage brandies; the Cognaçais counter by saying, with full justification, that in the case of distilled spirits, vintages are virtually meaningless. The Armagnaçais claim that single distillation in continuous stills lends more body and grip to brandy; the Cognaçais point out that their traditional double-distillation approach in small copper alembics (pot stills) makes for greater refinement and flavor focus. The Armagnaçais age their brandies in black oak from the Monlezun forest; the Cognaçais utilize the white oak from Limousin and Tronçais.

The bald fact is that cognac is simply too well established throughout the entire world to be derailed by the modest likes of armagnac, which is produced in only a tenth of the volume that cognac is. For every 100 bottles of cognac sold around the world, only 6 bottles of armagnac are sold. The term *cognac* is the most recognized French word around spaceship Earth.

Yet to its credit, Armagnac is but one of three officially demarcated brandy regions in Europe, along with Cognac and Jérez in Andalusia, Spain. To the surprise of many people, records show that brandy was being made in Armagnac at least two full centuries before the Cognaçais lighted the fires beneath their first pot stills. Of late, the U.S. market has been taking a longer, more studious look at these earthy brandies from the *département* of Gers in the southwest corner of France. While it will never altogether replace cognac in the hearts or liquor cabinets of brandy lovers, armagnac is nevertheless steadily claiming a wider audience as drinkers from Tokyo to London to Chicago search for new and exciting distilled-spirit experiences.

There are by my count about eight to ten armagnac producers and *négociants,* including Sempé, Larressingle, de Montal, Cerbois, B. Gelas, Samalens, Darroze, Laberdolive, Marquis de Caussade, and Janneau, who really stand out from the pack, producing world-class brandies that on their own merits can compete with any spirits, be they brandies or whiskies.

Legend has it that France's King Henry IV (1553–1610) had armagnac and garlic placed on his lips by his grandfather on the day he was born. He is said to have drawn "wisdom and strength for his whole life" from that experience. Indeed, after professionally tasting armagnacs for several years now, my hat is off to any infant who is able to withstand a jolt of armagnac right after the opening kickoff.

Armagnac's brandy is made in a warm, sunny region that lies about 100 miles south of Bordeaux and 40 west of Toulouse. The region, famed for the Musketeers and foie gras, is divided into three districts, in which a total of 40,000 acres are planted in vines: Bas Armagnac, Tenareze, and Haut Armagnac. Though *bas* means "lower" in French, it is the heady brandies of Bas Armagnac that are the best of the region. Not only is the volume produced less in Tenareze and Haut Armagnac, but so is the quality of armagnac compared to that of Bas Armagnac. The grape varieties that grow well in the region's fine sand and clay soil are *ugni blanc, colombard, folle blanche, jurançon,* and *picquepoul.*

Armagnac is traditionally distilled only once at low temperatures to maintain as much of the fruit character as possible. Whereas cognacs are double-distilled to achieve elegance and balance, armagnac's single distillation assures the drinker that they are enjoying the heartiest, most flavorful of French brandies.

The board that regulates production and aging requirements for armagnac, Bureau National Interprofessionnel de l'Armagnac, recently declared new maturation minimums for each of the designations of Gascony's brandy. Though these revised BNIA regulations lengthen the legal maturation periods, most of armagnac's brandy producers age their armagnacs longer than what the law states anyway. Nevertheless, the BNIA statute is welcomed by producer, importer, and consumer alike.

THE BNIA AGING REQUIREMENTS FOR ARMAGNAC

Category	Legal Aging Minimum	Actual Aging in Most Cases
VS	3 years	3–7 years
VO, VSOP, or Réserve ADC	5 years	5–15 years
Extra, XO, Napoleon, Vieille Réserve	6 years	6–40 years
Hors d'Age	10 years	10–50 years

B. Gelas 12-Year-Old Bas Armagnac 40% Alcohol

Medium-amber/dark-rum color; the sweet nose speaks of brown sugar, cookie batter, vanillin, sweet oak, and cocoa, but no fruit element whatsoever; the sweet, pruney flavor is countered by a pleasing citrus acidity that niftily completes the package; it owns a full-bodied, silky texture that supports the flavors ably; shows a glimpse of finesse; a solid, respectable, unassuming, and unpretentious armagnac.

RATING ★ ★ ★　　*Recommended*　　$$

Castarede VSOP Armagnac 40% Alcohol

Very pretty orange/russet/amber color, good purity; the nose is marked by a spicy, black-pepper note that dominates the bouquet even after 15 minutes of aeration—you'd expect a VSOP armagnac to offer more scope in the aroma than a mundane pepperiness—there's nary a trace of oak or fruit; the taste scores a few redemption points, however, as biscuity, plush, and sweetish flavors of oak, vanilla, and cheese almost rescue the unidimensional nose; the finish, while smooth, has a resiny, chemical taste that refuses to go away; poor nose, decent palate entry and midpalate, so-so finish, end of story; after evaluating it four times in the span of 60 minutes I felt comfortable rating it two stars.

RATING ★ ★　　$$

Cerbois 1985 Bas Armagnac 40% Alcohol

Medium amber, orange core highlights, a considerable amount of dark sediment settles in the well of the glass; the succulent aroma is laced with dark toffee, caramel, vanilla wafer, and spirity notes right from the starting gun—with aeration, a comely sour-fruit/raisiny echo emerges, which beautifully complements the candied surface smell; lively, spirity, smoldering flavors greet the palate—the midpalate is decidedly sweet, deeply fruity (raisins and plums), and toffee-like; the aftertaste offers a sensational candied-almond quality that tops off the experience with panache.

RATING ★ ★ ★ ★　　*Highly Recommended*　　$$

Cerbois 1962 Bas Armagnac 40% Alcohol

Medium-to-dark amber/black pekoe tea, lots of dark sediment floating about; this bouquet is mature and almost, but not quite, biscuity in the first go-round—with aeration, the vanilla/biscuity note opens shop in the second pass, developing into a dark toffee, maple, bacon-fat-like presence in the third nosing—ditto in the last pass; delicious, user-friendly, and bosomy at palate entry—the flavors range from walnuts to maple to candied almonds—there's some grapy fruit, but it plays a minor role compared to the honey/maple and candied nuts; the aftertaste is supple, endowed, and creamy; mature, mellow, and simply savory.

RATING ★ ★ ★ ★　　*Highly Recommended*　　$$$

Cerbois 1955 Bas Armagnac 40% Alcohol

Pretty, mature, deep amber/honey, orange pekoe tea tone, with orange core features, lots of sediment; the nose is astoundingly lively, considering that it's over four decades old—in the second pass, it expands into harmonious aromas of wood, rancio, spice, leather, and spirit—very little fruit to be found in this zesty bouquet—the last pass fails to unveil anything further; right from palate entry, I found this old thoroughbred to be luscious, sweet, candied, and only a bit oaky, to my surprise—the flavor focus is firmly on the brown sugar and honey notes; the finish is luxurious and long, highlighting the sweet oak; a highly attractive old-timer with plenty of pleasure yet to give.

RATING ★ ★ ★ ★   *Highly Recommended* $$$

Cerbois 1967 Bas Armagnac 40% Alcohol

Medium amber, rusty orange core highlights, minor sediment; the wood element in the nose dominates the first two nosings—in the third pass, I detect some butter and almonds—the last pass brings all the components together in a sweet-oak, leathery final statement; on palate, the subtle sweetness seems like it's more from the oak than from the fruit, which has almost disappeared completely by midpalate; the finish is pleasantly sweet, almost like brown sugar, and quite easy; it ends up being a viscous, husky armagnac with a supple woodiness, which dominates the entire mouth experience.

RATING ★ ★ ★   *Recommended* $$$

Cerbois 1965 Bas Armagnac 40% Alcohol

Medium amber/honey, vermilion core features, minor dark sediment; the nose is vibrant, heady, and notably nutty—in the second and third passes, a snappy, zesty, dry, nutty, nail-polish-remover-like quality emerges, then recedes—the final nosing is a chemical, medicinal mess; much better in the mouth than in the nose, this sweet, lip-smacking brandy is friendly at palate entry, then it turns sticky-sweet at midpalate; the finish is ripe, sweet, and long; this armagnac is all over the map, up, then down, in, then out—way too inconsistent and erratic for a recommendation.

RATING ★ ★ $$$

Cerbois 1974 Bas Armagnac 40% Alcohol

Medium amber, orange core features, pure; this nose is all oak resin out of the box—it doesn't develop much beyond that into the third pass—the final nosing hatches a very deep caramel-corn, almost oily, note that I liked; too lean, too understated, and too acidic in the mouth—I expected greater flavor impact and balance where, in fact, there was only resin—this armagnac needs more fruit to balance the oily, resiny, and acidic taste factors; drinkable, even average, a good nose, but wholly uninspiring on palate.

RATING ★ ★ $$$

Cerbois 1940 Bas Armagnac 40% Alcohol

Deep amber/nutbrown hue, tons of sediment chunks; the nose is shut down in the first pass—after considerable aeration time, the second pass doesn't open up that much save for a bit of cocoa and resiny oak—the third pass mirrors the second—the final nosing becomes a little questionable, since about all that's left aromatically is the stripped-down spirit; right from palate entry, it's obvious that this brandy has expired—it's far past its prime, in fact—no depth, no real character here, just flimsy echoes of past glory; it's drinkable, but with the lovely 1955 still showing so much vitality, don't bother with this ghost from the past.

RATING ★★ $$$

DE MONTAL Réserve Personnelle Armagnac 40% Alcohol

The deep-amber/iced-tea tone has great purity; the sweetish nose is ripe, buxom, and fathomless, as traces of fruit, fruit stone, old oak, rancio, chocolate-covered almonds, and pears produce one of the finest armagnac bouquets I've encountered—it owns that undefinable virtue that effortlessly incorporates maturity, underlying power, and finesse; on the tongue, this luxurious, full-bodied classic envelops the palate in a velvety robe of sweet, raisiny, caramel, and almost port-like flavors that are as dazzling and endowed as they are pointed and seamless; the finish offers a comforting, smoldering warmth and lasts an eternity; the most fulfilling armagnac experience on every sensory level that I've had.

RATING ★★★★★ *Highly Recommended* $$$

DE MONTAL 1965 Armagnac 40% Alcohol

Solid, medium amber/vermilion/rust color, pristine clarity; this nose is delightfully vibrant for a 30-year-old brandy—it boasts a pleasant fruitiness, the producer's trademark oakiness, and a caramel/peppery/heady aroma combination in the second nosing that becomes its meal ticket for the duration—I admired this oaky-sweet but not rich bouquet very much—what it lacks in opulence and heft, it makes up for in clean, crisp directness and tight focus; to my great surprise, the palate entry borders on being ambrosial, as overripe yellow fruit flavors bowl the taste buds over—the more contained midpalate features luscious, lip-smacking flavors of sweet oak, plums, raisins, and light toffee; the finish is plump; a paradoxical, but enchanting, armagnac.

RATING ★★★★ *Highly Recommended* $$$

DE MONTAL 1962 Armagnac 40% Alcohol

Medium-to-dark amber/amontillado sherry color, excellent purity; the full-speed-ahead, assertive, but not aggressive nose oozes mature wood/rancio and dried fruit, backed by a faint touch of spice—I categorize this bouquet as elegant, harmonious, and mature—in other words, it's not out to prove anything; on the palate, the harmony between acidity, fruit content, and alcohol is admirable and sturdily in place—the midpalate shows off the svelte but graceful texture and flavor in fine form; the aftertaste is caramelly, acceptably candied, and not in the least woody, which is a departure from the other De Montals; a well-made armagnac that is at its peak right now and for the next five to ten years; gorgeous.

RATING ★★★★ *Highly Recommended* $$$

DE MONTAL 1939 Armagnac 40% Alcohol

Light-brown/oloroso-sherry color, good clarity; the sweet, heady nose shows more than ample vivacity as appealingly piquant waves of nuts, spirit, and leather have a positive impact in the nasal cavity; in the mouth, the nut-meat quality expands into a dried-fruit/raisiny flavor that's waxy and even a bit oily by midpalate—the maturity aspect makes it nearly sedate on the tongue—neither opulent nor layered, this pre–World War II armagnac is nuanced, subtle, and deceptively potent, particularly in the sterling finish, which exhibited more than a little finesse and punch; I upgraded it to four stars after it appeared to pick up some steam with aeration; I ended up liking this old geezer very much.

RATING ★ ★ ★ ★   *Highly Recommended* $$$

DE MONTAL XO Armagnac 40% Alcohol

Really beautiful, medium amber/honey/bronze color, ideal clarity; this bouquet has all the elegance, complexity, and harmony that the VSOP lacks—it delights the nose as opulent, warm aromas of cheese, caramel, custard, and black pepper blend nicely into a unified fragrance that's both muscular and candied; the richness of the palate entry makes for a lovely taste overture—the texture is medium-weighted yet bountiful, and the flavors of toffee, vanillin/oak, and glycerine are layered and poised; the finish is surprisingly short and only mildly sweet, giving off slight waves of oaky flavor in the tail end; this XO lost some steam in the aftertaste, but it's still a nifty, chunky, and recommendable brandy.

RATING ★ ★ ★   *Recommended* $$$

DE MONTAL 1975 Armagnac 40% Alcohol

Brilliant burnished-orange/medium-amber color, unquestioned purity; the nose shows the De Montal penchant for resiny, mature oak and pear fruit—this is not a blockbuster bouquet, but rather a mannered, neatly manicured aroma that doesn't do more than it has to, but nevertheless exhibits confidence and style; medium-weighted, satiny texture; the warm, cozy palate entry is semisweet, then in midpalate an acidic tartness shows itself and tips the fruit/acid balance in favor of acid, making it seem lean by the slightly combustible finish; a good, solid armagnac that would have earned a fourth star had it shown more fruit for balance in the middle meaty part of the flavor.

RATING ★ ★ ★   *Recommended* $$$

DE MONTAL VSOP Armagnac 40% Alcohol

Lush, golden amber tone, perfect purity; the piquant nose reeks of vinous, woodsy, earthy, waxy, coconut-like aromas that are keenly pronounced, but not necessarily generous, from the first through the fourth nosings—a burlap-like, resiny woodiness emerges in the third pass, effectively adding to the assertive aromatic melange; the taste behaves in a more polite manner than the raucous nose, but I find the resiny quality present immediately upon palate entry—thankfully, the caramelly midpalate is completely free of the oily/woody influence, which suits me fine; the aftertaste is spirity and not a bit graceful or refined, but acceptably grapy and medium-long; a mediocre VSOP armagnac with a volatile nature that's like dynamite waiting for a match; try at your own risk; I wasn't crazy about it.

RATING ★ ★ $$

De Montal 1961 Armagnac 40% Alcohol

Medium amber color, some sediment is spotted floating about; the astringent nose reeks of grapefruit and pineapple in the first two nosing passes, then the astringency blows off, leaving behind a raisiny/overripe grape quality that reminds me strikingly of a Spanish Solera Brandy de Jérez—not the best of De Montal aromas—in the final nosing I experience an irritating tingling in the nasal cavity from the heavily spirited aroma—it seems that as this beast aerates, the alcohol becomes more pungent; flabby/fatty at palate entry—the bacon-fat flavor noted in the entry continues into the midpalate, where very little else appears to be happening; the finish is neither fruity nor oaky, just oily and nutty; perhaps the poorest overall showing of the De Montals.

RATING ★ $$$

De Montal 1960 Armagnac 40% Alcohol

The color is reminiscent of an amontillado sherry, a medium amber, with dull orange highlights, ideal purity; this nose is snappy, oaky, and toasty in the first nosing, then it turns benign and a bit weary by the third pass, giving off a grain-cracker/cardboardy aroma that is stale; the weariness noted in the latter stages of the aroma bleeds into the tired, some might say mature, flavor, which I found seriously wanting—the timid midpalate offers little other than smothered oak; the aftertaste is pleasant, but on the weak side; similar to the anemic 1961, I wonder if this brandy should even be on the market . . . especially at the lofty price.

RATING ★ $$$

Gerland VS Armagnac 40% Alcohol

Smashing, opulent, russet/copper, burnished color that's really a knockout in its clarity and tone; the stout nose reeks of cream, overripe grapes, light toffee, tea, and sweet old oak—it's pleasant enough and highly concentrated—off-dry to sweet; the entry flavor whispers "toffee," then at midpalate, it gamely says "more toffee," then in the aftertaste it bellows "SUPER TOFFEE"; it's a likeable, slightly over-the-top brandy, with a touch of heat on the tongue, but unfortunately it plays only a monotonous one-note melody; give it more dimension and/or balance and this could be a real looker; as it is now, however, nah.

RATING ★ ★ $$

Gerland VSOP Armagnac 40% Alcohol

Darker, more brown/tawny than the luminous VS; the sweet-oak bouquet is more settled down and graceful than the rambunctious nose of the VS—this aroma, while sturdy, is more perfumed and less eager to please—the third pass reveals a delightful toasty quality; it bothers me that in the mouth I note ample sweetness but scant substance and hardly any viscosity or depth—a brandy worthy of its price tag should offer ample flavor supported by adequate depth of character, acidity, and body—a great brandy should offer multilayered flavor, counterbalancing acidity, and several layers of depth; the feel of this brandy simply doesn't jive with the sweet-flavor element; while I don't find it offensive in the mouth, I can't ignore the missing major components of texture and depth of character; it's out of sync and therefore not recommendable in view of established standards.

RATING ★ $$

JANNEAU 1966 Armagnac 43% Alcohol

Equally lustrous color but of honey/topaz, with gold/light-brown highlights; the sweet, saucy, mature, zesty nose is laden with clearly discernable waves of oak and vanilla; beautifully structured, smooth texture; the handsome, refined, and married flavor components are still very vibrant—the midpalate is highlighted by black pepper, cocoa, and oak; there's even a pleasant warmth at the start of the medium-length aftertaste, then it settles down into a gentle finish; a top-notch armagnac all the way; retasted and upgraded.

RATING ★ ★ ★ ★   *Highly Recommended* $$$

JANNEAU Réserve de la Maison Grande Fine Armagnac 40% Alcohol

Sports a stunningly lustrous and rich topaz color, seeded in the core with copper highlights; the opulent, inviting, warm nose offers a somewhat brisk, incisive spicy quality that is supported by a decidedly oaky, vanillin spine; on palate, the zingy flavors of oak and spice leave little room for any other flavors; it finishes long and clean, with an unusual and totally rousing last-minute trace of tingly cinnamon; everything about this armagnac suggests great care in production.

RATING ★ ★ ★   *Recommended* $$$

JANNEAU VSOP Armagnac 40% Alcohol

Appealing topaz/orange color; a wee bit odd in the nose, which emits feinty, cooked, corn-husk, mashy, biscuity aromas, but nonetheless is correctly spirity; the nose isn't off-putting at all, you understand, it's just atypical; very masculine, full, and toasty flavors greet the tastebuds, then rapidly fade in the understated, whispy aftertaste; I was hoping for a guttier midpalate and finish after such a pronounced entry; average quality, but the taste, nose, and finish are not in harmony.

RATING ★ ★ $$

<u>LABERDOLIVE</u>

Pierre Laberdolive is one of the most respected grower-producers in the Armagnac region. Laberdolive draws from the vineyards of three domaines—Pillon, Jaurrey, and d'Escoubes—to make his superb single-vintage, single-estate armagnacs. As a testament to the grace of Laberdolive armagnacs, it's interesting to note that they are served in every three-star restaurant in France. No small feat.

LABERDOLIVE 1982 Bas Armagnac 46% Alcohol

The amber/honey/harvest-gold hue is just slightly turbid; the dazzling perfume rockets from the sampling glass in heady bursts of Brazil nuts, unsweetened coconut, and resin—it's a serious noseful by any measure, one that offers unusual breadth—I particularly admire the mature, resiny/oily quality that's especially evident in the final nosing; in the mouth, the velvety texture purrs like a Lexus as the subtle but solid flavors of pears and dried apricots, resin, and raisins come together in a damned impressive crescendo of harmony in the perfectly behaved, sumptuous finish; exquisite quality.

RATING ★ ★ ★ ★   *Highly Recommended* $$$

LABERDOLIVE 1976 Bas Armagnac 46% Alcohol

More luminous than the 1982—a vibrant, medium amber/honey color; this piquant fragrance is all nut city, baby—pecans, hazelnuts—but what supports the nut-meat layer is a brooding, profound foundational aroma of oak and grapes—it's a truly outstanding nose; flavorwise, I actually prefer, to my surprise, the more nimble 1982; 6 years older, this one shows more overall profundity and depth, but I also feel that it may perhaps be too young to be released—yet some of the taste elements seem muted to me and that's precisely why I say that it may be too green, even though it's 20 years old; the splendid aftertaste is intensely grapy and a total joy; I found the mid-palate too reined-in; I look forward to trying this brandy again in a decade.

RATING ★ ★ ★ ★   *Highly Recommended* $$$

LAPOSTOLLE XO Armagnac 40% Alcohol

Medium amber/tea color—it suffered from floating particles in each glass I poured, even after decanting; the bountifully generous bouquet has a delightful top layer of ripe apple, baked apple, caramel custard, and an underpinning layer of musty oak and woodsy aromas; the acutely sweet, charred flavor simply expands on the sugarcane-like aroma but in a much more concentrated way; by a long shot, one of the two or three sweetest armagnacs I've sampled—it gets buried in cloying tutti-frutti flavors that don't have enough acid in them to balance the honey/sugar/saccharine element; it's mildly pleasant if you like this kind of blunt, hammer-over-the-head style, but for my taste it comes off as being too manufactured and too cloyingly sweet to suit my taste; further, what's all that guck floating around?

RATING ★ $$

LARRESSINGLE

This excellent house was established in 1837 by Hyppolyte Papelorey, who operated the business for nearly six decades. It owns the distinction of being the first armagnac producer to sell its brandies in glass bottles rather than casks. In 1896, the company reins were handed over to Papelorey's son Gabriel, who jump-started the firm and dramatically accelerated its growth. One of the first major moves for Gabriel was to purchase an old fortress, the Chateau de Larressingle, which was completed circa 1250, and make it the symbolic and literal headquarters for the company. Today, the family still owns and operates Larressingle, combining the elegant wines of Bas Armagnac with the vibrant wines of Tenareze.

Larressingle Très Vieil 1934 Armagnac 43% Alcohol

I was astonished by the freshness of this six-decade-old senior citizen; the nose is delicate, but opulent and serious, with a rich floral undertone that lies beneath the top layer of mature spirit; on palate, it displays a genuine and appealing vitality that belies its age—nicely married flavors of prunes, apricots, and hazelnuts linger long after swallowing; no heat to speak of in the throat; extremely refined; my guess is that it will only improve with further aging and that's an inspiring thought, knowing how delicious it is right now.

RATING ★★★★   *Highly Recommended* $$$

Larressingle XO Grande Réserve Armagnac 43% Alcohol

Absolutely gorgeous, opulent topaz/orange-blossom honey color; the mature, lusciously rich, creamy, and medium-sweet aroma shows snappy scents of orange rind and roasted walnut; in the mouth, it has the fire of its sibling, the lesser VSOP, but the maturity of this smoky blend (15–20 years) magically offsets the heat with toffee, citrus, prunes, and caramel flavors that ultimately caress rather than torch the taste buds; this is one lovely armagnac worthy of anyone's liquor cabinet.

RATING ★★★   *Recommended* $$$

Larressingle Très Vieil 1960 Armagnac 43% Alcohol

Lustrous, amontillado sherry/topaz/medium brown hue, gold edge; the engaging nose of spice and flowers is followed by moderately intense flavors of ripe figs and tropical fruit—I liked the heady, sound aroma in particular; the lovely, rich texture floats on the palate; the piquant aftertaste ends with a slight, but pleasant warmth like smoldering embers in the fireplace; the impression is that this beauty is just now coming into its own; I would like to taste again in five to ten years; while very good, it doesn't offer the complexity or savoir faire of the great 1934.

RATING ★★★   *Recommended* $$$

Larressingle VSOP Armagnac 40% Alcohol

Very pretty bronze hue, perfect clarity; the fiery, potent, spirity nose goes a bit over the top in terms of alcohol thrust in the first three passes; on palate, I detected faint notes of caramel, nutmeg, and mandarin orange—again, the take-no-prisoners attitude of this VSOP made it rough in the mouth—pungent and aggressive, this armagnac will never be accused of being subtle; this is a cross-vintage blend of brandies no less than eight years old; ride 'em, cowboy.

RATING ★★ $$

Marquis de Caussade Extra S. P. Armagnac 40% Alcohol

Lovely chestnut/bronze color; the robust, sweet, toffee, and heavily oaked nose offers a generous hunk of roasted almond—the wood element becomes more pronounced in the last two nosings as a cheesy rancio aroma appears and sweeps the olfactory sense off its feet; the well-defined bittersweet chocolate taste at entry lasts all the way through to the tantalizingly long and sweet aftertaste; along the way luscious supplemental flavors of coffee bean, baked bread, and honey make themselves evident in stages, never overshadowing the very savory chocolate element, which I found irresistible; this sinewy thoroughbred owns plenty of stuffing and character, but doesn't club the drinker into submission; the elegance factor to me makes it rival some XO cognacs at a fraction of the price; the operative descriptive term here is "chocolate."

RATING ★★★★   *Highly Recommended* $$$

Marquis de Caussade 17 Ans Grande Age Armagnac 40% Alcohol

Marginally deeper amber/brown/bronze tone than the ten-year-old; this nose is less aggressive and more poised than that of the frisky "10 Ans" and shows melded, mature, and harmonious traces of soft sweet oak, tannin, chocolate-cake batter, and ripe white grapes—in a deep whiff I got a heady rush of manageable spirit perfume; a supple, delicious presence on the palate, with a medium body and silky texture—the harmony between the oak, the plump red fruit, and the sweetness level is masterful and accomplished; polished, svelte finish of pears and toffee; for those who mistakenly think that all armagnacs are only burly reflections of cognac, I suggest you try this well-endowed, but sophisticated charmer.

RATING ★★★★   *Highly Recommended* $$$

Marquis de Caussade VSOP Armagnac 40% Alcohol

Dashing topaz/medium amber color, highlighted by a sunset-orange/gold core; the meaty, full, but friendly nose of hazelnuts, oak, toffee, and tobacco leaps from the sampling glass; on palate, it shows a genuine off-dry to sweet richness that evolves nicely into a slightly candied, but very cheerful finish; whereas one normally expects a lion of a brandy from armagnac, this winner is a fatted lamb ready for quiet evening feasting; what it lacks in dynamic taste it more than makes up for in uncomplicated, direct, plump brandy pleasure; if you're just starting out in the world of armagnac or if you're searching for an approachable armagnac, stop right here.

RATING ★★★   *Recommended* $$

Marquis de Caussade 10 Ans Fine Armagnac 40% Alcohol

Beautifully clean, clear amber/vermilion color; the beguiling, assertive nose is of spiced baked apple, wood resin, faint cinnamon stick, hard candy, and peppermint—I really got behind the bouquet on this one at first, then felt a bit lukewarm about it after the third and forth passes because it seemed to lose some steam with extended aeration; the comely, ripe sweetness on the palate entry is wonderful, no doubt—at midpalate, the resiny oakiness takes the helm and steers this armagnac to a dry finish, at which point the tart baked-apple quality reemerges; muscular, young to the taste, and solid from top to bottom; Caussade is unquestionably one of Armagnac's most reliable producers.

RATING ★★★   *Recommended* $$$

Nicolas Napoleon Armagnac VS 40% Alcohol

Dullish, gold/hay, almost Sauternes-like color; the sharp, spirity nose is intensely stemmy, with potent backnotes of nail polish, cactus, and fusel oil (a congener that evidently didn't get eradicated by maturation or filtering)—strangely and disturbingly, this armagnac smells almost like an *añejo* tequila—in fact, Sauza Hornitos or Conmemorativo come to my mind in disbelief as I whiff it time and again; on the tongue, I detect only minor fusel oil, but considerable amounts of ripe red apple; the aftertaste is oily, sweet, and fruity and may be the best part of it; this poor devil doesn't know what it is; but, rest assured, I know what it is—a genuine mess; avoid.

RATING ★ $$

Samalens

Samalens is one of the most illustrious names in the armagnac industry. Founded in 1882 by Jean-Francois Samalens with but a single pot still, Samalens has for over a century produced many premier armagnacs that have been enjoyed from the smallest French countryside inns to the boardrooms of London and New York. The Samalens cellars are constructed in various levels for the 400-liter oak casks. The wood used is mostly black, an oak that is indigenous to the Armagnac district in Gascony. Today, Monsieur Samalens's grandsons, Georges and Jean, control the destiny of this fabled producer. They offer a trio of armagnacs to the U.S. market. The VSOP and the Relique Ancestrale come bottled in thick-glassed, rather cumbersome, scallop shell–shaped bottles, while the 1966 is offered in a more graceful rounded bottle that shows off the brilliant hues of this superb armagnac.

Samalens 1966 Vintage Millesime Bas Armagnac 44.5% Alcohol

Clear, gorgeous topaz/tawny color, dappled with rust/copper highlights, excellent purity; the sweet, full, candied bouquet is the most ponderous, welcoming, and compelling aroma of the three Samalens armagnacs—interestingly, the nose gives little trace of the high alcohol content; the maturity gathered during three decades of aging evidently allows for the evolved fruit component to mask the alcohol; absolutely divine and delicious on palate, with well-developed, but kicky flavors of apples and spice (cinnamon among them); finishes very long, with a mild hint of heat, a pleasant, quiet warmth rather than a tongue of flame; one of the premier armagnacs available at present in the U.S.; find, buy, and savor.

RATING ★ ★ ★ ★   *Highly Recommended* $$$

Samalens Relique Ancestrale Bas Armagnac 44% Alcohol

Luminous, clear, amber/orange color, perfect clarity; the generous, full, beguiling bouquet highlights ripe tropical fruit (especially guava and passion fruit), toffee, and spirit; has genuine presence in the mouth—while neither a graceful nor an elegant armagnac, this sinewy powerhouse awakens the taste buds with hefty amounts of orange, oak, and chocolate flavors; this is the perfect brandy when one is hankering for a bracing, but comforting

jolt of liquid warmth on a cold, dank, clammy winter day; it finishes well
with medium length.

RATING ★ ★ ★   *Recommended* $$$

SAMALENS VSOP Bas Armagnac 40% Alcohol

Dull, topaz color, with a surprising amount of microscopic, but nonethe-
less visible suspended particles in both sample bottles; the sweet-sour nose
is pleasant enough, offering savory hints of clover, honey, and lemon/lime
in the first two passes, then oak and tart grapes in the final nosings—I found
the nose disappointing and lacking in depth; spirity, tartly dry, and fiery fla-
vors command the taste buds upon entry—the midpalate calms down a bit
into an acidic/astringent brandy suffering from a serious fruit deficiency;
cocoa and caramel lead the long and appealing finish; problems stem, first,
from murky appearance and, second, from the stinging/astringent quality
on the palate; pluses are down to a mildly charming nose and an attractive,
candied aftertaste; hardly what I call a complete package, however.

RATING ★ $$

SEMPE

Even though Sempé was started only in 1936 by Henri Abel Sempé, it
quickly became one of the largest and most influential producers in Gascony. Monsieur Sempé began bottling his armagnacs when he was an en-
terprising teenager of sixteen. A mere two years later, he started marketing
his brand within France and continental Europe. Today, his daughters and
sons-in-law operate the business and guide the growth of the brand. The
Sempé family employs grapes from the Bas Armagnac and Tenareze districts, which are noted for their warm growing seasons and sand and clay
soils. Sempé owns only twelve hectares of vines, opting instead to purchase
grapes from other trusted growers. Sempé armagnacs are all single-distilled
and aged solely in Limousin oak casks. As of this writing in 1996, the company was reportedly experiencing financial difficulties. Whether or not this
situation will affect distribution, I know not.

SEMPE Impérial Réserve Baccarat Crown Armagnac 40% Alcohol

Rich, brilliant, medium amber/ocher/russet hue, the purity couldn't be
better; the chocolate/orange, soft, fresh, sweet-william/violet nose captured
my imagination and attention right in the initial nosing pass—completely
taken in by the grandeur of this brandy's perfume, I greedily inhaled my way
through the next three passes—a dazzler; in the mouth, it's very round, full
but delicate and gentle, showing nuanced flavors of pecan, nougat, and
caramel—hardly any wood exposes itself; the soft, velvety, almost creamy
texture wraps around the tongue; clean, luxurious aftertaste; outstanding
balance; upgraded after a recent second evaluation.

RATING ★ ★ ★ ★ ★   *Highest Recommendation* $$$

SEMPE Grande Réserve Prism Armagnac 40% Alcohol

Wonderful old Sauternes-like color, superb clarity; the sweetish, melony,
piquant nose offers many levels of fragrance as ripe yellow fruit leads to

caramel, which leads to oak/resin—a complex, masculine bouquet; on the palate, it's very restrained, with no heat/bite—the midpalate is deep, mellow, and intensely flavorful as waves of rancio, overripe grapes, and toffee dazzle the taste buds; it finishes extremely smooth, very elegant, handsome, subtle, slightly orangey; I pictured myself in front of the fire, stroking a snoozing canine while rolling this buxom beauty over the smitten taste buds; a heady, luxurious, paramount armagnac experience.

RATING ★★★★ *Highly Recommended* $$$

SEMPE 1965 Armagnac 40% Alcohol

Very dark, brooding brown/brackish color from extended wood-aging; the aroma was full, chocolatey, and tea-like in the first two passes, then it deepened in the final nosing as an English toffee scent took charge; this bosomy vixen is more rousing and complex on palate than reined-in 1973—at palate entry there's a slight, though not unpleasant, bite—the midpalate expands into a multilayered flavor panorama that includes grapefruit, marinated orange, tart red apple, cookie batter, and digestif biscuits—this is an all-out, full-throttle flavor experience of the first order; the medium-length, musty attic-like finish is at once disarming and thought-provoking; glory, hallelujah, I've seen the light.

RATING ★★★★ *Highly Recommended* $$$

SEMPE Extra Armagnac "The Crown of Louis XIV" Blue Limoges Decanter 40% Alcohol

Slightly paler than the XO in appearance; the bountiful nose bursts with perfumy cedar, fresh flowers, baked apples, and even a hint of old leather—a multilayered bouquet of impact, style, and substance; on the palate, the baked, melded flavors of herbs, fruit, honey, and oak come together in an altogether harmonious and satisfying fashion; this wonderfully extravagant Extra ends in a warm, honey-wheat-toast flavor that's remarkably delicious; no heat, no bite, just smooth sailing all the way from bouquet to aftertaste; the most sophisticated, elegant, and complete of the Limoges trio.

RATING ★★★★ *Highly Recommended* $$

SEMPE Napoleon Armagnac "The Crown of Napoleon" Green Limoges Decanter 40% Alcohol

Radiant yellow/goldenrod/amber hue; very full, assertive, and voluptuous nose of smoke, wood, and candied almonds; on palate, its innate armagnac vigor is a real pleasure as it tweaks the taste buds to full alert with piquant flavors of nuts, mild vanilla, and resinous wood; finishes rather softly, but long in the throat, with a parting flash of ripe-pear taste; all in all, a vivacious armagnac that, while uneven, reflects better-than-average quality nonetheless.

RATING ★★★ *Recommended* $$

SEMPE XO Armagnac "The Crown of Henry IV" Red Limoges Decanter 40% Alcohol

Slightly darker than the Napoleon, but with more of an orange tint; the elusive nose forced my olfactory sensors to chase it for nearly 15 minutes before much of a presence could be discerned—whereas the Napoleon's bouquet was immediately generous and outgoing, the XO's played a good game of hide-and-seek; what it lacks in the aroma, it more than makes up for in taste—this one provides an utterly luxurious ride into toffee/sherry/oak flavor country; the finish is extended and opulent; the candied-fruit element in the flavor is particularly sexy; funny how in the nose the coy XO is the exact opposite of the gregarious Napoleon; this one begins in a whisper but ends up rolling like thunder on the enchanted palate; another uneven, unpredictable armagnac that keeps you guessing; with more of a sustained bouquet, it would easily earn a fourth star.

RATING ★ ★ ★   *Recommended* $$

SEMPE 1973 Armagnac 40% Alcohol

Mature, burnished orange/autumnal gold color, good clarity; the lush, vanilla, chocolate, woody/resiny nose seems a bit weary to me in the first three nosings, then it comes alive in the last pass as the vanilla element goes into overdrive; on palate, it has a dried-pear quality that I liked, but there wasn't much depth beyond that—no heat or harshness; it finished nicely but too quickly, in clean waves of candy and wood.

RATING ★ ★ ★   *Recommended* $$$

SEMPE 1924 Armagnac 40% Alcohol

Handsome, cola-brown hue, with vermilion/rose highlights; the mature, self-contained nose offers roasted nuts, toasted wheat bread, mandarin orange, and lanolin—not my favorite bouquet, but a good one—its lack of generosity troubled me; in the mouth, the lovely, though slightly medicinal, oaky, cherry-like, caramel flavors suitably impressed my palate; the long, lovely finish ended up being its finest attribute; very earthy, ponderous, and good, but not earthshaking.

RATING ★ ★ ★   *Recommended* $$$

SEMPE 1908 Armagnac 40% Alcohol

Deep, very mature, tawny/cola-brown color, a tad dull; the nutty, almondy, sweetish, chocolatey nose started out awfully well in the first pass, then it abruptly turned south and vanished for the last three nosings—the contact with air evidently proved to be too stressful for the bouquet; on palate, the lush, shockingly piquant (considering its age), orange/vanilla flavors somewhat redeemed the spent bouquet; it finished short in a flurry of oak and resin—too woody for my taste; I believe that the fruit had simply dried up over time, leaving behind the oak and spirit influences.

RATING ★ ★ $$$

SEMPE 15-Year-Old Armagnac 40% Alcohol

Sexy, luxurious, vermilion/red grapefruit color, excellent purity; this chocolatey nose is considerably more complex than limp VSOP, exhibiting moderately complex aromas of grapes, old oak, cheese, and coconut; it owns a pleasant heat, a warming sensation in the mouth that I liked—unfortunately, this armagnac's flavors are surprisingly undeveloped, as the acid, fruit, and alcohol components just couldn't get together—each one takes its turn at the helm in the midpalate; pleasing, silky texture; the tart apple flavors in the medium-long finish made my mouth pucker; a disappointment.

RATING ★ ★ $$$

Sempe VSOP Armagnac 40% Alcohol

Pretty bronze/orange tone; the mild, melony, citrusy bouquet offers deep vanilla and caramel as underpinnings; the burning heat at palate entry didn't excite the tip of the tongue—the midpalate featured shockingly meek flavors of old oak, tannin, grape must, and citrus; the medium-long, way too timid finish didn't have the character to jump-start the midpalate; disappointing and ultimately the least inspiring of the Sempés.

RATING ★ $$

MARCEL TREPOUT

Marcel Trépout is an octogenarian who is still active in the business. The Trépout cellars are located in a twelfth-century monastery next to a narrow road that was used by the Romans. Monsieur Trépout is one of the few *négociant-éleveurs** remaining in Armagnac. He will not purchase an armagnac that has been aged in wood for less than six years. Once an armagnac is chosen, it is aged further in the Trépout cellars. The Trépout cellar stocks go all the way back to 1868. This type of living library assists Trépout and his son-in-law in maintaining consistent quality from bottling to bottling.

MARCEL TREPOUT 1971 Armagnac 42% Alcohol

An almost identical color to that of the XO; the slinky aroma is more layered and complex than the simpler XO, with lovely, solid notes of candied orange, paraffin, spice, and a dash of butterscotch; the sweet, fruity, grapy flavor delivers a most satisfying texture as it generously coats the entire mouth; the aftertaste builds on the delicious midpalate flavors by shifting the grapiness into passing gear; this is a beautifully crafted armagnac that more than deserves a try.

RATING ★ ★ ★ ★   *Highly Recommended* $$$

MARCEL TREPOUT XO Armagnac 40% Alcohol

Lightish amber/gold color; the remarkably nutty, off-dry nose focuses squarely on macadamia nuts and bittersweet chocolate—there's even a faint trace of orange rind—it's a very sexy perfume; in the mouth, the moderate complexity is nicely accentuated by delicate but firm tastes of guava, spirit (indicated by the slight heat in the throat), white grapes, and oak; the finish is rather lean and semisweet; while the bouquet is clearly the headlining element, it is overall a very appealing armagnac of more than a little charm and grace.

RATING ★ ★ ★   *Recommended* $$$

---

*A firm or person who purchases brandy already in barrels from independent growers/distillers and then matures and bottles it at their facility and under their own label.

AMERICAN BRANDY

For centuries the foremost brandies from France, namely, cognac and armagnac, have been the models for product quality, skill in marketing, and creation of image for the entire category. The wily and ingenious Cognaçais, in particular, have set the pace in the quest for global recognition. The brandies from other nations and other regions have, as a result, been forced to feed on the dust that has billowed up behind the rumbling Cognac juggernaut.

America's frontline, mass-produced brandies, the vast majority of which (over 90 percent) are produced in California, have long been perceived and depicted as awkward, glutinous, overly sweet concoctions, best utilized in gummy cocktails with embarrassing names like "Between the Sheets," "Corpse Reviver," "Bosom Caresser," and "All Dressed Up Like A Dog's Dinner." Rightly or wrongly, these high-volume brandies have been viewed as beverages that only the numb-of-palate would serve without the cloak of other ingredients.

The disturbing thing is, brandy production in this country is in fact a proud and well-established industry. Brandy was undoubtedly made by the Spanish missionaries, whose missions were either surrounded by or within close proximity of vineyards, which supplied the wines for consumption and sacramental use. While it's likely that brandy was produced in the missions as early as the 1700s, no proof has been unearthed to transform assumption into irrefutable fact. The initial American brandy producer is generally considered to be, oddly enough, a Frenchman by the name of Jean Louis Vignes, who reportedly made brandy in the latter half of the 1830s. But America's brandy industry didn't really shift into gear until the 1860s, when Almaden Vineyards, which was located in Madera, California, started to make brandy on a regular basis and in volume. Today, all the major mainstream American brandies are distilled in continuously running column stills and aged in wood for at least two years. Some are palatable; others are deplorable.

About fifteen years ago, a few pioneering distillers in California and Oregon began to dabble in the art of distilling wine in small copper-pot stills, in a process similar to that used by the Cognaçais. Today, the exciting efforts of these and other distillers are being increasingly promoted in the best restaurants and liquor shops of New York, Chicago, Boston, Washington, D.C., and even London and Paris.

Distillers such as Steve McCarthy of Clear Creek Distillery in Oregon, Miles Karakasevic of Domaine Charbay in Napa Valley, Bernard La Borie of Carneros Alambic Distillery in Napa Valley, Jorge Rupf of St. George Spirits in the East Bay, Randall Grahm of Bonny Doon Vineyards in Santa Cruz, and Hubert Germain-Robin and Ansley Coale Jr. of Germain-Robin Alambic Brandy in Mendocino County are offering world-class, double-distilled brandies and grappas from top varietal grapes as well as other types of fruit. These trailblazers have wrested the baton away from America's major brandy producers like Korbel, Christian Brothers, Gallo, and Paul Masson, and are now running in the race that has long been led by the Cognaçais. The truth is, the home team will never catch the Cognaçais in terms of volume, but they are steadily gaining in the area of quality.

As the collective American palate becomes more sensitive to the nuances and gentle turns of fine spirits, the American brandy industry, in particular at the ultrapremium "boutique" end, will, I predict, continue to expand and conquer.

Bonny Doon (California)

Wine buffs are familiar with the exploits of Santa Cruz, California, winemaker Randall Grahm, whose inventive concepts at Bonny Doon Vineyard have since 1981 introduced galefuls of fresh air to the occasionally stodgy and stagnant California wine industry. Mr. Grahm was one of the first California producers to experiment on a large scale with the traditional grapes of France's Rhone Valley *(syrah, grenache, mourvedre)*, thereby kicking off the so-called "Rhone Ranger" craze in the late 1980s, which offered a much needed alternative to California's tunnel-vision-bound industry. Going one step further, Grahm has in recent years tinkered in the art of distilling. Beginning with a quest for grappa, Mr. Grahm has expanded his eau-de-vie roster to include spirits made from pears, cherries, apricots, plums, and nectarines. Mr. Grahm's élan and zeal are unmistakably evident in these well-crafted eaux-de-vie. Indeed, a handful of Bonny Doon spirits rank as some of the best domestic brandies.

Bonny Doon Poire Eau-de-Vie 40.3% Alcohol (California)

Clear; the no-nonsense, sweetish perfume of overripe pears shows virtually no spirity face—a rather astonishing feat for an eau-de-vie; remarkably, as true to pears as the nose is, the taste is even more so, as waves of fresh, succulent, ripe Bosc pear flavors wash over and captivate the taste buds; it finishes in a full-flavored, semisweet manner; a number of other domestic eaux-de-vie have left a metallic, tanky aftertaste—not this one—it's luscious from stem to stern; top-notch quality.

RATING ★ ★ ★ ★ **Highly Recommended** $

BONNY DOON Cal Del Solo Prunus Eau-de-Vie 40% Alcohol (California)

(73% apricot, 26% cherry, 1% plum) Clear; absolutely glorious symphony of semisweet aromas ranging from ripe cherries to apricots (as expected) to citrus fruits to the bubblegum you used to get along with the baseball cards of the 1950s and 1960s—it's a veritable fruit-salad bouquet that's graceful, balanced, vivacious, clean, and, most of all, inviting; in the mouth, this zippy spirit seems dry at entry as the apricot fruitiness races forward, then in the finish the taste caresses the palate in a sweetish blanket of fruit flavor; a highly complementary concoction that's a total joy to drink.

RATING ★ ★ ★ ★ **Highly Recommended** $

BONNY DOON Cerise Eau-de-Vie 40.5% Alcohol (California)

Clear; beguiling, delicate bouquet of ripe black cherries offers the slightest nuance of anise in the background, but the spotlight remains squarely on the concentrated cherry aroma—a fabulous bouquet; the taste offers a full-bodied, full-throttle cherry flavor that leaves no doubt as to this eau-de-vie's fruit of origin; so far so good; unfortunately, following the immensely pleasing smell and taste experiences, the trouble started in the aftertaste, where a burning sensation dropped the final score; while it's proper for an eau-de-vie to display a bit of heat in the throat, this is too excessive not to mention; in spite of this failing, I still find this eau-de-vie to be recommendable on the strength of the vastly appealing nose and taste.

RATING ★ ★ ★ **Recommended** $

BONNY DOON 1978 Fine Potstill Brandy 45% Alcohol (California)

Rather dull, pale amber/light honey/gold color—not a dazzler on the outside; the pleasant, caramelly nose offers ample though hardly generous fruit and vanilla overtones—I detected no oak perfume to speak of; on the tongue, it's full and voluptuous, as skillfully layered flavors of mint, cake batter, butter, and sweet spirit lavish the contented taste buds; it finishes well endowed and sustained; the taste and finish outdistance and, in fact, redeem the mediocre aroma and limp appearance; give it more character in the bouquet and luster in the appearance and you'd have a recommendable brandy.

RATING ★ ★ $$

BONNY DOON Nectarine Eau-de-Vie 40.8% Alcohol (California)

Clear; a disappointing (since I adore nectarines) metallic, steely nose that only faintly suggests nectarines—it left me completely unimpressed even after affording it the full four analytical passes—I thought that the tanky quality might blow off, it didn't—it's more like a medicinal, sterile aroma than fresh fruit; on palate, the taste showed marked improvement in being true to the fruit of origin; the fruity flavor accelerated in the aftertaste; regrettably, the unattractive, cleaning-fluid nose does too much early damage to this eau-de-vie—it simply can't be retrieved.

RATING ★ ★ $

CARNEROS ALAMBIC (CALIFORNIA)

At Carneros Alambic Distillery in Napa Valley, everything that could be provided to make a superior and representative American brandy has been provided by the French owners, Rémy Martin, one of France's "Big Four" cognac producers. Located in the cool Carneros district of lower Napa Valley, this splendid facility was erected in 1982 and was the first alambic brandy distillery built in the States. The spanking-clean, cathedral-ceilinged distillery house boasts eight French-built copper-pot stills. Like their cognac siblings, Carneros Alambic brandies are double-distilled in small batches, which concentrates the flavors and aromas. Only one gallon of spirit is produced from every ten gallons of wine that is distilled. The barrel house is seconds away from the distillery. Inside, nearly 4,000 naturally cured, French Limousin oak barrels cradle the maturing brandies. The earthen floors maintain the necessary level of humidity.

Carneros Alambic has Managing Director Bernard La Borie to thank for their success. There are few people whom I've met in the spirits industry who can match Mr. La Borie's verve, vision, and positive energy. La Borie takes as much pride in presenting and marketing his brandies as he does in making them. The visitor's center includes a pot still model created for Carneros Alambic by George Lucas's Industrial Light & Magic special-effects company. The model depicts the process of distillation in a clear, effective fashion. Each visit ends with a sensory evaluation where the visitors can sniff their way through distilled examples of the six different grape types.

CARNEROS ALAMBIC QE Alambic Brandy 40% Alcohol (California)

Clear, pure, russet/honey/orange/medium amber tone; the delicate, polite, semisweet, but substantial bouquet gains momentum with aeration as measured waves of mild caramel, guava, black pepper, ripe red apple, cinnamon, and honey combine for an elegant aromatic treat; the mouth-feel of this brandy is creamy, round, and like crushed velvet; the entry is sweet and grapy, with a delightful warming quality that immediately designates it as an in-front-of-the-fire, sipping brandy—the straightforward, pear-like, honey-eyed, caramelized midpalate is so bosomy, fruity, and friendly that the novice might think it simple when, in fact, it's deceptively multilayered and concentrated; the finish is long, sweet, and almost viscous; a dynamite gift choice for those people who relish broad-shouldered, chewy brandies; Bernard La Borie's pinnacle achievement.

RATING ★ ★ ★ ★   *Highly Recommended* $$$

CARNEROS ALAMBIC XR Alambic Brandy 40% Alcohol (California)

A blend of *colombard, pinot noir, chenin blanc, palomino, muscat,* and *folle blanche* grapes; drop-dead gorgeous orange/amber color of tea and rich honey; the bouquet says "red apples" to me in the first pass, then it expands into grapes, leather, melon, and spice by the third pass—it's a study in understatement, but that's not to imply that it's deficient in complexity, because it most certainly is not; the flavor is its best attribute, as sweetish tastes of grapes, oak, and yellow fruit engage the taste buds in a friendly romp from entry through midpalate; fleetingly offering ripe fruit and a quiet heat, the finish goes regrettably limp after only 10–15 seconds; I liked it and I recommend it, but this very good brandy didn't inspire me the way that the superlative QE did.

RATING ★★★   *Recommended* $$$

Carneros Alambic Folle Blanche Brandy 40% Alcohol (California)

The brilliant, orange/copper hue dazzles the eye; though the delicate, tart bouquet is decidedly grapy, with a trace of unripened pear, I'm not wild about it because it doesn't give much of itself; in the mouth, this brandy takes off in elegant, ripe grape/red fruit waves of flavor that are composed and tidy—the second level of flavor reveals a buttery quality to which I favorably responded; the aftertaste is as understated and firm as the midpalate flavor; a sound, low-key brandy whose overall impression borders on elegant.

RATING ★★★   *Recommended* $$$

Carneros Alambic Special Reserve Brandy 40% Alcohol (California)

Lustrous, rich amber/orange hue, with subtle copper highlights—quite the stylish and inviting brandy eyeful—it's so lovely visually that you almost forget the next step of evaluation; the intense, grapy nose is savory, to be sure, but one-dimensional in its scope—yes, there are plenty of grapes present and accounted for in the fragrance, but nothing else that I could discern in terms of oak or fruit; in the mouth the unidimensionality continues until the sweetish aftertaste finally introduces a second sensory quality, namely, tobacco; all in all, I believe this brandy is too polite, too correct, trying too hard not to offend in its mission and therefore turns up short on pizazz, magnitude, earthiness, et cetera; a decent, totally acceptable, and average brandy effort—but brandy can't survive on appearance alone—great brandy provides a visceral experience—this one simply isn't at that stage; reevaluated for *Kindred Spirits* and upgraded.

RATING ★★ $$

Christian Brothers Brandy 40% Alcohol (California)

The deep, pretty topaz/tawny/orange color is impressive; the very soft, muffled, sweet, candied nose shows a confident but not overwhelmingly spirity foundation—it's more confection-like than grape-like, but inoffensive nonetheless; the firm, straightforward palate entry, surprisingly, is dry to off-dry in total contradiction to the supersweet nose—this hefty, viscous brandy goes too alcoholic from midpalate through to the aftertaste, which bites you in the throat; too sickly sweet and unctuous.

RATING ★ $

CLEAR CREEK DISTILLERY (OREGON)

Steve McCarthy is one of this nation's most talented distillers. McCarthy is a man with a vision—a vision of apples, raspberries, and pears dancing in consumers' heads. Production numbers are relative, but sometimes they're fun to consider, anyway. It takes up to 35–40 pounds of apples to produce one bottle of apple brandy, 40–45 pounds of pears (usually Bartletts) to make one bottle of pear brandy, and up to a whopping 75–80 pounds of raspberries to translate into one bottle of raspberry brandy. McCarthy harvests his pears while they are still green, leaving them in storage at his distillery to allow them a quiet period of ripening. Once the sugar reaches the desired levels, the pears are pressed, and the crushed fruit is inoculated with a yeast cultivated in Champagne. The juice ferments in temperature-controlled 2,000-gallon tanks, producing a "mash." The mash is next moved to McCarthy's copper-pot stills for distillation into a crystal-clear brandy of extremely high proof, somewhere in the gum-numbing neighborhood of 70% alcohol. The brandy is then matured in stainless-steel tanks for approximately two months before it is cut with water to 40% alcohol. McCarthy ages his apple brandy further in wood for at least two years, though nary a hint of oak can be discerned.

CLEAR CREEK DISTILLERY Eau de Vie de Pomme Apple Brandy 40% Alcohol (Oregon)

Aged in Limousin oak casks from France; pale straw yellow/apple juice hue; the nose is so delicate as to be feminine in its bearing—the notes of grass, apple, and spice are neither sweet nor tart, just ethereal in the first three passes—by the last nosing, the spice/apple-peel components shift into high gear, creating a heavenly aroma of succulent fruit that took my breath away; in the mouth, the grace noted in the bouquet grows into regal elegance as the apple element becomes more clearly defined at midpalate—just prior to the aftertaste, the taste of tart green apple is mesmerizing; the finish is long, but very soft and appley; this is Stephen McCarthy's best all-around distilling effort and must be considered an American classic.

RATING ★ ★ ★ ★ ★   *Highly Recommended* $$

CLEAR CREEK DISTILLERY Williams Pear Brandy 40% Alcohol (Oregon)

Bright, crystalline appearance, as it should be; the intense, unmistakable, succulent, ripe-pear aroma bursts forth from the glass as soon as it is poured; on palate, it's almost as if you've just bitten into the most luscious pear you've ever eaten—delicious, dry, pear, slightly minerally flavors carry through on palate with appealing sweetness in focused, delicate, and elegant aftertaste; this wonderful brandy captures the essence of pear as nimbly as any European producer.

RATING ★ ★ ★ ★   *Highly Recommended* $$

CLEAR CREEK DISTILLERY Kirschwasser 40% Alcohol (Oregon)

Clear appearance—devoid of any color whatsoever; the distinctive, phenolic, nonfruity aroma is of minerals, slate, wet pavement, and rain; pleasantly dry to off-dry, exceedingly subtle taste of underripe cherries—I hardly noticed the spirit at all, so nuanced is the alcohol; the aftertaste is as reined-in as the flavor, offering just the stingiest hint of cherry fruit; while I wasn't expecting a brimming-with-flavor fruit-salad brandy, neither was I anticipating so delicate, so serene a brandy—the longer it sat on my palate after tasting, the more I appreciated its low-key but sturdy presence—if you're looking for a brass-band type, ambrosial cherry brandy that bursts with ripe cherry fruit, pass up this one—but if you want to appreciate the feline delicacy of cherry flavor robed in a manageable spirit that plays like a string quartet, absolutely grab this brandy from Clear Creek—I appreciated it even more after the second and third samplings; recently reevaluated and upgraded.

RATING ★ ★ ★ ★   ***Highly Recommended*** $$

CLEAR CREEK DISTILLERY Grappa 40% Alcohol (Oregon)

Expected crystalline appearance; the leesy,* muscat, high-voltage, medicinal nose tweaks the olfactory sense with a potent, grapy/spirity rush—the nose also gives off a barely detectable backnote of stale mustiness that blew off after 20 minutes—the bouquet reminded me of one of my favorite French white wines, Muscat Beaumes-de-Venise; lush, keenly grapy, sweet, and focused flavors enchant the palate as the lees flavor underpins and guides the entire experience in an understated, but firm manner; the piquant, zesty, and flowery aftertaste is mildly hot and tingly on the tongue; I would have scored it even higher if not for the suspicious fustiness in the nose.

RATING ★ ★ ★   ***Recommended*** $$

CLEAR CREEK DISTILLERY Apple Brandy 40% Alcohol (Oregon)

Golden/tawny apple juice/apple cider appearance; extremely spirity, subtle bouquet, faint vanilla, tart-apple aroma—the nose closely resembles a Lowland single-malt Scotch whisky in its gentlemanly bearing and captivating fruitiness—the nose markedly opened up after 15 minutes in the tasting glass, producing a round, tart, and fragrant bouquet that was irresistible; the potent entry is snappy and zesty—the apple flavor turns a bit tart at midpalate; the lovely appley finish is totally dry and short; this brandy would be ideal with pungent orange-colored cheese; I urge lovers of single-malt Scotches to seek out this impeccably made brandy.

RATING ★ ★ ★   ***Recommended*** $$

CORONET VSQ Brandy 40% Alcohol

The light amber/harvest-gold hue shows perfect clarity—an attractive brandy; the nose could not be described as being generous, assertive, or expressive as meek aromas of gum, mild tangerine, grapes, and spirit struggle to make their way out of the sampling glass—a gelding of a brandy bouquet; in the mouth, the situation improves only slightly as a mild grapiness makes a brief appearance in the midpalate—otherwise I taste spirit, maybe a dash

---

*In production terminology, lees are the astringent, mushroomy-smelling residue that's left behind in the bottom of an aging barrel after a mature wine or brandy has been removed.

of caramel, but that's as far as this uninspired, characterless brandy travels; it actually tastes manufactured.

   RATING ★ $

CREEKSIDE VINEYARDS

These brandies were sampled in 1991. Since then the ownership has changed hands. There may be some bottles of these brandies occupying space on retailers' shelves, but probably not very many.

CREEKSIDE VINEYARDS Grappa 40% Alcohol (California)

Clear-water appearance; the correct, distilled-spirit aroma is very fresh, estery, and intensely pear-like, with background hints of pink grapefruit and peaches; the exceedingly refined and gentle entry advances in richness at midpalate with lavish, tangy flavors of grapes and spice; the finish is clean, with full-blown flavors of spirit and lees; most impressive is the balance that never allows the spirit to override the splendid *zinfandel* and *cabernet sauvignon* fruit; an excellent, stylistic, and unique offering; good show.

   RATING ★ ★ ★ ★   *Highly Recommended* $ $

CREEKSIDE VINEYARDS Apple Brandy 40% Alcohol (California)

Pretty amber/yellow color; the tart apple-pie-like nose is appealing, if unidimensional; on palate, this brandy is not even close to being average—it suffers badly from a total lack of character, complexity, or depth of flavor—surprisingly, it offers scant evidence of the tart, crisp fruit quality that one rightly expects from an apple-based spirit—what you do taste is some scrawny spirit on the tongue but that's about it; predictably it has a nondescript aftertaste; back to the drawing board on this one; it should never have been released to begin with.

   RATING ★ $ $

CREEKSIDE VINEYARDS Grape Brandy 40% Alcohol (California)

Attractive, amber/honey color; aggressive, sweet, citrusy, woody nose that proudly touts its spirit; after enjoying the extroverted, punchy aroma, the flavors are surprisingly muted and downright timid up to the pleasing, grapy, coffee-like aftertaste; I see some genuine potential here, but the flavor part of this experience definitely needs some giddyap—as it stands, the flavor prevents the nose and the finish from soaring—I don't mean to imply that this brandy is unpleasant or offensive—I do mean to point out its woeful deficiency of guts and a general lack of character in the flavor department; needs work.

   RATING ★ $ $

DOMAINE CHARBAY (CALIFORNIA)

Miles and Susan Karakasevic are throwbacks to another era, a time when "small" meant "better." Talkative, proud, and keenly intelligent, Mr. Karakasevic comes from a long line of master distillers—eleven generations, to be exact. He clearly doesn't have his sights set on becoming the Gallo of boutique distillers; he's too realistic for reveries like that. It's more important to him to produce very limited quantities of extremely high-quality brandies and liqueurs, made in his own tiny alembic still.

DOMAINE CHARBAY Grappa di Marko 45% Alcohol (California)

Crystal-clear appearance; the full-throttle, aldehydic nose of grape must, freshly mown hay, and freshly cut flowers provides a rollicking banquet of intensely fresh garden aromas, tightly wrapped and irresistible; in the mouth, the highly concentrated, raisiny flavor is sweet right from the opening bell; the aftertaste is extravagant, long, and fruity; it left no doubt in my mind that this is one of America's premier grappas, one with all the style and flavor you could hope for.

RATING ★ ★ ★ ★ **Highly Recommended** $$$

DOMAINE CHARBAY Calvad'or Apple Brandy 45% Alcohol (California)

Golden/honey color; the nose is delicate, with ripe-apple perfume, but it's not what I'd call memorable—it's really a rather thin and anemic aroma; in the mouth, it's proper in every way and the flavor is mildly attractive in a ripe-red-apple sense, but there's nothing beyond that superficially pleasant apple taste—no sense of depth from oak or maturity; the aftertaste is as meek as the bouquet; without a doubt, my least favorite of this formidable line of domestic brandies and liqueurs; I'd like to see more depth of aroma and flavor, as in true Calvados.

RATING ★ ★ $$$

E & J Brandy 40% Alcohol (California)

Attractive, clear amber color; full-blown, gum-like, minty, ambrosial, spirity, fruit-basket nose, highlighted by banana and apricot—throw in a hint of slate as an afterthought; decidedly velvety on palate—the texture is quite astonishing considering the affordable price tag; appealingly dry in the mouth; hardly a blockbuster in terms of character, but it handles itself extremely well from entry to the mild, caramelly, persistent finish, finally ending with a slight trace of pineapple, spice, and lemon peel; considering that Gallo makes as much of this brandy in one day as the small-fry distillers make in one year, I was impressed.

RATING ★ ★ $

E & J VSOP Brandy 40% Alcohol (California)

Fine, pale amber/honey tone, excellent purity; the nose offers not-so-subtle notes of citrus, pineapple, caramel, coconut, and cotton candy—it's an overly sweet, candied bouquet that would have been more pleasing if someone had thrown the switch on the sugary/caramel perfume earlier than they obviously did; right off the bat, a syrupy sweetness assaults the palate—turn down the volume, people—the midpalate offers little more than caramel/nougat candy flavor, no grapiness, nonexistent acidity; ditto the aftertaste; while it's not offensive, it most definitely is way too sticky sweet from palate entry through midpalate; probably would be pleasant on-the-rocks with a healthy twist of lemon to cut the sugar; the regular bottling of E & J Brandy is actually better because it's not as cloying as this gooey concoction.

RATING ★ $

GERMAIN-ROBIN (CALIFORNIA)

Since 1987, Hubert Germain-Robin, whose family had been producing cognac in France's Charente *département* for over two centuries prior to being purchased by gigantic Martell, has been offering some of the most meritorious grape-based brandies this country has ever produced. The base of operations for Germain-Robin is an uplands ranch in the rugged coastal mountains of Mendocino County, 100 miles north of San Francisco. Using *colombard, pinot noir,* and *gamay beaujolais* grapes instead of *ugni blanc,* the hometown favorite variety of the Cognaçais, Germain-Robin and his partner, Ansley J. Coale Jr., are at the forefront of domestic brandy making. They met in 1981 when Coale gave a lift to the hitchhiking Germain-Robin and his wife.

The choice of the grape varieties was crucial in the evolution of these wonderful spirits. The white *colombard* grape has long been utilized in the Charente, though mostly in a second-tier role to *ugni blanc. Colombard* is recognized as producing a lean, tart, high-acid wine that is perfect for distillation into brandy. The surprise comes from the use of red *gamay beaujolais* and *pinot noir.* Coale and Germain-Robin adamantly argue that the *pinot noir* adds elegance and the *gamay beaujolais* lends smoothness and bouquet. Their pot still was originally located in an old, abandoned distillery in Cognac. After a bit of refitting and patching up, they transported it to Coale's ranch. Production is predictably meager—a scant 80 barrels yearly, which translates roughly into 2,600 cases of brandy.

Because of the diminutive size of the operation, virtually all phases of production are done manually. Hubert Germain-Robin personally makes every barrel of brandy himself, taking close to half a year to produce the 80 barrels. Certainly, the uniqueness and smallness of the Germain-Robin operation is part and parcel of the charm. There is no doubt in my mind that Germain-Robin brandies are not only America's finest but they compete with the best from Cognac.

GERMAIN-ROBIN Pinot Noir Single-Barrel Brandy 42.7% Alcohol (California)

Light amber/golden hay color; the estery, spicy, herbal, acetate, solid, but restrained, almost ethereal nose has intriguing backnotes of grape pomace, melon, and tangerine, but hardly a trace of oak—a keenly sophisticated, lightish nose that reminds me very much of a Fins Bois cognac; the mouthfeel is so seductive that I don't want to swallow it, not because it doesn't taste wonderful, but because the texture is so sublimely silky—the feline, sexy flavors of burnt almonds, resin, and grapes come together as elegantly and harmoniously as any domestic brandy I've sampled; this complex but polite classic finishes gracefully; there is only one regret—only 47 cases were produced; I believe that this is the greatest American grape-based brandy ever made.

RATING ★ ★ ★ ★ ★   **Highest Recommendation** $$$

GERMAIN-ROBIN Shareholder's Blend No. 4 Alambic Brandy 40% Alcohol (California)

Straight amber/honey color; the mesmerizing, multilayered, pineapple, and coconut nose is very delicate at first, then with aeration picks up a spicy oakiness; the focused, off-dry, serious, concentrated flavors are of sweet oak and toffee; this superlative brandy displays the round, generous, nutty, and flowery personality that is frequently associated with cognacs from the Borderies district in the Charente *département* of southwestern France; hands down, one of the sleekest noncognac brandies I've tasted; a great find; seek out and enjoy.

RATING ★ ★ ★ ★   **Highly Recommended** $$

GERMAIN-ROBIN Reserve Alambic Brandy 40% Alcohol (California)

Lovely orange/bronze color with rust highlights; the elegant, refined, sedate, and altogether luscious aromas of vanilla, banana, and cream lay a banquet for the olfactory sense—simply a great bouquet; a bountiful, but silky mouth-feel; the caramel, off-dry flavors are beautifully and skillfully composed into a harmonious, spirity presence that is simultaneously firm and classy; this beauty is what brandy making in the U.S. should be and hopefully will be for years to come; excellent aftertaste, which is superbly balanced, refreshing, and faintly sweet; sincere and deserved kudos.

RATING ★ ★ ★ ★   **Highly Recommended** $$$

GERMAIN-ROBIN XO Select Barrel Reserve Alambic Brandy 40% Alcohol (California)

Made from approximately 80% pinot noir brandies; medium amber hue, good clarity; the delicate nose is shy at first, then with aeration it offers a moderately snappy grapiness that's alluring—beneath that layer is a spicy, vinous foundation that's so faint most admirers won't even notice it—I've enjoyed other more expressive Germain-Robin bouquets more than this one; once on the palate, this subtle thoroughbred takes off like Seabiscuit with firecrackers tied to its tail in the fifth race at Pimlico—the nuanced tastes of ripe grapes and old oak are complemented beautifully by soft white cheese at the midpalate—it's a truly sublime flavor that rivals my all-time G-R favorite, their now sold-out Pinot Noir Single-Barrel brandy of a while ago; had the nose been more generous, it would have won a fifth star.

RATING ★ ★ ★ ★   **Highly Recommended** $$$

GERMAIN-ROBIN Zinfandel Grappa 43.4% Alcohol (California)

Ricetti Ranch—distilled in 1994; water-clear, impeccable purity; the brazen hussy aroma leaps from the glass—it's all unbridled pomace, cotton, seeds, and fruity fresh-off-the-still fragrances, wrapped in a delectably disarming package that by the final nosing neither assaults nor bullies; in the mouth, it's like taking a cluster of ripe Zinfandel grapes and devouring them right off the vine—the flavor is sweet, clean, very heady, but controlled to the point of being elegant and fully focused on the grape; the finish is a total winner, as a crushed-violet feel takes hold of the palate and surprisingly delicate, plump, grapy tastes take it home.

RATING ★ ★ ★ ★   ***Highly Recommended*** $$$

GERMAIN-ROBIN Old Vine Zinfandel Grappa 43.7% Alcohol (California)

Totally clear; emits an intensely grapy, stainless-steel, gummy-bear bouquet that's not in the least jarring or pungent—considering the alcohol level and the very nature of grappa, that's unusual; on palate, this extraordinarily graceful and genteel grappa is a study in flavor nuance, with supple and complementary layers of citrus, sweet cake frosting, ripe apricots, and pomace; the aftertaste is sleek, clean, round, firm, but low key and mannered; I never thought I'd hear myself call a domestic grappa "elegant," but there's always a first time for everything.

RATING ★ ★ ★ ★   ***Highly Recommended*** $$$

GERMAIN-ROBIN V43 Single-Barrel Alambic Brandy 41.6% Alcohol (California)

100% pinot noir; light amber/golden/apple cider–like color, with evidence of microscopic suspended particles (grape must?) that would go unnoticed to all but the most anal-retentive imbibers, like yours truly, who are petty enough to point out such insignificant things; the light-as-a-feather bouquet is soft, tart, and refined, with heady, astringent scents of orange peel, grape skins, and, strangely, flannel—I wasn't in awe of this aroma; as is usual for a G-R alembic brandy, it's the combination of texture and taste that garners all the rating stars—the texture is firm, finely structured, and deliciously silky, while the defined, agile tastes of oak, burnt nuts, and grapes crescendo nicely in an aftertaste that's graceful, pleasingly tart, and moderately long; only 462 bottles of this beauty available nationwide.

RATING ★ ★ ★ ★   ***Highly Recommended*** $$$

GERMAIN-ROBIN Single-Barrel V16 Alambic Brandy 42.9% Alcohol (California)

Made from 100% French *colombard* grapes, the second most important variety in France's Cognac region from the seventeenth century up to the phylloxera devastation in the middle to late nineteenth century—the grape that was first among equals in the pre-phylloxera era was the fragrant *folle blanche;* pure, light-to-medium amber/harvest gold hue; this nose is delightfully zesty, vivid, and dry to off-dry in its opening salvo—aeration and swirling open it up quite a bit as grapy, vanilla-wafer, and citrus notes leap forward—even after 30 minutes in the glass, the bouquet remains agile, one-pointed, and keenly fresh; it begins shyly at palate entry, then punches the accelerator and zooms forward tastewise, with succulent, off-dry, intensely fruity flavors that are nicely balanced by a soft-edged acidity—the midpalate is off-dry to sweet and very biscuity and peach-like; the finish is a tad timid, but medium-long and off-dry.

RATING ★ ★ ★ ★   ***Highly Recommended*** $$$

GERMAIN-ROBIN Special Cigar Lover's Blend Alambic Brandy 40% Alcohol (California)

Amber/brown color; the citrusy nose has oodles of tropical fruit, especially pineapple, guava, kiwi, and mango, upfront and in your face—all this enchanting fruit is supported by a sturdy foundational layer of tobacco smoke, new oak, and a soft grapiness—it's a civilized, highly stylized bouquet that leans heavily to the fruit side of the aroma chart; astonishingly, once in the mouth, I instantly recognized why distillers Ansley Coale and Hubert Germain-Robin designated this particular blend specifically as their "cigar lover's" companion—it's moderately sweet, potent, firm (but not chunky), smoky, and fruity—all the complementary elements to cigar enjoyment; the finish is feline smooth and succulent; a rare brandy that's purposely geared to a certain consumer; the fact that I'm not a smoker myself, however, won't dissuade me from having some after dinner at regular intervals.

RATING ★ ★ ★ ★   ***Highly Recommended*** $$$

GERMAIN-ROBIN Fine Alambic Brandy 40% Alcohol (California)

Pale orange/amber color; piquant, remarkably buoyant, perfumed, fruity nose, accented by vivacious pear and apple-like qualities; the very tart, mouth-puckering, smoky, tobacco, keenly citrusy flavor relies way too much on that acidy crispness; the palate showed little of the delightful appley-peary fruit promised in the authentically pleasant nose; if the fruit were extended for the taste buds as nicely as it was for the olfactory sense, this brandy would be an instant winner; as it presently is, it is so austere as to be astringent and regrettably one-dimensional; tasted several times with the same impression—I can't understand why this brandy is so markedly inferior to all the other Germain-Robin spirits.

RATING ★ ★ $$

JACQUIN'S Five-Star Brandy 40% Alcohol

Skimpy, pale color—a muted harvest gold; the feinty, leathery, musty, pungent nose has an off-putting sweaty and stale quality that left me cold; the pleasant, if different, palate almost redeems the peculiar aroma by offering tasty, defined flavors of raisins, ripe apples, and coffee; it finishes smoothly with a ripe-fruit, off-dry tail; clean up the malodorous nose and you might have a decent domestic brandy.

RATING ★ $

KORBEL Brandy 40% Alcohol

Lively, clear light amber/honey color; the rather shy, simple bouquet of spirit and grapiness is coy and unevolved; the aromas are thrown to the side as the silky texture and elegant flavor completely captivate the palate; easily the most grapy and classy brandy of the inexpensive, mass-produced domestic brandies—a downright tasty brandy by any standard, imported or domestic; the fresh, vigorous flavor is rich and creamy, then turns intensely raisiny, but gentle in the satisfying, extended aftertaste; would even have scored higher if the nose had been more pronounced.

RATING ★ ★ ★   ***Recommended*** $

Paul Masson Grande Amber Brandy 40% Alcohol

The label states that this brandy has been matured in oak for three years; the appearance lives up to this brandy's name, as an opulent, lively, medium amber/marigold/orange hue impresses the eye, superb clarity; the nose emits a pleasant grapy, dry-cheese-like, and generally fruity aroma that, while hardly a dazzling experience, is nevertheless quite enjoyable in an uncomplicated way; the palate entry is smooth, clean, correct, and tart, then a keen sweetness enters the picture at midpalate; the finish is medium-long, piquant, and well structured; if this domestic brandy had possessed more depth of character and scope in the flavor department, I would gladly have given it a third star and a recommendation.

RATING ★ ★　　$

St. George Spirits (California)

St. George Spirits is the realization of distiller Jorg Rupf's dream. Rupf opened his distillery in 1982 in Alameda, California, directly across the Bay from San Francisco after doing postdoctoral work at University of California–Berkeley. Born in Alsace, France, Rupf spent his childhood in the Black Forest assisting his grandfather in the making of family brandies. After spending time as an attorney in what was then West Germany's Ministry of Culture, Rupf brought his family's distilling expertise and passion with him when he landed in California. His mission: to make eaux-de-vie and fortified dessert wines from fruit grown on the West Coast that rival the great fruit brandies of Alsace, northern Switzerland, and western Germany, like Massenez, Ova, Jean Danflou, Trimbach, René de Miscault, and Retter. Rupf offered his inaugural bottling in 1984. Starting a fruit brandy distillery in a traditionally beer-drinking country that at the time was in the midst of a "wine revolution" must have caused more than a few sleepless nights for Rupf. Bucking the odds, however, he has prevailed for over a decade and a half.

St. George Spirits Kirsch Eau-de-Vie 40% Alcohol (California)

Clear to the eye; like the Kirsch Royale, the nose acquits itself very well indeed, as the red Montmorency cherry element overrides any cherry-pit minerally/slaty/phenolic bitterness that almost always seems to show up in any cherry spirit; in the mouth, the feel is solid and round, while the sweet cherry fruit flavor is firm and compelling; the delightful finish shows a dab of heat in the throat, which I liked, since it wasn't a three-alarm job; it's a nicely crafted spirit in which the subtle aftertaste lingers on and on.

RATING ★ ★ ★ ★　　*Highly Recommended*　　$

St. George Spirits Grappa of Zinfandel 40% Alcohol (California)

Clear; a robust, steely, passing-gear nose of ripe grapes, grape must, seeds, and bark—this nose is so basic and elemental that it's irresistible; flavorwise, it enters the palate sweetly as the pedal-to-the-metal grapiness plays it to the hilt—by midpalate a vinous, brambly quality gets thrown in for balance and takes it all the way to the easy, delectable aftertaste, where there's a slight flicker of heat; made from the wet pomace of Sonoma County and Napa Valley grapes.

RATING ★ ★ ★ ★ **Highly Recommended** $

ST. GEORGE SPIRITS Grappa of Traminer 40% Alcohol (California)

Clear as spring water; the nose is audaciously viney, vegetal, weedy, lemony, and even spiced with ginger root—a charismatic, quirky bouquet that even reminds me a bit of root beer and roses on the second and third passes—easily the most intriguing and layered nose of the St. George spirits; in the mouth, the lemon-peel taste greets the taste buds at palate entry, then a fine, sweetish grapiness takes the wheel and keeps on driving through to the sublime, snappy, zesty finish; a sound grappa that keeps you guessing as to its origins; I liked the overall uniqueness of it more than any one quality; made from Santa Maria Valley *gewurztraminer* grapes.

RATING ★ ★ ★ **Recommended** $

ST. GEORGE SPIRITS Williams Pear Eau-de-Vie 40% Alcohol (California)

Clear appearance; the focused, laser-beam-like pear fragrance has a fine balance between tartness, alcohol thrust, and fruit essence—it's a clean, firm nose that showcases the fruit without losing sight of its distilled-spirit mission; on palate, it starts out in an almost sedate manner, offering a mild taste of ripe Bosc pear, then inexplicably and startlingly it explodes in the throat, going rough, raw, and harsh, finally overheating in the rocky finish; all the gains made in the nose are lost by midpalate; while I don't think it's totally without virtue, I can't even consider recommending it, because it spins out of control after the palate entry and, certainly, no spirit can live solely on the charm of its bouquet; made from Bartlett pears.

RATING ★ ★ $

ST. GEORGE SPIRITS Framboise Eau-de-Vie 40% Alcohol (California)

Properly clear; the nose initially speaks of barely ripe raspberries, with background touches of gum, damp vegetation, oil, and brambles—as the bouquet mingles with air, the raspberry component advances from minimally ripe to abundantly ripe—it's a bouquet that shows some promise; similar to the Williams Poire, once in the mouth, it disappoints—I found it oily, creamy (which it shouldn't be), and lacking in grace up until the aftertaste; to its credit, it didn't bite at all in the finish, and, clearly, the aftertaste ends up being its finest quality—unfortunately, there's not enough substance or virtue there, however, to redeem its evident shortcomings; while not unpleasant, it simply falls well short of a recommendation if for no other reason than it's so inconsistent; a good spirit is one that's steady all the way through; made from Meeker raspberries grown in Oregon and Washington.

RATING ★ ★ $

PISCO–SOUTH AMERICA

H ardly known outside of South America, except in locations where Peruvians and Chileans have migrated, pisco is a distilled spirit made from wine, usually from the highly aromatic and orange-like grape variety known as *muscat*.

ALTO DEL CARMEN Reservado Pisco 40% Alcohol (Chile)
Very pale straw color; made from 100% *muscat* grapes and aged in 200-liter American oak barrels for six to eight months; the bouquet is completely focused on the sole grape of origin—it owns that seductive, sweet-sour, orange-blossom scent that's so closely associated with *muscat*; in the mouth, it's pure, medium-bodied, tart at entry, then off-dry to semisweet in mid-palate—it's in the midpalate that the exotic, spicy fruit takes hold of the taste buds and rides them in a gallop through to the aftertaste; this is a truly delicious spirit that has only the slightest traces of distillate rawness and carloads of fruity flavor and aroma; excellent job.

RATING ★ ★ ★ ★   *Highly Recommended* $

CAPEL Reservado Pisco 40% Alcohol (Chile)
Clear appearance; the nose is soft, bubblegum-like, herbal, a bit spicy (cinnamon), and fruity in a dry, tart manner; the taste is pure, gum-like, off-dry to semisweet, and very acceptable; though made from a blend of *mus-*

cat, Pedro Ximenez, and *torontel* grapes, it definitely displays a distillate, oily/fruity face rather than a wine/fruity persuasion, or even a fortified or aromatized wine demeanor; it's pleasant and easy to quaff; I can envision good applications as an aperitif on-the-rocks with a twist of lemon or lime.

RATING ★★★   *Recommended* $

South African Brandy

South African wine producers have been making brandy for over three centuries. Although it suffered from a dubious reputation over the years, South African brandy was given new life in the 1920s with the introduction of a Brandy Board, which meted out production standards and regulations. Today, the Cape brandy industry is dominated by one company, Ko-operative Wijnbouwers Vereinging van Zuid-Afrika, or KWV.

KWV 10-Year-Old Brandy 38% Alcohol (Republic of South Africa)
Pretty, luminous orange/light amber hue, perfect purity—seems awfully light for so old a brandy from a hot climate; even after ten minutes and furious bouts of swirling, this bouquet remained subdued in comparison to its two younger and more expressive siblings—the little that it did display showed decent balance between acid, wood, and fruit—if you purchase it, just don't expect a rollicking aroma; this brandy comes to full flower in the mouth as supple, gentlemanly, off-dry to sweet flavors of soft, old oak and ripe grapes make for a very pleasant taste experience; mannered, undemanding, but extended finish.

    RATING ★ ★ ★   ***Recommended*** $$

KWV Three-Star Brandy 43% Alcohol (Republic of South Africa)
Good color, light-to-medium amber/honey/orange tone, good clarity; the nose is acceptably heady/spirity, with barely detectable backnotes of sweet oak and honey—the inherent aromas have a difficult time breaking

through the alcohol ceiling; quite sweet right from palate entry, but there's very little in terms of substance after the opening round of sweet, ripe grapes; overly sweet aftertaste; drinkable, to be sure, but too simplistic and deficient in depth and dimension to be recommended—a sweet lollipop of a brandy that's designed for brandy beginners.

RATING ★★ $

KWV VSOP Brandy 40% Alcohol (Republic of South Africa)

Gorgeous, deep orange/medium amber/pekoe tea tone, great purity; the full nose shows some elements of caramel, roasted almond, and honey in the initial two passes, then it tones down and narrows its scope—what's left in the third and fourth nosings is a reticent, spirity grapiness and that's about all; the very sweet entry approaches the danger zone for brandy sweetness, but doesn't quite cross into it—at midpalate, although the intense sweetness makes an attempt at opulence, it falls short due to a lack of acidity and over-all definition; very woody, honeyed, and drinkable, but the near-cloying sweetness makes me wonder what shortcomings are being concealed.

RATING ★★ $

CALVADOS–FRANCE

L ittle is known and bare concern is shown about apple brandy in the U.S. Yet the U.S. is one of two major sources for the distilled spirit made from apple cider. In America, brandy made from apples is called *applejack*. The other apple brandy, and clearly the superior of the two, comes from France's Normandy region and is referred to as *calvados*. The region's premier apple brandies are given the designation of *Calvados du Pays d'Auge.*

Calvados has been around for centuries. In fact, when the Vikings came rumbling through Normandy, circa 1000 A.D., they took a strong liking to the local spirit made from the vast orchards of the district. It's said that the Normans themselves routinely enjoyed a glass of calvados in the middle of a meal to aid digestion and to clear the palate for the remainder of the feast. The production process is similar to that of other brandies in that the cider made from the apples is distilled twice in pot stills and then aged in oak barrels, in this case from the forests of Limousin. Most are aged for less than ten years, but some are held back for as long as four or five decades before bottling. The older versions can display remarkable similarities in color (from the oak) and character to cognacs.

CALVADOS DU PRIEURE 40% Alcohol

Immensely appealing, vibrant gold/honey/amber hue; the gloriously tart, baked-apple nose is full and juicy, but delicate, showing scant trace of spirit/alcohol—it actually reminds me of baked apple pie; on the palate, a rich, cinnamon sweetness envelops the tongue in a most enjoyable manner;

the keen appley flavor is right on the mark; the aftertaste is clean, silky, and smooth, showing just a smidgen of tingle on the sides of the tongue; nicely done from the snappy start to the engaging finish; I thought this wonderful brandy delivers the message of Calvados articulately and with style.

RATING ★ ★ ★ ★   ***Highly Recommended*** $

Daron XO Calvados Pays d'Auge 40% Alcohol

Markedly darker in color than the Fine—it's a pretty amber/honey hue with orange highlights, proper clarity; this nose shows more heft as off-dry to sweet, biscuity, wine-like aromas come up from the glass—yes, there's an apple presence, but it's intertwined with oak, light tannin, cake batter, and hard-candy aromas; in the mouth, the decadent, mature tastes of spiced apple, baked apple, oak, vanilla, orange peel, and sugar cookies make this a genuine treat; the tart finish is very long, concentrated, and supple.

RATING ★ ★ ★ ★   ***Highly Recommended*** $$

Daron 1955 Calvados Pays d'Auge 40% Alcohol

Flat, medium amber color, with a yellow/gold core, pure; the bouquet immediately offers up a great woodiness that nicely supports the sour-apple headlining aroma—a luscious, light toffee/butterscotch note comes on board after about ten minutes of aeration—this aromatic deepening made it a memorable calvados fragrance; lip-smacking good, this hearty, heady winner is acceptably prickly, sweet-sour, and loaded with oaky depth and layering—the flavors just keep unfolding the longer it's in the mouth; the aftertaste is sweet, appley, and almost biscuity rich; genuinely lovely.

RATING ★ ★ ★ ★   ***Highly Recommended*** $$$

Daron 1971 Calvados Pays d'Auge 40% Alcohol

Medium-to-dark amber/honey tone, with copper core highlights, pure; the nose is very toasty, like baked apples sprinkled with cinnamon through all four nosings—the oak comes into play in the third pass, adding a clean, resiny backnote; after swirling, this ropy calvados clings to the glass's interior walls like paint; on palate, it's lean, feline, intensely tart, and pointed at entry—at midpalate, a fruity sweetness enters the picture as the spiritiness picks up its pace, leaving behind a bit of tingling on the tongue; the aftertaste is heady, appley, and very fine; not a blockbuster, but a tidy, compact, direct winner.

RATING ★ ★ ★   ***Recommended*** $$$

Daron 1970 Calvados Pays d'Auge 40% Alcohol

Medium amber, with orange core features, pure; the bouquet is quite sour and acidic, with very little of the toastiness found in the 1971—the apple factor is more pronounced, however, in this svelte beauty; in the mouth, I found it somewhat dumb at entry, then it expanded quickly on its way to midpalate, where it displayed a mouth-puckering tartness before going moderately sweet in the finish—it tasted much rounder on the third sampling as it became deeper with aeration; I marginally preferred this 1970 to the slightly thinner, but very good, 1971 from Daron.

RATING ★ ★ ★   ***Recommended*** $$$

Daron Fine Calvados Pays d'Auge 40% Alcohol

Light gold/straw/flaxen color, excellent purity; the nose is vivacious and assertive, but fine-tuned and accessible, with slender hints of paraffin, sour apple, and flowers; in the mouth, its firm texture generously coats the tongue as alluring flavors of citrus, ripe apple, banana, and vanilla wafer (from the oak casks?) meld beautifully by midpalate; the aftertaste is clean, off-dry, and remarkably long.

RATING ★ ★ ★   *Recommended* $ $

HÉROUT

The Hérout Fils family ages all their ciders for a minimum of two years before distillation. But what makes them stand apart from their competitors is the fact that Hérout distills their calvados only once, which gives them a fuller body than most others. This is a very small operation that lives off of only 20 hectares of orchards, which supply 14 different varieties of apples.

Hérout Hors d'Age Medaille d'Or Calvados 40% Alcohol

Gold/honey color; the sour-apple candy bouquet is both prickly in the nose cavity (due to its lively spirit) and delicately fruity—a most distinctive and intriguing nose; dry, minty as it enters the mouth, acutely appley and tart but not overly astringent, sharp, or bitter on the tongue—at midpalate there's a sublime touch of caramel that grows warmer as the dry finish endlessly rolls on; the taste of apples lingers very long; a truly remarkable apple brandy whose elegance and complexity approach VSOP cognac territory.

RATING ★ ★ ★ ★   *Highly Recommended* $ $ $

Hérout 1977 Calvados 40% Alcohol

Darkest color of the three Hérouts—a definitive amber hue, with minute suspended particles floating about; the spirit ends up being the grand marshall of the nose parade, with just a very subtle hint of tart, green apples and caramel; an eye-opening entry of apples, vanilla biscuits, and calm, composed spirit; evolves at the back of the throat into a stately brandy that doesn't overstay its welcome; medium-long aftertaste; the only flaw is a clear taste of cardboard midway through the flavor; rich and rewarding.

RATING ★ ★ ★   *Recommended* $ $ $

Hérout 1958 Calvados 40% Alcohol

Yellow/amber color; the invigorating, piquant, vivacious nose speaks of ripe apples, gentle spirit, and a tinge of wild flowers and wet grass; on palate, it's most cognac-like in terms of bearing, feel, and complexity; the appley flavor has pretty much dissipated, but what's left behind is a soft, warm, mildly caramelized brandy of elegance and charm; strangely, the only time a graceful hint of apples appears is in the firm finish, way at the back of the throat; the only problem is a waxiness at the entry; other than that very minor irritation, I genuinely admired this lovely and satisfying brandy.

RATING ★ ★ ★   *Recommended* $ $ $

OTHER EUROPEAN BRANDIES

ASBACH URALT 40% Alcohol (Germany)

Deep harvest-gold color—a very pretty appearance by brandy standards; the forward nose is candy sweet, vanilla-cake-frosting-like, and slightly metallic, though not unpleasant in the least—after a third pass, I pick up an ethereal hint of raw apple—I keep envisioning coffee cake or Danish pastry for some reason as I sniff it; now the bad news—all the appealing qualities enjoyed in the aroma flee from the ungainly, awkward, and astringent flavor, which shows not one iota of fruit, balance, wood, firmness, or suppleness—this ends up being a horror show in the mouth; I can't figure out what went so wrong with this brandy; after a visually pleasant beginning and a good, but not great, bouquet, all sense of direction seems to have been lost; the final result is an acidic, harsh disaster.

RATING ★ $$

DESCHAUX VSOP Napoleon Brandy 40% Alcohol (France)

Solid amber color; the nose I find a bit hard and angular—in other (and doubtless better) words, there's no sign of smoothness, sophistication, or roundness—there is, however, a blunt acidic edge to the aroma, which, while not sharp or harsh, does give off some pointed tartness—with 20 minutes of aeration, the nose still doesn't improve; on palate, it's embarrassingly skimpy, overly acidic (to the point of being downright harsh), tediously short on charm, and virtually tasteless except for a quick burst of cigar smoke and tar; who escaped with the fruit? this gnawing brandy tastes like the grape wine was distilled once or twice too often; take a pass.

RATING ★ $

De Valcourt VSOP Napoleon Brandy 40% Alcohol (France)

Rich, vibrant, amber/orange color, pristine clarity; the luxurious nose is all butterscotch, English toffee, caramel, cream, and new wood, with scant evidence of grapes, acidity, or other fruit; in the mouth, the lush, almost syrupy texture swathes the tongue with suave, melded, sweetish flavor of sauteed butter, violets, oak, and light coffee; the finish is mildly sweet but surprisingly timid and short considering the plump nature of the texture; the lack of acidity and the fact that the concentration dissipated so dramatically in the aftertaste worked against it being rated higher; this brandy is produced by Augier Robin Briand et Compagnie in the Cognac region of France—it is not, however, considered a cognac because it is distilled in a column still rather than the small alembics traditionally utilized in the production of cognac.

RATING ★★★   *Recommended* $

Fassbind Framboise Raspberry Brandy 40% Alcohol (Switzerland)

Clear as spring water; zesty, alcoholic, head-snapping, stemmy nose of fiery raspberry—not the kind of nose that you could leisurely sniff for hours on end, since the alcohol fumes are too intense, too piercing even after 15 minutes of being in the glass—the pungency in the aroma at last settled down into a mellow fruitiness after 30 minutes—question: What consumer will know enough to wait that long?—it enters the mouth dry and fruity, rests on the tongue calmly, quietly, and gracefully, then smoothly shifts into overdrive in the dynamic, fully fruited, but bone-dry aftertaste that's a genuine knockout; after a so-so bouquet, the flavor and finish brought home the bacon.

RATING ★★★   *Recommended* $$

Jacopo Poli L'Arzente Brandy 10 Years Old 43% Alcohol (Italy)

Pale amber/golden yellow color, with an interior touch of green, perfect purity; aged in Limousin, Allier, and Slavonian oak casks for ten years—the grape is *trebbiano*; the elegant, but deceptively potent, bouquet is assertive, rounded, grapy, butterscotchy, and resiny sweet in the first two nosings—later on, hints of paraffin and lanolin add to the serene complexity—a stellar aroma that's ideally balanced; on palate, the entry thrust is lean and fruity, then it quickly fills out at midpalate in generous, endowed flavors of cocoa, oloroso sherry, vanilla, sweet oak, and ripe fruit—the mouth presence is borderline semisweet/sweet and, not for a moment, heavy or cloying; the finish sees the return of the butterscotch quality; lovely, controlled, compact.

RATING ★★★★   *Highly Recommended* $$

Raynal VSOP Napoleon Brandy 40% Alcohol (France)

Bold, stunning, copper color; the nose is like roasted nuts, citrus (tangerine?), spice, and even some herbs; on the palate, it's nicely balanced between lip-smacking fruit and the acid counterpoint; the texture is silky and sure-footed; the mild aftertaste is smooth and grapy, with a tail end of heat that borders on being too vigorous; but, clearly, the overall impression is of a soundly produced, properly aged brandy that's as comfortable served neat in a snifter as it is mixed into a cocktail; I can't think of a more pleasing (or more affordable) everyday imported brandy; bravo.

RATING ★ ★ ★   *Recommended* $

RAYNAL Réserve Extra French Brandy 40% Alcohol (France)

Superb, rich, medium amber/tea/orange/rust/copper-penny hue; the generous nose is biscuity, almost yeasty, leathery, and coffee-like—I enjoyed it right from the first pass through the succulent last nosing—there are oaky, smoky, tobacco-like elements that are refined and inviting; it's sweet at palate entry, really almost caramel-like, and then it takes on more of an oak, ripe yellow fruit character at midpalate; the aftertaste is balanced between fruit, wood, and sweetness and is quite long; I rode the rating fence on this well-made brandy, wanting to give it a fourth rating star, but the elevated, intense sweetness bordered on being too impactful; nevertheless, a solid, chewy, muscular brandy that's a good buy.

RATING ★ ★ ★   *Recommended* $

VECCHIA ROMAGNA Riserva Rara Oltre 15 Anni 40% Alcohol (Italy)

Old amontillado sherry color of russet/topaz, with pretty highlights of copper—quite a beguiling eyeful; the forward, caramelized bouquet is pleasantly sweet, biscuity, and leathery with a wonderful cake-frosting quality—an inviting nose, which is more friendly and rewarding than it is complex or ponderous; oddly neutral tasting at entry, then succulent, high-octane flavors of brown sugar, ripe grapes, and milk chocolate caress the entire palate in a pillow of soft spirit; ends as amiably as it began in an easygoing, generous aftertaste that's completely unpretentious; what it doesn't offer in august character it ably supplies in delectable flavors and approachability; very nice job.

RATING ★ ★ ★   *Recommended* $ $ $

VECCHIA ROMAGNA Riserva 10 Anni Brandy 40% Alcohol (Italy)

Made from *trebbiano* grapes; the brilliant orange/bronze/amber hue is most appealing, ideal clarity; the nose is intensely grapy and remarkably fresh, almost like grappa—it shows moderate wood, ample caramel, and a slight touch of nail polish remover—it's not my favorite bouquet of the three brandies from Giovanni Buton; in the mouth is where this brandy shines brightest as citrusy, clean, and crisp tastes sparkle on the tongue—while there isn't great depth here, there is enough flavor and texture layering to lend better-than-average character and, hence, satisfaction; the aftertaste is medium-long, astringent, grapy, and delightful; high marks for the appearance, palate presence, and finish.

RATING ★ ★ ★   *Recommended* $ $

VECCHIA ROMAGNA Etichetta Nera Brandy 40% Alcohol (Italy)

Made from *trebbiano* grapes; rich, deep amber/honey color is augmented by a trace of orange in the core, perfect purity; the curious bouquet has none-too-subtle hints of spice and paraffin overlapping the grapy spiritiness—the second and third nosings reveal pickled cucumber, peppermint, and dried fruit—it's a zesty, idiosyncratic, aromatic melange; on palate, the off-dry to sweet flavors include caramel, toffee, and a bit of wood-influenced vanilla—it's lean and almost austere in terms of body; the finish is too quick and borders on being overly astringent; the nose provides the most pleasure in this average brandy.

   RATING ★ ★ $$

BRANDY AND GRAPPA–ITALY

For centuries, grappa was the peasant's daily drink in the villages of Italy. It was often scorned as being "firewater," unfit to imbibe by people with discerning tastes. But as fashion inevitably changes, grappa has become one of the most exciting distilled-spirit categories at the moment and, I hope, for many moments to come. Grappa is made from the pomace—the grape skins, seeds, stems, and pulp that are left behind from the making of wine. The pomace is pressed again and the juice is fermented and distilled, creating a high-alcohol spirit that is the limpid, fragrant essence of the grapes. The new stylistic wave of Italian grappa is toward more palatable, fresher grappas and away from the traditional style, which was known in the past to melt down fillings, take paint off boats, and flush plumbing free of all debris.

ANTONELLA BOCCHINO

Antonella Bocchino is a fourth-generation maker of grappa. Her ancestors founded the family business back in 1898. When the baton was passed to Antonella and her older brother Carlo, Antonella soon embarked upon a personal mission to create a new, more delicate, and aromatic style of grappa. In 1985, she began her tedious and often frustrating trek of experimentation. Her initial goal was to introduce some of Italy's rarest grapes into the grappa arena. As time went on, she likewise started to experiment with distilled fruit from indigenous fruit trees. That dabbling led her to do research on producing brandies from flowers as well, a long-forgotten tradition.

Soon Antonella was toying with the distillation of the oils from the petals of orange and lime blossoms, roses, violets, and irises. Learning how to deal with nature's most delicate elements, knowing when to have the flowers picked exactly at the most advantageous moment, took many sleepless nights and numerous hours of research. After three years of trial and error, Antonella discovered the formulas that allowed the maximum essence to come forth from her distillates in a way that expressed the very soul of the berries and flowers. Whether or not you like grappas doesn't matter when it comes to these incredibly fine spirits. If you have come to think of grappas in incendiary terms, try these, which are redefining the category.

AB Collection Bacche di Corbezzolo 43% Alcohol

Crystal clear; by far, one of the two or three most memorable, fresh-picked, and unique berry aromas I've ever experienced in a spirit; the perfumed, succulent fragrance is so well endowed and firm that you almost can't help but envision the hillsides of Canelli, Italy; the nose comes closest to ripe California strawberries, or, better, strawberry puree; I also experienced a keen, snappy peppermint quality on the palate that temporarily dominated, then faded into the background in the concentrated berry finish, which was long, but soft; I really felt as though I had eaten some just-picked, ripe berries right off the vine; a spirit experience that transcends all others.

RATING ★ ★ ★ ★ ★   *Highest Recommendation* $$$

AB Collection Fiore di Rosa 43% Alcohol

Crystalline, fresh-water appearance; the nose is stunningly fresh, sweet, perfumed, and boasts a still-on-the-stem scent of roses—nosing this thoroughbred is like strolling through an English garden; the heart-of-the-rose flavor dazzles the taste buds, but never overpowers them—the flavors are sedate, mellow, concentrated, and miraculously delicious; finishes on little cat's feet with echoes of roses lasting for minutes; this is what nectar and essence are all about—a unique distilled experience of the first order unlike any other I've had.

RATING ★ ★ ★ ★ ★   *Highest Recommendation* $$$

AB Collection Grappa di Moscato d'Asti 45% Alcohol

Spring-water clarity; the piquant, leesy, whistle-clean, dry, slate/shale, minerally, round aromas gently tweak the nose in all four passes; medium-to full-bodied; satiny texture; the lively, vivid flavors of citrus (alternately orange, lime, and pink grapefruit) coat the palate; the dry, extended aftertaste evokes ripe grapes, pomace, and spice; what is most appealing about this toothsome grappa is its ideal balance between chic sophistication and open, somehow rustic naturalness; it goes light years beyond the old-time masculine firewater image of grappa, which has become something of a caricature, and transports grappa to its next evolutionary step, which is a flavorful spirit that is refreshing, lush, and, most important of all, approachable; in my opinion, women in particular should love this spirit.

RATING ★ ★ ★ ★ ★   *Highest Recommendation* $$$

BANFI Grappa di Moscadello (Italy) 45% Alcohol

Very pale straw/yellow color; the racy, sexy, intense lead-pencil, ever-green, viney, fresh-water, perfumy, semisweet nose captivates and charms the nose; the full, round, concentrated, grapy flavor holds court in the mouth, then dismisses it in the gentle, soft, grapy, and, dare I say, mellow aftertaste; I was not at all overpowered by the elevated alcohol; beautifully balanced acid/fruit/alcohol components; minutes after spitting out, there was still a delicious ripe-grape flavor; well made.

RATING ★★★   ***Recommended*** $

BANFI Grappa di Brunello (Italy) 45% Alcohol

Slightly deeper in pale, yellow/green color than the Banfi Moscadello; the heady, seriously spirity nose has an able supporting cast of anise, orange blossoms, asparagus, and lees; this nose seems more refined and floral than the forward, herbal Moscadello; satiny, smooth on palate, with an intriguing flash of cotton candy at the tail end; drier, fleshier than the Moscadello in terms of flavor and feel; an awfully pleasant spirit by all accounts; finishes fruity, but dry; where the Moscadello exhibits vigor, the Brunello shows finesse; I like them equally for reasons as different as they are.

RATING ★★★   ***Recommended*** $

BORTOLO NARDINI Riserva Grappa 50% Alcohol

Pure, yellow/gold, like a *premier cru* Chablis, some infinitesimal bits are noted; this is a brazenly traditional grappa nose, one with guts and a cheese-like surface layer—beneath that, the spirity/heady foundation layer of pomace keeps this bruiser on course; shockingly sweet in the mouth, this head basher transforms itself into a pussycat by midpalate as the streamlined, winey, grapy flavors combine in a harmonious presence that leads to the unbelievably soft and polite finish; I could barely believe the shift in gears from the bonecrusher nose to the mannered taste; there is some acceptable, smoldering, embers-like heat in the throat.

RATING ★★★★   ***Highly Recommended*** $$$

BORTOLO NARDINI Rue-Flavored Grappa 42.8% Alcohol

Spitting image of a new-vintage German riesling—straw yellow/green tone, some minute suspended particles are seen; the nose is definitely not the selling point—it's mushroomy, musky, stinky, and skunky on the surface, but below that lies a strangely alluring tobacco-leaf, intensely vegetal (broccoli, brussel sprouts) aromatic layer that reminds me most of unsmoked cigarettes; on palate, Nardini has more elegance than the other rue-flavored grappa that I've evaluated, Candolini—in this grappa, the mushroomy/ weedy flavor actually complements the spirit because there's a subtle sweetness to it; the finish features the unsmoked cigarettes and a delicate sweetness; skip the bad-ass nose and proceed right to the tasting.

RATING ★★★   ***Recommended*** $$

CANDOLINI Grappa Ruta (Rue Flavored) 40% Alcohol

Clear, with just the palest shade of green—has a rut plant floating inside; the rubbery, pencil-eraser, weedy, overgrown garden nose leaves me as cold as a January day in Fairbanks—it's simply unnecessary, in my opinion, to adulterate the natural, grapy, pomace-like bouquet of grappa—but, hey, what do I know? I liked the taste of the New Coke back in the 1980s; the taste is leagues ahead of the aroma as bitter, herbal, undeniably fresh, even delicate (this is grappa?) enchant the taste buds; the finish is meek, leaving behind the slimmest taste of herbs; the mellow flavor and character saved the day for this otherwise mediocre grappa; it's difficult to speculate, but I wonder what this grappa tastes like without the shrubbery.

RATING ★★ $$

CERETTO Zonchera Nebbiolo 45% Alcohol

Fresh spring-water clarity; owns a minerally, slate-like bouquet that has background scents of lead pencil, dried herbs, and seaweed; on the palate, one loses the mineral-like quality as the succulent, semisweet flavor shifts into a minty mode that is appealing from entry through the extended, grapy finish; what begins as a steely, austere grappa in the nose ends up being a warm, fruity grappa in the taste and finish; a somewhat confusing spirit in its quick directional change, but, in spite of that, it's a dashing grappa nonetheless; the pomace came from *nebbiolo* grapes grown on Ceretto's 12.5-acre Zonchera vineyard in La Morra.

RATING ★★★ *Recommended* $$$

CERETTO Brunate Nebbiolo 50% Alcohol

Clear, with minor bits of sediment harmlessly floating about; fresher and more expansive in the nose than the more mannered Zonchera—the lovely bouquet is round, melony, and very alluring; regrettably, the pronounced mintiness in the flavor completely overshadows any other taste element, leaving it unidimensional in the flavor department; the aftertaste goes soft and sweet in the throat; this grappa's trio of main parts, the nose, taste, and finish, simply didn't come together for me, acting as though they were separate entities rather than members of a team; while moderately delectable and most assuredly drinkable, it bothered me that I found so little harmony; grape pomace was taken from Ceretto's illustrious Brunate vineyard; only 1,500 bottles produced.

RATING ★★ $$$

GAJA Costa Russi Nebbiolo Grappa 45% Alcohol

Lovely, opulent, clear, goldenrod color, which is Sauternes-like in how it captures and reflects daylight; this is *nebbiolo* nectar in a glass; the monumentally fresh, piquant nose gives off aromas of lees, lead pencil, herbs, and green olives at the first pass, then, as it evolves with aeration, emits a keen grapiness that is a joy to behold; on palate entry, a refreshing burst of totally dry, astringent fruit changes over rapidly to a lusciously spirity, semidry flavor of grapes and dried fruit; it finishes semidry, with a remarkably long and chiseled flavor of anise and minerals; one of the most elegant, pure grappas I've sampled; a must buy for the grappa-initiated and followers of the genius of Angelo Gaja.

RATING ★ ★ ★ ★ ★   **Highest Recommendation** $$$

GRAPPA DI CAPEZZANA Riserva 43% Alcohol

Looks like a mature Montrachet in its rich golden/sunset-yellow hue; its atypical nose coyly tantalizes the olfactory sense with semisweet, chewy aromas of green olives, dried flowers, cotton fabric, and overripe tropical fruit—it's an intriguing nose that requires some coaxing, but it's worth the extra work; the serene, sweet, well-behaved, and remarkably grapy flavor delighted my palate from entry to the long, fruity finish; a top-flight grappa that, despite its 43% alcohol level, is so well crafted it almost drinks more like a potent wine than a distilled spirit; a simply splendid grappa that should definitely be sought out.

RATING ★ ★ ★ ★   **Highly Recommended** $$$

GRAPPA DA VINACCE di Sassicaia 42% Alcohol

Deep gold/straw color, absolute clarity; the fat, muscular nose shows hardly any spirit whatsoever, but is brimming with scrumptious fruit and nut aromas, including roasted almonds, grapes, banana, and even ripe tropical fruit—with aeration, the plumpness gets scaled back to a one-pointed, juicy, highly perfumed fruitiness—I really adored this bouquet; in the mouth, this viscous, succulent, flavorful beauty shows mature, melded signs of orange peel, ripe table grapes, and garden herbs all wrapped in a sweet, semithick texture; the mouth presence is stunning; one of my all-time favorite Italian grappas—a breathtaking example that totally dismisses the commonly held belief that grappa is invariably brutish; bravo.

RATING ★ ★ ★ ★ ★   **Highest Recommendation** $$$

GRAPPA DI ORNELLAIA di Merlot 42% Alcohol

Lovely rich gold/wine color, with moderate, harmless sediment and particles evident; the piquant, zesty nose leaps from the glass in stirring waves—this sassy bouquet settles down with aeration as the punchiness evolves into a more genteel, round fragrance of grape must, vines, green olives, vegetables, and linseed oil—an intriguing, dry, oily, even captivating nose of many faces and dimensions; the taste is wildly different from the aroma in that an unexpectedly feline, candied, sweet flavor of ripe grapes and hard candy enchant the palate right through to the long, citrusy aftertaste; a dazzling grappa with two distinct personalities that are gratifyingly compatible.

RATING ★ ★ ★ ★   **Highly Recommended** $$$

JACOPO POLI Sarpa di Grappa 43% Alcohol

Crystal clear; *sarpa* means "pomace"; no sweetness to be found in this bouquet, but that's not to say it lacks ripeness, because it doesn't—the piercing ripeness has more of an astringency and a sap-like quality than opulence or fruitiness—this is a rugged aroma of grape skins, pulp, and seeds, not sweet juice—an old-style grappa nose; yet on palate, the sublimely sweet, ripe, fruity, glycerine taste warmly greets the taste buds—the change of direction is startling, but welcome—the midpalate features rare richness and bounteous fruit through to the aftertaste, where a flame of heat licks the throat, then recedes; a memorably superb grappa experience; a noble spirit whose greatness builds as you drink it.

RATING ★ ★ ★ ★ ★   *Highest Recommendation* $

Jacopo Poli Grappa Amorosa di Merlot 43% Alcohol

Spring-water clarity; the nose is inviting, lean, and pointed—the first pass reveals a delicate pomace theme that doesn't overpower the olfactory sense—the freshness factor is alluring through all four nosings—the final nosing introduces a minerally aromatic backnote; on palate, the entry sets my taste buds tingling, but that sensation rapidly gives way to a satiny, off-dry fruitiness that comfortably rests on the tongue—pointed, but polite, flavors of grape must and vegetation are buttressed by a finely threaded texture that caresses the palate; the delicacy of this grappa shoots down any blanket statements that depict all grappas from Italy as being feral libations.

RATING ★ ★ ★ ★   *Highly Recommended* $ $

Jacopo Poli Grappa Amorosa di Torcolato 43% Alcohol

Unblemished clarity; this peculiar bouquet has a slightly nail-polish-like, acetate opening salvo, which later defers to a ripe, acidic grapiness that I more favorably responded to—the final pass sees a partial return of the nail-polish scent; in the mouth, this grappa takes off like a rocket as sweet palate-entry flavors of yellow fruit and grapes disarm the taste buds—the midpalate flavor is full, meaty, and totally satisfying; the impeccable nature of the mouth presence pulled this grappa up from three stars to four; delicious, but I suggest that you don't waste time sniffing it—go right for the taste sensation.

RATING ★ ★ ★ ★   *Highly Recommended* $ $

Jacopo Poli Chiara di Moscato Immature Grape Brandy 43% Alcohol

Spring-water clear, minor bits floating about—all right; as one would expect from the lovely, underrated (at least in the U.S.) *muscat* grape, the bouquet is a cornucopia of plump, citrusy aromas that leap from the glass at the pour—by the second and third passes, the nose has become an off-dry bouquet of flowers, especially orange blossoms—there's even a bit of pumpkin seed peeking out in the final nosing; in the mouth, the succulent, fat taste of ripe *muscat* grapes makes my day—it's balanced, however, as a core of acid anchors the mouth presence, allowing the fruity surface flavor to strut its stuff; long, leisurely, and delicious aftertaste; the outright star of the three Jacopo Poli Chiaras; genuinely luscious.

RATING ★ ★ ★ ★   *Highly Recommended* $ $

Jacopo Poli Grappa Amorosa di Vespaiolo 43% Alcohol

Perfect purity; this charmer is perfumy and citrusy—it reminds me slightly of pineapple and tropical fruit—a cherry-stone aroma enters into the picture in the third pass—the final pass loses much of its fruitiness as acetate begins creeping into the bouquet; the mouth presence is well-knit, as the seductively velvety flavor of rich fruit is balanced by a strong acid spine—

the finesse displayed by the flavor is laudable; it finishes sweetly and quietly on a dried-fruit note.

RATING ★ ★ ★   *Recommended* $ $

JACOPO POLI Grappa Amorosa di Pinot 43% Alcohol

Clear, but the only one of the Poli grappa amorosas with minute bits of barely discernable sediment; the nose is piquant and moderately prickly in the first two passes, showing only distant echoes of grapiness—it's more a stemmy/grape-skin nose than a graceful, juicy bouquet—though let's not forget that it's a grappa, not a fine still wine—the very last nosing brings an off-dry berry scent that added a smidgen of charm to this otherwise mundane bouquet; subtle, potent, and creamy in the mouth—I largely forgave the lackluster nose because of the viscous, rich, unabashedly sweet, concentrated flavor; an outstanding mouth presence from entry to finish; too bad that the nose is so woefully banal.

RATING ★ ★ ★   *Recommended* $ $

JACOPO POLI Chiara di Fragnola Immature Grape Brandy 43% Alcohol

Clear, but showing considerable pulpy sediment; the nose is more wine-like than brandy-like at first—I pick up very little of the spirit/alcohol—past that initial winey thrust there's not a whole lot of aroma to grasp; it reminds me more of a sweet, young, dessert wine than a full-fledged grappa—the grapy flavor is concentrated and almost jammy in its sweetness—the round, plump texture elevated it to recommendable status; sweet, thick aftertaste, which features the red-grape jamminess.

RATING ★ ★ ★   *Recommended* $ $

JACOPO POLI Chiara di Tocai Rosso Immature Grape Brandy 43% Alcohol

Clear, just infinitesimal bits; even with ample aeration and plenty of swirling in the glass, the most this young brandy offers odorwise is very faint, grapy, viney scents—nothing more over the course of four nosings; it's a bit raw at entry, then it smoothes out at midpalate and displays enough grape intensity to be mildly pleasant; the finish is as monotonic as the taste; not the pick of the Jacopo Poli Chiara litter.

RATING ★ ★ $ $

JACOPO POLI Grappa Amorosa di Cabernet 43% Alcohol

Ideal purity and clarity; the nose is seriously stemmy and vinous and altogether boring—even with intense swirling and ample time out of the bottle, this aroma doesn't want to evolve—perhaps it doesn't have the tools to reach beyond the rudimentary pulpy/seedy odor of a country village grappa; the palate entry is a tad sharp, but that's okay, nothing outrageous or out-of-line—the midpalate offers a pleasant, but hardly sterling, semisweet grapiness and that's all—the texture is medium-full and silky; the finish is vinous; the one Poli Grappa Amorosa I was looking forward to the most left me as cold as ice.

RATING ★ ★ $ $

Lungarotti Grappa di Rubesco 45% Alcohol

Crystal clear; one of the most seed-like bouquets in the category—the off-dry nose imparts a zesty, clean fragrance of anise and licorice, layered on top of a pleasant autumn-forest aroma; on palate, the feline smoothness of this ambrosial grappa goes against the party line of what grappa is traditionally supposed to taste and feel like; the flavor, while undeniably sweet, is nevertheless vivacious, grapy, and keenly fresh, not the slightest bit heavy-handed; another titan of the new, leaner generation of grappa—compellingly drinkable, fresh, and very nimble; made from the pomace of *sangiovese* and *canaiolo* grapes.

RATING ★★★★ **Highly Recommended** $$

Marchesi Di Gresy 1988 Grappa Martinenga 42% Alcohol

Crystalline, water-like appearance; the very compelling, focused, laser-beam, cocoa, semisweet, raisin-bran-cereal-like aroma is simultaneously assertive and smooth; stunningly fine-wine-like in bearing; the cocoa quality continues on palate as hints of citrus, mostly tangerine, emerge at the back of the throat; this sleek grappa finishes masterfully in waves of chocolate/orange slices and ripe nectarines; the quality and character of the *nebbiolo* grape really comes through; stately and refined.

RATING ★★★★ **Highly Recommended** $$

Mastroberardino 1987 Grappa Novia Greco di Tufo 45% Alcohol

Spring-water clarity; the nose jumps at you with concentrated, vegetal, and herbal aromas of juniper, basil, rosemary, clover, mint, and grass; the taste has a stately, elegant bearing as controlled, sweet flavors of grapes, cedar, and berries politely engage the palate; medium-long finish; while I'm not as excited about it as some of the other grappas I've evaluated, I do appreciate its graceful, amiable style and feel that it is recommendable.

RATING ★★★ **Recommended** $$$

Mastroberardino 1987 Grappa Novia Taurasi 45% Alcohol

Clear; similar to its sister grappa, the Greco di Tufo, in its highly vegetal fragrance aspect, though it seems to rely more on an earthier, sweeter underpinning; on palate, its inherent grapiness is beautifully drawn out in layers of ascending flavors; it's sweet, make no mistake, but it's also immensely fresh, crisp, and clean in the throat; the aftertaste is sublime, integrated, sweet, mildly grapy, and gentle; a diplomatic, suave, well-heeled grappa.

RATING ★★★ **Recommended** $$$

Michele Chiarlo Vinacce di Moscato d'Asti Grappa 42% Alcohol

Ideally clear and pure; the nose is raucous, stemmy, and cardboard-like—in the second and third nosings, pungent aromas of pomace, black pepper, green vegetables, wet earth, and artichoke hearts keep the nasal passages full and occupied; while I didn't care for the vegged-out bouquet, I did take a serious liking to the smashing taste, which opens sweetly at entry, then goes deliciously grapy at midpalate; it possesses the unmistakable thumbprint of the *muscat* grape variety in the remarkably extended, orangey aftertaste; the lasting impressions are those of citrus fruits and grapes; it won me over hugely in the mouth.

RATING ★ ★ ★ ★   **Highly Recommended** $$

MICHELE CHIARLO Vinacce di Gavi Grappa 42% Alcohol

Crystal clear; this nose is beguiling and intriguing right from the assertive, pomace-like, wet-wool-like opening—with aeration, the bouquet develops into a concrete-solid, concentrated perfume that's long on grapes, stems, and pulp, and short on sweetness; in the mouth, the round, supple sweetness puts the spotlight on ripe white grapes at entry, then goes almost grainy/doughy on its intense path to the midpalate point, where it turns grapy-sweet again; the finish is ripe, sweet, but austere; very palatable.

RATING ★ ★ ★   **Recommended** $$

MICHELE CHIARLO Vinacce di Barolo Grappa 42% Alcohol

As clear as the water from a mountain stream in the spring snow-melt; I wasn't bowled over by this aroma, which highlights cardboard and sweet pomace from the first nosing to the last—in the background lurk elusive scents of flint and apple—not a standout bouquet; on palate, it's pleasantly understated at entry, then it surges forward with a grapy thrust that's both satisfying and elegant; the finish is subdued and semisweet; a well-mannered grappa whose greatest asset is its civility.

RATING ★ ★ ★   **Recommended** $$

PIAVE Plum-Flavored Grappa 40% Alcohol

Clear; the perfumy bouquet is a luscious, highly concentrated combination of ripe black plums, sweetened coconut milk, tangerine, and grape pomace—it's a sweet nose that borders on being a liqueur—while Piave sits on a categorical fence as to whether it's a true grappa or an off-dry to sweet liqueur, I responded very favorably to the ambrosial but not-in-the-least cloying aroma; the sweetish taste mirrors the aroma to a tee—intensely fruity, with plums, coconuts, tropical fruits, and glycerine leading the way; medium-weighted; the finish is sweet, spirity, but refreshingly clean; a grappa that really stands on its own.

RATING ★ ★ ★ ★   **Highly Recommended** $$

SARTORI Grappa Delia Valpolicella 40% Alcohol

Crystal clear, completely devoid of color; the piquant, paint-thinner, nail-polish-remover, seed-like, minerally nose didn't exactly jump-start my olfactory sense; surprisingly mild on palate, with rather muted, sweet, but agreeable flavors of ripe apples and peaches, plus just the barest hint of chocolate; medium-length aftertaste; genial, but middle-of-the-road.

RATING ★ ★ $$

TENUTA IL POGGIONE Grappa di Brunello 45% Alcohol

Clear, water-like appearance; lovely, understated, sweet tropical-fruit nose, with a dash of spice and peppermint in the background; abundant, luscious, ambrosial, but dry flavors that sing on the palate; it has a lush, opulent feel to it that is very alluring; finishes clean, but round and almost fat; the alcohol never overshadows the delicate flavors; superbly balanced; the garden-fresh/herbal aftertaste is very extended; bravo.

RATING ★ ★ ★ ★   *Highly Recommended* $$

BRANDY AND BRANDY DE JÉREZ–SPAIN

Centuries before cognac was being made by the people of what are today the Charente and Charente-Maritime *départements* in west-central France, the inhabitants of Spain were experts in the art of grape distillation. Having learned the magic formula from history's acknowledged distillation masters, the Moors, who occupied Spain for over seven centuries, the Spanish were adept at capturing the soul of fermented grape must in the chambers of alembics (pot stills) as early as the thirteenth century A.D. Recorded history offers proof that a Catalonian doctor, Arnau of Vilanova, regularly employed alcohol in his treatments during that century. Doctor Arnau even composed a treatise on distillation, which was considered the definitive manual on the practice through the next century.

With the ouster of the Moors from the Iberian Peninsula in 1492, the Spaniards accelerated their brandy-making endeavors, especially in the southern province of Andalusia. The part of Andalusia in which brandy making became a primary industry was located south of Seville in and around the sherry town of Jérez de la Frontera. But the modern era of Spanish brandy is considered to have begun only in the mid-nineteenth century; when the custom of aging the spirit in the same system as that used for sherry, the Solera system, was started.

At the close of the twentieth century, no country produces more brandy than Spain. The Spaniards' ardor for their own brandy is nothing less than amazing. During the decade of 1975 to 1985, brandy producers sold an average of 162 million bottles *every year just within the borders of Spain.* Astonishingly, they annually sold only 22 million bottles in foreign markets. And brandy outsells sherry within Spain two to one.

The brandies of Andalusia, known collectively as Brandy de Jérez, account for nine-tenths of Spain's total production of grape brandy each year. The region of Catalonia, near Barcelona, is responsible for most of the balance. Even though the grapes for Brandy de Jeréz are grown, fermented, and distilled north of Andalusia in La Mancha, they are considered as natives of the south because they are matured, blended, and bottled in Jérez. The only grape variety used in making the wines that eventually become Brandy de Jérez is Airén.

While many brandy snobs in the past sneered at Brandy de Jérez ("too fat, too sweet, too chunky"), the tide has turned, as more people have tried them. Yes, they are significantly more robust than cognac, or even armagnac. But to my way of thinking, they are quite simply different interpretations of a fundamental theme. Like armagnac, they are distilled only once, which accounts in part for their feral nature. Another factor that sets them apart from all other brandies is that they age in old sherry butts (casks), which most definitely influence their demeanor. The sherry accent is especially notable when the brandy has been aged in a butt that used to carry oloroso sherry. While I admire and greatly enjoy cognac and armagnac, I'm a huge fan of the Solera Gran Reservas because they offer muscular, robust, no-nonsense brandy experiences that are like no other. They have their place, in particular, after dinner with cigars in dark wrappers.

There exist three official classifications of Brandy de Jérez as recognized and regulated by the Consejo Regulador, the governing body that watchdogs the industry. They are:

Brandy de Jérez—Solera: These brandies, by law, must be aged in wood for at least six months. The lion's share of the Solera brandies available in the marketplace are aged for around a year.

Brandy de Jérez—Solera Reserva: The next rung up on the Brandy de Jérez ladder. Must be aged in wood for at least a full year, though most are aged for up to two and a half years.

Brandy de Jérez—Solera Gran Reserva: Though most of these tony classics are wood-aged for an average of eight to ten years, some more, the legal definition dictates that they must age for a minimum of three years in cask. These are the best of the best.

CARDENAL MENDOZA Solera Gran Reserva Brandy de Jérez
45% Alcohol

No wallflower this one; the piquant, opulent, intense, multilayered nose owns concentrated flavors of orange rind, roasted nuts, and peppermint; on palate, this rich, heavy-weighted, noticeably sweet brandy has many dimensions in terms of taste—the top layer has cocoa and toffee, while the foundational layer boasts prunes, cream sherry, oak/vanillin, and caramel; the influence of sherry is unmistakable, particularly in the lengthy, fleshy finish; this is Brandy de Jérez at its peak; one of the great *digestif* experiences available.

RATING ★ ★ ★ ★   *Highly Recommended* $$

CARDENAL MENDOZA Non Plus Ultra Solera Gran Reserva Brandy de Jérez 40% Alcohol

This deep-brown/mahogany stunner looks like cola or cream sherry; the all-business nose springs out of the glass in charred/smoky waves of burnt sugar (crème brulée), cane sugar, molasses, and old oak—there's scant evidence of grapiness, sumptuous sweetness, or ripe fruit—just mainline toastiness; in the mouth, the flavor opens up with a roasted-nut, semisweet salvo that lasts well into the midpalate, whereupon a minute trace of raisiny grapiness is detected along with a splash of off-dry oloroso sherry; the finish is medium-long and very roasted, showing a dark caramel-like flavor; please take note that I did not prefer it to the regular bottling of Cardenal Mendoza, even though it costs more than twice the price; do what you will with that observation, but I tell you that it's nowhere near being twice as delicious.

RATING ★ ★ ★ ★   ***Highly Recommended*** $$$

CONDE DE OSBORNE Solera Gran Reserva 40.5% Alcohol

Fabulous, deep amber/tawny color, with gold edges; the nose brims with a lusciously fragrant butterscotch aroma, which is supported by sexy scents of musk, honey, pears, butter, walnuts—do you want me to continue?—this sensationally multileveled bouquet is irresistible; on palate, the semisweet flavors highlight oloroso sherry, light English toffee, overripe grapes and very old wood; it finishes sweetly, but not overly so, in a smoky, tobacco-like flourish that also smacks of cream; a delicious, generous, well-crafted brandy by any standard.

RATING ★ ★ ★ ★   ***Highly Recommended*** $$

FELIPE II Solera Reserva Brandy de Jérez 40% Alcohol

Produced by Agustin Blazquez; medium amber color, good clarity; the nose is sweet, like cinnamon apples or pears, showing no sign of grapes, sophistication, or finesse, just a candied, ripe-yellow-fruit clunker; in the mouth, I'm surprised by its *gentillesse* and elegant demeanor; the aftertaste is sweet but not cloying, fruity (citrus especially), and even a bit toffee-like; it nearly pushed itself into recommended territory on the strength of its pleasantly plump mouth presence; it's as though the nose and taste/finish are of two brandies; bizarre, but decent.

RATING ★ ★ $

GRAN DUQUE D'ALBA Solera Gran Reserva Brandy de Jérez 40% Alcohol

Cola color/golden rim, with red highlights in the core; fat, the buttery, opulent, PX-sherry, spirity, woody, sugar-maple, multidimensional pedal-to-the-metal nose requires a day and a half by itself to properly define the myriad components; clean, velvety texture; the incredibly rich, caramel, toffee, fiery, road-tar flavors explode on the palate, then curiously calm into an unforgettable aftertaste that features a wide array of flavors, including bittersweet chocolate and oranges; the addition of Pedro Ximenez sherry before bottling comes to the fore in the dramatic finish; the to-die-for super-premium Spanish brandy par excellence; one of the world's greatest, most complete, most virile brandies, period; this view allows for the opinion that such a feral, fiery brandy would never win favor in the camp of those who prefer delicacy to power—what do I care? pass the Duque; tasted more than I care to say; upgraded to its proper place at the head of its class.

RATING ★ ★ ★ ★ ★   **Highest Recommendation** $$

LEPANTO Solera Gran Reserva Brandy de Jérez 40% Alcohol

Wonderful, luminous, orange/honey color; the expansive, generous, fruity, slightly sherried, piquant nose is simultaneously alluring and assertive; by a country mile the most feline, dare I say "cognac-like," Solera Gran Reserva available; that's not to say that it lacks the traditional SGR guts, because it has plenty of that; the off-dry palate sings with mellow fruit, then fades neatly into a medium-length and -strength aftertaste that concludes on a tarry, tobacco note; it's the lightest, most sedate, and best behaved of the SGRs and a total pleasure to savor as an afterdinner treat; noble Lepanto is a true velvet hammer—though it carries the big stick, it walks very softly indeed.

RATING ★ ★ ★ ★   **Highly Recommended** $$

MASCARO Don Narciso 8- to 10-Year-Old Brandy (Catalonia) 40% Alcohol

Marginally deeper amber than the VO; the nose is nothing short of sublime as heady notes of dark toffee and butterscotch enchant my olfactory sense—underneath it all lies a biscuity oakiness that's devilishly alluring; in the mouth, it's ideally balanced, as satiny, succulent flavors of chocolate, coffee with cream, rancio, and dark English toffee curl around the willing taste buds; easily ranks with the best from Jérez, but is really more akin to a small-house, small-production VSOP cognac; bravo, Mascaro.

RATING ★ ★ ★ ★   **Highly Recommended** $$

MASCARO VO 3-Year-Old Brandy (Catalonia) 40% Alcohol

Standard-issue amber/orange color; the toasty, roasted nose is firm but not aggressive, indeed almost elegant (this is Spanish brandy?)—the sexy bouquet emits measured waves of vanilla wafer, clove, and nut meat; on the palate, it's sinewy to the feel and semisweet to the taste—the flavors are of overripe grapes, white-grape raisins, and caramel—nary a hint of oak; the aftertaste is very smooth and goes all-out sweet in the seductive tail end; quite a different animal than the viscous, beefy brandies from Jérez; this one hints coyly of cognac.

RATING ★ ★ ★   **Recommended** $

MERITO Brandy de Jérez Solera 40% Alcohol

Pretty, standard-issue Brandy de Jérez light brown hue, with russet highlights; even tasting blind, there was no mistaking the country of origin of this brandy—brandies from the Jérez district in Andalusia all possess a peculiar burnt scent that's emblematic of the region's brandy style—high-octane, kippery, alcoholic, and ripe-to-overripe aromatic and taste characteristics; this little brother of my all-time favorite Brandy de Jérez Solera Gran Reserva, the imposing and splendid Gran Duque d'Alba, is fully concentrated on the palate, very toasty, with honey-wheat flavors and not-so-subtle hints of Pedro Ximenez sherry; it finishes long and solid; it's anything but elegant, yet it does possess some fundamental brandy charm in an overall package that's pleasant but pedestrian.

RATING ★ ★ $

MIGUEL TORRES Imperial Brandy Reserva Especial 40% Alcohol

Rich orange/copper/medium-to-deep-amber color; the sweet, biscuity nose could come from none other than a Spanish brandy because of its robust, punchy, fruity, caramelized, rancio bouquet that snugly fills the nasal cavity—interestingly, in contrast to the sherry-influenced Solera Gran Reserva Brandies from Jérez in the south of Spain, this aroma leans more in the direction of acidic fruits (citrus and tropical) rather than overripe grapes—analogously, this brandy is more a baritone, while the majority from Jérez are bass (the great Lepanto Solera Gran Reserva is the sole baritone in Jérez); it's weighty in the mouth, as flavors of roasted nuts, honey-wheat toast, light caramel, spice, and applebutter race headlong from entry through to the long, sweet, but tart aftertaste; Torres Imperial is a very sound, well-crafted, double-distilled brandy made from 100% *parellada* grapes and aged in French oak for more than eight years.

RATING ★ ★ ★   *Recommended* $$

PEDRO DOMECQ Carlos I Solera Gran Reserva Brandy de Jérez 40% Alcohol

Sorrel, tea-like color; vigorously heady, spirity aromas of orange rind, butterscotch, and almonds make their delectable presence known in the bountiful and compelling nose; light- to medium-weighted; proper distilled-spirit bearing in the mouth, imparting moderate heat/bite; smooth, but almost utilitarian flavors—this one was difficult for me to score in light of my unabashed ardor for Spanish brandy, because, while I genuinely admired it, I didn't get passionate over it, as no particular virtue jumped out to seize me or my imagination; I was actually mildly disappointed in the taste after appreciating its very appetizing nose; my overall impression was favorable, to be sure, but while some people might say it is well balanced, I feel its downside is more a lack of follow-through on the promise of the nose; tasted at least a half dozen times both in Jérez and the U.S.

RATING ★ ★ $$

ROMATE Solera Reserva Brandy de Jérez 40% Alcohol

From the producer of Cardenal Mendoza; delightfully deep amber/amontillado sherry color; the luscious, biscuity nose speaks of burnt almonds, oloroso sherry, and bread dough; the creamy taste of milk chocolate and prunes is remarkable; yes, it's got full-throttle sweetness; no, it's not cloying to my taste; my dilemma stems from how it should be classified—on the one hand, it's almost like a liqueur, while on the other it's most definitely a brandy—it could go either way; I believe that there would be many critics of this brandy because of its unctuousness—undoubtedly some people would even wonder what's in it; my feeling is that this baby brother of the great Cardenal Mendoza Solera Gran Reserva has been doused with a healthy portion of either cream or Pedro Ximenez sherry; so, is a brandy such as this why the Cognaçais sneer at Spanish brandy? very possibly, very probably; but the fact remains that it tastes splendidly; this is the best Solera Reserva Brandy de Jérez I've evaluated.

RATING ★★★   ***Recommended*** $

TERRY Primero Solera Gran Reserva Brandy de Jérez 40% Alcohol

Deep amber, with russet, autumnal highlights; the sedate nose is compelling, warm, and spirity, with a backnote of apricot and peach; in the mouth, the richness level is remarkably higher than its two far-less-charming siblings; the flavors are balanced, savory, and elegant, with vanilla, cream, and ripe apricot leading the way—the taste actually reminds me of a childhood taste, namely, that of Creamsicles, the orange and vanilla ice cream bar; Primero's aftertaste is medium-long and laced with an orangey sweetness, which is pleasant and not a bit cloying or overbearing.

RATING ★★★   ***Recommended*** $$

TERRY 1900 Solera Reserva Brandy de Jérez 40% Alcohol

Slightly deeper, richer, amber color than the Centenario; the lemon-peel, vanilla-wafer, biscuity, doughy nose is doused with a judicious use of caramel—there's potential here; on palate, a nonsticky sweetness like top-grade English toffee rules the roost all the way from entry to the long aftertaste; the finish betrays oloroso sherry, most likely from the oak aging vessel; while I'd never classify this as a stylish or elegant brandy, it does deliver a moderate amount of straightforward, concentrated flavors; average on its very best days.

RATING ★★ $

TERRY Centenario Solera 40% Alcohol

Amber/brown color, with a yellow/gold rim; the pungent, aggressive, citrusy, almost lanky, metallic nose is off-putting and off-balance; the palate entry is stingingly tart; at midpalate it displays a one-note flavor of caramel, period; the quick, uninspiring finish hints mildly of lemons and tangerines; barely drinkable, this is a brandy sorely lacking in finesse and breeding; its best use would be as a mixer; typifies how many consumers worldwide perceive Spanish brandy—top-heavy and chunky; comes imaginatively packaged in yellow bottle netting, referred to in Spanish as *malla dorada*.

RATING ★ $

VETERANO Solera Brandy de Jérez 40% Alcohol

The producer is Osborne; rich, amber/orange tone—absolute clarity; the frisky, pungent nose emits a citric acid, caramel, almost medicinal aroma that has a smoky, burnt, pipe-tobacco background scent—the manufactured bouquet isn't a high point; right from the palate entry the sweetness level is off the charts and then proceeds to slash and burn its way through midpalate, becoming docile in the soft, pillowy finish that is this insipid brandy's only shining moment; it's a cloying, overripe, overproduced, and rough brandy; don't even think of it.

RATING ★ $

EAUX-DE-VIE, FRUIT BRANDIES, AND CRÈMES–EUROPE

au-de-vie (oh-duh-vee) is French for "water of life." Eaux-de-vie are the crystalline brandies made from the wine of grapes or other fruits. Some countries classify them as "fruit liqueurs," and others describe them as "fruit brandies," but in both cases they are simply the pure distilled essence of fruit without the skins, seeds, pulp, or stem. Thus, the aromas and flavors involved are frequently intense and, on occasion, spectacular. Eaux-de-vie fall usually in the 40–45 percent range in alcohol content. Since they are as clear as spring water, their potency can take the unsuspecting imbiber by surprise.

The larger portion of eaux-de-vie are created by distilling fermented fruit. Others are produced by a system referred to as *maceration* (meaning, "to soak"), in which fermented fruit is steeped in neutral spirits for weeks at a time to gradually and gently extract the fine characteristics of the fruit without submitting it to the rigors of heated distillation. Eaux-de-vie are always looked upon as *digestifs,* or afterdinner drinks. The regions/countries that produce the hallmark eaux-de-vie are Germany's Black Forest district, France's Alsace district, Austria, and Switzerland's German-speaking areas. The distillers in these locales have been crafting eaux-de-vie for centuries and, as a result, have elevated the skill to an art.

I have also included in this section the dense, highly concentrated, and sweet crèmes—the viscous, liqueur-like fruit brandies that are lower in alcohol (normally 16–20 percent) and are often used in mixed drinks or poured over sorbet or vanilla ice cream. Crèmes are frequently found in the same sections as eaux-de-vie at liquor merchants.

Eau-de-vie terms to be aware of:

framboise = raspberry　　　　　*slivovitz* = blue plum
mure = mulberry　　　　　　　*fraise* = strawberry
mirabelle = Mirabelle/yellow　*myrtille* = bilberry
　plum　　　　　　　　　　　*kirsch/Kirschwasser* = cherry
quetsch = Switzen/blue plum　*coing* = quince
prunelle = sloe　　　　　　　*poire* (Williams) = pear

BACCATE DE PECHE DE VIGNE (Peach) 18% Alcohol (France)

Feminine, orange/honey color, with soft pink highlights; the most aromatic and perfumed of the Baccate line; the mouthwatering bouquet that glides up from the tasting glass is right on the mark, emitting juicy, ripe peaches all the way down the line; delicate on palate, the driest of the line; as opposed to some eaux-de-vie, this extraordinary winner relies more on finesse than authority, spirit, or sweetness; the finish is long, dry, and very classy; best of the Baccate show without a doubt.

RATING ★ ★ ★ ★　　　*Highly Recommended*　　$

BACCATE DE MURE (Blackberry) 18% Alcohol (France)

Attractive, madeira-like, mahogany color, with rich garnet highlights; I loved this perfumed, ripe-blackberry, minerally nose; in the mouth, the syrupy, jammy, need-a-spoon texture is incredibly sumptuous—the delicious blackberry flavor actually had me envisioning the wild blackberries that profusely grow outside my house in late summer; carries enough acidity in its bone structure to effectively balance the intense, fleshy fruit; beautifully made from stem to stern; an absolutely near-divine experience; bravo.

RATING ★ ★ ★ ★　　　*Highly Recommended*　　$

BACCATE DE FRAMBOISE (Raspberry) 18% Alcohol (France)

Pretty, light ruby color with flecks of crimson; it owns a disarmingly fragrant and heady raspberry-preserve nose that wafts from the glass; the sublime flavor component is totally true to the fruit—the spirit is in the background, as intense, but refined raspberry essence gently swathes the palate; beautifully balanced, enmeshed fruit/acid/alcohol components, which are gorgeous, generous, and luscious; two varieties of raspberries are used in the making—the Lloyd George for its sensational color and the Rose de Plombière for the bouquet; find it and buy it.

RATING ★ ★ ★　　　*Recommended*　　$

BACCATE DE CERISE (Cherry) 18% Alcohol (France)

Cherry/brick red, Burgundian color; the minerally, wet-gravel, cherry-pit, cola-nut, ripe-cherry bouquet is horrible—no other word for it; this loser is disgustingly viscous, almost like cherry Jello just prior to gelling; on palate, the severe, steely, kernel-nut quality is strikingly similar to that of cheaper amarettos; I don't feel that the fruit content is sufficient to counter the particularly annoying mineral/flinty quality that so thoroughly dominates the palate; the aggressive aftertaste merely continues the minerally onslaught; my taste buds never had a chance; born of the *cerise de Montmorency* and *cerise noire de Chalon* cherry types; to be technical, yeeeccchhhh.

RATING ★ $

BACCATE DE CASSIS (Black Currant) 19% Alcohol (France)

Inky, deep blood-red color, a dead ringer for young vintage port; very thickly textured because of double crème process—so syrupy that it clings to the bowl of the tasting glass like a man hanging onto a life raft; the vegetal, minty, musty, attic-like, dog-kennel, earthy, downright malodorous nose assaults the olfactory sense like General Patton's troops making a frontal charge; the tasty, concentrated berry, very unctuous flavor just doesn't have enough depth to redeem the disturbingly offensive, locker-room nose; way off base; I can't even imagine this bow-wow being used in cooking or over vanilla ice cream; only wild berries are used as opposed to commercially grown; maybe that's the problem; this is a serious mistake.

RATING ★ $

CAPOVILLA 1992 Prugne Selvatiche Distillato a Bagnomaria 41% Alcohol (Italy)

Clear as rain water, pure; the vibrant nose is intensely pruney in the first pass, then it settles down into a yellow fruit softness that I liked enormously—there's nothing showy or extravagant here; in the mouth, the flavor starts small and tart, then it steadily builds to a stunning, sweet, ripe-fruit crescendo at midpalate; the aftertaste diminishes gradually, as delicate, ripe prunes dominate; this flavor experience is like a camel's hump with the zenith at midpalate; delicious, reined in, and stately.

RATING ★ ★ ★ ★   *Highly Recommended* $ $

CARTON Crème de Cassis de Bourgogne 19% Alcohol (France)

Very pretty, purple hue, with pink/cherry edges; the texture is syrupy, even ropy in its extreme viscosity; the assertive nose is true to the fruit, vinous, herbal, woodsy, and lands somewhere between dry and off-dry—though only 19% alcohol, I detect some of the spirit aromas between the thick layers of fruit and fresh herbs; the bracing sweetness of double creaming at palate entry settles down into a more manageable ambrosial taste by midpalate but make no mistake, the concentration of cassis is daunting; the aftertaste is surprisingly low key, only mildly sweet, and delicious; makes an outstanding topping to ice cream or sorbet; try a few drops in Champagne or sparkling wine to make a smashing Kir Royale.

RATING ★ ★ ★   *Recommended* $

DETTLING Kirschwasser 41% Alcohol (France)

Clear; the nose is all sour cherry and tartness as the acid backbone lords over the fruit component—to the good, there's hardly any interference by the alcohol at all; in the mouth, the flavor of cherries is balanced by keen acid and a freshness that are most appealing—what I felt this fine eau-de-vie lacked most was a lushness, an opulence in texture that sets apart the world's benchmark fruit brandies; on the other hand, I believe that among the most difficult to like eaux-de-vie are those made from cherries, and that being the case, Dettling should be applauded.

RATING ★ ★ ★   *Recommended* $$

ETIENNE BRANA Framboise Raspberry Brandy 45% Alcohol (France)

Very pale straw/flaxen color, excellent clarity; the nose is commanding, solid, and assertive without being aggressive or overbearing—it's a bouquet chockful of extremely ripe red raspberry perfume, which displays that beguiling sweet-sour quality found in all the upper-echelon framboise from around the world—by the fourth nosing, I found the sweetness dominating the acid tartness, but I didn't mind; in the mouth, the elegance of the ripe flavor and the firmness of the bosomy texture teamed up to make an eau-de-vie that was nothing short of exquisite and superb; a joyful, spirity warmth decorates the medium-long aftertaste; go out and find it.

RATING ★ ★ ★ ★   *Highly Recommended* $$

ETIENNE BRANA Poire Williams 44% Alcohol (France)

Like the framboise, very close to being as clear as spring water but not quite—I also noticed some minor suspended particles floating about; clearly, the master distiller at Brana believes in big, forward bouquets as, like the framboise, this direct, nose-filling aroma wastes no time in greeting you—its juicy, sweet, ripe perfume that stayed powerful right through the final nosing; on the palate, the taste is fourth-gear pear and little else except a mild spirit bite at the back of the tongue; the finish is medium-long, clean, and warming; while I think this poire is very good indeed, I didn't believe it to be as magical or endowed as its august framboise sibling; picky, picky, picky.

RATING ★ ★ ★   *Recommended* $$

ETTER Poire Williams 42% Alcohol (Switzerland)

Clear, unblemished; this sleek bouquet races from the sampling glass, requiring no aeration whatsoever—gorgeous, plump, and tart, this quintessential vamp defines what poire eau-de-vie is about—it's ripe pear essence, stripped bare, in aromatic overdrive; the mouth presence is swank, confident, deeply flavorful, layered, true to the fruit, and utterly mesmerizing; the aftertaste is remarkably extended, opulent, clean, and simply grand—I can't imagine a better, more sensuous poire, domestic or imported; go out and badger your local liquor merchant until he or she orders this classic.

RATING ★ ★ ★ ★ ★   *Highest Recommendation* $$

ETTER Kirsch Buger 41% Alcohol (Switzerland)

Limpid, pure; the exotic, highly alluring bouquet is spicy and not nearly as pit-like (seedy smelling) as so many other kirsch liqueurs on the market—the fruit-meat element really comes to the fore in this firm, sure-footed bouquet; in the mouth, it's almost creamy, which is unusual for a pitted-fruit essence—the sterling flavor of ripe red cherries is framed within an opulent texture that regally rests on the tongue; the aftertaste is dead on target, long, lush; a veritable cherry jubilee.

RATING ★ ★ ★ ★   *Highly Recommended* $$

ETTER Pomme Gravine 41% Alcohol (Switzerland)

Clear, perfectly pure, the sexy nose offers an exquisite mix of understated green apple, paraffin, and spice (a feathery touch of cinnamon, apple's most complementary spice companion)—the cleanliness of the waxy bouquet impressed me; in the mouth, it's like satin texturewise—the lovely delicacy of the crisp apple flavor is the highlight here—there's a flash of heat on the tongue at midpalate; the aftertaste is mannered, but hardly subdued, as a rich taste of apple bids adieu to the taste buds.

RATING ★ ★ ★ ★   ***Highly Recommended*** $ $

ETTER Pflumli Prune 41% Alcohol (Switzerland)

Lucid, immaculate; the assertive nose is astringent, akin to the acidic peel of red fruit, and very kernel-like—I'm admittedly not a card-carrying member of the Society of Prune Admirers, so keeping my prejudices at bay while judging this eau-de-vie wasn't simple, but I found that I genuinely liked this spicy, zesty essence very much; the sweet flavor is richer and more expansive in terms of ripe red fruit than I expected—it borders on being downright succulent—indeed, my lips were nearly smacking as I tasted it on the fourth and final go round—fortunately I taste alone very early in the morning.

RATING ★ ★ ★ ★   ***Highly Recommended*** $ $

ETTER Framboise Himbeere 41% Alcohol (Switzerland)

Crystal clear, immaculate; the focus of this laser-beam nose is strictly red raspberry—acknowledging this should come as no surprise, since framboise is red raspberry spirit, the intensity of the bouquet is what's so notable—in addition, there's a backnote of vines/leaves/vegetation that balances the concentrated fruitiness; on the palate, this deft, delicate beauty dazzles the taste buds with waves of ripe raspberry splendor and richness; the finish is very long, succulent, sweet, and true to the fruit; a silky beauty that rings with purity and finesse.

RATING ★ ★ ★ ★   ***Highly Recommended*** $ $

ETTER Quitte Coing 41% Alcohol (Switzerland)

Clear, pure; not being that familiar with the hard-fleshed fruit known as quince, I found this exercise to be a new experience; the snappy, bordering-on-piquant bouquet is enticing and reminds me most of the seed-like, herbal aroma found in a pitted fruit—it's a delicate, stone-dry, fresh perfume that I found delightful; in the mouth, the silky texture wraps around the tongue as the tropical fruit (guava, banana, especially), mildly tart, nuanced flavors charmed the taste buds without overpowering them; the finish is sedate, medium-long, and not its strong suit; a solidly good eau-de-vie, but not the key to enlightenment that the other Etters are.

RATING ★ ★ ★   ***Recommended*** $ $

GABRIEL BOUDIER Josie Framboise 18% Alcohol (France)

Deep crimson color; the profound, exceptionally lush, ripe-raspberry nose charms the olfactory sense right under the table; it's pleasantly sweet on entry, then surprisingly it goes off-dry at midpalate, as the fruit's acid takes charge, perfectly accenting the keen fruitiness; not in the least jammy, awkward, or overbearing; delightful, true-to-the-fruit, very drinkable; finishes long and lovely; this is really a voluptuous mouthful of succulent fruit.

RATING ★ ★ ★ ★   *Highly Recommended* $

GABRIEL BOUDIER Cassis 20% Alcohol (France)

Inky, opaque, purple color; the extremely viscous, ropy texture coats the glass's sides like a blanket; I found the typically minty, juniper, cooked-vegetable, pine-cone, cassis nose singularly unappealing for the simple reason that it's too resiny/oily/kernelly; the jammy, intense cassis flavor is better than the totally repugnant nose; the finish is syrupy, sweet, and chunky; I missed the point—somebody please enlighten me.

RATING ★ $

JACOPO POLI Stagione di Lamponi Raspberry Brandy 43% Alcohol (Italy)

Clear, pure; this beauty is the knockout nose of the three Jacopo Poli fruit brandies—the intense, concentrated, scoop-out-with-a-spoon bouquet is all ripe raspberries and vines—I loved this generous, expansive, true-to-the-fruit source, tart-like aroma; in the mouth, the taste is graceful and elegant rather than explosive or effusive—that understatement catapults it into the higher rating terrain than its good, but unspectacular siblings, the pear and the cherry; the aftertaste highlights the tart side of raspberries at first, then it goes ambrosially succulent in the tail end; lovely, corpulent, and well crafted.

RATING ★ ★ ★ ★   *Highly Recommended* $$

JACOPO POLI Stagione di Ciliege Cherry Brandy 43% Alcohol (Italy)

Clear, pure; there's no mistaking the fruit source of this nose—it starts out as a cherry-pit aroma and develops into a handsome, low-key cherry fruit bouquet that's piquant and firm; exceedingly pleasant, though not gifted on palate—the entry is tart, acidic, but it never loses sight of the fruit—by mid-palate, an austere, tart/sweet, fruitiness dominates; the aftertaste is tart, but not sour; a nice, sinewy fruit brandy without an ounce of flab on it.

RATING ★ ★ ★   *Recommended* $$

JACOPO POLI Stagione di Pere Pear Brandy 43% Alcohol (Italy)

Clear, with some minor transparent bits floating about; the nose is indeed pear-like, but moderate in its strength—there is a spirity side to this fruit brandy, as well as a touch of oily wax; not a blockbuster in the mouth taste-wise, but satisfying nonetheless—what I like most about the mouth presence is a sense of "grip," it really hugs the palate—the pear flavor is very ripe, but not overly sweet or succulent—it has a solid acid foundation; the aftertaste is lean, but long; not an inspired pear brandy, but very good, very drinkable.

RATING ★ ★ ★   *Recommended* $$

RENE DE MISCAULT

Alsace is famous as the source of some of the finest eaux-de-vie in Europe. Virtually all of the Alsatian eau-de-vie producers are also winemakers. Located on the France–Germany border at the eastern side of the Vosges Mountains, Alsace is approximately 70 miles long, running north and south, but a mere 1 to 2 miles wide. It has some of the lowest rainfall in all of France because of the nearby mountains and, therefore, it is one of the regions with the most sustained sunshine. Alsace has flipped back and forth between French rule and German rule for centuries. The Germanic influence is unmistakable, for this is a wine region where Riesling and Gewurztraminer are king. What makes the eaux-de-vie of Miscault so interesting is the breadth and depth of their offerings. Not only does Miscault dabble with fruit, they also produce spirits from vegetables like celery and roots like ginger. I found them all extremely intriguing and totally different from other eaux-de-vie that I've tried.

RENE DE MISCAULT Poire William 43% Alcohol (France)

Clear; the ripe-pear perfume zooms up from the sampling glass in impressive fashion—the fragrance is as intoxicating as it is seductive; topflight, pedal-to-the-metal bouquet; this spirit's subtlety, finesse, and elegance are all astounding and wonderful to behold—the sweet, ripe-pear flavor has incredible staying power on the tongue; the balance between the concentrated fruit, razor-sharp acidity, and manageable alcohol is a textbook example of how to make eau-de-vie; simply a superior spirit.

RATING ★ ★ ★ ★ ★   *Highest Recommendation* $$

RENE DE MISCAULT Framboise Sauvage 43% Alcohol (France)

Clear; this savory perfume is delicate, but hardly coy, in its gentle bearing—there's absolutely no mistaking what kind of fruit this is; now, at last, here's the type of full-bodied eau-de-vie that gets my motor running—the tidal waves of raspberry flavor are mesmerizing, sweet, bosomy, and long-lived; the finish only amplifies the majesty of the midpalate; only one word adequately describes it, "scrumptious"; this baby cooks.

RATING ★ ★ ★ ★   *Highly Recommended* $$

RENE DE MISCAULT Ginger 43% Alcohol (France)

Clear distillate appearance; intensely aromatic, almost stinging perfume of fourth-gear ginger, spice, and citrus (lemon mostly)—the first pass was rough, but subsequent whiffs were magical, vigorous, and snappy—this aroma is a wild one; a one-note song, flavorwise, warbling "ginger, ginger" all the way home to the zesty finish; scores big for freshness, vivacity, and being true-blue to its source; problem is, what do you do with ginger eau-de-vie? I'm open to suggestions; wisecracks are the most welcome.

RATING ★ ★ ★   *Recommended* $$

RENE DE MISCAULT Réserve Céleri 45% Alcohol (France)

Clear; this exotic nose is piquant, vegetal, peppery, and true to its source—celery; it seriously reminds me of a Bloody Mary I once knew, or, better yet, a can of just-opened V-8 juice; the palate is all chili pepper and high-flying celery flavor, I mean, it's dead on the mark from entry through aftertaste; again, while I greatly admire the distilling skill of Miscault in producing such a faithful spirit, I ask in all sincerity: If I buy this eau-de-vie, how in the blazes do I use it? why would anyone pay forty dollars for a veggie eau-de-vie? am I being too harsh, too cynical? am I missing the point? of course not.

RATING ★★★   *Recommended* $$

Rene de Miscault Marc de Gewurztraminer 45% Alcohol (France)

Clear; the rubbery, musty (as in grape must), pomace, dry aroma is tanky and unexciting—not the one I'd go for if I were buying; the sweet, luscious taste so easily eclipses the rubber-sole nose that I'm amazed—the flavor speaks articulately of grapes in a controlled, focused manner; it's a reined-in marc that showcases the concentrated spicy/fruitiness of one of my favorite *vitis vinifera* grape types; the aftertaste is sweet, mannered, and medium-long; a rating star was lost, however, because of the compost, attic-like nose.

RATING ★★★   *Recommended* $$

Rene de Miscault Réserve Kirsch 45% Alcohol (France)

Clear; the firm, direct nose is predictably all cherry—black cherry, to be more precise—it's a dry, clean, and authentic bouquet; the taste is bountiful, but so tart as to be close to sour; while I admire the obvious craftsmanship that went into the making of this dry but fruity eau-de-vie, it leaves me stone cold all the same—a personal lack of enthusiasm for kirsch shouldn't take away, however, from the clearly evident skill of the artisan, hence the favorable rating.

RATING ★★★   *Recommended* $$

Rene de Miscault Vieille Prune 43% Alcohol (France)

Pale gold/straw, white-wine-like hue; the nose is dry, astringent, yet intensely fruity, plummy, and pleasant—it's spirity, but not overwhelmingly so—it has a nice balance to it; the ripe, plummy flavor is outdone only by the viscous texture—the taste is round, full, and mildly fruity; neither a blockbuster nor a tower of fruit intensity, but an able, workmanlike, faithfully true spirit just the same.

RATING ★★★   *Recommended* $$

Rene de Miscault Réserve Quetsch 45% Alcohol (France)

Clear; a highly spirited, phenolic, and bone-dry nose that's lanky, steely, and devoid of any charm whatsoever—not my cup of eau-de-vie; the taste is pungently spicy, zesty, candy sweet, yet paradoxically tart in the aftertaste; I guardedly liked the flavor, hated the nose, and was lukewarm to the erratic, but pleasant, finish; on balance, however, not recommendable.

RATING ★★ $$

Rene de Miscault Myrtille 43% Alcohol (France)

Clear; the dry, mechanical nose smells like the inside of a kitchen decorator's showroom—you know, that new plastic, linoleum-floor odor—to say the least, this bomb will not be inducted into my aroma hall of fame; the flavor on this one, while inoffensive, isn't even mildly appealing and in no way can redeem a nose that only Bob Vila or Martha Stewart could appreciate; write this one off.

RATING ★ $$

RETTER Himbeer Raspberry Nectar 43% Alcohol (Austria)

Clear; the fragrant, sweet-sour bouquet is a glorious mix of ripe red raspberry and not-fully-ripened strawberry scents—there's even a slight piquancy to it as it aerates—it's not a luxurious, blockbuster nose as much as it is a refined, feminine, but direct bouquet that spotlights the acute tartness of the fruit—one of my favorite eau-de-vie perfumes of all time; in the mouth, the taste is so ideally balanced between natural acidity, alcohol, and the sublime fruit element that I can't imagine it getting any better than it already is; my personal category standard for raspberry eaux-de-vie.

RATING ★ ★ ★ ★ ★   *Highest Recommendation* $$$

RETTER Waldheidelbeer Forest Blueberry Nectar 43% Alcohol (Austria)

Clear; the piquant, charcoal-like nose astonished me with its atypical posture in the first nosing pass—by the critical third nosing, which allows time for aeration, the aroma gracefully shifted to an ethereal, ripe fruitiness that was nothing less than bewitching; the flavor is so vibrant, focused, intense, and balanced that it's almost difficult to describe adequately—the softness and refinement of the fruit is sensuous, supple, firm, defined, and exact; the aftertaste echoes the flavor and lasts for an extended period; simply put, this is a mind-blowing distilled spirit experience of the first rank.

RATING ★ ★ ★ ★ ★   *Highest Recommendation* $$$

RETTER Gravensteiner Apple Essence 40% Alcohol (Austria)

Predictably clear and clean in appearance; the saucy, zesty nose is gregarious, as assertive but refined scents of wood smoke, fresh ripe apples and apple peel compete for dominance in the fragrance; the tart, tightly knit flavor entry cleanses the palate; by midpalate, a curious smoky quality emerges, buttressed by the core flavor of ripe apple; the finish is surprisingly rich, deep, and extended; delicious all the way to the end.

RATING ★ ★ ★ ★   *Highly Recommended* $$

RETTER Hirschbirne Pear Essence 40% Alcohol (Austria)

Clear; the amount of lusty spice in this bouquet amazed and delighted me—the supple pear quality is the foundational aroma, to be sure, but playful, complementary scents of cream, spring leaves, and garden herbs make for an engaging aromatic package; in the mouth, it provides both a touch of ripe-pear richness, with an acidic, spirity edge that I liked immensely; this Hirschbirne possesses the depth of character that the more cavalier Retter Williams-Christ lacks.

RATING ★ ★ ★ ★   *Highly Recommended* $$

Retter Marillen Apricot Essence 43% Alcohol (Austria)

Clear; the compelling nose grabbed my attention from the first instant as sweet, no-nonsense, succulent apricot meat mingled with the subtler hints of spirit, honey, and spice—this is a top-notch, lightning-bolt bouquet that alone is worth two stars; in the mouth, the nectar-like apricot taste is framed by a welcome acid edge that balances the fruit intensity in smashing form; the aftertaste is supple, off-dry to sweet, and the ideal topper to an extraordinary spirit experience.

RATING ★★★★ **Highly Recommended** $$

Retter Sour Cherry Nectar 43% Alcohol (Austria)

Clear; the scrumptious bouquet is slightly candied, minty, tart, and bubblegum-like, emitting a gorgeous cherry perfume that I did not find totally sour—on the third nosing a viney, seed-like quality emerged; in the mouth, the cherry flavor is delicate and refined, with no hint of elevated alcohol except in the refreshing, mildly acidic aftertaste; one of the finest cherry eaux-de-vie I've sampled because the focus is so squarely on the cherry meat, not the bitterness found in the skin or the pit as is so often the case of other, lesser cherry eaux-de-vie; bravo.

RATING ★★★★ **Highly Recommended** $$$

Retter Williams-Christ Pear Essence 40% Alcohol (Austria)

Clear; the nose is upfront, true to its fruit source, clean, and decidedly sweet, with a dash of nutmeg thrown in for good measure, in the mouth, it owns an opulence that's quite irresistible—the overripe pear flavor is balanced by a solid acid spine, making it one of the more easily drinkable pear eaux-de-vie I've sampled in a while; better than average.

RATING ★★★ **Recommended** $$

Retter Vogelbeeren Elderberry Nectar 43% Alcohol (Austria)

Clear; the pine-like nose at first put me off, then after second and third nosings, I warmed up to it—by the fourth nosing the bouquet reeked unabashedly of jasmine blossoms; on the palate, the flowery/piney taste eventually gave way to a bitter berry flavor that grew more palatable and sweet with time; by the succulent aftertaste I liked the taste, which was unusual for me, and thought it ultimately recommendable; the smoothness of the texture, in particular, I found lovely.

RATING ★★★ **Recommended** $$$

Retter Brombeer Blackberry Nectar 43% Alcohol (Austria)

Clear; the bubblegum-like nose is delightful and cavalier in the initial nosing, then with aeration this bouquet gets serious, and by the fourth nosing the fragrance has a vinous, cardboard-like quality that approaches being medicinal—it has a surprisingly low fruit quotient, however, which concerned me; on the palate, it's delicious, as the sweet fruit element that was lost in the bouquet makes itself known at last; the aftertaste is plump, fruity, and long; the elegance found so abundantly in the taste and finish rescued it from an unsatisfactory ranking.

RATING ★★★ **Recommended** $$$

RETTER Macintosh Apple Essence 40% Alcohol (Austria)

Clear as spring water; the off-dry to sweet bouquet is very friendly and appley, with only a mild spirity quality; the flavor is delicate in its demeanor as fine, almost creamy (apple sauce?) tastes of ripe apples gain steam by mid-palate after beginning in a rather quiet way at the entry; the finish is clean, subdued, but surprisingly lengthy; a true-to-the-source eau-de-vie whose finest virtue is its fragile delicacy.

RATING ★ ★ ★   *Recommended* $$

RETTER Original Apple Cuvée Essence 40% Alcohol (Austria)

Crystal-clear appearance—nothing more needs to be said; the bouquet is appley, but with intriguing side hints of fabric, vanilla extract, and, most interestingly, malted grain—it's perhaps the most atypical aroma for an apple distillate that I've come across; in the mouth, it's keenly tart, almost sharp, in fact, at palate entry, then it settles down by midpalate into a spirity, lackluster eau-de-vie whose charm and character eluded me for the most part; while not at all unpalatable, it simply left me wanting much more than it seemed capable of supplying in terms of overall sensory satisfaction.

RATING ★ ★ $$

RETTER Holunder Rowanberry Nectar 43% Alcohol (Austria)

Clear; the snappy, forest-floor, anise-like, intensely herbal, cedary, almost medicinal, and steely (like steel wool) bouquet didn't have me singing even after four separate and thorough nosings; once in the mouth, however, the tart berry flavor came close to redeeming the metallic nose; the finish was clean, but the steel-wool, vegetal, viney qualities reintroduced themselves in the tail end of the aftertaste, closing the coffin lid on this one for me.

RATING ★ $$$

TRIMBACH Prunelle Sauvage Grande Réserve 45% Alcohol (France)

Spring-water clarity; made from the sloe plum, the nose is extremely seed-, or, more appropriately, pit-like and is very similar to a kirsch aroma—I found this bouquet to be more alluring than any cherry eau-de-vie, however, because it's spicier (pepper? cinnamon?), zestier, and more fruit-like than medicinal, as so many kirsch liqueurs seem to be; the flavor entry is sweet-sour and vigorously plummy, then the midpalate goes sweet and creamy, offering a glowing-embers-like warmth in the splendid finish; one of the finest eau-de-vie experiences I've enjoyed; an absolute "must buy" item.

RATING ★ ★ ★ ★ ★   *Highest Recommendation* $$

TRIMBACH Kirsch Grande Réserve 45% Alcohol (France)

Clear as rain water; the nose bolts from the sampling glass like a three-year-old-thoroughbred from the gate on Derby day—it's a racy, fruity, seed-like kirsch bouquet that falls squarely between cherry fruit meat and the bitterness/oiliness of the cherry pit—I call it a draw; in the mouth, the cherry fruit clearly commands as succulent, sweet, robust and spirity waves of flavor wash over the palate; the sweet, charming, exciting aftertaste keeps the fruit in the driver's seat; what I liked so much about this sensational kirsch was that the spirit component was never lost in the maze of ripe fruit—there was never any doubt that it was an eau-de-vie; superlative, my choice as the number-one kirsch in the marketplace.

RATING ★ ★ ★ ★ ★   Highest Recommendation $ $

TRIMBACH Mirabelle Grande Réserve 45% Alcohol (France)

Clear; the spicy, vanilla extract, clove nose is feather-light, seductive, mildly sweet, and opts more for tart acid purity than fruit heft; while other Trimbach eaux-de-vie bouquets catapult from the glass, this slinky number wafts up gently in measured waves—a beauty in the aroma department; the flavor is unabashedly sweet and plummy, but it's supported by an arrowstraight acid backbone that nicely accents the plum rush; the finish is cleansing, refreshing, totally harmonious, and sports the trademark Trimbach spirity warmth at the back of the throat; a revelation.

RATING ★ ★ ★ ★ ★   Highest Recommendation $ $

TRIMBACH Framboise Grande Réserve 45% Alcohol (France)

Crystal clear; the nose has everything going for it—smoothness, purity of fruit, the sweet-sour balance that routinely shows up in the great eaux-de-vie, substance, and a harmonious teaming of fruit, acid, and alcohol—it simply doesn't get better than this in the fragrance arena; the flavor only improves upon the stunning bouquet as the aromatic virtues come to fruition on the palate—the focus on the raspberry fruit is astonishing, mesmerizing; the finish is ultraclean, sweet, and complex; a clinic on framboise making.

RATING ★ ★ ★ ★ ★   Highest Recommendation $ $

TRIMBACH Poire William Grande Réserve 43% Alcohol (France)

Clear; the nose is round, bountiful, and oozes with sexy pear fragrance, leaning more to tartness than to sweetness or ripeness; in the mouth, the spirity flavor explodes on the tongue as a fourth-gear pear taste completely dominates the palate—it's a dazzler on the palate; the aftertaste seems infinite, as the marriage of tart fruit and spirit form an ideal union; a prime eau-de-vie example of form following name; seek it out.

RATING ★ ★ ★ ★   Highly Recommended $ $

WHITE SPIRITS

This large and diverse primary spirits category is ruled by the "translucent four"—gin, vodka, rum, and tequila. I purposely group them together into one broad category because, with the exception of the oak-aged rums and a handful of *añejo* tequilas, their appearances, as a rule, run from crystal clear to foggy silver to pale straw. White spirits are painted by the industry's marketing geniuses as the breezy, less serious counterpoints to the seemingly weightier libations that traditionally have been known as the "brown spirits," namely, brandy and whiskey. I think it's time to reexamine the role of white spirits.

Although white spirits are perceived by the drinking public at large as being lighter and more agile than the browns, that's hardly true in all cases. When you compare a sturdy white like Stolichnaya vodka, which can take the paint off your schooner, to a surprisingly ethereal brown spirit such as that from the Glenkinchie Distillery, a Lowland single-malt Scotch, 99 out of 100 people would choose the Stolichnaya as the heavier spirit, provided they were tasting both without being able to see them. Message: You can't always tell a spirit by its color.

Also affixed in the minds of consumers and even most liquor-industry people is the befuddled concept that white spirits are only meant to be enjoyed as warm-weather beverages and mixers, while brown spirits are to be dusted off only when the sun starts setting before 6:00 P.M. Such antiquated rules-of-thumb are the playground of nitwits. I'm as content to savor a brandy after a supper in June as I am sipping a gin-and-tonic before dinner in January. Write your own rules. Be daring. F. Scott Fitzgerald is credited with saying, "Life has no second act." Enjoy the drinks you like when you like.

Historically, white spirits are some of the oldest distilled spirits of all. Rum and vodka, especially, have their origins in ancient epochs. Some historians believe that distillates made from sugarcane were making people smile in Asia, India, and Indonesia long before the time of Christ. And vodka, the elixir of Czarist Russia and the aristocracy of medieval Poland, has been around, at least, for seven centuries.

So, although white spirits may not yet have the cachet of brandies like cognac or of whiskies like single-malt Scotch and single-barrel bourbon, they most certainly deserve to have better placement. I can think of few drinks—brown, blue, green, or amber—that provide as much sensory satisfaction as a shimmering, straw-colored, 100% blue agave *añejo* tequila, or a fine, honey-hued, oak-aged rum from the Caribbean region, or a clear, robust Russian vodka, or a creamy English dry gin that slithers down the throat like crushed velvet.

WHAT TO LOOK FOR IN WHITE SPIRITS

Purity.

All gins and vodkas, as well as silver (white) rums and white tequilas should be crystal clear, devoid of color or tint, and have no suspended particles floating about. Amber and dark rums should resemble brandy in color (gold to amber to brown) and be free from particles. *Reposado* and *añejo* tequilas should be particle-free and, in the majority of cases, have color, running from a soft pale-straw tint (almost like that of lemon juice) to gold-amber.

Aromatic and Flavor Properties.

- Gin should emit lovely, faintly sweet aromas and flavors highlighted by botanical, delicate bursts of flowers (primarily juniper) and spice (mostly coriander). Inferior gins smell and taste overly sweet or too flowery or overly botanical, as in the floor of a wet forest.
- The better vodkas are very subtle, even elusive in smell and taste, giving off mere whispers of charcoal, dry grain, or a slate-like quality. Poor-quality vodka is frequently intensely grainy or semisweet.

- Silver (white) rums should be clean smelling and tasting as well as slightly sweet. Amber and dark rums at their best should provide aromas and flavors of molasses, vanilla-caramel, and wood. The darker rums of renown are typically complex, concentrated, balanced, and heavier in body than all other white spirits. Poor dark rums are smelly, overly sugary or honeyed, and cloying in the mouth.
- Top-notch tequilas smell and taste of flora, dried herbs, with a touch of salt. The older, wood-aged *reposados* and *añejos* can have a dash of oakiness. Bad tequilas have the sour smells and tastes of locker rooms, wet fabric, and general mustiness (rotten mushrooms, especially).

Finish.

- Gin should offer a silky, mildly off-dry aftertaste with no burn or bite whatsoever.
- Vodka, in its finest showings, ends up totally dry, almost mineral-like in the finish. Even a little sharpness is acceptable in the tail end of a vodka aftertaste, so long as it doesn't leave the throat raw.
- Rum should be the sweetest ending of all the white spirits, though never syrupy or cloying. The darker styles should also throw in a mellow touch of wood.
- The best tequilas glide down the throat almost like a fine brandy, smooth, seamless, and elegant. When it bites at the back of the tongue, look for an alternative or an older tequila.

GIN

The first gins were produced in Holland in the 1600s. Back then, gin was simply a distilled grain spirit that was flavored with juniper berries, which were believed to have positive effects on ills of the bladder and kidney. The drink was dubbed *genièvre* by Dr. Franciscus de la Boe (a.k.a. Dr. Sylvius of Leyden), a Dutch physician and professor who by the majority of accounts is credited with gin's discovery. The name eventually evolved into *genever* and *geneva*.

British soldiers returning from the Continent years later brought back *geneva* samples to England, and a love affair commenced. Brits began distilling their own gin, and the rest is alcoholic beverage history. In seventeenth- and eighteenth-century England, gin became so popular that the government was forced to legislate controls on production because of the misuse of it by much of the population. In an ill-advised course of action (or perhaps, in desperation), the British Parliament's Gin Act of 1736 taxed distillers, who in turn had to hike up the cost to their customers. The legislation put gin out of reach to the masses and, consequently, the masses rioted. Additionally, in response to the taxation, numerous illicit stills appeared, producing inferior and often dangerous gin that cost a fraction of the purer legal spirit. Undaunted by the rivers of poisonous gin and prohibitive legislation, the citizenry of England continued to guzzle gin at frightening per capita rates. So, in 1756, the distillation of corn was outlawed completely in England. This measure led to further civil turmoil, and by 1760, the law was repealed.

By the mid-1700s, estimates put the number of so-called "grog" shops at a whopping 7,000 . . . just in London alone. The grog shops, or "gin palaces," as they were also referred to, were the public houses that served gin to paying patrons. Gin was scorned in society circles as the stupifier of the plebes. It took decades for gin to gain respectability in salon London. But once it became accepted by the gentry, gin was considered an indispensable tipple throughout the whole of England.

While the Dutch style of gin is sweet, London Dry Gin, which was introduced approximately a century ago, is bone-dry and is the preferred gin of England. Today, the phrase "London Dry Gin" is merely the name of a style of gin and doesn't necessarily indicate the place of origin. London Dry Gins can be legally made in Peoria, Illinois, and labeled as such.

Contemporary gins have a neutral-grain base. The herbal flavor of gin comes from the addition of botanicals, which can include any of the following: juniper berries, coriander seeds, aniseed, caraway seeds, orange peel, cardamom, licorice root, cinnamon, fennel, ginger, almonds, and orris root.

The major differences in the quality of gin are attributed to three factors: the quality and purity of the base spirit, the distillation technique used, and the individual mixture of the botanical flavorings. Producers jealously guard their own formulas.

BEEFEATER London Dry Gin 47% Alcohol (England)

Clear, ideal in its purity; one of the classiest, lushest, roundest gin bouquets in existence—spicy (coriander) and fruity—amazingly focused, the laser-beam-like aroma of juniper berry is immensely appealing, fat, and marvelous; delicious multiple layers of flavor develop on the palate; at entry, a stone-dry, minerally flavor opens up, ultimately giving way to a midpalate taste of defined juniper berry; the medium-long aftertaste takes you home in a savory, off-dry manner; doubtless this is one of the most stylish, downright succulent gins in the marketplace; slinky, sexy, and a joy to quaff; purchase in mass quantities.

RATING ★ ★ ★ ★   *Highly Recommended* $$

BOMBAY Sapphire London Dry Gin 47% Alcohol (England)

Clear and pure, not the sapphire blue hue that many people think it is— the blue tint belongs only to the bottle; a zesty, piquant aroma of juniper berries, peppermint, eucalyptus, and even faint echoes of cinnamon; this medium- to full-bodied gin has loads of pungent, prickly flavor elements, especially a briary, juniper, outdoorsy freshness that's really captivating; the elegant finish is full, clean, and flecked with spice; doubtless one of the top gins from the U.K.

RATING ★ ★ ★ ★   *Highly Recommended* $$

BOMBAY Dry Gin 43% Alcohol (England)

Properly clear, ideal clarity; sports a very clean bouquet that shows subtle touches of coriander, juniper berry, and citrus—but it's nowhere near the glorious nose of the big-hitting Bombay Sapphire; perfectly fine, more than acceptable on palate, as moderately creamy flavors of juniper, vanilla bean, and spice make their way along the taste path in good fashion; not the stuff of genius, but a better-than-average gin all the same.

RATING ★ ★ ★   Recommended $$

BOODLES British Gin 45.2% Alcohol (England)

Translucent, ideal purity; the nose has a zesty snap of juniper on the surface, supported by a foundational aroma of coriander seed that stays lurking in the background through all four nosings; in the mouth, it's medium-weighted, crisp, and just a tad too acidic to be rated more than three stars; the aftertaste is impressively smooth and satiny; the splendid bouquet and vixen-like finish are connected by a mouth presence that's middle-of-the-pack and, frankly, surprisingly pedestrian; in its defense, Boodles makes one of the savoriest gin-and-tonics you'll ever have, especially if you don't overdo the tonic.

RATING ★ ★ ★   Recommended $$

BRADBURN'S English Gin 47.4% Alcohol (England)

Properly limpid, excellent clarity; the production method is interesting because each of the botanicals (juniper berries, coriander seed, and citrus) used for flavoring are added individually in three sequential distillations—the result is one of the gin category's two or three most alluring bouquets, one that is zesty and spicy rather than plump or creamy (like Tanqueray, Bombay, and Beefeater); the citrusy taste is dry and impressively lively, even prickly, on the palate as vibrant, but stately and fully endowed, flavors of seeds, pine/cedar, citric acid, and juniper occupy the taste buds; the aftertaste is medium-long and highlights the citrus element; what it lacks in overall finesse it more than makes up for in strength of character; not designed for the crowd that relishes the plush, creamy style championed by Tanqueray or Beefeater, this is a heady, spicy, pedal-to-the-metal gin that marches to a different drummer—probably a kettle drum.

RATING ★ ★ ★ ★   Highly Recommended $$

CORNEY & BARROW London Dry Gin 47.3% Alcohol (England)

As crystal clear as one would expect; the intensely perfumed, herbal bouquet could only be of British origin—it's a heady, sweetish, fresh herb garden of a nose that I found about as ravishing as a gin bouquet can hope to get; in the mouth, it's medium-weighted and deliciously endowed with lively, creamy flavors of tart berries, cedar/pine, and (strangely) creamed spinach; the aftertaste is low key, slightly hot in the throat (which nearly dropped it down to four stars) and very extended for a gin; to my taste, this utterly spectacular gin shows stunning similarity to Tanqueray in the bouquet, Beefeater in the texture, and Bombay Sapphire in the flavor—luckily for us, Corney & Barrow takes the best from all of these illustrious gins and wraps them in one outstanding package; the world's finest gin, period.

RATING ★ ★ ★ ★ ★   Highest Recommendation $$

FLEISCHMANN'S Distilled Dry Gin 40% Alcohol (USA)

Clear, excellent clarity; the nose is quite grainy and minerally, with hardly a trace of botanical influence; the flavor is ruled by a licorice-like component from stem to stern; a lackluster, rudimentary, unidimensional gin suited mostly for bar mixing for indiscriminate people; has as much personality as its appearance has color.

RATING ★ $

GILBEY'S London Dry Gin 40% Alcohol (USA)

Clear, brilliant, and pure; a slightly sweet, pleasantly plump, and inviting nose that's piquant, spirity, and spicy—the peppery, coriander bouquet shows loads of zest; offers a definite berry-fruit element on the palate that vanishes in the dry finish; starts out with considerable pizazz, but ends up very minerally, flat, and neutral; the flavor and aftertaste simply don't fulfill the promise found in the attractive nose, which is left holding all the charm; use for mixing purposes only.

RATING ★ ★ $

GORDON'S London Dry Gin 40% Alcohol (USA)

Clear, correct purity; the reserved, moderately spicy, and desert-dry aroma is mildly intriguing, particularly in its peppermint quality—the lovely mintiness captured my attention immediately; very satiny, smooth bearing on the palate; soft, even demure flavors of mint, fruit, and licorice are pleasant and well balanced, if meek; it finishes on a nice, dry, black-licorice note; give this gin more depth of character in the aroma and midpalate and you'd have a recommendable item; as is, it's a perfectly average mixing gin.

RATING ★ ★ $

GREENALL'S Original London Dry Gin 47% Alcohol (England)

Clear, superb clarity; one of the nicer, leaner, noncreamy noses of the British gins, most of which (Tanqueray, Beefeater, Corney & Barrow) seem to display a dairy-like quality in the aroma—this attractive bouquet speaks of cedar, spice, and juniper berries, wrapped in a crisp, direct package; in the flavor department, Greenall's is dry, hard, and mineral-like, qualities that I like in a gin, a spirit that should never be flabby or viscous; the aftertaste is quite short but whistle-clean; a compact, tidy gin, Greenall's does the job without the grandeur and extravagance of some of its British competitors.

RATING ★ ★ ★   *Recommended* $

NOTARIS V. O. Genever Moutwijn 35% Alcohol (Holland)

Very pale yellow/straw color (like a Muscadet white wine from the western Loire Valley), excellent purity; the grainy/dry cereal bouquet transports me back to the countless mash tun rooms I've passed through in Scotland, Kentucky, and Tennessee—the nose is all about wheat and barley (strikingly similar to Wheat Chex brand cereal) that's steeping in water; I like the taste, but it's quite tame—the concentrated graininess is the whole show here and, really, I'm not sure in what circumstances the average consumer would ever think of pouring this malty, wheat-like spirit; it's a libation that smells and tastes exactly like new spirit that's been drawn off the still; Notaris V.O. is a novelty best saved for quirky collectors—it will never be a mainstream product because most people will never know when to serve it.

RATING ★ ★ ★　　Recommended　　$$

SEAGRAM'S Extra Dry Gin 40% Alcohol (USA)

Clear; one of the more individualistic noses in the gin category—highly pronounced, come-hither, distinct orange-peel, cinnamon, and lilac qualities hold court over other fruity components—I greatly admired the off-dry bouquet; unquestionably the fullest tasting of the domestic gins; the orange peel and cinnamon carry over onto the flavor, then a nifty, spicy hint of coriander develops in the stone-dry finish; best part of this handsome package, though, is the fleshy, fruity, full-blown nose; little wonder to me why this is one of the most popular distilled spirits in the U.S.; perfectly good on-the-rocks or in a cocktail.

RATING ★ ★ ★　　Recommended　　$

SIR ROBERT BURNETT'S London Dry Gin 40% Alcohol (USA)

Clear; the pungent, assertive, lavish, juniper-berry, fruity, slightly metallic aroma is very generous and alluring; on palate, the mild metallic quality fades quickly after entry and a pleasing herbaceousness takes over in midstream; the aftertaste goes fruity, then dry, then unfortunately reverts back to the metallic quality that it can't seem to shake; while acceptable overall, I found myself feeling disappointed in this gin after liking the assertive bouquet; mysteriously much better as a mixer than straight; evaluated three times—upgraded on the last go-round, as the slaty/steely quality seems to have been eliminated.

RATING ★ ★　　$

SOMERS British Gin with Citrus Flavour 35% Alcohol (England)

Clear; the nose is highly perfumed, with appetizing notes of tangerine, tangelo, lemon peel, pine nuts, and, of course, juniper berries—I think it's one of the more enchanting bouquets in all of white spirits; on the palate, it's silky, citrusy, juicy, tart, and medium-bodied—the lower alcohol level makes it thoroughly easy to quaff and the citrus bite makes it quite the refreshing mixer; I see endless possibilities as a mixer, like in fruit punch, for instance; a dashing, sophisticated, and totally fun gin.

RATING ★ ★ ★　　Recommended　　$

TANQUERAY Special Dry English Gin 47.3% Alcohol (England)

Clear, ideal purity; a delicate (but not for a moment wimpy), citrusy nose in which the tiniest hint of ideally balanced juniper berry and spice emerge—"stately" is the most apt term I can think of to describe the fleet, dry, sure, and seductive aroma; on palate it tasted and felt like double cream—how can that possibly be accomplished in a neutral-grain spirit?; a remarkably sensuous, impeccably crafted spirit that luxuriously glides down the throat—no heat, no edge, just liquid crushed velvet; gin heaven in a green bottle; the finish is predictably understated, but full, dry, and very, very extended; along with Corney & Barrow, the standard against which all other gins must be judged; upgraded to classic status after five tasting evaluations.

RATING ★ ★ ★ ★ ★   ***Highest Recommendation*** $ $

Rum

um is the name of the popular distilled spirit that is the result of the distillation of the fermented mash of sugarcane or its byproducts, especially molasses and cane sap. Sugarcane is a towering, prolific, perennial grass, which flourishes in warm, humid climates. It's speculated that the earliest alcoholic libations may have been made in the South Pacific, southern China, or India from the sap of sugarcane, which has a tendency to ferment without the aid of human intervention. Upon his return from his expedition to India in the fourth century B.C., Alexander the Great told of the spirits made from sugarcane, the "reed that gives honey without the help of bees."

Christopher Columbus introduced the reed to the islands of the Caribbean on his second voyage to the New World in 1493. Sugarcane found a friendly environment in the tropics of the Western Hemisphere and was quick to take root. With the creation of plantations in the Greater and Lesser Antilles, sugarcane became a staple cash crop by the dawn of the seventeenth century. Entire communities sprang up around the plantations as the demand for sugar and molasses skyrocketed with the expansion of the colonial Americas. Rum became the preferred distilled spirit in the North American colonies by the end of the seventeenth century and an indispensable cargo aboard the vessels of the English.

All rums are created from basically the same formula. Sugarcane reeds that have been freshly harvested are pressed to obtain their juice. After being decanted and filtered, the juice is then boiled to vaporize the water, creating a viscous syrup, cane syrup. The syrup is next placed into a centrifuge, which, at the speed of over 2,000 revolutions per minute, crystalizes the sticky syrup's sugar. What's left behind after the removal of the sugar crystals is dark brown molasses. The molasses is fermented for 24 to 48 hours, then distilled twice, either in continuous running column stills or small pot stills. Rums are never distilled at higher than 190 proof. Though the most prized rums come from the region of the Caribbean, rums are produced in virtually any country in which sugarcane is cultivated.

The word "rum" or "rhum," as it is sometimes spelled, is thought to have been derived either from the seventeenth-century West Indies term *rumbullion,* which was a term used to describe the raucous antics of a person who imbibed too much, or from the Latin derivative for sugar, *saccharum.*

There exists no international rum commission, to my knowledge, that regulates production or defines categories. Each country pretty much creates its own styles and classifications. Every country's rum distillers make both light and dark rums. The lights (a.k.a. white, silver) are rarely matured in oak casks (Puerto Rican rum is a prime exception). The darks (a.k.a. gold, oro) usually have some wood-aging, routinely about six months to two years. Black rums are aged longer in oak casks, frequently up to four years or more. There are also spiced rums and the great collection of rums that have been aged in oak casks for extended periods of a decade or more. A handful of these "reserves" and "estate bottlings" are the cognacs of the tropics and should be savored in wine glasses as you would a fine brandy.

The best rums come from the islands and countries of Puerto Rico, Martinique, Barbados, the U.S. Virgin Islands, the British Virgin Islands, Haiti/Dominican Republic, Jamaica, Venezuela, Nicaragua, and Guatamala.

RUMS OF PUERTO RICO

Since a staggering 85 percent of all the rums sold in the U.S. hail from the island of Puerto Rico, it's perfectly fitting to expound a bit on them. Puerto Rico is a good-sized island, 110 miles by 35 miles, and is the easternmost of the Greater Antilles. The terrain is remarkably varied, ranging from beautiful beaches to undulating hills to elevated rain forest to rugged mountains. The island was discovered on Columbus's second voyage in 1493. Drawings found on cave walls in the interior regions indicate that Puerto Rico (Spanish for "rich port") has been inhabited for at least two millennia. Ponce de Leon was made governor in 1508 as Spain expanded its influence in the New World. For centuries the island was the site of numerous battles, as competing empires inevitably overlapped there.

For centuries rum has been a major source of revenue for Puerto Rico. Before the World War I, the island grew most of its own sugar cane. But as the country modernized and production costs of both labor and energy soared, the old sugar plantations closed down. Today, as much as 87 percent of the molasses used to make Puerto Rican rum is imported from Jamaica and the Dominican Republic.

Rum's fermentation formula consists of three parts water to one part molasses. Fermentation is temperature controlled at 86–90 degrees Fahrenheit. Puerto Rican rums are distilled in large, continuously running patent stills rather than small pot stills for two reasons: Patent stills are more cost efficient and they produce lighter, drier rums. All Puerto Rican rums must be aged by law for at least one year in oak casks. The darker *añejos* and *reserves* are aged for considerably longer periods, some for up to a decade or more. Distillers can use additives up to 1.5 percent of the total volume to enrich the bouquet and flavor. Sherry is the most commonly used additive, with cognac being the second most used.

The trio of rum distillers I've had the pleasure of visiting with were industry giant Bacardi, the world's largest rum producer; minute, family-owned Edmundo B. Fernandez; and medium-sized Serralles. Bacardi's plant has a surreal, amusement-park feel to it, with visitors being bussed around on surrey-covered trams. Viewing their long, clanking bottling lines is a main attraction. Taking into account their production numbers and the size of the market they must service, their rums are very palatable. Going from massive, fastidiously organized Bacardi to the laid-back, backyard production facility of Edmundo B. Fernandez is both disconcerting and refreshing. Operated today by Manuel Fernandez, the distillery produces the most elegant rums on the island, labeled "Ron del Barrilito" (Spanish for "rum from the barrel"). Fernandez himself greets you in an unassuming, almost self-effacing manner and puts you immediately at ease. Walking about the barn-like distillery takes approximately ten minutes. The two Barrilito rums are in the class of the great oak-aged rums of Pampero from Venezuela.

Last, but certainly not least, was Serrales, whose representatives I met at their beautiful museum, El Museo Castillo Serrales in Ponce, Puerto Rico's largest city in the south. With Master Blender Sylvia Santiago, I tasted through the various brands in the Serrales stable. They include Don Q, the best label, Palo Viejo, Ron Llave, Captain Morgan, and Granado. A chance to make my own blend, which ended up being dubbed "Ron Bow-Wow," compelled me to express my appreciation of Ms. Santiago's skill.

APPLETON **Dark Rum 40% Alcohol (Jamaica)**

Looks remarkably similar to an older cognac in its medium amber/dark honey tone with copper highlights; nosing it blind, it could be mistaken for an old calvados or a non-French brandy—its regal bearing is immensely alluring, as baked scents of spiced apples, almonds, sugarcane, caramel, and oak tannin meld beautifully into one harmonious aromatic thrust; in the mouth, I was unprepared for the intense smokiness of the off-dry, astringent taste—other flavors, mostly black pekoe tea, tannin, and macadamia nut took control at midpalate; the finish highlights the tea component; a unique and challenging rum experience.

RATING ★ ★ ★ ★   ***Highly Recommended*** $$

APPLETON **Estate VX 5-Year-Old Rum 40% Alcohol (Jamaica)**

Superb purity and warm amber hue; the toasty, roasted bouquet is dripping with bittersweet brown-sugar/molasses scents, which seem to grow in strength with each nosing—it's a fine, even delicate bouquet that shows background hints of citrus peel and spice; on palate, what strikes me the most is the satiny texture and medium to full weight—it caresses the tongue like a warm winter blanket; the finish is firm and toasty; wow.

RATING ★ ★ ★ ★   ***Highly Recommended*** $$

BACARDI Añejo Rum 40% Alcohol (Puerto Rico)

Amber/orange color; oak-aged from one to six years; smoky, butterscotch, slightly medicinal nose; oaky, vanillin, floral flavors are very smooth and toothsome on palate; the aftertaste is hot and biting at first, then a syrupy molasses flavor and feel take over, soothing the relieved taste buds; it's startlingly VSOP-armagnac-like in terms of bearing, aroma, and texture; Bacardi Añejo has truckloads of raw, feral, spirity flavors—it's unabashedly short on finesse but admirably long on passionate tropical-fruit flavors and stimulating aromas; I admired the unruly, raucous, free-spirited quality of this aggressive, take-no-prisoners rum; if someone held a gun to my head and told me to choose between this ruffian and the more composed and serene Bacardi Gold Reserve that I also rate three stars, I do believe that I'd reach for the Añejo.

RATING ★ ★ ★   *Recommended* $$

BACARDI Gold Reserve Rum 40% Alcohol (Puerto Rico)

Golden/amber/nutbrown color; oak-aged from one to six years; pineapple, intense, pungent, caramel, vanilla aromas abound in the nicely balanced nose; the silky, sedate, oily, focused, semidry flavors of orange rind and dark caramel possess genuinely alluring finesse; the finish is rather timid after a fast rush of spirit in the midpalate; it leaves an overall impression of great care in production; correct, savory, and elegant, but seems locked in third gear.

RATING ★ ★ ★   *Recommended* $

BACARDI Light Rum 40% Alcohol (Puerto Rico)

Clear as water; oak-aged at least one year; semidry, pedestrian, somewhat metallic, gravelly, mildly candied, slate-like nose; medium-weighted on palate; minerally, peppery finish; boringly neutral on its own, but in all fairness that's not its purpose in life—this rum is meant to be mixed with anything and everything from Coke to tonic to citrus juices to fruity tropical drinks to cake; ho-hum.

RATING ★ ★ $

BACARDI Black Rum 40% Alcohol (Puerto Rico)

Beautiful bronze/ochre/cola color; oak-aged from one to four years; decidedly sweet, molasses, candied-nut nose, which develops an unbaked bread dough quality after a few minutes of aeration; unexpectedly limp entry onto the palate, then candied flavors accelerate modestly to a sweetly pleasant midpalate, ending with an aftertaste of black coffee; good overall, but not as sumptuous in the nose or taste as its appearance leads you to believe; upgraded.

RATING ★ ★ $

BACARDI Limon Rum 35% Alcohol (USA)

Clear; the nose is heavily citrused so as to completely conceal any resemblance to rum—nosed blind, it could be guessed to be yet another citrus-flavored vodka; on the palate, it tastes like lemon/lime soda (with a 35% alcohol kick) as the tart lemony front taste is backed by a sweet sugarcane foundation; the aftertaste is decidedly sweet and the lemon flavor lasts long; its best applications, I think, would simply be either as an on-the-rocks drink or as a mix in a citrus punch; the Bacardi name and its drinkability will more than likely make this rum a success with the twentysomething set.

RATING ★★ $

BARBANCOURT Estate Réserve 15-Year-Old Rhum 43% Alcohol (Haiti)

Like the other Barbancourts, double-distilled in pot stills; aged in oak casks for 15 years; darker still than the eight-year-old, it dazzles the eye with its gorgeous, medium amber/honey gold/orange-pekoe-tea color, resembling a Speyside single-malt Scotch; the extraordinary bouquet outdistances the eight-year-old in terms of overall complexity, confident depth, and the influence of wood—very mature, settled-in, and sublime—aromatically, the most brandy-like of the three Barbancourts; the deep, brown-sugar/honeyed taste is rivaled only by the equally heavenly (but virtually impossible to locate) Clement 1952 from Martinique—so smooth, it's sinful—so ripe and sweet, it's decadent—a true benchmark rum that's as elegant as brandy and as complex as a blended Scotch; it blew me away, period.

RATING ★★★★★   *Highest Recommendation* $$

BARBANCOURT Réserve Spéciale 8-Year-Old Rhum 43% Alcohol (Haiti)

Aged for eight years in white oak barrels; very close in appearance to the four-year-old, though this beauty has more orange tint to it, ideal clarity; the nose is biscuity, mature, pleasantly sweet, with nuanced touches of vanilla extract, lanolin, and oak—by the last pass, after 15 minutes of aeration, the alcohol element really exposes itself as it pushes through the cane sweetness and oak; on palate, the taste is so lip-smackingly luscious that I can't imagine adulterating it with ice, water, or mixed-drink ingredients—think of honey, nougat, chocolate walnuts—a fat, chewy, whopping-good flavor that's assertive, but not aggressive; no wood to speak of in the candied finish; a voluptuous, well-endowed, deep-dish rum.

RATING ★★★★   *Highly Recommended* $

BARBANCOURT 4-Year-Old Rhum 43% Alcohol (Haiti)

Matured in oak for four years; very pretty, medium amber/gold color, superb purity; the nose is pungent, round, and sweet in a controlled way—no syrupiness or cloying sweetness whatsoever—as expected, the most heady/spirity and punchy of the three Barbancourt aromas, since it's the youngest; the fullness of the texture is impressive—there's a seductive, almost rancio-like (cheesy) quality in the midpalate that's there doubtless because of the oak effect—delicious and atypical—molasses, black pepper, and wood resin all contribute something to the honeyed-flavor impact; the resiny/honey quality lasts long into the finish; a very solid, structurally firm rum.

RATING ★★★   *Recommended* $

BLUEBEARD'S Authentic Spiced Rum 35% Alcohol (U.S. Virgin Islands)

Wonderfully bright, clear, clean, amber/golden color; astringent, softly spirity, markedly herbal nose that offers three distinct levels of aroma—the first is dried apricot, the second is a mild herb/floral quality, and third is a hint of sweetish sugarcane; this baby really hums on the palate with zesty, tangy flavors of sugar, red pepper, paprika, and cola nut; finishes with a touch of heat in a vivacious, carefree, and flavorful way; a fun rum as a mixer but that's about it.

RATING ★★ $

BRUGAL Añejo Gran Reserva Familiar 40% Alcohol (Dominican Republic)

Stunning, beguiling ochre/auburn/umber color that beautifully picks up the light—in terms of appearance one of the prettiest rums I've sampled; the heavenly, multifaceted nose speaks of butter, controlled spirit, sweet oak, hazelnuts, and the finest English toffee; on palate, all the sensory delights promised in the color and the nose are fulfilled in a balanced, stately manner; off-dry flavors of caramel, molasses, dark honey, and bittersweet chocolate combine in a harmonious way; the extended, sweet finish has a flash of butterscotch; like Pampero Anniversario from Venezuela and Ron del Barralito Two Star from Puerto Rico, it's simply too good to mix and should be served like a cognac or brandy in a small wine glass; it rivals many VSOP-level cognacs in terms of elegance, aromatic charm, and flavor intensity.

RATING ★★★★   *Highly Recommended* $

BRUGAL White Label 40% Alcohol (Dominican Republic)

Clear; the sweetish, sugarcane nose has a very pleasant piquancy to it—an absolute knockout on the palate, as incredibly rich vanilla, coffee-cake, and cola flavors take the taste buds captive—my taste buds serenely surrendered in a "we have met the enemy and we are theirs" fashion; this beauty finishes concentrated, long, and sweet, but very clean—no fat, no flab, never cloying; the aftertaste reminded me most of vanilla wafers; the texture is shockingly bountiful for a white rum; looks like a white rum but tastes like an oak-aged *añejo*; doubtless one of the choicest white rums in the marketplace.

RATING ★★★   *Recommended* $

BRUGAL Gold Label 40% Alcohol (Dominican Republic)

Luminous, orange pekoe tea color; the restrained, plummy nose barely peeks out from the glass; has a soft, mushy, pillowy texture that's plump rather than crisp and focused; on palate, the dry caramel flavor comes on strong and stays long, but comprises the entire taste repertoire; I was disappointed with this rum after being so favorably impressed by its sibling, the white label; to my way of thinking, the dark should have been even more opulent and purposeful than the white, but such was not the case; make no mistake, this is a good rum, but in view of the other two exemplary rums from Brugal, it's the runt of the litter.

RATING ★ ★ $

CACIQUE Ron Añejo 40% Alcohol (Venezuela)

Average amber/gold color; the nose shows some feintiness, smokiness, old leather, and tobacco; it turns nicely sweet on the palate, especially in the lovely, long, cocoa-like finish; while technically sound and correct within accepted rum parameters, it lacks the depth of character and opulent presence of other highly memorable rums from Venezuela, in particular, those of Pampero; it relies too heavily on its sweetness, failing to expand from that theme into genuine complexity; didn't show that well as a mixer.

RATING ★ $

CAPTAIN MORGAN Private Stock Spiced Rum 40% Alcohol (Puerto Rico)

Truly gorgeous color of medium amber with orange core highlights, perfect purity; the nose is very different from the regular bottling of Captain Morgan in that it's much more mature and less spicy—while I didn't necessarily prefer it to that of the younger bottling, I did appreciate its suppleness; in the mouth, the clear presence of wood in the form of vanilla extract makes for a sumptuous taste experience—the spices don't overlap with the sweet, sugary rum, but complement them nicely; the aftertaste is extended and offers flavors of butterscotch and oloroso sherry; I'd serve this lipsmacking rum on-the-rocks with a healthy twist of lemon or lime.

RATING ★ ★ ★ ★   *Highly Recommended* $

CAPTAIN MORGAN Coconut Rum 27.5% Alcohol

Crystal clear; the sassy nose instantly blurts out "piña colada" in a distinct, sweetened aromatic blast that's really delightful—with the exception of flavored vodkas, I've never been a proponent of flavored spirits, but I found this rum to be unusually pleasing; the taste is only mildly sweet and correctly focuses on only one subject, coconut; here's an example of an affordable, fun item that's good for mixing with cola or fruit juice, but could also be enjoyed on-the-rocks; its biggest asset is the sumptuous bouquet—two stars just for the nose; as tasty as the spiced original. (*Note:* I tried Captain Morgan Coconut Rum in a piña colada that relied solely on the CMCR for the coconut element rather than using coconut juice and that was a mistake, so keep coconut juice in your piña colada recipe even when you're using this rum.)

RATING ★ ★ ★   *Recommended* $

CAPTAIN MORGAN Original Spiced Rum 35% Alcohol (Puerto Rico)

Slightly darker than the Bluebeard's—a rich honey color; lush, egg-cream, sweet, nutmeg, coriander, and cinnamon aromas caress the olfactory sense with hardly any sense of spirit—a classy, spicy, and honeyed nose; this creamy rum makes no effort to conceal its sweet molasses foundational taste; further down the palate, honeyed flavors dominate the backseat spiciness and low-key spirit; the texture is velvety; the long, tropical-fruit-like aftertaste shows just the slightest bite; mission accomplished from top to bottom.

RATING ★ ★ ★   ***Recommended*** $

CASTILLO Spiced Rum 35% Alcohol (Puerto Rico)

Pretty Sauternes-like, golden hay color; the sweetish, tutti-frutti nose is mildly spicy, but hardly zesty, showing a bit too much sugar candy and vanilla extract for my liking; in the mouth, however, the vanilla that was over-accentuated in the bouquet really becomes the major flavor asset and supports the rummy, fruity foundation taste; the aftertaste is very pleasant and offers a smidgen of astringent bite in the tail end (not enough to detract); not as polished as the superior Captain Morgan, but decent nevertheless.

RATING ★ ★ $

C. J. WRAY Dry Rum 40% Alcohol (Jamaica)

Predictably clear; the off-dry bouquet is unappealing, if slightly phenolic, owning a pencil-eraser quality that's a little unsettling; on palate, questions regarding the nose are somewhat resolved in a wave of herbal/vegetal flavors that are reminiscent of cedar/pine and smoke; the aftertaste is on the sweetish side of the scale, as a sexy flavor of coconut announces itself; I ended up sitting on the rating fence over this rum, not liking the nose one bit but finding the palate and finish more than agreeable; a good mixer; recently upgraded to a more suitable score.

RATING ★ ★ $

CLEMENT RUMS (MARTINIQUE)

The Clément rum reviews were taken from barrel samples that were sent to me while negotiations were taking place between the producer and a highly respected U.S. importer. Lamentably, the talks never came to fruition. As of the writing of *Kindred Spirits*, I do not know if these sensational rums have ever made their way into the U.S. If they have reached an agreement with an importer and you are lucky enough to spot them in your local liquor store, or if you travel to the isle of Martinique, take, at least, one nanosecond to buy them.

CLEMENT 1952 44% Alcohol (Martinique)

Luminous, dazzling—an eye-opening, crisp, and clearly defined orange/amber color; the sweet, understated nose offers ripe fruit, caraway seed, oak, cream, and walnuts, all in just the right amount with one never stepping on the toes of another; on palate, the mannered flavor components show the benefit of four decades of aging; the refinement and ethereal quality of the various flavor elements have melded into a single taste of such harmony that, and I can say this without the slightest hesitation, Clément 1952 is the finest, most regal, and profound rum experience I've ever had; this spirit is on the same level as XO-level cognac; bravo and hats off to Jean-José Clément, grandson of founder Homère Clément.

RATING ★ ★ ★ ★ ★   ***Highest Recommendation*** $ $ $

CLEMENT 1970 44% Alcohol (Martinique)

Attractive honey/amber color with orange/vermilion highlights—no sediment; a serious, spirity, armagnac-like nose, which showcases an impeccably married array of feinty aromas, including basil, coriander, dried flowers, and chocolate-cake batter; the focus of the semisweet, biscuity flavor is like a laser beam and as fine as an old-vintage armagnac, with its chewy, fleshy texture; one of the most brandy-like rums I've ever tasted, period; the finish is composed, elegant, and very soft, without the faintest hint of heat or bite—it simply charmed the daylights out of me from start to finish; "regal" is a term I use more for wine than for spirits, but here is that singular case when the word is perfectly apt.

RATING ★ ★ ★ ★   ***Highly Recommended*** $$$

CLEMENT 15-Year-Old 44% Alcohol (Martinique)

Luminous orange/amber color—no sediment; heady, sweet, estery, perfumed, and melded aromas of cola and molasses are buttressed by underlying fragrances of ripe pears, pink grapefruit, cardboard, and sweet, old, sherried oak—a very complex nose to say the least; this rum takes off on the palate, as focused, mature, beautifully orchestrated, VSOP-cognac-quality flavors of grapes, walnuts, orange rind, and toffee come together in a graceful package; the finish serves to further highlight the balance between power and delicacy; a bona fide race horse that leaves most other rums eating its dust.

RATING ★ ★ ★ ★   ***Highly Recommended*** $$$

CLEMENT Blanc 50% Alcohol (Martinique)

Absolutely clear; offers an intensely grainy, mashy, corn-husk, cereal-like nose at first pass, going off-dry, nutty, and significantly medicinal with aeration; on palate, it exhibits above-average richness in both texture and taste; the sweet, creamy flavors of vanilla bean and coconut meat cloak the ample alcohol, making the taste an extremely pleasurable experience; the very long aftertaste recalls cotton candy at the county fairs of yesteryear; an altogether lovely white rum whose charm and zesty personality are disarming; I would have scored it four stars but for the unimpressive, medicine-chest nose.

RATING ★ ★ ★   ***Recommended*** $$

CLEMENT 10-Year-Old 44% Alcohol (Martinique)

Very pretty honey/amber color, which is without sediment; husky, chunky, molasses-like nose, which with aeration shows deeper levels of candied almonds and oak; much more evolved and subtle on palate than the sugar-coated six-year-old; this ten-year-old is sweet, make no mistake, but its maturity corrals the sweetness so that other flavor components, like sherry, butter, and mint, are allowed to contribute to the whole impression; it ends on a pleasantly refined and polite note; while it's not what I'd term a memorable blockbuster of a rum, it's amiable, user-friendly, and above average.

RATING ★ ★ ★   ***Recommended*** $$

CLEMENT 6-Year-Old 44% Alcohol (Martinique)

Stunning, lustrous orange/amber color, which is totally devoid of any sediment—the riveting appearance alone elevates the score; the nose is sedate but sure-footed, emitting restrained, astringent aromas of black pepper, lemon peel, dill, and basil—with ten minutes of aeration, the bouquet takes on a sweeter, charcoal-like quality that is more appealing than its more obvious upfront, phenolic scent; with palate entry, the concentrated, mocca-like, syrupy sweetness obliterates all other flavors in its path; the aftertaste provides more of the same molasses, black coffee, and a numbing sweetness; while good, this rum runs the risk of being too cloying to people with low thresholds for sweetness.

RATING ★ ★ $$

COCKSPUR VSOR 40% Alcohol (Barbados)

A vast improvement in appearance over the limp Five-Star—the VSOR proudly displays a pretty dark gold/amber color, but is still rather light considering that it's blended from rums that have been aged in wood for at least eight years; subdued, sugarcane nose; the highlight of this rum is in the toasty, oaky, mature, round, caramel-like flavor that's well endowed and tightly knit; highlight number two comes in the sublime, roasted-almond, lemony aftertaste, which seems endless; a sound, better-than-average rum that hardly shows any resemblance to its shockingly inferior sibling.

RATING ★ ★ ★   ***Recommended*** $

COCKSPUR Five-Star 40% Alcohol (Barbados)

Ordinary amber color; unexciting aromas of ripe melon, cinnamon, and hay gently greet the nose—not an evolved bouquet; very soft, medium-bodied, polite bearing on the palate; very fleshy texture; different, moderately medicinal, off-dry flavors of tobacco smoke and cereal seem to fight for dominance in the mouth; ends up sweet in a rush of honey and chocolate flavors that are quite nice but that don't provide enough pleasure to redeem the lackluster nose and unharmonious entry flavors; while inoffensive, I really disapproved of the flabby texture and unfocused demeanor of this rum.

RATING ★ $

CRISTAL Aguardiente 32% Alcohol (Colombia)

Clear; the snappy bouquet shouts out "black licorice" as the pungent fragrance of anise wipes out everything else—and, I wonder, if this is a sugarcane distillate (what's anise doing in it?); in the mouth, it's smooth but neither creamy nor plump in texture; while I believe I should be experiencing something different and possibly good, my taste buds remain underwhelmed and bored by the one-note quality of the muffled taste of anise; ditto with the finish; it's not in the least bad, just a snoreburger of a spirit; I'm not sure how I'd serve this spirit.

RATING ★ ★ $

CRUZAN Premium Diamond Estate 4-Year-Old Rum 40% Alcohol (U.S. Virgin Islands)

Gorgeous, orange/medium amber color—perfect clarity; the high-voltage nose gallops from the glass in piquant, zesty aromas of egg cream, vanilla extract, white chocolate, and new oak—it's a terrific rum bouquet that's more vivacious than profound; on the palate, it's whistle-clean, slightly oily, and jam-packed with oak tannins and vanilla overtones; it finishes quietly but firmly; while it would be unfair to place this fine rum in the same ring with heavyweight champs like Barrilito, Clément, Pampero, or Brugal, this is a very strong, very stylish, middleweight rum that has plenty of appeal; don't expect a vision of the great beyond when sipping this rum, but do expect more than ample satisfaction.

RATING ★★★   *Recommended* $

CRUZAN Dark-Dry Rum 40% Alcohol (U.S. Virgin Islands)

One of the lightest "dark rums" I've yet seen—shows a timid, bland, wheat color; very much like its Light sibling, the nose is exceedingly shy—but when finally coaxed out, the bouquet is actually quite charming in its low-decibel sweetness; a pleasant, one-note rum in which sugarcane molasses is the name of the game from start to finish; it's definitely better and has more stuffing than the Cruzan Light; its taste is clean and straightforward; an acceptable, serviceable, middle-of-the-road dark rum.

RATING ★★ $

CRUZAN Light-Dry Rum 40% Alcohol (U.S. Virgin Islands)

Crystal clear; this is a rum that will never be famous for its expansive nose—it's so coy and minimalist that it hardly exists at all—I got the barest impression of vanilla, that being the inadequate sum total of the aroma department; on palate, it's quite chunky, even top-heavy in its sweetness; it finishes long, heavy, and sweet; technically it's okay, but in style it's way too lumbering, showing no snap, balance, or crispness; indeed, the Hulk Hogan style makes something of a joke of the terms "Light-Dry" that are splashed across the label, because it's neither.

RATING ★ $

CRUZAN Clipper Spiced Rum 40% Alcohol (U.S. Virgin Islands)

Pale yellow/gold color; enthralling, piquant nose of clove, vanilla extract, and whipped cream—it's like a dessert; while the bouquet set an appetizing table, the hot, peppery flavor failed to come through with a suitable meal; I found the mouth-feel thin and the taste too heavily reliant on the spice; the finish tries too hard to clean up the table; prior to tasting it, I would have laid odds on a recommendation by virtue of the sexy aroma; disappointing, a bust.

RATING ★ $

DON Q Cristal Rum 40% Alcohol (Puerto Rico)

Water-clear; faint but evident hints of bing cherries and chili peppers—quite an ambrosial nose really for a base-level light rum; very clean, fresh at entry to palate, charcoal taste at midpoint, backs off quickly to a medium charcoal, bitter finish; far from neutral; a slightly better light rum than Bacardi Light; use only as a mixer.

RATING ★ ★ $

Don Q Gold Rum 40% Alcohol (Puerto Rico)

Very soft, peach-like color; stone-dry, rich, generous, oaky, vanilla extract nose; keenly dry in the unique entry; the midpalate is reinforced by a pleasantly bitter flavor that makes the tongue tingle; finishes a bit too harshly at first, then settles down in a minor, dry-flavor crescendo of light caramel; okay as a mixer.

RATING ★ ★ $

Don Q 151 75.5% Alcohol (Puerto Rico)

Clear, wheat-colored appearance; assertive, spirity aroma (though not of nose-killing intensity) that displays an attractive underpinning of sweet, ripe fruit; gobs of alcohol grip that takes no prisoners in the mouth; the initial impression is one of mild caramel, then comes the hammer of spirit that crushes any flavor, leaving the entire mouth begging for mercy as my oral thermostat goes haywire; like industrial-strength, five-alarm chili; the stratospheric alcohol obliterates any sense of flavor enjoyment; unless you enjoy having your mouth torched like a warehouse for insurance purposes, leave this blistering firewater on the shelf; I can envision no practical purpose for this stuff.

RATING ★ $

Flor de Cana Grand Reserve Rum 40% Alcohol (Nicaragua)

Aged seven years; a slightly darker orange/amber/tea hue than the Black Label; the nose is quite pronounced and assertive right from the initial whiff—it has a keen sugarcane foundation that nicely supports top-layer scents of vanilla wafer, pine needles, and candy; one of the smoothest, silkiest palate entries in the rum category; it's easily the sweetest of the line, with smoky backup tastes of sweet oak, honeydew melon, and pears; it finishes as classily as it started out on the tongue; an elegant spirit from Central America.

RATING ★ ★ ★ ★   *Highly Recommended* $

Flor de Cana Gold Rum 40% Alcohol (Nicaragua)

Aged three years; yellow/gold/medium amber appearance; this nose is much zestier, sweeter, and spicier than the round, succulent white Flor de Cana Extra Dry—it really betrays wood in the resiny quality that wafts up from the sampling glass—the third pass introduces a showy butteriness; the flavor is surprisingly dry as it first enters the palate, then the hard-candy sweetness takes over and keeps the taste buds duly entertained all the way through the soft, warm, buttery finish; makes a much better-than-average mixer.

RATING ★ ★ ★   *Recommended* $

FLOR DE CANA Black Label Rum 40% Alcohol (Nicaragua)

Aged five years; the eye-catching orange/amber color has honey/russet highlights; the nose of this rum is much more subdued than the vigorous Gold, yet I discern a sense of power in the layers of sweet-sour aromas; this is by a mile the most different of the Flor de Canas in that its strength is of a silent kind that, at first, is deceptive, then it makes itself known in spades in the throat; the flavors are tightly wound and laser-beam-like in their focus; the most winning element is the supple, muscular aftertaste, which offers bits of oak, molasses, and honey wheat.

RATING ★★★   ***Recommended*** $

FLOR DE CANA Extra Dry Rum 40% Alcohol (Nicaragua)

Aged three years; pale, off-white, cream-soda-pop color; one of the richer, creamier noses for a white rum that I've evaluated—it emits a heady, provocative, off-dry perfume of unsweetened coconut meat that's extremely alluring if you're willing to spend the time coaxing it out—I doubt the vast majority of rum drinkers are patient enough to properly nose a rum; low key on the palate as the creaminess welcomes the taste buds; the aftertaste is clean and off-dry; the less-than-thrilling flavor and aftertaste left the nice aroma hanging; strictly a mixer.

RATING ★★ $

GOSLING'S Black Seal Dark Rum 40% Alcohol (Bermuda)

Very deep amber/honey-brown hue with gorgeous scarlet highlights; the complex, multilayered, provocative nose emits soft scents of plum brandy, quinine, juniper, cedar, grape must, sugarcane, and wood resin—it's anything but a sweet bouquet and leans in the direction of tartness/bitterness—there's even some butterscotch way in the back; to my surprise, the sand-dry taste of quinine dominated at palate entry, then an intensely spiced midpalate flavor grabbed hold of my taste buds and refused to give them back until the finish, in which a subtle sweetness of cane brought the whole experience to closure; I liked the razor-sharp spiciness right at dead-center midpalate.

RATING ★★★   ***Recommended*** $

JUMBY BAY Proprietor's Rum 43% Alcohol (Antigua)

Pale gold color; I noted some suspended particles, so I changed glasses just in case—unfortunately, the second well-rinsed glass also showed strange, elongated strands of God-knows-what floating about, so they definitely came from the sample bottle; the nose was moderately spicy, with a kicky, pleasing note of orange rind; on palate, this intensely astringent, peppery, and zesty rum explodes on the tongue, giving it a wee spirity jolt; the aftertaste settles down into a serene, citrusy taste that's truly delightful; would have scored much higher and been recommendable but for the problematic appearance; strong suit is as a mixer.

RATING ★★ $

MOUNT GAY Eclipse 40% Alcohol (Barbados)

Really beautiful amber tone, pure; the nose is slightly nutty, intensely sugary, and even a bit oaky in a resiny kind of way—this agile bouquet turns biscuity by the third pass, almost like vanilla wafer—a dynamite, expressive, and graceful aroma; in the mouth, the taste mirrors the virtues found in the nose, except for the oakiness, which disappeared; clean, gently sweet aftertaste, which lingered forever; solid, gentlemanly, even stately.

RATING ★ ★ ★   ***Recommended*** $

Myers's Platinum White Rum 40% Alcohol (Jamaica)

Clear as water, excellent purity; the pronounced nose is plump, round, sugarcane-sweet, even spicy and a bit fruity—one of the better white-rum bouquets—very true to its source; tasted next to the disappointingly timid Myers's Original Dark, I have to say that I preferred this lovely, well-balanced white—harmonious, sweet flavors of egg cream and confectioner's sugar are touched with citrus essence in the throat; quick, sweet finish; if you like a sweet core to your rum, go for this Jamaican beauty.

RATING ★ ★ ★   ***Recommended*** $

Myers's Original Dark Rum 40% Alcohol (Jamaica)

Gorgeous, oloroso-sherry-like color, all bronze/russet/copper shades; citrusy, astringent, slightly piquant, perfumy, unusual nose, which is surprisingly dry to off-dry and flecked with hints of black pepper, cayenne, anise, and most surprising of all, cabbage; in the mouth, this rum is semi-sweet, sedate, and understated, with a cocoa underpinning that accelerates into full-throttle chocolate in the aftertaste; I expected more punch and oak influence from such a dark rum; to be sure, it's proper in every way, but it didn't thrill me to the bone; the appearance garnered lots of points, but no distilled spirit can live on looks alone.

RATING ★ ★ $

PAMPERO RUMS/VENEZUELA

The following Pampero rums are more than noteworthy. Pampero is the second largest rum producer in the world, exceeded only by Bacardi. Pampero wood-ages its premium "Special Reserve" rums in 55-gallon American white-oak casks for as long as six years. This extended contact with oak lends an astonishing mellowness, in particular, to the Pampero Añejo Deluxe and the Añejo Aniversario, which in my opinion are certainly two of the most luxurious rums currently available in the U.S. market. Pampero's commitment to wood-aging has, according to sources from Pampero, made it the world's largest aged-rum producer, with over 300,000 barrels quietly resting in its enormous cellars at Ocumare, Venezuela.

Pampero Ron Añejo Deluxe 40% Alcohol (Venezuela)

Pretty, but a much more serious shade of topaz/bronze/light brown than the color of the Gold, with gilded orange highlights; absolutely luscious, multilayered bouquet of flowers, hard candy, vanillin (from oak), and spice; full, round, crushed-velvet texture; the cocoa and spice flavors dominate on entry—at midpalate the tongue is treated to a velvet-hammer hit of sugarcane molasses; the admirably elegant aftertaste is clean, dry, and sleek; a quiet, sinewy powerhouse; outstanding quality.

RATING ★ ★ ★ ★   *Highly Recommended* $$

PAMPERO RON Añejo Aniversario 40% Alcohol (Venezuela)

Extraordinary deep, burnished-orange/cola-brown color; nose of great, if controlled, strength and complexity, laced with raisins, walnuts, ripe tropical fruit (especially guava and passion fruit), and peppermint; it has the stately texture and bearing of a very old family-reserve cognac—this stunning thoroughbred is so delicious on its own, served neat, that I can't conceive of using it as a mixer—why dilute such elegance?—it finishes smoothly and serenely; I would immediately place this on my *digestif* serving tray squarely alongside my favorite brandies, ports, cream sherries, and whiskies; as stylish and elegant a distilled spirit as you can hope for.

RATING ★ ★ ★ ★   *Highly Recommended* $$

PAMPERO RON Premium Gold Rum 40% Alcohol (Venezuela)

Yellow/bordering-on-gold color; generous, firm, slightly burnt nose of oranges, caramel, and honey; off-dry to mildly sweet, the tasty, direct flavors of oak, cane sugar, toasted honey-wheat bread, and charcoal generously coat the palate; the long, lovely finish is hearty without being fiery or rowdy; the 24 months of oak-aging is clearly evident on the mellow, feline palate; I tasted it neat for the purposes of evaluation, but later on Pampero Gold made the best rum-and-Coke I've ever had; bravo, Pampero.

RATING ★ ★ ★   *Recommended* $

PIRASSUNUNGA 51 Cachaca 40% Alcohol (Brazil)

Clear as a bell, visually; the malodorous nose reminds me, with sincere regret, of somebody's three-year-old sneakers—has one of the oddest distilled-spirit aromas I've come up against—it's a little bit cooked asparagus, mezcal, wet cardboard, wet Fido, and that dank aroma that's often found under sinks that leak; tastes somewhat better than it smells—a mildly sweet, exceedingly basic white spirits whose application and reason for being elude me completely: The press sheet says it's the number-one-selling *cachaca* (rum) in Brazil—no wonder they spend so much time in the sun; it's supposed to be a mixer, but why spoil the taste of fruit juices or whatever with this stuff? avoid.

RATING ★ $

PUSSER'S BRITISH NAVY Admiral's Reserve 47.75% Alcohol (British Virgin Islands)

Very pretty, luminous honey/amber hue, touched with flecks of copper; the nose has the same salty, seaweedy, astringent twang of the other Pusser's—clearly, they are related by aroma alone—scant evidence of sugarcane, molasses, or wood is detected; a definite improvement in taste over the lighter version, but still light years away from being recommendable; the flavor, while mildly pleasant, still strangely seems manufactured; there's hardly any trace of natural sugarcane or molasses distillate—just the slightest hint of wood; canned fruit in the aftertaste; you'll hear no chorus of "Hail, Brittania" coming from here.

RATING ★★ $

PUSSER'S BRITISH NAVY Rum 40% Alcohol (British Virgin Islands)

Attractive chardonnay-like golden color—each pouring kept throwing curious brown-colored particles—I'm absolutely positive that the glassware wasn't the problem, because I changed glasses three times to make sure that the unwanted sediment was coming from the bottle; the atypical nose is astringent, acutely vegetal, verging on medicinal, saline, and kippery—a peculiar, improper, and outrageously unwelcome fragrance for a rum; all the oddball elements found, and thoroughly disliked, in the nose regrettably show up in the chemical-like flavor and the completely disagreeable aftertaste; no wonder Britain no longer rules the seas; this stuff is awful, pure and simple; avoid.

RATING ★ $

RHUM J. BALLY 1982 Agricole 45% Alcohol (Martinique)

One of the most comely, vivacious shades of orange/amber in the entire category; the off-dry, seductive, and coy nose emits delicate scents of cinnamon, nutmeg, orange peel, and lemon peel—an immensely appealing bouquet in a cavalier sense, as the ripe fruitiness of the bouquet, which makes it resemble a Speyside single malt, alone makes it worth the search; a bit of spirit heaven on earth in the sublime flavor, which features vibrant echoes of tart citrus, green apple, clover honey, saddle leather, tobacco, raisins, vanilla extract, and sherry; though it's a compelling, complex, and multilayered rum, it never loses sight of rum's inherent fun side; exceptional quality.

RATING ★★★★   *Highly Recommended* $$

RHUM J. BALLY 1970 Agricole 45% Alcohol (Martinique)

Average amber color, minor dark particles are noted; the low-key nose is mature, estery, but somewhat sweaty on the surface—underneath it's showing nice scents of cocoa, vanilla, and ripe peaches—the confounded nose has me going in two directions, liking it and disliking it simultaneously, which isn't exactly an encouraging sign; the classy flavor very nearly redeems the perplexing nose and questionable appearance by coming off as elegantly as a VSOP cognac—up top, flavors of toffee and cake batter flow over subtler flavors of ripe apple, spirit, and citrus; serene aftertaste; an extremely difficult rum to score because I didn't feel that the flavor and finish, while admirable, were sound enough to completely overlook the obvious problems in its rollercoaster aroma and unappealing appearance.

RATING ★★ $$$

RHUM J. BALLY 1975 Agricole 45% Alcohol (Martinique)

The slightly dull bronze color is ruined completely by unfortunate, repellent, stringy sediment, which killed this rum for me before I even nosed or tasted it; the cereal-like, off-dry nose of cooked vegetables and pencil eraser was a major disappointment after the extraordinary 1982 Bally;

pleasant on palate, but clearly not what one hopes for in terms of depth of character, appearance, or bouquet for the price; simply unacceptable in virtually all departments; nexxxxxxxt.

RATING ★ $ $ $

RHUM MARTINIQUE Vieux 7-Year-Old Agricole 47% Alcohol (Martinique)

Pale gold/flaxen/hay color, which showed infinitesimal suspended particles; feinty, perfumed, exotic, sweet, this most inviting nose is comprised of several levels of aroma, including leather, peppermint, sherry, oak, cocoa, and honey-wheat bread—a delectable and gorgeous bouquet by any standard; it's rather aggressive and spirity on the palate, then it quickly turns soft, toasty, and sweet in the back of the throat; the finish is friendly, soothing, plush, and sweet in a ripe-fruit way; the nose is so sexy and diverse that it almost carries the whole experience, but once on the tongue this gentlemanly rum shows great presence; bottled in Paris.

RATING ★ ★ ★ ★   *Highly Recommended* $ $

RHUM MARTINIQUE Blanc 3-Year-Old Agricole 54% Alcohol (Martinique)

Crystal-clear appearance; very intriguing nose that initially brings to mind the malty/yeasty/cereal-like aroma of Scotch whisky distilleries, then with ample aeration time the bouquet settles into a more predictable and appropriate scent of off-dry spirit, with an enticing and zesty backnote of cinnamon; on palate, it's a bracing, firmly structured, sweet rum that opens cleanly with convincing assertiveness; the spirit is evident throughout the entry and midpalate, then it mellows gracefully into a rich, semisweet, floral rum; it ends elegantly with no heat or burning; bottled in Paris.

RATING ★ ★ ★   *Recommended* $ $

RON DEL BARRILITO Two-Star Rum 43% Alcohol (Puerto Rico)

Warm, honey/bronze color; oak-aged a minimum of four years; straightforward, softly spirity nose, with harmonious layers of sweet aromas, including pecans, tobacco, butterscotch, wood, and smoke—by considerable margin, the most complex nose of any Puerto Rican rum and certainly one of the top five bouquets in the category; lush, semidry flavors of double cream and burnt almonds greet the happy taste buds, then gently fade into a concentrated midpalate flavor of English toffee; the aftertaste is very mellow and medium-long, politely not overstaying its welcome; best served in a wine glass to take advantage of the heavenly, brandy-like nose; hands down, the premier rum from this lovely island.

RATING ★ ★ ★ ★   *Highly Recommended* $ $

RON DEL BARRILITO Three-Star Rum 43% Alcohol (Puerto Rico)

The most alluring Puerto Rican rum in terms of appearance—clear, deep bronze/topaz core hue, with bright golden edges; oak-aged a minimum of six to ten years; a spirity, highly individualistic, peculiar, atypical, buttered-popcorn nose that is anything but sweet or rum-like; mature, advanced, quite dry flavors of dark toffee and melted butter at entry give way to cocoa, dried apricot, and stone flavors that, although completely complementary, lack the smashing charm and vivacity of the Two-Star; finishes admirably in a mild praline style, which is very warm and extended; some people have argued with my decision to rate the Two-Star higher than the Three-Star Barrilito—my feeling is, fine, you kids just go right ahead and buy up all the Three-Star, leaving me and those of like mind with more of the Two-Star— I'll laugh all the way to the bar.

RATING ★ ★ ★   *Recommended* $$$

Ron Botran Añejo 40% Alcohol (Guatamala)

Eye-appealing deep amber hue; the creamy, dusty, piquant nose is quite lusty and vivacious, offering delectable scents of candied almonds and spice; in the mouth, a pleasant oakiness settles on the tongue—there's a quick, inoffensive flash of heat, but that passes and the taste buds are left with a middle-of-the-road *añejo* rum experience that's nice, but hardly the stuff of legends.

RATING ★ ★ $

Ron Botran Light Dry 40% Alcohol (Guatamala)

Clear; standard-issue white-rum nose of vanilla, egg cream, and spice, though I detect a steely, metallic aroma lurking in the background; substantial, full, varnish-like, almost aggressive on the palate as the dry egg-cream flavor surges forward, then drops from sight in the finish; the vague steeliness I noticed in the nose came rushing forward at palate entry—it simply pulls up too harshly in the first stages in the mouth—no finesse or restraint to be found here; by the third tasting pass it's almost undrinkable; steer clear.

RATING ★ $

Ron Botran Oro 40% Alcohol (Guatamala)

Light-to-medium amber color; the citrusy/spicy nose almost comes off like a spiced rum—overall, however, it's an appealing bouquet; on palate, there's a hint of harshness that underlies the toasty, typical gold rum taste; the aftertaste shows a bite that detracts from the overall experience; an awkward, gangly rum that's terribly short on charm and purpose; nowhere near the stylish elegance of the classy Flor de Cana Gold from neighboring Nicaragua; this one and its insipid white sibling should be put back on the drawing board.

RATING ★ $

Ron Llave Oro Supremo Rum 40% Alcohol (Puerto Rico / Bottled in U.S.)

Pale orange/honey/gold color; in the bouquet department, it's a carbon copy of the Blanco Supremo but with a suntan—dull, flat, and uninspiring; at least, this Gold shows more substance on the palate than its vapid white sibling—indeed, it actually exhibits decent character in its sweet, molasses/honey midpalate, which then develops a genuine chocolatey creaminess in the finish; put more stuffing in the aroma and I'll recommend it.

RATING ★ ★ $

RON LLAVE Blanco Supremo Rum 40% Alcohol (Puerto Rico / Bottled in U.S.)

Clear; tame, predictable nose of sugarcane without much else to offer; it burns the tongue slightly before you notice any flavors—not an auspicious beginning; after that, this middle-of-the-road rum simply follows the White Rum Formula 101 and accomplishes nothing out of the ordinary; I'd like to say more about it, but I can't find anything to talk about.

RATING ★　　$

RON MATUSALEM Golden Label Rum 40% Alcohol (Puerto Rico)

Very pale, honey gold/light amber, good purity; the nose is almost as pale as the color—even after four rigorous nosings and a full quarter hour of aeration, the best that this bouquet could do was send up a flare of wan, dry to off-dry, brown-sugar-like flavor—the bouquet offers nothing in the way of dimension, layering, or depth; skip the nose and proceed directly to the flavor, which is intensely sweet and almost smoky—the taste is much better than the gutless, paper-thin aroma—in general, I took a shine to the mouth presence; the finish is sweet and a bit charcoal-like; a serviceable mixer.

RATING ★ ★　　$

RON MATUSALEM Carta Plata Rum 40% Alcohol (Puerto Rico)

Crystal-clear, ideal purity; the bouquet is flat, faint, and stingy, giving off nothing but a wimpy cane aroma—"meek" puts it too mildly; tastewise, Matusalem Carta Plata is no better a Puerto Rican white than those from Bacardi, Don Q, or Ron Rico, all of which lack substance and panache—this does have some flesh to it, but not enough—it starts off being off-dry, then goes sweet at midpalate, offering a flinty taste; now-you-see-it, now-you-don't aftertaste; to be used only as a mixer when a rum taste isn't required.

RATING ★　　$

RON RICO Gold Label Rum 40% Alcohol (Puerto Rico / Bottled in U.S.)

Honey/amber color; the piquant, snappy nose of nutmeg and butterscotch is framed by alcohol—this nose is no wallflower—I say this in admiration since many of the high-volume gold rums come off sappy-sweet—Ron Rico Gold's scent has real pizzazz and more charm than a number of other popular golds; on the palate, the pleasing zestiness continues, as the off-dry taste is fresh and clean and not the least bit syrupy; it finishes nicely in a subdued, mellow manner; good show.

RATING ★ ★ ★　　*Recommended*　　$

RON RICO Silver Label Rum 40% Alcohol (Puerto Rico / Bottled in U.S.)

Clear; standard-issue white-rum nose—bland, slightly candied, with a delicate sugarcane aroma; another of the paint-by-the-numbers white rums that litter the shelves of liquor stores across America; there's simply nothing worthwhile to describe; it's not that it's bad, it's just that this white is as boring and faceless as at least five other basic white rums.

RATING ★　　$

Ron Rico Spiced Rum 32.75% Alcohol (Puerto Rico / Bottled in U.S.)

Light amber/flaxen/pale wheat-field color; the nose says only one thing to me—the unmistakable aroma of cotton candy found at a July county fair—where's the spice, I wonder; tastes like malted milk; I'm completely confused now, I'm supposed to be evaluating a spiced rum, except that it smells like cotton candy and tastes like malted milk—pass the Tums; definitely the least charming and least spicy of all the spiced rums I've sampled; take a pass.

RATING ★ $

Ron Rico Spiced Rum & Cola 5% Alcohol (Puerto Rico / Prepared and Canned in U.S.)

Predictable cola color; the spicy, ginger/cinnamon/vanilla extract quality helps immeasureably here—it's much more pleasant and carefree than the flabby, insipid Rum & Cola; I have to say right out that I really liked this one's lively, happy nature—it's refreshing, zesty, spicy, and not overly sweet; it would be nice on picnics or at the beach; if you desire such a marketing conceptualist's concoction, skip the other two and zone in on this one.

RATING ★ ★ ★   *Recommended* $

Ron Rico Rum and Cola 5% Alcohol (Puerto Rico / Prepared and Canned in U.S.)

Cola color; it has a sweet, sweaty aroma that's puzzling, quite frankly, and anything but appealing (why would it and, further, how *could* it emit such a malodorous scent?); tastes flat, dull, and totally uninteresting—make mine a full-strength rum-and-Coke, *por favor;* if this wasn't a bad sample, this concept should have been left on the drawing board.

RATING ★ $

Ron Rico Rum & Tonic 5% Alcohol (Puerto Rico / Prepared and Canned in U.S.)

Clear; the lime/citrus/quinine aroma shows only a dash of alcohol—the fragrance is quite steely, almost metallic and minerally, which is common and completely acceptable when quinine is involved; in the mouth it's fresh, off-dry, and limey—the quinine is a mere background element—no alcohol taste to speak of, but I guess that's the whole idea behind these rum sodas; though it's marginally better than the bombastic Rum & Cola, I still personally wouldn't rush out to buy it, but I think that there's an audience somewhere for it—probably sitting around in singles bars.

RATING ★ $

Ron Viejo de Caldas 40% Alcohol (Colombia)

Pretty orange/amber color; the nose is abysmally horrible and musty, reminding me of rotting mushrooms and boiled cabbage, sulphur, and a gymnasium locker room after "the big game"; to make matters worse, all the unsavory components that destroy any sense of pleasure in the nose pop up in the flavor and the vile aftertaste; a rum disaster that should be avoided at all cost.

RATING ★ $

Royal Oak Select Rum 40% Alcohol (Trinidad)

The pale amber appearance has the same light golden tint as tupelo honey, the purity is ideal; the aroma is a bit prickly as the spirit charges aggressively from the glass—the background aromatic notes hint of mint, gum, and cotton candy—there's really little of interest or dimension in this wan, basic bouquet; at palate entry, a candied sweetness greets, but fails to impress, the taste buds—at midpalate a decent, if rudimentary, cane sugar taste holds court—unfortunately, further depth of character simply doesn't develop; the finish is meek, at best.

RATING ★ $

Strummer's Fruited Rum 31.5% Alcohol (Jamaica / Bottled in U.S.)

Bright orange/Scotch-like color; profuse, tropical-fruit nose of pineapple, mango, and passion fruit—a vibrant, pungently appealing aroma; in the mouth, a brisk pineapple flavor surfaces and is balanced by the rum's stony dryness; the aftertaste leans toward the woolly, cottony feel of the rum spirit, where the fruit suddenly seems to be only a memory, except for a hint of banana; this rum is markedly different from the spiced rums that it's being positioned against and hence I question how it's being marketed; very palatable for mixing purposes.

RATING ★ ★ ★   *Recommended* $

Stubbs Queensland Dry White Rum 42.5% Alcohol (Australia)

Clear; the fetching nose is fruitier (ripe peaches and nectarines) than most other white rums—in addition, it hints vaguely of aniseed, an intriguing and characterful bouquet; I wish that the individuality and character I discerned in the nose had carried over to the flavor and aftertaste; it's more satiny than most other white rums, but the fruitiness simply fell off the table after the nosing and for that it lost enough points to drop it below a recommendable score; after a very promising start, the grossly disappointing middle and aftertaste finished it off.

RATING ★ $

Toucano Cachaca Rum 40% Alcohol (Brazil)

Fino-sherry-like/flaxen/pale straw color—very pretty, actually; this exotic rum is made from the first press of sugarcane, not molasses, and it shows in the interesting aroma that has a dozen things happening simultaneously—I pick up lead pencil, dill, brine/salt, corn husk, rubber, and even steamed asparagus—the unforgettable nose alternately reminds me of ten-year-old Laphroaig single-malt Scotch whisky, dill pickles, rubber erasers, and manzanilla sherry—it's like an entire liquor store in one bottle; I was warned not to judge it tasted neat and they were so right—it's smoky, powerful, off-dry, root-like, and pungent; so I mixed it with fresh lime juice and added one teaspoon of sugar on-the-rocks—voilà! its destiny was fulfilled as a mixed drink.

RATING ★ ★ ★   *Recommended* $

VENADO Especial Aguardiente 36% Alcohol (Guatamala)

Clear appearance; the nose on this one is unpleasantly sweaty in the first nosing, then it clicks into a delicate nutty posture after the third pass—it's nowhere near as spirited a nose as the Cristal from Colombia; on the palate, it's slightly soapy and not well defined, and I can't seem to shake this gut feeling that there's something unhygienic about this cane spirit; the aftertaste is limp and flabby; the malodorous bouquet is a huge shortcoming from which it never recovers; it's simply a dud of a product, period.

RATING ★ $

VODKA

One of the more prevalent misconceptions concerning the white-spirits segment of the distilled-spirits category is that vodka is devoid of aroma and flavor. Nothing could be further from the truth. This erroneous notion was fueled in large part by a successful advertising campaign of a popular vodka, namely Smirnoff, during the 1950s and 1960s. The clever and effective gist was that this limpid spirit left you "breathless," implying that since it itself possessed no discernable characteristics it would not be detected on the breath of the imbiber.

This misinformation has been compounded by the U.S. government, which officially describes vodka in Subpart C, Section 5.22, Item 1 of the U.S. Standards of Identity for Distilled Spirits as "a neutral spirits, so distilled, or so treated after distillation with charcoal and other materials as to be without distinctive character, aroma, taste, or color." In typical bureaucratic fashion, they scored on only one of four points: Vodka does not, in fact, have color.

At tastings that I've conducted that have featured six or seven premium and ultrapremium vodkas, the participants have always been astonished at the vodkas' broad spectrum of aroma, texture, and flavor. The most robust and hearty varieties are those from the Russian Federation and Poland. Holland's vodkas are very textured and off-dry to sweet, while the vodkas that hail from Scandanavian countries are agile and ethereal. None, except the cheapest plonk brands that you can purchase for $7.99 for the 1.75 magnum, is without individuality.

Vodka is an old Russian noun that means "little water," having evolved from *zhizenennia voda* (water of life). Historians have deduced through writings dated in the twelfth century A.D. that vodka was commonly available during that period both in Poland and Russia. The first vodkas were, in all likelihood, produced from these regions' most plentiful natural products, potatoes and beets. While today, the overwhelming majority of vodkas are made from cereal grains (predominantly, rye, corn, and wheat), a handful of German and Polish distillers still employ the spud to make their vodkas. There's very little difference between potato vodka and grain vodka.

In the first few centuries of vodka's existence, it was used by distillers in the production of cosmetics, perfumes, and vile-tasting panaceas, potions that were probably flavored with spices, honey, roots, or herbs to make them somewhat more palatable. Vodka became the libation we know today in the early decades of the 1800s, with the introduction of filtering through bits of charcoal. Running the high-alcohol, raw distillate through charcoal eliminated most of the impurities that, until that landmark discovery, made the spirit barely drinkable. In the contemporary vodka distillery, one and a half pounds of vegetable charcoal are used to filter one gallon of spirit. A few vodka distillers use quartz crystals to filter their spirits. The proofs for mainstream vodkas generally range from a low of 70 to a high of 100.

Very few vodkas are aged in wood barrels, and most are bottled almost straight from the filtration. Stårka, the exception, is a style of vodka matured in old wine casks for up to a decade. The biggest development in the last decade in mass-marketed vodkas doubtless is the remarkable popularity of flavored vodkas, like *pertsovka* (pepper), *okhotnichya* (herbs and honey), citrus (lemon/line, orange, pineapple), and berries (black currants, cranberries).

Vodkas are made in numerous countries, including the U.S., Canada, Iceland, the Low Countries, Scandanavia, England, Japan, Israel, Turkey, and even China. As the best-selling spirit of all across the globe (approximately 35 million cases are sold annually just in the U.S.), vodka is currently available in more than 200 nations. Not bad for a beverage that's supposedly as vacant as the furthest reaches of the universe.

ABSOLUT Kurant Vodka 40% Alcohol (Sweden)

Crystal clear; the intense, highly concentrated, laser-focused, weedy, vinous, sweet-sour black-currant nose is a one-way ticket to the currant patch—the concentration is remarkably seductive; on palate, there's a little more diversity in the flavor arena—in addition to the fourth-gear black currant, there's a smidgen of ripe black raspberry; very nice balance between the ripe fruit, fruit acidity, and distillate; while many people might see this lovely vodka as the ultimate mixer with berry juice, I really believe it's best served straight on-the-rocks with a twist of orange.

RATING ★ ★ ★ ★   *Highly Recommended* $

ABSOLUT Citron Lemon Vodka 40% Alcohol (Sweden)

Absolutely pristine in appearance; the lovely, clean, and intense tangerine aroma is full and squeaky tart; on palate, it's high-octane Seven-Up and undeniably delicious; a crisp, razor-edged lemon taste dominates in the light, pleasantly tart, and irresistibly fresh aftertaste that goes on forever; terrifically tasty and tangy; the wonderful taste dashes any cynicism that it's just a vodka novelty; bravo, Absolut.

RATING ★ ★ ★ ★   *Highly Recommended* $

ABSOLUT Peppar Pepper Vodka 40% Alcohol (Sweden)

Clear as spring water; the saucy, piquant, jalapeno-pepper, Tabasco-sauce, almost *añejo*-tequila-like nose simply doesn't quit—it just keeps coming at you in waves; *arriba!* this snappy, sassy critter sneaks up on you in the finish, with a sudden burst of medium heat that warmly fades in the throat; makes a superb Bloody Mary base; ends up being more spicy, as in "herbally," than strictly peppery, as in "vegetal."

RATING ★ ★ ★   *Recommended* $

ABSOLUT Vodka 40% Alcohol (Sweden)

Crystal clear; the aroma is barely discernable—nondescript, really; light-bodied, but exceptionally smooth, silky, and well-mannered on the palate; mildly alcoholic; no bite or heat to speak of; moderate licorice flavors save it from being wimpy; creative advertising aside, it's easy to understand this pleasant, user-friendly vodka's popularity; clearly produced for the masses, not for the strict or fanatical vodkaphiles.

RATING ★ ★ $

ATTAKISKA Vodka 40% Alcohol (Alaska/USA)

Ideally clear; the tarry, anise aromas are moderately appealing; owns a substantial, medium-weighted texture; after being pleasantly snappy and zesty at palate entry, it inoffensively nibbles at the taste buds along the way to the finish; middle-of-the-road vodka whose sole claim to fame is that it's from the forty-ninth state.

RATING ★ ★ $

BURNETT'S Vodka 40% Alcohol (USA)

Crystal clear; the leafy, herbal nose is really lovely in an understated way; on palate, there's an initial harshness, which quickly vanishes, leaving a charcoal-like flavor that's stone-dry and quite nice in the mouth; a good, solid, more than serviceable vodka that's a worthy challenger to the best midrange domestics.

RATING ★ ★ ★   *Recommended* $

CELSIUS Scandinavian Vodka 40% Alcohol (Denmark)

Predictably crystal clear; quite appealing in the nose, as crisp, grainy, behaved aromas gently rise from the glass—on my second pass, I discover with regret that the fragrance has significantly fallen off; in the flavor department, the opening salvo is correct, even pleasant, but once it begins the journey past the tongue, it starts to bite, claw, and burn in the throat; I downgraded the score from two stars to one because of this uncontrollably fiery finish.

RATING ★ $

DANZKA Danish Vodka 50% Alcohol (Denmark)

Clear; this bouquet is even more shut down than the 40% alcohol version—with some vigorous swirling, however, a metallic aroma peeks out and changes over to a fat, easy grainy quality; on palate, a disarmingly sweet, even succulent, entry is followed swiftly by a full-bodied flavor of dry cereal (oats?)—the taste has something going for it; the aftertaste isn't nearly as deft or consequential as the palate flavor, but it will do; with some patience, this is a solid spirit; the question is, do most consumers care about patience or quality that much when it comes to vodka? I think not, because of vodka's "tasteless-odorless" image (remember the tagline "It leaves you breathless"?).

RATING ★ ★ ★ **Recommended** $

DANZKA Citron Lemon-Flavored Vodka 40% Alcohol (Denmark)

Clear; this sedate nose runs on a freshly sliced lemon scent all the way, but what I like most of all about it is its feline delicacy; while certainly not in the formidable flavored vodka league of either Stolichnaya Limonnaya or Absolut Citron, this feathery, citrusy, fresh vodka does possess a tangible charm from its whispy start to the velvety finish; if you'd prefer to stay away from the powerful, masculine presence of Stoly Limonnaya, try this velvety, well-mannered flavored vodka; it's Mel Torme to Stoly's Axl Rose.

RATING ★ ★ ★ **Recommended** $

DANZKA Danish Vodka 40% Alcohol (Denmark)

Clear as water; the subdued, restrained nose is miserly with any odors at all—the sole scent that I pick up is a spicy graininess—with time under its belt, a bit of vanilla bean is detected in the third nosing; the satiny texture is first rate and perhaps its finest attribute; the flavor is very smooth, if somewhat muted; it finishes medium to full and silky—no heat to speak of; a decent, but altogether unexciting vodka of modest virtue.

RATING ★ ★ $

DENAKA Vodka 40% Alcohol (Denmark)

Crystal clear; boasts a full, pungent nose, with alluring, sweetish scents of egg cream and rubber pencil eraser; the full-throttle, assertive sweetness at palate entry evolves into an almost maple-syrup-like flavor just before the clean, extended aftertaste takes over; just the blowsy ticket for vodka fans in search of a candy bar in their glass; a rousing, unruly, unfocused, but totally likable vodka, to say the least, but may be too far gone on the sweetness spectrum for some people; I liked its swashbuckling demeanor.

RATING ★ ★ ★ **Recommended** $

FINLANDIA Vodka 50% Alcohol (Finland)

Clear; clean, tightly wrapped, and spirity nose, which is off-dry and herbal (anise) on the surface, but has an undercurrent of fruity sweetness; this one does a bungee jump from the glass onto your palate, with huge, creamy, biscuity flavors that are alternately feisty with spirit and suave with creamy flavor; the fire it gives off at the back of the throat is more warm than stinging; it finishes cleanly, firmly, and in a semisweet mode, with more than a hint of corn-husk taste; good show; one of the best, most assertive, deeply flavored, but elegant vodkas you'll find.

RATING ★ ★ ★ ★   ***Highly Recommended*** $

FINLANDIA Vodka 40% Alcohol (Finland)

Completely clear; appealing, off-dry nose of herbs, wood, milk, cooked white rice, and cereal; one of the more elegant, well-knit, and structured vodkas around; no one flavor element leaps out at you, so skillfully blended is it; I can't help but wonder, though, if it isn't a tad too haughty and homogenized; I thoroughly liked its classiness, but I didn't feel I could go crazy for it; all coolness and finesse but scant passion; an outstanding mixer.

RATING ★ ★ ★   ***Recommended*** $

FINLANDIA Cranberry Vodka 30% Alcohol (Finland)

Has the appearance of brick-red cherry juice or, better, a Provence rosé color; the nose is an appetizing blend of cranberries and red-apple scents—there's nary a hint of alcohol in this mild, pleasantly fruited bouquet; at entry, I didn't at all care for the cranberry/vodka marriage, though by the third taste evaluation it began to make minor inroads with my palate; the red fruit/grainy flavor is off-dry and seems to be higher than the stated 30% alcohol; the finish is smooth, slightly bitter, and medium-long; though I purchased this bottle for evaluation, I wouldn't buy one for consumption.

RATING ★ ★ $

FINLANDIA Pineapple-Flavored Vodka 30% Alcohol (Finland)

Pale-straw/hay color, ideal purity; the reluctant nose is limp, phenolic, and uninviting, showing a stingy perfume of canned, not fresh pineapple—at the third nosing a startling creosote-like (overly smoky, chemical) aroma appeared—I certainly couldn't characterize this tinny, petroleum-like, dour bouquet as being lively, fresh, or alluring; I was sorry to have tasted this bow-wow at all—it's so bad that I couldn't convince myself to perform my normal four tasting passes, so with great trepidation I ran through two and that proved to be two too many, as the midpalate was tanky, skunky, metallic, and putrid; how lousy was this vodka? it makes Finlandia's Cranberry look like rare nectar; don't even think of buying it, especially if you like pineapple.

RATING ★ $

GORDON'S Citrus Vodka 40% Alcohol (USA)

Clear; the sweet-sour, steely nose is all about lime and nothing else; in the mouth, it's clean, refreshing, citrusy, and more sweet than it is tart, kind of like limeade—in fact, there's an appealing taste of grain that I liked very much that underpins the citrus flavoring; the crisp aftertaste highlights the lime element once again; while it's not in the class of the superb Stolichnaya Limonnaya or Absolut Citron, Gordon's Citrus is a very good vodka and a stark, welcome contrast to its sibling, the disastrous Wildberry.

RATING ★ ★ ★   ***Recommended*** $

GORDON'S Pepper-Flavored Vodka 40% Alcohol (USA)

Water-clear, perfect purity; in the initial pass, the bouquet comes off like the pungent aroma of a cap pistol going off, that smoky, leaden, gunpowdery aroma that sets the nostrils flaring—by the third nosing, the bouquet settled in and showed some zesty red and black pepper spice; on the palate, I found the pepper element a touch too pronounced for my taste and though I think this vodka might be perfect for mixed drinks like a Bloody Mary, it will never make it on its own; the aftertaste was probably its strong suit, as nicely spiced flavors rested comfortably in the throat; the minor leagues compared to Stolichnaya Pertsovka (four-star rating) or even Absolut Peppar (three-star rating); a decent attempt, but at the end of the day not recommendable.

RATING ★★ $

GORDON'S Wildberry Vodka 30% Alcohol (USA)

Clear as spring water; the sweet nose leans in the direction of tutti-frutti bubblegum as unharnessed waves of red berry aromas wash over the olfactory sense—a smell that took me back to the Chicago summers of my youth, opening up packages of Topps baseball cards and inhaling the sugary-sweet odor of the hard, powdered slab of pink gum; on the palate, the cloying sweetness of this awkward concoction is simply over the top for my taste—what has this to do with vodka?—this is like kiddy vodka; get this syrupy garbage out of here.

RATING ★ $

KETEL ONE Vodka 40% Alcohol (Holland)

Pristinely clear; the balanced nose of mild spirit and richness doesn't reach up and grab you, but it's a pleasing bouquet just the same; Ketel One exhibits genuine presence on palate as the sweet, mild spiciness accelerates at the midpalate, making the tongue tingle; the finish is marvelously long, mannered, doughy, round, citrusy, and only moderately sweet; one of the classiest, most complex, and multilayered unflavored vodkas in the marketplace; a superlative mixer; tasted eight times, upgraded after the fifth evaluation.

RATING ★★★★   *Highly Recommended* $$

LASKA Vodka 40% Alcohol (Czech Republic)

Clear; the faint nose is almost totally closed down at first pass, then after vigorous swirling, a creamy (is this vodka?), flowery, vanilla-bean-like bouquet emerges and charms the daylights out of my sense of smell; on palate, the unexpected creaminess builds and greets the taste buds in waves of butter, honey, and smoke by the time it reaches the back of the tongue; the same flavor qualities continue on into the soft aftertaste; this beauty is definitely worth a search for confirmed vodka aficionados.

RATING ★★★   *Recommended* $

LUKSUSOWA Vodka 40% Alcohol (Poland)

Clear; the earthy, elemental, understated nose betrays the potatoes that it's made from; very subdued initially on palate, with low-key, off-dry entry flavors that go bubblegummy sweet in the nice, simple finish—the finish then vanishes completely; this is a too-polite, middle-of-the-road vodka; no match for its far more muscular countryman, Wyborowa.

RATING ★★ $

Majorska Vodka 40% Alcohol (USA)

Predictably clear; the let's-get-busy nose explodes in intriguing aromas of milk chocolate, cola nut, fresh-cracked walnut, and charcoal; who would have guessed that a standard-brand domestic vodka would show so much punch in the bouquet? in the mouth, it's as sweet as most Dutch vodkas and makes me curious about whether or not a sweetening agent like corn syrup has been added; certainly, it's not as complex as Stolichnaya or as elegant as Finlandia or Tanqueray Sterling, but for an inexpensive vodka, Majorska acquits itself surprisingly well.

RATING ★★★   *Recommended* $

Moskovskaya Osobaya Vodka 40% Alcohol (Russian Federation)

Clear as water, but it has some minute suspended particles floating about; the bouquet is standard issue and nothing to write home about—it hints at grain mash, but is so meek that the nose is a wash—proceed directly to the taste; the questionable appearance and sheepish aroma are cast aside once this snappy, piquant-tasting vodka hits the palate in zesty, spicy flavors of grain and egg cream—I loved the buxom feeling of it on the tongue—the peppery character is disarming and potent, as it should be for a Russian; with vodkas becoming increasingly polite and neutered nowadays, it's a delight to taste one from the old school.

RATING ★★★★   *Highly Recommended* $

Nikolai Gold Vodka 40% Alcohol (USA)

Water-clear, pure; the nose is timid and slightly flowery—nothing much beyond that; the taste is smooth but bland in the first sampling—by the second mouthful, a pleasantly tart, charcoal-like taste really perked up my taste buds; after a banal aroma and an initially wimpy flavor, Nikolai stepped up to bat, down two strikes, and smacked a double to the left-field wall; hardly the stuff of white-distillate genius, but I had to admire how it got itself out of the hole and made a play.

RATING ★★★   *Recommended* $

Priviet Vodka 40% Alcohol (Russian Federation)

Mineral-water-clear; the bouquet is feeble on all four nosings, which surprises me, since it's Russian—it manages only a meek, rudimentary grain scent that could be knocked over with a blown kiss; in the mouth, the taste is far more evolved and charming than the weak-in-the-knees bouquet implies—it's seductively creamy texturally and offers a deep mashy flavor at midpalate; in the finish, a lightning bolt of heat is duly noted; an atypically well-behaved vodka from the land where vodka is used to ward off the cold more frequently than are furry hats.

RATING ★★★   *Recommended* $

ROYALTY Vodka 40% Alcohol (Holland)

Crystal clear, pure; this nose is typical for a vodka from Holland in that it highlights a marshmallow sweetness that's pleasant and inviting—this Dutch vodka bouquet is not as complete as the splendid aroma of Ketel One, also from Holland; the solid mouth presence is its strong suit—the sweet, developed, mashy flavor is totally convincing and pleasant; it even provides a gentle bite in the aftertaste; an admirable import.

RATING ★★★   *Recommended* $

SKYY Vodka 40% Alcohol (USA)

Crystal clear; very pleasant, delicate, and enticing nose of sugarcane, corn mash, malt, and even some cocoa—only a slight hint of graininess; without question, the most satiny domestic vodka; the palate entry is so subtle that it isn't until the second tasting that I come to appreciate the refined cocoa and grain qualities; this is not a vodka for those people who desire the intensity of staunch, hearty vodkas like Stolichnaya or Wyborowa; it is ideal for spirit lovers who prefer refined, feline vodkas; my trepidation, however, is that this vodka is so nuanced that people may, in their haste, unknowingly depict it and prematurely dismiss it as being a lightweight when that's not the case; it's a chocolatey, understated vodka that requires some time to get to know.

RATING ★★★   *Recommended* $

SMIRNOFF Black Vodka 40% Alcohol (Russian Federation)

Clear; the nose is heady, creamy, nougat-like, and boldly appetizing—this is a take-no-prisoners bouquet that shows more power than finesse at first, but in the fourth nosing presents the taster with an unusual, but captivating, oiliness, like almond oil; for all the muscle detected in the nose, the taste goes a different route, the route of elegance and supple presence on the tongue—at midpalate there's even a flash of richness that diminishes in the sweet finish; the feisty rival of Stolichnaya Cristall, Smirnoff Black furthers the legend of true Russian vodka in fine form; triple-distilled in small batches in copper-pot stills and filtered through charcoal of 100% Siberian silver birch—bravo; sampled four times, upgraded on the last evaluation; it shares with Stoly Cristall, the honor and distinction of being one of the two best vodkas in the world.

RATING ★★★★★   *Highest Recommendation* $$

SMIRNOFF Citrus Twist Vodka 40% Alcohol (USA)

Clear; this citrusy nose leans heavily toward lemon rather than lime or orange—the lemon thrust easily overshadows the aromatic grain base; I thought that this taste showed a smidgen more grace than the Gordon's Citrus, wherein the grain factor is more evident—this citrus taste really showcases the tart lemon component, almost like classic lemon meringue pie; I ended up liking it more and more with each pass; nice job.

RATING ★★★   *Recommended* $

SMIRNOFF Vodka 40% Alcohol (USA)

My least favorite vodka for one simple reason—it has no discernable character or backbone; the mildly peppery aroma (and that's a stretch) is its lone best feature; featherweighted, ethereal, some might say emaciated, body; the dry, crisp, clean but pitifully muted flavors are barely perceptible; this can't even be considered an entry-level vodka; for those people who prefer not to taste alcohol . . . or anything else, for that matter; dullsville.

RATING ★ $

STOLICHNAYA Cristall 40% Alcohol (Russian Federation)

Clear; the subdued but potent nose gradually gathers steam as stirring aromas of rose petal, dry cereal, and double cream swell in the second nosing pass—the mannered, opulent scents come to full blossom in the third nosing; this is one of the firmest and most confident vodkas I've sampled—it doesn't try to impress, it just does; the flavor is remarkably similar to milk chocolate when you take a sip of a half ounce or so and let it sit on the tongue; the finish is semisweet, full-bodied, and lusciously touched with vanilla/white-chocolate qualities that are simultaneously subtle and satisfying; top-notch all the way; easily a classic; sampled a dozen times and recently upgraded to its proper status.

RATING ★ ★ ★ ★ ★   *Highest Recommendation* $$

STOLICHNAYA Ohranj Orange Vodka 35% Alcohol (Russian Federation)

Clear; the fresh navel-orange perfume bursts forth from the glass in the same way as when you first break the skin on a ripe juicy orange—it's a sweet, highly delectable bouquet, almost like a Creamsicle; the orange flavor is so well defined that you hardly notice the spirit—it actually tastes like a Screwdriver, the classic mixed drink in which vodka is mixed with orange juice; the aftertaste is refreshing, citrusy, superb, and very extended; it ranks right up there with both of the other Stolichnaya flavored blockbusters, the great Limonnaya and Pertsovka; if I'm in the mood for flavored vodka, I just simply reach for any of the Stolis—the matter's that cut and dried.

RATING ★ ★ ★ ★   *Highly Recommended* $

STOLICHNAYA Limonnaya Lemon Vodka 40% Alcohol (Russian Federation)

The sample I tried was a sunshiny yellow/green color; I understand that at present there's no trace of color; keenly fresh, tonic-quinine water, lemon-bitters nose that reminded me of every European *en suite* bar I've ever encountered; has remarkable bearing on the palate—wildly refreshing, but the texture is opulent; the luscious lemon, flowery flavor dashes all the way from entry to aftertaste; so savory that I'd stay with it unmixed, on-the-rocks; too bad it's been denuded of its luminous color; I loved it; unequivocally one of the two or three best flavored vodkas I've ever tasted.

RATING ★ ★ ★ ★   *Highly Recommended* $

STOLICHNAYA Pertsovka Pepper Vodka 35% Alcohol (Russian Federation)

The aged-cognac, racy, copper/rust color is beguiling; the toasty, off-dry, subtle, surprisingly unaggressive nose is actually elegant in its demeanor;

like its lemon sibling, Pertsivka is the height of flavor/alcohol balance; lushly textured, medium-bodied; the organic spiciness warms the gums and tongue as the red pepper flavor enlivens the taste buds rather than scorches them; eccentric, delicious, and bountiful, this sumptuous vodka is a treat all on its own, but do try it in a brazen Bloody Mary.

RATING ★ ★ ★ ★   **Highly Recommended** $

STOLICHNAYA Vodka 40% Alcohol (Russian Federation)

Perfectly clear; the potent, kicky, piquant, heady aroma borders on being medicinal, but never loses its luster and panache; lusty, deep, licorice, and herbal flavors stimulate the taste buds from palate entry to the combustible finish; this tough vodka has old-style swagger; certainly, no wallflower; the alcohol is evident, especially at midpalate; exactly what one expects from a Russian vodka—hammer and guts; the acknowledged pet of vodka connoisseurs.

RATING ★ ★ ★   **Recommended** $

STROVIA Vodka 40% Alcohol (Russian Federation)

Predictably clear; it possesses a pleasant, sweetish aroma that's clean, round, and mashy—the bouquet's focus is on a creamy, sweet cereal-grain note rather than oil or fruit, the two other characteristics commonly found in vodka; it's sweet in the mouth right from entry through the warm midpalate to the full, supple aftertaste; only the slightest trace of bite emerges near the finish; overall, it's a tasty, well-made vodka that's remarkably fresh and sweet.

RATING ★ ★ ★   **Recommended** $

TAAKA Platinum Vodka 40% Alcohol (USA)

Clear and pure; it smells suspiciously similar to the Nikolai Gold, which is produced by the same New Orleans–based company, Sazerac, in their Leestown, Kentucky, distillery—the Sazerac people assured me, however, that they, indeed, are unique vodkas—at any rate, they are twins aromatically; on palate, I do see the difference—Taaka is noticeably creamier and more viscous than the Nikolai and finishes with a supple, intensely mashy, wet-cereal taste that's silky smooth; a good vodka either for mixing or on-the-rocks.

RATING ★ ★ ★   **Recommended** $

TANQUERAY Sterling Vodka 40% Alcohol (England)

Complete clarity; rich, grainy, estery, semisweet-to-sweet nose, which hints of peaches and green melon—a lovely bouquet, which vanished after 15 minutes of aeration; owns the voluptuous, creamy constitution so emblematic of Tanqueray; the roundness and generosity of the sweet, cake-batter-like flavor is undeniably attractive; the aftertaste is slightly candied and very extended; definitely good enough to serve neat and icy cold in a small, tulip-shaped glass.

RATING ★ ★ ★   **Recommended** $

TANQUERAY Sterling Citrus Vodka 40% Alcohol (England)

Crystal clear, absolute purity; the nose emits the expected amount of tart, lemony aroma—beyond that, there's really nothing to report on; in the mouth, it surprisingly lacks the firm, structured presence of the unflavored (three-star) Tanqueray Sterling and promotes more of the lemon/lime than the base vodka—it should be the other way around, with the flavoring accenting the base spirit—way too much emphasis is placed on the citrus flavoring; while drinkable, it's not up to the usual Tanqueray standards; use as a mixer.

RATING ★ ★ $

TARKHUNA 40% Alcohol (Georgian Republic)

Interesting, unusual, crystalline, and extraordinarily comely pale blue/turquoise color that reminds me of the tropics—doubtless one of the most singularly attractive hues in the distilled-spirit category; the unabashedly lusty nose is filled with an intense herbaceous piquancy, which is obviously the infusion of the *tarkhuna* herb—this addition sways the aroma in a new direction for vodka; a distinctive and supple vodka that on the palate shows a pungent herbal face, but underneath has an austere, steely, grainy quality that's immensely appealing; regrettably, to my taste, it throws off way too much heat and bite in the finish, which hurts the final rating—as a result, I'm placing it in the Recommended group rather than the Highly Recommended, where it began; if vodka lovers are looking for a new, high-quality treat, one that's unique and delectable, try Tarkhuna—not for mixing, however, where it didn't show well at all; and watch out for that fire-in-the-hole finish.

RATING ★ ★ ★   *Recommended* $

WODKA WYBOROWA Vodka 40% Alcohol (Poland)

Crystal-clear appearance; the attractive aroma is sweetish, almost nutty, floral, and even a tad minty, particularly in the third and fourth nosings, where it really came alive; the texture is medium- to full-bodied and quite satiny; on palate, the charcoally flavors are deep and alluring in a smoky way; there's a faint bite in the throat just to let you know it's there, but it's not unpleasant at all; falls well within the traditional eastern European style, which showcases both guts and finesse.

RATING ★ ★ ★   *Recommended* $

TEQUILA AND MEZCAL

O f all the alcoholic beverages to come forth from Mexico, including its fine beers, so-so brandies, atrocious wines, and excellent liqueurs, none are more charismatic or dashing than tequila and mezcal. With the festive and dramatic methods of drinking tequila, like slamming, to the floating agave worms that inhabit some brands of mezcal, the two spirits have taken firm hold in America. Even the labels are a hoot: Grave, mustachioed *pistalleros* adorn some labels, while bullfighters evading dramatically posed bulls decorate others. But it's what's in the bottle that counts, and by all accounts, tequila and mezcal are here to stay.

Tequila and mezcal are similar distilled spirits, but are produced from different families of the spiky agave plant. (To date, over 400 varieties of agave have been classified by botanists.) Tequila comes primarily from the tequilana-blue agave, a member of the amaryllis family, while mezcal comes from maguey. Of the two distillates, tequila is considered superior.

Tequila is so called because it comes from distilleries located in or near the town of the same name in the mountainous state of Jalisco. Tequila is the type of ramshackle, dust-choked town that you see in movies, the type of town where the ribs on every dog stand out to be counted. The town is flanked by the two main growing districts for blue agave, the pastoral plains of Amatitan and the elevated fields that surround the village of Arandas. These growing areas provide the perfect arid environment and silicate-based soil in which blue agave thrives. There are about 35 tequila distilleries in operation in the area.

Tequila is made from a lip-puckeringly sour drink, a fermented, milky beverage made from the juice of the agave plant. Hernando Cortés and his conquistadors discovered that the Aztecs had been imbibing such a drink for generations when they plundered Mexico in the sixteenth century. The blue agave's head, or inner core, termed the *piña,* looks like a pineapple with a thyroid problem. It's not uncommon for blue agave heads to weigh in at over 125 pounds, with some as heavy as 175. Agave plants take a decade to reach the point of maturity, when harvesting is necessary. The *piñas* are harvested by *jimeadors,* men with low centers of gravity and arms like Popeye. The ripe heads drip with syrupy-sweet sap, called *aguamiel,* which means "honey water."

The *piñas* are transported via trucks to the distillery, where they are cut in half. While being steamed in ovens for up to a full day, the agave heads ooze the sappy, viscous *aguamiel,* which is collected. Fermentation of the *aguamiel* is completed in huge wooden vats over the span of two to three days. The fermented juice is then twice distilled in traditional copper-pot stills.

Mexican government regulations, which are among the most notoriously flexible in the hemisphere, state that tequila must be made up of a minimum of 51% blue agave. The balance of the blend can be the distillate from sugarcane or other (you don't want to know) sources. While it would be churlish and unjustified to imply that all tequila producers make used-car dealers look like social workers, I urge you to buy the tequilas that state "100% Blue Agave" on the label whenever possible. Likewise, make certain that you can locate a registration number, which always begins with the letters NOM (for Norma Oficial Mexicana de Calidad), on the label, usually printed in the lower corners. The registration number is the official Mexican seal of authenticity.

The white/silver (Plata) and gold (Reposados) categories of tequilas are nearly always cut to 80 proof (40 percent alcohol by volume), though some of the rarer *añejos* are offered at higher proofs. White tequilas, which are pleasantly approachable, are bottled straight from the holding tanks after the distillation process. Gold tequilas, which are uniformly more complex than the whites, are normally matured in redwood casks for about half a year. The majestic and smooth *añejos* are aged in oak for at least 12 months, with some producers aging them for two or three years. The wood-aging allows the tequila's intensely herbal qualities to settle down and meld with the mellowing influence of the wood, producing alcoholic beverages of unique and impressive character.

To be sure, tequila is a solitary, yet versatile animal. Comparisons of tequila to any other type of distilled spirit are risky at best. Tequila has proven to be an outstanding mixer, most often as the herbal, punchy, mouth-puckering foundation for margaritas. Tequila can be served straight, immediately preceded by lime and salt. At the *añejo* stage, chilled tequila can even be enjoyed neat in a tumbler or a wine glass.

Mezcal is more rambunctious than tequila. The rough-and-tumble mezcals originate in Oaxaca in southeastern Mexico. Contrary to common belief, the infamous worms *(gusanos)* are found only in some mezcals, never in tequilas. The fact is, tequila producers long ago disavowed the practice of popping grubs into their booze.

CAMINO REAL Gold Tequila 40% Alcohol

Dirty-dishwater appearance; it begins painfully limp in the nose, with the barest traces of fabric and pepper; in the mouth, it picks up some vegetal tastes and even some roundness; middle-of-the-road tequila that's fine for mixing, but that's the extent of it.

RATING ★ ★ $

CASTENADA Gold Tequila 40% Alcohol

Pale straw/hay hue; I wanted to vomit soon after inhaling this aromatic disaster—the headlining scent reeks of sweat on the putrid surface and citrus/grapefruit underneath—so vile that I didn't want to proceed; surprisingly, on palate, things improved, as decent flavors of chocolate and caramel almost, but not quite, redeemed the wicked bouquet; the last impression in the aftertaste makes this oddball seem almost manufactured and totally unnatural; treat this one like a rat that's carrying the bubonic plague.

RATING ★ $

CHINACO Añejo Tequila 100% Blue Agave 40% Alcohol

Looks more like an amber single-malt Scotch than what one normally thinks of as a tequila appearance, devoid of the suspended particles that plague the Blanco and Reposado; the atypical nose has brandy-like notes of caramel and oak that act as window dressing for the agave core aroma— many people wouldn't ever guess in a blind tasting that this perfume belonged to a tequila—this bouquet has sherry and/or whiskey written all over it; the sweet, dark toffee/caramel taste (and deep color) makes me project that Chicano Añejo has to have been matured either in old sherry casks or old bourbon casks; an entity and a law unto itself, Chinaco Añejo is the tequila to imbibe if you like sherry, brandy, or bourbon; bravo.

RATING ★ ★ ★ ★   **Highly Recommended** $$

CHICANO Blanco Tequila 100% Blue Agave 40% Alcohol

Clear, slightly pale-straw tinge, with numerous suspended particles floating about; the mild nose is inviting, intensely vegetal and earthy in the first two nosings, then a succulent sweetness emerges in the third pass—in the last nosing a pronounced note of dill bedeviled me—I found this nose very seductive; in the mouth, it's mannered at entry, surprisingly sweet at midpalate and delivers some old-fashioned agave octane in the aftertaste; the smoothness of the texture is a delight and, I believe, is the primary signature feature of this svelte tequila—the next impressive virtue is the flash of dill in the aroma.

RATING ★ ★ ★   **Recommended** $$

CHINACO Reposado Tequila 100% Blue Agave 40% Alcohol

Pretty, light yellow/straw/green color of a white wine whose main grape is *riesling,* a regatta of suspended particles is found cruising around; this nose is much more focused and impactful than that of the Blanco—piquant, sensuous aromas of agave, dill-pickle/brine, spirit, green chili peppers, and fresh garden herbs vie for attention without stepping over one another; ex-

ceedingly smooth on palate and, while very good, I was expecting more giddyap in terms of flavor depth and variety—don't allow my fastidiousness and
picayune nature to deter you from this very nice, oily, and salty tequila
(though the stuff floating around drives me to distraction); this is one that
definitely has a mind of its own.

RATING ★ ★ ★   Recommended $$

JOSE CUERVO 1800 Tequila 40% Alcohol

Medium honey/amber/orange color; the sweet, piquant, woody, well-
endowed nose is notably deep and inviting right from the very first nosing
and, to its credit, remains sound, punchy, and attractive; a brandy-like
tequila; it enters the mouth sweetly with a pronounced caramel-like flavor
and remains sweet, warm, and luscious all the way to the very sweet, almost
candied aftertaste that brings oloroso sherry to mind; I can't help but won-
der with this level of sweetness if a sweetening agent has been added to it;
sipping neat seems more appropriate for this tequila, especially in light of
the elevated sweetness and unusual toastiness; a different tequila animal al-
together; even with my questions about it, it's very good from appearance
to aftertaste.

RATING ★ ★ ★ ★   Highly Recommended $$

JOSE CUERVO Tradicional Reposado 100% Blue Agave Tequila 40% Alcohol

Pale-straw/flaxen/white-wine tone, some miniscule suspended particles
evident; this is the finest aroma of the José Cuervos—buttery, vegetal,
squeaky clean, mildly salty, and perfumy, this bouquet soars right from the
first pass and keeps right on trucking through the last nosing—a superb,
benchmark tequila nose that's on par with the Herraduras and Sauza Hornitos; on palate, the cleanness of it is totally charming—the delicate, mannered flavors of bittersweet chocolate, coffee, and hard candy make this effort my favorite of the Cuervos; nimble, semisweet Tradicional couldn't be
more different in style and character than the biscuity, woody, brandy-like
1800 if it tried; both are superlative tequilas.

RATING ★ ★ ★ ★   Highly Recommended $$

JOSE CUERVO Especial Gold Tequila 40% Alcohol

Pale yellow color; the pleasingly rich, dry, some might say opulent, nose
of garden-fresh herbs, cactus, and artichoke heart enchant the olfactory
sense, not with elegance but with directness; on palate, the velvety texture
greets the taste buds; nicely balanced flavors of herbs, especially anise, mild
licorice, plus a bit of tar keeps the palate alert; it finishes as agreeably as it
began in the nose; best to drink neat, but refreshing and tasty in margari-
tas.

RATING ★ ★ ★   Recommended $

JOSE CUERVO White Tequila 40% Alcohol

Has a Chablis-like color; the moderately intense, direct, agave, herbal,
prickly, dill nose is only mildly accounted for—it's a rather lazy bouquet that
never seems to take shape; in the mouth, it's another matter, as generous,

broad strokes of earthy, evergreen minty flavors gently coat the tongue; the correct, refined finish of juniper, black pepper, and anise, with a tangy licorice tail tops off the experience; an acceptable, middle-of-the-pack White.

RATING ★★ $

Dos Reales Añejo Tequila 40% Alcohol

The deep amber color reminds me of a Highland single-malt Scotch; it's so unctuous and rich in the nose that it's almost more a brandy than a tequila—what has been added to this to make it so opulent?—in the mouth it's creamy, sweet, dense, and caramelized; the finish is very extended and deep; it's so stylized and managed that I can't help but think that the earthy/minerally/vegetal element that makes tequila so luscious is lost in the haze of caramel and sugarcane; a difficult one to score because, while it tastes fine, I can't put a lid on my suspicious nature.

RATING ★★ $

Dos Reales Plata Tequila 40% Alcohol

Clear, pure; the assertive nose leaps from the sampling glass in heady waves of vegetation, wet earth, and diesel fuel; the second and third passes unveil a saline, green-chili-pepper burst of aroma that tweaks the nasal cavity; on palate, the diesel-fuel quality greets the taste buds at entry, then it shifts into a minerally/slaty/flinty mode at midpalate; the finish is minerally and a little sharp; too manufactured, too flinty, no evidence of style or grace—a big-it-out tequila, at best.

RATING ★ $

Encantado Mezcal de Oaxaca Lot 1 40% Alcohol

Clear as water, ideal purity; the nose has vegetal, pungent aromas that bring to mind a number of incongruous and seriously unpleasant things, such as burnt matches/sulphur, burning tires, artichoke hearts, kerosene, and metal—this is not a bouquet that one brings home to mother; it tastes only slightly better than it smells, which is about as nice as I can force myself to be regarding this swamp water from south of the border—to put it another way, it's vile; the tequila producers of Jalisco would be wise to buy up all the Encantado and pour it alongside the better Reposados and Añejos as a comparison of mezcal and tequila—it could be a marketer's bonanza; my suggestion for those eight people who have Encantado in their house is to, first, beat it with a stick, then throw it out the window and say, *"buenos noches";* here's hoping that "Lot 2" is, at the minimum, drinkable.

RATING ★ $$

Fonda Blanca Gold Tequila 40% Alcohol

Hazy appearance; the bouquet is intensely fruity in the first three nosings, then the pear/peach quality fades with aeration and completely vanishes by the last pass; on palate, the awful mouth presence tastes like gasoline and rusted metal—a nightmare that doesn't even deserve a single star; through the entire evaluation I had the urge to utter, "Fill 'er up."

RATING ★ $

GAVILAN Gold Tequila 40% Alcohol

White-wine color; the bouquet is pleasantly fruity as ripe aromas of pear, apricot, and orange keep the olfactory sense occupied—it's a bountiful nose that I liked very much; now the bad news—in the mouth, this tequila unravels totally, as oily, impure flavors of diesel fuel, iron, and sweat immerse the horrified palate—a new standard in lousy, offensive tastes; I won't even describe the aftertaste, just in case you're eating while reading this; I begrudgingly grade this tequila with a lonely star in recognition of the okay appearance and lovely, but wasted, aroma; I had the strangest feeling that Gavilan and Fonda are related, kind of like tequila's version of the Manson family.

RATING ★ $

GUSANO ROJO Mezcal with Agave Worm 40% Alcohol

Flat, dirty water, dull color, slightly cloudy, undetermined suspended particles (worm parts?), an unappetizing, repulsive appearance; obnoxious, downright malodorous, putrid, unsmellable nose; undrinkable; some of the most awful, bitter, unsavory flavors I've ever come across in 15 years of professional tasting; if this mess is one of those "acquired taste" cases, call me a cab, 'cause I'm outta here; I didn't even want to give it one star.

RATING ★ $

HERRADURA

Guillermo Romo de la Peña, the owner-operator of 225-year-old Tequila Herradura, insists upon using agaves that have been farmed on his own property. Herradura tequilas are produced from only 100% blue agaves, the best variety for making the spirit. Señor Romo has led a small movement to have all tequilas be 100% blue agave. Herraduras have absolutely no additives in them, such as caramel for coloring. The soft amber tint of Romo's older tequilas comes naturally from the oak barrels in which they are aged. He likewise espouses estate-bottling, which, as in the case of top-drawer wines, indicates that the plant source was grown, fermented, aged, and bottled all on the Herradura property. Such strict control and integrity, which are unheard of in the unbelievably unsavory tequila industry, assure the consumer of the highest possible quality.

Bill Romo's outspoken character and stated positions have not made him popular with the two industry giants, José Cuervo and Sauza. They vehemently disagree with Romo's estate-bottling and 100% blue agave stands, which they believe are neither cost-effective nor realistic for the larger producers. The heated debate is sure to continue into the next millennium.

HERRADURA Añejo Estate-Bottled 100% Blue Agave Tequila 40% Alcohol

Pale gold color; the gloriously juicy nose bursts forth from the sampling glass with attention-getting scents of pears, apricots, peaches, herbs, and pulp—in fact, like the Herradura Gold, the bouquet is astonishingly wine-like in its bearing; on palate, the entry is actually salty, then that fades and a sensuous fruitiness emerges at midpalate; the aftertaste is extremely sexy, round, and extended, as various and disparate tastes of citrus, cream, grapes, green beans, and dill all somehow get together into a workable flavor crescendo in the throat; the busiest, most ambitious tequila I've sampled; it's hard to keep tabs on all the different flavors and aromas, but that's all the fun; recently upgraded after repeated evaluations.

RATING ★ ★ ★ ★ ★ **Highest Recommendation** $ $

HERRADURA Special Old Añejo Estate-Bottled 100% Blue Agave Tequila 40% Alcohol (Available only in Mexico)

Gold/light amber color; the intriguing cardboard, rose-petal, vanilla, anise, and citrus nuances in the seductive, highly perfumed nose are as delicate and well crafted as any XO-level cognac or Speyside single malt—this world-class aroma is unforgettable; peculiar and spectacular overtones of cane sugar on entry, then the taste changes over to a combination of ripe green apple and apricot that together provide the most delightful taste I've encountered in the tequila category; it finishes luxuriously full in a flourish of cocoa-like sweetness that's stunningly luscious; I put this opulent, complex, meaty, but classy and stylish thoroughbred at the head of the tequila class along with the regular *añejo* bottling; a classic, a prototype, and a benchmark for the industry.

RATING ★ ★ ★ ★ ★ **Highest Recommendation** $ $

HERRADURA Silver Estate-Bottled 100% Blue Agave Tequila 40% Alcohol

Clear appearance; the piquant, heavily herbal nose of dill, licorice, anise, and bay leaf is topped off with a zesty, spirity lift; on palate, this tangy, gutsy tequila really fills the mouth with tingly sensations—the semisweet, head-lining flavor of bittersweet cocoa is drawn against background tastes of citrus and herbs; it finishes in a slightly more restrained manner than how it started out, giving off savory flavors of fresh garden herbs; doubtless the Rolls Royce of silver tequilas and better than many *reposado* and *añejo* tequilas from competing distillers.

RATING ★ ★ ★ ★ **Highly Recommended** $ $

HERRADURA Gold Estate-Bottled 100% Blue Agave Tequila 40% Alcohol

Pale straw hue, the color of a California Sauvignon Blanc; much softer in the nose than the pungent silver—gives off lovely, sweet-sour, round aromas of green olives, seaweed, flowers, and basil—I loved this sensuous fragrance; the elegance factor found in the nose carries over into the graceful, feline texture, which behaves almost more like a wine than a tequila; in addition to the silkiness, very subtle flavors of orange peel and tangerine prick the taste buds; what I found most appealing, however, was the creamy finish—it ends so nimbly and harmoniously that you find yourself wanting it to continue on all night; a superb, sophisticated distilling achievement.

RATING ★ ★ ★ ★ **Highly Recommended** $ $

MONTE ALBAN Mezcal with Agave Worm 40% Alcohol

Pale gold color; the steely, metallic, nail-polish, green-olive/briny, soy-sauce-gone-bad nose approaches being vile; the very different, bitter, severe, burnt-match/sulphur, charcoal flavors oddly enough don't seem that offensive after a third and fourth tasting; the sulphury aftertaste quietly lingers; for all its flaws, the sharp charcoal quality inexplicably grew on me; I upgraded it.

RATING ★★ $

MONTEZUMA Gold Tequila 40% Alcohol

Harvest-gold hue; one of the more banal, nondescript aromas in the category—there's so little to deal with in terms of aroma, it's ridiculous; ditto in the mouth; this vapid tequila reminds me strikingly of the Castanada Gold; avoid even as a mixer—garbage.

RATING ★ $

OLÉ WHITE Tequila 40% Alcohol

Devoid of color; the metallic, mild, light, steely, typically vegetal nose offers scant charm—very little excitement here; the mouth presence actually has echoes of milk chocolate upon entry, then the chocolate unfortunately fades in a flash to fresh vegetable juice (V-8) at midpalate; little finish if any to speak of; run-of-the-mill; a bar well offering.

RATING ★ $

PATRON Añejo 100% Blue Agave Tequila 40% Alcohol

Pale yellow/honey tone, perfect clarity; this nose is far more advanced and generous than the Silver, as roasted/toasty aromas of nuts, pine/cedar, and fruit (especially nectarine) enchant the olfactory sense—the nose is worth two stars on its own; on palate, the gracefulness found in the aroma continues as measured, semisweet flavors of bittersweet chocolate and coffee bean come to the forefront at midpalate; the aftertaste is supple, almost stately, and very satisfying; an excellent *añejo* as a slammer with lime and salt.

RATING ★★★★   *Highly Recommended* $$

PATRON Silver 100% Blue Agave Tequila 40% Alcohol

This Silver has been highly touted by some writers, but I confess that I miss the point—it's better than average, to be sure, but it's not the key to nirvana like some of the ill-informed would have you believe; clear; the nose is nicely balanced between fruit, roasted peppers, and spirit; on palate, it shows good viscosity and ample amounts of butter, boiled green vegetables, and resin; the aftertaste is seriously long and meaty; a solid performer.

RATING ★★★   *Recommended* $$

PORFIDIO Añejo 100% Blue Agave Tequila 40% Alcohol

One of the stupidest bottles I've ever seen—I won't tell you what it is—find it and have a good laugh; pale amber tone; the nose rockets out of the glass in musty waves of mushroom, old attic, bacon fat, and steamed vegetables—while my notes might not sound appetizing, the fact is, this bouquet is seductive and earthy—I can almost smell the soil of Jalisco; the vegetal/bacon-like splendor continues in the sexy taste, as fruity, round, and immensely charming flavors enchant the taste buds; the finish is ultraclean and sleek; highly stylistic and top-notch all the way; I'd bathe in it.

RATING ★ ★ ★ ★   ***Highly Recommended*** $ $

Porfidio Añejo Single-Barrel 100% Blue Agave Tequila 40% Alcohol

Marginally darker in appearance than the regular *añejo;* this nose is disappointing right from the sound of the gun, as smelly aromas of cactus and airplane glue greet the olfactory sense in the first two passes—it recovers somewhat in the third nosing as the glue fades and earthy/pine/evergreen scents move in and stay through the final pass; on palate, it's as dry as the Sahara at entry, then it takes a sharp left and becomes sweet, almost like a cheap vodka, at midpalate; the aftertaste is sweet and uncomfortably atypical for the category; a serious letdown after the glorious regular *añejo;* what happened?

RATING ★ ★ $ $

Sauza Hornitos Reposado 100% Blue Agave Tequila 40% Alcohol

A very pale straw/flaxen color; the distinct, elegant, concentrated, semidry, peppery, cardboard, salty, and pulpy nose offers several layers of intriguing aromas—if you stick with the nose long enough, you even discern soft licorice and anise way in the distance; almost wine-like in its bearing on the tongue—it starts snappily on the palate, then turns full-weighted and elegant at midpalate, with soft, semisweet flavors of peaches, apples, pears, and black pepper; it finishes like warm, crushed velvet; this is a top-flight, full-throttle tequila that delights the drinker from stem to stern.

RATING ★ ★ ★ ★   ***Highly Recommended*** $

Sauza Conmemorativo Añejo Tequila 40% Alcohol

White-wine-like appearance of straw yellow, with green highlights; the decidedly winey nose emits nuanced hints of earth, yeast, esters, salt, and chalk; it has a potent, semidry, spirity, wine-like bearing on palate, then citrus flavors burst forward onto the back of the tongue—really delicious and succulent just before the high-flying, orange, pineapple, banana finish that's wonderfully fruity and alone is worth the price of the bottle; a graceful mouthful.

RATING ★ ★ ★ ★   ***Highly Recommended*** $

Sauza Tres Generaciones Añejo Tequila 40% Alcohol

Like the superlative Conmemorativo, the 3G's also has a white-wine-like appearance, but owns a deeper straw/yellow color that is flecked with gold highlights; it's less salty, but strikingly similar to the Conmemorativo in the nose except that it's a notch or two more advanced in the richness department; on palate, the supple, citrusy, pineappley flavors are very understated, quietly potent, and downright sensational; the aftertaste is sophisticated, but surprisingly austere; simply a wonderful tequila that makes a fantastically tasty margarita.

RATING ★ ★ ★ ★   ***Highly Recommended*** $ $

EL TESORO DE DON FELIPE Añejo Tequila 40% Alcohol

Simply one of the four or five best tequilas to be found, period; handsome light-amber hue, excellent purity; the nose is profound yet direct, as layered aromas of herbs, asparagus, butter, cream, and fruit dazzle the olfactory sense—a stunningly complex bouquet that's been a benchmark in my evaluations; in the mouth, it's as graceful and powerful as a great cognac, but with that zesty, vegetal tequila hip-hop that's irresistible when it's done right; the finish is very extended and displays as much finesse as it does muscle; one of the finest white-spirit experiences to be had.

RATING ★ ★ ★ ★ ★   ***Highest Recommendation*** $$

EL TESORO DE DON FELIPE Silver Tequila 40% Alcohol

Clear appearance, correctly pure; aromawise, this stallion is rivaled only by the Herradura Silver in complexity, density, and elegance—shockingly mature, melded scents of orange rind, pineapple, and hard candy light up the marquee in this reined-in bouquet—you almost feel that it's going to explode; in the mouth, the suppleness and grace of the vegetal, off-dry flavors are rewarding and memorable; the finish is medium-long and clean; one of the two best silvers in the marketplace.

RATING ★ ★ ★ ★   ***Highly Recommended*** $$

TORADA Reposado Tequila 40% Alcohol

A clear, flaxen/hay-like/light amber/honey color; it's far more rounded and customary than its white sibling in the woody, keenly vegetal nose; in the mouth, the smooth, very silky texture is accented with tasty charcoal, and sweet-oak flavors that are anything but dry; a pleasantly smoky, almost caramel-like, sweet finish that lasts long and is very easy on the throat; nice job.

RATING ★ ★ ★   ***Recommended*** $

TORADA Añejo Tequila 40% Alcohol

Yellow/goldenrod color; the lean, intense fresh-asparagus, corrugated-cardboard nose has a slight, dried red-chili-pepper background aroma to it that I favorably responded to; on palate, the semisweet, straightforward, uncluttered, leafy flavors of peppers and almonds get the job done tastewise; it has hints of caramel and sweet oak in the inoffensively biting aftertaste; Torada Añejo doesn't feign being a blockbuster, but does show a solid, refined presence all the same; excellent in margaritas.

RATING ★ ★ ★   ***Recommended*** $

TORADA White Tequila 40% Alcohol

Crystal clear, no color to address; the strange, unsettling aromas of rubber pencil eraser and cooked vegetables inhabit a mildly assertive nose; the exceedingly smoky, cooked, oaky flavors are followed by a stinging, zesty aftertaste that is surprisingly rich and semidry; I nearly ended up recommending this high-spirited offering, because it showed some character in the midpalate and finish, but the mildly "off" nose is the problem.

RATING ★ ★ $

EL TORO Gold Tequila 40% Alcohol
Light yellow/flaxen hue; the somewhat peppery, spirity, assertive nose is kickier than that of the White; on palate, the smooth, floral, developed flavors of herbs, hay, and broccoli are correct, but too pedestrian for a recommendation; the pleasantly sweet, simple finish is mildly graceful and full; better than the wimpy White all the way around.
RATING ★ ★ $

EL TORO White Tequila 40% Alcohol
Clear, no color; the benign, herbal nose is flecked with dill; in the mouth, the moderately appealing, vegetal flavors offer a firm bite and plenty of textural grip; the sweet aftertaste finishes long; on the whole, a mildly satisfying, uncomplicated, low-key, and easy quaff; can see its best application in margaritas that aren't necessarily meant to impress a large group or party.
RATING ★ $

EL VIEJITO Reposado Tequila 40% Alcohol
Pale yellow/light straw color; the pungent, cactus-like (makes sense only if you've ever had the pleasure of eating baked cactus plant), acidic, tofu, herbal, and sour-pickled nose packs some punch; it's spirity and clean on palate entry, then goes mildly sweet in the throat and in the extended, very tasty, acutely herbal finish; nice job; decent on its own, but better in margaritas.
RATING ★ ★ ★   *Recommended* $

EL VIEJITO Añejo Tequila 40% Alcohol
Light gold color; the full, round, moderately complex nose speaks of dill and sweet, dried herbs in the first three passes, then mysteriously dies in the last nosing; on palate, the clean, focused, forward, concentrated flavors of smoke, Dijon mustard, and the ever-present dill impress the taste buds, especially in midpalate after they've gained some momentum; nicely balanced between herbs/sweetness/alcohol; heady, weighty feel; has a disappointingly quick finish; quite tasty on its own with or without the customary lime and salt.
RATING ★ ★ ★   *Recommended* $

WHISKEY

Whiskey is the frequently glorious, sometimes wretched, and virtually always amber- to brown-colored distilled spirit made from grain, water, and yeast. The preeminent whiskies are manufactured in the countries and regions of the world that traditionally have grown grains in abundance, in particular, barley, wheat, rye, and corn. The four most notable whiskey-producing countries are Scotland, the U.S. (the central states of Kentucky and Tennessee are the headliners), Canada, and Ireland. Yet, to be sure, other countries grow or purchase grain, ferment and distill its mash, age it in wood, and affix a label on the bottle that identifies the distillate as whiskey. Second-tier producers, whose whiskies are showing genuine promise, are Japan and Australia. Third-tier whiskey-making nations include Germany, the Czech Republic, and India.

I have over the last decade chosen a definite path for my whiskey sojourn. For evaluation purposes, my focus has been set squarely on the whiskies that hail from Scotland, the U.S., Canada, and Ireland. My reasons are as simple as my tasting notes are numerous: One, the whiskies from this quartet of countries have had the most impact in both historical and socioeconomic respects; and, two, these four nations are the countries whose whiskies are the most readily available in the North American and U.K./European markets, where most of my readers reside. In addition, these countries produce 15 or 20 whiskies that must be included among the finest distilled spirits currently made on the planet, so the concentration is warranted.

The term *whiskey* evolved from the Gaelic words *uisge beatha* (pronounced, oos-gah bay-thah) and, later, *usque baugh* (oos-keh baw). (Gaelic, which is still spoken in the outer islands of the Hebrides and in the remotest hamlets of the Highlands as well as in western Ireland and Wales, is a dialect of the Celtic tongue.) The terms both mean "water of life." In the late Middle Ages, a bastardization was *usky* (oos-kee), which later evolved into "whiskey." The Latin-speaking Christian monks, who more than likely introduced the art of distillation first to Ireland, then later to Scotland, referred to the potent liquid as *aqua vitae*, which also means "water of life."

Whiskey is a term that has two correct spellings, according to the Oxford English Dictionary. "Whiskey" (with the "e") is utilized by the majority of distillers in the United States and Ireland, while "whisky" (sans the "e") is employed by Scottish and Canadian producers. I've asked various people in the whiskey trade why this discrepancy, which causes minor fits of confusion, exists, but I've yet to receive a convincing reply. "That's just how things have developed" is a paraphrase of the usual response.

Historians are moderately confident (and well-worn fables are dead certain) that the Christian monks who returned to Ireland after tours of duty spreading the word of Jesus through the wilds of the European continent and the Middle East brought back the skills of fermentation and distillation, skills that were, by the end of the Dark Ages, commonplace in the abbeys and monasteries of Europe. The advancement and perpetuation of all alcoholic beverages were the province of the monasteries and the aristocracy during the worst days of plague, invasion, and political and social upheaval in the centuries that spanned A.D. 500 to 1500.

Using resources that were close at hand, namely, grain and water, the Irish monks, in all probability, made the first primitive whiskies to fend off the dank climate of clammy Eire as well as for medicinal purposes. Spirits had from their inception been considered a restorative, an almost mystical presence of warmth in the throat and chest that warded off the chill of the environment and made the often harsh reality of daily circumstance easier to bear. By the twelfth century A.D., whiskey making was well established in the cold encampments of Ireland. Eight centuries later, whiskey is the soul of every pub in Ireland's and Northern Ireland's cities and countryside.

Crossing the North Channel from what is now Northern Ireland to the Scottish mainland, perhaps on the Mull of Kintyre, a finger of land that dangles off the southwest coast of Scotland, the monks brought their holy water in one hand and their drinkable whiskey in the other to an inhospitable land that featured fieldstone huts heated by clods of peat; unremittingly in-clement weather; and rugged men decked out in wool skirts that bore the colors of their clan. The Scots embraced whiskey with a gusto that has never since been matched. For a minimum of 200 years prior to the discovery of North America, both the Scots and the Irish made and consumed their "usky" with staggering zeal. They perfected their cottage-industry techniques to the point of transforming distillation into an artisan's craft, an art form that would, in the age of colonization, capture the collective palate and imagination of almost the entire globe.

In the colonial America of the 1600s, whiskey wasn't among the most popular libations. Rum, distilled from the sugarcane molasses imported from the islands of the Caribbean, madeira, and beer were the leading bracers of the day. Since the coast-hugging early colonies were not ideal grain-growing locales, whiskey's basic ingredient, cereal grain, was lacking. It wasn't until the colonists started moving westward into the frontier regions of Pennsylvania, western Virginia, and western Maryland, where soil types and topographies allowed for grain cultivation, that whiskey making became a viable activity. Since farming was the foremost occupation in the 1700s and 1800s, the colonists were no strangers to the manifold potential of grain.

With further movement west into the Ohio River Valley in the late eighteenth and early nineteenth centuries into what is now Ohio, Kentucky, and Tennessee, whiskey distilling in America took permanent root. Today's bourbons, blended whiskies, rye whiskies, corn whiskies, and Tennessee sour-mash whiskies were born courtesy of the flocks of Irish, German, and Scottish immigrants who settled in the sheltered glens and river valleys of the New World's heartland. These people weren't pioneers only in carving out a new nation, but also in forming an industry that years later would compete with the whiskey juggernauts of Ireland and Scotland.

To the north, first- and second-generation Canadians, many of whom were of Scottish descent, set in motion the Canadian whisky industry in the late eighteenth century in the land stretching from the town of Windsor on Lake Erie east to Toronto and Kingston on Lake Ontario. The cradle for whisky production in Canada's infancy, 200 years later the province of Ontario remains the primary source, along with the cities of Ottawa (Ontario) and Montreal (Quebec). In the early years, Canada's whisky roster included the million-dollar names of Hiram Walker and Joseph E. Seagram, who poured and shaped the foundation of the industry.

THE FIVE FUNDAMENTAL STEPS TO MAKING WHISKEY

Whiskey's ingredients—grain, water, and yeast—are relatively easy to procure in most of the industrialized world. The differences in various whiskies come from the method of distillation (pot still, which produces small volumes, versus patent still, which produces huge volumes, plus the number of distillations), the types of yeast used (each strain of yeast imparts a unique flavor all its own), the kinds of wood employed for aging (oak is by far the most prevalent variety, because it is more easily fashioned into barrels than other woods and also because it has the right porosity), the size of the barrel, the length of time allotted for barrel-aging, the water source (different innate chemicals, microbes, and mineral compounds in water contribute to whiskey's aroma, texture, and flavor), and, most important, the type of cereal grain(s) used (barley, corn, wheat, rye, oats).

Each of these factors will be touched upon in the opening segment of the following sections or in the individual tasting notes. The reality is that all the elements come into play singularly or in combination within the same rudimentary blueprint, the nearly identical sequence of production events that are responsible for virtually every whiskey made in the world.

Malting/Cooking: When barley or rye are the primary grains, they are partially germinated, then dried in kilns to promote enzyme action for the mash. After drying, the malted grain is milled into a grist for mashing, the next stage. When corn or wheat is the base cereal, cooking is the first step. Cooking forces the molecular cellulose membranes to disintegrate, thereby allowing the starches to blend together in preparation for mashing.

Mashing: This crucial phase happens in the production of *every* whiskey. Mashing brings closure to the process of malting or cooking, depending on the type of grain involved. Mashing prepares the grainy liquid for fermentation by transforming the innate starches into sugar. In this sequence, the malted or cooked grain is placed in large vats and steeped in warm water. Mechanical arms, which resemble rakes, rotate, mixing the mash. The sugary liquid is most often referred to as "wort."

Fermentation: Fermentation, which takes place in a separate vessel, is a natural biochemical process that transforms the sugars into alcohol. The process is initiated by the action of yeast cells. This tumultuous, bubbling stage is nothing more than the yeast cells' feasting on the sugars of the mash. After fermentation, the liquid is, for all intents and purposes, beer, and is referred to as such in Kentucky and Tennessee. The Scots and Irish call this aromatic liquid "wash." The alcohol level at this point is anywhere from 5 to 8 percent.

Distillation: Distillation is what separates spirits from either wine or beer. In the distillation process, the fermented liquid is boiled, either in copper-pot stills or in tall, continuously running patent stills. Alcohol boils at a lower temperature than water, 173.1 degrees Fahrenheit, to be precise. Distillation separates the alcohol from all other properties in the fermented liquid, including water. The spirit vapors rise from the boil and are cooled in condensers. The vapors revert to liquid form with cooling. That translucent liquid is alcohol. The distillates that end up being whiskey are distilled two, sometimes three times. Whiskey spirits coming off the still after two distillations generally range from 68 to 80 percent alcohol. In addition, they are as clear as mineral water and pungently floral to the smell.

Maturation: This is the most romantic phase of whiskey production. Maturation in wood casks or vats mellows the distillate and imparts some of the wood flavor into the whiskey. Whiskey also takes on its amber-to-brown tint in the barrel, an influence both of the wood and oxidation. Different countries or regions legally dictate minimum periods of wood-aging. Scotch whisky, for example, must by law be aged for a minimum of three years. In the U.S., federal law dictates that bourbon must be aged for at least two years. Oak is the most widely used kind of wood because it's durable, relatively plentiful, easier that harder woods to shape into casks, and has the right porosity for the aging of whiskey. In order for whiskey to mature and evolve, a small amount of contact with oxygen is necessary. Since oak is porous, oxygen seeps through the staves and mingles with the developing spirits, allowing them to mellow and soften. Conversely, whiskey vapors penetrate the wood and escape through the action of evaporation. The longer the whiskey rests in the barrel, the less remains, through evaporation. In warm climates, as in Kentucky and Tennessee, evaporation can snatch up to 3 or 4 percent of the volume annually. In cooler climates, as in Ireland and Scotland, evaporation loss is normally about 2 percent a year.

Some producers, most notably, the bourbon distillers of Kentucky, age whiskey in brand-new white-oak barrels whose interiors have been deeply seared. Other producers, especially the Scots and Canadians, mature their whiskies in oak casks that have formerly been utilized to age other alcoholic beverages. Used sherry casks, which give off wine-like, often sweet flavors, and used bourbon casks, which impart candied, caramelized, vanilla-like tastes, are the most widely employed.

In the age of social consciousness, it's appropriate to urge vigilant moderation and individual responsibility. But, it's likewise important to keep in sight the fact that whiskey has and does give immeasurable pleasure, delight, and comfort to millions of people around the globe. Whiskey has been the inspiration for countless quotes, ditties, toasts, and prose over the centuries. No one, however, has captured the glory and the spirit of whiskey with more verve and eloquence than Scotland's most beloved poet, Robert Burns, who wrote,

> Let other Poets raise a fracas
> 'bout vines, an' wines, an' drunken Bacchus,
> An' crabbed names an' stories wrack us,
>   An' grate our lug;
> I sing the juice of Scotch bear can mak us,
>   In glass or jug.
>
> O thou, my Muse! guid auld Scotch Drink,
> Whether thro' wimplin worms thou jink,
> Or, richly brown, ream owre the brink,
>   In glorious faem,
> Inspire me, till I lisp an' wink,
>   To sing thy name!

What to Look For in a Whiskey

Purity. All whiskies, whatever their country of origin, should be free of suspended particles. Neither should any whiskey be turbid. Likewise, they should display a warm glow when held against a light. Some single-malt Scotch whiskies can be very pale in color—a sort of straw-like, white-wine tinge. Most Scotch whisky malts and blends run the normal whiskey-appearance gamut of that of the Canadian, Irish, and American whiskies—

light amber to honey to chestnut brown. Bourbon, the premier whiskey made in the U.S., sometimes has a suggestion of burnished red.

Aromatic and flavor properties.

- Scotch whisky, the most complex of whiskies, should, first and foremost, be grainy in the aroma and the taste. Depending on the style and/or the region it comes from, additional positive elements include woodiness, a dry to off-dry fruitiness, and mild to moderately potent smokiness due to the use of peat in the kilning of the barley malt. A Scotch whisky is having problems when it smells and tastes stale, musty, metallic, or sulphury, like a burnt match. A single malt aged in old sherry casks is usually on the sweeter, heavier side of the spectrum, while those aged in old bourbon casks are slightly drier and on the lighter side.
- Bourbons and Tennessee whiskies are commonly sweeter than Scotch because of the high percentage of corn, a sweet grain, as well as the use of charred barrels, which when the char level is deep can impart sweetness. Sweet, however, doesn't mean cloying or honeyed or syrupy, any or all of which can signal problems. The best American whiskies have balanced influences from the grain, alcohol, acid, and wood. Bourbons typically emit a vanilla or caramel-like aroma and taste. Tennessee whiskey leans to the smoky side.
- Irish whiskies vaguely resemble lighter Scotch whiskies in their overall bearing. A sound whiskey from Eire will be very smooth, mildly cereal-like, and drinkable.
- Canadian whiskies are, on average, the most approachable of all whiskies. This easy-drinking moniker is due to the fact that the most prevalent grain is corn, an easy, sweet, and friendly smelling and tasting cereal. A Canadian whisky is questionable when it appears to be too sticky-sweet.

Good-to-great whiskies all give off a warming sensation in the mouth. A few of the whiskies that are labeled "barrel strength" or "cask strength," meaning that they have not been diluted with water to reduce the alcohol level, may impart a slight burning feeling either on the tongue at entry or in the throat at the finish. That doesn't necessarily make them bad, they're just very potent. Add an ounce or two of water to cut their strength, thereby making them more approachable and aromatic.

Finish. The aftertaste in virtually all good-to-great whiskies is mellow, balanced, and polished, never biting, fiery, overly sweet, sour, or stale. The whiskey should coat the tongue and throat with a pleasing richness, spearheaded by the grain, followed by secondary elements, such as the wood influence.

✳

SCOTCH WHISKY

My fondness for Scotch whisky goes far beyond the actual liquid itself. As I have described in the Introduction, Scotch was the catalyst for my becoming a spirits journalist in the first place. The Scots themselves are, I think, the most hospitable and the most refreshingly candid of all the people that I deal with on a professional basis. Over the years of visiting Scotland, I've made friends in all areas of that great country. I feel as at home in the glens of Speyside as I do in the Hudson Valley. If I could, I'd split in two and continue living near New York City while simultaneously sitting in the library of the Craigellachie Hotel near Macallan talking fly fishing with the local gillies. Scotland is the most bewitching country in which I regularly travel, not because it is the most mysterious, but because it is the most honest. I feel clean and renewed whenever I'm in Scotland. My head is clear and my heart is full. Back home, when I'm longing for the sightings of red deer in the Cairngorms or a misty ferry ride across to Skye from the mainland, I pour myself a dram of Scotch whisky and settle in with my musings. Each dram of Scotch (my friend Duncan Christy once said, "I think, therefore I dram") has in it the crystalline water, grain, carefully cultivated yeast, and very air of this most pristine of lands. Scotch whisky's scope of aromas, colors, flavors, and textures provide one of the most fertile landscapes of discovery in all of distilled spirits.

There exist two fundamental types of Scotch whisky, grain whisky and single-malt whisky. Single malt is a whisky that comes from one distillery (the "single" part of the equation) and is made from only malted barley (the "malt"). Distilled in individual batches in small, onion-shaped, copper-pot stills, single-malt Scotches are mesmerisingly idiosyncratic. Unquestionably, one of the primary allures of single-malt Scotch *is* each whisky's unique-ness. Of the nearly 100 malt distilleries that are still in operation, the single-malt whiskies of no two are exactly alike. The pot still method is the origi-nal whisky making process and is, by its very nature, labor-intensive. Pot stills need constant care and attention by stillhouse workers and copper-smiths, who take extraordinary measures to perfectly duplicate each ding, crease, and dimple when a still is being replaced with a new one. Distillery managers swear on the souls of their grandchildren that the imperfections in the pot stills influence the flavor of the whisky. How can you argue with centuries of experience?

Single malts range from being the most feral and lusty of whiskies (Laphroaig 10 and Lagavulin 16 from Islay) to the most serenely elegant (Glenlivet 12 and Macallan 18 from Speyside). But the scores of single malts that lie in between cover an astonishing range of individualistic per-sonalities, some benevolent, others rowdy. After evaluating hundreds of distilled spirits from every category, I've concluded that single-malt Scotches are not only the most complex of whiskies, but likewise the most complex distilled spirit, period. The sole spirit that approaches single-malt Scotch's stature, density, and sensory latitude is XO-level cognac, which, like single malt, accurately reflects its place of origin.

To illustrate, in single malts from the western Hebrides (Islay, Skye), you can actually taste, smell, and feel the influence of the Atlantic Ocean. The salinity of the coastal atmosphere invades the oak casks and imparts a briny quality to the whisky. In Grande Champagne cognac, you can taste, smell, and feel the flintiness and mineraliness of the calcareous soil. Only these two types of spirit offer that kind of detectable elemental experience.

Grain whiskies are made from corn or wheat, not malted barley, and are distilled in factory-like facilities. The type of still used is the patent still, which never stops running except for cleaning. Continuously operating patent stills are more cost-efficient than pot stills and are designed for high-volume lots. The concept for the continuously running still was developed in the 1820s and perfected by Aeneas Coffey in 1831. (Patent stills are still sometimes referred to as Coffey stills.) Grain whiskies are, as a general rule of thumb, more homogenized and uniform in aroma, texture, and flavor than single-malt whiskies.

Blended Scotches, such as Johnnie Walker, J & B, Cutty Sark, Dewar's, Famous Grouse, and Chivas Regal, are combinations of single-malt and grain whiskies. As many as forty to sixty varieties of whisky can go into the making of one blended whisky. Blended Scotches were invented in the mid-dle of the nineteenth century to help meet the growing demand for Scotch whisky as the British Empire blanketed the globe. The existing malt distil-leries of the day simply couldn't meet the demand. Single-malt whiskies were deemed too potent for the general populace in any regard, and, so, milder versions, the Scotch blends, were introduced with alarming and in-stant success. For the last century, blended Scotch whiskies have been the cash cow of the Scotch industry. In fact, most malt distilleries allocate the vast majority of the whiskies they distill for blending, not for bottling as sin-gle malt. Single malt comprises a mere 3–5 percent of worldwide Scotch whisky sales in any one year.

On the lecture circuit, I've found that single-malt snobs freely and without sufficient reason thumb their noses at Scotch blends. I find that regrettable for the reason that many of the ultrapremium blends rival single malts in their bearing and complexity. Some, such as Royal Salute, J & B Ultima and J & B J.E.T., Pinch 15, Johnnie Walker Gold, Usquaebach Deluxe 8, and Usquaebach Reserve, even surpass some of the lesser single malts in overall drinking pleasure. Don't make the mistake of cavalierly dismissing blended Scotch whisky. You'll be missing out on some of the best whisky experiences you'll ever have.

UPDATING THE SCOTCH WHISKY REGIONS

For many years, the standard party line has been that there are four classic whisky regions in Scotland—the Lowlands, the Highlands, Islay, and Campbeltown. This facile rendering is woefully obsolete. It misrepresents the topic and does no justice to the malt whiskies. To help make the subject of single-malt Scotch at once more precise, intriguing, and explicit, I've broken down the the original four regions into nine geographically defined districts.

Speyside. Scotland's premier malt whisky area, formerly included in the old Highlands appellation, more than deserves to be recognized as its own district. I define this wide region as spanning from the city of Inverness in the west to the village of Turriff in the east, from the city of Elgin in the north to the village of Tomintoul in the south. Green, lush Speyside is nourished by a network of rivers and streams, including the rivers Spey, Avon, Findhorn, Deveron, Bogie, Fiddich, Livet, and Lossie. Over 40 malt distilleries inhabit this pristine, bucolic district. It is doubtless the finest area in the world for making whisky. The range in styles is as broad as the amount of real estate involved. Therefore, contrary to many people's beliefs, I must state unequivocally that there exists no definable "Speyside style."

Northern Highlands. The wild, coast-hugging area running from Loch Ness and the city of Inverness in the south all the way directly north to the coastal town of Wick. Usually, the whiskies are broad-shouldered with the tang of sea salt.

Eastern Highlands. The mountainous area bordered by the city of Aberdeen to the east and to the north, to the city of Perth to the south, and to the Grampian Mountains to the west. A large, picturesque district that includes some outstanding distilleries.

Western Highlands. Boundaries are the coastal city of Fort William to the north, the Atlantic Ocean to the west, and to the south the coastal town of Oban. The malts are, on the whole, muscular and peaty.

Central Highlands. Sometimes referred to as "The Midlands." The area borders the imaginary line drawn west to east, from Glasgow to Edinburgh in the south, north to Perth.

Islay. The legendary, gum-numbing malts from this district come from eight distilleries located on a breezy, virtually treeless isle off the central coast of mainland Scotland. The heartiness of the malts is a function of both the sea air and the heavily peat-influenced water sources.

Islands. Included in this maritime district are the whisky-making islands of Mull (west), Skye (west), Jura (west), and the Orkneys (northeast). There is no common aspect to the malts.

Lowlands. The entire agricultural, softly contoured area south of the Glasgow–Edinburgh line. There is uniformity to the Lowland malts, in that they are each very soft-spoken, lightish, and quaffable.

Campbeltown. Once a bustling coal-producing area, now quiet and rural. Two distilleries still supply malts, though one, Glen Scotia, is closed. The other, Springbank, is one of the best distilleries in the world.

RANKING SCOTLAND'S MALT DISTILLERIES

The 1855 Classifications of the prime chateaux of the Médoc and Sauternes/Barsac districts within Bordeaux were landmarks in the history of French wine, because in ranking the producers they informed the drinking public as to which chateaux were the most reliably sound, vintage after vintage. While some industry observers have claimed the Bordeaux classifications to be antiquated and akin to a sort of caste system, they have nonetheless served as the primary touchstones of the public's perception and appreciation of red and white Bordeaux wines for a century and a half. Based on their success, other Bordeaux districts have had their chateaux graded. The Classification of the Crus Bourgeois of the Médoc (revised in 1978) and the Classification of St. Emilion (revised in 1985) are fitting examples.

Whether one agrees with such individual rankings by authorities is irrelevant. What does matter is that a qualitative foundation for an important segment of the French wine industry was laid, and, as a result, both consumers and all the Bordeaux producers have benefited. These classifications and their revisions have helped wine drinkers from around the world sift through some of the 7,000 chateaux that inhabit greater Bordeaux. The rankings are simultaneously an anchor and a beacon. An anchor, in that they lend gravity to the region, and a beacon because such a tabulation stirs interest in the minds of the public.

Over the years that I've been keenly evaluating single-malt Scotch whisky, my notes and impressions, both from the strictly controlled tastings in my own facility and from hundreds of on-site tastings, have defined an unequivocal pecking order in the hierarchy of producers. In no way am I asserting that this classification should be viewed as anything more than one person's personal set of rankings. However, I likewise point out that since I've spent more time tasting and learning about single-malt Scotch than any other libation since 1988, my observation point is unusual, varied, and unique. I offer this classification neither to step on toes nor to repay kindnesses, but to shed some beams of unbiased light onto an industry that is largely controlled by a handful of enormous companies who are perceived to serve only themselves and not necessarily the greater good of the industry as a whole.

My rankings are built upon three interdependent factors: first, consistent quality, time and again, bottle after bottle, of the single malts of the individual distilleries; second, the number of rated or sampled whiskies of different ages, whether they are merchant bottlings, private-society bottlings, or distillery bottlings; and, third, how the distillery is viewed by its industry peers, as ascertained by me through the scores of interviews and casual conversations in which I've been involved.

My goal is to periodically revise and add to this classification, as warranted. Please note that not every malt distillery, open or closed, is represented.

Malt Distillery of Scotland Classification—1997

★ ★ ★ ★ ★ *Scotland's Finest Malt Whisky Distilleries*

Bowmore	Clynelish
Highland Park	Longmorn
Macallan	Springbank

★ ★ ★ ★ *Scotland's Superb Malt Whisky Distilleries*

Aberlour	Auchentoshan
Balvenie	Caol Ila
Cragganmore	Dalmore
Glenfarclas	Glenlivet
Glenmorangie	Glen Rothes
Glen Scotia	Knockando
Lagavulin	Mortlach
Singleton of Auchroisk	Strathisla

★ ★ ★ *Scotland's Very Good Malt Whisky Distilleries*

Aberfeldy	An Cnoc (Knockdhu)
Ardbeg	Balblair
Balmenach	Benriach
Bladnoch	Braeval (Braes of Glenlivet)
Dallas Dhu	Dalwhinnie

Dufftown

Glen Deveron

Glenfiddich

Glen Grant

Glen Spey

Glenugie

Isle of Jura

Linkwood

Miltonduff

Port Ellen

Royal Brackla

Scapa

Tamdhu

Glenallachie

Glenesk

Glengoyne

Glen Ord

Glenturret

Inchgower

Laphroaig

Littlemill

Oban

Rosebank

Royal Lochnagar

Speyburn

Tamnavulin

★★ *Scotland's Good Malt Whisky Distilleries*

Ardmore

Bunnahabhain

Dailuaine

Fettercairn

Glencadam

Glendullan

Glen Keith

Glenlochy

Inchmurrin

Old Pulteney

Talisker

Tomintoul

Tullibardine

Bruichladdich

Cardhu

Edradour

Glen Albyn

Glendronach

Glen Garioch

Glenkinchie

Glen Moray

Mannochmore

St. Magdalene

Tobermory

Tormore

★ *Scotland's Subpar Malt Whisky Distilleries*

Ben Nevis

Glenglassaugh

North Port

Glenburgie

Glen Mohr

Tomatin

I have not, as yet, gathered sufficient data on the following 24 obscure, new and/or closed distilleries for them to be included at the present time. They will be added as my exposure to them evolves:

Aultmore	Banff
Benrinnes	Benromach
Ben Wyvis	Blair Athol
Caperdonich	Coleburn
Convalmore	Craigellachie
Deanston	Glen Elgin
Glenlossie	Glentauchers
Glenury Royal	Imperial
Inverleven	Kinclaith
Ladyburn	Lochside
Millburn	Pittyvaich
Strathmill	Teaninich

Blended Scotch Whiskies

100 PIPERS Blended Scotch Whisky (Bottled in U.S.) 40% Alcohol

Medium amber/harvest-gold color; not what I'd term rich or deep in the nose by any measure, but for what it is—an inexpensive, low-end blend— it's not a bad bouquet—there are actually detectable hints of oak and vanilla; in the mouth, it goes toasty and charcoally to the extreme, then snaps at your tonsils with burning heat as it exits; 100 Pipers has admirable body, a mediocre bouquet, and an unacceptably scorching presence on the palate; a rude Scotch whisky.

RATING ★ $

BALLANTINE'S Gold Seal 12-Year-Old Blended Scotch Whisky 43% Alcohol

Light gold/harvest-yellow/goldenrod tone; the nose is much more balanced than its younger sibling, the Finest, emitting a graceful, mature, unhurried bouquet of small grain, light peat, hard candy, and pear brandy; on the palate, this handsome, almost stately blend offers elegant, manageably sweet, fully married tastes of malt, light wood smoke, mature oak, and even a slightly bitter citric acid nip in the throat, which I liked for the sake of balance; the aftertaste is silky-smooth, but short-lived; an alluring, rock-solid blend overall.

RATING ★ ★ ★   *Recommended* $$

BALLANTINE'S Finest Blended Scotch Whisky 43% Alcohol

Light-to-medium amber color, which, though not cloudy, is woefully dull; the nose is well endowed, intensely grainy, like cereal with honey—it offers no traces of peat, smoke, or wood—still, it's a decent, solid, no-frills, one-note blended Scotch aroma; in the mouth, it's blatantly sweet, bordering on syrupy sweet, full, round, succulent in a grainy rather than fruity or floral way; the sugary finish is a continuation of the midpalate experience; this is a blend that, while acceptable to me, dangerously flirts with too high a reading on the sweetness meter; I personally didn't mind the overdrive sweetness, but many people would, I'm afraid; the two stars are bestowed with this important caveat—this is a highly stylized blend that may simply be too sweet for some whisky lovers.

RATING ★ ★ $

BUCHANAN'S Deluxe 12-Year-Old Blended Scotch Whisky 43% Alcohol

Attractive medium-amber color; the well-endowed nose speaks of sweet oak, chocolate, oloroso sherry, and vanilla, all erected upon a firm, corn-like, grain whisky foundation; this 12-year-old really comes off grainy on the palate with full-throttle flavors of cereal, cooked mash, and malted barley— I wrongly anticipated that it would go all-out sweet in the mouth because it abruptly changed directions and temporarily went astringent and peaty before recovering its sweetness; in the creamy finish I found it desirably sweet once again; a mature, intriguing blend with lots going for it.

RATING ★ ★ ★   Recommended $$

CHIVAS REGAL 12-Year-Old Blended Scotch Whisky 43% Alcohol

A luxurious gold/amber color; the enchantingly sweet and delicate nose is soft and refined, emitting mature, bountiful aromas of pears, apricots, and, heather; the palate entry is smoky, then the roasted, peaty, smoky qualities accelerate in the throat, where they seem to cascade in a complex, vanilla, butterscotch aftertaste that unobtrusively lingers a very long time; the intricate flavors are beautifully melded and somehow keep evolving at the rear of the tongue; Chivas's top-notch character is at once powerful and understated; hats off to the Chivas master blender; this is Scotch blending at its near-best.

RATING ★ ★ ★ ★   Highly Recommended $$

CLUNY Blended Scotch Whisky (Bottled in U.S.) 40% Alcohol

Correct amber/honey, blended Scotch whisky hue; the milquetoast nose of amber waving grain is strikingly similar to that of another inexpensive blend called Queen Anne—this has the identical tutti-frutti, sappy, candied flavor that's uncomfortably reminiscent of that horrible blend; the body is relatively firm, while the flavor has a resiny, sap-like, maple-syrup bend that's simply awful; a bush-league whisky that barely deserves one star.

RATING ★ $

CLUNY 12-Year-Old Blended Scotch Whisky (Bottled in Scotland) 43% Alcohol

Impressive, deep amber/honey color, with orange highlights; moderate amounts of character are present in the two or three aromatic layers of barley malt, vanilla extract, ripe pear, and bread dough—overall, a decent, substantial bouquet that gives you something to clasp onto; starts out neutral at entry, then turns on the dry malt, finishing off-dry and slightly spicy and hot in the throat; I was disappointed in the unpolished, sharp, and uninteresting taste and aftertaste, neither of which came close to fulfilling the promise found in the nose.

RATING ★ $$

CUTTY SARK Imperial Kingdom Blended Scots Whisky 43% Alcohol

Not available in the U.S.; pretty gold/hay/amber hue; the superb, dry to off-dry bouquet offers soft, rich, heavenly scents of peat, red fruit (plums), and malted barley—I have no idea what percentage of single malt this lovely blend is, but I'll take a stab and guess at least 35–40%; it's so buttery on the palate that you can almost envision it being spread on your morning toast—it's an absolutely delicious presence in the mouth; it deftly finishes with rounded-off flavors of creamy butter and nuts; this bottling stands easily as the best whisky that Cutty Sark produces; a stellar whisky!

RATING ★ ★ ★ ★   *Highly Recommended* $$

CUTTY SARK 12-Year-Old Blended Scots Whisky 43% Alcohol

Firm green/gold/yellow color; the dry nose is very shy initially, but after 15 minutes of aeration finally it emerges in sedate aromas of oak and cereal; this Cutty tastes very nice indeed on the palate as raisiny, buttery flavors envelop the tongue; there's even a brief flash of pleasurable, smoldering warmth in the woody finish; hardly a bulldozer (as one would expect), but well structured and firm; a good, undemanding dram, which exhibited more than enough panache, especially in the flavor, to be recommendable.

RATING ★ ★ ★   *Recommended* $$

CUTTY SARK 18-Year-Old Blended Scots Whisky 43% Alcohol

Handsome, deep amber hue; the added maturity really stands out in the sensuous, dry bouquet, where there's even a faint hint of saltiness/peatiness; has plenty of smoke at the palate entry, then goes oaky and peaty in the sweet, fruity, and altogether dazzling finish; it's a real mouthful of beautifully blended, old Scotch, no doubt about it; it's gentlemanly, but not in the least wimpy; an excellent, classy dram that should be picked up on your next trip to the U.K.—it's not available in the U.S.

RATING ★ ★ ★   *Recommended* $$

CUTTY SARK Blended Scots Whisky 43% Alcohol

Pale yellow/hay/gold/autumnally colored; the frail, sweet, grassy nose echoes the delicate appearance as featherweight scents of oatmeal and toasted cereal hold court on the palate; it's pleasantly oily to the feel; this popular blend gently glides onto the tongue and then ethereally departs by way of the throat, leaving behind mildly sweet taste impressions of candied almonds; takes the wind out of the sails of the uninformed who decry the overly robust nature of all Scotch whiskies; this, along with J & B Rare, is the most polite and fleet-footed of blended Scotches—but for my personal taste it's way too pale, meek, and spineless—certainly the weak sister when compared to the other fine blends from Cutty Sark.

   RATING ★ $

DESMOND & DUFF 12-Year-Old Blended Scotch Whisky 40% Alcohol

   Strong, firm amber color; the creamy, caramel, opulent, sticky-bun nose is lively, sassy, and delectably sweet—might be too over-the-top sweet for some purists; the flavor is not as sweet as the aroma—I pick up a pekoe tea or coffee-like quality that's nice and toasty; the finish goes back to the sweet mode, but is also slightly oaky, with vanilla-wafer and dried-fruit backnotes; I came quite close to recommending this blend, but two qualities prevented me from doing so—first, the finish jacked up the sweetness level almost to distraction and, second, there ended up being an unpleasant harshness at the very end of the aftertaste—my throat felt raw after the evaluations, which ended up being a whopping negative.

   RATING ★★ $

DEWAR's 12-Year-Old Blended Scotch Whisky 43% Alcohol

   Medium amber hue, excellent clarity; the nose speaks of freshly mown hay, light peat, and earthy hints of dried bitter orange—it's a dry to off-dry bouquet; on palate, it's light, but offers long flavors of pipe tobacco smoke, roses, hard candy, and black pepper; the aftertaste is medium-long and a tad smoky.

   RATING ★★★   *Recommended* $$

DEWAR's White Label Blended Scotch Whisky 43% Alcohol

   Firm amber color, superb purity; the nose is too meek for me, showing flashes of earth, dirt, very light peat and smoke, and pears—all the fragrances are so fleet that there's nothing to grip on to; in the mouth, White Label is mannered, perhaps overly so as it displays scant character—the tastes of sweet malt, sweet corn, oats, and dough are perfunctory and forgettable; the finish is medium-long and highlights the cereal; snooze-o-rama.

   RATING ★ $

DUGGAN's 12-Year-Old Blended Scotch Whisky 40% Alcohol

   Attractive, light-to-medium amber color with gold/orange highlights, absolute purity; the nose is inviting and shows a bit of a nip if you inhale too deeply (as, of course, I did, almost blowing off the top of my head)—the focus is all grain, as sweet, dry cereal aromas capture the brain's attention—there are lovely backnotes of spice (cinnamon) and juniper; immediately at mouth entry I detected a smoky, intensely tart, grain-like thrust that builds at midpalate, then turns sweetish, plump, and well mannered in the aftertaste; an intriguing, complex, multifaceted blend that hasn't lost a step of vivacity in its dozen years of aging; a leading Scotch blend.

   RATING ★★★★   *Highly Recommended* $$

DUGGAN'S Dew Blended Scotch Whisky 43.3% Alcohol

Flat, amber/gold color, superb purity; the nose is more a middleweight than a heavyweight and is exceedingly pleasant, echoing, at least for me, more of a grassy, clean Lowland malt style than Speyside, Highland, or island; in the mouth, the smoothness is like a lake on a calm day—what the mouth presence lacks in profundity it counters with drinkability—it's sweet to the taste and offers subdued but complementary background flavors of chocolate, honey, and sweet oak; the finish is clean, gently sweet, and surprisingly long; walks with the better premium Scotch blends.

RATING ★ ★ ★   *Recommended* $

FAMOUS GROUSE Gold Reserve 12-Year-Old Blended Scotch Whisky 43% Alcohol

Very attractive, amber/gold with a tint of green at the edge, immaculate purity; the prickly nose might put off some of the weak-in-the-knees set, but I liked the high octane bouquet that highlights a candied-fruit (apple, pear) aroma—the nose's foundation is a marriage between acid and spirit—this lusty blend's bouquet isn't afraid to come out swinging in the first round—the nose alone is worth a couple of rating stars; on palate, the whisky calms down at entry, going off-dry to sweet in a woody, caramelly fashion—the mid-palate gets charged up as the prickliness reemerges; estery flavors of mint, flowers, and light caramel dominate the finish in which there's no evidence of heat or bite; considerably more enjoyable, smooth, and round than the regular bottling.

RATING ★ ★ ★   *Recommended* $$

FAMOUS GROUSE Blended Scotch Whisky 40% Alcohol

The most popular pour of Scottish pubs; amber/tawny color; irresistibly friendly, open, casual, soft, round nose of barely discernable peat, ripe fruit in a clearly evident majority of grain whisky; on palate, it goes down with great ease; amiable, simple, smooth, fruity flavors abound; disarming, long, sweet, caramel finish; FG doesn't pretend to be a ponderous whisky; it accomplishes with charm what it set out to do—to provide a carefree, Saturday afternoon dram; can't go wrong with it under most circumstances; while totally average and correct, I don't like it enough to bestow a third star on it; a no-brainer blend.

RATING ★ ★ $

GLENDROSTAN Blended Scotch Whisky 43% Alcohol

Pale gold color; the soft-spoken, but round, grainy nose is simple, clean, crisply off-dry, and correct; an ethereal blend that's very sweet to the taste, but neither cloying nor syrupy—in fact, it's an entry-level blend that's almost feminine in its character; in the mouth, the taste reflects the uncomplicated character of the bouquet; the aftertaste is where it loses its poise, as a perceptible bite sneaks up on you; I was going to score it as a two-star Scotch when the hot, bothersome finish dropped it down a notch.

RATING ★ $

GRAND MACNISH Blended Scotch Whisky 43% Alcohol

Clean, clear, goldenrod color; the generous, cereal-like, cooked mash, toasty nose unmistakably betrays the high percentage of grain whisky in the blend; it's exceedingly smooth, gentlemanly, off-dry, but light to a fault at palate entry—oily, sweet flavors touched with lanolin and walnuts dominate at midpalate; it finishes as cleanly and well balanced as it began in a pleasingly easy, carefree way; most certainly not a blend that one would characterize as being either complex or thought-provoking, but its honest, friendly, bountiful manner is admirably brought across in a satisfying fashion; a perfectly sound mixing Scotch; retasted and upgraded.

RATING ★★　$

HAMASHKEH Blended Scotch Whisky (Kosher) 40% Alcohol

Pretty, medium-rich amber/orange tone; the very pleasant, honeyed aroma is ripe and fruity—quite inviting; on the palate, an assertive, honey/molasses sweetness dominates the taste to the point of exclusion; the aftertaste is predictably sweet and borders on being overly candied—candied almonds, to be precise; it's pleasant and inoffensive and might serve ably as an entry-level Scotch or, better yet, as a mixing Scotch; while there are no technical flaws to speak of, the flavor character relies too much on the sweetness aspect and, hence, the whisky comes off as monotonic, listless, and uninspiring after starting out well in the nose; retasted and downgraded.

RATING ★　$

INVER HOUSE Rare Blended Scotch Whisky 40% Alcohol

Pale yellow/hay color; pungent, forward, intensely malty, earthy nose, with a faint background hint of grain-whisky sweetness; decidedly sweet, light-bodied in the mouth; Inver House fades too quickly in the finish, leaving a benignly thin layer of malty flavor in the throat; retasted and downgraded because of the sweetness, which was in overdrive.

RATING ★　$

J & B J.E.T. 12-Year-Old Blended Scotch Whisky 43% Alcohol

Pale amber, excellent clarity; the first nosing won me over instantly, as grainy, off-dry, succulent scents of cereal, oats, and yellow fruit lead the inning off with a triple—the subtlety and grace of the bouquet are exhibited best in the beautifully balanced pairing of sweet grain and bitter smoke—a dazzling, understated fragrance that ranks with the best in blended Scotch; in the mouth, the harmony achieved in the blending provides a superior flavor experience—creamy, mannered, but hardly restrained flavors of sweet oak, honey, oloroso sherry, and caramel highlight this sleek winner; the aftertaste is extended, citrusy, and off-dry; quite simply a top-notch, affordable winner.

RATING ★★★★　*Highly Recommended*　$$

J & B Ultima Blended Scotch Whisky 43% Alcohol

This unique blend, conceived and completed by the former Justerini & Brooks master blender Jim Milne, is made from 128 Scotch whiskies, 116 malts (96 of the 98 malt distilleries still in operation plus 32 that are closed down) and 12 grain whiskies; the pale amber/golden honey color is not as vibrant or deep as I'd expected, but it's pure; the sweet, sturdy, but soft bouquet reeks of mash in the first nosing, then it settles down into a homogenized, cereal-with-sugar nose by the third pass—in the last nosing it's impossible to pick out any one or two defining attributes—if anything, Ultima's fragrance leans to Speyside, but don't put that in ink; in the mouth, there's a flame upon entry, then steamed-white-rice and toasty flavors come into play at midpalate; the clean finish is where this Scotch whisky hodgepodge does its best work, as sweet, cereally, oily, and mature flavors, at last, show flashes of harmony; so, is Ultima the mother of all Scotch blends?—it's as close as anyone will ever come; and, is Ultima currently the best blended Scotch? no way, not as long as there's Royal Salute to be had—in fact, as nice as Ultima is, I believe that Jim Milne's swank J.E.T. runs neck-and-neck with it.

RATING ★ ★ ★ ★   *Highly Recommended* $$$

J & B Select Blended Scotch Whisky 40% Alcohol

Substantial, medium gold/hay color; the nose is a sexy, piquant melange of aromas, headlined by hints of Islay peatiness, Lowland sweetness, and Speyside elegance—it's a sensual, sherried bouquet (the blend was aged in sherry casks for part of its maturation phase), which classily incorporates the best of Scotland's whisky regions; on palate, the range of flavor is narrower than the range of aroma, as the nutty, fino sherry quality is nicely accented within the grain-whisky structure of sweet corn; finishes cleanly, then goes smoky in the tail end; this savory blend is light years ahead of the leaner, lighter, and much fruitier J & B Rare in the sensory gratification department.

RATING ★ ★ ★   *Recommended* $

J & B Rare Blended Scotch Whisky 43% Alcohol

One of the palest Scotches of all—a lemon/green color that reminded more of dry white Bordeaux than Scotch whisky; feathery-soft, very fruity, pencil-eraser, pleasantly sweet nose, which offers a bit of of anise and licorice as well; goes down awfully well on the palate as benign flavors of ripe fruit, sweet corn, and malt mildly enchant, but never overwhelm, the taste buds; the aftertaste is medium-long and echoes the frivolous taste; while it takes no chances or prisoners in its cautious style, it's acceptable as an entry-level Scotch; yet I still find Rare too ethereal, too vacuous to recommend.

RATING ★ $

Johnnie Walker Gold Label 18-Year-Old Blended Scotch Whisky 40% Alcohol

Light amber/orange color, good purity; the malty nose sings with cocoa, buttered nuts, and very soft fruit, even a note of paraffin; the oily mouth presence is really exceptional, as an ultraclean, but bosomy texture forms the foundation for the sweet and estery flavors of ripe pears, grain mash, and oak—the sheer elegance of the mouth-feel is alone worth three stars; the aftertaste exposes a peppery, almost candied backnote that may be too sweet for some Scotch drinkers; tasted side-by-side with the three times as expensive Johnnie Walker Blue (three-star rating) and preferred hands-down over the Blue; 15 whiskies are included in this old blend, which was first developed in 1920—the heart and soul of JW Gold is the malt from the Northern Highlands distillery, Clynelish—other malts involved include Cardhu from Speyside, Talisker from Skye, and Royal Lochnagar from the Eastern Highlands; the finest Johnnie Walker blend in the marketplace—a genuine dazzler.

RATING ★ ★ ★ ★   *Highly Recommended* $$

JOHNNIE WALKER Black Label 12-Year-Old Blended Scotch Whisky 40% Alcohol

Absolutely luminous deep-amber color with stunning copper/sunset highlights—by a country mile, one of the four or five most eye-catching blends; the salty, high-octane, pungent Talisker imprint comes out freely in the nose, but carries with it the unflappable confidence of age; the medium-bodied, slightly salty flavor has bucketloads of refinement, much more so than the mundane Red Label; on palate, it begins dry and peaty but ends semisweet in the long, ripe apple, grapy, and malty aftertaste; a class act all the way.

RATING ★ ★ ★   *Recommended* $$

JOHNNIE WALKER Blue Label Blended Scotch Whisky 40% Alcohol

Lively medium-amber hue, with harvest-gold highlights; the gentlemanly peach- and apricot-like forward nose is finely layered, with foundational aromas of black pepper, wood smoke, glycerine, and a soft, lilting peatiness—by no means is this bouquet a blockbuster—it's reserved, even restrained, but warm, inviting, and complex, with a moderately sweet roasted-cereal perfume; the taste begins rather sweet and oaky/vanilla, then throws a rolling wave of peat smoke that carries the taste buds all the way to the extended, civilized finish; a handsomely made, polite, and mildly oily blend that's definitely a *digestif*-style sipping whisky; a prudent, seamless blend that's more a Mercedes than a Land Rover; JW Blue, while very good, still didn't inspire visions of the Great Beyond and, most importantly, I seriously question the wisdom of the ridiculously overinflated price tag.

RATING ★ ★ ★   *Recommended* $$$

JOHNNIE WALKER Red Label Blended Scotch Whisky 40% Alcohol

Commonplace amber color; the nose is very sturdy, seaweedy, and piquant, clearly directed more toward a salty Hebrides style than a Speyside style—the guiding hand of dashing, tony Talisker is indelibly planted; on palate, the iodine/seaweed presence leaps out at you; the flavor then goes soft, silky, and feline in the peaty, kippery finish; a moderately attractive, assertive but mannered blend that ably comes through with some measure of Scotch delights; a better mixer than a neat Scotch; I personally think that the blend seems thinner than it was even a decade ago, though frankly I've never cared for JW Red; okay, but too pedestrian and boring.

RATING ★ $

Martin's VVO Blended Scotch Whisky 40% Alcohol

Good clarity, firm amber/light-honey tone; I changed sample glasses twice and poured different batches to discern if the mushroomy, musty, off-odor was from my glasses or from the whisky—I concluded definitely that it's the whisky—major points off for the skunky, musty bouquet; paper-thin in the mouth, showing a bit more virtue in the flavor, but still it's a flimsy, see-through blend that offers no stuffing whatsoever—this lemon isn't even close to being pleasant; the raspy, jagged finish burns slightly; nowheresville, continue moving past it when you see it on your liquor merchant's shelf; the VVO must stand for Very, Very Offensive.

RATING ★ $

Muirhead's Blended Scotch Whisky 40% Alcohol

Dullish, medium amber/dark straw hue—strangely, the light from my evaluation lamp is diffused in this fuzzy appearance; typical sweetish, candied, sugary, cereal-grain, whisky bouquet that shows little in the way of dimension or depth—it's all upfront, no nuance, no subtlety; the taste is a mirror image of the aroma—a sweet, hard-candy, sugar-on-morning-cereal flavor that's not unpleasant, but way too simplistic and superficial all the same; in view of its clear lack of substance and charm and after two retastes, I chose to downgrade it to one-star territory.

RATING ★ $

Old Smuggler Blended Scotch Whisky 40% Alcohol

Gold/amber color; the pleasantly zesty, perky, piquant, floral, maize-like nose is more grainy than fruity, but exhibits some genuine pizzaz; the full, rich, graceful bearing and generous flavors impressed my palate; the mouth-puckering finish is terrific, as waves of charcoal, English toffee, and caramel combine in a focused effort; one of the more harmonious inexpensive blends I've tasted; buy by the magnum.

RATING ★ ★ ★   *Recommended* $

Original Mackinley Blended Scotch Whisky 40% Alcohol

Rich gold/amber color; in the assertive, fragrant, dry nose of dry cereal (in particular, shredded wheat and puffed rice) there's a trace of smoke that lends a degree of robustness; it ably carries itself onto the palate in a remarkably sweet and elegant manner that's balanced but not aggressive; the satiny texture is a total joy; well-defined flavors of cocoa, sweetened cerreal, and a bit of vanilla make this one of the better blends I've tasted; the aftertaste is sweet, compact, and substantial.

RATING ★ ★ ★   *Recommended* $

Passport Blended Scotch Whisky 40% Alcohol

Pale straw/yellow color; the pedestrian nose reminds me of unbuttered popcorn and has meek additional scents of black pepper, wet fabric, very mild peat, and corn grain; it starts out dry and somewhat harsh at palate entry, then shows a flash of corn sweetness but not a lick of complexity or flavor range; the finish is sweet, simple, and fat; beyond that, there's nothing much to expound on; pass on it in favor of the better inexpensive blends, which are readily available.

RATING ★　　$

PIG'S NOSE Blended Scotch Whisky 40% Alcohol

Interesting, burnt-orange color, with reddish highlights; the heavy iodine, estery, corn husk/corn mash nose is dominated by the grain spirits, which, I would guess from the aroma, is composed mostly of maize rather than wheat; it's a zesty, tangy, tongue-tingler in the mouth, as sweet, very smoky, and tobacco-like tastes arrest the palate; quite smooth and sweet in the quick, but potent finish; after my third evaluation of this blend I have to admit that, despite its weird name, I was surprised and impressed with the character—I certainly liked it more after not sampling it for about three years—perhaps the most recent blend is of a higher quality; the painfully silly name comes from the insightful assessment that the whisky is as soft as a porker's proboscis.

RATING ★★　　$

PINCH THE DIMPLE 15-Year-Old Blended Scotch Whisky 43% Alcohol

Engaging amber/orange color; the serious, assertive, aldehydic, dry nose offers subtle hints of hay, cooked rice, corn husk, iodine, and toasted cereal; Pinch shifts into overdrive once on the palate as voluptuous tastes of smoke, iodine, and soft peat come together in a graceful, well-coordinated dance of flavor; it ends rather smokily with a sweet, toffee tail; no question but that the 15 years of aging really makes the difference in this medium- to full-bodied Scotch, in which the various components complement each other beautifully; a prime example of the glories of blending; the artistry of the Haig & Haig master blender shines in this succulent, distinguished whisky; hats off to this one; one of the top ten blended Scotches available in the marketplace.

RATING ★★★★　　*Highly Recommended*　　$$

QUEEN ANNE Blended Scotch Whisky (Bottled in U.S.) 40% Alcohol

Standard-issue amber/honey color; exceedingly soft nose of grain whisky—a downright timid, grainy aroma that will never be used to launch a thousand ships; on the palate, it shows a cloyingly candied flavor that puts a lock on the taste buds and throws away the key; somebody should fire the chap in control of the caramel additive—he's gone hog wild in this insipid, sickeningly sweet, totally boring blend; what are they trying to cover up with the sweetness, I wonder; maybe Queen Anne expired from this bathtub moonshine and so it's been named in her dubious honor; a disgrace, no other word for it; suspiciously identical in almost every aspect to Cluny.

RATING ★　　$

ROYAL SALUTE 21-Year-Old Blended Scotch Whisky 40% Alcohol

Produced by Chivas Bros.; firm, medium amber color, perfect clarity; the nose was backward and dumb during the first nosing, then it opened up incrementally over the next three passes—what was there was a fetching, mature breath of Speyside, that magically refined, floral, beautifully structured, finesse-filled bouquet of the world's greatest whisky district—when it's in full flight, it's a gorgeous, memorable perfume; decadent, satiny on the tongue, it gives off splendidly ripe and balanced flavors of dried fruit, lightly peated malt, old oak, and dry cereal at entry, then at midpalate a succulent, candied sweetness and embers-like warmth mesmerize and bedazzle the taste buds; the aftertaste is luxurious, sweet, and wonderfully refined; I have, at long last, found my five-star blended Scotch; Royal Salute is the ideal marriage of maturity, elegance, and quiet power; this is the finest blended Scotch whisky in existence—a prototype and a benchmark.

RATING ★ ★ ★ ★ ★   *Highest Recommendation* $$$

SCORESBY Rare Blended Scotch Whisky 40% Alcohol

Tawny/honey color; the softly fragrant nose offers aromas of sweet corn and cream; the pleasantly candied, piquant, peaty, tea-like flavors are nicely balanced and married; medium-weighted, silky texture; medium-fast finish of malt and ripe fruit; a good, if very average blend, but I find it easy to understand why this affable brand has enjoyed great success in the U.S. market in the last few years.

RATING ★ ★ $

SOMETHING SPECIAL 12-Year-Old Blended Scotch Whisky 40% Alcohol

Lively amber/orange color; there's something strangely sour in the grainy, tart green-apple nose—I think the problem lies squarely on the observation that there's hardly any evidence of single-malt fragrance—the sour, cornhusk, grain-whisky aroma leaves no room for anything else to emerge; as lackluster as the overbearing nose is, the flavor displays genuine single-malt depth, as waves of peat, oak/vanilla, wheat toast, cedar, and cinnamon treat the taste buds to a multileveled flavor experience; it finishes very long, sweet, and stately; forget the nose and proceed right to the sipping.

RATING ★ ★ ★   *Recommended* $$

SPEY CAST Deluxe 12-Year-Old Blended Scotch Whisky 40% Alcohol

Solid, dark gold/amber color; the low-key nose gives away very little even after vigorous swirling and ample aeration time—a mildly sweet, biscuity, candied, spirit-cake aroma is all I pick up; it begins very sweet and intensely candied at palate entry and remains so through the aftertaste, which offers a background taste of orange peel; goes too far off the sweet scale for me to take it seriously; additionally, the concentrated, syrupy sweetness makes me wonder about what, if anything, was added to punch up the sugar meter; a Scotch that makes me go, hmmmmmm?

RATING ★ $$

SPEYSIDE 21-Year-Old Blended Scotch Whisky 43% Alcohol

Rather ordinary amber color; nose-tweaking, phenolic aromas of freshly mown hay and rice pudding hold court in the astringent, somewhat medicinal nose, which seemed younger than its 21 years; after the less than enthralling appearance and nose, this agile blend really kicks it into overdrive on the palate as intense, deep, and completely melded flavors of oak, glycerine, lanolin, sherry, and candied almonds stormed the beach of my taste buds, which happily surrendered; forgiving the label, which pretentiously states "The Best Whisky in the World" (what, they never heard of single malts called The Macallan 18-year-old or Cragganmore 12-year-old or blends such as Royale Salute?) it's evident that this is one of the better Scotch blends available in the U.S.; a scrumptious whisky whose flavor and aftertaste are so compelling that they convincingly redeem the lackluster appearance and pedestrian nose.

RATING ★ ★ ★ ★   *Highly Recommended* $$$

Stewart's Cream of the Barley Blended Scotch Whisky 40% Alcohol (Available only in the U.K.)

Pretty gold/amber color; the delightfully sweet, perfumed, mown-hay-like nose displays a decidedly potent, malty, floral inclination; firm and generous in the mouth, with sweet, creamy flavors of malt, yet I felt there was something missing in the flavor; the exceedingly smooth but virile finish gives off a pleasant bite in the throat; this one almost has the whole package—power, smoothness, and presence—what it sorely lacks is a dynamite, satisfying midpalate experience; tasted at the Glencadam Distillery in Scotland.

RATING ★ ★ ★   *Recommended* $$

Usquaebach Deluxe 8-Year-Old Blended Scotch Whisky 43% Alcohol

Brilliant, light amber/orange hue, perfect clarity; I liked this round, toasty, spirity, almond-like, slightly piquant bouquet very much, more for its prickly zest than for its depth of character, which is not inconsiderable—the final nosing pass revealed a kicky, caramel-corn/Cracker Jack aromatic wave; this is a vibrant, muscular mouthful right from the entry, as sweet, toffee-like, caramel-candy flavors rule from the outset, eventually settling down by midpalate and finally turning grapy in the gentlemanly aftertaste; sturdy, sweet, heavily malted, and throat-warming—I loved every moment.

RATING ★ ★ ★ ★   *Highly Recommended* $$

Usquaebach Reserve Blended Scotch Whisky 43% Alcohol

Gorgeous, vibrant, honey/amber color; one of the most beguiling noses in the entire blended-Scotch-whisky category—perfumed, multilayered opulence, accentuated with roasted almonds, butter cream, sweet oak, and vanilla combine in a wonderful symphony of fragrance; luxurious, sweet, elegant, concentrated flavors of pepper, coffee, and sherry dazzle the taste buds; the sublime midpalate and long, heavenly aftertaste are remarkably balanced, supple, characterful, and graceful; after tasting scores of blended Scotch whiskies over the past ten years, I've concluded that this one runs with the elite; seek out and buy.

RATING ★ ★ ★ ★   *Highly Recommended* $$

Usquaebach Original Blended—Stonecrock Flagon 43% Alcohol

On the heels of my highly favorable reviews of the Usquaebach Reserve and Deluxe comes the older (18–27 years) version in the Stonecrock Flagon;

luxuriously opulent, golden honey tone; the finely scented, succulent nose evokes juniper berries, light peat, a hint of sherry, and spirit-marinated fruit—not aggressive in the least; upon entry to the palate, there's no mistaking the richness of the oaky/peaty flavor as it rolls over the tongue, but it's at the midpalate stage that this sensational whisky takes flight, with charcoally, spicy, tobacco-like tastes that reach far into the sublime aftertaste; in terms of quality and satisfaction it's every bit as grand as the superb Reserve and the decadent Deluxe; the blend is 85% malt/15% grain whisky and aged in sherry oak.

RATING ★ ★ ★ ★   ***Highly Recommended*** $$$

USQUAEBACH Special 12-Year-Old Blended Scotch Whisky 40% Alcohol

Available only in Japan; medium amber/light honey tone, right-on-the-money clarity; I found the nose on this curious 12-year-old to be disappointingly muted on the first two nosings—after 30 minutes of aeration, it begrudgingly woke up in the third pass, sending off pleasantly malty, dry-cereally, heathery/flowery aromas, with very subtle backnotes of peat smoke and maritime brine; the lean texture took me by surprise—it doesn't own the expected fleshiness for which I've come to admire Usquaebach whiskies; flavorwise, I picked up angular, rather monotonic tastes of sour grain and esters—the lackluster mouth presence left me totally cold; the finish is medium-long and grainy; by a wide margin, the least impressive offering to date from this stellar Scotch *négociant*.

RATING ★ ★ $$

WHITE HORSE Blended Scotch Whisky 40% Alcohol

Attractive, warm honey/gold color; the sweet, fruity nose leans to smoky peat more so than any other major production blend; a meaty, fleshy, substantial whisky that's semisweet on palate and ends seriously with a ripe fruit, sweet oak, and mildly peaty aftertaste that leaves a pleasing, comforting imprint of warmth; perfectly delightful when served neat or as a mixer; easily my favorite of the standard, inexpensive blends; a superb, friendly, generous whisky, which rivals and indeed even outshines some of the superpremium blends and a handful of single malts at a quarter of the price; unquestionably one of Scotch whisky's greatest all-around values.

RATING ★ ★ ★ ★   ***Highly Recommended*** $

WILLIAM GRANT'S Family Reserve Blended Scotch Whisky 43% Alcohol

Standard, pretty amber color; this nose is definitely of a Speyside bent—plump, oily, and semisweet, with layers of rubber, biscuit batter, and honeyed oatmeal; unmistakable familial influence of the Glenfiddich and Balvenie single malts in the comely, nectar-like flavor; tastes of almonds, toffee, chocolate, and vanilla extract abound from palate entry through to the lovely, candied aftertaste; I was admittedly smitten with this succulent and amply endowed blend, which offered truckloads of flavor and true complexity.

RATING ★ ★ ★   ***Recommended*** $

Single-Malt, Pure-Malt, Single-Grain Scotch, and Special-Bottling Grain Whiskies

ABERFELDY 1978 Central Highlands Single Malt 43% Alcohol—Whyte & Whyte Label

Pale yellow/flaxen color; on the first nosing, it comes off as being moderately robust, candied, honey-like, weedy, but not quite fruity in the assertive bouquet, then with 20 minutes of aeration, a fruit assault hits the nose like a beach invasion—the end result is a very appealing aroma; this malt rolls onto the tongue like a purring Bentley gliding down the M25—it's a gorgeous palate entry that's equal parts finesse and power; the midpalate goes to industrial-strength smokiness, the plume of smoke obliterating all other flavors; the finish is chunky, pleasingly sweet, and succulent, a genuine winner that simply needs some time in the glass to develop.

RATING ★ ★ ★ ★   *Highly Recommended* $$$

ABERLOUR 25-Year-Old Speyside Single Malt 43% Alcohol

Gorgeous, deep amber/chestnut mature color; a teeth-curling, potent single malt that rumbles like thunder in the tasting glass; the heady, sweet malt, oak cask aromas gracefully waft up from the glass in measured, but confident waves; very satisfying, satiny on palate, with a robust, honey/sugarcane foundation; seemingly endless, ripe tropical-fruit finish; the sherry component is evident from the first nosing pass through to the extended aftertaste; a scarce limited edition, consisting of only 10,000 bottles worldwide; one of the finest 25-year-olds around and most appropriately served alone as a *digestif*; evaluated six times, scored with four stars four of those times.

RATING ★ ★ ★ ★   *Highly Recommended* $$$

ABERLOUR Antique Very Fine Aged Speyside Single Malt 43% Alcohol

Tasted at the distillery; not available in U.S.; a very attractive dark amber/burnt-orange tone, perfect purity; the nose is intensely fruity, especially red fruit, but also shows ample evidence of oily, resiny oak in the foreground—it's a round, supple, and highly spirited bouquet that has been kissed by sherry oak more than once; on palate, I believe the Antique to be the most elegant of the Aberlours that I've sampled—the fruit once again steals the show from entry to finish, but beneath the surface fruit lies a sturdy, mature, oak base flavor that supports the entire experience; the aftertaste is very full and spicy, with a dash of vanillin/oakiness thrown in for good measure and some balance; for those single-malt aficionados who think that Macallan and Singleton are the only sherry-influenced Speyside blockbusters, try any Aberlour.

RATING ★ ★ ★ ★   *Highly Recommended* $$$

Aberlour 10-Year-Old Speyside Single Malt 43% Alcohol

The Aberlour Distillery is one of Scotland's most modern and fastidiously clean; deep, rich amber/clover honey hue, brilliant clarity; this is a first-rate Speyside single malt, aged both in old bourbon and old sherry casks; this beefy 10-year-old owns a luxurious, bountifully rich, almond-like bouquet, which is delightfully piquant—the use of sherry casks is clearly evident in the wine-like, heady aroma; in the mouth, soft, malty undertones, concentrated fruitiness, multilayered complexity, and even a vague hint of spearmint play games on the tongue; the long, generous finish confirms the sherry presence; for admirers of Speyside's meatier, thicker expression.

RATING ★ ★ ★   *Recommended* $$

Ardbeg 1974 Islay Single Malt 43% Alcohol—The Signatory Series

Attractive, strong amber/orange hue; ahhh, that sea-breeze, peaty, salty bouquet that could only come from an Islay malt—this saline aroma has loads of perky iodine to prick the nose cavity—I love it because it so accurately mirrors the environment of Islay and also because it's under control—while some Islay malts bludgeon you to death with peat smell, this one doesn't; the intense smokiness on the palate, however, may be too punishing for some Scotch drinkers—this is a taste that's reserved only for the most ardent fanatics of Islay "peat reek"; the smoke/peat element dominates from palate entry through to the beguiling, sweet (cherry?), pipe smoke aftertaste; a brawny, rugged mouthful, to be sure, but one that does it with style and balance.

RATING ★ ★ ★   *Recommended* $$$

Ardmore 12-Year-Old Speyside Single Malt 56.2% Alcohol—The James MacArthur Series

Vibrant, medium straw/gold/white-wine appearance; the concentrated, grainy, mashy, steamed-rice, and corn-husk aromas dominate this agreeable, if unmemorable, nose; a heavy-handed maltiness/peatiness comes through on the astringent palate; after aeration, the second pass offered a finish that displayed a fleeting sherry/fruit element, then proceeded to get searingly hot, burning the throat in a less than graceful exit; take a pass on this rock 'em, sock 'em fire eater.

RATING ★ $$$

Auchentoshan 18-Year-Old Lowland Single Malt 43% Alcohol

Author's note: The correct pronunciation is "aw-ken-taw-shen." From the most elite distillery in the Lowlands comes this medium-amber-hued stunner; its bouquet is alluringly soft, but regal and firm, as scents of dry cereal with sugar, sweet oak, and yellow fruit bathe the olfactory sense in authentic splendor; on palate, it's as sleek and sensuous as in the smell—well-proportioned flavors of lightly toasted malt, honey-wheat bread, and dried fruit bedazzle the taste buds; the finish is compact and deep; another sterling performer from this top-notch distillery; no longer available in U.S.

RATING ★ ★ ★ ★   *Highly Recommended* $$$

Auchentoshan 21-Year-Old Lowland Single Malt 43% Alcohol

Triple-distilled; the goldenrod/amber hue is gorgeous, even voluptuous; the sweet, maple-sap nose is peppery, zesty, and piquant—I greatly admire this frisky nose because it possesses the feline charm that comes only from Scotland's Lowlands and, in particular, from Auchentoshan, which for my money is the prototypical Lowland malt distillery—no other region in Scotland produces such a seductively feminine bouquet, or should I say perfume?; in the mouth, the sweet vivacious (this is a 21-year-old?) flavors of toffee, oak, and vanilla (from bourbon casks?) are approachable, warm, and deep, but not ponderous; white pepper and toffee dominate the savory aftertaste; my top choice as the quintessential Lowland single malt; it doesn't get better.

RATING ★ ★ ★ ★   *Highly Recommended* $$$

Auchentoshan 10-Year-Old Lowland Single Malt 43% Alcohol

Triple-distilled; sound, golden/hay/light amber appearance, ideal purity; the diverse aromas include ginger, citrus, minerals, ale, and corn—it's a youthful bouquet that's showing a bit of awkwardness, but it's still one of the best 10-year-old aromas you can find; in the mouth, oily, rich tastes of blueberries, heather, pears, and apricots are present and accounted for; the aftertaste is deliciously oily and waxy; a sweet, willowy malt that's a showcase for the Lowlands.

RATING ★ ★ ★   *Recommended* $$

Auchentoshan Select Lowland Single Malt 40% Alcohol

Triple-distilled; intense, wine-like yellow tone which is strikingly reminiscent of either a big vintage Montrachet or an average vintage Sauternes; this is a young (5- to 7-year-old) malt, but I would have guessed it by the color and the immaturity of the distillery-like nose—by that I mean that the aroma clearly still has more of the distilling influence than the oak-aging influence; the uncomplicated nose is all flowers and barley malt; the taste is decidedly sweet and so succulent that if you're alone you want to smack your lips—suffice it to say, I was alone; the candied finish is quicksilver fast and thus disappointing; an ideal starter kit for malt-maven wannabes; veterans of the malt game will want something more challenging.

RATING ★ ★ $

Balblair 10-Year-Old Northern Highlands Single Malt 57% Alcohol—The Gordon & MacPhail Series

Deep, amontillado-sherry-like, tawny/amber/copper hue; the atypical nose puzzles me right off the starting block—what is it I'm smelling?—it's sweet, but neither candied nor fruity—it's slightly phenolic (meaning medicinal), but without astringency, which is normally associated with the medicine-chest aroma—I detect low levels of malt, rice, and oats, backed by a very faint whiff of citrus, especially yellow grapefruit and later on even a dash of dry, yeasty fino sherry; holds court on the tongue with a fleshy, fat texture and varied sweet tastes ranging from ripe grapes to candied apples to peppermint to cocoa to smoke; it finishes strongly in the throat as a butter-cream candy flavor brings it home—in the tail end of the aftertaste this unusual malt shows a flavor/feel quality usually found only in very old cognacs, namely, the renowned *rancio;* what a memorable ride this special bottling provides.

RATING ★ ★ ★ ★   ***Highly Recommended*** $$$

BALVENIE

Balvenie is the sister distillery to Glenfiddich, which is literally right next door. Both are owned by William Grant & Sons. The correct pronunciation is "bal-vee-nee."

BALVENIE 10-Year-Old "Founder's Reserve" Speyside Single Malt
43% Alcohol

Brilliant, luminous, medium amber/honey tone—absolute clarity; the bountiful, estery, citrusy, malty Speyside bouquet that's long been a personal favorite of mine continues to enchant, as solid, floral/fruity scents show just the right balance—seems more mature than a 10-year-old in the elegant, wine-like nose; in the mouth, the succulent fruit flavor is ripe and sweet, but not in the least bit cloying—the midpalate sensation introduces a dash of smoke, but the main event in the flavor is the sweet-malt/citrus combination, which guides the taste buds along into the refined, well-behaved, medium-long finish that is simply luscious; a top-notch Speyside favoring grain and fruit, especially citrus/tangerine, in a whisky that oozes finesse; my pick for the leading candidate as Scotland's premier 10-year-old single malt.

RATING ★ ★ ★ ★   ***Highly Recommended*** $$

BALVENIE 12-Year-Old "Doublewood" Speyside Single Malt
43% Alcohol

Author's note: The "Doublewood" designation means that the malts involved in this bottling were first matured in old bourbon casks, then transferred to sherry casks for further aging. Dark amber color with a trace of orange in the core; this pronounced, sassy, bacon-fat aroma is far different than that of the more understated Founder's Reserve—peppery, slightly peaty, smoky components amply contribute to the zesty, sherry quality of this superbly balanced nose; the heightened level of richness (due undoubtedly to the sherry oak) is evident right from palate entry as a vanilla cream/caramel flavor, so reminiscent of oloroso sherry, delights the palate— at the midpalate point, the vanilla cream turns into a sweet malt flavor that lasts well into the endless aftertaste; this is a round, full-bodied, well-endowed, toffee, sweet smoke Speyside that's taken the best virtues of both types of oak barrel and made the most of them.

RATING ★ ★ ★ ★   ***Highly Recommended*** $$

BALVENIE 15-Year-Old Single-Barrel Speyside Single Malt
50.4% Alcohol

Author's note: Only 300 bottles per individual cask—every bottle is numbered and each cask is identified on the label. Rich, deep amber hue and excellent clarity. The sweetish, heady nose explodes from the glass as much from the elevated alcohol as from the piquant, honeyed oak element—like a bugler sounding reveille, it's a rousing, aggressive, bulldozer of a bouquet that picks up steam with aeration; in the mouth, this vivacious malt begins its taste journey in a predictably rambunctious manner, again the alcohol making itself known immediately—by midpalate it settles down somewhat into a biscuity, full-bodied, honey/sherry Speyside that is round and oaky but neither mellow nor sublime; the finish is clearly its strong suit, as the alcohol diminishes enough to allow the other, more pleasing flavor components of vanilla, sherry, and even cream to emerge; I salute William Grant for having the guts to offer a single-barrel malt, even if at the end of the day I prefer the 12-year-old and the 10-year-old.

RATING ★ ★ ★   Recommended $$$

BEN NEVIS 27-Year-Old Western Highlands Single Malt 54% Alcohol—The James MacArthur Series

Author's note: The correct pronunciation is "ben neh-vis." The amber/honey-gold color is very attractive; the nose is fruity, forward, and assertive, with toffee/sherry aromas upfront, but underneath lies an oily, coconut core that's inviting and delicious—so much for the good news; unfortunately, the malt is so strenuously showcased in the flavor that little else seems to be happening—there's simply no room for any other flavor element; the aftertaste shows a sweet element of lanolin, but that too falls beneath the wheels of the malt/wet-cereal juggernaut; too much of a one-note melody for me.

RATING ★ $$$

BENRIACH 1976 Speyside Single Malt 40% Alcohol—The Spirit of Scotland Series

Honey/amber/orange appearance; an immediate and firm aroma of white-grape raisins hits the sense of smell straight on, followed by lesser scents of pears, bananas, and peaches—it's one of the fruitiest single-malt noses I've experienced; this ambrosial malt delivers in a big way on the palate, as firm, sure-footed flavors of toffee, oak, vanilla, passion fruit, and mango combine perfectly; the finish is semisweet, honeyed, and altogether charming.

RATING ★ ★ ★ ★   Highly Recommended $$$

BENRIACH 10-Year-Old Speyside Single Malt 43% Alcohol

Author's note: Part of the Heritage Selection from the House of Seagram. The correct pronunciation is "ben-ree-ickh." Light-to-medium amber/ harvest-gold hue, perfect clarity; the soft, but intriguingly prickly nose has jalapeno pepper, black pepper, and malt extract in abundance—what's so interesting is that while this paradoxical nose is pillowy soft, there's still a zesty piquancy to it that I found very alluring—it kept my attention; the sweet, grainy flavor focuses almost exclusively on the malt component, leaving behind any fruitiness—the warming, mashy, toasty flavors that occupy the taste buds and the olfactory cavity are well integrated and vibrant; the finish is clean, firm, and cereal-like in its sweetness; this is a relatively youthful single malt and I can't help but wonder what a 12- or even a 14-year-old version would be like; in any event, this solid 10-year-old easily pleases.

RATING ★ ★ ★   *Recommended* $$

BLADNOCH 1980 Lowlands Single Malt; Alcohol n/a—Whyte & Whyte Label

Author's note: The correct pronunciation is "blad-nok." Pretty light amber/yellow gold color, excellent clarity; the engaging nose of butterscotch, hazelnut, walnut, citrus, and nougat is piquant and attention-getting—this Bladnoch doesn't even approach being grassy or floral, the usual pair of fragrances that are frequently associated with malts from the Lowlands—for a Lowlands malt, this aroma is a blockbuster; there's measured heat at palate entry, then the spicy flavors swing around into an oaky/vanilla/nutty mode that is light-to-medium in body; the midpalate turns caramelly sweet; it finishes compactly and firmly, no loose ends or extravagant parting gestures; a genuinely superlative malt from Scotland's southernmost malt distillery.

RATING ★ ★ ★ ★   *Highly Recommended* $$$

BOWMORE

The Bowmore Distillery, located on the western Hebrides island of Islay, is in my top echelon of Scotland's whisky operations. Of the eight licensed distilleries on Islay, Bowmore claims to be the oldest, citing establishment in 1779 by David Simpson. The Bowmore distillery rests in the town of the same name and is situated on the Loch Indaal inlet in the dead center of Islay. Bowmore is intensely community-minded. A few years ago, an indoor, year-round swimming pool was constructed for the townspeople. If you ever visit dank, blustery Islay, you'll comprehend how significant a gift that pool is. Bowmore whiskies are miles apart in style from both the husky, peat-laden filling-crackers that are made on the island's southeastern edge (Laphroaig, Lagavulin, Port Ellen, and Ardbeg) and the light- to medium-bodied, more gentlemanly single malts of Bunnahabhain, Caol Ila, and Bruichladdich to the north. With the exception of one, Bowmore's exquisitely made single malts lie somewhere in between. Describing Bowmore's house style in a few words, I'd say that their single malts are elegant, classy, and mouthfilling. They possess the poise of Speyside's best with the muscle of traditional Islay malt.

BOWMORE 30-Year-Old Islay Single Malt 43% Alcohol

Brilliant, luminous, medium-deep amber/burnished-gold color, perfect clarity; the complexity and breadth of the nose are staggering—it opens with succulent, oily, briny waves, then in the second pass it adds iodine—the third and fourth passes are multilayered and as profound as any Bowmore aroma—the overlapping fragrances dance in perfect harmony—one of the two or three greatest Islay bouquets; in the mouth, the melded, expansive, and elegant tastes of oak resin, sweet malt, sea air, brine, oloroso sherry, cake batter, cocoa, and caramel dazzle, but don't bulldoze the taste buds; the finish is long, sexy, oily, and intensely sweet; easily deserves to be a five-star malt; sampled blind in a flight that included Bowmore 17, 22, 25, and La-gavulin 16.

RATING ★ ★ ★ ★ ★   *Highest Recommendation* $$$

Bowmore 25-Year-Old (Distilled 1968) Islay Single Malt 43% Alcohol

Deep amber/honey tone; the juicy, ripe, red apple, wine-like, peppery nose is so well integrated and defined that I feel it's a textbook example of how an Islay single malt should smell in the optimum circumstances—the extraordinary richness and depth of character are perfectly complemented by background notes of salt air and peat; tastewise, I believe from my own evaluations that the only other Islay malt that compares and probably even tops this 25-year-old beauty by the slimmest of margins is Black Bowmore; the entry is of orange peel, tangerines, oloroso sherry, sweet oak, resin, chocolate toffee, honey, pipe smoke, red cherry, and mild, subdued peat; the aftertaste is as smooth as glass and as warm as smoldering embers; doubt-less one of the finest single malts to be found in the mainstream marketplace and easily worth every penny; an utterly sensational, perfect Islay malt.

RATING ★ ★ ★ ★ ★   *Highest Recommendation* $$$

Black Bowmore 1964 Islay Single Malt 48% Alcohol

Immensely eye-catching oloroso-sherry color of walnut brown edged with gold; this blockbuster, pruney nose promises sherry on all levels—it's sweet, direct, perfumed, woody, and magical; a note of caution: It definitely needs a few drops of water, because of the intensity of the sherry oak influ-ence; on palate, this classic sings as easily as Ella Fitzgerald swinging into Cole Porter's "Night and Day"; the sherry is potent, to be sure, but it's never for a moment clumsy or cloying; the rich extract is mind-boggling; it fin-ishes in an unhurried wave of ripe grapes, vanilla, honey, and cocoa; my choice for the malt I want if ever I'm trapped on a desert isle; one of the nine or ten greatest distilled-spirit experiences I've had.

RATING ★ ★ ★ ★ ★   *Highest Recommendation* $$$

Bowmore 17-Year-Old Islay Single Malt 43% Alcohol

Majestic orange/bronze/amber color; this is one of Islay's most elegant, piquant, and sumptuous bouquets, at once graceful and brawny, sublime and racy—to my way of thinking, this is one of Islay's two or three sexiest noses; in the mouth, this sinewy 17-year-old is silky, firm, sweet, sherried, elegant, and succulent, without the least hint of bite or harshness; the fin-ish is round and focused, as a sweet oakiness dominates in an extended af-tertaste; one of the two best Islay delights in the 16- to 18-year range (La-gavulin 16 being the other).

RATING ★ ★ ★ ★   *Highly Recommended* $$

Bowmore 21-Year-Old Islay Single Malt 43% Alcohol

Pretty medium-amber color; the astoundingly piquant, downright sassy, peppery, head-snapping, iodine nose fills the nostrils faster than a chicken running from Colonel Sanders—this salty, peaty aroma takes no prisoners—

it's the type of feisty island Scotch bouquet that you either love or hate—well, me Bucko, my sentiments come down squarely on the love side if for no other reason than it so accurately tells the story of what Islay is all about—sea breeze and peat; it's only for a flash in the palate entry that the sherry influence shows its face, then just as quickly the sherry is dramatically overtaken by an intense sweet smokiness that grabs control of the wheel and floors it to the finish line; in a wonderful twist, the sherry reemerges in the infinite aftertaste; a supple and truly exciting single malt that runs with the best from the island.

RATING ★ ★ ★ ★   *Highly Recommended* $$$

BOWMORE 22-Year-Old Islay Single-Malt Scotch 43% (Scotland)

Stunning, medium amber/orange/honey color, perfect purity; this sinewy nose has the trademark Bowmore aroma that marries finesse, a manageable amount of salty sea breeze, and understated power—the initial pass is dry, then the aroma goes off-dry in the second and third passes as a notably seductive nuttiness takes hold on the surface—the last nosing underlines the Islay pedigree as the briny quality comes to the forefront; on palate, the brine/iodine character plays the lead in a way that doesn't overshadow the maltiness, nuttiness, or richness—the midpalate is opulent and shows just a quick fiery flash of heat; the keynote speaker in the aftertaste is definitely the sea breeze; not as grand as the 25-year-old, but still a superlative Islay malt that delivers the Bowmore message with style.

RATING ★ ★ ★ ★   *Highly Recommended* $$$

BOWMORE 1988 Islay Single Malt 45% Alcohol—Whyte & Whyte Label

Very pale yellow/flaxen hue, perfect clarity; the appetizing bouquet owns the aromatic trademark of Bowmore, a bridled Islay saltiness balanced by a Speyside-like elegance; assertive, but mannered aromas of light peat, brine, and steamed asparagus team up beautifully in this zesty nose; on the palate, the zestiness translates initially into a tart, tight, peppery entry, then by midpalate the sweet, medium-weighted, almost creamy flavor leans more to finesse than to muscle; the finish is extended, off-dry to sweet, mildly fruity, and, in a word, luscious.

RATING ★ ★ ★ ★   *Highly Recommended* $$$

BOWMORE 10-Year-Old Islay Single Malt 43% Alcohol

Gorgeous, brilliant amber/new-copper-penny color that captures both the light and the eye; this sinewy malt owns the gracefully sweet, but briny, grain nose I've come to associate only with Bowmore malts—obviously the aromatic balance isn't as evolved as with the solid 17- and 21-year-olds, or the stupendous 25-year-old Bowmores, but it's a splendid, clean, and succulent bouquet nevertheless, leaving many other 10-year-olds in the dust; on the palate, the ripe, mashy entry is decidedly sweet and malty, with a faint hint of salty seabreeze coming in by midpalate; the intense finish is a bit hot in the throat but not enough to knock off points.

RATING ★ ★ ★   *Recommended* $$

BOWMORE Legend Islay Single Malt 40% Alcohol

Gold/amber hue; the dead-giveaway nose of peat, briny salt air, wet wool, and smoke tell me only one thing, "Islay"—the problem here to me, however, is an all-too-evident lack of complexity, an ungainly youthfulness that's still green and immature—it's not a pleasant bouquet, just immature; highly medicinal in a sweet manner on the palate, the tastes of peat, salt, wood, and smoke simply haven't melded together into a harmonious unit, most probably because they haven't been given the time in oak to do so; this is my second tasting of this "no age stated" single malt, and my initial impression, which was unfavorable, was only bolstered by this second, more careful, controlled environment evaluation; I feel that a mistake (the only one Bowmore has made, to my knowledge) has been made by Bowmore in rushing unfinished single malt into the marketplace; the miracle of Glenfiddich, the world's largest selling malt and the original no-age-statement entry, won't be repeated by whiskies that aren't ready for consumption.

RATING ★ $

BRAES OF GLENLIVET (BRAEVAL) 1979 15-Year-Old Speyside Single Malt, Single-Barrel (Sherry) / Cask Strength; 59.2% Alcohol—Whyte & Whyte Label

Author's note: Operated by Chivas Bros., which is owned by Seagram, this rare bottling comes from an obscure malt distillery located in Speyside, whose malts are used exclusively (at this point) in blends, especially Chivas Regal and Royal Salute. The piquant nose is catapulted from the glass, propelled by the cask-strength alcohol (I can't even stick my nose into the bowl of the glass without it being shot off) in highly unusual scents of butterscotch, parchment, cotton linens, charcoal, smoke, fennel, oil, and more—it's the most astounding and confounding single-malt bouquet I've encountered in eight years of serious evaluations; the keen fire found burning at the palate entry could easily turn off the uninitiated, but for veteran and adventurous malt drinkers this husky, oily, remarkably intense, atypical Speyside malt offers one of the most memorable rides available; the butterscotch element in the aroma and taste is indelibly etched in my sensory recall file; what an experience.

RATING ★ ★ ★ ★   *Highly Recommended* $$$

BRORA 1972 Northern Highland Single Malt 40% Alcohol—The Spirit of Scotland Series

Author's note: Brora is a resort/golfing town on the north coast and likewise is a former name of the Clynelish Distillery. Painfully small amount remaining in scattered markets in the U.S.; pretty dead-on amber/orange tint, great clarity; there's a wallop of brine in the first nosing that had me labeling it an Islay malt when in fact it's from a now-closed Northern Highlands distillery that sits on the coast, hence the bracing sea breeze, saline aroma; sweet to the taste with backnote flavors of lemon peel, caramel, cooked rice, seaweed, and popcorn—it's an incredible melange of flavor that willingly confronts the taste buds—I admired and was not intimidated by its aggres-

siveness; the surprisingly timid finish stays with the sweetness, finally showing a tad of ripe fruit; what a dashing, daring mouthful.

    RATING ★ ★ ★ ★   ***Highly Recommended*** $$$

BRUICHLADDICH 1969 Islay Single Malt 43% Alcohol—The Signatory Series

    Author's note: Pronounced "brook laddie." Luminous amber/green color;
again, that unmistakable badge of seaweed, brine, peat, and iodine so closely
associated with Islay single malts flies into your face from the sampling
glass—and I draw attention to this only with the most complimentary of in-
tentions; the moderately sweet, woodsy tastes of juniper, evergreen/pine,
and oak are enchanting after the kippery bouquet; it's a strange, but completely convincing, combination of aroma and flavor; the finish is mature,
melded, and mildly sweet; a dandy of a vintage single malt and one that I
wouldn't mind having in my liquor cabinet.

    RATING ★ ★ ★   ***Recommended*** $$$

BRUICHLADDICH 15-Year-Old Islay Single Malt 43% Alcohol

    Almost identical, but slightly paler golden honey hue as the 10-year-old;
this aroma is much more assertive, richer, and downright fruity than the 10,
with charming components of rose petals, new car leather, sweetened coconut, ripe guava, and hints of oloroso sherry; I'm such a shameless fool
for 15- to 18-year-old single malts—aromatically this winner hit the spot;
on palate, I find more brininess than the 10, plus a bit too much heat perhaps at midpalate—it leaves my tongue tingling; the aggressive, acidic, medicinal flavors of iodine, tobacco smoke, seaweed, and soy sauce take command into the finish, which is very, very long and astringent; a clean, lean
Islay machine.

    RATING ★ ★ ★   ***Recommended*** $$

BRUICHLADDICH 10-Year-Old Islay Single Malt 43% Alcohol

    Strangely, this 10-year-old's color is marginally darker than either the 15-
or 21-year-old Bruichladdichs—"How could that be?" my inquiring brain
inquires; owns an exceedingly pleasant papaya, honeysuckle, floral, estery
nose, which barely hints of Islay brine—I like this settled, confident, fresh-
garden bouquet; in the mouth, it opens rather lamely, almost muted at entry,
then leaps forward with fourth-gear bursts of succulent, sweet, light toffee,
peppermint, and orange-blossom honey; the aftertaste leans toward the toffee element, but it's also vegetal, leafy, earthy, woodsy, and salty; a nice, lightish, unassuming dram.

    RATING ★ ★ $$

BRUICHLADDICH 21-Year-Old Islay Single Malt 43% Alcohol

    Amber/gold/honey color; the nose of this mature malt is far more elusive
than either the 10- or the 15-year-old—finally after too much aeration labor
from my side, I coaxed out traces of cream, nail polish, and lanolin; it starts
out crisp, briny, and clean in the mouth, then it breaks down into a sherry-
a-thon of overly sweet, almost cloying tastes, which approach liqueur sta-

tus only in the aftertaste; clearly on the downside of its chemical life cycle; adding insult to injury, it's even harsh and biting in the finish; nexxxxxxxxxxxt.

RATING ★ $$

BUNNAHABHAIN 1964 Islay Single Malt 46% Alcohol—The Signatory Series

Author's note: Pronounced "boo-nah-ha-ven." Medium yellow/straw/gold; I can't mistake the salty, maritime, island influence in this vigorous, zesty nose—the piquant, spicy, sassy, iodine character is so emblematic of fabled Islay malts; the snapping, crackling freshness on the tongue is delightful— well-structured flavors of oak, toffee, ripe fruit, and spirit are beautifully or- chestrated; the finish is medium-long and semisweet; the saline element in the nose moves to the shadows in the taste and the aftertaste, allowing the wood and fruit qualities ample room to stretch; Bunnahabhain at its classy best.

RATING ★ ★ ★   ***Recommended*** $$$

BUNNAHABHAIN 12-Year-Old Islay Single Malt 43% Alcohol

Deep goldenrod/almost amber color; its supple nose displays little of what we have come to expect from an Islay malt, as just a vague hint of peati- ness emerges through the rather odd coupling of sweetness and salt; no io- dine/peat monster here, which should put glee into the hearts of those who shudder at the thought of the Lagavulin-Laphroaig tag-team duo; forthright, slightly briny, heated flavors dominate the taste buds on entry, then de- murely fall away as this malt's more subtle, honeyed charms take the helm; quick, quiet aftertaste; decent, but unexciting.

RATING ★ ★ $$

CAOL ILA 1974 Islay Single Malt 61.1% Alcohol—The Signatory Series

Author's note: Pronounced "cull ee-lah." Very pale yellow/green, Sauvi- gnon Blanc–like color; the curious, sweet-sour nose juggles the biscuity, lemony, salty, and leathery aromatic components very deftly; as different from the chunky, lumberjack malts from Islay distilleries such as Ardbeg or Laphroaig as Mike Tyson is from Alan Alda—while very potent, this Islay gem walks a different path, a fruitier, more grainy path that makes the fla- vor seem quite gentle despite the high alcohol—it's an absolute delight; this is not to say that it's devoid of any briny aspect, because there most certainly is one—it's simply reined-in in favor of the outstanding fruit component; the balance between acid, alcohol, fruitiness, and oak is utterly superb; a masterfully crafted single malt of the first order.

RATING ★ ★ ★ ★   ***Highly Recommended*** $$$

CAOL ILA 1979 Islay Single Malt 46% Alcohol—Whyte & Whyte Label

Extremely pale straw/flaxen color; the nose is an enchantress, which emits come-hither scents of salty/brine, vinous vegetation, and a delicate but firm semisweet cereal quality in the distance—this bouquet is like a slinky siren calling out to sea; on the palate, it's fine, evolved, semisweet to sweet, medium-bodied, and deceptively potent, as wonderfully seductive tastes of fresh malted milk, very mild peat, smoke, cream, and light English toffee mesh perfectly; the finish is elegant but solid, showing the best face of the malted-milk quality; on the same superb level as the lovely 1974 bottling; one of Islay's best kept secrets and destined to become a personal favorite, likewise the distillery.

RATING ★ ★ ★ ★   *Highly Recommended* $$$

CAOL ILA 1980 Islay Single Malt 46% Alcohol—Whyte & Whyte Label

Very pale yellow/straw hue; aromatically, this could be nothing else but an Islay single malt, as tantalizing waves of zesty seaweed, wood smoke, and oil vigorously shake hands with the olfactory sense—my only complaint with the bouquet is a detectable back odor of cardboard; the properly medicinal flavor is all seeds, sweet oak, seaweed, brine, and wood smoke—it tastes like the bottle was laid open in front of the fireplace all night, so smoky is it; medium-long finish; strict Islay aficionados only need apply.

RATING ★ ★ ★   *Recommended* $$$

CAOL ILA 12-Year-Old Islay Single Malt 60.2% Alcohol—The James MacArthur Series

Pale straw color, which strikingly resembles a barrel-fermented chardonnay gold; carries with it the briny, sea breeze, iodine nose that one expects from an Islay malt; underneath it all lies a highly peated, phenolic, foundational aroma—also shows just the barest hint of biscuits; a full-flavored malt whose elevated alcohol by no means overshadows the "peat reek," seaweedy taste; surprisingly, it finishes in a sweet flurry of oak, plums, and sherry; indeed, my lips and tongue were tingling from the alcohol; not for the weak of knees, but definitely for the sensitive of taste.

RATING ★ ★ ★   *Recommended*

CARDHU 12-Year-Old Speyside Single Malt 40% Alcohol

Proper amber/gold color; the feinty, cheesy, garden-fresh, almost wine-like bouquet is one of Speyside's most delicate and restrained—I like it, but do not love it; very light touch in terms of both body and flavor; after Glenfiddich and Glenlivet, Speyside's most nimble featherweight malt, though Cardhu doesn't possess anywhere near the elegance or complexity of Glenlivet; almost ethereal sweet flavors of candy, ripe fruit, and pastry; the finish is vivacious, long, and sweet; designed not to be ponderous, Cardhu is another good first-step single malt for beginners.

RATING ★ ★ $$

CARSEBRIDGE 28-Year-Old Grain Whisky 54.7% Alcohol—The James MacArthur Series

Light amber/tawny color; subtle, rather coy nose even after 30 minutes of aeration—has a faint almond quality that turns buttery on the third pass—you have to work a bit too hard to coax this bouquet out—I hate that; while it's faultily timid in the aroma department, the taste bolts from the starting gate like Sea Biscuit with a hot foot in huge, rolling waves of malt, cocoa, rye cracker, and oatmeal, with honey tastes that overwhelm the taste buds as they wash over them; it closes on a warm, toffee note; this old gray beard is handsomely crafted and would score even higher save for the lackluster nose; the ride that the flavor takes the taste buds on is very memorable, but this whisky is flawed; downgraded on a second evaluation.

RATING ★ ★ $$$

CLYNELISH 1965 Northern Highlands Single Malt 50.7% Alcohol—Whyte & Whyte Label

Author's note: Pronounced "kline-leesh." Considerably darker than the 1980 (see below), this three-decades-old malt casts a classic medium amber/bronze malt color, absolute clarity; the nose is an evolved, fully melded, remarkably harmonious bouquet seeded with alluring scents of lightly peated malt, sea air, honey, and wood—it's an irresistible, mature aroma that could only be from coastal Scotland; a miracle on the palate, this deep, endowed, but nimble malt is in so perfect a place right now flavor-wise that I place it without hesitation in the top 20 malts I've ever tasted—layers of sweet wood, tobacco (pipe) smoke, ripe red fruit, brown sugar, and sweet malt treat the taste buds to an amazing, but wholly understated and self-confident, malt experience; the endless finish is all wood; hats off to the enormously talented distillers at Clynelish—they are perhaps Scotland's best-kept-secret distillery and one of my six favorites.

RATING ★ ★ ★ ★ ★   *Highest Recommendation* $$$

CLYNELISH 22-Year-Old Northern Highlands Single Malt / Cask Strength 58.64% Alcohol (Rare Malts Selection)

Pale amber/gold color, great purity; the intriguing aroma incorporates a moderate maritime/saline/iodine front note, which is backed by a peppery spiciness on the second pass—I've always admired the island/Highland fragrance of Clynelish—this particular bouquet is scrumptious; on palate, the cask-strength alcohol level doesn't really make itself felt until the smoldering fireplace finish—the palate entry is surprisingly refined, as mildly peated flavors of toffee, mint, brine, and cocoa compete for dominance all the way to midpalate, where the brine crosses the finish line ahead of the other elements; may be too powerful, too feral for some people, but I love it; to my mind, Clynelish is, along with Longmorn in Speyside, the best un-known and underrated malt distillery in Scotland.

RATING ★ ★ ★ ★ ★   *Highest Recommendation* $$$

CLYNELISH 1980 Northern Highlands Single Malt Cask Sample; Alcohol n/a—Whyte & Whyte Label

Vibrant yellow/straw hue; the big-time nose is laden with a savory oaky/vanilla note that lords over the secondary aromas of sea air, cedar, mint, and bay leaf; it's pleasantly sweet right from the palate entry through to the meaty, oily finish; along the way full, no-nonsense flavors of mint, oak, and toasty malt keep the palate amply entertained; there's a smoldering fire in the oaky aftertaste that gently warms the throat; this is a dynamite northern Highlands dram that captures the maritime ruggedness of its place of ori-gin with style and finesse. .

RATING ★ ★ ★ ★   *Highly Recommended* $$$

CRAGGANMORE 12-Year-Old Speyside Single Malt 40% Alcohol

Author's note: This plum distillery is acknowledged within the Scotch whisky industry itself as being the creator of true "distiller's whiskies," and deservedly so. This bottling is part of the Classic Malt Collection. Bronze color; blockbuster, multilayered nose of unbelievable depth, cleanness, and complexity—all at once one detects underlying peatiness, fresh heather, spice, sweet malted barley, ripe fruit, plus hints of caramel and coffee; the prototypical bouquet alone is worth the price; the olfactory concentration carries over into the sublime smoky flavors on palate; it finishes long, smooth as silk, and full; easily one of Speyside's most regal malts; a grand achievement in distillation.

RATING ★ ★ ★ ★   **Highly Recommended** $$

DAILUIANE 1971 Speyside Single Malt 40% Alcohol—The Spirit of Scotland Series

Author's note: Pronounced "dal-oo-ain." Lightish amber/burnished gold hue; this feinty nose is nonaggressive, but emits a pleasant piquancy that spotlights old saddle leather, yeast, cooked vegetables, and a pinch of black pepper—an intriguing, low-decibel bouquet that whispers rather than shouts; the close-to-the-vest demeanor continues into the taste, as understated, sweet flavors of chocolate, mint, and honey impress the palate; finishes on little cat's feet; an unassuming, quiet, but lovely single-malt experience that's almost feminine in its approach.

RATING ★ ★ ★   **Recommended** $$$

DALLAS DHU 1974 Speyside Single Malt 43% Alcohol—The Signatory Series

Medium amber/yellow/straw color; the astringent nose calls to mind nail polish remover, iodine, peat, and old-time, pretutti-frutti cough medicine—a highly idiosyncratic nose that many seasoned single-malt aficionados relish—I like and I understand it, but I don't swoon over it; peat and heather, heather and peat on the tongue and that's about all there is to say about this oily flavor; shows a pleasant butteriness in the finish, which is its best moment—it goes out warmly and on an amiable note; at the end of the day it's a monotonic, middle-of-the-road malt at best, which, if it offered more dimension beyond the mouth-puckering peat, would be average.

RATING ★ $$$

DALMORE 12-Year-Old Northern Highlands Single Malt 43% Alcohol

Author's note: Another of Scotch whisky's best kept secrets—a truly outstanding Northern Highlands distillery. One taste and you'll be convinced that this meaty, hearty Northern Highlands malt deserves to be a part of your whisky collection; a no-nonsense, sherry-influenced, malty nose that starts the taste buds gyrating; a bona fide mouthful, loaded with mandarin orange, jasmine, tea leaves, and toffee, but that's just the beginning of the palate, which is fully textured and expansive but neither clumsy nor cloying; the finish is abnormally lengthy, highlighted by the mandarin orange; there's only one way to enjoy this beauty and that's as a *digestif*, served neat or with a few drops of water; may be too much for lovers of much softer Lowland malts; sampled at least ten times; upgraded after the second evaluation.

RATING ★ ★ ★ ★   **Highly Recommended** $$

DALWHINNIE 15-Year-Old Central Highlands Single Malt 43% Alcohol

Pale gold color; racy, sleek nose, highlighted by mature, toasty, vanilla-like qualities that are appealingly harmonious; upon entry, this lovely malt shows its Central Highlands origin with a heathery/flowery flavor, then in midpalate a satisfying, spirity, ferocious bite takes over and doesn't relent until the soothing, fruity, peaty finish kicks in; a gentlemanly malt on the surface, but with a hidden Mr. Hyde streak that peeks out midway on the palate; an intriguing, rewarding malt experience.

RATING ★ ★ ★   **Recommended** $$

DEERSTALKER 12-Year-Old Speyside Single Malt 43% Alcohol

Author's note: This is a specially labeled bottling from the Balmenach distillery, which, while not well known to consumers, is a highly regarded distillery by whisky producers. The distillery is located in a beautiful, contoured part of Speyside known as the Haughs of Cromdale, a notorious locale famous for its illicit whiskies prior to the era of licensing, which began in the early 1820s. Goldenrod tone, ideal purity; the bouquet is a winner, as ample amounts of oak, toast with jam, black pepper, geraniums, jasmine, and brandy/wine-like elements congregate to form a sexy, high-grain, floral, and very appealing nose; shows plenty of stuffing in the texture; at entry, astringent flavors of tobacco and peat smoke eventually give way to roasted malt, oak, corn husk, and bland English digestive biscuits—the smokiness at palate entry concerned me, but I fancied the midpalate richness and complexity; the aftertaste mildly reprises the smoke; I liked this malt quite a lot and would have given it a fourth star had it not been something of a rollercoaster ride.

RATING ★ ★ ★   **Recommended** $$

DUMBARTON 1961 Grain Whisky 46% Alcohol—The Signatory Series

The green/gold hue is quite white-wine-like; a remarkably vivacious 35-year-old nose, which articulately speaks of ripe raspberries and heather—it's likewise prudently touched with honey and oak, not to mention rose petals and a dash of vanilla toffee—a genuinely engaging, well-preserved, floral, honeyed aroma whose waning power is offset by sweet, calm maturity; enters the palate serenely, clearly showing its age—delicate, feathery tastes of sweet oak and candied fruit quickly fade into a memory in the finish; it gave all that it had in the nose, then vanished by midpalate, leaving only a faraway echo in the aftertaste.

RATING ★ ★ $$$

EDRADOUR 10-Year-Old Central Highland Single Malt 40% Alcohol

Author's note: Edradour is one of the prettiest distilleries in all of Scotland and has the distinction of being Scotland's smallest malt distillery, with a crew of only three men. Pronounced "ed-rah-dowr." Exceedingly pretty, tony, vibrant amber/medium brown hue; the moderately assertive nose offers a pleasing array of complementary aromas, namely, malted barley, toffee, mint, evergreen, and even a dash of pineapple; the overly toasted flavor quality didn't impress me, but on the whole it's a pleasant, one-track single malt whose Central Highland demeanor is mildly engaging; the aftertaste is perhaps its best moment, as toffee, chocolate, and walnut flavors combine for a bang-up finish.

RATING ★ ★ $$

GLEN ALBYN 1980 Northern Highlands Single Malt 43% Alcohol— Whyte & Whyte Label

Exceedingly pale, with just the barest tinge of straw color; the behaved, almost feminine nose calls to my mind freshly picked apples and a wet forest floor on the top odor layer and mint and mushrooms on the foundational aroma layer—it's a benign but not necessarily passive bouquet that requires some patience and persistence; in the mouth, the sweet, smoky entry is compelling and quite luscious; by midpalate the taste mellows into a glycerine-like flavor that borders on being too sweet; the finish is long and very supple as burnt-toast flavors coat the throat; I walked a fence on this one as to whether or not to recommend it; after a third tasting I decided to give it the nod, mostly because of the intriguing fragrance and the smashing entry.

RATING ★ ★ ★   *Recommended* $$$

GLEN DEVERON 5-Year-Old Speyside Single Malt 40% Alcohol

Lightish amber/gold hue—very good clarity; the spicy, cinnamon, nutmeg, dry-cereal nose startled me on the initial nosing—a highly stylized, distinctive malt nose—the bouquet is a unique combination of rice pudding, barley malt, and spice cake—I came around to it in a big way by the third nosing; in the mouth, it's remarkably smoky and sweet for such a single-malt youngster—the vigor found in the mouth-feel is quite irresistible; the aftertaste is lively, off-dry to sweet, and medium-long; an exciting Speyside discovery that outpoints Glenfiddich as a single-malt whisky.

RATING ★ ★ ★   *Recommended* $

GLENDRONACH 12-Year-Old Speyside Single Malt (Sherry Cask) 43% Alcohol

Deep amber/honey/orange color; the phenolic (medicinal) nose speaks more of sweat and barley than it does old sherry casks—I detect a warm, toasty, charcoal mustiness that is moderately pleasant, but on the whole this aroma is uninspiring; it's left to the taste to betray the contact with sherry casks as a fourth-gear oloroso sherry twang passes the aroma in the fast lane—then on my second pass, a potent smokiness matches the pace of the oily sherry flavor; in the end I found this single malt too uneven to recommend; I especially found the nose lacking; it's a single malt in search of an identity, in my opinion; time in sherry casks during the maturation period doesn't necessarily put a lock on superior quality, as some distillers seem to think.

RATING ★ ★ $$

GLENDULLAN 1983 Speyside Single Malt 60% Alcohol—Whyte & Whyte Label

Pale, rather dullish yellow/silver hue; the nose reeks of cracked corn, black pepper, and malt—it's hard to discern the levels of bouquet because the cask-strength alcohol makes it difficult to deeply inhale—it's a potent concoction, one that most assuredly is not for novices; in the mouth, it's loaded with gritty, highly malted, rocket-fuel punch that even I find way too overpowering—when it's served neat, which is how I normally evaluate any spirit, I can't seem to get past the alcohol—a few drops of water help minimally, but I still feel frustrated that I can't detect much in the way of flavor; the finish is peppery, semisweet, and not as difficult to deal with as are the explosive nose and taste; a flamethrower of a whisky whose alcohol level requires cutting by at least 5%, in my humble opinion.

RATING ★ ★ $$$

GLENFARCLAS

One of my favorite Speyside distilleries for buxom, meaty, sherry-influenced malts. The name means "valley of the green grass."

GLENFARCLAS 1959 Speyside Single Malt 50.2% Alcohol—Whyte & Whyte Label

Deep amber/oloroso sherry tone—some suspended particles noted; the nose is notably complex, but polite, as melded, heady aromas of spirit, cherries, oak, egg cream, dark toffee, and orange rind keep the sense of smell busy; it's magical in the mouth, as subtle, perfectly married, succulent tastes of sherry, spirit, caramel/toffee, coffee, and nougat treat the taste buds to an exhilarating flavor adventure; the aftertaste is silky-smooth and medium-long, but as sweet as the finest nut candy; a 35(+)-year-old marvel that's at its peak right now; do what you have to do to find it; the combination of maturity, elevated but controlled alcohol, intense flavor and aroma, and overall breeding make this a classic.

RATING ★ ★ ★ ★ ★   *Highest Recommendation* $$$

GLENFARCLAS 105 8-Year-Old Speyside Single Malt 60% Alcohol

Batten down the hatches, Elmira, this one's a-kickin' in the door; almost full-cask strength at 120 proof, making it strong enough to burn the heels off your Florsheims; goldenrod/sunshiny hue; the brassy, defiantly forward nose is steeped in unrelenting smells of spirit, candied fruit, fresh flowers, and even some walnuts; on palate, its amazing sweetness, ripeness, and vigor take no prisoners, bulldozing the taste buds until they cry "uncle"; the viscosity is such that one could term it "heavy"; its blazing finish is extended and shows remarkable hints of prunes and candy; a single-malt horse of a very different and pleasingly distinctive color, though its teeth-curling potency makes it not for the weak-of-knees; I responded positively to its brute honesty and, despite its imposing strength, found it quite a delicious whisky to boot.

RATING ★ ★ ★ ★   *Highly Recommended* $$

GLENFARCLAS 12-Year-Old Speyside Single Malt 43% Alcohol

The brilliant, luminous color of golden amber/honey brown is beautiful, fine purity; the nose is sassy but buxom, as assertive, piquant aromas of clover, wintergreen, orange, pineapple, and vanilla bean wow the olfactory sense; texturewise, it's plump and oily; on palate, the nectar-like flavors of ripe plums, root beer, and bananas are sensuous and vivacious; the finish is loaded with sherry notes; the robust only need apply.

RATING ★ ★ ★ ★   *Highly Recommended* $$

GLENFARCLAS 15-Year-Old Speyside Single Malt 46% Alcohol

Gorgeous amber/light-brown color; the sweet, honeyed, vastly alluring nose offers layer upon layer of sensory impression, including heather, sherry, and ripe fruit; what a mouthful, brimming with banana, sherry overtones, even some toasted nuttiness; considering its alcohol level, it's amazingly smooth, balanced, and drinkable neat, which I feel is most appropriate for this substantial type of single malt; the finish, where the sherry wood really stands out, feels like crushed velvet and tastes of flowers; again, one of those malts that perfectly marry power and finesse; this is one to definitely snare at your local retailer.

RATING ★ ★ ★ ★   *Highly Recommended* $$

GLENFIDDICH

The most widely known name in single-malt Scotch. A venerable distillery whose malts are on the lighter side of the Speyside scale.

GLENFIDDICH 15-Year-Old Speyside Single-Malt Scotch / Cask Strength; 51% Alcohol

Lovely, light-catching, light amber/golden yellow tone, ideal purity; considering that it's cask strength, the nose is totally disarming and well-behaved as biscuity, creamy, and even buttery waves waft up from the sampling glass—with aeration, this nuanced enchantress displays its Speyside elegance with increasing intensity; on palate, the entry is intensely sweet, candied, and grainy, then the flavor levels out at midpalate, as seriously delicious, but fine and ripe, tastes of honey, toffee, and nuts impress the taste buds; the only time the elevated alcohol is felt is right before the aftertaste, as a sleeping tiger of alcohol rolls over and growls softly under its breath; the customary finesse and agility of Glenfiddich is finally given an edge with the introduction of this malt; it rivals the splendid, but much plumper, 30-year-old for the lead in the Glenfiddich derby.

RATING ★ ★ ★ ★   *Highly Recommended* $$$

GLENFIDDICH 30-Year-Old Speyside Single Malt 43% Alcohol—Silver Stag's Head Edition

Solid, medium amber/clover honey color, superb purity; the nose is surprisingly earthy, spicy, and sweet, with subtle backnotes of sage and rosemary—the punchiest bouquet of the Glenfiddichs; on palate, this sleek malt tweaks the taste buds with a snappy, herbal entry, then goes fat and winey-sweet at midpalate—definitely a sherry shading here; the aftertaste is very supple, quite sweet, and very extended—in fact, it seemed to go on forever; excellent, expansive, mature, and fully melded effort.

RATING ★ ★ ★ ★   *Highly Recommended* $$$

GLENFIDDICH 21-Year-Old Speyside Single Malt 43% Alcohol—Wedgwood Decanter Edition

Very pretty appearance, a warm gold/light-honey color, excellent purity; the nose is ripe, typically ethereal for the brand, and intensely floral (heather? roses?)—I really took to this bouquet's nuanced demeanor; in the mouth, while not as grand or generous as the 30-year-old or even the 15-year-old/cask-strength bottling, the flavors are tight, compact, and direct—there's nothing wasted here, all very tidy and straightlaced—the flowery quality is transferred from the bouquet to the flavor; the finish shows a barely discernable flash of sherry oak alongside a sweet, fruity final flavor.

RATING ★ ★ ★   *Recommended* $$$

GLENFIDDICH Special Old Reserve Speyside Single Malt 43% Alcohol

Pale, flaxen color, unblemished clarity; the nose is a study in simplicity and cleanliness—each of the four passes confirmed its aromatic steadiness—the fact that there was no diminishment in the bouquet with time and aeration impressed me—delicate aromas of flowers, sweet malt, and cereal with sugar tell the entire story; on palate, it's amazingly agile, yet polite—no one flavor quality takes charge in this youthful malt (I was told while I was at Glenfiddich that this malt is normally about eight years old); the aftertaste is ethereal and floral/earthy; the quintessential starter single malt.

RATING ★ ★ $$

GLEN GARIOCH 15-Year-Old Eastern Highlands Single Malt 43% Alcohol

Look-alike of the Glen Garioch 12-year-old; this singular nose is woody, piquant, peaty, and pine-needle-like, with equal supporting parts of resin, oak, and toasted cereal; this malt's taste has Highland written all over it; concentrated peatiness, sweetness from the oak (a dash of sherry wood, perhaps?), and a heavily malted flavor base; the aftertaste is smoky, moderately peaty, and, to my surprise, even a bit fruity and flowery; a solid, no-nonsense, in-its-prime malt that evokes a sense of the past, when the term "compromise" never entered the vocabulary of a distiller.

RATING ★ ★ ★   *Recommended* $$

GLEN GARIOCH 21-Year-Old Eastern Highlands Single Malt 43% Alcohol

Slightly richer amber color than the 15-year-old; the nose initially emits a caraway-seed, rye-bread bouquet, then gently shifts into a lovely, complex, sweet oakiness that is dazzling; one of the more intriguing Highland flavor experiences in that it shifts gears three times from entry to aftertaste; at entry, it's so plump, sweet, and juicy that I thought for a moment it might be over-the-hill—then by midpalate, a warm, smoldering, compelling, nut-like richness took over; in the finish, it shows some fire beneath the sweet, sublime, but solid layer of flavor; not so much better than the supple 15-year-old that it merits another star, but close; I would not call this a particularly complex malt, but it's a good one, with some time left on its ticket.

RATING ★ ★ ★   *Recommended* $$$

GLEN GARIOCH 12-Year-Old Eastern Highlands Single Malt 43% Alcohol

Marginally richer amber than the 1984; this atypical bouquet is vegetal and seed-like in character at first pass—I detect a weak scent of aniseed and peat—the second and third nosings don't develop further, but I liked the nose very much—shows the woodsy side of Highland malts that you don't often encounter; the entry taste is piney, sweet, and ripe—the midpalate goes smoky/peaty (what is it with this distillery and smoke?) and sharp; the aftertaste carries along some of the razor-sharpness, which I didn't like or appreciate at all; a middle-of-the-road Highland malt of modest virtue that gets let down in the finish.

RATING ★ ★ $$

GLEN GARIOCH 1984 Eastern Highlands Single Malt 43% Alcohol

Medium amber, unexceptional color; the nose is remarkably smoky (cigarette), antiseptic, and mushroomy—beyond these three upfront elements, I don't detect an underpinning aroma—perhaps there's nothing more to it; the concentrated smokiness goes all out on the palate entry, then subsides as a sweet oakiness assumes control all the way through to the appealing, if benign, aftertaste; a medium-bodied, intensely smoky malt whose youth may work against it because it's too young to have developed much in the way of finesse or subtlety; in a robust Highland malt, ten years is still an adolescent period, in my opinion; I don't think that it should be on the market.

RATING ★ $$

GLENGOYNE

This distillery touts the fact that it employs no peat in its kiln drying process, resulting in a very approachable, fruity malt-whisky style. Approximately 33% of its oak casks are old sherry casks.

GLENGOYNE 1969 Vintage Reserve Unfiltered Central Highlands Single Malt 47% Alcohol

Very pale amber/flaxen hue—good clarity for an unfiltered whisky; the dazzling aroma is saturated with sweet yellow fruit notes, a touch of sherry, honey, brown sugar, oak, and a unique herbaceousness—even at 47% alcohol, this is a satiny-smooth, fully integrated, sublimely sweet, and grainy nose that's easy on the olfactory sense; the taste is loaded with intriguing flavors of ripe golden apple, peppermint, and sweet oak from palate entry to midpalate—a keen taste of sherry oak makes itself known in the clean, alluring, medium-long finish; this is an opulent, bountiful Highland malt, one that I consider to be the best Glengoyne I've evaluated; bravo.

RATING ★ ★ ★ ★   *Highly Recommended* $$$

GLENGOYNE 17-Year-Old Southern Highlands Single Malt
43% Alcohol

Gold/honey color; what a difference five years make when it comes to complexity; much more serious nose than the Glengoyne 12-year-old; the nose gives off an acute, laser-beam perfume of barley malt, with a barely perceptible trace of sherry, which stands in the shadows; delicious, full-bodied entry, laced with sherry, pepper, and herbs; the orange/citrus finish is warm and very extended, with a soft bite as it fades into a slightly candied memory; a grand, marked advance in complexity from its demure, younger sibling.

RATING ★ ★ ★   *Recommended* $$$

GLENGOYNE 12-Year-Old Southern Highlands Single Malt
43% Alcohol

Author's note: This 12-year-old has been replaced by an as yet unreviewed 10-year-old bottling. Golden-hued; sweetish, round, fruity, simple, to-the-point nose, which feigns neither legendary status nor ferocity; in mouth it's a very charming malt, indeed, but take note that it's not one to be pondered for very long—understand that I point this out not in a derogatory vein at all; this tasty malt is very well made in the typically low-key Central Highland fashion that makes for an excellent starter malt as one ascends, if one desires, the Highland complexity ladder; as agreeable and average an everyday malt as one could find.

RATING ★ ★ $$

GLEN GRANT Speyside Single Malt 40% Alcohol

Resembles a white Bordeaux/Sauvignon Blanc–based wine so pale yellow that it couldn't get better purity; the gregarious, assertive, estery nose is abundantly fruity, highlighting tropical fruit, in particular, and has nicely developed backnotes of rose petals, apples, and citrus—I took to this buoyant, vivacious Speyside bouquet immediately; though it's not a powerhouse on the palate, this agile malt nonetheless shows ample grip and texture, which both guide the flavor of rich barley malt, sweet, resiny oak, honey, and vanilla all the way through to the lip-smacking finish; a solid, if unspectacular, malt that provides one of the better entry points for neophytes and a comfortable, affable old friend for seasoned malt imbibers; enormously popular in the U.K. and Italy—difficult to locate in the U.S. market.

RATING ★ ★ ★   *Recommended* $$

GLEN KEITH 1983 Speyside Single Malt 43% Alcohol

Author's note: Part of the Heritage Selection from the House of Seagram. Medium gold/amber, pure appearance; this nose is all cereal, malt, and mash, with a grainy sweetness that's pleasurable and direct—this isn't a bouquet of layers and nuances, but rather one that's honest and uncomplicated; the taste begins in a delectably sweet, mashy manner, then abruptly turns astringent in midpalate, going prickly and hot in the aftertaste, where

I taste traces of gunpowder; what began as a recommendable malt turned into a two-star entry because of the regrettable change of direction at the middle point of the flavor experience; the attractive nose kept this malt afloat; I frequently steer consumers who have little experience with single malts but want to learn more about them in the direction of this agile, undemanding whisky.

RATING ★★ $$

GLENKINCHIE 10-Year-Old Lowland Single Malt 43% Alcohol

Author's note: Part of the Classic Malt Collection. Clear, sunny-gold/flaxen color; round, inviting, exceedingly delicate aromas of spice and hay—an outstanding, vibrant nose; dry on entry, then goes phenolic (medicinal) and sharp on the tongue; the subdued aftertaste is smoky and lean, lingering nicely for several minutes; a Lowland malt that unfortunately goes disappointingly astringent in the mouth after a mesmerizing, come-hither bouquet; far from the splendor of other Lowland malts like Auchentoshan or Rosebank.

RATING ★ $$

GLENLIVET

One of the true prestige names in the world of distilled spirits, not just Scotch whisky, Glenlivet is owned by Seagram. Perhaps the most elegant of all Speysides, the Glenlivet 12-year-old is a benchmark of finesse. About a third of the distillery's aging vessels are sherry oak, a feature that shows up especially in the grand 18-year-old bottling. This was the first distillery to be licensed under the newly drawn laws for distilling in 1823. The distillery was licensed in 1824. The Glenlivet 12 is the largest-selling single malt in the U.S. marketplace.

GLENLIVET 21-Year-Old Speyside Single Malt 43% Alcohol

A notch deeper than the splendid 18-year-old in color—there's no hint of gold here, but lots of layered amber/clover honey, perfect purity; I couldn't imagine a more sensuous and elegant Speyside bouquet than this huskily mature aroma that focuses squarely on the sherry-cask influence in the first two passes, then moves on into a flowery/herbal stratum with nuanced backnotes of flint and shale—the final nosing exposes the malt component in heavenly sweet, even biscuity scents that beautifully top off the aromatic part of the program—truly lovely; in the mouth, the satiny texture is confident in its maturity and ably forms the foundation for the multilayered flavors, which include off-dry sherry, tangerine, rose petal, and a bit of loose, unsmoked tobacco; this memorable beauty concludes on a semisweet note, almost like a piece of expensive English toffee that quietly rests, melting in the throat; simply, one of the greats from Speyside.

RATING ★★★★★   *Highest Recommendation* $$$

GLENLIVET 12-Year-Old Speyside Single Malt 43% Alcohol

Rich gold color; nosing this thoroughbred is like walking into a florist's shop—heather, evergreen, and sweet-william alternate, teasing the olfactory sense, but there's more to it than flowers, there are also a hints of caramel, soft oak, and cookie batter; on palate, it explodes with tingling flavors of apricots and pears, finishing strongly with a rush of buttery cream; make no mistake, this is one of Speyside's definitive malts and deserves its enormous popularity in the U.S.; deceptively complex, Glenlivet 12 is one of the classiest, most sophisticated malts.

RATING ★ ★ ★ ★   *Highly Recommended* $$

GLENLIVET 18-Year-Old Speyside Single Malt 43% Alcohol

Deep, opulent, harvest-gold/amber hue; the cake-batter, cinnamon/spicy nose is a total joy—three distinct aroma levels enchant the olfactory sense—the foundation aroma is zesty, mature, elegant, malted barley—the next layer is sweet oak, mint, and honey—and the surface level is estery, dried rose petals; in the mouth, this confident, surefooted malt holds court with firm, fully melded flavors of oloroso sherry, vanilla, candied almonds, and dried apricot; the aftertaste is full, extended, and crammed with nutty, toffee flavors that really steal the show from the midpalate flavor; one of the most memorable finishes in the entire Scotch category.

RATING ★ ★ ★ ★   *Highly Recommended* $$$

GLENLOCHY 25-Year-Old Western Highlands Single Malt / Cask Strength 62.1% Alcohol (Rare Malt Selection)

Pale yellow/flaxen hue; the nose makes too much of the cask-strength alcohol in the first pass because it's difficult to get around it—the second and third passes unveil lovely ripe pear, mild peatiness, and graininess that are admirably controlled and nicer than the nastily aggressive fumes found in the first nosing—if you come across this malt, do yourself a favor by allowing it 5–10 minutes of aeration before nosing it; in the mouth, the lack of textural substance and flavor allows the lofty alcohol content to run amok, making it seem very harsh and combative from palate entry through to the unbridled finish, which features way too much heat; the problem with this pugnacious malt is so clear that it's ridiculous—the elevated alcohol has nothing to counterbalance it; United Distillers should have known better than to release this out-of-control malt.

RATING ★ $$$

GLEN MOHR 1978 Northern Highlands Single Malt 43% Alcohol— Whyte & Whyte Label

Light yellow/hay/pale gold hue; what strikes me most is the citrus/pineapple quality of this snappy, intensely fruited nose—a deep second whiff confirms the tartness originally detected, but adds an attractive note of sweet oakiness, which develops during aeration and swirling; the palate entry is sweet-sour, with atypical, botanical tastes of high-flying new oak and bark, then it turns bittersweet, resiny, seed-like, and even sap-like by midpalate; I didn't care at all for the herbal, weedy, leafy, and vinous finish; distinctive and different, but it still left me feeling uninspired.

RATING ★ ★ $$$

**GLEN MHOR 1965 Northern Highlands Single Malt 56.4% Alcohol—
The Signatory Series**

The gorgeous XO cognac–like amber/sunset orange is a real standout; the sturdy, meaty, directed nose shows aldehydic elements of spice, black pepper, and barley malt, which are all married to the clearly evident alcohol—no bite here, though; the potent, spirity, fourth-gear, off-dry flavor highlights smoke, tobacco, and old leather in a John Wayne barroom brawl manner; it has a hard, brittle feel to it, sacrificing suppleness and grace in favor of might and muscle; the aftertaste is almost ale-like, so yeasty and malty is it; I really couldn't decide even after four passes at it whether or not I liked this unruly hooligan; one of the most quizzical tasting experiences I've ever had with a single malt; my doubts trouble me.

RATING ★ $$$

GLENMORANGIE

Glenmorangie is the best-selling single malt in Scotland. The distillery produces a mere 38 barrels of whisky per day. Glenmorangie is the sole distillery in all of Scotland that doesn't offer its single-malt whisky to blending houses. Rather astonishingly, the company has had only four distillery managers since 1898. 1993 was Glenmorangie's 150th anniversary year. Glenmorangie is gaelic for "valley of great tranquility" and is pronounced "glen morange-ee" as in "orange." The distillery mainly uses American bourbon barrels, but is renowned for experimenting with different types of oak casks, including casks that formerly aged port, red Bordeaux, and madeira. Glenmorangie owns the loftiest pot stills in the Highlands at 16 feet 10¼ inches. Legend says the taller the pot still, the more delicate the whisky. The distillery is located north of Inverness in Tain and is one of the northernmost whisky distilleries in Scotland.

**GLENMORANGIE 18-Year-Old Northern Highlands Single Malt
43% Alcohol**

Good, firm honey hue; a distinctively delicious, multilayered nose of peat, iodine, black pepper, heather, pastry, oak, and caramel-like sweetness and depth—one of the more complex and inviting Northern Highlands single-malt noses—this is one of those rare items that could be recommended solely by virtue of the fragrance; in the mouth, I find this to be one of the most colorful and intriguing malts I've evaluated—its taste spectrum is amazingly broad, ranging from fruity to peaty to flowery to wine-like to citrus; in the aftertaste all the various parts blend beautifully into a harmonious ending; as many times as I've tasted Glenmorangie 18, I have yet to grow tired of its various flavor components—in fact, it seems like I always notice something new; one of the most compelling single-malt experiences to be had.

RATING ★ ★ ★ ★   ***Highly Recommended*** $$$

GLENMORANGIE 1971 Northern Highlands Single Malt, 150th Anniversary Limited Bottling Edition; No Alcohol Declaration

Good, solid, yellow/straw/amber color; the nose is soft, but firm and crammed with roasted almond, pear, peach, caramel candy, and a touch of alcoholic bite—it's a delicate nose, really, at which I'm more than a little surprised; on palate, this race horse launches into full gallop as round tastes of almonds, dark toffee, and ripe tangerines all meet at the superb finish; this is the Northern Highlands at their sweet, classy best; while I've long been an ardent fan of Glenmorangie's 18-year-old, I believe that this 23-year-old whisky beats it by the slightest of margins—I say this as a person who is not ordinarily a great admirer of malts that are older than 22–23 years.

RATING ★ ★ ★ ★   ***Highly Recommended*** $$$

GLENMORANGIE 12-Year-Old Sherry Wood Finish Northern Highlands Single Malt 43% Alcohol

Rich, light-to-medium amber/harvest gold hue, ideal purity; this nose offers a dry, saddle leather–like opening aroma, followed by marked aromas of ripe yellow fruit, honey, and even a dash of very mild vanilla—the touch of sherry oak is noticeable, if barely so—I kept returning to this mysterious bouquet, attempting to define it further, but it proved elusive, yet totally compelling; in the mouth, there's no mystery, no coyness as downright succulent, sweetish tastes of light caramel and vanilla frosting mix harmoniously with the astringent woodiness, making for a terrific midpalate malt experience; the aftertaste is where the sherry element is obvious; to me, the clear winner among Glenmorangie's wonderfully innovative Wood Finish program; bravo, lads.

RATING ★ ★ ★ ★   ***Highly Recommended*** $$

GLENMORANGIE 12-Year-Old Madeira Wood Finish Northern Highlands Single Malt 43% Alcohol

Lightish amber color, good purity; the nose is notably apple-like in the first two passes—with time and aeration, a zesty spiciness comes about in a mannered rather than prickly way—this is not a blockbuster bouquet, but its acidic/cottony underpinning makes it extremely clean and manageable; its best face is shown on palate as a peppery, gently malty, and crisp flavor cleanses the tongue in fine form—the midpalate is beautifully structured and direct—there's not much in the way of flavor layering, but the straight-ahead honesty is engaging; the aftertaste is slightly vegetal, cereally, and very seductive; nicely done; aged for 12 years in old American white oak (from the Ozarks) Bourbon casks, then finished in old Madeira casks before bottling.

RATING ★ ★ ★   ***Recommended*** $$

GLENMORANGIE 10-Year-Old Northern Highlands Single Malt 43% Alcohol

Very pale straw/hay/flaxen color; this agile 10-year-old possesses a round, warm, bountiful, harvest-time-in-the-orchard nose that I greatly fancy—it's not as complex as it is compelling; the evidence of bourbon wood-aging is unmistakably identified in this handsome, graceful, medium-bodied malt—it's the intensity of the floral quality that tips me off; on the palate, underlying tastes of smoke, nectarine, tangerine, and mild pepperiness grandly entertain the taste buds; the aftertaste is piquant and very spirited; one of Scotland's five best 10-year-old single malts; holds an enormous amount of drinking pleasure.

RATING ★ ★ ★   *Recommended* $$

GLENMORANGIE 12-Year-Old Port Wood Finish Northern Highlands Single Malt 46.5% Alcohol

Very attractive medium amber/light brown/honey/orange color; a very different malt nose, offering wine-like hints right from the first nosing along with subsequent passing scents of apple, spice, and even soft cheese; but it's on the palate that this unique animal comes out to play, as firm flavors of sweet malt, cocoa, oak resin, and bourbon crescendo at midpalate, then gently, gradually fade into a mellow, winey, malty, vanilla finish that's delightful and medium-long; bravo to the 16 men of Tain who are willing to share their adventures with us and who aren't afraid to stretch their talents by experimenting with aging single malt in various types of previously used oak barrels; while I still place Glenmorangie's fabulous 1971 at the top of the heap, I did genuinely like this malt.

RATING ★ ★ ★   *Recommended* $$

GLEN MORAY 12-Year-Old Speyside Single Malt 43% Alcohol

Straw yellow color; the welcoming bouquet speaks volumes about corn husk, fennel, malt, and even pine—it's a soft, comfortable nose that's open, engaging, and companionable; in the mouth, the lightish, unassuming flavors are sweet at palate entry, then go minty midway through the taste experience; the aftertaste introduces touches of cigar smoke, herbs, and smoke; clearly, this malt's strong suit is its delightful fragrance, which is neither particularly grainy/dry nor fruity/sweet, but rather some pleasant place in between; a good, moderately complex, to-the-point dram for beginners and Scotch veterans alike.

RATING ★ ★ ★   *Recommended* $$

GLEN MORAY 15-Year-Old Speyside Single Malt 43% Alcohol

Richer, darker than the 12-year-old—a very pretty amber/light honey tone; the phenolic, gamey nose isn't anywhere near as interesting as that of the 12—astringent scents of cardboard, cinnamon, and citrus hold court, leaving little room for grain, wood, or fruit aromas; the bitterness I detect in the taste element could hardly be considered a virtue; somewhere along the way, this malt has imploded; the finish has a sharp, razor-like bite to it that seals the coffin shut in my book; hasn't one iota of the charm of the better-than-average, if younger, 12-year-old; don't take the chance—take a pass.

RATING ★ $$

GLEN ORD 12-Year-Old Northern Highlands Single Malt 40% Alcohol

Solid, medium amber/light honey color, excellent purity; the bouquet is compact and concentrated on the malt component—the second pass reveals pleasingly sweet notes of vanilla and glycerine—the third and fourth nosings don't expand beyond the sweet malt theme established in the opening salvo; once in the mouth, it's clear that this is a malt to be tasted and savored, not overly sniffed—medium-weighted, it displays a round suppleness that's highlighted by an intense maltiness that comes off sweet and a tad oaky/resiny—my guess is that the primary oak was old bourbon cask, because of the vanilla-wafer backnote taste, especially in the finish; not as bighearted as some of its Northern Highlands neighbors (Clynelish, Glenmorangie, Dalmore), but a structurally sound and charming malt.

RATING ★ ★ ★ $$

GLENROTHES

One of those obscure distilleries that's a quiet, still undiscovered gem—undiscovered because there's so little of it available in single-malt bottlings. It's also one of the most respected distilleries within the community of malt distillers. That being the case, the vast majority of its whisky goes for blending purposes. What little is on the market as a single malt is absolutely dazzling.

GLENROTHES 1966 Speyside Single Malt 53% Alcohol—Whyte & Whyte Label

As dark an amber/brown as the oldest XO cognacs I've seen; the tidal waves of all-out oloroso sherry rival the older Macallans in scope and intensity—the depth of fruit perfume is no less than astonishing—ditto the compelling oak component—an imposing, fathomless bouquet that may be over-the-top for admirers of more agile Speyside malts (i.e., the floral/heathery/long-on-elegance cadre led masterfully by Glenlivet and Knockando)—but if decadent, sweet (but not over-the-top) opulence rings your pleasure chimes, do what you have to to locate this unrestrained treat; rich, sweet, brandy-like on the tongue (especially the bigger Solera Grand Reservas from Jérez, Spain); so thick you can almost scoop it out with a spoon or put it over vanilla ice cream; the total experience is very special and unusual, meant only for the most radical sherry-cask malt lovers . . . like yours truly.

RATING ★ ★ ★ ★ ★   *Highest Recommendation* $$$

► GLENROTHES 1979 16-Year-Old Speyside Single Malt 43% Alcohol

Light/yellow/amber/honey color; the bouquet is generous, as scoops of green-apple fruit, spring garden, fresh herbs, sweet malt, and lanolin charm the nose—it's more nimble than the fragrances of other Glenrothes bottlings I've evaluated, which have run to the opulent, dark, and muscular leanings; in the mouth, the agility found in the bouquet becomes transformed into an ambrosial, creamy, buttery, coconut-milk taste and texture that had my taste buds doing handstands (metaphorically speaking, of course)—the midpalate is citrusy, but mildly sweet and floral, with luscious backnotes of chocolate, toffee, and vanilla; the aftertaste is medium-long and citrusy; a slinky elixir that is aged to near perfection.

RATING ★ ★ ★ ★   *Highly Recommended* $$$

GLENROTHES 1975 Speyside Single Malt 43% Alcohol—Whyte & Whyte Label

Medium gold color; the downright sweet, oloroso sherry explosion in the expansive, generous, almost overpowering nose gets your attention in a hurry—this is a big, bruising, winey, overstuffed package that keeps pace with the headlining, musclebound Speyside sweeties like Singleton, Aberlour, and Macallan; on the palate, it comes off rather tame and one-dimensional after the rollicking, fourth-gear bouquet; from start to finish, it's a sweet and simple number tastewise; I can see how this juicy, sherried style will go over big with the growing fan club of sherry-wood single-malt fanatics; comes close to pushing the sweetness buzzer too vigorously.

RATING ★ ★ ★   *Recommended* $$$

GLENROTHES 12-Year-Old Speyside Single Malt 43% Alcohol

Deep gold color; in the aroma, this malt carries the sweet Speyside aroma banner of dried fruit, flowers, and muesli-like cereal nicely; unmistakably Speyside in the mouth, as savory tastes of ripe fruit, soft oak, and tobacco converge into a fresh-fruit-salad finish that's buttressed by a clean, crisp acidity; decent, if uninspired, aftertaste; an appealing, sturdy, yet not overpowering single malt.

RATING ★ ★ ★   *Recommended* $$

GLENTROMIE 12-Year-Old Highland Malt 43.4% Alcohol

Lightish amber/gold color; clumsy, medicine-chest nose that's neither tart nor sweet at the start, then mellows out somewhat with 10–15 minutes of vigorous aeration—the iodine core component that emerges over time makes me think that it's more of an Islay than a Highland malt—a pitfall for a nose like this is that for the uninitiated the aroma is stinky rather than iodine-like; light to the taste and feel, but shows very nice semisweet, smoky flavors of ripe pears and toasted honey-wheat bread; it finishes gracefully as the savory flavors gently fade in the throat; after puzzlement over the awkward aromatic beginning, this malt really won me over with its style and finesse.

RATING ★ ★ ★   *Recommended* $$

GLENTURRET 15-Year-Old Eastern Highlands Single Malt 40% Alcohol

Sunshine yellow/golden color captures the eye; highly aromatic, very complex nose of wet leaves/damp earth, toffee, spice, and, oddly, even some road tar; the oily, handsome, take-no-prisoners texture is arresting and sublime; on palate, this beauty really cooks, as flavors of ripe fruit, smoked almonds, and malted barley take turns charming the taste buds; the aftertaste is wide-open, full, sexy-smooth, and delivers some moderate heat at the back of the throat; loaded with character and pizazz.

RATING ★ ★ ★   *Recommended* $$

GLENTURRET 1979 Eastern Highlands Single Malt 43% Alcohol— Whyte & Whyte Label

Dull, corn-yellow/white-wine tone; owns a curious caramel/popcorn nose that goes weedy, vegetal, and musty/woodsy after five minutes of aeration—I like the nose primarily because it's so different and kind of funky/musty/attic-like, but not in the least sour or off-putting—the smell is like when you open your class yearbook after about a decade of not looking at it; in the mouth, it's substantial, nicely textured, and nutty/sweet, like candied almonds; the aftertaste is medium-long, sweet, malty, and quite snappy; I didn't find it a profound single malt, but nonetheless it's a handsome, charmingly quirky dram all the same.

RATING ★ ★ ★   *Recommended* $$$

HIGHLAND PARK

One of two distilleries in the Orkney Islands, and the better of the two. In fact, this is one of the six best distilleries in all of Scotland. The distillery is located near the gray-stone town of Kirkwall. The malts are among the most highly regarded within the circle of distillers. The standard distillery bottling of 12-year-old malt is one of the best bottles of whisky to be found.

HIGHLAND PARK 12-Year-Old Orkney Islands Single Malt 43% Alcohol

Amber, gold color; sherry makes its sweet presence known immediately in the multidimensional nose, which likewise has copious amounts of room for oranges, leather, and smoke; this utterly sensational malt sings and zings on the palate as the sherry races to the front just ahead of peat, mild brine, and heather; it's a photo finish, the peat winning by a nose in the incredibly satiny aftertaste that goes on for infinity; this is a glorious malt, a sinewy race horse that always goes the distance; one of my top ten malts without any hesitation; find and hoard at all cost; tasted at least 15 times; a genuinely great single-malt experience.

RATING ★ ★ ★ ★ ★   *Highest Recommendation* $$

HIGHLAND PARK 1985 Orkney Islands Single Malt, Cask Sample; Alcohol n/a—Whyte & Whyte Label

Pale amber/corn yellow tone; the nose is vibrant, heady, spirity, and oozes with ripe fruit and flowery/estery notes that I find irresistible—a classic bouquet and one that most certainly upholds and even enhances the standard set by Highland Park 12-year-old; the mouth-feel is so round, complex, honeyed, and rock solid that I almost find myself swooning over it—this is the stuff of whisky-making genius; harmonious, vivacious flavors of heather, cream, caramel, and oloroso sherry captivate the taste buds; even with the bracing, burning-embers-like fire in the aftertaste, it garners five stars without breaking a sweat, because whisky, from anywhere, simply doesn't come better than this astounding spirits achievement.

RATING ★ ★ ★ ★ ★   *Highest Recommendation* $$$

HIGHLAND PARK 1986 Orkney Islands Single Malt 43% Alcohol— Whyte & Whyte Label

Light amber/gold tone, excellent purity; the graceful, off-dry bouquet points more to the fruity/floral elegance of Speyside than to an island-sea-breeze salinity—the nose is soft, supple, but demure and rather elusive; the expressive taste, however, is another matter entirely, as decidedly sweet, succulent, cereal-like, and ripe-fruit flavors explode on the tongue—there's enough embers-like warmth to go around and even a peppery spiciness in the aftertaste; so loaded with finesse that you feel honored drinking it.

RATING ★ ★ ★ ★   *Highly Recommended* $$$

INCHGOWER 12-Year-Old Speyside Single Malt 59% Alcohol—The James MacArthur Series

Light-to-medium flaxen hue; the fragrant, granola-like, estery nose features raisins, grapes, flowers, and toasted-cereal scents, all neatly wrapped in a lovely, perfumed, contained bouquet that's a joy to sniff; the taste offers two distinct layers of customary Speyside flavors—the more obvious layer is stuffed with pepper, heather, hay, and flowers, while the piquant underpinning layer is a celebration of oak, vanilla, amontillado sherry, and malt; goes a tad sharp in the aftertaste, but overall shows very well; this is one of the more feline Scotches available.

RATING ★ ★ ★   *Recommended* $$$

INVERGORDON 10-Year-Old Single-Grain Whisky 43% Alcohol

Rather dullish straw/yellow color; the inviting nose is fragrant, friendly, and sweet in every pass—it offers delightful scents of cream and sweetened coconut in the last two nosings—one of the most luscious grain whisky aromas around; on palate, it's simple, lean, and clean, with sweet flavors of honey, biscuits, yeast, and spice—a round, amiable taste experience; a splendid entry-level Scotch that delights in an honest, uncomplicated way.

RATING ★ ★ ★   *Recommended* $

INVERGORDON 7-Year-Old Highland Single Grain 40% Alcohol

Pale straw color, pure; the fetching nose is round, delicately sweet, but with a curious minerally, lead-pencil-like backnote that comes out in the second pass, then gives way to a concentrated caramel-corn/grain aroma in the last nosing; on palate, the ethereal texture keeps the taste light and easygoing—no one flavor feature dominates the palate experience; the grainy sweetness makes a strong statement in the aftertaste, which ends up being the most expressive feature; definitely lighter and less characterful than the 10-year-old version; good, but not recommendable.

RATING   ★ ★

ISLE OF JURA 10-Year-Old Isle of Jura Single Malt 43% Alcohol

Luminous golden/tawny color; the roasted-nut, toasted-bran-cereal nose is full, straightforward, and quite luscious—I admired the no-nonsense bouquet on this island malt—no pretense, no coaxing required—it just comes right out to say hello; Jura 10 owns more of a round Highland character and texture than traditional seaweedy/iodine island leanings; the unabashedly sweet flavor is simple, which I consider to be its greatest asset; it's really a pleasure to taste an uncomplicated but flavorful malt; outstanding medium-bodied malt both for neophytes and for single-malt veterans who desire an unaffected dram.

RATING ★ ★ ★   *Recommended* $$

KNOCKANDO 1980 Distilled / 1994 Bottled Speyside Single Malt 43% Alcohol

Author's note: One of the classiest, if unsung, Speyside malts. The distillery rests on one of the prettiest bends of the River Spey. Pronounced "nock-an-doe." Ordinary gold/amber malt color; very mellow, but supple, nose of barley malt, oak, mild toastiness—a low-key, understated aroma of quiet depth—a "still waters" bouquet whose subtle strength might elude the novice; here's a serious Speyside malt whose flavor leans heavily to the smoky/sweet/elegant style that's long been the hallmark of the region; class act all the way from the sinewy nose to the endowed, complex finish; a top-flight malt running with all cylinders open.

RATING ★ ★ ★ ★   *Highly Recommended* $$

KNOCKANDO 21-Year-Old Speyside Single Malt 43% Alcohol

Deep honey-brown/amber tones; the fully developed nose is laden with oaky/vanillin notes that overtake the grain component in the first two passes—by the third nosing, a honey aroma gets added to the mix; on palate, the mature grain sweetness teams up with the oakiness to form a palate experience that is fat, but never cumbersome or overbearing; the aftertaste adds a dash of smoke to the plumpness, and everyone goes home happy.

RATING ★ ★ ★ ★   *Highly Recommended* $$$

KNOCKANDO 18-Year-Old Speyside Single Malt 43% Alcohol

Very attractive, medium amber/honey color; the aroma is mature and confident as subtle waves of nuts, toffee, barley malt, and banana come together in a harmonious, if understated, manner that's in keeping with the Knockando style that traditionally highlights finesse and gentle smoke; the flavor is as self-assured as the bouquet—biscuity, cookie-batter-like tastes pamper the taste buds; in the throat, there are touches of lanolin and vanilla as the wood element finally makes an appearance; a well-mannered, well-rounded, captivating, and comfortable old Speyside that deserves to be sought out.

RATING ★ ★ ★ ★   *Highly Recommended* $$$

KNOCKANDO 12-Year-Old Speyside Single Malt 43% Alcohol

Medium gold/greenish color, admirable purity; bouquetwise, there's a flowery, vegetal lean that's rather elusive in each nosing pass—I yearned for more single-malt expression—after 12 years in oak casks I want more from the aroma; in the mouth, the suppleness is complemented perfectly by a malty sweetness that is the epitome of Speyside malts—this 12-year-old saves its best moments for the palate—in fact, it's nothing short of delicious;

the finish shows a quick flash of peppery heat, which I liked; give me more gusto in the bouquet and a fourth rating star is sure to follow.

RATING ★ ★ ★   Recommended $$

LAGAVULIN

An Islay legend, which is now part of the Classic Malt Collection. Another of the more highly regarded malts within the Scotch whisky community, Lagavulin reveals its excellence in the balance it achieves between strength and elegance. Pronounced "lag-gah-voolin."

LAGAVULIN 16-Year-Old Islay Single Malt 43% Alcohol

Beautiful amber/light-topaz color; the aroma defines the descriptive term "iodine" when applied to malt whisky, but don't be fooled because there's much more happening in this memorable nose than pungent iodine—the nose also offers many subtle layers of oloroso sherry, smoke, and heather, but you have to dig down to reach them, which is all part of the fun; on palate entry the sea breeze/saltiness plunges immediately to the forefront with a seaweedy flavor that says "Islay" all the way; the fiery, oily midpalate suggests tea and toasted cereal, finishing long, lean, and sinewy, with a stately flavor of sweet smokiness; doubtless this brawny malt is not for everyone, but when I think of the most distinctive single malts, this hallowed legend automatically flashes across my mind's screen; an incredibly complex whisky that one must work up to gradually if one is ever to fully appreciate it.

RATING ★ ★ ★ ★   Highly Recommended $$

LAPHROAIG 1977 Islay Single Malt 43% Alcohol

Author's note: Lagavulin's neighbor and one of the most notorious single malts of all, because of its medicinal flavor. Pronounced "laff-royg." Medium amber/light brown hue, good clarity; this peaty, salty, oily, medicine-cabinet nose could only come from one place on the planet, southern Islay in the western Hebrides—but what's so interesting to me is that while this nose advertises Laphroaig, it does so with much more finesse and bearing than even the splendid 15-year-old bottling—yes, it says sea and peaty water, but it doesn't bludgeon you with them, taking the mellow, mature approach that I appreciate; in the mouth only a few seconds, I can tell that this is the finest Laphroaig available—the flavor is grainy-sweet and balanced, with focused, rich oloroso-sherry notes that elevate this distillery to new heights; the finish is measured, sweet like sugar-on-cereal, and totally captivating; a "must have" malt for all admirers of Islay malts; one last word—fans of the take-the-paint-off-your-boat 10-year-old would do well to check out this elegant beauty.

RATING ★ ★ ★ ★   Highly Recommended $$$

LAPHROAIG 15-Year-Old Islay Single Malt 43% Alcohol

Virtual look-alike to the pretty 10-year-old; this nose shows a marked degree of positive evolution from the Hulk Hogan approach of the 10—in comparison, it's almost graceful, offering mature, well-knit, calm scents of oak and fino sherry—there's still oodles of peat, but my nose cavity isn't aflame like it was with the cantankerous 10; in the mouth, this oily beauty has an interesting and varied array of flavors, as warm, compelling tastes of salty pretzels, amontillado sherry, chestnuts, cheese, and oak keep the palate intrigued but never overpowered; it finishes boldly, but elegantly; bravo; to me, there's absolutely no question but that the 10-year-old should be shelved; taste these two Laphroaigs side-by-side and then ask yourself if I'm wrong.

RATING ★ ★ ★   Recommended $$

LAPHROAIG 10-Year-Old Islay Single Malt 43% Alcohol

Bright, lustrous, honey-gold color; this, to me, is the most immediately identifiable nose in the realm of Scotch whisky—beast-like, phenolic, wheel barrels of iodine, sea salt, nonstop peat and kippers—and as if the medicinal tidal waves aren't enough, beneath them lies a thin layer of fino sherry—is this loutish nose too much? why am I reaching for a rifle?—on palate, the peat reek is so thick I almost have to scrape it off my tongue with a spatula; the three-alarm smokiness leaves scant room for anything else—I wonder if there *is* anything else in terms of flavor—maybe it's just peat, smoke, peat, smoke; I appreciate the damn-the-torpedoes character of this burly brat, but if I were stranded on that proverbial island with only one single malt, Laphroaig 10 most definitely would not be my choice; make sure you have a whip and a chair handy after you open this beastie; my biggest objection to this malt is, what does a newcomer to malts think if they happen to try this five-alarm malt before tasting other, tamer, more elegant malts? do you lose that person forever?

RATING ★ $$

LINKWOOD 15-Year-Old Speyside Single Malt 40% Alcohol

Sampled on site; the appearance of this luminous beauty is a clean, sparkling bright honey/amber, perfectly pure; the bouquet is round, toasty, and grapy sweet—the concentrated fruitiness must be the result of sherry oak—no other influence can encourage that type of ambrosial intensity—whatever the case, it's a luscious aroma; in the mouth, the sweetness becomes more like brown sugar/molasses/honey than overripe grapes or other fruit—it glides down the throat as easily and regally as a swan floating on a calm lake surface—this is a heady, refined malt that goes a long way in satisfying; plump, but not overly fat or cheesy aftertaste; wow.

RATING ★ ★ ★ ★   Highly Recommended $$

LITTLEMILL 8-Year-Old Lowlands Single Malt 43% Alcohol

I was a little taken aback and unprepared by the paleness of the appearance, absolute clarity; the nose is very delicate and floral, even grassy and a bit vegetal, but inviting and polite all the same—a textbook Lowland bouquet of manners and loveliness; on palate, it's notably candied and runs the risk of being too sweet—it's more a grainy/mashy sweetness than a fruity sweetness—by midpalate, the sweet element settles down enough to let a bit of malty/husk-like/almost-beer-like yeastiness to enter the fray; mild, fast finish; worked for me.

RATING ★ ★ ★   *Recommended* $$

LOCH DHU 10-Year-Old Speyside Single Malt 40% Alcohol (Mannochmore Distillery)

Author's note: This black-coffee-colored malt comes from the Mannochmore Distillery (Speyside), which was founded in 1971, only to be closed in 1985. The highly unusual dark-brown/black hue comes from the used bourbon casks that were severely recharred after they were reassembled in Scotland; the muted bouquet is extremely sweet, bordering on unctuous, and very smoky—in the second pass I detect bits of molasses and cardboard—considering the burnt-to-a-crisp state of the aging casks, I'm surprised at the acquiescence of the aroma even after 20 minutes of aeration and swirling; the smoky palate is seriously sweet, as layers of vanilla bean, brown sugar, and molasses coat the tongue—the midpalate reminds me of oak-aged rum from the Caribbean in the toasty, sweet, almost syrupy fashion; the aftertaste is, you guessed it, sweet as the dark-caramel taste races to the fore and stays with you long after the final sip; while all right, it was simply too sweet for me—beneath all the goo, I'll bet there's a decent Speyside; tasted next to Black Bowmore, which blew it off the table.

RATING ★ ★ $$

LONGMORN

This beauty is part of the Heritage Selection from the House of Seagram. This is not my first encounter with this legendary and highly regarded malt, since each time I'm in Scotland I enjoy a dram, but this is my initial formal evaluation of it under ideal tasting conditions. One of my favorite malts, bar none.

LONGMORN 15-Year-Old Speyside Single Malt 45% Alcohol

Lightish amber/harvest-gold color, excellent clarity; one of the top five Speyside bouquets, period—amazingly complex, layered, and seductive, as balanced and comely aromas of caramel, violets, malt, glycerin, honey, and cereal mash completely captivate the sense of smell; the taste and mouth presence are as close to perfect as any malt I know of—ripe, sweet, fleshy flavors of grain, sweet oak, butter, cream, and wood resin are harmoniously melded into one spectacular taste sensation; the finish is long, gentle, soothing, yet powerful and in control; one of Speyside's benchmark malts and an insider favorite of the Scotch industry; a Speyside that deserves to be as beloved as Macallan or Glenlivet.

RATING ★ ★ ★ ★ ★   *Highest Recommendation* $$

LONGMORN 1981 Speyside Single Malt, Cask Sample; Alcohol n/a— Whyte & Whyte Label

Very pale straw hue; the disarming nose is a friendly duel for dominance between flowers and nuts at the first nosing, then it develops further into a creamy, malty perfume that's quintessential Speyside and nothing but—an elegant, well-appointed bouquet; in the mouth, it's the fast lane to creamy, supple textures and flavors of heather, concentrated barley malt, cereal sweetened with honey, and caramel; the finish is silky-smooth, mannered, clean, and very long; a luxurious single malt that's so seamlessly made that the complete enjoyment of it is effortlesss.

RATING ★ ★ ★ ★   *Highly Recommended* $$$

MACALLAN

The Macallan Distillery ages its malts in old sherry casks from the time the casks are filled with new spirit off the pot still to the time of bottling. Single-malt Scotch doesn't come any better than these Macallans.

MACALLAN 18-Year-Old Speyside Single Malt 43% Alcohol

A smidgen darker than the 12-year-old; one of my favorite noses in the Scotch whisky category—a leisurely, lingering, mesmerizing, sweet bouquet of malted milk, double cream, almonds, heather, worn leather, and, of course, oloroso sherry—so disarming, inviting, and plump that the nose alone is reason enough to purchase it; splendidly decadent on the palate—it both feels and tastes like sweet creamery butter—estery flavors of rich, long-aged sherry, spearmint, ripe peaches, and pears caress the enthralled taste buds; the creamy finish goes on forever; you don't drink Macallan 18, you devour it; this seductive Speyside malt, to me, represents the quintessence of whisky making, no matter the place of origin; only a handful of single malts approach the majesty, grace, and panache of this sleek, willowy malt; one of the paramount distilled-spirit experiences the world has to offer.

RATING ★ ★ ★ ★ ★   *Highest Recommendation* $$$

MACALLAN 25-Year-Old Speyside Single Malt 43% Alcohol

Darker than its younger siblings, with a slightly more pronounced copper-penny tint; this nose unexpectedly offers more toasty-cereal than fat-sherry qualities, even with the more advanced age—it's resoundingly supple, emitting gentlemanly waves of black pepper, dried leaves, tobacco, and even biscuits; while in terms of flavor this exceptional Scotch is indeed more complex than the peak-experience 18-year-old, it's not quite as awesome in structure, leaving it just a breathy shade behind the more vigorous Macallan 18 in terms of overall sensory satisfaction—I'd hate to have to stake my life on the difference, however; on the palate, it's perhaps the most stately and elegant of any single malt I've ever judged; an extraordinary array of fruit and herb flavors delight the palate no end; the aftertaste is extremely regal and long; the stuff of genius.

RATING ★ ★ ★ ★ ★   *Highest Recommendation* $$$

MACALLAN 12-Year-Old Speyside Single Malt 43% Alcohol

Brilliant, luminous amber/orange/honey color; very sexy, musky nose of spice, nectarine, lanolin, tannin, and cream, all supported by that unmistakable and unshakable foundation of sherry, which is the customary trademark of Macallan; it wastes no time with formalities or coyness at palate entry as the stylish, wine-like sherry quality leaps right out amidst other succulent tastes of ripe blueberry, bell pepper, sweetened coconut, and peppermint; the aftertaste is fathomless and endless and only mildly sweet, providing the ideal and satisfying denouement to what is simply the best 12-year-old single malt around; by all means, don't miss it.

RATING ★ ★ ★ ★   **Highly Recommended** $$

MORTLACH 22-Year-Old Speyside Single-Malt / Cask Strength 65.3% Alcohol (Rare Malt Selection)

Author's note: This Speyside distillery was founded in 1823 and deserves more recognition. Solid, medium amber/light honey hue; considering the notably high alcohol level, this bouquet is directed, fresh, malty/cereally, and totally delightful, showing elegant backnotes of brown rice and candied almonds—a tour de force nose that's remarkably balanced and restrained; in the mouth, this sensational malt is supple, brazenly sweet, and succulent, offering layer upon layer of texture and flavor—at midpalate, the caramel/toffee/dark-chocolate combination is met halfway by a malty underpinning, which doesn't overplay its hand; the aftertaste is extended and sweet; a superb malt, whose cask strength was, I admit, beginning to wear me down by the final tasting pass, so don't underestimate its potency; in any case, this sweet malt deserves a long look.

RATING ★ ★ ★ ★   **Highly Recommended** $$$

MORTLACH 1983 Speyside Single Malt, Cask Sample; Alcohol n/a— Whyte & Whyte Label

Pretty gold/yellow, white Burgundy color; I love this kicky, pungent, corn-husk, vegetal, peppery nose because it's not trying to be proper or correct or true to form—it's compelling, straightforward, intensely malty, and cereally; it starts out in the mouth with a flash of prickly heat that surprisingly is neither offensive nor overwhelming—the fire is extinguished by midpalate, as this complex, full-bodied malt shifts gears, offering toasty, malty, opulent flavors that fondle the taste buds; the finish is full, buxom, succulently sweet, and medium-long; a dandy Speyside from an overlooked, underrated distillery.

RATING ★ ★ ★ ★   **Highly Recommended** $$$

NORTH BRITISH 1964 Grain Whisky 46% Alcohol—The Signatory Series

Pale amber hue; the nose offers considerable evidence of oak, as mellow, harmonious aromas of fino sherry, cocoa, pine sap, and molasses converge into one sweetly perfumed fragrance; what starts out succulent and savory at palate entry turns into a peculiar, manufactured, cardboard, pencil-eraser taste by midpalate and runs wild all the way to the finish line; this is a major disappointment after the nose scored very high—the wheels simply came off of this carriage halfway through the journey; nothing more to say; skip it.

RATING ★ $$

OBAN 14-Year-Old Western Highlands Single Malt 43% Alcohol

Author's note: This bottling is included in the Classic Malt Collection. Brilliant, gold/amber hue; the piquant, aggressive, heady, well-knit, and directed nose reeks of peat, cream, and smoke—definitely an aroma that serves notice; the bold, robust, peat-reek entry and midpalate change into an oaky, intensely smoky aftertaste, which is extended, stone-dry, and approachably potent; the amazing smokiness continues for 5–10 minutes in the throat; not that you need a whip and chair to corner this single malt from the Western Highlands, but it doubtless has more than ample guts and character.

RATING ★★★ ***Recommended*** $$

OLD FETTERCAIRN 10-Year-Old Eastern Highlands Single Malt 43% Alcohol

Pale yellow/flaxen/moderate gold color; feathery light nose, which brims with ripe tropical fruit, shadowed by a faint hint of butterscotch; in the mouth, Fettercairn 10 is invitingly light and mellow on palate—so ethereal that definitive flavors are hard to discern, but what I did find was a dry, delightful, butter-and-nut quality in the rather long finish; a nimble, entry-level, appetite-stimulating, Eastern Highlands dram all the way; not, however, an easy single malt to find in the U.S.; only the most fanatical liquor merchants carry it.

RATING ★★ $$

ORIGINAL OLDBURY SHEEP DIP 8-Year-Old Pure Malt 40% Alcohol

Very pale/golden color; the proper and pronounced malty nose is slightly doughy and biscuity; on palate, the spirity but soft flavors rapidly give way to a smoky aftertaste that completely disappears after 30 seconds; a ghost of a Scotch whisky; so light and airy that it should be served only in a cocktail or on-the-rocks or with soda; no ponderous, thought-provoking malt, this one; in the end, I didn't like it one bit; no guts.

RATING ★ $

PORT ELLEN 1974 Islay Single Malt 43% Alcohol—Whyte & Whyte Label

Very pale yellow/lemon-juice color; a different, a more aggressive shade of Islay—a moderately peated, oaky, Band Aid–smelling bouquet that includes vanilla bean and atypical grape-must/grappa undertones—overall in the nose, it's a hard-punching, but ultimately alluring, malt; ditto on the palate—a rambunctious, unruly, medicinal, whip-and-chair type of Islay beast that's tamed only by a healthy splash of mineral water; nevertheless, it carries the briny, frank stamp of Islay so nobly that I find it impossible to resist.

RATING ★★★★ ***Highly Recommended*** $$$

ROSEBANK 8-Year-Old Lowlands Single Malt 40% Alcohol

Author's note: A highly regarded Lowland malt, whose distillery closed down in 1995. Not as majestic as Auchentoshan, but sound, dignified, and affable. Good, solid, medium amber/topaz hue, ideal purity; the nose speaks of freshly mown hay and/or grass—one of the most garden-like malt aromas that I've come across—it's fresh, airy, and delightful; in the mouth, the feathery texture doesn't provide much of an underpinning for the flavor, but some nuanced tastes of fino sherry, tomatoes, and herbs come through by mid-palate; interesting, stony/flinty aftertaste.

RATING ★★★ **Recommended** $$

ROSEBANK 1974 Lowlands Single Malt 43% Alcohol—The Signatory Series

Triple-distilled; very pale straw color; this nose has a grassy, leafy, spring-meadow-like quality that is infectiously fresh and nimble, like a feather floating on a morning breeze—there are faint aromatic touches of ripe melon and grapes to complement the earthy, clean grassiness—no doubt about it, it's a really lovely, sedate, prototypical Lowland nose; the flavor is civilized and genial, with a mild heather scent—it's an unassuming, keenly floral taste that honors politeness and shuns bravado; the aftertaste is exquisite in its serenity, clean, and warming; while it will never be a rival to the majesty of fellow Lowlander Auchentoshan, this feminine 1974 is a sound and representative Lowland single-malt experience.

RATING ★★★ **Recommended** $$$

ROYAL BRACKLA 1978 Speyside Single Malt 43% Alcohol—Whyte & Whyte Label

Almost as clear as spring water; a resoundingly perfumy, estery nose with highlights of melted butter, rubber pencil eraser, airplane glue, lanolin, heather, and even the odd touch of clove—for all its peculiarity I really took to this saucy, multilayered, complex, and compelling nose—an endearing oddball; in the mouth, it goes down so easily that it's scary; taste-wise, there's a whole new menu of flavors to choose from including chocolate, egg cream, mild white cheese, and spice; the vivacious, herbal aftertaste is as friendly and passionate as the fourth-gear bouquet and midpalate presence; awfully good, from the kicky fragrance to the textured finish.

RATING ★★★★ **Highly Recommended** $$$

ROYAL BRACKLA 1972 Speyside Single Malt 40% Alcohol—The Spirit of Scotland Series

Brilliant, light-catching honey/amber color, with flecks of orange; a remarkably fresh (for its age) aroma greets the olfactory sense, as delicate scents of corn husk, honey, grass, and malt vie for early dominance; the sublimely sweet, ripe flavors of buttered almonds and oak headline the taste display in this well-heeled, classy single malt—the flavors are very spry, considering this whisky is nearly two and a half decades old; the enchanting aftertaste is round, warming, sweet, and, most of all, polite; as genteel a single malt as I've ever judged; quality doesn't always have to come wrapped in neon; the best term to describe it is "stately."

RATING ★★★ **Recommended** $$$

ROYAL LOCHNAGAR Selected Reserve Eastern Highlands Single Malt 43% Alcohol

Author's note: An overly expensive limited edition. Attractive, rich chestnut-brown hue, perfect purity; the baked, winey, high-flying oloroso sherry aromas are pleasant, but hardly enchanting; this malt is warm, inviting, very smooth on palate, boasting a silky oloroso texture and mild berry-like fruitiness; the burning leaves, charcoal-like, oaky/resiny aftertaste is moderately alluring; the big question is—is it worth its hefty price tag ($160 to $180) when compared to other big-gun single malts? the realistic answer is *absolutely not;* there is no logical reason for the extreme pricing of this handsome, but ultimately merely better-than-average single malt.

RATING ★ ★ ★   *Recommended* $$$

ROYAL LOCHNAGAR 12-Year-Old Eastern Highlands Single Malt 40% Alcohol

A sound, if uninspiring, Eastern Highlands single malt, noted for its somewhat restrained, slightly woody aromas; on palate, it's full-bodied, with piquant flavors of peppermint, heather, chocolate, and toffee—in the midpalate, it shows an appealing balance between alcohol, maltiness, and fruitiness; the aftertaste gives faint echoes of stylishness and elegance, but at the end of the day this ends up being an average Highland malt.

RATING ★ ★ $$

SINGLETON OF AUCHROISK 1983 Speyside Single Malt 43% Alcohol

Very attractive and pure bronze/honey/amber tone; the estery bouquet is round, welcoming, warm, more fruity than grainy, and shows deeply layered hints of wine (from the sherry casks, no doubt), candied apple, and paraffin—it's a sweet, oily nose that could almost be taken for a brandy by the untrained drinker; the mouth entry is notably creamy and oily as semi-rich flavors of citrus, apple, old oak, and banana coat the palate; the aftertaste is quite extended, mildly sweet, and apple-like; with little perceptible variation, this latest bottling capably maintains the buxom, oloroso sherry, Singleton style established early on by the mid-1970s versions; tasted alongside the 1975, 1976, and 1981 bottlings, this amiable, toothsome 1983 most resembles the 1976; a fleshy, full-bodied treat for sherry-cask aficionados.

RATING ★ ★ ★ ★   *Highly Recommended* $$

SINGLETON OF AUCHROISK 1981 Speyside Single Malt 43% Alcohol

A gorgeous, deep amber/mahogany/tawny hue, with dazzling orange highlights; the generous nose is laden with ripe banana and cherry fruit, mild oakiness, and a hint of sweet spice; whoaaaaaa—the heavy texture envelops the palate as straightforward, sweet flavors of egg cream, *palo cortado* sherry, and vanilla-chocolate take hold of the entrance taste buds; finishes awfully well, sweet, chewy, and round; ride 'em, cowboy, this one won't be broken easily.

RATING ★ ★ ★ ★   *Highly Recommended* $$

SINGLETON OF AUCHROISK 1976 Speyside Single Malt 43% Alcohol

Has more red in the color than the other bottlings; a virtual carbon copy of the 1975 in the nose—the fasten-your-seatbelt amounts of sherry and wine aromas keep your attention; on palate it's velvety smooth, well-defined, and chunky/chewy; the fourth-gear sherry-cask overtones from beginning to finish are bridled; masterfully crafted; worth the search, worth the money, and then some; this is outstanding, sherry-influenced whisky making surpassed only by the Macallan.

RATING ★ ★ ★ ★   *Highly Recommended* $$

SINGLETON OF AUCHROISK 1975 Speyside Single Malt 43% Alcohol

Shiver me timber, matey, this is what buxom Speyside single malt is all about; the deep honey/amber color has red highlights in the core; there's an exceedingly mellow, rich, oloroso-sherry banquet taking place in the nose; on palate one discerns pear/peach fruit, soft maltiness, an almost toffee-like quality that is both laden with power and elegance; intensity and purpose coincide in the full-bodied texture; slight spearmint and coffee meld in the sweet, utterly behaved aftertaste.

RATING ★ ★ ★ ★   *Highly Recommended* $$

SPRINGBANK

As one of the more idiosyncratic malts, one bottling may be spicy, the next may be oily or salty, but each of them is meticulously crafted and sensational. The distillery, which was established in 1828, also has the reputation of being erratic in its production schedule. For all its quirkiness, Springbank has survived where other distilleries on the peninsula have failed. Before a mass of closings after World War I, Campbeltown boasted over 30 operating distilleries. I urge readers to grab any bottling of Springbank that can be located.

SPRINGBANK 1975 Campbeltown Single Malt 55.8% Alcohol—Whyte & Whyte Label

By vivid contrast with the crystal-clear 1989 edition, this appearance is a honey brown, burnished gold; the nose takes your head off if you aren't cautious—this racy, raucous, unbridled aroma evokes the sea in a way few others do—it's the kind of high-octane brininess/spiritiness gallop right out of the sampling glass that may actually be too much for the uninitiated—on the other hand, who cares?—this deceptive beauty absolutely sings on the tongue, as mature sherry notes blend perfectly with the salty-air component in a heady marriage of flavor—I call it deceptive, because at first look it's a rampaging powerhouse, but once it's in the mouth, the settled, multilayered flavors and finish are elegant and loaded with finesse and character; memorably great.

RATING ★ ★ ★ ★ ★   *Highest Recommendation* $$$

SPRINGBANK 1989 Campbelton Single Malt, Cask Sample; Alcohol n/a—Whyte & Whyte Label

Water-clear—hardly a trace of any pale color whatsoever; power-packed, very heady, piercingly briny, even slightly tanky/stinky and with no alcohol-by-volume figure given, I guess by smell alone that it hovers between 50% and 56%; the take-no-prisoners flavor owns one of the most unique fruit characteristics I've yet encountered—it brims with an overripe tropical-

fruit quality that's simply smashing from palate entry through to the unabashedly sweet, but mildly salty, finish; a monster in the glass that would
inch toward five-star country but for the stale tankiness in the bouquet.

   RATING ★ ★ ★ ★   ***Highly Recommended*** $$$

SPRINGBANK 12-Year-Old Campbeltown Single Malt 59.8% Alcohol—The James MacArthur Series

   A tawny/amber/amontillado sherry–like hue that stands out from other
Springbank malts, which are often pale straw/light gold in color; at first nos-
ing, I think of wine, then the medicinal, seaweed, iodine, and peat compo-
nents surge to the front—a dramatic, spellbinding, powerhouse aroma,
which consists of at least three distinct levels—wine, salt, then fruit; on
palate, it's distinctive and highly idiosyncratic—this is a sinewy, Scotch-
cruiser-weight single malt, jam-packed with generous, high-flying walnut,
cream, butter, dark toffee, mint, and oak flavors, all peacefully coexisting in
a remarkably sublime package; long, leathery, peaty finish, with a hint of bite,
nothing serious; a superb whisky.

   RATING ★ ★ ★ ★   ***Highly Recommended*** $$$

SPRINGBANK 23-Year-Old Campbeltown Single Malt 53.7% Alcohol—The James MacArthur Series

   Pretty straw/gold color; aromatically, as different from the 12-year-old
Springbank as Scotch whisky is from fortified wine—this fantastic, semisweet, voluptuous nose is made up from glycerine, apples, peaches, pears,
and sweet oak—it's so harmonious you almost don't need to taste it—
smelling it seems reward enough; this supple malt is finely tuned on the
palate—it slinks down the throat in a fat wave of nutty, creamy top-layer flavors, which are buttressed by a rich, honeyed, wheat-like base flavor; the
heat in the finish knocked some points off, but overall this is a fabulous
Scotch whisky ride, well worth taking.

   RATING ★ ★ ★ ★   ***Highly Recommended*** $$$

STRATHISLA

The distillery was founded way back in 1786, making it the oldest distillery
in Speyside. Before it became a fully licensed distillery in the 1820s, it was
a fully operational farm distillery, which supplied whisky to the surround-
ing community. Its water source has been used either for brewing beer or
for distilling for over six centuries. It's also the heart of Chivas Regal.

STRATHISLA 12-Year-Old Speyside Single Malt 43% Alcohol

   Radiant, orange/iced tea/amber hue, perfect purity; dry waves of deeply
aromatic, perfumed malt cereal, sweet oak, toffee, and cocoa wash over the
delighted olfactory sense in this splendidly elegant and characterful bou-
quet, which I inhaled in greedy gulps—this is northern Speyside aroma at
its graceful best; in the mouth, the grainy/woody sweetness is actually suc-
culent and ripe, buttressed by a supple textural base; the wine-like sweet
note lasts well into the aftertaste, which is long in tenure and finesse; a
Speyside gem that leans to the luxurious side of the chart.

   RATING ★ ★ ★ ★   ***Highly Recommended*** $$

STRATHISLA 25-Year-Old Speyside Single Malt 40% Alcohol—The Gordon & MacPhail Series

Rich, orange/amber color; what impresses my olfactory apparatus initially is the silky-smooth, resiny oakiness—beneath the wood, however, lies yet another layer of aroma, specifically, a mature maltiness that's medium-sweet, well-endowed, and immensely appealing; on palate, the supple, round flavor abounds with oloroso sherry, grapes, vanilla extract, and cream—it's a potent, chewy taste whose sherry preeminence might be a turn-off to appreciators of the austere, grainy single-malt style; for a professed lover of sherry, however, this ripe, Rubenesque beauty is precisely what my Scotch doctor ordered.

RATING ★ ★ ★ ★   *Highly Recommended* $$$

TALISKER

Talisker is the sole distillery on the picturesque western Hebrides island, the Isle of Skye, and its salty malt is a key component of the Johnnie Walker blends, especially Johnnie Walker Red and Black. This bottling is now part of the Classic Malt Collection.

TALISKER 10-Year-Old Isle of Skye Single Malt 45.8% Alcohol

Very pretty, solid medium-amber/harvest-gold tone; the decidedly sea-weedy/briny, power-packed nose also offers soft peatiness, heather, and maltiness; the round, smoky, commanding, oily, iodine, burnt-almond flavors on palate literally leave the taste buds tingling; muted briny/salty, ocean-influenced finish; tasted at least a dozen times over the years; my notes and scores over the last two years have rated it lower than in the previous years' tallies; Talisker shows sound maritime/island character, but, to my taste, it lacks the air of depth and scope that pushes an average whisky into noteworthy territory.

RATING ★ ★ $$

TAMDHU 10-Year-Old Speyside Single Malt 40% Alcohol

Charming, rich, honey/amber color; oodles of ripe, sweet, sherried, fragrant, toffee aromas gently waft from the glass; on the palate, succulent, sweet, ripe-peach, and pineapple flavors disarm the sense of taste in a laid-back way; finishes whistle-clean in a mildly candied wrapping of honey and caramel; a truly lovely, mannered, low-key, rather simplistic single malt whose good-natured demeanor and sexy sweetness are very compelling; while some admirers of sinewy, racy, teeth-busting single malts may find it banal, I like its reserved, self-assured, steady bearing; comes off as being a tortoise, not a hare; before you question that comment, remember who crossed the finish line first.

RATING ★ ★ ★   *Recommended* $$

TOBERMORY Isle of Mull Single Malt 40% Alcohol

Sampled at the distillery—no statement of age; the warm harvest-gold hue ends up being the best thing about it; I found the bouquet totally lacking in charm and depth—so ethereal as to be nearly nonexistent—only timid notes of faraway peat and cereal with sugar make themselves known; in the mouth, a bit of saltiness greets the tongue, then astringent/acidic flavors of dry cereal, sour milk, and flint take over; the finish is medium-long and very dry; left me cold.

RATING ★ $$

Tomatin 10-Year-Old Speyside Single Malt 43% Alcohol

Very alluring, clear amber color; the intensely ripe, fruity, and perfumed nose is appealing, showing scents of berry, raisins, and fino sherry; the palate entry is clean, rich, sweet, and quite lovely, then it badly stumbles in midpalate by getting shockingly harsh and abrasive, burning the tongue and throat in the process; the finish somewhat regains the whisky's composure by ending on a mundanely pleasant note of cinnamon; this malt needs some help—the unacceptably nasty flavor leaves the nose's promise completely unfulfilled and shifts too much recovery work to the aftertaste, which, though nice, hardly has enough character to fully redeem the turpentine, kerosene-like midpalate flavor; a perplexing disappointment.

RATING ★ $$

Tomatin Speyside Single Malt 1966 43% Alcohol—The Signatory Series

Pretty amber/clover honey color; the unusual vegetal bouquet left me cold—green pepper, broccoli, and cigar tobacco are the upfront aromas—this is underpinned by a cereal-like, cooked-vegetable quality that seemed to have nothing to do with Scotch whisky—this hound is over-the-hill chemically, pure and simple; like plunging into a freezing mountain lake on a scorching July day, the cloyingly sweet taste is actually startling to the unsuspecting palate—there's no preparation, no gradual buildup to this unpleasantly fleshy experience; the finish is fat, candied, and way too sweet and cloying; this confused, erratic single malt doesn't have a clue; avoid.

RATING ★ $$$

Tullibardine 10-Year-Old Southern Highlands Single Malt 40% Alcohol

A very attractive malt that exhibits a deep harvest-gold tone, very good purity; the straightforward bouquet emits a mildly sweet/doughy aroma of honey wheat all through the four passes—I'm intrigued and disappointed that the nose doesn't reach beyond the bread-like quality; on palate, there's much more complexity and depth than in the nose, as round, supple flavors of figs and dates are supported by foundational flavors of oatmeal and dry cereal; the aftertaste is clean, simple, and undemanding; a decent before-dinner dram.

RATING ★★ $$

Usquaebach 15-Year-Old Highland Pure Malt 43% Alcohol

Stanley J. Stankiwicz, the Scotch wizard behind the sterling Usquaebach blended-Scotch labels, has produced another drop-dead winner in this sublimely opulent Highland pure malt, a 100% barley malt whisky; gorgeous, deep amber/honey hue, some suspended particles evident; the round, supple nose offers seductive scents of off-dry sherry, oak, honey, oak-aged rum, custard, candied fruit, and banana; decidedly, but not overly, sweet on the tongue as voluptuous, warm flavors of vanilla, honey, dry cereal with sugar, malt, and cake frosting make this a substantial and bracing taste experience; the finish is big, sweet, and very smooth, with just a flash of heat; while it may be too broad-shouldered and biscuity for malt lovers who relish lighter Speyside or Lowland malts, I responded to its heft very favorably; I wouldn't mind seeing the suspended-particle situation corrected, however.

RATING ★ ★ ★ ★   *Highly Recommended* $$$

WOLFE'S GLEN 10-Year-Old Highland Single-Grain Scotch Whisky 40% Alcohol

Distilled and matured in oak barrels at Invergordon Distillery, Scotland; the very pale straw-green color is a white-wine knock-off, perfect purity; the designated single grain is wheat grown in the Scottish Highlands—as a result, the nose has an intriguing cereal-with-fruit quality that's mildly sweet, bordering on biscuity—it's an appealingly easy aroma that doesn't have the smoke, peat, wood, oil, or intensity of the bigger blends or most single malts from the islands, Highlands, and Speyside; it's friendly, slightly plump, and sweetish on palate—mild, mellow tastes of oatmeal and toasted cereal keep the flavor experience rudimentary, but pleasant; the finish is clean, surprisingly long, and acceptably sweet; a solid starter Scotch or, simply, a good quaff for those people who don't feel the need to ponder their whisky.

RATING ★ ★ ★   *Recommended* $$

The Scotch Malt Whisky Society Single Malts

In my continuing coverage of Scotch whisky, I've been introduced to an organization called The Scotch Malt Whisky Society, which buys single casks of old single malts from distillers. These cask-strength malts are for sale through mail order to the Society's paying membership. Started in 1983 in Great Britain, the SMWS is open to membership in the U.S. through its American chapter. For an initial first-time membership fee of $139.00 plus tax (annual fees after that are $75.00), the new member receives one bottle of single malt immediately, and quarterly mailings describing the other malts that are available. To receive the malts, the member simply orders them using the enclosed order form or by calling the toll-free number, 1-800-990-1991. The malts are packed and shipped quickly to the member's local retailer, ready for pickup and supreme enjoyment.

I've visited The Vaults, the four-story, stone home of the SMWS, in the Leith section of Edinburgh. My trip included long conversations with the principals and their staff, as well as a chance to taste possible new bottlings with the panel that decides which malts are good enough to be included in the SMWS catalogue. Many of the samples submitted by distillers are rejected, but what passes muster is bottled and offered to members through the newsletter. Composite notes of each new selection are offered for the membership. Single malts purchased by SMWS members are neither diluted nor chill-filtered, thereby leaving the whisky's natural components to stand or fall on their own.

So, the pressing question remains of these and other private bottlings (sometimes called "merchant bottlings," including Gordon & MacPhail, Cadenhead, The Signatory Series, The James MacArthur Series, and Whyte & Whyte): Are they better than the regular distillery bottlings of single malts? Or to phrase it another way, is an uncut merchant or private society version of, say, Lagavulin from Islay finer to the taste than the distillery bottling you pick up off your local retailer's shelf?

My answer is: It depends. Each merchant or private-society bottling has to stand on its own, since the majority are single-barrel offerings. A particular cask of Lagavulin can show extraordinary qualities that might well be lessened by the normal routine of dilution and chill-filtering. This virgin malt may be the truest expression of Lagavulin. But then, because each cask is so different, another may be too overpowering, too idiosyncratic to the lover of Islay malts, who will be better off with the distillery bottlings, which offer a consistency and reliability that aren't found in the merchant or private-society bottlings. The very nature of distillery bottlings guarantees a sense of continuity for the consumer, with no surprises, no variations. Merchants and private societies who buy and bottle their own offerings aren't necessarily driven by or interested in reliability as much as they are concerned about supplying highly individualistic malts to adventurous souls who are intrigued by the single-malt odyssey and who are willing to plunk down hefty dollars to seek out these gems.

Simply stated, there's ample room for both distillery bottlings and these out-of-the-ordinary bottlings. Certainly, because of the extremely limited supply alone, the SMWS could never challenge the standard bottling market. And indeed, I feel that the distilleries benefit from the modest operations of the SMWS, which educates consumers about the sensory delights of Scotch whisky.

SCOTCH MALT WHISKY SOCIETY Cask 53.5 Caol Ila Islay Single Malt 64.8% Alcohol

Gold/hay/straw color; in the salty bouquet—I trust my nose enough to instantly recognize what must be an Islay malt—the burning-embers-like peat element is very well-behaved and actually sweet and slightly oily—the elevated alcohol level is zesty, but manageable; the mouth-feel is oily and fastidiously clean, as mammoth waves of flavor wash up on the palate's shore—pungent, modestly enticing tastes of seaweed and wood smoke; all told, this is not the kind of medicine-chest Islay savage that requires a pistol whipping, but an intensely fragrant malt whose saline flavor isn't quite up to the level of the nose; okay, but too spirity for my taste.

RATING ★ ★ $$$

Scotch Malt Whisky Society Cask 6.16 Glen Deveron Speyside Single Malt 58.3% Alcohol

Orange blossom honey/amber/light topaz color; this meaty nose talks of sweet oak, vanilla, egg cream, and old-fashioned orange Creamsicle in the ripe-berry-fruit and wood-laden bouquet; on palate, the fruited entry gives way to moderate fire at midpalate, then the raisiny, pruney, absolutely stunning fruit component kicks back in with a flourish, providing a chewy, engrossing aftertaste that's medium-long, warm like a smoldering fire, piquant, and totally luscious—pears emerge in the tail end of the finish; my socks were rolling up and down; a sensational, vanilla-wafer-like malt.

RATING ★ ★ ★ ★   *Highly Recommended* $$$

Scotch Malt Whisky Society Cask 86.5 Glen Esk Single Malt 64.3% Alcohol

Sturdy, yellow/gold color; on the first pass, the nose is slightly off-putting, sour, mildly rotten-egg-like and certainly, one of the least desirable noses of the SMWS samples—then on the second nosing pass the aroma becomes much rounder, kinder, and markedly oaky—the aeration blew off the rotting/putrid smell within ten minutes; on palate, this Jekyll and Hyde malt turns into a malted-milk, creamy, sweet whisky with succulent flavor elements, including dry oloroso sherry, prunes, and honey; the finish is opulent, viscous, and fruity, with a trace of tobacco smoke; a wee bit erratic and shaky at the start, but then it composed itself and finished admirably well; watch out for the alcohol—sample with a few drops of mineral water.

RATING ★ ★ ★   *Recommended* $$$

Scotch Malt Whisky Society 77.2 Glen Ord Northern Highlands Single Malt 65.2% Alcohol

The moderate harvest-gold hue runs between pale and medium deep; the nose initially is pungent, chalky, and minerally, then it turns up the volume on the maltiness and oiliness, ending up like green olives; the bracing power of this alcoholic beast is unleashed in the heated aftertaste; but before you arrive there, you first must pass through taste sentinals of delicious red fruit, butter, and cream; the finish might be too imposing for some Scotch fans, so beware; treat this husky, bristling hound with respect.

RATING ★ ★ ★   *Recommended* $$$

Scotch Malt Whisky Society Cask 99.2 Glenugie Eastern Highlands Single Malt 60% Alcohol

A beautiful topaz/amontillado-sherry color; the sensational aroma oozes glycerine, honeydew melon, vanilla extract, brown sugar, and the sexy kiss of an off-dry oloroso sherry cask—my guess is that this concentrated, deeply bronzed malt saw more sherry cask than bourbon in its maturation period, if indeed it saw any bourbon at all; in the mouth, it rolls over the tongue read-

ily and luxuriously—a glorious but uncomplicated malt of monster proportions—malt, sherry, wood, and fruit, all richly wrapped in a warm, sexy
structure; I place this sinewy beauty up in my all-time favorite private-
bottling malts.

RATING ★ ★ ★ ★   *Highly Recommended* $$$

SCOTCH MALT WHISKY SOCIETY 99.5 Glenugie Eastern Highlands Single Malt 63.9% Alcohol

Slightly darker honey/amber color than the 99.4 bottling of Glenugie;
the malty/honey nose is similar to that of the 99.4 but far more confident
and straightlaced—it stays firm and steady at every pass; on palate, this
beauty takes hold of the taste buds and won't let go, as opulent flavors of
ripe watermelon heart, vanilla, chocolate cake frosting, and coffee with milk
all combine in a harmonious, slightly hot aftertaste that's a humdinger; this
is a full-blown malt that delivers the goods in an unfaltering fashion that's
far removed from its volatile brother, the schizoid 99.4; what's so intrigu-
ing about tasting these two side-by-side is the illustration of how different,
how totally unique each barrel of Scotch whisky is, even from the same dis-
tillery; a sexy, luscious beauty.

RATING ★ ★ ★ ★   *Highly Recommended* $$$

SCOTCH MALT WHISKY SOCIETY 99.4 Glenugie Eastern Highlands Single Malt 64.4% Alcohol

Rich honey color; fittingly, the honey appearance is buttressed by a honeyed opening aroma, followed by a minty, evergreen, vegetal scent that's hard
to pinpoint—the fourth and final pass reveals an unpleasant whiff of wet
cardboard and mold—with aeration, this nose has unraveled in the sampling
glass; what charm was lost in the deteriorating nose is recovered momen-
tarily in the mouth, then mysteriously is lost again in a heat wave of searing
alcohol; the finish is sweet and fruity and quite lovely, but I find it too ex-
hausting to keep up with this peculiar malt, which could be voted the Grand
Marshal of the inconsistency parade.

RATING ★ ★ $$$

SCOTCH MALT WHISKY SOCIETY 49.4 St. Magdalene Lowland Single Malt 62.8% Alcohol

Very pale—a white-wine-like straw/yellow color; the nose emits a tad too
much cough medicine and vegetation for me at first, then goes sweet and
melony by the third pass, ending up like cotton candy at the county fair—
what a queer ride; perhaps the most vegetal/floral of all the SMWS malts
I've tasted; the finish travels through a very warm, alcoholic stage before set-
tling down into a sexy, sensual sweet-apple-pie finale that doubtless is its
finest attribute; overall, it's not one I'd shell money out for, but it still pro-
vides one of the more interesting single-malt experiences for a Lowland
malt.

RATING ★ ★ $$$

SCOTCH MALT WHISKY SOCIETY 17.6 Scapa Orkney Islands Single Malt 55.1% Alcohol

Very pretty gold/yellow hue; the nose is as finely appointed as any SMWS selection I've experienced—it speaks volumes about elegance without forgetting about strength and character—it's rich, but neither overpowering nor cloying—it's filled with a keen stuffing of citrus, going slightly bitter in the final whiff; on the palate, though, is where this handsome single malt shines brightest, as wave after wave of zesty barley malt flavor comforts and envelops the taste buds; there's a slight brininess in the aftertaste that bows out quickly to the sweet apricot-like flavor that carries you home; I loved this well-defined, multilayered malt because it depicts how grace can be paired beautifully with power in one memorable swallow; outstanding quality at any price.

RATING ★ ★ ★ ★   ***Highly Recommended*** $$$

AMERICAN WHISKEY

I t's my opinion that, next to Scotland, the world's finest whiskies are produced in the United States. While Scotland is responsible for a greater number of superlative whiskies, the distillers of Kentucky and Tennessee are closing the gap. With the introduction over the last ten years of America's crème-de-la-crème whiskies, specifically, the impressive single-barrel and small-batch bourbons from Kentucky and Pennsylvania and the ultrapremium Tennessee whiskies, the whiskies of the United States have catapulted forward in terms of worldwide status. This new breed, which, oddly enough, echoes how whiskey was made and offered in the U.S. in the nineteenth century, has gone a long way toward serving notice that American distilling will take a back seat to no one. In a way, I feel that the distillers of the U.S. owe a debt of gratitude to the Scots, for it was only when the American producers observed the consuming public's warm and enthusiastic embrace of the single malts from the Highlands and islands of Scotland toward the end of the 1980s that they comprehended the desire for greater quality and the willingness to pay for it.

In colonial America, rum, not whiskey, was a staple item. This was largely because little grain was grown along the coast of eastern North America in the latter decades of the seventeenth century and the early part of the eighteenth century. In addition, sugarcane molasses was plentiful, since at the time trade between the colonies and the developing countries of the Caribbean was vigorous. The colonists, few of whom possessed the skills or the stills to make spirits, simply distilled the mash of the sugarcane molasses to produce rum, which they mixed into everything imaginable. America's first still was operated by a Staten Island, New York, gent by the name of William Keith, who busily stoked his first still fire around 1640.

America's whiskey saga didn't take root until the colonists began moving westward in the mid-1700s into what were then the wilds of western Virginia, western Maryland, the Carolinas, and Pennsylvania. These frontier areas offered environments that were conducive to the cultivation of cereal grains, and, as history has shown, where cereal grains are planted, whiskey is almost always sure to follow. This migration, coupled with the massive infusion of immigrants from Ireland, Scotland, and Germany, three countries rich in distilling tradition, marked the dawn of America's whiskey age.

By the late eighteenth century, whiskey making on the local level had been thrown into high gear on the westernmost outskirts of colonial settlements. In 1791, however, the U.S. Treasury, under the guidance of Alexander Hamilton, imposed an excise tax on all distilled spirits as well as stills to help pay off the debt incurred in the war for independence. By 1794, disputes between farmers, who at the time did most of the nation's whiskey distilling, and excisemen, whose job it was to locate the stills and collect the tax, became so heated that President Washington, who himself owned a pot still that was operated by a Scotsman, was forced to send troops into western Pennsylvania to quell the revolt. After the display of federal muscle, the situation calmed without serious bloodshed, and taxation remained in place.

In the meantime, however, scores of the most disgruntled of the Pennsylvania farmers packed up their pot stills and moved to Kentucky, which was then still a part of Virginia. This vast, untamed area was ideally suited for the growing of grain, especially corn. When the farmers combined their corn mash with the local crystalline, iron-free water, purified by the limestone shelf that lay beneath the area, the foundation was laid for generations of families to earn their living from whiskey making. By the turn of the nineteenth century, the whiskey that was being produced in Bourbon County, Kentucky, was fancied all along the settlements that used the Mississippi River as their primary connection to other communities. Calls for "Bourbon Whiskey" were heard echoing in the taverns and roadhouses of New Orleans, Natchez, Baton Rouge, and St. Louis. The name stuck, and the whiskey flourished. Bourbon was destined to become the spirit of America, which it did officially in 1964 by an Act of Congress.

As business boomed, so did crackdowns by tax collectors. Records show that in 1894 the registered number of distilleries in Kentucky alone hovered near 600. That same year saw almost 500 suits filed against Kentuckians for tax violations. The downside of the stiff taxation was the inevitable rise in the making of illicit whiskey, which was called "moonshine," "white lightning," and "white dog."

Following World War I, the Women's Christian Temperance Movement teamed up with Minnesota representative Andrew Volstead to push the Eighteenth Amendment, which made the production, shipment, and consumption of alcohol illegal, through Congress. At 12:01 A.M. on January 17, 1920, the pouring of whiskey stopped until 1933.

The repeal of Prohibition occurred in the throes of the Great Depression. The whiskey industry in the U.S. slowly revived, but considerable damage had been done. Many distilleries never reopened. With the hostilities of World War II soon to follow, it wasn't until the late 1940s that production was back to full strength. The 1950s, 1960s, and 1970s were outstanding decades for growth for the whiskey industry as brands like Jim Beam, Wild Turkey, Old Grand Dad, Early Times, and Jack Daniel's became not only popular whiskies at home, but symbols of America's strength and prosperity abroad.

The 1980s offered another challenge, with a rise in health-conscious consumers, as well as a burgeoning interest in lighter beverages and wines. But the industry has recently turned a corner and American whiskey is once again flexing its muscles both domestically and around the world.

BOURBON

What makes a whiskey a bourbon? Federal law dictates what defines a bourbon: First, the whiskey must be comprised of at least 51 percent corn. The corn content of most bourbons actually ranges from 60 percent to 75 percent. If the corn content rises above 80 percent, it is then, according to federal law, considered corn whiskey. Other grains that are commonly used in a bourbon blend are barley, wheat, and rye. A distiller's rule-of-thumb dictates that the higher the corn content, the lighter the whiskey. Rarely are rye and wheat used together as supplemental grains, because they are not compatible. Bourbons are viewed within the industry as being either rye bourbons or wheat bourbons, even though corn always makes up the largest percentage of the grain used, because the supplemental grains have a greater influence on the final fragrance and taste. Rye imparts a spicy, sassy flavor, while the contribution of wheat is characterized as being dense or textured.

Second, bourbon must be aged in new, charred white-oak barrels for a minimum of two years. The barrels are American white oak from Missouri, Indiana, or Kentucky. They range in size from 50 to 66 gallons. Most bourbons age longer than the two-year minimum, with a rare few aging for up to two decades. There are four levels of char, graded one (the lightest toasting) to four (the deepest penetrating char). The deeper the char, the more intense the color, aroma, and flavor of the bourbon. By level three, the sap starts to caramelize. This result, which contributes a vanilla-like flavor, is referred to as the "red layer." The cask ends up being a crucial contributor to the overall character of any premium or ultrapremium bourbon.

Third, by law, the whiskey cannot be distilled higher than 160 proof (80 percent alcohol).

Fourth, bourbon can be cut only with water to reduce the alcohol level. Distillers claim that the best water for reduction is the same water that is used for distillation.

Interestingly, although bourbon is most frequently associated with the state of Kentucky, it can be legally made and labeled as such anywhere within the U.S. States that currently produce or have in the past produced bourbons include Virginia, Illinois, Pennsylvania, and Indiana.

Tennessee is the second most illustrious whiskey-producing state in the Union, even though only two distilleries remain in operation, Jack Daniels in Lynchburg (population 361 plus two mosquitoes in July and August) and George Dickel in Tullahoma (population 18,000).

Tennessee's whiskies are routinely referred to as "Tennessee sour mash" rather than bourbon because, first, Tennesseans do not want their whiskies to be aligned with those of rival Kentucky and, second, the spirits do not quite fit the legal requirements laid down for bourbon. Because of the custom of filtering them through ten-foot-high vats filled with sugar-maple charcoal before being transferred to oak casks for aging, Tennessee whiskey is legally different from bourbon. The charcoal filtering system is known as the Lincoln County Process.

There must be something to the charcoal filtering, however, because one Tennessee sour mash's case sales worldwide annually top 4 million. That whiskey is Jack Daniel's Black Label No. 7, a whiskey that I've seen being poured in as disparate locales as Paris, London, Singapore, New York, and Nashville. The mainline whiskey created by "Mister Jack" is as familiar an American icon as Levis, Nikes, Coke, or Michael Jordan's No. 23 Chicago Bulls jersey.

Since I've traveled through these states visiting the distilleries and talking it up with the lovely people, I'm delighted—no, thrilled—that American whiskies are entering a new era of recognition. These are some of the very finest distilled spirits one can purchase. You will want to take advantage of this remarkable period of availability and choice.

AMERICAN WHISKEY

A. H. HIRSCH 16-Year-Old Pot Still Straight Bourbon 45.8% Alcohol

Lustrous, rich medium-amber/sunset-orange with copper/russet highlights; the tight, compact nose has sensuous fragrances of spiced orange, walnut, corn husk, a touch of resin, and, most prominently, nougat—while it's anything but expansive, the bouquet subtly draws me in, forcing me to inhale deeper—in the process, the layers of aroma unwrap like the delicate skins of an onion—it's a seductive and coy bourbon nose; in the mouth, this robust but polite bourbon confidently offers happily married tastes of caramel, oats, toffee, wood smoke, maple syrup, oak, controlled alcohol, and raisins; there's even a slim, winey trace of sweet sherry in the sublime, firm, heady aftertaste; clearly, a superlative bourbon that stands head and shoulders above the pack.

RATING ★ ★ ★ ★ ★   *Highest Recommendation* $$$

A. H. HIRSCH 20-Year-Old Pot Still Straight Bourbon 45.8% Alcohol

Made at the Michter's Distillery located in Schaefferstown, Pennsylvania, in 1974 in a small pot still; stunningly fantastic color of copper-penny/rich amber with ocher highlights; the bouquet is spirity, heady, and a bit prickly in the initial two passes, then by the third nosing it settles in and expels luscious aromas of mint, oak, ripe banana, ripe guava, nut meat, and brown sugar—it ends up being a mannered, stately bouquet that betrays the employment of the pot still method through its more than ample complexity, style, maturity, and breeding; I loved the opening salvo of controlled heat at palate entry, then the silky-smooth texture ushers in perfectly melded flavors of sweet oak, red fruit, maple, spice, and grain mash; the aftertaste is round, direct but polite, and very long; I found this 20-year-old bourbon every bit as grand and idiosyncratic as the five-star 16-year-old; these two Pennsylvania bourbons rank with the world's best whiskies; the most stylish tandem that America has to offer.

RATING ★ ★ ★ ★ ★   *Highest Recommendation* $$$

ANCIENT AGE 100 Bottled-in-Bond Kentucky Straight Bourbon 50% Alcohol

Author's note: "Bottled in Bond" is a labeling practice that indicates that the whiskey was produced by one distillery in one distilling season, was bottled at 100 proof (50% alcohol), was matured in charred new-oak barrels for at least four years, was stored and bottled in a Treasury Department–bonded warehouse, and had no excise tax paid on it until it was taken out of the warehouse and shipped. As is often erroneously perceived, the Bottled in Bond designation is NOT necessarily an assurance of superior quality. Golden/amber, winey hue; the lofty alcohol content is neatly masked beneath aromas of sweet and succulent ripe red apples and Anjou pears—in the background I detect scents of black pepper and toffee; the flavor elements are remarkably subtle and synchronized in view of the alcohol—gorgeous, compelling, yet mannered tastes of ripe peaches, apricots, and pears completely disarm the taste buds; it finishes in a surprisingly low-key fashion as an unexpected taste of key lime concludes the experience; I was blown away by the balance of this remarkable bourbon, as not once did the alcohol intrude upon the enjoyment of the delicate fruit components; seek out and buy.

RATING ★ ★ ★ ★   *Highly Recommended* $

ANCIENT AGE Barrel 107 Special Edition 10-Year-Old Kentucky Straight Bourbon 53.5% Alcohol

Fabulously rich orange/honey/amber color that offers russet/copper interior highlights; the sublime nose initially smells of sweet oak and vanilla, but a wave of warm alcohol follows and quickly exits (it is barrel strength, after all), then all that is topped off by honey, chocolate-covered cherries, and cream sherry—it's an incredibly busy, perfumed bouquet that even bests some of the ultrapremium (small-batch and single-barrel) bourbons currently en vogue; on palate, it's a potpourri of egg cream, vanilla, sweet oak, cream sherry, cake batter, cocoa, and honey flavors that are fat, chewy, and velvety—this whiskey isn't as profound as much as it is simply delicious and fun to sip.

RATING ★ ★ ★ ★   *Highly Recommended* $

ANCIENT AGE Preferred Blended Whiskey 40% Alcohol

Rather dullish, dusty amber/brown color; the cereal-like, corn husk, oatmeal aroma is pedestrian and flat, but oddly is mildly pleasant in its malty toastiness—it also hints of sweet oak without being candied or cloying; on palate, the entry is flat, but once it coats the tongue the friendly, warm, sweet-corn, honey-wheat flavor is savory; finishes medium-long, malty, and sweet; one of the better blended whiskies I've tasted, though it took me a second and third pass to take a shine to it; once I got past the mediocre nose and appearance, the flavor and aftertaste went a long way to win me over.

RATING ★ ★ ★   *Recommended* $

ANCIENT AGE 90 Kentucky Straight Bourbon 45% Alcohol

The brilliant, luminous, rich clover-honey hue is really bedazzling to the eye, making it an inviting bourbon; with swirling, the vigor of this oily nose leaps from the glass, as layers of almonds, lanolin, butter, and coconut come together in a harmonious manner; the flavor is like a laser beam on the tongue—totally focused, it excites the taste buds with waves of nuts, creamery butter, and off-dry, underripe fruit elements that balance beautifully in the congenial finish; this one is a dandy, straightforward, clean, and all there.

RATING ★ ★ ★   *Recommended* $

ANCIENT ANCIENT AGE Kentucky Straight Bourbon 45% Alcohol

Next to the Barrel 107, the lovely "triple A" possesses the deepest amber/dark-honey color of the Ancient Age–labeled whiskies; normally aged for about ten years in wood; potent, piquant coffee, tea-leaf, and cocoa aromas make this atypical nose stand out from the rest of the Ancient Age lineup—leafy and bean-like are the two descriptors that say it all; the intense bean-like quality marches onward in the delicious flavor, which goes waxy, sweet, ripe, and oaky in the exceptional aftertaste; a mature, fully present, svelte, concentrated bourbon whose surefootedness and grace are comforting and appealing; the slightly elevated alcohol level is never an issue in this well-crafted whiskey that deserves recognition.

RATING ★ ★ ★   *Recommended* $

ANCIENT AGE Kentucky Straight Bourbon 40% Alcohol

The clean, lively, and bright light-honey/yellow-hay color shows off goldenrod highlights in the core—very pretty to look at; almost wine-like in its aromatic scope, this grapy, citrusy nose is lean, limber, and forward in an estery way; in the mouth, the austerity detected in the nose continues on, in fact, a bit too much so, as the whiskey's abrasive acidity dominates the scenery; it finishes cleanly, but without any lift, stuffing, or sophistication—surprisingly, I found it less palatable than the Ancient Age Preferred Blended Whiskey; too acidic on the tongue—move past this one to others from this line.

RATING ★ $

BAKER'S 7-Year-Old Kentucky Straight Bourbon / Small Batch 53.5% Alcohol

Author's note: Baker's is the most cognac-like American whiskey in the marketplace and should be viewed as a digestif *to be served neat in a wine glass. A really superb and unique taste treat. Part of Jim Beam's Small Batch Bourbon Collection.* Warm, deep amber/nutbrown/tawny color; the nuanced aroma offers subdued, somewhat muted aromas of cherries, vanilla, caramel candy, and cola nut—remarkably, I could keep my nose in the glass for long periods even with the potency of the alcohol; downright regal on the palate as characterful flavors of roasted nuts, ripe banana, ripe pears, vanilla from the oak, and hints of old wine treated my taste buds to a genuine bourbon hootenanny; the sweet finish is medium-long and has a banana-like tail; the potency is properly harnessed, leaving the luscious flavor elements to entertain lavishly.

RATING ★ ★ ★ ★   *Highly Recommended* $$

BASIL HAYDEN'S 8-Year-Old Kentucky Straight Bourbon / Small Batch 40% Alcohol

Author's note: One of the four bourbons in Jim Beam Brand's Small Batch Bourbon Collection. Golden/yellow/amber color; lovely, aromatic, sweet nose of glycerine, honey, and peppermint—though only 40% alcohol, prolonged nosing brings out a fieriness that pinches the olfactory sense; peculiar, but utterly beguiling floral flavors of violets and roses dominate the palate at entry, then mysteriously go completely flat at midpalate; the aftertaste is too short and sweet, with simple notes of spice and apple; this is an ungainly, inconsistent type of bourbon that shows spurts of real potential, but then retreats to heavy-handed tactics; hardly offensive, but average and too unfocused for its own good; obviously, the weak link in Jim Beam's Small Batch Collection.

RATING ★ ★ $$

BENCHMARK Single-Barrel Kentucky Straight Bourbon 47% Alcohol

The richness of the deep-amber/dark-honey color dazzles the eye, ideal purity; the buxom, sweet-cereal, slightly candied, corn-like bouquet has "bourbon" written all over it—it's a powerhouse nose whose thrust lies mainly in the caramelly, fruity perfume rather than in the alcohol or wood elements; in the mouth, the vanilla/oaky sweetness is very pronounced, but manageable—the oak element flows calmly with the corn sweetness in a midpalate display of luxurious flavor; the finish is medium-long and cakefrosting-sweet; on the plus side, the lofty alcohol component never interferes with the flavor or the aftertaste; a fat, concentrated, jammy, unashamedly syrupy bourbon that I liked primarily because it's so brazen; a word of caution, however, it's so over-the-top in terms of sweetness and ropy texture that it could easily be perceived as being out of balance; tasted four times; I brought it down to three stars from four after my second blind tasting of it; a controversial style.

RATING ★ ★ ★   *Recommended* $$

BLANTON'S Single-Barrel Kentucky Straight Bourbon 46.5% Alcohol; Barrel No. 444, Rick No. 9, Warehouse H—Bottled in Oct. 1993

Author's note: This was the first single-barrel bourbon to be offered and is still one of the favorites. Markedly lighter in appearance than the Barrel 74, Rick No. 25—burnished-gold/medium-amber hue; quite grainy/cereally in the first nosing, then turns really fragrant as toasty aromas of biscuits, cookie batter, oak resin, and herbs vie for the attention of the olfactory sense in the rollercoaster third and fourth nosings—this bouquet is much more vigorous and unruly than the Barrel 74, Rick No. 25, bottling; shows a good fruit presence on the tongue that's multilayered and graceful; the finish is svelte, crisp, and estery, showing very little oakiness, sweetness, or vanilla; this is the more interesting of the two bottlings I've formally sampled in that it's more complex and challenging to the taste buds.

RATING ★★★★   ***Highly Recommended*** $$

BLANTON's Single-Barrel Kentucky Straight Bourbon 46.5% Alcohol; Barrel No. 74, Rick No. 25, Warehouse H—Bottled in Dec. 1994

Gorgeous topaz/dark-amber/dark-honey color; the lightly herbal, grainy, piquant aromas offer faint hints of caramel and fruity sweetness; in the mouth, roasted-almond, charcoal-like warmth neither overpowers nor fades on palate; beautifully balanced; exceedingly elegant, sublime finish; a sound, supple afterdinner bourbon that should be served only in a wine glass.

RATING ★★★   ***Recommended*** $$

BOOKER's Bourbon Kentucky Straight Bourbon / Small Batch 61.1% Alcohol (Some bottlings up to 63% alcohol)

Author's note: Booker Noe is the grandson of James Beauregard Beam, a.k.a. Jim Beam, perhaps the most famous name in the history of bourbon. Mr. Noe is likewise the master distiller for Jim Beam Brands, Inc. Whereas most bourbons are first cut with water, then filtered prior to bottling, Booker's Bourbon is neither diminished nor filtered. It comes at you, and I mean comes at you, literally straight from the barrel. This is no ordinary bourbon. This is the real stuff, direct from the distiller to your innards. At its inception, a mere 100 cases of Booker's Bourbon were bottled. The ensuing demand from collectors, connoisseurs, and the simply curious has so far outstretched all predictions. Justifiably so. Brilliant orange/bronze/iced-tea color, with copper/russet highlights; the potent, heady, spirity, rubbing alcohol, sweet, tangy nose is fiery, but when inhaled in small doses it exhibits superb depth and an oaky/resiny crispness that's alluring; the bar-the-door-Katie flavor thrust on palate is startling, as high-flying flavors of wood, smoke, and wine command the surviving taste buds; what I admire most about this incredible whiskey is its endless aftertaste of fruit and nuts—it simply doesn't quit and gets mellower as time advances—consequently, it's one of the most memorable finishes in the bourbon category; not designed for the faint of heart, this swashbuckler really howls and should be experienced by any person interested in distilled spirits; I strongly recommend a dash of mineral water before, during, and after.

RATING ★★★★   ***Highly Recommended*** $$$

CARSTAIRS White Seal Blended Whiskey 40% Alcohol

Attractive gold/amber color; the whiskey aromas that one expects to smell appeared to be all but vanquished through, I would guess, the process of overblending—in the vain attempt of making an easy-drinking whiskey, the distiller seems to have sacrificed any semblance of bouquet; unfortunately, this harsh, astringent, virtually flavorless whiskey is anything but a tonsil charmer; what it is, is an eye-popping flamethrower whose unbridled alcohol seared my gums; this nasty stuff tastes like it's straight from a backwoods still; no other way of putting it, but this is low-grade hooch.

RATING ★ $

EAGLE RARE 10-Year-Old Kentucky Straight Bourbon 50.5% Alcohol

Gorgeous amber/chestnut-brown color, with vermillion/rust highlights, perfect clarity; the zesty nose rises from the glass gracefully—there's a whole lot of shakin' goin' on in this camphor-like nose as succulent, woody, dark toffee, and nut-meat aromas keep the olfactory sense working O.T.—a simply grand bouquet that epitomizes what full-throttle bourbon is all about; in the mouth, this brazen hussy of a whiskey hot-wires the taste buds as the charged flavors of vanilla extract, spearmint, and caramel set the tongue tingling; the aftertaste is peppery and vivacious, eventually settling down into a sweet, oaky, dare I say, maple syrup, mode that's positively dynamite—this bourbon is not for the squeamish or the weak-kneed.

RATING ★ ★ ★ ★   *Highly Recommended* $

EAGLE RARE 15-Year-Old Kentucky Straight Bourbon 53.5% Alcohol

Available in the Japanese market only; rich, amber/orange/mahogany-brown hue—good clarity; the nose is notably less rambunctious than its younger, scamp-like sibling, the Eagle Rare 10-year-old—but what's lost in vigor is more than made up for in mellow presence and depth of character—the especially charming candied-almond aroma is nothing short of dazzling—this is a showstopper of a bouquet; on the palate, it cradles the tongue in toasty, silky waves of moderately sweet flavors and texture—the sophisticated flavors run from concentrated cereal grain to coffee to caramel candy to tobacco smoke; the aftertaste leaves the tongue feeling prickly enough to acknowledge the elevated alcohol level; give me a touch less high-octane heat in the throat and it flirts with getting a rare fifth rating star.

RATING ★ ★ ★ ★   *Highly Recommended* $$$

ELIJAH CRAIG

A prominent and widespread, but unsubstantiated, fable claims that a Baptist minister, whose name was Elijah Craig, discovered the wood-aging process, the charring of the oak cask, that has become an integral part of bourbon production. This whiskey has been named in his honor.

ELIJAH CRAIG 18-Year-Old Single-Barrel Kentucky Straight Bourbon, Barrel No. 007; 45% Alcohol

Very deep amber/tea-brown/burnt-orange tone, ideal clarity; the no-nonsense bouquet lets it be known in the first pass that this is a serious bourbon—there's an astringent oakiness that's crisp, clean, and very direct—I loved the no-frills, straight-ahead approach of the nose—enticing notes of corn husk (which is dominant), buttered popcorn, resin, lead pencil, and a subtle hint of caramel—dynamite; the mouth presence is divine, showing equal parts elegance and command as layered, fat flavors of old oak, cream, almonds, vanilla extract, and smoke all meet at midpalate and carry through to the soft but fiery aftertaste; my throat felt like it was glowing during the finish; a well-endowed, husky bourbon that rates damn near five stars.

RATING ★ ★ ★ ★   *Highly Recommended* $$

Elijah Craig Kentucky Straight Bourbon 47% Alcohol

Pretty tea color, flecked with orange/copper highlights; classy, refined, multidimensional nose that includes hints of coffee beans, vanilla, oranges, ripe pineapple, and moderate sweetness; on palate a dry, alluring cola flavor dominates early then gives way to a concentrated, smoky, charcoal, slightly fruity midpalate; the long, engaging finish has a gentlemanly fieriness that addresses the spirit in an eloquent voice; enjoy neat or with a few drops of water.

RATING ★ ★ ★   *Recommended* $

Elmer T. Lee Single-Barrel Kentucky Straight Bourbon 53.5% Alcohol

Proper, pretty, light-to-medium amber appearance; the elevated alcohol is nicely harnessed, allowing other faintly aromatic qualities like pencil eraser, fresh flowers, and mild spice to entertain the olfactory sense—it's a surprisingly sedate bouquet; the initial taste pass seemed limp, but the second vaulted easily over the bar as lush, round, succulent, full-bodied, heavily oaked flavors of lanolin, butter, cocoa, and toffee treated the palate to a sizeable feast; the aftertaste is sweet, cream-sherry-like, and potent but generally well-behaved; the high alcohol is never a problem in this well-crafted, but slightly too chunky and chewy winner.

RATING ★ ★ ★   *Recommended* $$

Evan Williams 1987 Single-Barrel Kentucky Straight Bourbon, Barrel No. 051; 43.3% Alcohol

Brilliant, luminous, translucent ocher/honey/medium-amber color; the nose seriously reminds me of paraffin in the first pass, then it expands in the second nosing, showing grassy, vegetal, hay-like scents that are delicate, yet assertive in their demeanor—the final two passes expose a vinous, entertaining, and complex bouquet devoid of fruit or wood; in the mouth, it takes a right turn away from the earthy/leafy bend toward a lovely, warm, chocolatey sweet taste that's like smoldering embers at the back of the tongue; I liked this sumptuous 1987 bottling more than the fine 1986 (three-star quality); the midpalate and the comfortable finish pushed it into four-star territory; smashingly good and satisfying.

RATING ★ ★ ★ ★   *Highly Recommended* $$

Evan Williams 1986 Single-Barrel Kentucky Straight Bourbon, Barrel No. 013; 43.3% Alcohol

Attractive, medium amber/harvest-gold hue with orange edges—there are suspended particles of undetermined origin noted; the nose is mildly sweet, with a pungent caramel-corn-like top layer that's a seductive "come hither" asset—beneath that lies a more acidic, resiny, oaky, cherry-pit-like layer, which is definitely the foundation of this lightish, but beguiling, bouquet; the resiny quality first noticed in the aroma carries over in spades into the flavor, especially at the palate entry, when a crisp, almost astringent taste nearly makes my lips pucker—the midpalate is grainy and medium-bodied; the finish brings home the intensity of the grain in warm waves of lingering, smoldering flavor, particularly in the throat.

RATING ★ ★ ★   *Recommended* $$

Evan Williams 7-Year-Old Kentucky Straight Bourbon 45% Alcohol

Attractive, lustrous deep amber/bronze color; a generous, direct aroma of spirit gently pinches the olfactory sense as fragrant, sweetish, ripe, round scents of flowers, oak, fruit, and evergreen delight the nose; succulent, estery, sweet flavors of ripe grapes, honey wheat, coconut, almonds, and cream blanket the palate; the finish is very smoky, clean, and full-bodied; clearly a solid bourbon that's as satisfying tastewise as it is pleasurable to look at.

RATING ★ ★ ★   *Recommended* $

Gentleman Jack Rare Tennessee Whiskey 40% Alcohol

The dazzling, lively, medium amber/orange/honey color is really impressive in its clarity and richness; the toasty, oaky, oily, smoky nose is fat, sassy, and buttery, indeed almost creamy in its opening salvo—with aeration (20 minutes) the nose settles into a two-tiered, complex bouquet of walnuts on top, bolstered underneath by a honeyed foundation—a grand, bountiful whiskey nose by any measure; on palate, this savory mouthful of spirit takes off like the space shuttle in a rainbow of feinty/estery flavors, ranging from old saddle leather to loose tobacco to coffee to raisins; the finish is a tad too biting and heated at first for my tongue, then it mellows out into a sherried, oily, almondy tail in the throat; the awesome complexity and multilayered nature of this superb whiskey are astonishing; it gallops with the best that American distillers have to offer; also, it's the first new whiskey from Jack Daniel's in more than 100 years.

RATING ★ ★ ★ ★   *Highly Recommended* $

George Dickel Special Barrel Reserve 10-Year-Old Tennessee Whiskey 43% Alcohol

Author's note: This whiskey is part of the Bourbon Heritage Collection.
Medium-amber/light-honey color; the bouquet is rather restrained in the initial nosing and only shows a bit of itself even after vigorous swirling and aeration; once the nose does guardedly emerge, soft waves of sweet grain mash and vanilla wafer tease the olfactory sense; this is much more a drinking whiskey than it is a sniffing whiskey in that its finely tuned character displays itself amply in deliciously sweet tastes of molasses, corn syrup, and honey-wheat toast; the aftertaste is almost tart, short-lived, and owns just enough heat in the throat to knock its score down one notch from four to three stars; even with the slight glitch in the finish it's a very pleasant whiskey, particularly on the tongue at entry and the midpalate point.

RATING ★ ★ ★   *Recommended* $ $

Hancock's Reserve Single-Barrel Kentucky Straight Bourbon 44.5% Alcohol

Handsome, medium-deep, amber/orange hue; the perfumy bouquet leans in the direction of grain rather than fruit as soft waves of malted milk, oatmeal, and dry cereal dominate the nose, aided by a solid dose of sweet oak that brings up the rear; the opulent, generous, lavish flavors envelop the purring taste buds in a blanket of balanced sweetness—this bourbon cooks on the palate in a well-orchestrated symphony of flavors, including cocoa, cake batter, and peanut butter, all neatly packaged in a delightful new-oak tanginess; the sweet-sour, biscuity aftertaste bites a wee bit too much in the throat, but overall this is a splendid, full-bodied bourbon whose utterly charming nature should encourage the development of a fanatical following at home and abroad.

RATING ★★★★ **Highly Recommended** $$

HENRY McKENNA 10-Year-Old Single-Barrel Kentucky Straight Bourbon, Barrel No. 009; 50% Alcohol

The richness of the orange/copper-penny color is dazzling; the upfront, sweetish bouquet offers moderately tantalizing aromas of leather, spice, orange blossom, honeysuckle, and grain—it's not an outstanding nose in range or depth, but it's workmanlike and honest all the same; it's on the palate that this combustible bourbon struts its best stuff, as two-alarm flavors of charred oak, sweet corn, light toffee/caramel, and spice (in the background) nicely offset the spirity foundation; there's a sudden rush of heat in the midpalate that I liked more in the second tasting than the first; once the fire is extinguished, the aftertaste turns mellow; much better than the wimpy regular bottling.

RATING ★★★ **Recommended** $$

HENRY McKENNA Kentucky Straight Bourbon 40% Alcohol

Amber color; definitely a vegetal nose of dead-on corn husk and mash at first pass, then after further sniffing one detects secondary aromas of wood and honey; regrettably, this one really left me cold in the flavor department; I found the taste unexciting and one-dimensional, but it almost redeemed itself in the savory, spicy, full, and warm finish; too little, too late, however; an average score could have been above average if the flavor had shown more complexity, style, and substance.

RATING ★★ $

I. W. HARPER Gold Medal 15-Year-Old Kentucky Straight Bourbon 40% Alcohol

Author's note: This whiskey is one of the five bottlings included in the Bourbon Heritage Collection. Light-to-medium amber/autumn-gold color; the nose comes right at you in the first pass, then turns biscuity and mature, showing superb balance among the components of sweet oak, traces of clove, sugarcane, and maple syrup; it's a decidedly sweet bouquet that reminded me most of light caramel candies; once on the palate, this nimble whiskey starts out off-dry at entry, then shifts to an appealing, crisp sweetness, not too far removed from ripe red apples; at a manageable 80 proof, it envelops the mouth rather than assaults it; the finish is agile, clean, but short-lived, exhibiting a final taste of tropical fruit just before it fades from view; there's hardly any grain presence at all in this easy-drinking bourbon; tasting it blind, I mistakenly guessed it to be much younger than it is.

RATING ★★★ **Recommended** $$

Jack Daniels Old Time No. 7 (Black) Tennessee Whiskey
43% Alcohol

Attractive orange/amber hue; the nose emits earthy, oily/resiny, mineral-hard, road-tar aromas, with faint background hints of leather and pepper-mint; the serious, tart, off-dry, and smoky flavors are lean yet muscular, leaving behind lovely traces of hard candy in the whistle-clean and medium-long aftertaste; the highlight of this venerable whiskey is the terrific finish, which coats the throat in a charcoal and honey buffer; unfortunately and surprisingly, the finish alone isn't enough to get this American institution recommended—the blue-collar bouquet is simply too resiny, and the flavor, while nice, hardly inspires.

RATING ★ ★ $

Jim Beam 4-Year-Old Kentucky Straight Bourbon 40% Alcohol

Pretty amber/orange color; pleasantly spirity, kicky, perfumy nose of vanilla wafer, cocoa, and peaches—an altogether engaging, round, sweet bouquet that's simultaneously aggressive and easy to like; irresistibly sweet flavors of caramel and smoke greet the palate, then turn astringent, though never hot, in the very long, crisp aftertaste; I liked this zesty bourbon most of all for its honest, sweet, and captivating bouquet; not a Mercedes sedan, but a reliable old Ford truck.

RATING ★ ★ ★   *Recommended* $

Knob Creek 9-Year-Old Kentucky Straight Bourbon / Small Batch
50% Alcohol

Author's note: This bourbon is part of the Small Batch Bourbon Collection. Terribly pretty medium-amber color, flecked with orange highlights; the semisweet, round, full-bodied, voluptuous, toasted nut and grain nose is very intense, but manageable—on my second nosing pass, I picked up ex-ceedingly lovely background aromas of peaches and hard candy—one of the deepest, most bountiful aromas in the bourbon category; once in the mouth, this musclebound, husky bourbon nipped my taste buds with a burst of entry heat—the three-alarmer subsided quickly into a smoldering campfire in the throat, as scrumptious and unusual flavors of raisins, lime, kiwi fruit, and grapefruit held court on my tongue; one of the most singular and richly textured bourbons currently available.

RATING ★ ★ ★ ★   *Highly Recommended* $$

Maker's Mark Limited-Edition Kentucky Straight Bourbon
50.5% Alcohol

Author's note: Truly, one of the great whiskies available from anywhere at any price. Made by one of the more engaging personalities in the bourbon busi-ness, Bill Samuels. The color is brilliant amber/orange, the purity level is top-notch; I adore this supple, muscular, caramelized, "totally bourbon" bouquet as much as any bourbon out there—it displays an entire arsenal of aromas, exotic and endowed, from Christmas spices to cream to dried fruit (plums, I think); on palate, the svelte sophistication alone is worth the price, as mannered tastes of vanilla extract, oak resin, and apple rind combine in a harmonious midpalate that ushers in the sublime aftertaste in style; sexy, sumptuous, and crammed with concentrated aromas and flavors.

RATING ★ ★ ★ ★ ★   **Highest Recommendation** $$$

MAKER'S MARK Kentucky Straight Bourbon 45% Alcohol

Radiant orange/bronze color, with russet highlights; sweet, sublime, ambrosial, keenly fruity nose with vanilla, chocolate fudge, buttermilk, and hazelnut underpinnings; impeccably balanced; roundly textured; one of the more elegant bourbons—a Rolls Royce Silver Shadow whiskey, to be sure; settled, melded, mature flavors of shredded tobacco, fruit, caramel, and pine serenely converge at the back of the palate; the slinky, smooth, feline, dry, and muscular finish hints of sweet smoke and dark caramel; unquestionably, one of the best bargains in American distilled spirits and renowned the world over.

RATING ★ ★ ★ ★   **Highly Recommended** $

OLD CHARTER Proprietor's Reserve 13-Year-Old Kentucky Straight Bourbon 45% Alcohol

Author's note: This bourbon is included in the Bourbon Heritage Collection. Medium amber/honey appearance; I found this intriguing, off-dry nose emitting atypical but wholly convincing botanical scents of pine, cedar, and juniper, in addition to granola, rye bread, honey, and toasted oak—what impressed me more than anything about the bouquet was its stateliness and grace—it didn't fall back on sweetness alone in order to shine—this is a smashingly sexy aroma; on the palate, it was well-behaved, balanced, succulent, and elegant—I even admit to a bout of minor, discreet lip-smacking so good was it on the first tasting pass—the off-dry, bosomy, oily flavor offered melded, mature, confident tastes of oak, dry cereal, and buttered popcorn that were nuanced and dazzling; the aftertaste is woody and medium-long, offering an unusual final taste of black pepper; this is one hell of a fine old bourbon.

RATING ★ ★ ★ ★   **Highly Recommended** $$

OLD FITZGERALD Very Special 12-Year-Old Kentucky Straight Bourbon 45% Alcohol

Author's note: This bourbon is included in the Bourbon Heritage Collection. Medium amber, verging on deep amber color; the open, friendly, even generous bouquet brims with oaky, roasted-walnut, candied-almond, and maple-syrup aromas—I found this nose to be more blue collar than many other bourbons, but it's remarkably charming and ended up being one of my favorite bouquets; the upfront and gregarious qualities enjoyed in the nose were amplified in the uncomplicated taste—the flavor entry is sweet, only slightly oaky, and altogether compelling—by midpalate I picked up succulent flavors of dried fruit, black pepper, and oak resin (that trace of oiliness); the moderately sweet finish is clean, not the least bit hot or biting, and quite extended.

RATING ★ ★ ★ ★   **Highly Recommended** $$

OLD FITZGERALD 1849 8-Year-Old Kentucky Straight Bourbon 45% Alcohol

The strong, solid color is medium amber, with orange core features, great purity; the nose is keenly acidic at first, then it smoothes out and shows plump, candied scents of caramel, light toffee, and nougat—by the fourth pass, most of the stuffing has vanished; on palate, it's round, medium- to full-bodied, and chockful of exotic flavors, including pipe smoke and sweetened coconut—at midpalate the flavors explode on the tongue, mak- ing it tingle; the finish is very extended and luxurious; a hidden treasure of a bourbon.

RATING ★ ★ ★ ★   *Highly Recommended* $

OLD FORESTER Bottled-in-Bond Kentucky Straight Bourbon 50% Alcohol

Gorgeous, luxurious tawny/amber/honey color—really one of the more striking bourbons appearance-wise; the nose is very subdued, but solid nonetheless—it emits wispy scents of maple, pine, and caramel in sweet, soft waves—almost like it doesn't want to offend anyone by being aggressive— curiously modest for a 100-proof whiskey; in the mouth, it shows good bal- ance and round, chewy, uncomplicated flavors of sweet oak, dark caramel, and sweetened oatmeal; the finish is firm, with just a mere touch of heat in the tail end; the high proof is deftly kept in check until the aftertaste; a South- ern gentleman of a bourbon; good job.

RATING ★ ★ ★   *Recommended* $

OLD FORESTER Kentucky Straight Bourbon 43% Alcohol

Medium-deep amber/bronze; the piquant bouquet is laced with sweet corn and the unmistakable fingerprint of rye—the high-profile rye element makes it resemble a top-form Canadian whisky more than most bourbons— since I admire the whiskies from tundraland, for me this is a plus; the palate has vanilla written all over the entry, then it turns fruity and acidic at mid- palate; in the final, it turns regrettably bitter in the throat—a second and third pass revealed the same downhill path after the bountifully pleasing aroma; it just couldn't maintain the momentum begun by the bouquet; this is a ven- erable old distillery whose frontline offering should be better.

RATING ★ ★ $

OLD GRAND DAD Kentucky Straight Bourbon 43% Alcohol

The very pretty and pure orange/copper color is classic bourbon; the nose is full-throttle grain, sharply sweet-sour and woody with dashes of spice and caramel—I liked this no-razzle-dazzle bouquet a lot; at palate entry, it begins rather meekly, then in an explosive midpalate it bursts forward with biscuity, vanilla-wafer, and white-chocolate tastes that capture the attention of the taste buds—riding a wave of manageable heat into the punchy after- taste, OGD mellows out in the throat after about 30 seconds; this is what premium bourbon is all about—direct, almost reckless whiskey enjoyment that's a touch sweet, a bit warm, and appealing all the way home.

RATING ★ ★ ★   *Recommended* $

OLD GRAND DAD 114-Barrel-Proof Kentucky Straight Bourbon 57% Alcohol

Beautiful, deep topaz/bronze/orange hue, with very attractive amber highlights; as expected, potent and heady in the nose, but also astringent, pepperminty, and zesty—not what I'd term a deep or complex bouquet— just straight on, fists cocked, and ready; on palate, it shows much more grace and gentility than in the pugnacious aroma, as well-defined, tightly focused sweet flavors of oak, pears, apricots, and dark caramel lead the taste buds to a moderately hot, though hardly unpleasant finish, where in the very tail end, the warm, rich flavor of oak-influenced vanilla completes the sensory impression.

RATING ★ ★ ★   **Recommended** $$

OLD OVERHOLT 4-Year-Old Straight Rye Whiskey 40% Alcohol

Handsome amber/honey hue, with gold core highlights, great purity; the nose is very delicate in the first pass, then it accelerates in the second nosings, as notes of sage and nutmeg are detected lurking in the background— the third pass finds the grain/rye spiciness in full bloom; in the mouth, the zesty rye taste sweeps past the palate entry and goes right for the midpalate in overdrive—the comely rye-bread twang is buttressed by a dry-cereal quality, which seems to be the foundation—nice touches of yellow fruit and mashy sweetness enter into the picture on the final tasting; the finish is surprisingly dry; not as grand as the Wild Turkey Rye.

RATING ★ ★ ★   **Recommended** $

OLD WILLIAMSBURG No. 20 Kentucky Straight Bourbon 50.5% Alcohol

Standard-issue medium amber color; the herbal nose packs a pulled punch as the elevated proof gently tweaks the nose cavity—it offers a mild, grainy perfume once you peek past the alcohol; the taste is where some brownie points are collected as warm, off-dry to sweet, round, corn-husk flavors pick up the pace from the timid aroma; it finishes politely, with no heat or bite whatsoever; as in the case of the green 80-proof version, I think that another year (or two) in oak would make this a much better bourbon.

RATING ★ ★ $

OLD WILLIAMSBURG Kentucky Straight Bourbon 40% Alcohol

Light, limp, amber color—comes off as being dullish; the nose offers scant evidence of life—just a frightfully faint glimmer of nondescript grain—not exactly an auspicious start; on the palate, this slender, immature whiskey is as awkward as a teenager that's experiencing growing pains—in my estimation, this whiskey has been bottled about a year, maybe two, too soon— it hasn't filled out—it still has the echo of virgin spirit in its voice and thus could use more time mingling with charred American oak; is this purposely a rush job? I doubt it—I think that it's simply an error in judgment that such an ill-prepared whiskey is being touted to consumers; what's unfortunate is that this kind of whiskey turns the inexperienced consumer off to bourbon before they've had a chance to sample a properly aged one; avoid.

RATING ★ $

Old Williamsburg No. 20 Kentucky Straight Bourbon, Barrel Proof 51.5% Alcohol

A more brilliant orange/bronze hue than the 101-proof No. 20; strikingly similar on virtually every single sensory level to the 101-proof version; if it wasn't for the mean bite found in the torrid finish of this barrel-proof edition (the 101-proof version had no bite at all, which I found to be one of its finer virtues) I doubt that I could tell the difference between the two; this one is a bona fide flamethrower that should, in my humble opinion, have some adjustments made to reduce the searing heat; has way too much giddyap in the aftertaste; that glaring error cost it a star.

RATING ★ $

Rebel Yell Kentucky Straight Bourbon 45% Alcohol

Luminous, light brown/amber/topaz tone, perfect clarity; I found the nose a bit over-the-top in terms of the concentrated sweetness and overripe fruit in all four nosings; on palate, it fared better, as deep, intensely fruity and caramelly flavors treated the taste buds to solid flavors and a medium-weighted, but viscous, texture; the biscuity, near-opulent aftertaste picked up where the midpalate left off, with very pronounced candy/nougat-like flavors lasting for a very long time on the tongue.

RATING ★ ★ ★   *Recommended* $

Old Rip Van Winkle Kentucky Bourbon 15 Years Old 53.5% Alcohol

By a hair, the deepest orange/amber tone of the Van Winkles; the potent nose is a harmonious marriage of power and grace as a heavily oaked presence underpins the entire nosing experience—the depth of character in the bouquet is impressive—a substantial layer of friendly spirit lies on top of bittersweet-chocolate, candied-pear, ripe peach, and caramel fragrances—it's a whiskey connoisseur's bonanza; on palate, the dried-fruit/estery flavor enchants the taste buds at entry—midpalate flavors include vanillin from the oak, tropical fruit, kiwi, bubblegum, and even raspberries; the finish is clean, extended, and warming without a rush of alcohol.

RATING ★ ★ ★ ★   *Highly Recommended* $$

Van Winkle Special Reserve Kentucky Bourbon Lot B, 12 Years Old 45.2% Alcohol

The light amber hue is the lightest color of the Van Winkles; the piquant, heady nose is alive with round, comely scents of vanilla wafers, citrus, red-grape must, sweet oak, bubblegum, kiwi, spiced apple, and pears—this is a complex, sassy, take-no-prisoners bouquet that owns a delightful snap when you inhale deeply on it; the taste/texture component is melded, rich, and chocolatey—not an ounce of flab exists on this sleek, sinewy bourbon—the cocoa/chocolate taste element is balanced beautifully by the oak/char component; the aftertaste is long, opulent, and spirity; it's so well crafted that you're barely aware of the alcohol level; an elegant, stately, understated bourbon that reminds me faintly of a VSOP cognac.

RATING ★ ★ ★ ★   *Highly Recommended* $$

Old Rip Van Winkle Kentucky Straight Bourbon 10 Years Old 45% Alcohol

Clean, medium amber color; the nose wastes no time in distributing ample amounts of charm—firm, sweet, atypical scents of ripe pineapple, baseball-card bubblegum, rose petals, vanilla, sweet corn, molasses, and ripe nectarines entertain the olfactory sense in "come hither" fashion—the nose is a shameless tease; in the mouth, this zesty whiskey opens fast, clean, friendly, and biscuity sweet, then inexplicably goes flat in midpalate—the taste just simply drops out of the picture—I sampled this whiskey four times in an attempt to recheck my experience concerning the midpalate lapse—curiously and disappointingly, the bottom dropped out each time—I have no explanation for it; the aftertaste rebounds with the splendid biscuity vanilla and sweet-corn qualities ascertained in the nose; with the exception of the midpalate lull, this is a sound, simple bourbon.

RATING ★ ★ ★   ***Recommended*** $$

Pappy Van Winkle's Family Reserve 20-Year-Old Kentucky Straight Bourbon 45.2% Alcohol

Beautiful, opulent, burnished brown/orange tone—good clarity; the bouquet is soft, grainy, and almost malty, with sweet plum pudding and fig notes that are impressive for their maturity—it's a slightly weary bouquet, however; the texture is buxom, viscous, and multilayered, while the flavor points to very mature sweet oak, mild spice, dried herbs, and even a dash of candied apple not unlike an old calvados; the woody finish leans in the direction of brandy as well, perhaps a broader-shouldered variety like a Brandy de Jérez Solera Gran Reserva like Cardenal Mendoza; this intriguing bourbon, although clearly on the downslope of its evolution, nevertheless viably belies the dictum of people (I used to be one of them) who hold that bourbon is never drinkable after 8–10 years in cask.

RATING ★ ★ ★   ***Recommended*** $$

Old Rip Van Winkle Kentucky Straight Bourbon 10 Years Old 53.5% Alcohol

A darker, more coppery/orangey amber than the 45% alcohol version; the heightened alcohol is apparent immediately in the first good whiff, as a more astringent road is taken in the aroma—this is not to imply in the least that this bouquet is less alluring—what comes out here is more wood, more resin, more finely tuned depth than the more affable sibling—make no mistake, this is a heady, top-flight, more typical bourbon bouquet; on the palate, the focused, warm flavors of tropical fruit, spirit (which approaches harshness), and resin dominate the picture—and I didn't at all care for the flavor, since the resiny quality gained in strength, eventually becoming a liability by midpalate; the finish lacked charm, as the resiny/oiliness took hold and wouldn't let any other flavor qualities into the arena; what began so well plummeted downhill disturbingly fast after palate entry.

RATING ★ ★ $$

Rock Hill Farms Single-Barrel Kentucky Straight Bourbon, Barrel No. 60; 40% Alcohol

Medium amber/chestnut-brown color; the nose is quietly, make that, deceptively, powerful as sweet, warm, estery, fruity aromas of peaches, baked apples, and grapes underpin the oaky, vanilla, and chocolate frontline scents; the decidedly polite flavor likewise offers two distinct levels of enjoyment—the more obvious, divinely sweet layer consists of creamy, nutty, oaky flavors, while the more subtle foundational layer offers a toasted-cereal, sour, mash, spirity, corn-husk-base flavor; owns an absolutely sterling finish of toffee, cocoa, and sweet oak; an impressively mannered, even stately whiskey of the first rank; single-malt Scotch whisky outshines in no way this supple bourbon.

RATING ★ ★ ★ ★   *Highly Recommended* $$

Seagram's Seven Crown American Blended Whiskey 40% Alcohol

Lovely, medium amber/burnt-orange hue, perfect clarity; this uncomplicated bouquet is brazenly sweet in a candied/caramel way that makes it seem more opulent than it, in truth, is—it's a pleasing, workmanlike aroma; on the palate, the pronounced sweetness grows in intensity as the medium-rich texture coats the palate; while it's not as nimble or alluring as the Seagram's VO Canadian, it's still a suitable choice for mixed drinks calling for affordable blended whiskey.

RATING ★ ★ $

W. L. Weller Centennial 10-Year-Old Kentucky Straight Bourbon 50% Alcohol

Author's note: This great bourbon is part of the Bourbon Heritage Collection. It owns a really dark, deep honey/umber color, which borders on red/brown; the nose is challenging—it's a remarkably mature aroma for a 10-year-old, in fact, nosing it blind, I estimated it to be older—the bouquet was neither aggressive nor fat, what it was, was nutty, oily, off-dry, nuanced, and firm—while not the most flamboyant of bourbon noses, it is one of the two or three most composed, elegant, and complex; in the mouth, this breathtaking thoroughbred soars, as surefooted, moderately sweet, and luscious flavors of molasses, dark chocolate, nougat, and nut meat totally disarm my taste buds; it lies regally on the tongue without the slightest hint of being 100 proof; the aftertaste is a striking balance of finesse and strength; a velvet-hammer-type of bourbon; I'm happy to report that this is one of America's greatest whiskies, period; buy several bottles, because they won't last long on the shelves of your liquor merchant.

RATING ★ ★ ★ ★ ★   *Highest Recommendation* $$

Wild Turkey Kentucky Spirit Single-Barrel Kentucky Straight Bourbon, Barrel No. 10, Rick No. 9, Warehouse D; 50.5% Alcohol

Eye-popping, fetching, orange/deep-amber color, perfect purity; the seductive nose is like a faraway siren calling out to you—the subtle layers of grain, pepper, biscuits, cake batter, spirit, ripe apples, saddle leather, pecans, and caramel are astoundingly harmonious, almost restrained, but always surefooted, regal, and potent—this is a bouquet that deserves to be approached and savored slowly; in the mouth, this is one of the monumental tastes in American distilled spirits—at palate entry, layer after layer of flavor, including vanilla extract, candied almonds and walnuts, succulent red fruit, and fine old wood are beautifully enmeshed; the finish is warm, toasted, biscuity, lush, and exquisite; whiskey doesn't get better than this.

RATING ★ ★ ★ ★ ★ **Highest Recommendation** $$

WILD TURKEY Straight Rye 50.5% Alcohol

Brilliant orange/bronze/amber color; rich, lovely, balanced, sexy, sweet nose of vanilla, spice, perfume, dare I say, sherried, aromas—a genuinely enchanting nose that evokes memories created by the best Canadian whiskies in terms of approachability and creaminess—sweet-oak, honey, and toffee flavors envelop the taste buds like a warm cloak of velvet; one of the plumpest, most drinkable, and sensuous American whiskies I've sampled; maybe too fat and chewy for some purists, but who cares? the high alcohol is not a problem and never overshadows the richness of flavor or the satiny feel; an opulent, sweet finish tops off this delightful whiskey treat; one of American whiskey's best-kept secrets; find it, buy it, savor it.

RATING ★ ★ ★ ★ **Highly Recommended** $

WILD TURKEY Rare Breed Straight Kentucky Bourbon, Barrel Proof; 54.8% Alcohol

Luminous, lovely, autumnal topaz/medium-amber color; refined, gently spirited, oaky, raisiny, ripe nectarine aromas waft up from the glass in a deceptively potent manner—this is a classical, prototypical bourbon nose; considering the alcohol level, on palate entry Rare Breed is rather subdued, with subtle flavors of citrus, tart apples, and spice—the alcohol builds in the back of the throat, finally releasing loads of pent-up heat in the long, luxurious, attention-getting aftertaste; I would dilute this full-throttle powerhouse with a few drops of spring water to stimulate the bouquet; I also suggest that it be served in a small tulip-shaped wine glass, not a tumbler or a snifter, to funnel the aromas; I would have scored it even higher had it not been for the flamethrower finish; nevertheless, it's definitely worth seeking out to add to your ultrapremium bourbon collection.

RATING ★ ★ ★ ★ **Highly Recommended** $$

WILD TURKEY 8-Year-Old 101 Straight Kentucky Bourbon 50.5% Alcohol

Amber/tangerine color; the extra alcohol immediately states its purpose in the highly spirited nose, but the foundational aromas of this savory bourbon offer the taster considerably more stuffing than its gutless 40%-alcohol sibling; the various and complementary components of fruitiness, oak, biscuit, and old saddle leather emerge in the dry nose as well as the flavor; these elements climax in a wonderfully warm, caramel, medium-length finish; an above-average, broad-shouldered bourbon that provides plenty of flavor and texture in the mouth, then astonishingly settles down and simply glides away in the charming, but disciplined, aftertaste.

RATING ★ ★ ★ **Recommended** $

WILD TURKEY Straight Kentucky Bourbon 40% Alcohol

Clear, amber/goldenrod color; full, pleasantly spirity, corn-husk, mashy, cereal-like nose that is reminiscent of fallen autumn leaves; exhibits a very easy, dry, but somewhat neutral tasting presence from entry through to mid-palate, then develops an interesting, semidry aftertaste that offers different levels of flavor, including burnt almonds, molasses, and a hint of oakiness; a banal bourbon overall, one that could definitely use more character in the nose, flavor, and finish.

RATING ★　　$

WILSON American Blended Whiskey 40% Alcohol

Correct, standard-issue, light amber hue, dotted with dull orange high-lights; throws off a grainy, cooked-cereal-like nose, which emits a touch of nail-polish-remover scent as well as steamed rice—oddly, the nose is more banal than offensive; high-voltage sweetness attacks the palate from the get-go—in fact, this whiskey is one of the most candied I've evaluated, though it's skimpy both in body and texture; the aftertaste is loaded down with a severe cane sugar and glycerine flavor (is it caramel additive?) that obliter-ates any other flavor possibility; a cheap, one-note whiskey mongrel from who knows where and who knows what and, further, who really gives a damn, Scarlett; the unintentionally funny label sports two preposterous phrases that have no relation to each other ("Regardless of price no better whiskey in the world" and "That's all") as well as a bizarre multicolored de-piction of the Earth as seen from outer space; beam me up, Scottie, but I'll pass on the Wilson's.

RATING ★　　$

WOODFORD RESERVE Distiller's Select Kentucky Straight Bourbon Labrot & Graham Distillery 45.2% Alcohol

Luminous, very pretty, medium amber/honey color, good clarity; the nose is especially biscuity, vanilla-wafer-like, and grainy-sweet with a firm underpinning of tannin and plump spirit—later nosings expose a highly de-sirable fruitiness (plums, grapes)—considering that this small-batch Bour-bon is less than seven years old, on the nose it shows a real maturity and el-egance in the front nosings right after the pour; at palate entry, an appreciable richness in the form of honey/caramel greets the taste buds—lying beneath the surface is an immature bite that becomes more pro-nounced at midpalate—the youthful heat might bother the uninitiated; in the aftertaste, the heat wave continues to the point of making the tongue tin-gle; this is surely not an entry-level Bourbon due to the bite of spirit, but seasoned Bourbon lovers will acknowledge this whiskey's *joie de vivre* and precocious temperament.

RATING ★ ★ ★　　*Recommended*　　$$

Irish Whiskey

L iving in the long shadow cast by Scotch whisky are the savory whiskies from Ireland. Even though whiskey is believed to have been invented on the Emerald Isle in the latter stages of the First Millennium, Irish whiskey is erroneously viewed by many of the world's whiskey drinkers in the final years of the Second Millennium as the wan, rustic, and pitifully inferior distant relation of the more cultured whiskies of Scotland. But the dismissal of Irish whiskey hasn't always been *de rigueur*. England's King Henry II and his army were enchanted with Irish whiskey in the twelfth century, and Russia's Peter the Great, the illustrious eighteenth-century czar, reportedly said, perhaps somewhat confusedly, "Of all the wines, the Irish spirit is the best."

Around the turn of the twentieth century, Irish whiskey basked in the sunshine of unprecedented popularity not only in Ireland but in the United Kingdom, continental Europe, and the United States, as well. But hurt by the negative impact of, first, the market-flooding of Scotland's lighter, nimbler blended Scotches and, then, the closing of the American market because of Prohibition, Irish whiskey tumbled out of the consciousness of all but its most fervent admirers. Scotch whiskey became the talk of the town after Prohibition was repealed and even more so after the World War II. Sadly, Irish whiskey has remained in what amounts to a total eclipse ever since.

With an air of caution, I report that there are some minor signs of life with the recent U.S. market introductions of two Irish single malts, one from Bushmills and one from Tyrconnell. These entries into the upper-echelon whiskey sweepstakes are significant because they show that the Irish want to play in the high-stakes game with their neighbors. However, with single-malt Scotch and ultrapremium American whiskey enlarging their individual market shares every year, it's difficult to see how the Irish can level the playing field altogether.

Ireland's premier whiskey maker (whiskey with an "e") is the Old Bushmills Distillery, nestled in the tranquil hamlet of Bushmills in County Antrim. The Bushmills distillers have been producing their wonderfully debonair whiskies in this northernmost outpost since 1608, the year they were officially licensed. Bushmills is the world's oldest whiskey distillery on record. Fine Irish whiskies are also made in Tullamore (County Offaly) in midland Ireland and in the south near Cork. Dublin boasts the Jameson Distillery, the only true rival of Bushmills, which was opened in 1780.

Irish whiskies are distilled three times, exactly like those from Scotland's Lowland region. Triple distillation makes for extra smoothness, aromatic freshness, and easy enjoyment. Irish whiskies are all of that and more, for within their approachable framework they also possess significant complexity and depth.

Since its land is perfectly suited for the growth of barley, it is little wonder that whiskey and beer should have such prized places in the social scheme that is Ireland's. Pub life *is* the way of life in this enchanting country and has been so for many centuries. In a nation that is too frequently rended by hatred and violence, a dram of whiskey can be a unifying force.

Old Bushmills Millennium 1975 Single Malt, Barrel Sample; 43% Alcohol

Golden, white-wine color, which resembles a fresh vintage Premier Cru Chablis; the round, soft-spoken nose is tart, like harvest-time apples, on the surface, but underneath lie solid layers of leafy, grassy, floral aromas that ably address the maturity factor—this regal beauty is already over 20 years old, but smells as fresh and vibrant as a whiskey half its age; in the mouth, a peachy, raisiny upfront flavor leads the taste band down Broadway—the backnote flavors of oak and bittersweet chocolate, however, actually make this palate as special as it is—they anchor the whole experience, giving it gravity and focus; the aftertaste returns to peaches; it shows lots of room to grow even more, but it's splendid as it is.

RATING ★ ★ ★ ★   *Highly Recommended* $$$

Old Bushmills Blended Irish Whiskey 40% Alcohol

Pretty, light amber tone, golden core highlights, superb purity; the fragrant nose is keenly malty and mashy, with backnotes of flowers and wet earth; in the mouth, it's nicely balanced, a bit tart, and generous as well-defined flavors of yeast, dough, toasted barley, and lanolin keep the taste buds happy; the finish is medium-long and very smooth; an unassuming, polite dram.

RATING ★ ★ ★   *Recommended* $

Black Bush Blended Irish Whiskey 43% Alcohol

Highly malted/mashiness/graininess, mildly sweet, sherry foundation in ever-changing nose; the luscious, medium-weighted texture supports the flavors of mature oloroso sherry and pine nuts; Black Bush offers uncommon approachability, due no doubt to triple distillation; the soft, medium-length finish is touched with ripe apples; takes its place among the world's better blended whiskies.

RATING ★ ★ ★   ***Recommended*** $ $

BUSHMILLS 10-Year-Old Single Malt 40% Alcohol

Flaxen/gold color, with curious green/blue highlights in the core—a fascinating color for a malt whiskey; the dry, delicate, almost beer-like nose is slightly smoky and offers underlying scents of barley malt and soft, old oak; on the palate, the burnished richness is subtle and refined as flavors of apple, lemon, and barley come together nicely; the finish is semisweet and dark-toffee-like; clearly, it's a sedate, restrained single malt whose gear shift remains firmly planted in "low"; I liked it increasingly, though, as I tasted it four times over the course of 30 minutes—it's a supple, understated malt that requires some element of patience, but it's well worth the wait.

RATING ★ ★ ★   ***Recommended*** $ $

JAMESON 1780 12-Year-Old Special Reserve Blended Irish Whiskey 40% Alcohol

Superb clarity—medium amber/clover-honey color; the nose immediately beckons as plump waves of spice, cream, sweetened cereal, oak, and honey wash across the sense of smell—it's an inviting, even sumptuous nose that easily ranks as one of Ireland's best; on the palate, the generous virtues found in the aroma expand and develop further as the husky, sweet flavors of wood, cereal, and cream take on a roasted-nut quality that's truly delicious; the finish is very long, sweet, and woody; this is a bosomy whiskey that's packed with double-barrel aromas and flavors; one of my favorite drams from Eire.

RATING ★ ★ ★ ★   ***Highly Recommended*** $ $

JAMESON Blended Irish Whiskey 40% Alcohol

Light-to-medium amber—excellent clarity; the nose emits an unnerving bit of nail polish remover in the first nosing pass, to the point that I changed glasses, pouring anew, but to no avail—with aeration, however, the ethyl acetate quality gradually blew off, leaving behind a crisp, tart, baked-red-apple aroma that was shadowed by a vegetal quality; in the mouth, Jameson shows its best face as clean, tart, edged flavors of oak, vanilla extract, red apple, and grain combine for a very pleasant, straightforward taste experience; the aftertaste is semisweet, medium-long, and almost caramel-like; in the finish this whiskey remains agile, giving off fleeting flavors of grain and a hint of smoke; almost didn't make three stars because of the so-so nose, but the taste and the finish were sound enough to pull it through to recommended territory.

RATING ★ ★ ★   ***Recommended*** $

JOHN POWER & SON Blended Whiskey 40% Alcohol

The beautifully lustrous, brilliant orange hue is very fetching; the dry, woodsy, herbal nose owns intriguing aromas of mushrooms, wool, acorns, corn husk, and freshly rained-on soil—musty and attic-like, it's not what I'd call an appealing bouquet, since I find scant evidence of whiskey element in it; it begins dry on the tongue, then shockingly changes gears at the back of the tongue, as syrupy, candied flavors bludgeon the taste buds with cloying sweetness; it ends up hot with a strange jalapeno-pepper-like aftertaste; a remarkably awkward, raucous, and out-of-sorts whiskey whose unpredictable negatives and twists and turns far outweigh the overwhelmed positives; pretty to look at, but anything more than that spells disaster.

RATING ★ $

KILBEGGAN Blended Irish Whiskey 40% Alcohol

Soft golden tone; the peculiar nose reminds me of damp fabric, especially cotton—in the background I detect the scent of mild spiciness that emerges with aeration and that finally overwhelms the wet-cotton/damp-fur smell—I wasn't ga-ga over this bouquet; it's on the palate that this nimble whiskey shines as exceedingly pleasant, sweetish tastes of corn, honey wheat, and light toffee make themselves known in a harmonious manner; medium-long, sweet aftertaste; I was ready to give it three stars to honor the taste and aftertaste, until I went back to sniff it one last time—I found to my dismay that the unappealing damp fur smell had returned, outgunning the spice; so I find myself sitting on the ratings fence with this one.

RATING ★★ $

TULLAMORE DEW Blended Irish Whiskey 40% Alcohol

Pure, crystal clarity, yellow/honey/medium-amber hue; the nose approaches being ambrosial so intensely fruity is it—alluring estery, ripe, and sweet scents of tropical fruits, most predominately tangerine backed up by guava, orange rind, and kiwi, make for an unusual but totally captivating whiskey perfume—there's barely a trace of graininess; the sweet palate entry gives way to a midpalate off-dry firmness that spotlights caramel, toffee, woody flavors—it's succulent and feather-light on the tongue, but strangely the concentrated fruitiness isn't evident in the taste; the finish is clean, medium-long, sweet, and squarely focused on the caramel/toffee component; an easy, uncomplicated, and undemanding Irish dram.

RATING ★★★   *Recommended* $$

TYRCONNELL Single-Malt Irish Whiskey 40% Alcohol

Attractive, medium amber tone with good clarity; this nose has a trace of the Kilbeggan damp fabric in it at first, then that quickly blows off—it develops into a soft, citrusy, mildly grainy, delicately floral fragrance that's almost fragile in its bearing—I ended up liking this bouquet after 20 minutes of evaluation; in the mouth, it's medium-bodied, almost plump in texture, and shows off lovely, well-behaved flavors of sweet, toasty malt; it's an approachable, smooth-tasting whiskey that finishes in a gentlemanly way, with only the slightest hint of burn; a good combination of drinkability, manageable complexity, and affordability.

RATING ★★★   *Recommended* $$

CANADIAN WHISKY

Unlike the governments of Scotland, Ireland, and the U.S., that of Canada as a matter of policy has chosen not to impose strict production or ingredient guidelines on their whisky (no "e") producers. Thus, there exist for the producers of Canadian whisky few regulations with regard to which grains are to be utilized, the variety of wood cask employed for maturation, or distillation proof levels. The sole stipulations are that they employ "cereal grains" and age their whiskies in wood barrels for at least three years. If it sounds like buying Canadian whisky might be akin to squirrel hunting on a moonless night while blindfolded, that's hardly the case. While few specific details concerning Canadian whisky production are made known by distillers, Canadian whiskies are considered to be among the most agreeable of all.

Here are the bare-knuckle facts, which aren't easy to come by, regarding Canadian whisky: The trinity of grains used by the distillers in Canada are barley, corn, and rye, with corn and rye taking turns in the lead position, at least from my investigation and research. Barley and rye are used in both malted and unmalted forms, depending on who's doing the distilling. Misconceptions among the public and even the trade that all Canadian whiskies are either 100 percent rye or predominantly rye are rife, but off the mark. With few exceptions, these sweet, affably light whiskies, some of which are distilled twice and others three times, have whiskies and/or spirits made from other grains, including barley malt, added to them, along with neutral spirits. All Canadian whiskies are, to my knowledge, distilled in continuously running patent stills. An unknown number of Canadian distillers, though they are understandably reluctant to discuss the matter, add flavorings, such as oloroso sherry or fruit wines. This practice is performed in order to add depth to the aroma and flavor of the whisky.

Most of the popular Canadian whiskies range in age from six to eight years, while the higher-ticket whiskies are often older than a decade. Canadian whiskies are reduced to the 40–43 percent alcohol range after being distilled all the way up to but not over 190 proof (95 percent alcohol). Virtually all Canadian distillers mature their whiskies in previously used white-oak casks, including old bourbon, brandy, and sherry casks, which are highly desirable because of the customary Canadian distillers' method. Treated casks are preferred because they impart flavor, color, and a mellowing effect.

History points out that two liquor industry giants, Hiram Walker and Joseph E. Seagram, have long steered the Canadian whisky boat. Hiram Walker, an American born in Massachusetts in 1816, is often credited with being the first visionary behind the Canadian whisky industry. Indeed, the perennial popularity of the brand Walker created, Canadian Club, lends support to that belief. Walker was, no doubt, a man of purpose who understood that by operating his whisky business outside the boundaries of the U.S., he could build his company in a more friendly economic environment but still sell his goods in the U.S. marketplace.

Seagram also started as the concept of a single man, Joseph Emm Seagram. As their evaluations and ratings bear out, Seagram's Crown Royal and Crown Royal Special Reserve must be considered as two of the premier whiskies in the pantheon of Canadian whisky. The story goes that iron-willed Sam Bronfman, whose family bought into the Seagram company, himself created the first blend of Crown Royal in honor of the visit of King George VI and Queen Elizabeth to Canada in 1939. Though it should be taken with a hefty chunk of salt, Bronfman, so the tale goes, snorted his way through over 600 whiskies before settling on the final blend. Apparently, Bronfman's legendary meticulousness regarding distillery quality control and production practice bordered on the fanatical. But, stories of such stringent standards appealed to the masses. As word of Bronfman's tough and ambitious stewardship spread, trust in Seagram products became instilled in the consumers.

Alberta Springs Blended Canadian Whisky 45% Alcohol

Medium amber/orange/honey color; the lovely, sweet, rye bread, black-pepper-scented bouquet is quite charming—there's a light musty-attic-like odor way in the back that doesn't in any way detract from the overall nose impression; in the mouth, its sweetness level is extremely high, a bit too much, a tad too cordial-like from entry through to middle palate, then it turns fruity, cereally, and burnt in the sweet, comfortable aftertaste, with only the mildest sting; to my taste, I found the charred, caramelized sweetness too potent, but to tasters who relish this direct, sugary style it might work.

RATING ★★ $

BLACK VELVET Blended Canadian Whisky 40% Alcohol

Soft, hay/flaxen color; the inviting, moderately sweet nose has nuanced elements of vanilla extract and egg cream; on the palate, delicate flavors of butterscotch, rye, and citrus border on being timid; the delightful, smooth, satiny, warm finish has no alcoholic bite whatsoever and little in the way of depth; strains to be elegant and classy, but the grossly understated character doesn't make the recommendation cut.

RATING ★★ $

BUSH PILOT 13-Year-Old Single-Cask Canadian Whisky 43% Alcohol

Has the pale yellow/straw color of a Grand Cru Chablis; the nose is quite coy at first, then gains momentum with aeration—I detect delectably soft hints of ginger, seedless rye bread, candied almonds, and sweet oak—it's a delicate, though not flimsy, bouquet, one that's more a teaser than a floozy—but it should be pointed out that in its delicacy lies a true but reticent complexity that might easily be overlooked by the whisky neophyte, so be aware; what makes this an instant legend is the flavor, which rockets onto the palate with a stunning opening salvo of controlled heat, followed by semisweet, biscuity tastes of ripe fruit, amontillado sherry, rye, and vanilla wafer; the slinky, understated aftertaste is melony, elegant, and classy; though totally different, it competes with the Crown Royal Special Reserve as Canada's foremost whisky; it's so soft and smooth, you just want to sip it, glass after glass; drink neat in a wine glass for maximum effect.

RATING ★★★★★   ***Highest Recommendation*** $$

CANADIAN CLUB Classic 12-Year-Old Blended Canadian Whisky 40% Alcohol

Delicate-looking, mature, medium amber/orange hue, ideal clarity; the bouquet is behaved, but not shy—aromatic waves of tropical fruit, honey, old oak, and sour mash politely mingle—it's a confident, graceful nose that clearly was fashioned for elegance; ultimately, though, it's in the mouth that this beauty does its best work, as melded, sweet flavors of grain, sugar frosting, and wood come wrapped in a velvety texture; the aftertaste shows a perfect balance between finesse and quiet power, with a hint of banana in the tail end; a knockout whisky from Canada.

RATING ★★★★   ***Highly Recommended*** $$

CANADIAN CLUB Blended Canadian Whisky 40% Alcohol

Hay/honey color; the creamy, mashy nose is much more authoritative than most other Canadian whiskies I've sampled; off-dry in the mouth, with a tight focus on cola nut, smokiness, wood, burning leaves, and caramel; nowhere near as candy sweet as other well-known Canadians; the grain element holds court over the fruitiness from start to finish, but in an appealing way; absolutely charming aftertaste of mild spirit, orange rind, and rich toffee; doesn't run with the pack; hats off for originality.

RATING ★★★   ***Recommended*** $

C. C. CITRUS Blended Canadian Whisky and Natural Citrus Flavor 35% Alcohol

The pale yellow/white-wine appearance immediately sets it apart from all other Canadian whiskies, very good clarity; I have to admit that even though I had reservations about the concept when I caught wind of it through the grapevine, the sprightliness of the bouquet charmed me in a nanosecond—the lemony zest dominates the aroma through all four passes—because the citrus is controlled, though it's not in the least overbearing or sour; on palate, the lemon impact is more pronounced than if a twist were tossed into regular CC, but I find the combination balanced enough to recommend—I'm glad to say that the whisky is not overwhelmed by the citrus; whisky purists will doubtless turn a blind eye to this hybrid, but I say try it first before you form a final opinion; an innovative and contemporary idea that may just convert people who normally wouldn't try whisky.

RATING ★ ★ ★ $

CANADIAN MIST 1885 Special Reserve 8-Year-Old Blended Canadian Whisky 40% Alcohol

Very pretty, pale amber/harvest-gold, excellent purity; the nose is very seductive, as prickly, zesty scents of spicy rye grain, fennel, new wood, paraffin, cocoa, and cooked mash perk up the olfactory sense—by the third pass the aroma settles down into a biscuity, leathery bouquet that's more dry than sweet; in the mouth, the entry is intensely grainy and husk-like, then by mid-palate crisp, oily, off-dry to sweet tastes of chocolate malt and sweet oak take charge; the aftertaste highlights the wood and leaves a wee burn on the tongue; while this medium-bodied, nicely crafted Canadian is not as buxom as Crown Royal, Canadian Club Classic, or Gooderman's Rich & Rare whiskies, it exhibits the snappy, spicy side of grain in a manner that's completely desirable and very drinkable.

RATING ★ ★ ★   ***Recommended*** $$

CROWN ROYAL Special Reserve Blended Canadian Whisky 40% Alcohol

Rich, amber/orange/light brown color; has a gorgeous, decadent bouquet, which offers round, fragrant scents of mint, new oak, sweetened coconut, guava, and orange pekoe tea—unquestionably, it's the finest, most complex nose in the Canadian category; at palate entry, the tart flavor is almost wine-like, so fine is it—then comes the engaging elegance of a classic blend, as layers of flavor, including ripe pears, banana, walnuts, and molasses crescendo into a splendid aftertaste, which is very extended and shows a wee bit of mandarin orange at the very end; an altogether great whiskey that has it all and freely spends it—classic bearing, opulent aromas and flavors, and a slam-bang finish; this beauty and Bush Pilot are Canada's premier whisky efforts.

RATING ★ ★ ★ ★ ★   ***Highest Recommendation*** $$

CROWN ROYAL Fine Deluxe Blended Canadian Whisky 40% Alcohol

Pretty, medium amber color, ideal purity; the deceptively soft, but potent, sugarcane aroma offers faint hints of esters, caramel, oak, and English toffee—this is an elegant, understated nose that almost doesn't seem whisky-like at all; the fineness continues on the palate, which is highlighted by a satiny smoothness—complexity merges neatly with overall finesse; as one would expect from a superpremium blend, no one feature dominates; quietly classy and composed; Crown Royal doesn't feign being a blockbuster.

RATING ★ ★ ★   *Recommended* $

GOODERMAN'S RICH & RARE Blended Canadian Whisky 40% Alcohol

The deep honey/topaz color is much richer than the majority of Canadian whiskies; the hi-toned, woodsy, cedar, cinnamon, snappy, leathery aromas gently waft from the glass—Gooderman's has one of the most complex and multilayered noses of the Canadians; clearly, a Canadian thoroughbred, the silky, sensuous texture is exquisitely balanced; unabashedly delicious, opulent flavors of pine and black pepper mingle ideally with a soft fruitiness; this truly lovely whisky has in great abundance what Canadian whisky is famous for—mellowness, full flavor, and easy drinkability; bravo.

RATING ★ ★ ★ ★   *Highly Recommended* $

HARWOOD CANADIAN Blended Canadian Whisky 40% Alcohol

Pretty, luminous amber/honey color; the inviting, mildly oaky nose is doused with firm scents of cola nut, vanilla extract, orange blossoms, honey, and rye—a forward, unabashedly sweet bouquet that I found immensely likable; the focused flavor, which showcases off-dry flavors of oak, rye, maize, black pepper, and spice, is dead serious in its mission; the finish is medium-long, nutty, off-dry, but slightly dull; my overall impression of this rather austere, medium-bodied Canadian is very favorable; a great mixer.

RATING ★ ★ ★ ★   *Highly Recommended* $

JAMES FOXE Blended Canadian Whisky 40% Alcohol

Yellow/gold, Sauternes-like color; the biscuity, sweet nose highlights the grain to the nth degree—a pleasant, simple bouquet; the slight heat upon palate entry quickly dies out as candied lemon and melon tastes take center court; there's a delightful hint of caramel candy in the throat, then an appealing bittersweet warmth introduces the aftertaste and stays moderately long; a lighter, more feminine style of Canadian whiskey that's agile, zesty, and very charming.

RATING ★ ★ ★   *Recommended* $

SEAGRAM'S VO Blended Canadian Whisky 40% Alcohol

Yellow/honey color, with an amber/orange tinge; appetizing, honeysuckle, highly floral, malted milk, sweet, come-hither nose; feminine bearing on palate—candied, mellow flavors are not complex by any measure; however, this is one of North America's most drinkable and user-friendly blended whiskies by a mile; hard to find fault with such a benignly agreeable whisky, which, while simple and direct, is like a comforting old pal; offers an intriguing layer of spice in the aftertaste; the quintessential whisky mixer.

RATING ★ ★ ★   *Recommended* $

WINDSOR CANADIAN Supreme Blended Canadian Whisky 40% Alcohol

Crystalline, yellow/goldenrod color; mellow, mildly alcoholic/spirity, floral, peppermint in coy, restrained nose; lovely, balanced, firmly textured; round, very smooth on palate, highlighted by grainy (rye) sweetness that is very becoming; the caramel-like, ripe-apple finish is long and friendly; hardly profound, but serviceable.

RATING ★★ $

JAPANESE WHISKY

Scarcely ever acknowledged in the U.S. or in Europe are the Japanese whiskies, probably because bourbons and Scotch so thoroughly dominate our marketplaces. Prior to beginning their own distilled-spirits industry with the construction of the first distillery in 1923, the Japanese had long revered the whiskies of Scotland. The Japanese whisky industry, as a result, has been strongly influenced by the Scots' practices. But true to form and to their credit, the Japanese do things in big and efficient ways. In terms of sheer muscle, Suntory's Hakushu distillery now boasts the world's biggest malt-whisky annual production, at a whopping 55 million liters. And even as their own whisky industry is growing at home, their interests are expanding in Scotland as well. Tomatin, wholly owned by the Japanese company Takara, Shuzo, and Okura, is Scotland's largest malt distillery. The Japanese also own major shares in other Scottish distilleries, including those of the Morrison-Bowmore group, Bowmore, Auchentoshan, and Glen Garioch.

As far as Japanese whiskies themselves are concerned, they are imbued with faint echoes of the Spey and the Scottish hills of heather. Since space and natural resources are severely limited in Japan, grain and even peat for the production of whisky are imported from other countries. The Japanese's greatest indigenous contribution is their water, the spine of any distilled spirit.

After tasting these two savory whiskies from Suntory, which accounts for nearly 70 percent of the entire Japanese whisky industry, I see no need for the emulation of another country's whiskies. While not necessarily to-die-for, they each were more than adequate and ultimately were quite pleasant drams. Nevertheless, the fact remains that Scotch is Scotch, the pinnacle of whisky, and never will those environmental conditions be repeated. The Japanese will do well if they simply approach the subject by saying, "Here are our whiskies. What do you think?"

SUNTORY Royal Blended Whisky 43.4% Alcohol

Orange/amber color; fresh, spirity, fruity, mildly sweet nose; on palate, it comes alive with a bracing heatwave at entry, then calms down into a savory, elegant blend; finishes modestly on a quiet note of semisweet smokiness; tasted blind three times alongside blends from Scotland; if it possessed more guts and substance, I would probably bump up the score; while I can't give it a recommendation as it is now, it's an inoffensive blend that doesn't pretend to be more than it is.

RATING ★★ $

SUNTORY 12-Year-Old Pure Malt Whisky 43% Alcohol

Rich amber/tawny color; very aromatic, highly perfumed nose that features multiple layers of fruit (mostly ripened bananas), hazelnuts, and faint hints of vanilla extract; full-weighted mouthful; on palate entry, it shows a very appealing, potentially explosive caramel/toffee richness; unfortunately, the lovely candied quality fades rapidly at the back of the throat and after about 30 seconds the whisky seems to disappear completely in the whistle-clean, virtually nonexistent aftertaste; what's interesting is that on entry, this whisky gives the first impression of being a genuine powerhouse, but the flavors politely and disappointingly abandon ship before reaching port; I'd like to see greater staying power in the finish; has potential, however.

RATING ★★ $

LIQUEURS

Over the last two decades the liqueur category has devolved into the Barnum & Bailey segment of the alcoholic beverage industry, the one in which fatuous marketing yahoos and fast-talking brand managers have run off the cliff of good taste. It's the distilled-spirits quarter in which you'll encounter the most outrageous concoctions. Urged on by their marketing department gurus and a sense of one-upmanship, producers vigorously employ cutesy tricks and gimmicks, like color additives for dramatic hues, nontoxic flakes of gold and multiplying tartrate crystals, names as quaint as the liqueurs are cloying, and screwball bottle shapes, which drive liquor retailers up the wall because they disrupt the orderly stocking of shelves. Alas, in this category, there is no shame, there are no rules and, what's saddest, there's little connection to an illustrious past that stretches back in time to the last turn of the millennium.

Through all the tomfoolery and chicanery, one fact remains: The classic liqueurs, some of which have been in existence for centuries, provide some of the most sublime alcoholic beverage experiences of all. Even some of the newer liqueurs are far better than average, but it's hard to keep track of what's what when scores of new, neon-colored beverages are continually pouring, or should I say oozing, into the marketplace every year.

Like wine, brandy, beer, and whiskey, the creation of liqueurs was the province of the Christian monks of the Middle Ages. The neighborhood abbey frequently served as the general store, brewery, winery, distillery, hall of records, and hospital of the local community. Since the monks were often looked to for assistance when disease ran rampant, which it frequently did in the days before hygienic practices, they invented many primitive liqueurs as restoratives, medicines, and digestive aids to help soothe the ills of their congregations. The monks added secret combinations of honey, seeds, herbs, spices, roots, and bark to distilled-base spirits and offered them as remedies. Some worked, others didn't, but the alcohol did, at least, alleviate a portion of the hoi-polloi's discomfort. These early liqueurs were doubtless awful-tasting soups, but the monastic orders continued to perfect their recipes, and from these early concoctions evolved the drinks we enjoy today after a meal, including such classics as Benedictine and Chartreuse.

Relatively speaking, the production of liqueurs is quite simple. You need an alcohol base—which can be anything from grape brandy to whiskey to neutral-grain spirits to rum to fruit spirits—and you need flavorings. The number of flavorings used runs well into the hundreds, and they are generally categorized into the groupings of Barks, Roots/Spices, Herbs/Leaves, Flowers, Seeds/Beans, Fruits/Nuts, and Honey. The art of producing fine liqueurs lies in matching the right ingredients in the most complementary amounts.

Barks include such items as cinnamon, aloe, angostura, sassafras, sandalwood, and myrrh.

Roots/Spices include calamus, licorice, cloves, celery, turmeric, rhubarb, ginger, henna, angelica, and orris root.

Herbs/Leaves include marjoram, sage, anise, rosemary, tarragon, thyme, mint sprigs (in particular, peppermint and spearmint), coriander, tea leaves, dill, fennel, cocoa leaves, basil, clover, thistle, genip, hyssop, and melissa.

Flowers include ivy, lavender, rose, lily, camomile, orange/lemon blossoms, clove, cinnamon, saffron, and poplar.

Seeds/Beans include vanilla beans, coffee beans, kola nuts, aniseed, celery seeds, caraway seeds, mace, nutmeg, and the stones (pits) of cherries, peaches, plums, nectarines, and apricots.

Fruits/Nuts include all berries, citrus (frequently the skins), raisins, peppers, pimentoes, and all types of nuts, most prominently, almonds, hazelnuts, and walnuts.

Most liqueurs should be served at room temperature and in very small amounts, especially if they are intensely sweet, spicy, or pungent. Cordial glasses normally hold a mere ounce to an ounce and a half. Most are best served on their own or with ice cream or sorbet. Many liqueurs also show up in the recipes of cocktails and mixed drinks.

I can't help but wonder what a twelfth-century monk would make of After Shock, one of the newest and most flamboyant liqueurs.

WHAT TO LOOK FOR IN A LIQUEUR

This is the one distilled-spirits category where the rules accorded the other categories simply do not apply. There are no rules-of-thumb with liqueurs, because each liqueur is a virtual subcategory in itself.

AFTER SHOCK Cinnamon Liqueur 40% Alcohol (Canada)

A solid cerise color that resembles cherry Kool-Aid—the interior walls of the squat bottle have crystals, which I presume to be tartrate, lining them—I understand that these edible crystals are the big draw to the crowd of "shooter" enthusiasts; the nose is quite piquant, with waves of zesty, snappy cinnamon rising from the tasting glass, and there the good news ends; at the palate entry, the flavor is dangerously medicinal and predictably heavy on the cinnamon, but the texture is so viscous that I lost patience with it; in the aftertaste, I grudgingly started to come around to it as it changed in my throat from a syrupy, goopy mess into a clean, cinnamon mother lode; I can comprehend the attraction of this cordial and the other tongue-tingling shooters if one is 22 and adventurous; try it, then move on to the cordial category's genuine treasures.

RATING ★★ $

ALIZE DE FRANCE 16% Alcohol (France)

Charming, citrus/tropical-fruit, juicy, intensely aromatic nose; squeaky-clean, tart passion-fruit-juice flavor, which, thankfully, doesn't mask the cognac; cognac amply makes itself known on the palate, and increasingly so in the pleasingly light, fruit-salad finish; at a mere 16% alcohol, Alizé (pronounced ah-lee-zay) is a suitably light cocktail that presumably also makes a good mixer; but even just served simply on its own, it's a satisfying, warm weather, poolside quaff that is neither cloying nor frivolous.

RATING ★★ $

AMARETTO DI LORETO 28% Alcohol (Italy)

Dark topaz/vanilla-extract color; commanding, direct, wet-gravel nose, spiced with a lovely prune-like quality that really impressed me; medium weight and viscosity; rather timid entry, then picked up strength and direction on palate, leaving a pruney, apricoty, nutty, sweet, but not cloying aftertaste that won the accolades of my taste buds; after first having been rather lukewarm to amarettos, I'd definitely request this one for an after-dinner embellishment.

RATING ★★★   **Recommended** $

ANCIENT AGE Mint Julep Liqueur 35% Alcohol (USA)

Whiskey-like amber tone, good clarity; the mint element soars in the nose, leaving any evidence of bourbon behind—the bouquet reminds me most of Wrigley's Spearmint Gum, which shouldn't be looked upon as a compliment; clearly, the spotlight is on the flavor, which nicely marries the more reined-in zest of mint with straight bourbon richness in a delightfully sweet, but not overbearing package that lasts long into the finish; I suggest that after you pour it, you simply slug it back and skip the nose; hardly inspirational.

  RATING ★★ $

ARTIC Vodka & Peach Liqueur 25% Alcohol (Italy)

Clear appearance, but with a pale gold/flaxen shade; this fabulous nose isn't all ripe, juicy peaches because I do detect a slender thread of alcohol—but, as in the case of the Artic Melon, the ambrosial bouquet is so concentrated, if you closed your eyes you'd swear a sliced peach was being held beneath your nostrils—the aroma is nothing short of luscious; to me, it's clearly the best of the three Artic vodka liqueurs; the alcohol plays the ideal foil to the intense peachy taste; a truly splendid spirit.

  RATING ★★★★   *Highly Recommended* $

ARTIC Vodka & Melon Liqueur 25% Alcohol (Italy)

Clear, with the palest touch of gold, which must be due to the viscosity—it resembles fruit juice; the cantaloupe aroma is totally on the mark without the slightest hint of alcohol—a remarkably ripe bouquet that says it all; it owns a ropy texture that leaves long, lazy legs on the inside of the glass; the flavor mirrors the aroma—four-wheel-drive cantaloupe, with just the slimmest trace of alcohol showing up in the finish; it's a handsome, unique, and well-made liqueur that would serve the purchaser well either straight up on-the-rocks or in a bevy of summertime mixed drinks; runs rings around its closest rival, the sickeningly sweet Midori.

  RATING ★★★   *Recommended* $

ARTIC Vodka & Lemon Liqueur 25% Alcohol (Italy)

Same appearance as its siblings; this nose is more pointed than the sweet melon or juicy peach as one would expect with citrus—it's not as true to form either, not as lemony as I'd hoped, but attractive nevertheless; even though I like the taste of lemon, the flavor doesn't jive as gracefully as the melon or the peach, because it can't decide if it wants to be sweet or tart—as a result, it ends up being both, and for that confusion or lack of commitment I can't recommend it; though the flavor is mildly appealing, it makes me analyze too much and that's not what a liqueur is supposed to do.

  RATING ★★ $

B & B Liqueur 40% Alcohol (France)

Author's Note: The letters stand for Benedictine and Brandy. An offshoot of the legendary liqueur, Benedictine. Lustrous topaz color, with orange highlights; the engaging aroma is like strolling in a field of wild grasses and flowers in the springtime; the bouquet is so intensely clove-like as to be slightly medicinal; the brandy component is very well-behaved on palate as the sweet, aldehydic, dried herbal qualities dazzle the taste buds; the warm, friendly midpalate has a fast nip from the brandy; finishes elegantly and long; a sumptuous afterdinner feast for the palate, but it doesn't own the magic or the majesty of its progenitor, Benedictine.

RATING ★ ★ ★   *Recommended* $$

Bailey's Original Irish Cream 17% Alcohol (Ireland)

A downright luscious, intensely creamy, well-mannered drink from start to finish; the nose is spirity, cinnamon-stick-like, almost spearminty, decidedly milky; luxuriously textured, faintly spicy flavor generously coats the taste buds; English-toffee-like in finish; easy sipping; no question in my mind why this elegant beverage continues as the world's favorite Irish Cream.

RATING ★ ★ ★ ★   *Highly Recommended* $

Bailey's Original Light Irish Cream 15% Alcohol (Ireland)

Milkier than the Carolans Light in appearance—a rich beige color; the nose is more nutty than creamy, with a freshly-cracked-walnut fragrance that is delightful—nevertheless, the cream is the underpinning foundation; bodywise, however, there's no question this liqueur is perceptibly skimpier than the full-strength version; the taste is full of gusto, as spicy, pepperminty, and floral (jasmine?) qualities all vie for dominance over the cream; interestingly, whatever cocoa-coffee flavors there are, these are mere echoes compared to the fourth-gear spice/mint contingent; while mildly tasty, my palate tells me in no uncertain terms that this is a significantly diminished version of the excellent original; I like the nose, but the lightweight texture and flavors fail to win me over.

RATING ★ ★ $

Bartenura Amaretto Kosher 24% Alcohol (Italy)

Pale orange/amber color; the nose owns the correct levels of kernel, popcorn, and nuttiness to easily pass its second sensory test, but odorwise it lacks sumptuousness and the compelling nuttiness of the great amarettos, like Lazzaroni, di Saronno, or Giovanni Buton; in the mouth, I find it disappointingly timid, paper-thin, and altogether lackluster; it's not bad or improper, it's just without a sense of mission—perhaps it rings too much of being manufactured.

RATING ★ ★ $

Bartenura Sambuca Kosher 40% Alcohol (Italy)

Clear; the viney/seedy/vegetal nose is atypical for *sambuca,* showing oddball hints of jalapeno pepper and black pepper, in addition to the expected licorice-candy scent; the quality level rises dramatically in the flavor as the tasty, savory, and even snappy flavor of licorice seems to crackle in the mouth; the finish is full, clean, and true to the flavor; also noted and appreciated is the medium-to-full, viscous texture.

RATING ★ ★ ★   *Recommended* $

BAUCHANT Napoleon Liqueur 40% Alcohol (France)

Harvest-gold/apple-cider color; the lovely, orange rind/tangerine bouquet is tart yet round, plump, and juicy, with hardly a blip of alcoholic fume even at the 40% level; the feel is like satin; the taste is sweet, but not in the least cloying, and it owns a luscious marinated orange flavor that competes with the best orange/brandy liqueurs; this one has everything going for it and certainly being produced in the Cognac region *with* cognac only enhances the quality.

RATING ★ ★ ★ ★   *Highly Recommended* $$

BENEDICTINE D.O.M. Liqueur 40% Alcohol (France)

Author's Note: This illustrious herb liqueur was invented circa A.D. 1510 to combat malaria, which occasionally sprang up in the French region where the Fécamp Abbey, Benedictine's place of origin, stood for centuries before being destroyed during the French Revolution. Brilliant honey/medium-amber hue, with orange/yellow core features, pure and very ropy texturally; the delicately herbal nose is an unusual combination of concentrated earthiness and floral perfume—some people might accuse it of being medicinal, but I view it as being seductive and piquant, but not prickly—there's no other bouquet like it; on palate, the fullness of the texture coats the tongue but doesn't overpower it, as the sweet flavor of honey is balanced by the tartness of citrus peel and the mild bitterness of herbs such as basil, rosemary, and sage; the aftertaste is silky-smooth and extended; magnificent.

RATING ★ ★ ★ ★ ★   *Highest Recommendation* $$

BISMARK Goldwasser Cinnamon Schnapps 40% Alcohol (USA)

Clear, with 24-karat-gold flecks floating about; the predictable cinnamon aroma is extremely concentrated, piquant, and luscious as it crackles up from the sampling glass—on my third nosing, my head almost snapped back from the cinnamon snappiness after vigorously swirling—this is a wild one, buckaroos; on the palate, it surprisingly turns creamy, full-bodied, and, dare I say it, elegant—all the zippideedodah found in the raucous bouquet came to a screeching halt in the mouth, where its presence suddenly became like a languid, purring pussycat; the finish, like the taste, is round and easy; after taking a shocking turn down finesse avenue, this savory cordial rivals the category leader, Goldschlager, in terms of overall sensory gratification.

RATING ★ ★ ★   *Recommended* $

BORGHETTI Café Sport Espresso Liqueur 33% Alcohol (Italy)

Looks exactly like espresso, that brown-turning-to-black color, golden edges; ropy, syrupy texture; the nose is intense and malodorous, giving off sweaty, locker-room odors that turned off my sense of smell in a hurry—later passes saw this loser bouquet become like an ashtray filled with two-day-old cigarette butts—one of the most disgusting noses in memory; unfortunately, the taste all-too-accurately mirrors the old cig-butt part of the aromatic equation—a disaster; one of the singlemost sickening liqueurs I've been within 50 miles of in the last decade.

RATING ★ $$

BUCKSHOT Original Wild West Liqueur 50.5% Alcohol (USA)

Light amber color, good clarity; the aroma is kicky, heady with spirit, peppery (as in spicy hot peppers), with not-so-subtle touches of vanilla, cinnamon, peach, nectarine, and ginger—a wild, piquant, but ultimately disarming nose; in the mouth, the lead-pencil/slaty spiciness makes it clear to me why they named it Buckshot—it owns a very flat, stony, metallic, leaden taste at entry, then it turns delightfully fruity and sweet at midpalate as the peach/nectarine combination triumphs over the cinnamon/ginger; long, zesty aftertaste; in the "shooter," spicy-liqueur category, this product is doubtless one of the better entries.

RATING ★★★ **Recommended** $

CAPRINATURA Lemon Liqueur 36.15% Alcohol (Italy)

Milky, green/yellow color; the nose is one-note lemon, but it's downright sumptuous, ticklingly tart, and inviting—nothing more to add; in the mouth; it's properly tart, with a plump backnote sweetness—the lemon taste is more of the lemon-meat than lemon-peel variety and, as a result, isn't as bitter as you'd expect; the finish is long, manageably tart, and keenly citrusy; a very savory, warm-weather liqueur that would be splendid on-the-rocks with some soda water.

RATING ★★★★ **Highly Recommended** $

CAPUCELLO Cappucino Liqueur 14% Alcohol (Holland)

Milky-brown color; the bouquet is more nut-like at first than coffee-like—simple, no depth to speak of—then in the later passes, a nice coffee-bean fragrance makes itself known; in the mouth, it's very creamy and understated—flavors of coffee and milk play this one-note liqueur through to the aftertaste, wherein a slightly roasted, nutty quality survives in the throat for a long period; average, middle-of-the-pack quality.

RATING ★★ $

CARNEROS ALAMBIC Pear de Pear Liqueur 30% Alcohol (USA)

The fetching gold/amber hue is similar to amontillado sherry or VS-level cognac; the one-way-street nose goes only in the direction of perfectly ripe Anjou pears that have been doused with a trace of spice—a glorious nose for pear fanatics; the peary taste is so sublimely smooth and seamless that for a moment it's hard to believe that this is a real liqueur—it's more a viscous, syrupy pear nectar; along with the superb QE brandy, this is the best product to come forth from this distillery; bravo.

RATING ★★★★ **Highly Recommended** $$

CAROLANS Finest Irish Cream 17% Alcohol (Ireland)

Lovely beige color; satisfyingly delicious and aromatic; unquestionably the creamiest of the sampled brands; the potent honey/cream, cocoa-like aroma is a standout; the very silky, rich, viscous texture is almost like melting ice cream; the spirity punch on palate is balanced by the softness of double cream; long, not overly sweet finish; my favorite Irish Cream.

RATING ★★★★ **Highly Recommended** $

CAROLANS Irish Coffee Cream 17% Alcohol (Ireland)

Browner than regular Irish Creams, looking in fact very much like coffee and cream; the pungent bouquet has the unmistakable thumbprint of coffee and cream—so much so that it doesn't really smell like a liqueur; tastewise, the flavor of roasted coffee beans with subtle cream and whiskey components is beautifully orchestrated—the level of creamy sweetness is balanced by the coffee bitterness and the whiskey body; the finish ends up as a contoured taste experience that's delightful; the Carolans Irish Cream family has shown itself to be the most consistently good of any Irish Cream line.

RATING ★ ★ ★ ★   *Highly Recommended* $

CAROLANS Light Irish Cream 15% Alcohol (Ireland)

Correct milky, beige color; the subtle, welcoming aromas of milk chocolate and cream are nicely overlayed with an intriguing mint/almond scent; on palate, the taste is only moderately sweet (what a relief), highlighted by a cocoa/coffee/mocca quality rather than the cream element; the texture is only slightly leaner than the full-strength version; it finishes cleanly, again with the emphasis on the bean-like quality of the coffee component rather than the dairy contribution; while I'm admittedly not a maven of "light" spirits, Carolans Light Irish Cream is the exception—in fact, it's better than many standard cream liqueurs.

RATING ★ ★ ★   *Recommended* $

CAYMANA Banana Cream Liqueur 17% Alcohol (Ireland)

Has the off-white to yellowish hue of buttermilk or, for that matter, banana meat; like so many of the cream liqueurs made in Ireland, Caymana owns a spicy, gunpowder snap that acts as the overture for the main aromatic thrust, which, in this case, offers far more cream than banana, though with banana being one of the subtler fruit aromas, this comes as no surprise—it reminds me of the banana "smoothies" I used to make in my blender years ago; very pleasant on the tongue, not at all overly sweet, and again the cream component dominates from entry through to the velvety aftertaste; I can't imagine this liqueur ever being a huge seller or a regular afterdinner quaff, but for banana mavens it does have appeal.

RATING ★ ★ ★   *Recommended* $

CHARTREUSE (FRANCE)

Not until 1848 was Chartreuse made available to the general public. This classic liqueur was created by the Carthusian Order of Christian monks at their monastery near Grenoble, France. Invented to aid digestion, Chartreuse came to light in the outside world when it was served as a *digestif* to a band of French Army officers.

CHARTREUSE Green 55% Alcohol (France)

This old-world classic owns the most intriguing, clear, pale-green/yellow color—not the neon, Kermit green of, say, Midori; the mesmerizing nose is compelling, multilayered, and individualistic—it's an extraordinary collection of spirity aromas ranging from anise to licorice to basil to flowers to shrubs to spearmint, all of which dazzle and keep the olfactory sense busy; on palate, the very spirity, sweet flavors of candied banana, key lime pie, and peppermint go citrusy/astringent by midpalate, then curiously revert back to mellow, herbal/minty sweetness in the sublime, heavenly aftertaste; a one-of-a-kind liqueur of the first order, which is immensely pleasing; so well made that you never really feel the high level of alcohol; upgraded after my last evaluation of it.

RATING ★★★★★   *Highest Recommendation* $$

CHERRY HEERING Liqueur 23.5% Alcohol (Denmark)

Author's Note: This liqueur-brandy was invented by the Dane Peter Heering in the 1830s. Predictably, it displays a ruby-red color that's strikingly similar to a full-bodied red still-wine hue; the seed-like, vegetal, viney, leafy nose is somewhat medicinal and actually more like cherry pits than cherry fruit on the first pass, then on the second and third passes the cherry fruit emerges; while the nose failed to impress me, the concentrated, black-cherry flavor proved an instant hit with my taste buds—strangely, it's sweet without seeming sweet because the acid level is high enough to balance the fruit intensity; it finishes gracefully but confidently in a flurry of ripe-cherry taste that lasts long in the throat.

RATING ★★★   *Recommended* $

CHINCHON Dulce Anis Liqueur 37% Alcohol (Spain)

Author's Note: Produced by Gonzalez-Byass, one of Andalusia's premier makers of Brandy de Jérez (Lepanto) and sherry. Water-clear, superb purity; I was expecting a bouquet that would remind me of either sambuca or Pernod, instead I got one that called to mind damp earth (like your back-yard garden after a heavy rain), ground spices, and roots in the first pass, then, to my surprise, chestnuts, walnut shells, and the smoke of burning tires in the second and third nosings—hey, you think this job is easy?—while the funky nose admittedly left me confused and monumentally underwhelmed, the taste and texture were truly delightful, as well-mannered, sweet flavors of black licorice, black pepper, and herbs rescued this unusual Spanish of-fering from the one-star trash heap, which was the place it was headed after the nosing part of the program; the aftertaste is extremely long, mildly sweet, and softly licorice-like; one of the biggest turnarounds I've experi-enced in the liqueur sector; find it and you'll enjoy it.

RATING ★★★   *Recommended* $

CLEMENT Creole Shrubb Rum Liqueur 40% Alcohol (Martinique)

Viscous texture, honey color; robust, fat, ripe mandarin orange, lemon and sugarcane nose; surprisingly snappy and citrusy on the palate—it's sweet, but not in the least cloying—while hardly a complex liqueur, it is ir-resistibly delicious in its simplicity; it has a tea-like quality in the aftertaste that is direct, mildly bitter, and luscious; no razzle-dazzle, just straight-ahead sugar and citrus that are carefully balanced.

RATING ★★★   *Recommended* $$

Cocobay Chocolate & Coconut Schnapps 15% Alcohol (USA)

Clear-water appearance; pronounced coconut-meat aroma, with a subtle milk chocolate element—a fresh, sweet, scrumptious nose that is neither cloying nor candied; on palate, because the alcohol is a manageable and modest 15%, the appetizingly fruity coconut flavor dominates—the chocolate rides in the sidecar acting as a minor flavor influence; I thoroughly enjoyed this carefree, light, and very delectable cordial.

RATING ★ ★ ★   *Recommended* $

Coco Rhum Coconut & Puerto Rican Rum Liqueur 24% Alcohol (USA)

Clear as water, ideal purity; the sweet, cottony nose rides the coconut horse all the way around the track, leaving little room for other aromatic nuances, though I doubt they exist anyway; very pleasing on palate—the sweet coconut-meat component is held in check, making it very drinkable; I admit that there's no other dimension to this liqueur other than the pervasive coconut (the rum is nothing but a distant echo), but I liked the simplicity of it as well as the silky texture; a good addition to piña coladas.

RATING ★ ★ ★   *Recommended* $

COINTREAU (FRANCE)

This is the preeminent orange curaçao in the world. It was created in the mid-nineteenth century by the Cointreau family, who were confectioners and distillers in Angers. The story goes that on a trip to the Caribbean, one of the Cointreaus happened across native wild oranges. Instead of sending some back home on a long, hot voyage on which they would dry up, he sent back dried-up peels. Upon receiving this rather strange but highly aromatic shipment from his son, Edouard Cointreau experimented with various concoctions until he came up with the formula that we enjoy to this day.

Cointreau 40% Alcohol (France)

Clear in color, very pure; the crisp, acidic bouquet is all about orange peel and nothing else from start to finish—this seductively simple nose has no flash, no dash, yet it is exotic in its acute presentation of freshly cut oranges—this is a no-holds-barred aroma that lays it right on the line, saying, "I am orange peel, you are not"; the mildly bitter flavor reflects the nose, as the opulent, but remarkably fresh, taste of orange peel leaves no room for any other flavor, except maybe a faint hint of spice at the very end of the mid-palate; the finish is, you guessed it, all orange; one of the great cocktail components, especially in the making of dynamite margaritas.

RATING ★ ★ ★ ★   *Highly Recommended* $$

Copa de Oro Licor de Café 21% Alcohol (Mexico)

Very deep brown, almost opaque in the core; excellent, robust, dark-roasted coffee-bean nose that leaves no doubt as to its elemental origin—not sweet in the least; unfortunately, it's downhill from there faster than a popsicle sliding down an iceberg; the texture is curdled, dense, and ropy—

the disgustingly corpulent and awkward body loads onto the tongue as though it has a bill of lading; the taste is more cloyingly sweet than coffee-like; this gooey mess should be renamed "Licor de Azúcar," or sugar liqueur, since it tastes like 98% corn syrup and 2% coffee flavor; an unctuous, flavorless, and completely unacceptable liqueur that should be avoided; what started out so well in the aroma took a severe nose dive on the palate; putrid and awful.

RATING ★ $

CREME DE GRAND MARINER Liqueur 17% Alcohol (France)

Typical cream-liqueur, milky-beige/cafe-au-lait appearance; the overly tutti-frutti nose reeks of bubblegum, kiwi fruit, sour apples, and spearmint—a less than appetizing combination at these individual doses; the bubblegum sweetness is present throughout the entire taste experience and is impossible to shake off—only the flavors of sour apples and mint eventually come into play at the very end of the aftertaste; forget this one completely and reach for either the Baileys or the Carolans creams from Ireland if you have a hankering for a cream-based cordial.

RATING ★ $

CRYSTAL COMFORT Liqueur 36% Alcohol (USA)

Perfectly clear appearance; the appetizing, inviting nose of oranges, tangerines, and lemons leaps from the glass—the bouquet is like sauntering through an orange grove at harvest time; on palate, this spry, frisky spirit bursts with keen orange/pineapple/tangerine flavors, but is only off-dry as the acidity keeps the lid on any sweetness; even though I like Southern Comfort, that venerable old cordial (rated three stars), I prefer this agile, lean liqueur by a very slender margin because its fresh, clean demeanor and taste are more in harmony with what today's consumers are searching for in terms of mixers.

RATING ★ ★ ★   *Recommended* $

DER SAURE FRITZ Citrus & Lime Schnapps 30% Alcohol (Germany)

Clear and pure; the astringent, citrusy, limey, Seven-Up nose is clean, fresh, lively, but too soda-popish for my comfort; on palate, it's Seven-Up with 30% alcohol—I won't waste more time on it because it's not the type of product I'd ever purchase or recommend; however, in its defense, I will say that I see some warm-weather mixed-drink possibilities, especially with tonic water, ice, and a generous slice of lime.

RATING ★ ★ $

DEKUYPER Original Peachtree Schnapps 24% Alcohol (USA)

Clear as a schnapps should be; pleasantly sweet and fruity in the full-throttle nose, which features one thing and one thing only—you got it, ripe peaches; amazingly easy to quaff, Peachtree is all peaches—sweet, succulent, and omnipresent from start to finish; it's delicious, but there's really nothing more about it to analyze because it's about as one-dimensional a cordial as you'll find, period; but, make no mistake, what it does it does very well.

RATING ★ ★ ★   *Recommended* $

DeKuyper Amaretto 28% Alcohol (USA)

Brown-eye/chocolate color, with orange/russet highlights; the compelling, heady, intensely nutty nose is both forward and well-mannered; on palate, the sweetness is there but it doesn't numb the taste buds with concentrated sugar; ambrosial flavors of peaches, apricots, and hazelnuts make this a delectable domestic offering; finishes smoothly and long, with the nuttiness dominating; very nice job.

RATING ★ ★ ★   **Recommended** $

Devonshire Royal Cream Liqueur 34% Alcohol (England)

Chalky/milky beige appearance; the forward, spicy bouquet sings a song of cinnamon; on palate, spicy, herbal qualities mingle beautifully with cream and spirit—a sassy, minty spiciness dominates the midpalate until a wave of cream steps up in the long aftertaste; not as rich or creamy as either Carolans or Bailey's Irish Creams, but an above-average cream to be sure; what held Devonshire Royal Cream in three-star territory was its leanings to the spice/mint/herbal qualities rather than the silky cream—its producer may have overplayed his hand a bit.

RATING ★ ★ ★   **Recommended** $

Di Saronno Amaretto 28% Alcohol (Italy)

The topaz/orange/copper color is dazzling; the rather shy nose is composed of almonds, rusty sheet metal, and sweetness; upon palate entry it offers lush, roasted-almond, slightly peppery flavors that are not overly sweet on palate; the extremely appealing, moderately viscous texture generously envelops the entire palate; it elegantly finishes with a keen vanilla-extract aftertaste, which evolves further into a faint hint of mandarin orange in the throat; downright delicious afterdinner treat.

RATING ★ ★ ★ ★   **Highly Recommended** $

Domaine Charbay "Nostalgie" Black Walnut Liqueur 30% Alcohol (USA)

Beautiful, deep-chestnut/oloroso-sherry color; the nose is multilayered, exhibiting elusive, but scintillating scents of egg cream, nutmeg, and coffee beans that lie underneath the walnut surface aroma; the flavor at entry smacks of orange/chocolate, pineapple, and guava before accelerating into a serious but crisp walnut-tasting overdrive; the aftertaste is long, sublimely sweet, and true to the source; Nostalgie makes most of the other nut-based liqueurs I've sampled seem feeble, flabby, cloying, and over-the-top; this classic, concentrated nectar is the product of a passionate and proficient distiller; one of the finest, most memorable liqueurs.

RATING ★ ★ ★ ★ ★   **Highest Recommendation** $$

Domaine Charbay "Lara" Persimmon Liqueur 30% Alcohol (USA)

The gold/bordering-on-amber color is lovely; Lara's nose is one of the most elegant gems I've discovered in a decade and a half of professional tasting—it's crisp, tart, and heady without being overbearing—the spellbinding aroma is as true to its source as any fruit liqueur I've encountered—if the nose were to be scored on its own, I'd give it five stars; on palate, the flavor shows much more than just ripe, succulent persimmon as it reaches an almost pearlike quality in the throat; the finish is surprisingly short, as faint but indelible echoes of persimmon resonate in the throat; the medium-long finish tops off the experience; this is perfection in a domestic liqueur.

RATING ★ ★ ★ ★ ★   *Highest Recommendation* $$

DRACULA'S POTION Black-Currant & Cherry Schnapps 25% Alcohol (Germany)

The plum color is a ruby port look-alike; nosewise, it emits intense, fresh-ground black pepper, ginger, cinnamon/Dentyne, gunpowder/fire-cracker, and lead-pencil aromas that are simultaneously compelling and re-pulsive—I have never developed a taste for the acidic, peppery, minty fla-vor of black currants, but there's an elusive element in this schnapps that keeps me coming back to it; the ginger-snap/herbal quality overtakes every other potential flavor possibility, rendering this schnapps a one-note ode to ginger root; the aftertaste introduces some black currant, but where is the cherry that the label promises? not my cup of liqueur, thank you, but it could find some support with the collegiate set that guzzles Jagermeister and Goldschlager like they were Diet Pepsi.

RATING ★ ★ $

DRAMBUIE LIQUEUR (SCOTLAND)

According to legend, Drambuie was first made on the Isle of Skye from a closely guarded recipe personally passed down from Prince Charles Edward Stuart, Bonnie Prince Charlie, Scotland's ill-fated hero, to the Mackinnon clan, who harbored him after his miserable defeat at Culloden Moor at the hands of the British.

DRAMBUIE Liqueur 40% Alcohol (Scotland)

Amber/golden color; concentrated licorice, freshly ground black pepper, dill-seed, spicy, waxy aromas that all rest on top of a subtle but evident Scotch whisky foundation; a keen licorice taste dominates at palate entry, then recedes, leaving herbal/whisky flavors that carry the taste buds along all through the long, luscious finish; spirity? yes, but not overly so; ditto the sweetness factor; there's ample sweetness and viscosity but neither of these overshadows nor overpowers the flavorful herbal qualities of this virile (what else from Scotland?) liqueur; in Gaelic the word *drambuie* means "drink that satisfies"; that being the case, I'll succinctly wind up my review by saying, "Drambuie"; recently upgraded to classic status.

RATING ★ ★ ★ ★ ★   *Highest Recommendation* $$

DR. MCGILLICUDDY'S Vanilla Schnapps 24% Alcohol (Canada)

Mineral-water-clear, perfect clarity; the fat, almost chewy bouquet re-minds me of the sweet, syrupy cream soda I used to drink as a child—the focus is more on vanilla bean than vanilla extract and, as a result, the nose isn't cloyingly sweet—nice job; so silky-smooth on palate that it effortlessly glides down the throat—the taste also concentrates on vanilla bean—this kernel quality is bittersweet and admirably true to the source; while indeed, it is a one-note melody, Dr. M has struck the ideal pitch with that solitary note.

RATING ★ ★ ★ ★   ***Highly Recommended*** $

DR. McGILLICUDDY's Mentholmint Schnapps 24% Alcohol (Canada)

Clear appearance; the snappy, candied nose crackles with peppermint freshness—there's absolutely no mistaking what this is; the explosive, prickly flavor is of the pedal-to-the-metal variety—the one-note nature of it is peppermint candy and nothing else—the aroma doesn't feign subtlety or elusiveness, as it brings home the mint in the brassiest possible manner; the aftertaste is industrial-strength peppermint supremo; a remarkably vibrant cult following has made this liqueur amazingly popular in certain parts of the U.S.; the kinky name and clever package make it a fun item for less so-phisticated imbibers.

RATING ★ ★ $

EARL GREY English Liqueur 20% Alcohol (England)

Gorgeous red/tea color, with a golden rim; it would be difficult to miss the lemon in the sweet-sour nose, which does resemble Earl Grey tea that's been steeped for five minutes or so; while I fully comprehend that this drink is a liqueur, I still wish that it possessed more tartness/acidity to off-set the ooey-gooey, syrupy sweetness; to its credit, Earl Grey is very smooth on palate; the viscous texture makes it ooze out of the bottle; the nonexis-tent finish was a serious markdown; in spite of the pretty appearance, the over-the-top saccharine sweetness of this lopsided liqueur proved to be too insurmountable a negative.

RATING ★ $

ECHTE KROATZBEERE Wild Blackberry Liqueur 30% Alcohol (Germany)

A ruby port look-alike as a clear, crimson/ruby color enchants the eye; the viney, leafy nose speaks immediately of blackberries in a soft, creamy voice—the bouquet tweaks the nose just a bit with agreeable spirit; the fruit flavor explodes on the palate right at palate entry, leaving no doubt as to its blackberry origin—at midpalate a sweet and exceedingly pleasant jammi-ness emerges and stays in control through the low-key but concentrated af-tertaste; it evoked happy memories of picking blackberries long ago and far away.

RATING ★ ★ ★   ***Recommended*** $

EMMETS Ireland Cream 17% Alcohol (Ireland)

Standard-issue milky/chalky appearance; the cotton-candy, bubblegum-like, puzzlingly citrusy aroma ends up having an unsettlingly metallic/med-icinal twang in the third and fourth nosings—there are problems with this tin-can/medicine-cabinet aroma; moderately tasty on palate, offering a bit-tersweet chocolate flavor that easily and regrettably overrides the cream component; the chocolate/coffee finish is rather harsh; tasted four times be-fore rating was settled on; I found it hard to get past the can-factory aroma.

RATING ★ $

FERNET BRANCA Bitters Liqueur 40% Alcohol (Italy)

Dark brown/cola color; the cough-medicine-like bouquet thrusts bitter aromas of mint, herbs, and spices at you in waves that, after the first pass, become more manageable—I didn't dislike the astringent, mouthwash-like aroma, but neither did I particularly care for it; on palate, it's one of the worst libations I've taken into my mouth—bitter, astringent, metallic, salty, and herbal—in a word, horrible; in Italy, annual sales regularly top 1 million cases—it's drunk neat, on-the-rocks, or is mixed into espresso; not in my house.

RATING ★ $$

FRAGONARD Liqueur de Cognac X.O. 30% Alcohol (France)

Displays a luminous, amber, prototypical cognac appearance, though its viscosity is perceptibly thicker; the biscuity nose is semisweet and quite subdued as aromas of walnut and dried fruit push the cognac scent to the side; on palate, it's understated, silky-smooth, and sweet, but the sweetness is so well handled that it acts as the ideal counterpoint to the dryness of the foundational cognac; the finish is long, sweet, and mannered, with hints of egg cream and chocolate; everything about this sensuous liqueur is played down—a testament, I believe, to the skill and sensitivity of the producer.

RATING ★ ★ ★   *Recommended* $$

FRANGELICO Liqueur 28% Alcohol (Italy)

Lovely, luminous, golden-nectar/light-amber hue, excellent clarity; this classic liqueur bouquet is equal parts nut meat and butter, with a sprinkling of dried herbs—it's a potent aroma, one that engages the drinker immediately—but while it's strong, it isn't unruly, awkward, or even pungent; the lilting waves of hazelnut and butter continue on the palate; the finish showcases the hazelnut but only for a short time, since the aftertaste is too polite to overstay its welcome; focused, delectable, classy, stately; also a superb liqueur in cooking.

RATING ★ ★ ★ ★   *Highly Recommended* $

GAETANO Amaretto 21% Alcohol (USA)

Dark amber/topaz hue; the piquant nose is rubbery, like an inner tube, and modestly almond-like; a featherweight texturally; the nutty taste vanishes instantly before you really have the chance to evaluate it; the lame flavors can't seem to shake the bitter burning-rubber quality that dominates the dubious nose; the sole positive is the pleasantly sweet, fruity/almondy aftertaste; sampled blind four times, receiving consistent notes and scores.

RATING ★ $

GIOVANNI BUTON Sambuca 40% Alcohol (Italy)

Clear and viscous; the anise/licorice/caraway-seed aromas rule the piquant nose, but underneath there's an enticing layer of peppercorn that is vastly different from other superpremium *sambucas*—it is, by a long shot, the most perfumed bouquet in the *sambuca* subcategory; so classy on the tongue is it that it feels like silk; the anise flavor is underpinned by a pervasive dryness, which keeps the entire experience balanced in terms of sweetness, alcohol, and flavor; elegant, smart, chic, and obviously produced with enormous care; may not be seen everywhere, so ask your local spirit merchant to track it down for you—it's well worth the extra effort; it's the best *sambuca* made, period.

RATING ★ ★ ★ ★ ★   ***Highest Recommendation*** $ $

GIOVANNI BUTON Amaretto 25% Alcohol (Italy)

Luminous amber/orange/tea/harvest-gold color that is impeccably clean; the soft but endowed almond nose carries within it more than its share of vanilla bean; the satiny, unctuous (but not cloying) texture glides onto the tongue while a rich tidal wave of off-dry vanilla saturates the taste buds, backed up by firm flavors of almond, apple, and chocolate sauce; the aftertaste is sweet, long, and captivating; the amaretto standard-bearer; it's one of the finest cordials of any type I've evaluated; bravo, Buton.

RATING ★ ★ ★ ★   ***Highly Recommended*** $ $

GIOVANNI BUTON Gran Caffè Espresso 26.5% Alcohol (Italy)

By far, the prettiest of the coffee liqueurs—a stunning chestnut/mahogany hue plays host to a burnished-copper core and a brilliant golden rim—a resplendent eyeful; the coffee aroma is harnessed and subdued, but laden with rippling potency and vigor; the manageable viscosity coupled with the intense, espresso flavor make this one the pick of the coffee-based-liqueuer litter; the aftertaste is balanced, clean, and only off-dry as the concentrated coffee-bean flavor charms the daylights out of the palate—not once do you sense anything overbearing or overstated, so serene and well crafted is it; simply put, of all the coffee liqueurs I've evaluated over the last ten years this svelte beauty left the deepest impression.

RATING ★ ★ ★ ★   ***Highly Recommended*** $ $

GIOVANNI BUTON Crema Cacào 30% Alcohol (Italy)

Clear; the texture's so glutinous that I almost needed a knife to get it out of the bottle; wildly intense cocoa-butter/dark-chocolate nose that's surprisingly dry to off-dry, but very spirity and appealing; so sweet to the taste that my eyes crossed, but, like the intensity of chocolate truffles, in minute doses it's sinfully decadent and delicious; a slap-and-tickle cordial that's quite the bon vivant; the character of the cocoa bean is so focused from aroma through to the aftertaste that it's hard to resist if you have a hankering for chocolate; serve only in a customary small cordial glass on its wicked own.

RATING ★ ★ ★   ***Recommended*** $ $

GIOVANNI BUTON Amara Felsina 30% Alcohol (Italy)

The dark mahogany color resembles premium cream sherry; this intense liqueur has a strong bitters (as in quinine), highly astringent, Pepsi Cola leading edge in the aroma, which I ended up liking after the third pass; on the palate, the slate-like flavor is moderately bitter initially, then turns into a quiet, dry, herbal, cola finish; this is not a cordial I'd serve on its own; used as a mixer, however, when bitters are called for, I believe it would show very well; another possibility would be to try it over ice with a twist of lemon or orange and a splash of seltzer.

RATING ★ $$

GIOVANNI BUTON Coca 36.5% Alcohol (Italy)

The luminous yellow/green hue is like a lighter version of Green Chartreuse, one of my all-time favorite liqueurs; extremely ropy texture; the evergreen, woodsy, herbal nose is dry on first pass, then goes pleasantly cedary-sweet, almost like pine sap; it's so gelatinous on the tongue that the weight alone leaves a deep impression, literally; flavorwise, I detect only a passing hint of pine on the surface, but underneath there are fascinating echoes of kiwi, lime, tangerine, and sage; though the multilayered quality is remarkable, as is its faint similarity to Chartreuse, the sheer syrupiness is way too overpowering for my taste buds; made from the leaves of South American coca shrubs (*Erythroxylon* genus), whose inherent dangers are totally eliminated through the fermentation and distillation processes; I wanted to like it, but I ended up strongly disliking it.

RATING ★ $$

GODET Belgian White Chocolate Liqueur 15% Alcohol (Belgium)

Has the flat, off-white color of egg shells—also resembles fresh cream; the lactic nose is milky, chocolatey, not in the least sweet, and even offers a splash of vanilla bean in the background; on palate, it's feathery light in terms of alcohol punch, but velvety and creamy to the touch—the hands-down highlight flavors of this classy number are milk chocolate and cream; the finish is rich, creamy, and sweet, but never unctuous or overbearing; certainly one of the best two or three chocolate liqueurs I've evaluated; this is a sweetie that deserves your immediate attention, especially if you have a hankering for European chocolate.

RATING ★ ★ ★ ★   *Highly Recommended* $$

GODIVA Chocolate Liqueur 17% Alcohol (USA)

Cola-brown appearance; the sweet but acidic nose strongly hints of herbs, cocoa beans, nut meat, and even anise—the chocolate underpinning is surprisingly docile; what occurs next on the palate will be long remembered—the ultravelvety texture forms the foundation for one of the more noteworthy cordial flavors I've evaluated—the svelte dark-chocolate taste is sublime, balanced, not overly sweet, and wraps around the tongue as snugly as a Rolex around the wrist; a dazzlingly scrumptious cordial.

RATING ★ ★ ★ ★   *Highly Recommended* $$

GOLDSCHLAGER Cinnamon Schnapps Liqueur 53.5% Alcohol (Switzerland)

Clear, though I should point out that within the low-shouldered bottle are flecks of gold leaf—get the name tie-in?—the gimmicks never stop in the liqueur category, what can I say?—you can't whiff this one too long or too deeply for fear of sustaining whiplash, the tangy, punchy, cinnamon aroma is like a laser beam in its focus and potency; on palate, it's a sweet-sour cinnamon feast from wall to wall; no doubt that this double-barreled, well-crafted concoction is pig heaven for those quirky folks who get orgasmic over the most piquant of spices.

RATING ★ ★ ★   *Recommended* $

GRAND MARNIER Cuvée du Centenaire 1827–1927 Liqueur 40% Alcohol (France)

Medium amber with copper core features; the nose shows more cognac than triple orange as heady waves of spirit waft up from the glass—it's a great bouquet that exhibits as much mature power as it does supple finesse—this is a clinic on how to create the perfect liqueur aroma—exquisite balance; in the mouth, the opulence of the texture carries the flavor impact to the taste buds like a jewel—the orange taste is secondary to the old cognac; this pearl of a libation never gets old or tiresome as many times as I've had it; you could look up the term "liqueur" in the dictionary and you'd find a picture of this Grand Marnier there.

RATING ★ ★ ★ ★ ★   *Highest Recommendation* $$$

GRAND MARNIER Cuvée Spéciale 1827–1977 Cent Cinquantenaire Liqueur 40% Alcohol (France)

Strikingly similar to the Cuvée du Centenaire in every way, except for the flavor/texture/mouth presence, which is even more satiny and mellow—a defining moment in the world of liqueurs; the finish is round, buxom, syrupy, and semisweet as the cognac element bows to the triple orange; nothing short of perfection; it gives amazing satisfaction after a meal.

RATING ★ ★ ★ ★ ★   *Highest Recommendation* $$$

GRAND MARNIER Cordon Rouge Liqueur 40% Alcohol (France)

Yellow/goldenrod/orange color; the unmistakable, enchanting, and totally unique sweet-sour nose is kissed with mandarin orange and just the slightest suggestion of cognac; so supple, satiny, and smooth on palate that it leisurely glides down the throat; every chemical element—alcohol/acidity/fruit—is in perfect harmony with every other component here from start to finish; a true classic liqueur if there ever was one; a timely quaff of Grand Marnier is always comforting for the fond memories it rekindles; I can't imagine anyone not loving this exceptional *digestif;* it's a Bentley in an Escort world; tasted too many times to mention.

RATING ★ ★ ★ ★   *Highly Recommended* $$

GREENY Apple Schnapps 21% Alcohol (Germany)

Pretty, golden apple-juice/cider color; the tutti-frutti nose is all ripe apples, with estery/phenolic traces of bubblegum, pine, nail polish, and apricot—while this mixture may not sound too appetizing, the nose is really quite pleasant for a sweet, sappy aroma—in fact, it approaches being delicate and refined; on the palate, it borders on being sour-apple-like at entry, then picks up sweetness along the way to the finish; the aftertaste is like the fresh apple cider that I buy in the autumn at roadstands in rural Pennsylvania; against all odds and despite the poorly designed label, I thought this item to be a very appealing little number; serve well chilled.

RATING ★ ★ ★   *Recommended* $

Henri Bardouin Pastis 45% Alcohol (France)

The distinctive, green/yellow hue immediately tips off the nature of this beverage, excellent clarity prior to the addition of mineral water; the vibrant, heady bouquet is like licorice candy, sweet, sticky, and piquant—the zesty anise quality comes through more in subsequent nosings—it's a fresh, herbal, spicy aroma; to my taste, it's more palatable than Pernod—the intensely sweet-sour quality is surprisingly courteous—the headlining flavor of anise is supported by intriguing tastes of citrus peel and licorice; long, citrusy, tart aftertaste; turns a milky, opal-like white color with the addition of mineral water.

RATING ★ ★ ★   *Recommended* $$

Hiram Walker Sambuca 42% Alcohol (Italy)

Transparent and pure; the nose is disappointingly limp and weary with only the merest hint of aniseed or black licorice—by far, the meekest *sambuca* bouquet I've come across; it's syrupy-thick, ropy, and overly sweet on the palate; it's devoid of charm, balance, and elegance; whoever produces this liqueur for Hiram Walker should study the clear *sambucas* of Giovanni Buton, Strega, and Romana to see how the innate sharpness of aniseed can be tamed into one of the most beguiling of liqueurs; it's as though the flavor was injected with mega-amounts of corn syrup to cover other deficiencies; take a pass on this hideous lemon.

RATING ★ $

Irish Mist Liqueur 35% Alcohol (Ireland)

Appealing, crystalline tawny/orange color; the alluring, honey, parsley, leafy, wet-soil/garden-fresh nose is sensationally vibrant and prickly—to my surprise, the Irish whiskey takes a distant backseat; delicious, balanced, and sweet but never cloying; moderate viscosity; the focused herbal flavors lead the way at palate entry, then back off as the honey comes to the fore in midpalate, eventually giving way itself to mellow whiskey flavors in the elegant, classy, and understated finish; this is a prime example of a liqueur whose sweetness is prudently used as a calling card to the taste buds, not as a bludgeoning instrument; there's enough acidity and fundamental bite to balance the honey; bravo and a sincere tip of my tasting hat.

RATING ★ ★ ★ ★   *Highly Recommended* $$

Jacquin's Amaretto 28% Alcohol (USA)

Orange/amber color; the stinging, prickly, bitter, and spirity nose smells of citric acid, burning rubber, nuts, and minerals—it's an aromatic mess, no harmony, no direction; on palate, the tingly, biting, alcoholic quality in the bouquet abates, allowing a pleasant, almondy fruitiness to emerge; medium-weight, moderately thick; the aftertaste is subdued, sweet, and surprisingly pleasant; the flavor and aftertaste somewhat redeemed the awkward and unappealing aroma.

RATING ★ ★ $

Jagermeister Liqueur 35% Alcohol (Germany)

Very pretty, opulent cola hue that's been color adjusted with caramel; the zesty nose is direct, intensely herbal, citrusy, and almost medicinal, but alluring in an exotic manner—the herb (including thyme, rosemary, basil, parsley) quality is so profound that it's like walking into a Chinese herbalist's shop; quite sweet to the taste, it shows a cola-like element (Coke Classic, to be exact, which may be why it's so popular on campuses) right from the crack of the bat, then goes citrusy/herbal by midpalate; the citrus/herb evolves into a chocolatey aftertaste that is doubtless its best quality; a charming and quaffable shooter, but that's about it.

RATING ★ ★ ★   **Recommended** $

JOHNNIE WALKER Liqueur 40% Alcohol (Scotland)

Sports a fetching honey/hay/light-amber tone; the nose is unmistakably founded in Scotch whisky as a malty/grainy aroma supports more ethereal hints of sliced pears, ripe peaches, honey, cream, and cinnamon—it's a dashing, delightful fragrance in which the fruit component is clearly king; in the mouth, a citrusy/mandarin-orange element leaps out at palate entry, then recedes into a peachy quality that reins in the sweetness; the finish is polished, balanced, sophisticated, and positively yummy; for my money it runs with the whisky liqueur elite led by the estimable Irish Mist and legendary Drambuie—it differs in that it is decidedly fruity where they are herbal and honeyed.

RATING ★ ★ ★ ★   **Highly Recommended** $ $

KAHLUA Royale Cream Liqueur 17% Alcohol (Holland)

It should be specified from the outset that this yummy cordial is first and foremost a cream liqueur with a dash of Kahlua added and not Kahlua and cream—there is a vast distinction; resembles most other cream cordials, milky brown, like coffee and cream; very viscous; the nose is dominated by the rich cream, with barely a hint of the coffee-bean Kahlua influence in evidence—it's a pleasant, opulent, lactic, though hardly exciting aroma; after the predictable, chalky-brown appearance and banal, snooze-o-rama bouquet, the luscious, luxurious flavor and satiny texture catapult this liqueur into the big leagues in a hurry—the cream component rules all the way through the taste experience and is masterfully and judiciously complemented by the hint of Kahlua; the aftertaste is long and satisfying; do taste and finish alone deserve four stars? check the rating below for my answer.

RATING ★ ★ ★ ★   **Highly Recommended** $

KAHLUA Licor de Café 26.5% Alcohol (Mexico)

Rich brown/cinnamon color, with russet/ochre highlights; roasted-coffee-bean, somewhat metallic, disappointingly bitter nose; but wait—this thoroughbred really gets it into gear in the mouth; the flavor bursts with a luscious taste that beautifully balances the chocolatey semisweetness with the high-octane, lush coffee flavor—neither dominates, each complements the other in grand style; it finishes regally, richly, and chocolatey; a stylish, user-friendly, simply dynamite cordial that deserves its worldwide popularity in spite of its bitter aroma, which is redeemed by the well-endowed taste and lingering off-dry aftertaste.

RATING ★ ★ ★   **Recommended** $

KAHLUA **Almond Moo Moo 6.5% Alcohol (USA)**

Beige/chalky appearance; the nose on this "kiddie" liqueur is quite lovely in its sweet apricot/almond perfume, reminding me distantly of amaretto; it's milky on the palate, but the candied-almond charm carries this tasty morsel over the goal line; this one works for me and, no, I have not lost my mind; just forget the insipid name and try it.

RATING ★ ★ ★   *Recommended* $

KAHLUA **Mudslide 6.5% Alcohol (USA)**

Winner of the chocolate milk look-alike contest; the nose smells chalky, milky, and nutty and, curiously, almost comes off more like an Irish cream aroma than a coffee fragrance; the taste is sweet, milky/creamy, and rather bland all the way from entry through to the aftertaste; I picked up very little coffee component in this pleasant, but ultimately uninteresting offering— and most importantly, where's the Kahlua?

RATING ★ ★ $

KAHLUA **Milkquake 6.5% Alcohol (USA)**

I hope that I'm never called upon to tell the difference between this and the previous two premixes by appearance alone—this one is identical to the others; the bouquet and the taste are so close to the Mudslide that even side-by-side it takes all my evaluation powers to notice any differences except to say that I detect a smidgen more coffee flavor in this one than the Mudslide; again, not in the least offensive, but, well, milky, chalky, sticky-sweet, and boring.

RATING ★ ★ $

KALDI **100% Columbian Coffee Liqueur 28% Alcohol (Columbia)**

Opaque brown/dark-chocolate color, with a goldenrod rim—one of the darkest colors of the coffee-based liqueurs; offers an amazingly concentrated, potent, dry, black-coffee bouquet that is as focused as a laser beam; much drier than Kahlua on palate, robust, viscous Kaldi is a "must try" afterdinner elixir for espresso or Turkish-coffee lovers; considering the fathomless depth of coffee flavor, the expected bitterness in Kaldi is gratefully manageable; the off-dry finish seems a little tame after the raucous, bracing flavor at entry and midpalate; a genuine wake-up call; admittedly, it may be too heady and lusty for some people, but I thought it a nice counterpoint to Kahlua's mannered civility.

RATING ★ ★ ★   *Recommended* $

KAMORA **Coffee Liqueur (Mexico) 26.5% Alcohol**

Pretty, shimmering cola color, with a marigold edge; perhaps the nuttiest, beaniest aroma of the coffee-based liqueur group—the nose possesses a pleasant Macadamia-nut-meat quality that harmonizes ideally with the firm and arresting fresh-brewed coffee bouquet; the sexy texture is like crushed velvet on the tongue; Kamora packs slightly more overall flavor satisfaction than its higher-profiled competition; oodles of roasted-coffee-flavored stuffing mingles nicely with the ample, but understated, sweet-

ness; the aftertaste has a hint of cocoa and mint; a delightful cordial with a
reasonable price tag that runs rings around Kahlua.

RATING ★ ★ ★ ★   *Highly Recommended* $

KAMORA French Vanilla Coffee Liqueur 20% Alcohol (Mexico)

Medium brown/cola tone; the sexy nose emits seductive waves of French-
roast coffee beans, double cream, vanilla extract, and roasted almonds—one
doesn't have to be a coffee aficionado to appreciate this savory, svelte bouquet; the texture is unctuous and syrupy; I think that this beauty rivals its
delicious progenitor, original Kamora, in elegance and understatement; on
the tongue, it coddles the taste buds as tastes of vanilla bean, dark chocolate, and freshly ground black coffee come together in the delicate finish; I
like the fact that, while full-bodied, Kamora French Vanilla is neither cloying nor overwhelming in its richness-sweetness; a must item for vanilla
lovers.

RATING ★ ★ ★ ★   *Highly Recommended* $

KAMORA Hazelnut Coffee Liqueur 20% Alcohol (Mexico)

Darker in cola tone than the Kamora French Vanilla, Kamora Hazelnut
displays some copper highlights in the core; a knockout bouquet—nutty,
nougat, road-tar, licorice scents delight the olfactory nerves right from the
start; yes, it's syrupy, yes, it's rich, but the flavor elements of roasted nuts,
mild coffee, cocoa/mocca, and butter cream are craftily blended together;
the silky aftertaste is medium-long, sultry, and even a bit smoky in its controlled nuttiness; even a noncoffee drinker, like myself, can immediately take
a liking to this husky, but polite and friendly, liqueur.

RATING ★ ★ ★   *Recommended* $

KWV VAN DER HUM Liqueur 25% Alcohol (South Africa)

Attractive, copper/medium-amber color, ideal purity; the citrus-peel/
acidic bouquet calls to mind the bitterness of Campari to a minor degree
as well as pineapple and Chinese sweet-and-sour sauce—an intriguing
aroma, but I didn't find it especially inviting; it tastes almost exactly as it
smells—citrus meat and peel (tangerine/tangelo) lead the parade, followed
by flavors of sweet-and-sour sauce and pineapple; I liked the texture; while
I like tangerines, I didn't feel that this was tangerine heaven; a quaffable
liqueur, nonetheless.

RATING ★ ★ ★   *Recommended* $

LA GRANDE PASSION Liqueur 24% Alcohol (France)

Lightish and very pretty amber/orange hue; the sweet, sumptuous, perfumed, heady nose emits fragrant, seductive scents of candied apples, ripe
passion fruit, and fresh red raspberries, all supported by a brandy underpinning; comes across very velvety on the palate as succulent flavors of luscious tropical fruits are beautifully complemented by the unobtrusive spirit
base; the aftertaste is long, silky, and clean, never cloying, clumsy, or gummy;
one of the more elegant tropical-fruit liqueurs by a country mile; suited well
for mixing as well as being served chilled and neat.

RATING ★ ★ ★ ★   *Highly Recommended* $$

LAZZARONI Amaretto 24% Alcohol (Italy)

Vivacious gold/orange color; the pungent, sharp nose offers scents of almonds in the first pass, then concentrated, astringent, medicine-chest aromas in the second—it had me guessing; the remarkably delicious, pronounced almond/nutty/nougat flavor generously coats the tongue; it finishes like liquid satin, with the mature, satiny almond taste taking a backseat first to a citrusy tang, then ultimately to an astounding rose flavor at the back of the throat; hardly a trace of bitterness; an extraordinarily voluptuous *digestif* experience.

RATING ★ ★ ★ ★   **Highly Recommended** $$

LEROUX Irish Cream 17% Alcohol (USA)

A formula Irish Cream, but I wish they had found a better formula; no point in talking about such a slapdash product, whose producers are trying to cash in on a trend; ooey-gooey, overly sweet, cloying, wretched.

RATING ★ $

LICOR 43 Liqueur 34% Alcohol (Spain)

Rich, golden, Sauternes-like color; intense, single-barreled, assertive butterscotch aroma; on palate, the monotone aroma transforms itself into a rather one-note, very sweet flavor of vanilla, with just the barest hint of orange rind hiding in the wings; the orange/citrus flavor finally emerges in the extended and savory aftertaste; please note that this is an extremely sweet, viscous cordial, which is appropriately touted as a mixer; whether by design or not, the producers provide virtually no counterpoint to the numbing sweetness, and hence, for my taste, I could never enjoy this top-heavy liqueur on its own; I could, however, envision a number of worthwhile applications, as suggested by the importer, for instance, as a tasty addition to fruit salad or as a topping for ice cream or sorbet; indeed, I can see it as a useful item in the kitchen of an imaginative cook; but on its own, it's horrible.

RATING ★ $

LILLEHAMMER Scandinavian Berry Liqueur 21% Alcohol (Denmark)

Has the red-brick/cherry-juice look of a Grand Cru Beaujolais or a lesser Cru Burgundy; the bouquet is elegant, fruity to the beat of overripe red berries (it's produced from lingon berries), and more sweet than tart—it's a captivating nose that sports red-curranty, vinous, and leafy qualities; oh, baby, this liqueur really accelerates on the tongue as lovely, intense flavors of red berries swathe the palate in medium-bodied texture—the balance between the fruit element, the alcohol level, and the degree of sweetness is impeccably carried off; the finish is medium-long, delicate, very mannered, and much like a parting kiss; a first-rate, graceful beauty that absolutely deserves to be part of your collection.

RATING ★ ★ ★ ★   **Highly Recommended** $

LIQUORE GALLIANO 35% Alcohol (Italy)

The brilliant, almost neon-like, saffron-yellow/gold hue captures the vision of the taster immediately; the pungent, rustic nose is laden with woodland scents of roots (very much like root beer), herbs (thyme, rosemary, and basil), flowers (jasmine), kernels (pine nuts), and cedar—unquestionably an intriguing, pleasurable bouquet that keeps you guessing as you unpeel the earthy layers; unctuously thick and syrupy-sweet (much too syrupy for my taste); in the taste, Galliano replays many of the herbal characteristics identified in the nose; the finish is very sweet and long, with soft echoes of earth, woods, and vegetation in the tail end; megasweet, but mildly charming in extremely small doses.

RATING ★★ $$

LIQUORE STREGA 40% Alcohol (Italy)

The brilliant chrome-yellow/green hue compels the taster to gaze at it, awestruck by the remarkable color—aside from Chartreuse, the best yellow-green liqueur color I've seen; the prickly nose emits powerful waves of dandelion, anise, licorice, sunflower seed, pine sap, and spearmint—it's like walking into a natural-foods store; in the mouth, Strega feels and tastes like a spring day in the forest—there's something earthy and elemental about it that's appealing; spearmint, sap, and seeds in the flavor and the sweet aftertaste; it's a gorgeous, completely unique cordial of the first rank.

RATING ★★★★   *Highly Recommended* $$

MALIBU Liqueur 24% Alcohol (Canada)

Crystal clear in appearance; the ethereal, sweetened coconut fragrance is immensely appealing—there's no hint of any alcohol whatsoever in the enticing nose; for those consumers who are serious coconut nuts (like yours truly) this is the coconut mother lode; the crisp, laser-beam flavor is intense and focused on only one target—you guessed it; there's nary a hint of alcohol from the lovely palate entry all the way through to the svelte, clean finish; I see huge potential for creative, warm-weather mixed-drink concoctions, but I have to confess that I prefer Malibu simply on its own, chilled, no ice.

RATING ★★★   *Recommended* $

MANDARINE NAPOLEON Grande Liqueur Impériale 38% Alcohol (Belgium)

One of the prettiest liqueur colors—a brilliant amber/orange/honey hue that always seems to catch the light just right; the piquant, acidic, citrusy, spirity nose is ruled by the meat of mandarin orange; soft, silky texture; the sweet-sour entry is delightful, sound, and firm, then the orange gets in gear midway in tasting, ending tartly in an impressive flavor climax where the spirit is flawlessly melded to the fruit element; this is an outstanding liqueur by any measure.

RATING ★★★★   *Highly Recommended* $

MARCEL TREPOUT Liqueur d'Amour des Mousquetaires 35% Alcohol (France)

Brandy-amber tone; the heavenly nose reminds me at first of Grand Marnier, but then after I sniff it for a few moments I conclude that it's not as sweet as GM—this fantastic armagnac liqueur (the only one I'm aware of) offers concentrated, ripe scents of mandarin orange and butter—the bouquet is so refined and delicate that I could almost hear it crack—a breathtaking experience; the taste is one of the most divine brandy-based liqueur experiences I've had—it has everything—controlled sweetness, great delicacy, ideal acid/fruit balance, silky texture, and that extra charm that's indescribable when you reach this level of sophistication and excellence; my message is simple—find and buy.

RATING ★ ★ ★ ★ ★   *Highest Recommendation* $ $

METAXA Grande Fine Liqueur 40% Alcohol (Greece)

Significantly darker and richer in color than the other two Metaxas—a medium amber/medium brown color, superb purity; this bouquet is decidedly brandy-like, as succulent, heady, and spirity aromas of *muscat* grapes, almonds, oak, and caramel come together with style; on palate, the entry flavor is intensely grapy, then the taste turns compact and pruney, even raisiny, at midpalate, reminding me slightly of oloroso or palo cortado sherry; the aftertaste is very long, burnt, and brandy-like; and like its siblings, it rides the fence that separates brandies and liqueurs.

RATING ★ ★ ★   *Recommended* $ $

METAXA Seven-Star Amphora Liqueur 40% Alcohol (Greece)

Brilliant, opulent, amber/iced-tea color; this nose is sliced right down the middle between a sweet, herbal liqueur and a nut-like brandy—whatever it is, the bouquet is unique, pungent, herbal, earthy, caramelized, smoky, cheesy, and even musty; my palate, like my nose, is totally confused—this isn't a brandy, yet it's not a strict, by-the-book liqueur either; on the third tasting pass, my taste buds adjusted and treated it like a sweet, candied liqueur; I ended up cautiously liking it, but it demanded an enormous amount of work and patience; the aftertaste is sweet and herbal; I found it to be an acceptably nice liqueur, nothing more, nothing recommendable.

RATING ★ ★ $ $

METAXA Classic Liqueur 38% Alcohol (Greece)

Pretty, light amber/orange/tea color, perfect clarity; in the aroma, the unmistakable thumbprint of the *muscat* grape, an orangey/flowery scent, overrides the spirit fragrance, making the bouquet pleasant and wine-like; in the mouth, the sweet, grapy flavor is underscored by a firm texture, formed no doubt by the spirit base; the finish is lean, not overly sweet, and a bit lame—not much follow-through here; as good as the Seven-Star Amphora version, but not good enough to recommend.

RATING ★ ★ $

MIDORI Melon Liqueur 23% Alcohol (Japan)

Lime Jell-O color; the piquant, ripe melon, strawberry, piercingly sweet, spirity nose is more attractive if you only lightly sniff it, since deep inhalations draw out too much spirit; pleasant, if simplistic, melony flavors on palate generously coat the tongue and sides of the mouth; more a mixer in

exotic, warm-weather, tutti-frutti drinks than a straight, solitary indul-
gence—take my word for it, don't drink it straight; appropriately, Midori's
mixing strengths are what are encouraged by the producer.

RATING ★ $

MOLINARI Sambuca Extra 42% Alcohol (Italy)

Clear and extremely viscous—it coats the tasting glass like paint; the
heady, moderately herbal aroma, whose spiritiness pricks the sensors in the
nose cavity, is quite dry, but all on the table—not what I'd consider a wallflower nose; has all the correct *sambuca* components, but stylewise it's
pedestrian and heavy-handed compared to the likes of Giovanni Buton or
Romana; it displays scant elegance as it lumbers along from nose to tongue;
the main problem may have to do with the cloying heaviness in the texture;
it's sound, average, and moderately tasty, but in the end unexciting and un-
exceptional.

RATING ★ ★ $

MONTENEGRO Amaro 30.2% Alcohol (Italy)

Attractive, brandy-like, orange/medium amber tone, pure; the nose has
delicate notes of fruit pit (stone) and quinine—there's just the suggestion
of sweetness, but not the real thing itself—this aroma is all nuance and very
little substance; at palate entry, it appears as though there's a conflict between the quinine and the sugary sweetness—neither dominates—the latter stages of tasting offer an unexpected coconut-frosting taste that I liked,
being a fan of coconut; the only, if considerable, problem with this liqueur
is that full appreciation of it requires more time and patience than 99% of
the consuming public is willing to spend.

RATING ★ ★ ★   **Recommended** $$

MOZART Chocolate Liqueur 17% Alcohol (Austria)

Dark, creamy-brown appearance; the nose, which I didn't care for one
bit, is a strange, uneasy combination of nuts, chocolate, nougat, pencil
eraser, and rubber hose—this is anything but an attractive, compelling bou-
quet; in the mouth, things improve not one lick as the various flavors seem
to fight each other—it's not especially chocolatey, or nutty, or nougaty—
there's no direction, no focus, no charm for my palate to discern and ana-
lyze; if you want a chocolate liqueur, head straight for the Godet or the Go-
diva; if you get a bottle of this as a gift, throttle the gift giver.

RATING ★ $

OBLIO Sambuca 40% Alcohol (Italy)

Spring-water clarity, excellent purity; the solid, full, but not aggressive
nose features piquant, spirity aromas of anise and black licorice that di-
minish only slightly by the fourth and final nosing pass, in which flashes of
beans, seeds, cream, and citrus appear; a definite highlight is the ropy, but
not unctuous, texture that luxuriously coats the palate; flavorwise, the sweet,
delectable, and downright seductive mouth presence displays concentrated,
totally focused, and almost dense tastes of anise, licorice, beans, and spice;

the finish is very extended and satiny; a liqueur of uncommon balance, finesse, and flavor impact, bravo.

RATING ★ ★ ★ ★   *Highly Recommended* $

OBLIO Caffè Sambuca 35% Alcohol (Italy)

Lovely, chestnut/cola-brown hue; the semisweet, bitter bouquet leans heavily toward freshly ground, roasted coffee beans in the first two nosings, then adds cola nut in the third pass—the final nosing marries the coffee and cola in a pleasant, but ultimately bland, aroma that is neither of a full-time *sambuca* nor a coffee-liqueur nature—the split personality works against it aromatically; allowing that the aroma is not its best face, this combination of virtues works much better on palate, where its mission seems more clearly defined—in the mouth, it's obviously a *sambuca* with coffee flavor added—the licorice flavor forms the foundation on which the coffee taste is allowed to play; the aftertaste is manageably sweet and velvety; not a knockout, but still a better-than-average sweetie that developed nicely in the mouth.

RATING ★ ★ ★   *Recommended* $

O'CASEY'S Irish Country Cream Liqueur 17% Alcohol (Ireland)

Standard chalky/chocolate milk appearance; the charming, sweet nose is like marshmallows and cotton candy, with a faint touch of nutmeg; skip the pedestrian nose, however, because in the end it's the silky, creamy, spicy flavors that are the draw—so delicious is it that I place O'Casey's on equal footing with my two category favorites, Carolans Finest and Baileys Original Irish Creams—the concentrated cream element is the highlight; the ultradairy finish is as luscious as the flavor and very long lasting in the throat; this blockbuster is a serious player in the Irish Cream sweepstakes.

RATING ★ ★ ★ ★   *Highly Recommended* $

O'DARBY Irish Cream 17% Alcohol (Ireland)

Sound, if uninspiring effort; pleasant coffee bean-like nose; just slightly too sweet on palate, but, thankfully, the cream component isn't annihilated by spirit or sweetness as in others I've sampled; medium-long, but satiny finish that highlighted spice and chocolate in hand-to-hand combat; recently upgraded.

RATING ★ ★ $

O'MARA'S Irish Country Cream 15% Alcohol (Ireland)

Standard issue, Irish cream, milky tan color; viscous texture; the nose is understated in its creaminess and there's none of the usual spicy zest that most other Irish creams have—it's a limp and docile bouquet that doesn't seem to have a direction; in the mouth, the alcohol base is watery and skimpy—it doesn't have the normal spirit backbone that acts as the foundation for creams like Baileys and Carolans; tastewise, it's not even in the same ballpark as other Irish creams; dismal in every way. (Addendum: I later spoke with a producer spokesperson, who explained that the base alcohol was *wine,* not Irish whiskey or grain spirit; no wonder this lemon has no character.)

RATING ★ $

OPAL NERA Black Sambuca 40% Alcohol (Italy)

Midnight-black color, with purple/charcoal-gray edges and a ruby/crimson/blood core; owns a zesty, irresistible, alcoholic, but somewhat one-note nose in which anise holds court over all other fragrance possibilities; genuinely luscious flavor offers much more depth than the nose as the sweet, candied licorice taste is complemented beautifully by a pleasing bitterness in the aftertaste that balances the opulent syrupiness; ends very well and unalcoholic in the throat as the licorice flavor goes on and on; simply smashing; hey, I'm impressed.

RATING ★ ★ ★ ★   **Highly Recommended** $

ORAN MOR Malt Whisky Liqueur 40% Alcohol (Scotland)

Dull, turbid, honey/hay color, with yellow highlights; the frightfully metallic, spirited, but off-puttingly odd barnyard nose has little going for it; viscous texture; improves modestly on palate after the unfortunate aroma; grainy/maltiness combines nicely with a honey/nut flavor that pleasantly caresses the taste buds in a smoky cloak; does the flavor have enough stuffing to redeem the problematic nose? regrettably not; being an unabashed Scotophile, I was disappointed with this liqueur; some genuine potential here, but something has to be done to corral the savagely awkward nose and cloudy, unappealing appearance.

RATING ★ $$

ORIGINAL CANTON Delicate Ginger Liqueur 20% Alcohol (China)

The pretty gold color is negated by numerous floating bits of who knows what—ginger root?—I suggest to the producers that they step up their filtration efforts for the finicky consumers of the U.S.; the nose is more fruity than herbal, though the ginger does adequately come through past the honey and brandy aromas; in the mouth, the succulent ginger/honey taste is decidedly tasty, lasting long into the nimble finish; at a manageable 20% alcohol, it drinks easily and would, I project, be quite delicious with a twist of orange over ice; I'm simply not sure if there are that many ginger fanatics around the U.S.

RATING ★ ★ $$

OUZO by METAXA 40% Alcohol (Greece)

Clear and pure; the nose is an amazing banquet of aromas, ranging from licorice to aniseed to fennel—it's a well-mannered, even polite, aroma that shows admirable persistence throughout all four nosings—it changes slightly in the last pass, as more of the fennel scent takes the lead; sweet to the taste, Metaxa's Ouzo is smooth and nonabusive on palate, leaving just a wee tongue of fire in the heady finish; I liked it much more than I thought I would.

RATING ★ ★ ★   **Recommended** $

OUZO No. 12 40% Alcohol (Greece)

Clear as water, pure; in comparison to the nose of the Metaxa Ouzo, No. 12 introduces the element of mint (wintergreen) to the staple aromas of aniseed, fennel, and licorice—I liked the No. 12 bouquet marginally more than that of the Metaxa; wonderfully velvety on the tongue, this smooth talker is really luscious, offering harmonious tastes of aniseed and licorice—while Metaxa's Ouzo was brisker and more assertive on the palate, I responded more favorably to this silky, handsome winner; long, licorice-like finish.

RATING ★ ★ ★ ★   *Highly Recommended* $

PATRON XO Café Coffee Liqueur with Tequila 35% Alcohol (Mexico)

Looks exactly like cola—nutbrown with gold edges; the nose is unique, as the marriage of coffee and tequila creates a prickly, very spirity, and bean-like bouquet that goes a tad chalky by the third nosing—I simply didn't find this combination aromatically compatible; it tastes better than it smells, the intensely bean-like coffee flavor overriding the vegetal tequila taste—there's actually a bittersweet cocoa quality to the flavor that's very nice; the finish is sweet and rather quick for a liqueur—the tequila has a fast burst of flavor in the aftertaste; an interesting concept that works on the palate enough to get the recommendation.

RATING ★ ★ ★   *Recommended* $$

PEARLE DE BRILLET Liqueur 24% Alcohol (France)

Pretty, amber/honey/burnished-gold hue, good purity; the nose is like just-ripened pears, not sweet, not sour—I detect no spirit in the first passes—the literature claims that this delicately perfumed morsel is made from Pear Williams pears grown in Alsace and young eau-de-vie from Cognac—the eau-de-vie is aged for only one year in oak cooperage—it eventually develops into a pleasant, nicely fruited bouquet; on palate, the eau-de-vie finally comes into play as the subtle but sure foundation, on top of which the soft pear flavor is allowed to enchant the taste buds; the aftertaste is surprisingly long; a very pleasant, though hardly profound liqueur.

RATING ★ ★ ★   *Recommended* $

PERNOD Spiritueux Anise 40% Alcohol (France)

The classic name that has become synonymous with anise-based liqueurs; brilliant yellow/green hue, ideal clarity; the nose vaults from the glass in heady waves of anise, fresh garden herbs, carnations, fennel, and, most pungent of all, licorice—it's a lovely, fascinating, and exotic bouquet that's memorable; tasted neat, it's oily, bittersweet, and potent, with a well-defined note of licorice—with spring water added, Pernod turns milky, soupy, and opaque and tastes better, since much of the bitterness is diluted, leaving behind the concentrated anise flavor on its own; the finish is long, licorice-like, and sweet in both versions; not a spirit that I'd request in a bar or restaurant, but interesting all the same; Pernod is the legal knock-off of the now outlawed lethal spirit absinthe.

RATING ★ ★ $$

PRALINE Pecan Liqueur 21% Alcohol (USA)

Extremely viscous, pours out of the bottle like molten lava—so syrupy that it coats the sides of the glass like paint; attractive brown/oloroso sherry color; amazingly intense, burnt nuts, smoky, pecany nose comes off like

Turkish black coffee; the aroma is so remarkably nutty as to be overpowering; on palate, its pecans run amok; while I freely admit I'm not a fan of pecans, the flavor, which displays some sense of balance between sweetness and fruit, is better than the over-the-top nose; take a pass unless pralines/pecans really make your day; yyyeeccchhhh.

RATING ★ $

RETTER Pfirsich Peach Liqueur 26% Alcohol (Austria)

Medium amber/vermilion tone, perfect purity; the emphemeral, feminine, sweet, but not unctuous, bouquet speaks of the ripest, most succulent peach you've ever consumed (probably on that warm summer day long ago when you were a kid)—not the barest hint of alcohol gets in the way or competes with the mesmerizing fruit perfume—it's one of the most impressive aromatic experiences that I've ever had; in the mouth, the rich, ripe peach flavor can only be described as being quintessential—the serene beauty of it lies in the fact that it's both graceful and approachable; this breathtaking liqueur is neither ponderous nor multidimensional, but it is perhaps the liqueur truest to the fruit source that I've ever evaluated; monumentally brilliant.

RATING ★ ★ ★ ★ ★   *Highest Recommendation* $$

RETTER Cassis Johannisbeer Liqueur 26% Alcohol (Austria)

More a cherry-cola/coffee-brown than a plum/purple color, perfect purity—it reminds me most of a cream sherry in appearance; the reluctant nose is stemmy, seed-like, and not the least bit sweet or even off-dry, but it does emit a mild dose of black-currant fruit after ten minutes of aeration; while I'm admittedly not a devotee of anything relating to cassis, I can't deny that the flavor and texture in this silky liqueur are divine, mature, ideally tart at midpalate, with just the right finish of sweetness; in fact, the aftertaste even remotely hints of a lighter cream sherry, such as Emilio Lustau's Deluxe Cream; an outstanding discovery.

RATING ★ ★ ★ ★   *Highly Recommended* $$

ROMANA Della Notte Black Sambuca 40% Alcohol (Italy)

Fascinating black/gray color, with intriguing purple highlights in the syrupy core; the spirity, aniseed, apricot nose jumps out of the gate quickly and continues to pump out seedy/herbal intensity with every pass—I even notice a trace of citrus—it's an engaging, multilayered nose of self-evident depth; this sleek, sure black panther slinks down the throat with confidence; sweet? yes; subtle? terribly so; refined and elegant? you bet; this one offers one of the more complete cordial packages in the current marketplace; it even finishes with sexy fruit tastes of orange and cherry; this smoothie's on the prowl; absolutely delicious; go out and grab it.

RATING ★ ★ ★ ★   *Highly Recommended*

ROMANA Sambuca Classico 42% Alcohol (Italy)

Clear and very thick; the concentrated licorice-candy nose takes me back to childhood recollections of my mother devouring black-licorice whips like there was no tomorrow—it's a lovely, herbal, spicy, candied aroma consisting of several layers; dry to the taste, there's a minor letdown on the palate entry, where, for just a fleeting moment it gives off a diesel-fuel flavor, then the flavor quickly rebounds with anise/licorice on the tongue; the aftertaste is even, sure, and surprisingly dry; while not as supple as either the Della Notte or Opal Nera, this *sambuca* is savory and better than average nevertheless.

RATING ★ ★ ★   **Recommended** $

ROYALE CHAMBORD Liqueur de France 16.5% Alcohol (France)

Opaque, the color of ruby port; the nose is an awkward, viney combination of cassis, black raspberry, sunflower seeds, unopened attic, and wet cardboard—I thought the bouquet was stinky, stemmy, musty, and altogether unpleasant; it's quite another story on the tongue, however, as ripe, fully fruited flavors of black cherry, red raspberry, and plum offer a lush, smooth ride for the taste buds; the chunky, viscous texture is a plus; the ultraberry finish is soft, but firm, and medium-long; the terribly unappealing, seriously flawed bouquet works effectively against this otherwise enticing liqueur.

RATING ★ ★ $$

RUMPLE MINZE Peppermint Schnapps 50% Alcohol (Germany)

Clear; the nose is extremely delicate, as the understated, sweet, herbal peppermint fragrance wafts up from the sampling glass—considering the elevated alcohol, there's nary a hint of splashy or overbearing spirit—an altogether sublime, classy, and perfumed bouquet of the first rank; so sumptuous is the texture that it wraps around the tongue like a mink coat; the focused, laser-beam flavor of intense peppermint is so elegantly and deliciously presented that you don't even notice the alcohol; extended, mint-heaven finish; extraordinary quality from the nose through to the aftertaste; this is a must-buy item for any liqueur aficionado; it's magical.

RATING ★ ★ ★ ★   **Highly Recommended** $

SABRA Chocolate Orange Kosher Liqueur 30% Alcohol (Israel)

Very pretty appearance of cherry/amber/russet colors; the nose collapses in a heap of citrus, laundry soap, old sneakers, and men's-locker-room odors—curiously, the nose also has a bite that's amazingly disgusting and offensive—I detect not a single trace of chocolate or cocoa; while the nose is horrendous, the taste crawls up a notch on the quality scale as barely evident tastes of orange rind and dark chocolate finally make a showing, if grossly tardy; I'd long heard about the splendor and quality of Sabra, but I would be remiss not to report in no uncertain terms that this liqueur is a mess, an uncomely disaster, and one of the worst liqueurs I've evaluated over the last ten years; avoid as you would the Ricki Lake Show.

RATING ★ $

SAFARI Exotic Liqueur 20% Alcohol (Holland)

Possesses the attractive, vibrant orange/amber hue of a fine bourbon, but with a touch more orange; the ambrosial, tropical-fruit nose recalled my days of living in Hawaii over two decades ago—the bouquet is a turbo-charged, fuel-injected fruit salad, with acute emphasis on the mango component; on palate, this nimble liqueur achieves outstanding balance between sweetness, fruitiness, and acidity—the mango really steps forward in the taste, followed closely by a keen citrusy tang that adds a crisp pizazz; it finishes fresh, clean, and with good fruit concentration; what I admired most about this terrific liqueur is that it's not for a moment syrupy or cloying; tasty on its own or, I assume, in mixed drinks.

RATING ★★★   **Recommended** $

Sambuca Di Angela 42% Alcohol (Italy)

Properly clear; nicely structured aroma of licorice and aniseed, set in a sweet, though not cloying or clumsy, foundation; very viscous on the tongue, I mean, this baby is downright ropy, heavy, and oily; tastewise, it's very pleasant, with a correct jolt of aniseed, juniper, pine/cedar, and even orange/black pekoe tea; gives a quick hot flash in the aftertaste, but nothing that would detract from the overall impression—besides, I doubt seriously that most consumers would even pick up on the nanosecond of fire; good effort.

RATING ★★★   **Recommended** $

Sazerac Cocktail 30% Alcohol (USA)

Orange/amber color; I didn't like the minerally, old-attic, wet-cardboard nose at all—I kept hoping that some detection of the bourbon or the brandy would finally emerge to take charge of the bouquet, but that never happened; on palate, it markedly improved as the bourbon-brandy elements gratefully kicked into gear, providing a rather pleasant flavor experience; finishes well in a warm, semirich, almost citrusy fashion; not my cup of cocktail, but good as a mixer, which is its proper place.

RATING ★ $

Serrana Licor de Café 26.5% Alcohol (Mexico)

Deep molasses-brown/cola hue, with a gold/amber edge; the dry, beany nose here is a fascinating and delectable combination of coffee and roasted chestnuts; medium-to-heavy viscosity; another cloddy, lumbering, hammer-over-the-head coffee liqueur that beats the taste buds into a stupor with 25-pound bags of sugar; this one at least owns more coffee flavor than the hopeless Copa de Oro, but certainly not enough to break it into the ranks of Kahlua, Tia Maria, Kamora, or the sensational Buton; take a rain check on this one.

RATING ★ $

Sheridan's Original Double Liqueur—Black 26% / White 17%— Alcohol (Ireland)

I must have poured this wrong, because the two liqueurs in the stupid-looking attached bottles blended together in a coffee-with-cream color—I believe that the white liqueur is supposed to float on top of the black; after feeling taken in and unamused by the gimmicky quality of this concoction, I tasted the two liqueurs separately and liked them both, I then tasted them together and liked them even more; this is a richly decadent, unabashedly outrageous, and gimmicky cordial, but, hey, the taste, the aroma, the quality, and the quirkiness are there, and often it takes a trick to get people to try new items.

RATING ★ ★ ★ ★   **Highly Recommended** $$

Southern Comfort Liqueur 40% Alcohol (USA)

Amber/orange color; pungent, seed-like, citrusy nose that also reminds me of roses; pronounced orange/ripe peach flavors lead the way from palate entry to the extended aftertaste; sweet, yes, cloying, no; a definite mixer, or on-the-rocks cocktail specialty; very pleasant, easy-to-drink liqueur that has manners and is obviously well made; what I appreciate most about it is the fact that it doesn't bludgeon you with sweetness or viscosity.

RATING ★ ★ ★   **Recommended** $

St. Brenedan's Superior Irish Cream 17% Alcohol (Ireland)

One of the classier, tastier Irish Creams around; the charming, almost herbal, creamy aroma is delightful and sassy; it's richly textured; the finely balanced flavors of milk chocolate, spirit, and double cream are harmonious and sweetly expressive; an impressive, gentlemanly cordial with a lovely, soft finish.

RATING ★ ★ ★   **Recommended** $

Strega Sambuca 42% Alcohol (Italy)

Clear; the candied, licorice-whip nose provides a delightful kick for the olfactory sense—a pungent, sweet, coffee-bean bouquet that's very seductive and alluring; the full-throttle, viscous sweetness blankets the tongue upon mouth entry; by midpalate the anise/licorice flavor is in an orbit higher than the space shuttle—I mean to tell you that this robust, unctuous, no-apologies-here, fat liqueur pulls out all the taste and texture stops; not for everybody, to be sure, because of its strength, but if left alone with it for too long, I'd bathe in it; it runs with the best two or three *sambucas* currently available.

RATING ★ ★ ★ ★   **Highly Recommended** $$

Taam Pree Cherry Kosher Liqueur 24% Alcohol (USA)

Exceedingly pretty burnished-amber/copper color that's a dead ringer for a dry oloroso sherry; the seed-like, fruity nose is exotic and alluring as waves of ripe Bing cherries waft up from the sampling glass—it's an off-dry bouquet that's lovely and sedate; the sweet-sour flavor is nothing short of delicious, with tastes of ripe cherries coming wrapped in a semiviscous robe; the medium-length aftertaste is slightly smoky/earthy/musty and kernel-like; a savory, lip-smacking liqueur that's velvety, affordable, and luscious.

RATING ★ ★ ★ ★   **Highly Recommended** $

Taam Pree Banana Kosher Liqueur 23% Alcohol (USA)

Clear; it smells exactly like the banana taffy that I used to ingest in mass quantities as a child, so this is a trip down memory lane for me—the nose is like unripe bananas, but it's also steely and metallic; on the palate, the flavor leaves no doubt as to the type of fruit this liqueur is made of—it owns a medium-rich texture and a wholesome, clean, almost creamy-banana taste that's reminiscent of banana-nut cake or bread; I found it neither too sweet nor too dry; it's a pleasant balance of fruit, alcohol, and acid; it works.

RATING ★ ★ ★   *Recommended* $

TAAM PREE Blackberry Kosher Liqueur 20% Alcohol (USA)

Has a brick-red/medium-brown look of an old Côte de Beaune red Burgundy; the aroma is assertive and proper, exhibiting a keen, ripe blackberry fruit in a jammy, preserve-like manner—it even emits a vinous, briary scent that's quite captivating; intensely fruity on the tongue, it shows the jammy face of overripe blackberries in a low-alcohol arena that makes it quite quaffable; probably makes an excellent topper to vanilla ice cream or fresh blackberries.

RATING ★ ★ ★   *Recommended* $

TAAM PREE Kummel Kosher 35% Alcohol (USA)

Clear; the parchment-like, seed-like nose is not full-throttle caraway seed as one might expect, but a steely combination of caraway, bond paper, and lead pencil—in its dryness, the bouquet is quite nice, actually; on palate, the kernelly caraway flavor bounds to the forefront, leaving behind the mineral and cardboard flavors; though the alcohol is a hefty 35%, it's never really an issue on the palate impression or in the finish; nice job on this one.

RATING ★ ★ ★   *Recommended* $

TAAM PREE Pear Kosher Liqueur 23% Alcohol (USA)

Crystal clear; the faint aroma is only mildly pear-like and comes off more akin to white-grape raisins and baseball-card bubblegum—on the second pass, it throws off more sweet-pear fragrance; in the mouth, the taste is pleasant, sweet, and fruity, though I'm not sure that it's all pear, maybe cantaloupe, too?; whatever the case, the bland fruitiness, while inoffensive, isn't definitive or pleasing enough in any of the sensory areas to justify a recommendation.

RATING ★ ★ $

TAAM PREE Chocolate Truffle Kosher Liqueur 16% Alcohol (USA)

Deep brown/cola color that resembles a pruney Pedro Ximenez sherry; the off-putting nose is a malodorous mixture of burnt rubber, rotting almonds, black coffee, and the mustiness of an old attic that's just been opened—in short, it's like a wet-dog odor—in fact, this dog should never have been allowed to leave the kennel; the mildly chocolatey taste tries to make up for lost ground, but this battle was irretrievably lost in the loathesome, armpit aroma; a just plain awful, ooey-gooey concoction that probably sounded like a good idea in the marketing meeting, but in reality, it's horrible.

RATING ★ $

TAAM PREE Anisette Kosher 23% Alcohol (USA)

Clear; the dreary nose speaks of two incongruous things—licorice/anise and new sneakers—not the most appetizing combination, but there you go; the flavor is wafer thin and not concentrated at all on the tongue; the taste, quite surprisingly, is correct, but the watery texture defeats any flavor gains; the finish is like kerosene; don't strike matches around it, or wiser still, don't waste your time at all with this pathetic swill.

RATING ★ $

TIA MARIA Blue Mountain Coffee Liqueur 26.5% Alcohol (Jamaica)

The handsome auburn/bronze color is strikingly reminiscent of oloroso sherry; the steely, astringent nose is a bit too mild and passive for a coffee-liqueur profile; very elegant, classy demeanor, almost feminine on palate; the lightest body of this particular subcategory; exquisitely balanced, gentle coffee flavors are harmoniously joined by a sublime sweetness that carries through to the demure aftertaste; certainly the one coffee liqueur that one could drink the most of and for the longest period, though I can't say I preferred Tia Maria to its archrival Kahlua, and, in fact, I scored them equally; Tia Maria is so ethereal it could almost be served as an aperitif as well as a very gratifying *digestif;* very good quality.

RATING ★ ★ ★   *Recommended* $

TIRAMISU 24% Alcohol (Italy)

Black-coffee/cola-brown color; the espresso, coffee-bean nose is very pronounced, focused, and lovely; on palate, the coffee flavor temporarily takes a backseat to a candied-almond taste that's extraordinarily savory and sexy, then the aftertaste combines the coffee with the almond in a wonderfully sweet, lip-smacking crescendo that's totally irresistible; along with Kamora, easily one of the best coffee-based liqueurs I've evaluated; bravo.

RATING ★ ★ ★ ★   *Highly Recommended* $

TORRES Gran Torres Orange Liqueur 39% Alcohol (Spain)

Orange/pale copper/russet/amber color; the concentrated orange nose also offers some earthy, herbal, butter hints, even a touch of tannin (from the oak casks?)—but the aromatic headliner here is orange from start to finish; on the palate the laser-like citric-acid tartness nicely balances the sweetness, making it very quaffable and only light- to medium-bodied in texture; it concludes as it began, with ripe orange notes that don't seem to fade in the least throughout the aftertaste; while not as majestic as Grand Marnier, Cointreau, or Mandarin Napoleon, Gran Torres offers superb value all the same; Torres can even be used in margaritas in place of Triple Sec or Cointreau.

RATING ★ ★ ★   *Recommended* $

TRIMBACH Liqueur de Framboise 25% Alcohol (France)

The brick-like appearance closely resembles a youthful Côte de Nuits red Burgundy, like a Gevrey-Chambertin; the nose is ethereal and well-mannered, though not sedate, true to the fruit source, and only mildly sweet; in the mouth, the raspberry taste takes off like a skyrocket, as intense, sweet-sour, scrumptious waves of flavor cradle the palate—the flavor intensity and elegance carry over into the soft, fruity finish; a must-have item for red-raspberry freaks; dynamite as a warm-weather *digestif* or as an accompaniment to fruit salad, vanilla ice cream, or sorbet.

RATING ★ ★ ★ ★   *Highly Recommended* $$

TRIMBACH Liqueur de Poire 35% Alcohol (France)

Brilliant, Sauternes-like, yellow/gold color, perfect clarity; the nose of ripe pears is one-pointed in its mission and ends up being more tart than sweet—I was admittedly unmoved by the proper, but one-note, bouquet, however; it's in the mouth that this liqueur really reaches its potential as a rich, sweetish, but not overbearing afterdinner beverage; the finish is polite, sweet, and luscious; I would never have guessed after thoroughly nosing it over four passes that this captivating poire would end up with three stars, but the finesse and the power shown in the taste and finish scored telling points.

RATING ★ ★ ★   *Recommended* $$

TUACA Liqueur 35% Alcohol (Italy)

Light brown/honey color; the bouquet emits potent aromas of caramel, butterscotch, light toffee, coffee with cream, cola nut, hazelnut, oak, and a nice dash of spice—it vaguely reminds me of a Brandy de Jérez Solera Reserva at one moment and even a Speyside single malt at the next instant—maybe I'm finally losing my grip; in the mouth, it's pleasantly oaky, sweet but hardly cloying, as delicate, understated flavors of egg cream, butterscotch, and vanilla gently wrap around the tongue; the aftertaste is long, easy, and manageably sweet; I found it moderately appealing but inconsistent and befuddling, without the genuine depth of character or quality that would make it recommendable; it's a flashy, superficially decent, but, in the end, middle-of-the-road cordial.

RATING ★ ★ $

VANDERMINT Chocolate Liqueur 26% Alcohol (Holland)

Cola-brown color; the intense, semisweet chocolate, crisp, freshly cut spearmint nose also shows more than a smidgen of black coffee—an engaging aroma, indeed; I found more coffee/chickory taste than cocoa on the palate as the spearmint moved to the background in the flavor; the aftertaste is smooth, bean-like, and, to its credit, only moderately sweet; even though I'm not a coffee drinker, I bet that this silky, savory liqueur goes well with coffee; as far as a liqueur on its own, Vandermint is pleasant but as far from the level of Godiva or Godet as Geraldo Rivera is from good taste; I liked the bouquet more than the sappy, wimpy flavor; upgraded on the last evaluation.

RATING ★ ★ $

VILLA MASSA Liquore di Limoni 30% Alcohol (Italy)

Looks exactly like freshly squeezed lemon juice—pale yellow; the nose reminded me instantly of fresh lemonade, tart, clean, and inviting—admittedly, it's a one-note tune, but with a cordial such as this, it's unrealistic to expect layers of nuanced flavors (you want lemon, this has lemon); there's a heady rush of citrus flavor at entry that's simultaneously startling and enthralling—once it coats the tongue, you get the full benefit of its snappy flavor; moderately tart, some foundational sweetness, even an herbal twist in the crisp aftertaste; a superb, ice-cold shooter for those so inclined; I predict major success.

RATING ★ ★ ★ ★   *Highly Recommended* $$

WILD TURKEY Liqueur with Honey 30% Alcohol (USA)

Yellow/gold color; very sweet nose of rose petals, cinnamon sticks, bubble-gum, egg nog, and oranges—this could go on forever—suffice it to say, this liqueur displays an amazingly wide array of intriguing aromas; the cloying honey flavor dominates the palate, with just the barest hint of alcohol peeking out; while drinkable, the fourth-gear cotton-candy-like nose, ultragooey texture, and monotone honey flavor will never allow this liqueur to run in the big leagues with the other whiskey liqueurs, such as Drambuie and Irish Mist.

RATING ★ $

YUKON JACK Canadian Liqueur 50% Alcohol (Canada)

A distinctly white-wine-like appearance, a *cru* Chablis to be exact; mandarin-orange fragrance dominates the piquant, sweet, spirity nose; viscous, though not syrupy or clumsy, rich, satiny texture; potent, meat-of-the-orange flavor that is nicely married to the spirit, which is always evident; pleasant heat/bite at the back of the palate in citrusy, silky, long finish; quite luscious for a hearty afterdinner liqueur, where a little goes a long way; while sweet, YJ original has enough acid to balance the final package.

RATING ★ ★ ★   *Recommended* $

YUKON JACK Snakebite with Lime 45% Alcohol (Canada)

Sauternes-like color; the nose is heavily weighted in citrus and is slightly stinging as the 45% alcohol bolts from the sampling glass like a horse that's been given an electric shock—this nose will never be accused of being demure; in the mouth, I detect industrial-strength lime essence that overpowers all other flavor possibilities, so it ends up being a unidimensional samba; the finish merely echoes what's already been addressed in the citrusy nose and taste; it's not that it tastes bad, but even for a lime maven like me, I find the unbalanced emphasis on lime to be too forced, too heavy-handed—you just want to say, "All right already, I got the message"; I much prefer the regular Yukon Jack.

RATING ★ ★ $

YUKON JACK Black Jack Liqueur 50% Alcohol (Canada)

Inky, gray/black color brings to mind Opal Nera Black Sambuca; the stinging bouquet sports a mild aniseed/licorice quality that's supported by minty, herbal prickliness—don't inhale too deeply on this one, you may not recover for hours—the final nosing exposed the sweet licorice/cola/root-beer/candy component that I believe is supposed to be the headliner; on palate entry, there's a nanosecond flash of lemon-citrus, then it proceeds heavily into the licorice taste, as the highly charged, viscous texture coats the inside of the mouth like molasses; while I liked the aroma, the hammer approach in the taste and the finish made it unrecommendable.

RATING ★ ★ $

Fortified Wines

I've included fortified wines in this book because they are the bridge that connects the two continents of still wines and distilled spirits. Once distilled spirits (grape brandy, mostly) are added to wines for fortification, the wines cross a line over which they are never permitted to return. Their category, their physiology, their purpose, and their destiny are irretrievably altered. While the majority of fortified wines retain the blithe soul of a wine, they now encase that soul with a fleshier body that's more akin to that of a distilled spirit. In this hybrid stage, they deserve, in my opinion and experience, to be compared more to spirits than to still wines.

Their discovery was something of a propitious accident. Fortification was initiated not to add a new dimension to wine as much as it was to bolster a wine that was about to take a long ocean voyage. As shipping lanes developed and global trade evolved in the sixteenth and seventeenth centuries, many of the wines from western Europe became spoiled by the time they reached their destination. In response wine makers took to the practice of adding measures of brandy for the purpose of "muscling-up" a portion of their exported wines. The wines that were thus fortified usually withstood the rigors of crude vessel holds and wildly fluctuating temperatures much better than their unfortified counterparts. Interestingly, once the fortified wines made their way to the tables of roadside taverns and public houses, consumers often preferred them, with their firm textures and elevated alcohol levels, to the regular still wines. Consequently, an entire category—the realm of sherry, port, and madeira—was eventually created.

Today, many of the greatest libation experiences one could have inhabit the category of fortified wines.

What to Look For in a Fortified Wine

Purity. Some good-to-great fortified wines naturally show sediment, which is in fact composed of bits of the grape. The prime example is vintage port. It is entirely proper when a fine port from a declared vintage comes with a cloud of suspended particles. The simple solution is decanting, or moving the port from the bottle to a decanter for the purpose of a clear pour. The sediment settles in the well of the decanter and, with care and patience, the pourer can successfully transfer the port to glasses almost sediment-free. Sherry should never throw any kind of sediment, even the blockbuster sweet sherries. Madeiras normally don't have much sediment. If one does, one should decant it, like port.

Aromatic and flavor properties.
- Sherries have the broadest spectrum of aroma and taste in the fortified-wine category. Finos and manzanillas should be completely dry and offer stimulating charms, such as a yeastiness, doughiness, or underripe fruitiness. They should have a clean, acidy nip on the tongue. Manzanillas tend to be a touch salty. Amontillados are typically nutty yet dry. Olorosos are, by all traditions, intensely fruity, but dry to off-dry. Creams should be pruney or raisiny sweet, but never clumsy or overly heavy.
- Port's smell and taste should be concentrated, moderately sweet, and plum-like when it's "right." Being a wine first and foremost, port should be a balance of fruit, acid, and alcohol. The brandy that is added should never interfere with the naturally fruity nature of port. When port tastes moldy, musty, or overripe, it's probably too old. When port tastes too alcoholic, it signifies that the brandy has overcome the wine component. Toss it or take it back to the retailer.
- Madeira has the aromatic and flavor latitude of sherry and the intensity of port. The lighter, drier styles, like *sercial* and *verdelho,* offer

features of dried fruit and nuts, while the more profound styles, *bual* and *malmsey*, are typically pruney or raisiny.

Finish. All fortified wines should glide down the throat easily, leaving behind a mild fruitiness and/or nuttiness. Elements of wood are fine in the aftertaste as long as they don't overshadow the fruit.

SHERRY – SPAIN

The Jérez region of Spain is the home of sherry. This arid, sun-bleached land is located in the province of Andalusia's southern reaches. The sun shines for an astonishing 3,000 hours per year, which is more than in any other wine-growing area in continental Europe. An ancient wine region, the sherry district is nourished and bordered by two rivers, the Guadalete and Guadalquivir, and by the Atlantic Ocean. A trio of bustling towns—Jérez de la Frontera, Sanlucar de Barrameda, and Puerto de Santa Maria—form the rough geographic triangle within which is made the world's most versatile, and my favorite, fortified wine.

The region's eggshell-colored soil, known as *albariza,* is rich in calcium carbonate and thereby provides the ideal setting for the cultivation of the three great grape varieties that go into the making of sherry. *Palomino* is first among equals and the most widely planted grape type, followed by *Pedro Ximenez* and *moscatel.* Since rain is scarce, falling on average only seventy days a year, the absorbency of the *albariza* is key, because it retains moisture for the sustenance of the grapes during the dry growing season. Approximately 50,000 acres are planted over to grapes within the Jérez Triangle, and only grapes grown here are used for sherry.

The month of September is completely taken up with the harvest. *Palomino* grapes are collected first and are fermented first, producing wines that are low in sugar and acid. Next, the thicker-skinned *Pedro Ximenez* and *moscatel* are picked and laid out on straw mats for one to two weeks to ripen further under the early autumn sun before they are fermented.

To this juncture, the wine-making sequence of events is very similar to that in most other regions of the world. However, while in every other major wine-growing region new wine is shielded from oxygen by being placed either in sealed oak casks or stainless-steel tanks, the Jerezanos, by design, leave a gap of air in their 500-liter, American white-oak barrels. Rather than oxidizing, the new wine forms a natural layer of yeast on its surface the spring of the following year. This skin of yeast cells, which the Jerezanos call *flor* and which sometimes swells to three inches thick, acts as a natural barrier, a living shield that allows the wine to evolve at its own pace until it becomes a totally dry wine. The atmosphere in Jérez is thick with theories about why and how the mysterious *flor* might develop easily in one barrel and not in the cask adjacent to it. The reality is, no one knows for certain. The thicker the *flor*, the more likely the wine will end up being a light, crisp fino sherry. Thin *flors* mean that the wine will turn out to be an amontillado or an oloroso.

Sherry differs from port according to the point at which brandy is added. In Jérez, sherry producers mix in the grape brandy after fermentation has ceased. In Portugal, brandy is added during fermentation for the purpose of halting it.

After fermentation, the sherry is ready to be aged in a unique system of gradual maturation that was invented in Jérez. The *solera system* is carried out in the high-ceilinged, white-washed warehouses of Jérez, called *bodegas*. In each *bodega*, straight rows of casks are lined up in long processions, typically four barrels high. The top three tiers are referred to as the *criaderas*, while the bottom row is known as the *solera*. Sherry ages and evolves in a strictly-adhered-to set of stages in the *solera* system. From the barrels that constitute the *solera*, the oldest sherry is withdrawn and placed either in a tank for bottling or another barrel for further aging. Never is more than one-third of any barrel's contents removed. Then, sherry is siphoned from the row of casks directly above the *solera* and pumped, via hose, into the *solera* cask. Then, from the third row from the ground, sherry is withdrawn and added to the row directly beneath it. When the top row is ready to be added to, the new sherry is mixed into that *criadera*.

This progression continues until the sherries in each *criadera* eventually make it to the ground level, the *solera*. The procedure is simple and ingenious: The newer sherries, full of freshness and flavor, are sequentially married to the older sherries, which are mellow and deep. Many sherries are the results of 10–20 *criaderas*. The Jerezanos say that the old sherries educate the younger ones, while the young sherries lend vitality to the old ones.

Sherry producers shower consumers with an astoundingly broad menu of wine types and practical applications. Categories range from the best appetite stimulants to be found anywhere, manzanilla and fino, to the sweetest, most satisfying afterdinner treats, the magnificent Pedro Ximenez and Old East Indias.

THE STYLES OF SHERRY

Manzanilla: These ethereal, bone-dry, astringent, and tangy sherries come only from Sanlucar de Barrameda, the seaside town that rests at the place where the Guadalquivir River meets the ocean. Technically, manzanillas are a fino (15–17 percent alcohol). Their very pale color betrays their inherent lightness. But what makes manzanilla such a superb aperitif is the salty backnote in the aroma and flavor. This briny, saline quality exists courtesy of Atlantic sea breezes that flow through the *bodegas,* seeping into the barrel staves and affecting the flavor of the wines within. Unfortunately, because of their light weight, manzanillas have a terribly short lifespan and therefore must be consumed within a day or two after opening. Serve very chilled, at 40–45 degrees Fahrenheit.

Fino: The favorite sherry style in Spain, fino is the pale straw/hay-toned wine that in many instances emits a yeasty, bread-dough, or almondy nose and flavor. The alcohol level hovers at 15 percent on the low side to an unusual high of 17 percent. It's the quintessential before-dinner drink that prepares the palate for food more gracefully and thoroughly than any other alcoholic beverage in the world. Serve very chilled, at 40–45 degrees Fahrenheit.

Amontillado: Technically, amontillado is a medium-bodied fino. The hue of the majority of amontillados runs from light honey to medium amber. Always dry to off-dry, amontillados possess a bouquet and taste reminiscent of hazelnuts or roasted almonds. At its best, amontillado is one of sherry's most aromatic styles. As to pairing it with food, amontillado is polished and admirably adaptable, going well as an aperitif or with a soup course. It can even be served after dinner, with fruit and nuts. The alcohol level ranges from 16 to 18 percent. Serve at cellar temperature (48–55 degrees Fahrenheit).

Palo Cortado: A very rare and, therefore, routinely expensive sherry, the palo cortado begins life as a fino, then, for as yet unknown reasons, discards its *flor* to evolve into an amontillado, then, outgrowing that incarnation as well, ends up acting more like an oloroso. Palo cortado's stunning color is normally the rich mahogany/chestnut/sorrel tone of an oloroso, yet on the palate it behaves more like a well-endowed amontillado. Message: If you locate one, buy it and try it because, in most cases, the experience is well worth it. Alcohol range of 17–20 percent. Serve at cellar temperature (48–55 degrees Fahrenheit).

Oloroso: The most misunderstood sherry type of all. Most consumers think that olorosos are typically off-dry to sweet when, in reality, the truly best olorosos are dry to off-dry. The confusion probably is due to oloroso's richly grand appearance, which ranges from burnished gold to bronze to chestnut brown, and its opulent, intensely nutty, sometimes fruity aroma. In the mouth, the better olorosos define the word "velvety" and are among the most complex of all sherries. Alcohol usually ranges from 18 to 20 percent. Serve at room temperature as an afterdinner beverage, preferably with nuts.

Cream: This style generally has oloroso as the foundation, with varying amounts of Pedro Ximenez or Moscatel added to jack up the alcohol and residual sugar. Surprisingly, not all creams are sticky-sweet. Some of the finest are off-dry to lightly sweet. Colors range from ruby red to purple to cola-brown. Alcohol of 18–20 percent. To be served only as a *digestif* at room temperature.

Pedro Ximenez, Moscatel, Old East India: Three styles designed for those people who love adventure. Pedro Ximenez and Moscatel are named after the grape varieties from which they are made. Old East India is a style named after a dessert type of sherry that was shipped to India when the British still had colonies in the subcontinent. Along the way, it would become virtually black in color, very dense, and extremely sugary because of the heat of the tropics. All three styles are intensely sweet, syrupy in texture, and frequently smell and taste like raisins, prunes, chocolate-covered cherries, and even coffee. Colors run from dark chocolate brown to pitch black. An acquired taste, which once captured, is captured for life. Serve only at room temperature. Alcohol level is rarely lower than 19 percent, and is sometimes as high as 21 percent.

Almacenista: These specialty sherries come from small, hand-selected lots from private producers who don't have the time or resources to bottle and market their products themselves. So they sell them to Emilio Lustau, a prominent sherry *bodega* in Jérez de la Frontera, who prepares them, bottles them, and distributes them. They are often from very old *solera* systems. The name of the lot owner is always indicated on the bottle; they represent the sherry equivalent of estate-bottling. Some are incredible sensory experiences of the first magnitude.

ARGUESO Pedro Ximenez Sherry 18% Alcohol

Rich, chocolate-brown color; the focused, intense, pruney bouquet is equally assertive and opulent from the first nosing to the last—it presents an astounding density that is hyper-raisiny; Argueso's texture is properly lush and viscous for a 100% PX cream; the very sweet first taste evokes strong thoughts of orange/chocolate—on midpalate, the flavor changes back to prunes, then finishes cleanly and (surprisingly) meekly in a soft coffee/mocca whisper that echoes long at the back of the throat; one not to be passed by for PX aficionados.

RATING ★ ★ ★ ★   **Highly Recommended** $

DELGATO ZULETA Cream Sherry 17.5% Alcohol

Brownish/purple color; the expressive, expansive nose is highlighted by the unmistakable, plummy presence of Pedro Ximenez—it's a ripe, raisiny bouquet that's both pleasing and zesty; the soft, velvety texture gives way to moderately sweet flavors of ripe plums and nuts; the finish is medium-long and exceedingly pleasant—it's sweet without being cloying or syrupy; a better-than-average cream sherry that's uncomplicated and honest.

RATING ★ ★ ★   **Recommended** $

DELGATO ZULETA Amontillado Sherry 18% Alcohol

Lovely bronze color; it offers a very charming apple/almond aroma, which at first is closed off, then it opens in the third nosing; in the mouth, the off-dry flavors of hazelnut and vanilla are slightly creamy; the long, roasted-nut aftertaste is agreeable and clean; a decent, if uninspiring, effort from start to finish.

RATING ★ ★ $

DELGATO ZULETA Oloroso Sherry 18% Alcohol

Darker amber/topaz color than the Amontillado; the sweetish bouquet leans a bit too heavily to cotton candy for my liking, but it's not offensive; in the mouth, simple flavors of cocoa, coffee, and prunes do their best to keep the attention of the taste buds, but because of a lack of complexity, it's something of a losing battle; it's quite lush in its lengthy finish; commonplace, pedestrian, and definitely an afterdinner sherry.

RATING ★★ $

DELGATO ZULETA East India Cream Sherry 17.5% Alcohol

In appearance, a Coca-Cola replica—medium brown color, with gold rim; the peculiar, atypical, but quite appealing nose reeks of raw bread dough, fresh rye bread, and salty sea breeze—the Sanlucar influence lies right on top; on palate, it's medium-bodied, with a lightish viscosity—the semi-sweet, coffee, milk chocolate, and citrus flavors swim around on the taste buds without much focus; the aftertaste is long and reminiscent of vanilla extract; not what you'd altogether expect of an East India Cream; this one is drier, tamer, and more manageable than most others on the market.

RATING ★★ $

DELGATO ZULETA Fino Sherry 15.5% Alcohol

Straw-colored, but very pale; the tangy, almost sea-breezy, slightly manzanilla-like quality in aromatic bouquet is lively, fresh and stimulating; on palate, it's stone-dry and on the lightish/delicate side, with flavor hints of roasted chestnuts, salted peanuts, and yeast; while it's too lacking in fruit and acidic for me in terms of flavor, I did favorably respond to the bouquet.

RATING ★ $

DOMECQ

The Pedro Domecq firm, which is one of the region's and Spain's most venerated companies, was founded in 1730. The mouthwatering sherries labeled as "Pedro Domecq" are painfully rare, coming from the Domecq *bodega*'s oldest library *soleras*. The grapes have all been harvested from the hallowed Macharnudo vineyards, located in the most prized Jérez growing district. The Amontillado 51-la is blended from *soleras* that average *over 40 years of age*. The same is true of the sublime palo cortado, named Sibarita, a delicate but juicy cross between an oloroso and an amontillado, which actually should be served slightly chilled if you are serving it as an aperitif. One of the world's ultimate sweet-beverage experiences, the fabulous Venerable PX, comes from *soleras* with over two decades of aging time.

PEDRO DOMECQ Venerable Pedro Ximenez Sherry 20% Alcohol

Midnight-black core with chocolate-brown rim; it owns the unmistakable, pruney, raisiny, bittersweet chocolate, PX signature aroma—but it's how classily this buxom beauty presents it that's so enchanting; on palate, savage, authoritative flavors of raisins, prunes, and chocolate fudge rule the entry, then gradually, even grudgingly give way to a tobacco-like quality that takes over in the surprisingly benign finish; what I admire so much about this superb PX is that while it is brazenly rich, it is never cloying, clumsy, or overly heavy; granted, it is *very* sweet and one-half glass can keep anyone occupied for an hour, but it never clubs your tonsils into submission with sugar; it's easily one of the top two or three PX's that one could buy and one of the finest alcoholic beverages I've ever tasted; try it over vanilla ice cream; a magnificent, utterly unforgettable sherry.

RATING ★ ★ ★ ★ ★   **Highest Recommendation** $$

PEDRO DOMECQ Amontillado 51-la Sherry 20% Alcohol

The lustrous, warm orange/amber hue dazzles the eyes; the nose presents piquant, almond/walnut aromas that are well defined and muscular—the first nosing is damned impressive, as the intense nuttiness blocks out all other fragrance possibilities—a dynamite nose; the satiny texture envelops the tongue; medium-weighted, tightly knit body; its dry, full, multilayered, tangy flavors of ripe tropical fruit, nutmeg, and walnuts delight the taste buds; 51-1a is of such superior quality that it ably commands all your senses simultaneously; one of the most harmonious and utterly spectacular non-almacenista amontillado experiences to be had; a must for any cellar.

RATING ★ ★ ★ ★   **Highly Recommended** $$

PEDRO DOMECQ Sibarita Palo Cortado Sherry 20% Alcohol

I can't think of another sherry that has a more ideal or prototypical topaz-core/golden-edge color than this sleek, sinewy classic; the nose gently wafts from the bowl of the glass in waves of roasted walnuts, with substantial underpinnings of cedar, juniper, and herbs; even before tasting it, your olfactory sense signals your brain that this one is going to be a major-league thriller; on palate, it's medium-bodied, perfectly balanced, whistle-clean, and downright delicious as the walnut comes to the forefront, then recedes in a gentle herbal aftertaste that seemingly goes on forever; first rate all the way; a study of nuance and elegance.

RATING ★ ★ ★ ★   **Highly Recommended** $$

DOMECQ La Ina Fino Sherry 17% Alcohol

Pale straw/yellow color, which is absolutely clear; La Ina's snappy bouquet is one of my favorites in the premium fino category—its vivacity and freshness are completely captivating, showing subtle hints of yellow grapefruit, yeast, roasted almonds, spice, and even some bread dough; on palate, it's stone-dry, ethereally light, and mildly yeasty; the dry finish is gone in a flash; while La Ina's presence in the mouth floats somewhere between average and better than average in terms of satisfaction, it's one of the few wines I'd recommend based solely on the strength of the prototypical and immensely charming aroma; one of the better premium finos for appetite stimulation; a bit of irresistible Jérez in a *copita* glass; serve very cold at 40–45 degrees Fahrenheit as a cocktail.

RATING ★ ★ ★   **Recommended** $

DOMECQ Celebration Cream Sherry 17.8% Alcohol

The rich chestnut/tawny color, with gorgeous copper highlights, makes this the prettiest of the premium line of Domecq sherries; the lush, citrusy nose suggests an interesting melange of raisins, prunes, pears, nectarines, and candied nuts—first class all the way; not an overpowering, gooey cream, but an agile, medium-bodied, semisweet sherry that offers more than ample taste gratification; flavors of very ripe grapes, a touch of PX (Pedro Ximenez), and orange rind combine to make a delightful, affordable sherry experience; serve at room temperature.

RATING ★ ★ ★   Recommended $

DOMECQ Rio Viejo Oloroso Sherry 19% Alcohol

The suspect, cloudy, dull appearance smacks of poor storage since I've informally tasted this sherry on several occasions in Jérez, Spain—this is not the face I've come to know, hence I won't take points off for what is clearly an aberration; the aromas are showing true to form—solid, round, nutty, and dry (as olorosos traditionally should be—the all-too-common impression in the U.S. that olorosos should be sweet, buttery, and viscous is erroneous); the dry, indeed austere flavors abound in a lean nuttiness and oak, a delicate, feline taste, really; finishes gracefully as reserved flavors melt gently in the throat; I would serve this slightly chilled at 58–65 degrees Fahrenheit.

RATING ★ ★ $

DOMECQ Primero Amontillado Sherry 17.5% Alcohol

Limpid, dark gold/honey color, with amber highlights; not as expressive as the cracking La Ina, the Primero's nose is rather shy and closed at first pass, then meagerly opens with aeration into a floral, burnt, ripe-fruit, walnuty nose of modest proportions; not the kind of amontillado that excites me with regard to taste; wan, dry to off-dry flavors of nuts and grapes lead nowhere as far as I can judge; the aftertaste, which ended up being the best feature, is surprisingly sweet, balanced, and fruity; though it concluded on a very positive note, this wine was a disappointment to me early on; serve well chilled, at 45–50 degrees Fahrenheit.

RATING ★ $

DON ZOILO Solera Reservada Cream Sherry 19% Alcohol

Deep brown/chestnut color; after 15 minutes of aeration, the pruney, overripe grape, Pedro Ximenez nose finally emerges from the depth of the sampling glass; one of the better balanced creams I've tasted formally—on palate, it's medium- to full-bodied, with tightly knit but focused flavors of black raisins, ripe plums, and chocolate; the aftertaste is directed, chocolatey, and perfectly sweet; a delicious winner that's a well-behaved, even graceful cream . . . and that's almost a contradiction in that creams are often bruising, chunky, and viscous; a refreshing change from the beautiful, chalky, *albariza* vineyards of Andalusia.

RATING ★ ★ ★ ★   Highly Recommended $

DON ZOILO Manzanilla Sherry 15.5% Alcohol

Pale straw color; beautifully crafted, slightly salty, wheat/oat-like, piquant nose—the second pass picks up slivered almonds and lemon peel—overall a zesty, jaunty bouquet that I find alluring; on the tongue, it exhibits a light, feathery presence, with salty undertones; what disappointed me was the lack of freshness in the mouth-feel—it seemed tired and old; what happened to all of the aromatic elements that made the nose so appealing?; the bottom simply dropped out of this one in the overly lemon/citrusy flavor; too bad; it started out so promising; my guess is that this was an old bottle; manzanilla and fino must be served fresh, otherwise the delicate nature of each is lost; no excuses.

RATING ★ $

DON ZOILO Fino Sherry 15.5% Alcohol

Bright, sunny, yellow/straw color; this nose is more restrained and potent than the cavalier but charming manzanilla bouquet—the desert-dry, lemony aroma pervades the entire nosing experience, leaving little room for anything else to emerge; the citrus quality is so overblown in the flavor that you almost think you're drinking lemonade instead of fino sherry; curiously like the manzanilla, all the body vanished, unfortunately leaving behind truckloads of megalemon flavors that simply are too out of balance to make it a recommendable item; I again believe that this sample bottle is the victim of either poor storage or old age.

RATING ★ $

DON ZOILO Amontillado Sherry 18% Alcohol

Topaz/amber/brown color; I'm not sure where this aroma is going, but it's not pleasing to me even after the third pass—the natural nuttiness is secondary to an unpleasant, metallic/tanky quality that doesn't say a lot about the quality-control person at Don Zoilo; I hesitate to be so rude, but this shellac-like, mysteriously sour sherry is nothing more than a trumped-up, pumped-up fino that wasn't very good to begin with; it resembles nutty, supple, off-dry amontillado as much as I resemble Hillary Rodham Clinton; avoid.

RATING ★ $

DRY FLY Medium-Dry Sherry 20% Alcohol

Notably handsome color of chestnut/tawny brown, highlighted by autumnal vermillion and copper hues; the puzzling, nondescript nose goes nowhere even after 30 minutes of aeration; though the label specifies "medium dryness," the entry is simply dry, then the flavors go semidry at midpalate, as slightly bitter cocoa and coffee flavors take over; citrusy, orange-rind, pineapple, and hazelnut qualities come together in the aftertaste; a nice amontillado style that is clean and not overly nutty; quite atypical for an amontillado in that the nuttiness is toned down while the fruit is generous; a decent soup course complement.

RATING ★ ★ $

GONZALEZ BYASS

I'm totally confused by Gonzalez Byass, which was founded in 1870 by Manuel Maria Gonzalez Angel, because while I love their Brandy de Jérez Solera Gran Reserva, the great Lepanto, their pedestrian sherries leave me completely cold.

GONZALEZ BYASS Tio Pépé Fino Sherry 16.5% Alcohol

Tasted many times; standard-issue pale gold fino hue; the rich, yeasty, macadamia nut nose is completely dry and floral—it's definitely fuller than most fino bouquets, which normally tilt to the tartness end of the scale—it's one of my favorite fino aromas; the tart taste of green apple balances well with the alcohol and the yeastiness in a refreshing flavor package; the aftertaste is austere, clean, and fast; the unusual opulence in the nose fails to materialize later on in either the taste or the finish and that occurrence alone keeps this from being a recommendable fino—nevertheless, at the end of the day this is an average, well-made, stone-dry sherry that enjoys worldwide popularity; serve well chilled before meals.

RATING ★★ $

GONZALEZ BYASS La Concha Amontillado Sherry 19% Alcohol

Very pretty, tawny color, flecked with orange/vermillion highlights; unhappily, the off-putting, gasoline-like, intensely medicinal, herbal, almost synthetic nose turned me off big-time—I wasn't compelled to go further with this sherry, so unappetizing was the bouquet; while I abhorred the nasty nose, this unpredictable sherry came alive on the palate with off-dry, slightly bitter, but quite delicious flavors of tropical fruit, grapefruit, and tangerine; the finish is medium-long and also pleasant; this atypical amontillado shows all fruit and virtually no nuttiness to speak of; I was befuddled by it, hating it one minute and admiring it the next; no matter how much I appreciated the flavor and the finish, the gasoline-station/cod-liver-oil aromas in the disastrous nose could never in a million years make it recommendable.

RATING ★★ $

GONZALEZ BYASS Nectar Cream Sherry 20% Alcohol

Attractive chestnut-brown appearance; the rather hollow nose comes off being tinny rather than fruity or rich—some detection of prunes and raisins in the background, but up front it's mediocre at best; a lightweight cream in terms of texture and body; flavorwise it's average, showing a bit of Pedro Ximenez; definitely ho-hum; these sherries are totally inconsistent with the brandies offered by Gonzalez Byass.

RATING ★★ $

GONZALEZ BYASS Amontillado del Duque Viejo Sherry 21.5% Alcohol

This was an absolute mess as anything, let alone a sherry; light amber/tawny color; the delicate, almondy aroma with a marshmallow backdrop is elegant and refined—that's the good news; the bad has to do with the atrocious flavor of prunes gone completely rotten and sour; I strongly suspect a poor bottle and hope sincerely that that's the case, because this is one of the worst Spanish sherries I've sampled; I urge caution to the reader.

RATING ★ $$

GONZALEZ BYASS Apostoles Oloroso Abocado Sherry 20% Alcohol

Gorgeous mahogany/rich brown color; the arresting, if restrained, nose has several intriguing layers of aroma—roasted walnut, fruitcake, baked pear, and cola nut; unfortunately, the complexity of the aroma is nowhere to be found in the single-note flavor, consisting solely of sour apples—what's going on here?—sherries aren't supposed to taste like burning rubber; do you mean to tell me that bottles like this are circulating in the U.S. marketplace? if so, big trouble for this producer.

RATING ★ $$

HARTLEY & GIBSON Cream Sherry 19% Alcohol

I put this plummy thoroughbred right up there with the best creams in today's marketplace; the gorgeous coffee-bean/mahogany color has reddish/golden highlights in the core; the aggressive, ambrosial nose is simultaneously strong and elegant, emitting enchanting aromas of raisins, prunes, dark chocolate, and paraffin; the viscous texture underpins luscious, intense flavors of prunes, cocoa, and coffee; luxuriously long finish; high-end quality at a low-end price; no doubt the headliner of this cast; a superb sherry for any money.

RATING ★ ★ ★ ★   *Highly Recommended* $

HARTLEY & GIBSON Amontillado Sherry 17% Alcohol

The beautiful, clear amber color looks warm and inviting; correct, direct, roasted-almond, minor road-tar aromas lurk in the background shadows of this deceptively potent nose; in the mouth, focused, generous, almond flavors blanket the palate; it owns an unusually long, satiny aftertaste for an amontillado; top-flight wine making all the way; a natural with tomato-based soups.

RATING ★ ★ ★   *Recommended* $

HARTLEY & GIBSON Manzanilla Sherry 15% Alcohol

Extremely pale appearance; offers just a trace of saline/sea-breeze aroma—even flowers in the last pass; absolutely stone-dry—this sherry has, as one old California friend used to describe it, a "tongue-on-stone dryness"—other than that, it's mildly tangy/seaweedy on palate, with feather-light, kiss-and-run tastes of soy sauce, esters, and yeast; the slightly salty, quicksilver finish is whistle-clean; an able, if average, appetite stimulant.

RATING ★ ★ $

HARTLEY & GIBSON Fino Sherry 15.5% Alcohol

Very pale golden/straw color; the lovely, soft, slightly fruity nose gently tweaks the olfactory sense; desert-dry and light in the mouth—just what you want from a razor-sharp fino—pleasing, refreshing, faint nutty flavors, spiced with a tight, tart apple finish; well structured, nicely made, but lacking in the extra depth that makes an item recommendable.

RATING ★ ★ $

HARTLEY & GIBSON Oloroso Sherry 18% Alcohol

Inviting, deep mahogany color; the hard, austere, candied nose has a distinct (or is it odd?) walnut/caramel underpinning that seems rather stale; the surprisingly ethereal body is too thinly textured for an oloroso (I tasted it alongside three other comparably priced olorosos); in a weird moment on the tongue it was salty—decidedly nutty—the intense walnut finish is quite delicious; after a correct appearance but withered bouquet, it breaks down completely and irretrievably in the mouth; clearly the weak link in an otherwise strong product line; it left me with the impression that it didn't know what it wanted to be—an oloroso or an amontillado; the indecision plays against it; this one could use some polishing.

RATING ★ $

HARVEY'S **Rare Oloroso Sherry 17.5% Alcohol**

Gleaming, seductive, opulent, dark honey/topaz color, with russet highlights and an amber/gold rim—one of the prettiest olorosos I've laid my eyes on; the burnt, toasty, creamy, roasted-walnut nose has a restrained oak presence in the background; exquisite balance, viscous texture; on palate, the mature *solera* flavors of oak, caramel, polite Pedro Ximenez, and butter hold court until the long, biscuity aftertaste kicks into gear; this wonderful limited bottling honored the 500th anniversary of the discovery of the New World and approached the quality of the transcendental superpremium offerings of Valdespino, Lustau, and Domecq; comes handsomely packaged in an old-style low-shouldered bottle.

RATING ★ ★ ★ ★   *Highly Recommended* $$

HARVEY'S **Dry Cocktail Sherry 17.5% Alcohol**

Pale hay/cream-soda color, with alluring honey/gold highlights; the low-key, *flor*/yeasty aroma is engaging and sedate; on palate, the salty/sea-breeze flavor lends a manzanilla quality to it that's pleasant, but rather unidimensional, from entry to the proper, well-behaved finish; while this stone-dry, medium-salty, manzanilla-style sherry isn't allowed to stretch by design, it is nevertheless a perfectly acceptable, dry-aperitif choice when one desires to have an affordable and easy-to-find dry sherry in the house.

RATING ★ ★ $

HARVEY'S **Shooting Sherry/Oloroso 17.5% Alcohol**

Lush, mahogany/classic oloroso color, with honey edges; the nose is very coy and requires a tad too much coaxing, swirling, and time to finally expose itself—if it was a real showstopper, then that's one thing, but this nose is semisweet, cola-like, and very ordinary; it really comes alive in the mouth with succulent, sweet flavors of bittersweet chocolate, dark caramel, brown sugar, and molasses; the finish is full, clean, and sweet, but not overpowering; improve the nose and you'd have a very recommendable item that ounce for ounce is marginally tastier than the more popular, but more banal, Bristol Cream.

RATING ★ ★ $

HARVEY'S **Bristol Cream Sherry 17.5% Alcohol**

Alluring, exceedingly comely rust/orange color, with a goldenrod edge; appetizing, if one-dimensional, toasty, roasted-almond nose; on palate, it's sweet without being cloying, viscous, or heavy-handed; the agreeable flavor like the aroma is monotonal and simple, but tasty and user-friendly nonetheless; intensely nutty aftertaste; a solid, reliable, and decent mass-produced sherry that enjoys a high profile in over 100 countries worldwide; nothing daring or unique, but a suitable aperitif—could even by served on-the-rocks with a twist.

RATING ★★ $

HARVEY'S Amontillado Sherry 17.5% Alcohol

Brilliant orange/honey/amber color; while its lustrous appearance is very fetching, the peculiar nose is off-putting because of a wet concrete, stone-like aroma that sits atop any fruit or nut aroma—the nose is definitely a liability; on palate, the mildly nutty, appetizing flavor emerges from beneath the minerally odor and actually goes far to redeem the problematic bouquet; unfortunately, it finishes rather limply in a botched flurry of almond; too little, too late; while certainly most drinkable, this sherry is in need of a nose job and a stronger, more clearly defined finish.

RATING ★ $

HIDALGO Jérez Cortado Estate-Bottled Sherry 17.5% Alcohol

Very atypical manzanilla appearance—the tea/amber hue is more akin to an amontillado than a manzanilla—superb purity; the pronounced, mature nose has biscuity, sour-dough aromas that, again, cut against the traditional bouquet style of manzanilla—the third pass introduces pecans and caramel—there's no questioning its quality or ability to please, but I do wonder about its identification as a manzanilla; in the mouth, its moniker is earned and fulfilled as the mouth-puckeringly astringent taste brings along an intense *flor* (yeasty) flavor as well as a soft dash of brine; the aftertaste is properly salty, complex, and tart; I'd label it a "manzanilla-amontillado"; the sherries come from the family's oldest *solera,* which was established in 1792.

RATING ★★★★   *Highly Recommended* $

HIDALGO Amontillado Napoleon Estate-Bottled Sherry 17.5% Alcohol

Pure, amber/iced-tea tone; I found the nose a tad flat on the initial pass immediately following the pour—with aeration, it gradually opened up, revealing understated scents of *flor,* nut meat, and a trace of citrus peel—the delicacy of the bouquet could be mistaken for timidity by the uninitiated, so don't be fooled—afford it five minutes in the glass before sniffing it—patience is the watchword with this fragile beauty; on palate, the whistle-clean taste offers flashes of underripe grapes, bread dough, sea air, and almonds; the finish is long, citrusy, and tart; a slightly meatier version of the regular bottling manzanilla; sculpted, lean, and delicious.

RATING ★★★★   *Highly Recommended* $

HIDALGO Cream Napoleon Estate-Bottled Sherry 17% Alcohol

Medium-brown/light-cola color, excellent purity; the nose is in no hurry to develop, so like with the amontillado, be prepared to wait it out for a few minutes—allowing it a good ten minutes, the nose blossoms in agile, pointed aromas of prunes and Pedro Ximenez; on palate, the raisiny/PX taste is nimble and fleet of foot—no syrupy, cloying demeanor here—the medium-bodied texture is like crushed velvet; the finish offers notes of chocolate-covered cherries and Raisinettes; truly lovely, delicate, and manageably sweet.

RATING ★ ★ ★ ★   *Highly Recommended* $

HIDALGO La Gitana Manzanilla Estate-Bottled Sherry 15.5% Alcohol

Pale straw/green tint, it couldn't be more pure; the ethreal nose is a slice of sherry heaven—tart aromas of green apple, lemon peel, *flor* (yeast), and almonds enchant the sense of smell with delicacy and aplomb in all four nosing passes—a gem of a bouquet; on palate, the citrusy/doughy tartness greets the taste buds and immediately cleanses them—the goal of manzanilla, which is to stimulate and not overpower, is accomplished by this squeaky-clean, refreshingly tart, and altogether subtle winner; I would have given a fourth star had there been more of a salty/briny tang; nevermind, just go out and buy it to have on hand as a superlative aperitif; as with all finos and manzanillas, be sure to consume it soon after buying; this winner ages over the span of seventeen *criadera* sequences.

RATING ★ ★ ★   *Recommended* $

EMILIO LUSTAU

I vividly recall my visit to the Emilio Lustau *bodega* in 1987 because of the charm and poise of Manuel Arcila, Lustau's managing director, as he patiently poured every single sherry in the Lustau line for me. He knew that he was serving the world's most prestigious line of sherries, but rather than try to impress me with his own rhetoric, he graciously let the sherries speak for themselves and only then answered questions directly, politely, and concisely. And Lustau sherries speak volumes, if you know how to listen.

Emilio Lustau, sherry producer extraordinaire, was established in 1896, and today is the biggest family-owned and family-operated sherry maker in Jérez. The Lustau *bodega,* located at Plaza del Cubo in Jérez's enchanting old quarter, is one of my personal favorites. Cool and damp on the inside, the buildings are protected from the heat by thick walls constructed by the Moors. One edifice is thought to have been the headquarters for the Moorish city guard during their seven-century occupation of the district. The newest *bodega* is located north of the city limits in the vineyard of Nuestra Señora de la Esperanza. In 1990 Lustau struck up an association with another family-owned sherry producer, Luis Caballero. This union brought to Lustau an additional 170 hectares of prime vineyard acreage.

The following notes and ratings are from two mornings of evaluations at my office in the U.S., not from my trips to Jérez.

The Lustau Reserva Range. If I had to choose one brand line that represented the finest value not just in fortified wines, but in all alcoholic beverages, I'd vote for the Lustau Reserva Range line. Value simply doesn't come more elegantly presented than these incredible sherries. That they all retail for under $15 amazes me, for comparable wines in Burgundy, Bordeaux, Napa, Sonoma, Oporto, Piedmont, or Ribera del Duero routinely begin at twice to three times the price.

My recommendation: If you desire to learn about sherry, go out and purchase the entire Reserva Range. These seven sherries contain as much sensory information as most people would ever need to know about sherry.

About the wines: The ethereal Papirusa Manzanilla and Jarana Fino are bottled to order at 15.5% alcohol and are not refortified up to 17% like some finos and manzanillas. This procedure helps to maintain their savory freshness and delicacy. Once opened, they should be consumed within 48 hours. The wines in the *solera* from which the Emilin Moscatel is drawn from have an average age of 40–50 years. The San Emilio Pedro Ximenez comes from exceedingly old wines, hence its midnight color and intense character.

LUSTAU "Emilin" Moscatel Superior Sherry 17% Alcohol

Beautiful, deep chestnut/molasses/mahogany/porter-ale color; this bouquet is no wallflower—it comes straight out of the bottle roaring; the first and most impressive wave is of sweet bread pudding, then the dusty/musty second wave is of prunes, old saddle leather, and granny's attic—it's as incredible, totally unique, and disarming a bouquet as there is in the whole fortified-wine category; the flavor only heightens the already rapturous experience, as truckloads of succulent prune, tar, and red-grape raisin tastes enchant the panting taste buds; the aftertaste is extremely long—the moderately viscous, velvety texture coats the entire palate; the Emilin is as good as ultrasweet sherry gets, in my opinion; total decadence.

RATING ★ ★ ★ ★ ★　　*Highest Recommendation*　　$

LUSTAU "San Emilio" Pedro Ximenez Sherry 17% Alcohol

Mahogany/cola/black-coffee tone, edged with gold; the operative term in the aroma is "raisiny," as in raisins, raisins, and more raisins; the texture is thick, as ropy strands of glycerine cling to the interior wall of the glass bowl; in the mouth, the sublime, remarkably sexy prune/raisin flavor base and viscosity are numbingly sweet but mysteriously approachable all the same; one-quarter of a standard five-ounce wine glass would be an ample serving for afterdinner enjoyment; one of the ten most sumptuous and immoral alcoholic beverages that I'm aware of; this is a pinnacle achievement for the *Pedro Ximenez* grape variety; my favorite way of serving it is over French vanilla ice cream—after that combination you'll comprehend the real meaning of the phrase, "sweet dreams"; an incredible experience that I place as one of my all-time top beverage alcohol pleasures.

RATING ★ ★ ★ ★ ★　　*Highest Recommendation*　　$

LUSTAU "Capatez Andres" Deluxe Cream Sherry 20% Alcohol

Dazzling nutbrown/chestnut-cola color; the mesmerizing nose crosses back and forth from being intensely raisiny to deeply pruney, the elements of both being undeniable and dominant—after ten minutes of aeration, the bouquet emits fleeting traces of bittersweet chocolate and pipe smoke almost as an afterthought; on the palate, the semisweet to full-blown sweet raisiny quality takes over and runs with the ball through to the quick finish; the amazing thing about this cream is its agility—never is it cloying, clumsy, or syrupy—the medium body and moderately viscous texture make it eminently drinkable; the best cream sherry for under $12 in the world, period, case closed; it's at this fundamental level that Lustau rises above all other sherry *bodegas;* I've had the pleasure of enjoying this superior item many times over the last ten years and it still knocks me out; a longtime favorite that only seems to improve with time.

RATING ★ ★ ★ ★   *Highly Recommended* $

LUSTAU "Papirusa" Light Manzanilla Sherry 15.5% Alcohol

Pale gold/straw color; the dynamite nose launches from the sampling glass in robust waves of baker's yeast, lemon peel, peanuts, butterscotch, and chalk, with just the barest hint of sea air—the lemon-peel/butterscotch aromatic tag-team clearly dominates and actually grows in intensity with every nosing; it's so clean, tight, and compact in the mouth that I find myself smacking my lips—tastewise, desert-dry flavors of baked bread, citrus, and saltwater taffy give the taste buds all they can handle; the common perception that manzanilla is a skimpy, austere, skeletal sherry type gets tossed out the window with this stylish, solid offering; the Papirusa is a smart, snappy sherry that begs to be served very well chilled (42–48 degrees Fahrenheit) and solely as a smashing appetite stimulant before dinner, or as a cocktail sidekick to seafood or, even better, with *tapas,* the delicious Spanish finger foods; even though it's fleshier than most manzanillas, the fragility of its constitution, requires that the bottle be consumed within three to five days after opening and that it be kept refrigerated.

RATING ★ ★ ★   *Recommended* $

LUSTAU "Jarana" Light Fino Sherry 15.5% Alcohol

Medium gold/hay tone; the generous nose reeks of lemon juice, marzipan, flowers, white bleached flour, rye, and even a slip of ginger—it's perhaps the most multidimensional fino bouquet in the marketplace, bested only by the very good Valdespino Inocente—the big plus in the nose is this fino's remarkable freshness, I mean, it virtually crackles with acidic vigor; the mouth-puckering tartness holds court at the palate entry—the midpalate is unabashedly lemony and yeasty; it finishes in a refreshing, clean, and surprisingly extended manner; serve well chilled as you would a fine white Graves, a Chablis, or a Sonoma County, California, Sauvignon Blanc; food-wise, I'd use it exclusively as an aperitif with *tapas* or canapés.

RATING ★ ★ ★   *Recommended* $

LUSTAU "Los Arcos" Dry Amontillado Sherry 18.5% Alcohol

Eye-catching, brilliant amber/orange hue; it starts out a tad too vinegary in the first nosing, then shifts gears and goes pleasantly resiny/oily by the third pass—after 15 minutes of aeration I begin to pick up some nut meat—it's not an expansive or exciting nose by any means, but once it's had the opportunity to mingle with air, an alluring sturdiness impresses—it just needs some patience; in the mouth the Brazil-nut focus picks up a step or two and by midpalate a mildly bitter citrus taste emerges; the finish is off-dry and medium-long; I perceive this as a potentially satisfying and appropriate food wine with either vegetable consommé or even a spinach salad topped with red-wine vinegar and bacon; another ridiculously good value; I'd serve it just slightly chilled at around cellar temperature (48–55 degrees Fahrenheit).

RATING ★ ★ ★   *Recommended* $$

LUSTAU "Peninsula" Palo Cortado Sherry 19% Alcohol

Fabulous copper/amber hue, with luminous orange highlights—the prettiest of the Lustau Reservas; the nose is very shy at first, then gradually comes around in rather slinky, dry to off-dry waves of cedar, oak, raisins, and mushrooms—but even after a quarter of an hour's worth of aeration, the Peninsula's bouquet is still elusive; it's on the palate that this sherry becomes a winner, as it charges from the gate in a multilayered taste treat that ranges freely from toffee to tapioca to brown rice to crème brulée; the aftertaste is satiny-smooth and off-dry; an unusual sherry style that's as exotic as it is compelling; it's about halfway between amontillado and oloroso on the sweetness/texture scale; serve at room temperature.

RATING ★ ★ ★   *Recommended* $

THE LUSTAU RARE SOLERA SERIES

These five sherries represent what the Lustau people consider to be the upper tier of their regular offerings. The Rare Solera Series includes two especially intriguing sherries, the Old East India and the 1986 Vendimia Cream, which is the only vintage-dated sherry that I'm aware of. The Old East India is a chip off the madeira block. It's made in the style of the old madeiras that used to be sent on long, steamy voyages through the tropics in order to reach a particular level of richness/sweetness. While Lustau doesn't send its Old East India packing on a cruise, it does simulate such hot, humid conditions in one of its *bodegas*. The result is magical.

The 1986 Vendimia Cream comes from grapes—100% of the *palomino* variety to be exact—that were late-harvested in the fall of 1986. Made in a way similar to vintage port, its fermentation was halted at 5.5% residual sugar by the addition of brandy. The sherry was aged in small oak barrels and is unblended. It's the most unusual cream sherry I've ever sampled in that it's noticeably drier and lighter in color than most other creams.

The Escuadrilla Rare Amontillado is made from very old sherries, making it one of the best amontillados in the marketplace. The Emperatriz Eugenia oloroso, which has been hailed by other critics as a landmark sherry, I found very good, but hardly great. It's well worth noting, however, that one of the sherry *soleras* that contributes to the Eugenia is over a century old.

LUSTAU Old East India Sherry 20% Alcohol

Very close in color shade to the smashing Rare Cream Superior—a gorgeous chestnut/black-coffee brown; the nose, however, tells a totally different story, as the bouquet surprisingly comes off as being off-dry, even after ample aeration time—there are only the subtlest hints of dried prunes, pumpernickel/dark bread, cocoa, dark-bean-coffee espresso, and even some nut meat; but when all is said and done, it's the manageably sweet taste of raisins, vanilla frosting, and prunes that walk away with the experience; texturewise, it's thick, but hardly ropy or syrupy; the long aftertaste is a banquet of prunes and cocoa; the balance on this very sweet wine is so ideal that you barely notice the sweetness for the scrumptious flavor; a tour de force effort that ranks with the best in the entire fortified-wine category.

RATING ★ ★ ★ ★ ★   *Highest Recommendation* $

Lustau "Escuadrilla" Rare Amontillado Sherry 18.5% Alcohol

Amber/honey/orange hue; a glorious, exciting nose, studded with light caramel, English toffee, butter, almonds, unsweetened coconut, plus a trace of vanilla bean—this immaculate amontillado perfume is significantly more classic and characterful than the Los Arcos—this is a multidimensional bouquet that can be lazily sniffed for hours; in the mouth, it comes off delightfully oily and sinewy texturewise; the yeasty, off-dry entry taste evolves into a roasted-chestnut, toasted-almond flavor that's almost lemony/citrusy in the squeaky-clean finish; a refreshing, vivacious, and stately amontillado; the ravishing aroma alone is definitely worth two stars; outstanding.

RATING ★ ★ ★ ★   *Highly Recommended* $

Lustau 1986 Vendimia Cream Sherry 20% Alcohol

Colorwise, it falls on the light side of the cream-sherry color chart, looking more like an oloroso in its vibrant, handsome vermilion/orange/copper robe; the enchanting, atypical nose is loaded with concentrated raisin, oak, ripe-red-apple, ripe-pear, and even some walnut fragrances; on the palate, the medium-bodied texture couples nicely with the medium-sweet flavors of ripe grapes, sugar biscuits, and vanilla; it's lean style points to the fact that it's made from 100% *palomino* grapes rather than being a blend of *palomino* and *Pedro Ximenez;* so classy in its approach that it's almost like a late-harvest riesling or gewurztraminer; lovely and elegant from top to bottom.

RATING ★ ★ ★ ★   *Highly Recommended* $

Lustau "Superior" Rare Cream Solera Sherry 20% Alcohol

Medium-deep brown/chestnut hue, with a harvest-gold rim; the elegant nose (how many cream sherry bouquets can be termed "elegant"?) is sweet and delicately pruney; underneath the prunes lies a base layer of chocolate and cherry scents; the texture is only moderately viscous, making it accessible even for people who don't normally appreciate cream sherry; the luscious, harmonious flavors include dark chocolate, raisins, prunes, and cake batter that's been spiked—for some reason, its flavor reminds me of the Christmas holidays; the finish is well balanced, moderately long, with just the right level of sweetness; it redefines cream sherry; if you're searching for a cream sherry other than the customary jammy, chunky, numbingly sweet style, it's right here at a price that won't force you to sell the yacht.

RATING ★ ★ ★ ★   *Highly Recommended* $

Lustau "Emperatriz Eugenia" Very Rare Dry Oloroso Sherry 20% Alcohol

Traditional amber/brown oloroso color, but with gleaming russet highlights in the core—a most attractive appearance; the off-dry bouquet has a pronounced element of vanilla bean right upfront, then backs off into a raisiny, fruit-cake, honey-wheat-toast aroma that is simultaneously rich and fresh; dry to the taste as real oloroso should be, this beauty has a finely tuned, intensely focused flavor of candied apple from the palate entry through to the midpalate, then it goes tart in the supple aftertaste; while certainly better than average in the context of its category, I don't think it's the best value among the Lustau offerings.

RATING ★ ★ ★   ***Recommended*** $$

THE LUSTAU ALMACENISTAS

Lustau's racy almacenistas are drawn from extremely small lots of estate sherries. The estates are owned by private, independent sherry producers who sell their bottlings to Lustau, who prints the name of the originating *bodega* on the label. These excellent sherries are extraordinary wines and are really throwbacks to an era when all sherries were unblended and totally dry.

Understandably, there's some minor confusion about the number that appears on the Lustau Almacenista labels—the 1/143, 1/10, and the like. Let's take the Fino del Puerto 1/143 as an example. What the number means is that that particular sherry came from a stock that contained only 143 sherry butts (barrels that contain 500–600 liters of maturing sherry). By way of comparison, mainstream producers like Domecq, Gonzalez Byass, John Harvey, Wisdom & Warter, and so forth, have tens of thousands of sherry butts in their *bodegas*.

So special and rare are these sherries that Lustau has officially registered the name "Almacenista" with the *Consejo Regulador* (the Sherry Regulatory Council). The Almacenista designation can only be used when small lots of sherry are released to the care of Lustau by producers who have been approved by the *Consejo*.

FINO DEL PUERTO 1/143, José Luis Gonzalez Obregon, Sherry (Lustau) 15.5% Alcohol

Pale straw color; the yeasty, lemony, bread dough, delicately tart perfume is lively, keenly fresh, and altogether disarming in the first nosing pass, then softens and mellows with aeration as it becomes almost leathery/appley/flinty with time out of the bottle; it's so smooth from palate entry through to the fast-lane finish that it seems to glide gently onto the tongue and down the throat—it tastes of sour apples and orange rind; the aftertaste is austere, stone-dry, yet marvelously fruity, with green apples playing the lead; here's your quintessential aperitif; serve well chilled and with virtually any type of light foods—in fact, I could envision this superb wine being served throughout the entire meal, except for dessert.

RATING ★ ★ ★ ★   ***Highly Recommended*** $

MANZANILLA AMONTILLADA 1/21, Manuel Cuevas Jurado, Sherry (Lustau) 17.5% Alcohol

Surprisingly dark for a manzanilla—an amber/autumnal-gold hue that's almost more akin to an amontillado—so much so that if I couldn't smell or taste it, I'd guess it to be either an amontillado-fino or a lighter amontillado; the crisp nose is the briniest of any manzanilla I've sampled, giving off toasty hints of dried herbs, buttermilk biscuits, flowers, minerals, chalk (the *albariza* soil influence?), and even unsweetened coconut—it's the prototypical manzanilla bouquet, one that should be used in any wine appreciation class focusing on sherry; on the palate, it's so subtle, so understated, and so serene that unless you pay strict attention, the fine taste experience could flash right by—the tongue-on-stone dry entry is nutty, then the flavor goes salty/briny by midpalate; the aftertaste is lean, clean, and mouthpuckeringly dry; it's the most layered, svelte, and stylish manzanilla you can find; serve very well chilled (40–45 degrees Fahrenheit).

RATING ★ ★ ★ ★   *Highly Recommended* $ $

Oloroso "Pata de Gallina" 1/38, Juan Garcia Jarana, Sherry (Lustau) 20% Alcohol

Luminous copper-penny/russet/amber tone; this nose is fresh, minty, slightly honeyed but in no way sweet—I detect a second tier of flowers, spice, pine, and pears—there's an awful lot happening in this captivating, high-octane bouquet; off-dry and satiny at entry, the flavor then goes buttery, nutty, caramelly, and roasted by midpalate; the aftertaste is off-dry, medium-long, and seductively elegant; nosing it again after it's had 20 minutes of aeration, I pick up grapefruit, spearmint, and key-lime scents—this is a fabulous nose—one of the best, most complex on the Lustau scorecard; a discreet, deceptively potent, and highly distinctive sherry that's best served at cellar temperature (48–55 degrees Fahrenheit).

RATING ★ ★ ★ ★   *Highly Recommended* $ $

Amontillado Del Puerto 1/10, José Luis Gonzalez Obregon, Sherry (Lustau) 18.5% Alcohol

Medium amber hue; this nose is painfully shy, even after 15 minutes of aeration, swirling, and calculated coaxing—what finally does emerge is the image of an astoundingly delicate sherry, one that speaks in a whisper; there's more grip in the off-dry flavor, as mellow tastes of oak, apples, minerals, and grapes make themselves known in a harmonious crescendo at the midpalate; the finish is as calm as the nose and the taste, but I don't mean that in a negative way at all—this is simply a demure sherry that, I believe, might have an appreciative feminine audience—it's more a matter of sensory harmony and qualitative accord than a question of might or character—consumers, most definitely myself included, can sometimes confuse power for quality or virtue—in this case, serenity, quiet strength, and aplomb have their own place and charm.

RATING ★ ★ ★   *Recommended* $ $

Palo Cortado 1/50, Vides, Sherry (Lustau) 19% Alcohol

Beautiful, even stunning, rich amber/honey color; the assertive but simplistic nose speaks of oak, butterscotch, hard candy, and tea leaves—not a nose of genius; in the mouth, off-dry flavors of roasted chestnuts, ripe apples, pineapple, mango, kiwi, spice, and coffee with cream shift into gear effortlessly from palate entry to aftertaste; the finish is medium-long, off-dry, and very appley, especially spiced baked apples; a pretty wine with excellent balance between an emerging sweetness and a fruited core; a sound, unusual second-course wine choice that should be served at room temperature with tomato-based soup, any cream-of-vegetable soup, or spinach salad.

RATING ★★★ ***Recommended*** $$

Amontillado Fino 1/75, Alberto Lorente Piaget, Sherry (Lustau) 17.5% Alcohol

Brilliant amber color; the delicate nose is dry to off-dry and very toasty, but emits an evident staleness that translates into a laminated-cardboard-box quality that chops off a minimum of one rating star on its own; in the mouth, it's a firm presence that boasts a deliciously tart flavor of roasted almonds and dried tomato; the finish is solid and amazingly extended, but I'm underwhelmed by the lack of real flavor aftertaste—it's more a lingering presence of acidity than a taste I can hold on to or identify; don't get me wrong, it's not unpleasant, but singularly uninspiring compared to the other fantastic Lustaus; mediocrity really stands out in this august lineup; besides, in all fairness, the sample bottle may be slightly old; nevertheless, it's not recommendable.

RATING ★★ $$

Sanchez Romate Manzanilla Sherry 16.5% Alcohol

So pale as to resemble freshly squeezed lemon juice; the yeasty, biscuity, white-flour-like, sour-apple nose is dazzling—just a mere trace of sea-breeze saltiness appears in the perfumey bouquet; tastewise, this is one of the nicer, affordably priced manzanillas I've encountered; the delicacy of it is marvelous—it's almost fragile; the austere flavors are flinty, ultra-crisp, and clean, with lemon peel, slate, and minerals dominating the scene; the mildly briny, astringent aftertaste makes my mouth pucker; an excellent aperitif.

RATING ★★★ ***Recommended*** $

Sanchez Romate Fino Sherry 17% Alcohol

Standard-issue gold/straw fino color; shows a fruitier, more solid nose (as one would expect) than the ethereal manzanilla—I detect faint hints of pineapple, lemons, even figs in the fragrance; this is a round, mellow, totally dry fino with a barely discernable trace of *flor*/doughy/yeastiness; feels very comfortable on the tongue as the lemon element takes charge at the mouth entry, then gracefully bows out to pineapple and ginger; a very pleasant before-dinner quaff, indeed; by the slimmest of margins, however, I preferred the razor-edged saltiness of the Manzanilla.

RATING ★★★ ***Recommended*** $

Sanchez Romate Amontillado Sherry 17% Alcohol

Lustrous orange/russet/apple-cider hue—it's really a beautiful, classical sherry color; the ho-hum nose emits a correct, sweet, candied nuttiness that's only mildly engaging; while the bouquet is mediocre, the dry to off-dry flavor featuring sweet red fruit, candied almonds, and carob is delightful and easy and somewhat redeems the limp aroma; a touch sweeter than I like an amontillado to be, this sleek, slender sherry offers an abundance of fruitiness from start to finish; while a borderline product in terms of being recommendable, this sherry's simple charm finally swayed me to the positive side of the field; but if you have to choose from among the manzanilla, fino, and this amontillado, still grab the manzanilla.

RATING ★★★   **Recommended** $

SANCHEZ ROMATE Cream Sherry 17% Alcohol

Fetchingly attractive, worn-copper-penny/brown color; I detect prunes, prunes, and more prunes in the single-note song sung by the aroma; on palate, a potent, smoky taste component engages the taste buds, then the concentrated pruniness/plumminess blows away the smoke and what you're left with is a better-than-average, but rather lean and tightly wound cream sherry—one that never even hints at bludgeoning you with sweetness or syrupy texture; shows the genuine finesse and agility that the better creams always exhibit.

RATING ★★★   **Recommended** $

SANDEMAN Royal Corregidor Rare Oloroso Sherry 21% Alcohol

Stunning, light-mahogany/dark-honey color, rimmed with gold; low-key, soft-caramel, but very potent nose, where you can sense the power and pedigree that underlie this grand thoroughbred; quite simply one of the sleekest olorosos in the marketplace; a rare, medium-bodied, laser-beam-focused sherry triumph that articulately defines "oloroso"; the complex, superlatively balanced flavors of cream, dried tropical fruit, pears, and roasted nuts harmoniously converge in an unforgettable palate experience and aftertaste that leave the taste buds completely satisfied.

RATING ★★★★★   *Highest Recommendation* $$

SANDEMAN Imperial Corregidor Rarest VVO Oloroso Sherry 21% Alcohol

Dark brown/cola color; the coy, woodsy, mature nose requires some serious coaxing before it exposes itself; the semidry, raisiny flavor at entry hints of bittersweet chocolate, then goes moderately sweet in the finish; the finish advances softly and ponderously; not a blockbuster as one might expect, but the flavors of advanced *soleras* really take charge in the end, producing an extraordinary sherry experience—though I preferred the sinewy vigor of the Royal Corregidor over the noble maturity of the Imperial, this aged beauty offers sherry lovers a rewarding glimpse into the rich past of this legendary producer.

RATING ★★★★   *Highly Recommended* $$

SANDEMAN Royal Ambrosante Rare Palo Cortado Sherry 21% Alcohol

Exquisite, topaz/chestnut color, with yellow/orange edges—an absolutely eye-popping appearance; voluptuous, fresh-coffee-bean, cocoa aromas dominate, with a dash of vanilla in the elegant nose; on palate, I couldn't want a much more mellow flavor from any sherry—finely crafted, whistle-clean, nutty flavors abound, beginning semidry at entry, then going sweet in the remarkably sublime and extended finish; like the majority of the other Sandeman sherries, this exceptional Palo Cortado, the rarest of sherry styles, is the pinnacle of refinement and understatement—no over-the-top "statement" wine, just simple, delicious, affordable quality; bravo, Sandeman, this offering soars with the best of them.

RATING ★ ★ ★ ★　　**Highly Recommended**　　$$

SANDEMAN Royal Esmeralda Rare Amontillado Sherry 21% Alcohol

Deep, opulent topaz color, with a gold rim; luscious, focused, concentrated, assertive, burnt-sugar, roasted-almond/walnut nose that dazzles the olfactory sense; offers a sedate, surprisingly lightweight (considering the powerful nose) feel; immensely gratifying nutty/buttery flavors that have melded beautifully in the *solera;* the entire package opened up dramatically after 30 minutes in the glass; graceful, stylish aftertaste that is neatly balanced in terms of the fruit/alcohol/acidity ratio; very flavorful and lovely, but a bit too mannered and restrained overall, which is my sole criticism; my higher-than-average score demonstrates my overall admiration.

RATING ★ ★ ★　　**Recommended**　　$$

SANDEMAN Don Fino Light Dry Sherry 16.5% Alcohol

Clear, pale straw/golden color; an atypical, marvelously rich, biscuity nose for a fino—indeed, I found the bouquet to easily be in the top five fino aromas I've yet whiffed; desert-dry on entry, substantial weight, no wimpy "feline" fino here; the slightly clumsy, cheese-like midpalate fades a bit in the body department, then a lovely, dry, and lemony aftertaste comes to the rescue, gracefully closing the circle; good sherry making from the appealing start to the long, satisfying finish, with just the mildest flavor slip in the middle; seek out and enjoy as a scrumptious aperitif.

RATING ★ ★ ★　　**Recommended**　　$

SANDEMAN Armada Cream Oloroso Sherry 18% Alcohol

Orange color with bright yellow edges; the pleasant nose is rather one-dimensional in its evocation of ripe plums; much better, much richer on palate than the one-note nose promises; a mediocre frontline cream sherry that fulfills its limited potential in a workmanlike manner; maintains the suave Sandeman signature without the use of undue sweetness or muscles like some other mass-marketed creams; don't bother with it when there are so many other creams to be had.

RATING ★ ★　　$

SANDEMAN Character Medium-Dry Sherry 17.8% Alcohol

Engaging amber/honey color; lightish but direct and pleasing, multilayered aromas of light caramel, brandy butter, and unsweetened pineapple juice; smooth, light-bodied, profoundly citrusy/lemony entry and midpalate, then a roasted, toasty finish comes into play and stays quite long in the throat, finally ending in a tail that tastes like maple syrup; my overall impression was that of being let down, mostly because of the featherweight personality exhibited; though I fully comprehend this sherry's station as one that seeks to appeal to the widest possible audience, it's totally lacking in charm.

RATING ★ $

SANDEMAN Dry Don Amontillado Sherry 18% Alcohol

Gorgeous, rich amber/orange color; the correct, butterscotchy, chest-nutty, slightly spirity nose is well-behaved and straightforward, nothing coy or fancy here; the palate is heavily citric, which regrettably pushes the nutty fruit to the bleachers section; the aftertaste is quick, inoffensive, but wafer-thin—too light for my understanding of amontillado; sherry shouldn't be forced to live by appearance and correctness alone; I feel as though this sherry was reined-in during production for the sake of mass-market appeal; underwhelming and anemic; definitely the weak link of the cast.

RATING ★ $

VALDESPINO Inocente Fino Sherry 17% Alcohol

Pale gold/flaxen color; it owns full, meaty, no-nonsense aromas for a fino—it's a bouquet that's laden with pecans, *flor* (yeast), sourdough, and lemon; on palate, it's totally dry, very firm and commanding, but light, with hints of nuts and citrus; the ghost-like finish vanishes instantly, then curiously reemerges in a pleasant licorice tail; as with all finos and manzanillas, serve well chilled before dinner; one of my top two or three choices for fino.

RATING ★ ★ ★ ★   *Highly Recommended* $

VALDESPINO Amontillado Sherry 18% Alcohol

Gorgeous topaz/mahogany color; mildly salty, roasted almonds, vanilla extract in expansive, animated nose; beautifully structured all the way, satiny texture; full-blown hazelnuts explode on palate, then gently recede, leaving a savory aftertaste that is alternately visited by flavors of cola, vanilla, egg cream, and walnuts; easily one of the classiest amontillados available; get out there and track this one down.

RATING ★ ★ ★ ★   *Highly Recommended* $

WISDOM & WARTER Delicate Cream Solera 1902 Sherry 20% Alcohol

Iced-tea/tawny color; the aroma is unexpectedly semidry, nutty, and amontillado-like; immensely elegant demeanor in the mouth—more semi-sweet than sweet when compared to other popular cremes; it's hard to pin-point why I like this silky, lighter cream so much, especially when I have such a yen for blockbuster creams that have been jolted with heavy doses of Pedro Ximenez; the citrusy flavors of this beauty have enough tartness to balance the sugar content; a perfect sherry for those who do not appreciate viscous, strong-armed creams; I guess it all comes back to the label, which appropriately reads "Delicate"; clearly, the house style is long on finesse and drinkability.

RATING ★ ★ ★ ★   *Highly Recommended* $

WISDOM & WARTER Pale Fino Solera 1908 Sherry 17% Alcohol

Pale gold color; a bountiful nose for a fino, with hints of walnut, *flor* (yeast), and butterscotch—altogether lovely aromas; it's snappy, zesty, alive, and totally dry in the mouth; one of the fuller finos in terms of flavor directness and weight; it generously coats the palate with a substantial nuttiness; fast, toffee finish; excellent appetite stimulant to have with seafood *tapas* (finger foods); charming from stem to stern.

RATING ★ ★ ★   *Recommended* $

WISDOM & WARTER Extra Amontillado Solera 1912 Sherry
20% Alcohol

Lovely amber/golden color; the soft, restrained nose of roasted almonds and cola nut is nuanced and subtle; the mouth-feel is lean, clean, sleek; a lighter, feline amontillado style; flavors of honeyed nuts, mango, and passion fruit are slightly leathery on palate; it's drier than many amontillados currently available in the marketplace; a straightforward, elegant, yet mature and complex sherry that's very refreshing; I could easily see this handsome amontillado being paired with soups or fish dishes; seek it out.

RATING ★ ★ ★   *Recommended* $

MADEIRA

Madeira is the viscous, occasionally tooth-numbingly sweet, and always deeply flavorful fortified wine that is made on the island of Madeira. This vertical, tropical island lies 400 miles to the west of Morocco. Madeira, which means "island of woods," was discovered under tragic circumstances by a pair of ill-fated British lovers, Robert a Machin and Anna d'Arfet, in the early 1400s. The laws of feudal England dictated that subjects marry only within their social class. Since Machin was of inferior rank to his sweetheart, they were asked to renounce their passion. Instead, they fled England and set sail for the Mediterranean in Machin's small merchant vessel. But a violent storm blew them west, and they landed on uninhabited, uncharted Madeira. Exhausted from their journey and crestfallen at their fortune, they died there. Soon after, the Portuguese settled on Madeira. Although its mountainous terrain was heart-in-throat steep and thickly forested, land was cleared and grapevines were planted.

Madeira is made like no other wine. In the era before it was fortified, madeira was placed in 418-liter wood casks, called *pipes,* and sent on long voyages, which, because of the island's location necessarily passed through the tropics, to the New World. On these voyages, the wine, which was referred to as *vinho da roda,* which means "wine of the round voyage," was found to improve markedly, taking on a luscious burnt quality due to the baking it endured in the blazing tropical sun. Madeira is the only wine in the world that gets better when it is heated during the maturation stage.

In time, the Madeirense recreated the torrid conditions of the ocean voyages right on Madeira by erecting hothouses, which they called *estufas.* There, the madeira cooked for from three to six months in temperatures of between 95 and 120 degrees Fahrenheit. The fortification of madeira began in the eighteenth century, when wine makers discovered that the wines to which they added grape brandy were significantly more delicious than the unfortified wines. Since then, all madeiras have been fortified.

The various categories of madeira are: the 3-Year-Old, the fundamental madeira used for cooking purposes; Rainwater, which is a young three-year-old Verdelho; 5-Year-Old Reserve, where the premium madeiras begin normally with the name of the primary grape variety (usually about 85 percent of the total content) displayed on the label; 10-Year-Old Reserve and 15-Year-Old Reserve, some of the best madeiras; and Fresqueira 20-Year-Old, which identifies the vintage year. Vintage madeiras must be matured in oak casks for at least 20 years, and then age 2 years in the bottle before being released for purchase by the public.

Though madeira is considered legally a product of Portugal, in essence it is different from port. Madeira, when it is good, offers the opulent, pruney/plummy texture and taste of port, but with the diverse array of desert-dry to flamboyantly sweet styles found in sherry. *Sercial* is the most ethereal and dry type of madeira. *Verdelho* is a gold-colored madeira that's generally medium-dry. *Bual* is amber to brown in color, full-bodied, and moderately sweet. *Malmsey* is the island's most memorable wine, deep mahogany to chestnut in color, dense, intensely sweet, and long-lived.

BLANDY'S Malmsey 10-Year-Old Madeira 20% Alcohol

Mature, dark mahogany color, with ruby highlights; the very deep, intense, beguiling nose offers layers of walnuts, raspberry jam, vanilla extract, and baked bread—a genuinely beguiling bouquet that keeps opening up with aeration; texturewise, it's viscous without being clumsy or overbearing; the well-balanced flavors of plummy fruit, ripe bananas, molasses, and freshly roasted coffee beans are exceedingly ripe and round—it's stunningly sublime on the palate; so ideally mellow in the aftertaste that all the components are in perfect harmony; your mission, if you decide to accept it, is to find and buy.

RATING ★ ★ ★ ★   *Highly Recommended* $$

BLANDY'S Bual Medium-Rich Madeira 17.5% Alcohol

Stately, brown/cola color, with russet trim; the very fragrant, cedar/evergreen nose is meaty, generous, and gripping; medium-bodied, with moderate viscosity; the bittersweet-chocolate, chestnut, mocha flavors come wrapped in a silky, sexy texture that slinkily coats the palate; the toasty, nutty finish is medium-long and teases you with a hint of pineapple in the tail; while moderately rich, it's hardly what I'd describe as sweet; charming from start to finish.

RATING ★ ★ ★   *Recommended* $

BLANDY'S Malmsey Rich Madeira 17.5% Alcohol

Lovely, rich mahogany color; the toasty, cocoa, melted-butter, raisiny nose even emits a mildly floral (violets?) background aroma that I found delightful; in the mouth, lively, delicious flavors of caramel and prunes entertain the taste buds in a simple way; it finishes in a hurry, with the focused pruniness dominating; satiny texture, medium-bodied, with ample viscosity; very savory; good show.

RATING ★ ★ ★   *Recommended* $

BLANDY's **Sercial Dry Madeira 17.5% Alcohol**

Flat, slightly turbid, topaz/orange color, with yellow edge; musty, burntwood, flinty, dried-apricot nose that became more like corrugated cardboard as it aerated—not an auspicious start; bitter, sour, lemon/lime, limp, decaffeinated coffee flavors that failed to win over my taste buds even after four passes; coffee in the quiet, subdued finish; "dry" in wine terminology means "not sweet," not downright astringent and sour.

RATING ★ $

BLANDY's **Verdelho Half-Dry Madeira 17.5% Alcohol**

Clear, rich, topaz/copper color, with a goldenrod rim; the mild sulphur, sweet-sour, soy-sauce, and faintly nutty nose is barely smellable—the flinty aromas fade in and out; light- to medium-bodied; the domineering butterscotch and banana tastes ride high at entry, then become very timid in the aftertaste; fast ride, scant staying power; not much better than the meager Sercial.

RATING ★ $

BLANDY's **Rainwater Medium-Dry Madeira 17.5% Alcohol**

Pretty amber/orange color; the steely/metallic nose expands with aeration, showing hints of orangey perfume; light-bodied in texture; on palate, it's citrusy-sour, but not to the point of distraction—the deficient flavors vanish so quickly that you begin to wonder if you tasted anything in the first place; whither thou, O madeira?

RATING ★ $

COSSARTS **Duo Centenary Celebration Bual Madeira 20% Alcohol**

Deep brown color, with gold/green rim; the fathomless, moderately sweet, and multidimensional nose offers mature oakiness, vanilla-bean, caramel, and charcoal aromas in graceful form—one of the top madeira bouquets to come my way; liquid-satin texture, medium- to full-bodied—considering the ropy viscosity, it's not overly sweet—the well-mannered, smoky, tantalizing, dark-caramel, tobacco, charcoal flavors have come together in a lovely flavor offering; the longest and, by far, the best finish of the Cossart line; this is a delicious madeira that would be a worthy addition to any wine cellar or liquor cabinet.

RATING ★ ★ ★ ★   *Highly Recommended* $$

COSSARTS **Verdelho 1934 Madeira 20% Alcohol**

A small amount of sediment is noted in the almost clear, sumptuous mahogany color—what an alluring eyeful; the multilayered nose is very deep, as fold after fold of exotic aromas keep the nose guessing and reaching further—yummy whiffs of paraffin, hard candy, charcoal, wood, nutmeg, allspice, and bitters meld perfectly together in harmonious fashion; on the palate, it's remarkably fresh, clean, indeed vivacious—absolutely luscious, semisweet flavors of herbs, grapes, and spice entrance the taste buds; it finishes cleanly, albeit a bit meekly, with a mere echo of caramel flavoring; a truly venerable old madeira from a better-than-average vintage that still has plenty of pizzaz remaining; indulge yourself.

RATING ★★★★ *Highly Recommended* $$$

COSSARTS Rainwater Madeira 18% Alcohol

Dazzling topaz/light-brown color, with copper highlights in the core; the rather shy, benign nose needs to be coaxed out, then with aeration it delivers a neatly wrapped package of honey, citrus, and molasses; light- to medium-bodied, silky texture; on palate, the semisweet, concentrated, but easy flavors of macadamia nuts, orange rind, and pineapple are notably harmonious; the medium-length finish is understated; I really appreciated this madeira's restrained elegance; no one virtue stood out ahead of the others; a most pleasant fortified-wine experience.

RATING ★★★ *Recommended* $

COSSARTS #22 Malmsey Madeira 19% Alcohol

Rich mahogany color, with rust core highlights; the grapy aroma offers traces of raisins, freshly ground black pepper, mature oak, and a fetching spiciness—a sound, assertive bouquet that builds in intensity; medium-bodied, lushly textured; the engrossing flavors of creamy milk chocolate and tropical fruit aren't quite as evolved as the qualities of the aroma, but are delicious nevertheless; a focused, potent pruniness emerges in the extended, smooth, and sweet finish; nice job.

RATING ★★★ *Recommended* $

COSSARTS Special Reserve Malmsey Madeira 20% Alcohol

Deep chocolate-brown color, with lime green edge; this peculiar aroma offers cheesy, metallic, unsmoked-cigar, and sweaty scents—I was perplexed and put off by the weird aromas coming out the sampling glass; on palate, a major turnaround occurs as this baby hits the taste buds, running—the gorgeously opulent texture buttresses potent, mature flavors of ripe prune and butterscotch—to my amazement, the flavor successfully redeems the malodorous and curious nose; it finishes like a champ, with unctuous, long, sweet, velvety caramel flavors; a rare and clear case of overall quality overcoming an aromatic peculiarity.

RATING ★★★ *Recommended* $$

COSSARTS Viva Madeira 18% Alcohol

Lovely amber/orange/honey color; the assertive, brown-sugar, caramelized, softly sweet, fresh-flower-garden nose begins well, then grows feeble with extended contact to the air; on palate, it's dry, satiny, wonderfully smooth, and accented with roasted almonds—the almonds eventually take the flavor lead; this madeira owns a strong acid backbone, yet is light-bodied; finishes very clean, short, lean, and toasty dry; definitely a before-dinner beverage, served chilled at 50–55 degrees Fahrenheit.

RATING ★ ★ $

Cossarts No. 92 Bual Madeira 19% Alcohol

Pretty, medium-brown/mahogany color, with a yellow/gold rim; the slightly "off," steely, wet-sand, minerally, acidic aromas break loose from the glass in unruly waves—the nose has no pacing and little style; in the mouth, however, it's suave, classy, and medium-bodied; the coffee, mocca, bittersweet, light toffee flavors make up some of the ground lost by the aroma; sweetish, mild, quick to medium-length aftertaste of very ripe grapes and molasses; it just doesn't have enough in terms of consistent character to be recommended.

RATING ★ ★ $

Cossarts Malvasia 1933 Madeira 20% Alcohol

Turbid, sedimented, molasses/mud-puddle-brown hue, with limp goldenrod edges; this is an unfortunate, over-the-hill (or should it be under-the-hill?), sour-milk bouquet that's obviously tired and way too lactic and vinegary for its own good; ditto on palate; the fruit component has dwindled to shadow status—in other words, it's completely dried out; avoid as you would the plague.

RATING ★ $$$

Justino Henriques Malmsey 1964 Madeira 19% Alcohol

Very attractive, semiclear, autumnal brown/harvest-gold color; the somewhat coy nose offers faint and faded echoes of prunes and roasted almonds; by far, the most elegant of the Justinos in the mouth—the rich, full, supple flavors of butter, caramel, ripe grapes, and spearmint are harmonious and sweet but not cloying; the classy aftertaste has a mocca quality that is very beguiling; this moderately old madeira has a benevolent, confident presence; I would estimate that this endowed madeira has a good two to three decades of growth ahead of it; buy for lay-away.

RATING ★ ★ ★   Recommended $$

Justino Henriques Verdelho 1934 Madeira 19% Alcohol

Throws a sediment and should be decanted—moderately turbid appearance—dark honey/umber color; the lively, sweet, spicy nose of wax and cinnamon has real charm—I liked this 60(+)-year-old bouquet because it still's showing some feistiness; the caramelly flavor is still represented quite admirably from the Brazil-nut entry to the soft but persistent aftertaste, which highlights a smashing peanutbutter flavor; capably lives up to the critically acclaimed 1934 vintage; my guess would be that it has another decade to go before beginning noticeable chemical breakdown; all in all, a very pleasant quaff for an old buck.

RATING ★ ★ ★   Recommended $$$

Justino Henriques Bual 1964 Madeira 19% Alcohol

Coffee-brown, turbid color, with pretty umber edges; the strangely weedy, vegetal, boiled-cabbage nose is slightly rancid and altogether disagreeable;

the flavor jumps at you like a cat—astoundingly sexy, nimble, concentrated, toffee and cocoa flavors deeply impress the taste buds; the generous, stylish finish is full-blown fresh-roasted coffee; the taste and finish are so compelling that they alone seem worth a recommendation in spite of the dicey, highly suspect appearance and the downright lousy bouquet . . . but not quite; it's one of the toughest rating calls I've had to make.

RATING ★★ $$

JUSTINO HENRIQUES **Malmsey 1933 Madeira 19% Alcohol**

Cloudy, medium brown color, with a gold rim; the disturbingly cheesy, stinky, musty, fusty, old-attic aromas of overripe grapes and butter brittle are annoying, to say the least—this aroma died in the bottle about ten years ago; in the mouth, however, the full, round, smoky, quite sprightly flavors of hazelnuts and raisins almost redeem the malodorous nose; it finishes nicely with off-dry backnotes of grapes and lemons; the flavor rescued this old wine from a below-average score; it's clearly weary, but oddly there's still ample sensory enjoyment here; buy cautiously, with the understanding that most of its luster is long gone, never to return.

RATING ★★ $$$

JUSTINO HENRIQUES **Sercial 1940 Madeira 19% Alcohol**

Misty amber/brown color, with a deep golden rim and an inconsequential amount of sediment showing; the roasted-coffee-bean, stale aromas are unfortunately too fatigued to go anywhere but down; on palate, there's still some genuine potency in the pleasingly tangy taste—this particular grape simply can't be expected to withstand over a half century of time and still display the usual freshness and delicacy attributed to younger Sercials; while it does offer a surprising amount of character, it's too little, too late; 1940 was an especially fine year for delicate Sercial, and with patience the taster can discern some of that fading glory.

RATING ★ $$$

JUSTINO HENRIQUES **Verdelho 1954 Madeira 19% Alcohol**

Murky, dull, nearly coffee-with-milk/brown color, flecked by minimal sediment; the slightly medicinal, one-note nose of prunes doesn't develop beyond that even after 30 minutes of vigorous aeration; the flavors come alive on the palate as the entry betrays the *verdelho* grape in an astringent splash that evolves into a charming, off-dry roundness in the sour-apple aftertaste; I liked how this sassy madeira closed out, but serious points had to be taken off for the narrow nose and unbecoming appearance.

RATING ★ $$$

LEACOCK'S **Bual 10-Year-Old Madeira 20% Alcohol**

Deep brown/cola color, with a gold rim; the heavenly nose of raw bread dough, peaches, saddle leather, espresso, and dark honey showed remarkable balance and finesse—the first and second nosings were the ones with the greatest impact; glorioski, if you're a chocolate freak, I strongly urge you to hunt down a bottle or two of this cocoa-flavored stallion a.s.a.p.; medium-to full-bodied, crushed-velvet texture; the long finish features molasses, cocoa, and marshmallow; what great madeira is all about.

RATING ★ ★ ★ ★   *Highly Recommended* $$

LEACOCK'S **Superlative Rich 15-Year-Old Madeira 20% Alcohol**

Mature brown/gold color, with rust highlights; succulent, complex aromas of honey, maple syrup, and prunes are explosive in the toasty, ripe-melon nose—each nosing pass is surpassed by the next in terms of intensity; medium-weighted and obviously mature in bearing and texture—but, strangely, while it indeed is very good, it lacks the punch and overall presence of the more expressive, voluptuous, and disarming 10-year-old Bual—lovely, concentrated flavors of ripe pear, dark caramel, and oak coddle the taste buds prior to the regal, medium-length finish of caramel.

RATING ★ ★ ★   *Recommended* $$

PORT—PORTUGAL

lthough port may not be as versatile as sherry or as esoteric as madeira, it is nonetheless perceived by connoisseurs as being the most regal member of the fortified-wine family. When port dresses in its finest attire as a vintage port or aged tawny, it commands as imposing and impressive a collection of aromas, textures, subtleties, and flavors as any fortified or still wine. At its best, port provides one of the two or three most elegant and thrilling conclusions to a meal.

Allowing for the port-style wines that are made in many wine-making locations worldwide, port from Portugal, where it is referred to as *porto,* is the genuine article, the prototype, and the standard. Port-style wines from countries such as Australia, the United States, and South Africa are frequently toothsome and passable, but never do they approach the depth of character or inherent majesty of true port. That's not to say that someday they won't. But right now, at the end of the Second Millennium, ounce for ounce, it's no contest.

Wine has been made in Portugal since before the time of Christ. Circa 130 B.C., the Roman Empire absorbed what is now Portugal into their enormous sphere of influence. It's recorded that the Roman soldiers who occupied the region drank the table wines of the Lusitanians, the ferocious Celtic tribe who resided in the northern stretches of the area. In the eleventh and twelfth centuries A.D., Crusaders from the British Isles who passed through Portugal either going to or returning from the Holy Land reported on the region's delicious wines. Because of various confrontations with both France and Spain, the Portuguese enjoyed excellent relations with Great Britain, a bond that would later play a key role in the development of the port industry.

From the 1500s through the 1800s, England was herself squabbling off and on with France and Spain. The English have always appreciated good wine and spirits, so Portugal became a reliable supplier of wine during these centuries of turmoil. Indeed, records indicate that Portuguese wine from the Minho district had been shipped to England as earlier as the 1460s in exchange for cod, cotton cloth, and wool. In 1654 and 1703, trade treaties between the two countries further cemented the friendship.

During this era of mutually beneficial commercial traffic, the English found that the Minho vintners, whose simple wines were palatable but hardly profound, were unable to supply the rising demand for wine in Great Britain. Forced to seek out new sources for Portuguese wine, several British merchants searched near the seaport town of Oporto and learned of the more robust red wines made far inland in the wild territory of the Douro River Valley. A pair of merchants traveled into the rugged interior and, coming upon a monastery, reportedly purchased all the wine that had been produced by the monks. Before sending it off to England, they fortified it with some locally made grape brandy to ensure that it would survive the rigors of the river journey to Oporto and then the seafaring trip to England. In the ensuing 150 years, merchants and wine makers continued to tinker with this basic port-wine-making process.

With the rise in popularity of the Douro's wine, the British merchants moved their headquarters south to Oporto from the Minho. As word about the delicious red wine from northern Portugal spread throughout the European continent, merchants from Germany and Holland also opened field offices in Oporto. By the middle of the seventeenth century, the English had become the most influential and biggest foreign trade community in Portugal. By the end of the 1600s, many Port firms, or lodges as they are called, were established, and companies such as Taylor, Fladgate & Yeatman, Quarles Harris, Croft, and Warre were woven into the social fabric of northern Portugal.

Later, in the 1700s and 1800s, other English firms, as well as German, Dutch, and Portuguese, were added to the roster: Graham, Delaforce, Offley Forrester, Calem, Noval, Ferreira, Ramos Pinto, Sandeman, Fonseca Guimaraens, Dow, Smith Woodhouse, Cockburn, Robertson, Borges e Irmao. Port wine soon cascaded into England at such a furious rate that it became known as the "Englishman's wine."

Without question, the Douro River Valley is the world's most remote, inhospitable, primitive, and yet romantic world-class viticultural area. Visiting the Douro is like walking through a window of time. Coming from its source high in the interior mountains of Spain, the wild Douro gouges out an incredibly precipitous, serpentine river gorge on whose terraced overhangs of yellow-tinted, schistose soil rest the vineyards of *touriga naçional, touriga francesca, tinta cao, barroca, roriz,* and *mourisco* grapes, the varieties that are used to make port.

Blocked by the Serra do Marao mountains that stand 50 miles due east of coastal Oporto, the Atlantic's sea breezes never get the chance to kick up dust in the blazing hot Douro. From May through early October, this natural trough bakes in daily temperatures of 100–110 degrees Fahrenheit; from December through March, the hearty Douro denizens freeze from the bitter cold. Yet, through all the climatic tribulations, the Douro remains the world's choicest spot for the production of port wine. In the torrid growing season, the grapes ripen to outlandishly high sugar contents, making naturally high in alcohol the wine that eventually becomes port. To halt fermentation so that the alcohol levels don't rise too high, brandy is added in a ratio of 1:5 to the fermenting must. With the fermentation process stopped, the wine registers an alcohol level of approximately 20 percent and has some residual sugar remaining, which gives port its naturally sweet flavor.

Although port production takes place in the depths of the Douro, its maturation period in oak casks *(pipes)* occurs, for the most part, downriver in seaside Vila Nova de Gaia, which lies directly across the Douro from Oporto, to take advantage of the cooler, more humid climate. The rationale for this is that the milder climate allows the port to age more gracefully and unhurriedly than in the extremes of temperature of the Douro.

The port industry is one of the most strictly regulated alcoholic beverage industries in Europe. Three government-directed counsels watchdog the production of port from the growing of grapes and classifying vineyards to bottling and "declaring vintages," or publicly pronouncing particularly spectacular harvests.

STYLES OF PORT

White Port: Little known in the U.S. but very popular in France, this straw/white-wine-colored port style is made from the *malvasia fina, codega, rabigato, viosinho,* and *gouveio* grape varieties and is the only port that should be served chilled (45–50 degrees Fahrenheit) as an aperitif. The flavor range is remarkably broad, with some versions dry and others stickysweet. The sweetest are labeled "Lagrima," which means "teardrop."

Ruby Port: The prime all-purpose port style, which is popular in all parts of the world. Colored as the name implies. Matured in oak casks for rarely more than three years, ruby is customarily fruity, ripe, and fresh. Serve at cellar temperature (48–55 degrees Fahrenheit).

Tawny Port: Rarely more than three years old, tawnies have more of a burnished brown/red color than the rubies. They make a very good aperitif. The French, in particular, are great admirers of tawny port. Serve at cellar temperature.

Aged Tawny Port: My bet as the best-kept secret in the fortified-wine category. In its finest versions, tawny port is on par with vintage port in terms of depth of character and satisfaction. These are tawny ports that have been aged in cask for extremely long periods. They are offered in four ages of 10, 20, 30, and 40 years. Since these ports are blends, the age indication is the average age of the ports involved in the final mixture. This category is the supreme test of each lodge's master blender.

Colheita Port: The style is a single-vintage tawny port that is aged in cask for at least seven years (quite often much longer). The label must indicate the year that the grapes were harvested. The rarest of all port styles, Colheita is a precious treat. The industry leaders in this uncommon style are Niepoort and Burmester. Serve at room temperature.

Late-Bottled Vintage Port: A combination of ports from a single vintage, which have spent a minimum of four, but not more than six, years in barrels. This lackluster style was invented as a poor man's version of vintage port. They do not age further in the bottle as vintage ports do. Once purchased, they are ready to be consumed.

Crusted Port: Infrequently seen in the U.S. market, this obscure style is a late-bottled vintage derivative. A blend of several vintages, crusted port is matured for four years in the bottle. Being unfiltered, it ordinarily deposits considerable amounts of sediment into one's glass, hence the descriptive moniker.

Vintage-Character Port: Yet another attempt at making a blue-collar vintage port. Almost all are ruby ports that have shifted into overdrive. Vintage-character ports are blends of ports that range in age from four to six years generally and have heightened properties of ripeness and texture. What is confusing is that not all producers put the words "Vintage Character" on the label.

Vintage Port: This hallowed style is reserved for the best wines from the best vintages (the random "declared" vintages). They are ruby ports that are bottled only two years after the harvest. Not all producers declare vintage years, even in uniformly great years. The decision to declare or not to declare depends solely on the quality of the grapes from each lodge's best vineyards. Normally, vintage ports are potent and dense, with high levels of tannin and fruit concentration. They more often than not require 15 to 20 years of bottle aging to come to full flower. Some from legendary vintages, such as 1963 or 1977, require even longer periods, like five or six decades before they will reach their peak.

Single Quinta: Special bottlings, usually from undeclared vintages, of high-quality ports from a single estate/vineyard holding. Port's equivalent of "estate-bottled wines." The best rival the finest regular bottlings of vintage port. My personal favorite single *quintas* are: Quinta do Bomfim (Dow), Quinta da Cavadinha (Warre), Quinta da Corte (Delaforce), and Quinta de Vargellas (Taylor, Fladgate & Yeatman).

THE TWENTIETH CENTURY'S MONUMENTAL VINTAGES

THE SEVEN PEERLESS FIVE-STAR LEGENDS

1908 (declared by 26 shippers): A controversial vintage in that some experts rate 1912 higher. Don't believe it. This vintage is the pinnacle of the four outstanding pre–World War I vintages, offering viscous, brawny ports of fathomless color and elegance. Almost unbelievably, some are still showing well, that is, if you can find them. I tasted the Cockburn's in 1988 and scored it four stars. In its prime I bet that it would have garnered five.

1927 (declared by 30 shippers): Vintage of the century? If there ever is such an ideal, I wouldn't argue against 1927 being this century's prototype. Nearly all the lodges jumped on this one, which produced ports of impeccable character, the ideal union of finesse and power. Cockburn, Noval, Dow, and Graham are all still in top form.

1935 (declared by 15 shippers): Oft-debated vintage within port circles, mainly because relatively few lodges declared it. Not as fathomless as 1927 or 1912, but the wines accent port's delicate, fruity side. The growing season and harvest experienced excellent weather conditions.

1945 (declared by 22 shippers): Another candidate for century's premier vintage, no question. Massive, multilayered wines of unparalleled strength and depth. Drought was responsible for the mixed blessings of tiny production and sensational quality. Is it better than the stunning 1927 vintage? I wouldn't want to have to live on the difference. Graham and Taylor lead the pack in tandem, and both have a decade or two to go.

1963 (declared by 25 shippers): Doubtless the most classical post–World War II vintage. Round, generous, fruit-filled, plummy wines of wide girth, some of which are just now coming round to drinkability. But don't be fooled. Taylor, Graham, Sandeman, Fonseca, and Croft are just hitting stride. Most won't reach their peak until well after the clock strikes midnight, heralding A.D. 2000.

1977 (declared by 24 shippers): Finest vintage since 1963. Long way to travel yet in terms of development. Most wines are chewy, broad-shouldered, tannic, and opaque. Don't even think of opening any of them prior to 2000–2010.

1985: Samplings show that most '85s are luxurious wines of intense character, deep color, and impeccable breed. The incredibly luscious Graham '85 is the flagship. Most will peak well after 2015–2020. A vintage that has gotten better with time.

GREAT FOUR-STAR VINTAGES

1900 (declared by 22 shippers): What a way to begin the century. Not showing all that well now, since most wines were on the lightish side at the outset. Many are dried out. But, alas, still a milestone.

1904 (declared by 25 shippers): Another vintage that at present is highly suspect as to current drinkability. Like its famous predecessor, 1900, longer on finesse than durability.

1912 (declared by 25 shippers): Heavier than either 1900 or 1904, and, thus, still occasionally showing well, depending on the producer. Found only in auctions, if then, and a few specialty merchants.

1931 (declared by 6 shippers): Perhaps the biggest missed opportunity of the century by the port producers. Most shippers grimly acknowledge this fact. A great vintage, but because of ample reserves of '27 and the worldwide depression, producers played it close to the vest by not declaring. Pity. Quinta do Noval '31, which retails now for a staggering $1,000.00 per bottle, is considered the benchmark port of the vintage, if not the century.

1934 (declared by 12 shippers): Passed over in favor of the bigger 1935, but a great vintage nonetheless.

1955 (declared by 26 shippers): Best vintage of the overall lackluster 1950s by a country mile. At their peak now.

1960 (declared by 24 shippers): The other high-quality post–World War II vintage that is drinking very well right now. Overlooked because of its calendar proximity to the awesome 1963s. Some excellent values if you do some careful comparison shopping.

1970 (declared by 23 shippers): To some, should probably be included in the "legend" category. Ports of exceptional richness and fruit extract, developing nicely, but still require time in bottle.

1983: These are massive, highly concentrated wines that are perfect for cellaring now through 2020. The Cockburn and the Dow are awesome.

1991: Extremely fine wines. The majority of lodges declared this vintage, while some chose to sit on the sidelines in favor of the 1992s. These are muscular, tannic, raisiny, jet-black beauties that won't begin to approach their peak until 2010–2015.

1992: The handful of lodges that declared this vintage may get the last laugh, since the wines are showing remarkably well at the time of this writing. These are uniformly chunky, inky-purple, and astonishingly fragrant. The richness factor of the '92s is what separates them from the more sinewy '91s.

1994: Huge potential. Most lodges will declare this monster vintage. Keep an eye on this one. Barrel samplings have indicated that in time, this vintage may have the character to break into the five-star category. At the time of publication, it's most resembling the graceful, but tannic, jammy blockbusters from 1977.

ADRIANO RAMOS-PINTO Quinta Do Bom Retiro 20-Year-Old Tawny Porto 20% Alcohol

Burnt-orange/typically tawny color, with brick-red highlights; the open, inviting, approachable, chocolate-covered-cherries nose gains in strength, richness, and fruitiness with aeration; on palate, it's light- to medium-bodied; the roasted-almond flavor dominates the sweet-sour entry and mid-palate, then softly fades in the finish, where a smoky, dried-fruit quality assumes control; a delightful, savory aged tawny in the lighter vein; after a third sampling, this tawny's greatest achievement is its sublime balance; along with the fantastic 30-year-old tawny, it's the best that this house has to offer.

RATING ★ ★ ★ ★   *Highly Recommended* $$

ADRIANO RAMOS-PINTO 30-Year-Old Tawny Porto 20% Alcohol

Brownish/light-cola color, a flat, uninteresting appearance; the nose is shy in the first two passes, then in the third pass a butterscotch/caramel/toffee-candy surface fragrance appears—this presence is underlined by an oaky potency that is mature and dense; this graybeard port reaches its zenith on the palate, as feline, svelte flavors of tropical fruit, raisins, sweet oak, walnuts, and vanilla cake frosting combine in a memorable midpalate taste extravaganza—the medium-bodied, slinky texture is a huge plus; the aftertaste is silky-smooth, layered, sweet, and unbelievably long; deeper, more compact, and concentrated, but just as majestic and downright delicious as the 20-year-old Bom Retiro Tawny from the same producer; a big-time, totally captivating aged tawny; wow.

RATING ★ ★ ★ ★　　*Highly Recommended*　　$$

ADRIANO RAMOS-PINTO Quinta da Urtiga Single Quinta Porto 19.5% Alcohol

Crimson/purple hue, very pretty; the lovely nose is round and biscuity, showing off seductively sweet, peppery aromas of chocolate cake batter, chocolate-covered cherries, freshly ground black pepper, and strawberries—a sexy, come-hither bouquet that's only moderately assertive; the chocolate presence is really pronounced at palate entry, then the flavor turns a little bitter at midpalate—the lack of fruit in the mouth is surprising, given the berry/cherry elements noted in the bouquet; the aftertaste exhibits flashes of red fruit as well as tannin, but no bitterness; I presume that this is a blend of different vintages from the one estate, hence no vintage designation; a borderline three-star port.

RATING ★ ★ ★　　*Recommended*　　$$

ADRIANO RAMOS-PINTO 1991 Vintage Porto 20% Alcohol

Nearly opaque purple/crimson; the bouquet is bountiful, sweet, ripe, and has a wonderful banana-like underpinning that I find compelling—it's not a blockbuster 1991 vintage nose, like those of Cockburn, Quinta do Vesuvio, or Taylor Fladgate's Vargellas, but it's warm, supple, and welcoming; in the mouth, this medium-bodied port is more cocoa-sweet than fruit-sweet and offers lovely backnote flavors of toffee candy and nougat; the tannin level is marked but not massive; the finish is clean and highlights the chocolate element so evident throughout the entire palate phase; a good, moderately dense vintage port, which if it showed more, might well have ended up a four-star winner; as it is, it's above average.

RATING ★ ★ ★　　*Recommended*　　$$

ADRIANO RAMOS-PINTO 1983 Vintage Porto 20% Alcohol

Very deep ruby color, with a garnet/cherry rim; long, long legs drape the bowl of the glass after swirling; the lusciously sweet, ripe-black-cherry, boysenberry nose slowly lures you in; medium-weighted; on palate, the explosive, concentrated prune and tobacco flavors are wrapped in a silky, smooth texture that coats the throat all the way down; nice, skin-tight finish that neither leaves too soon nor stays too long; I don't see the makings of a particularly long-lived vintage port here; but in the meantime, this is awfully pleasant drinking in the near term, that is, now through 1999.

RATING ★ ★ ★　　*Recommended*　　$$

ADRIANO RAMOS-PINTO Fine White Porto 20% Alcohol

Extraordinarily brilliant umber/orange/honey color, which captures the eye; the clean, semisweet, exotic, honey/almond nose has layers of bread dough, prunes, guava, and vanilla bean; lush, well-structured, focused plum and roasted-almond flavors lavish the palate; it finishes long, with a lovely pear-nectar, pineapple, biscuity flavor; without question, one of the finest white ports I've sampled; because of the sweetness, I wouldn't serve it as an aperitif, but as a *digestif;* a downright savory and vastly elegant discovery.

RATING ★ ★ ★   *Recommended* $

ADRIANO RAMOS-PINTO Lagrima White Porto 20% Alcohol

A hair darker than the Fine White port, with a touch more orange hue; the intense nuttiness (primarily hazelnuts) in the nose is almost sherry-like at first, but then with aeration develops further into dried flowers and prunes; the palate is even more alluring than the nose, with accelerated flavors of light caramel and plums; it's more candied than the Fine White, but just as tasty in a more streamline, austere, astringent way; finishes medium-long and semisweet.

RATING ★ ★ ★   *Recommended* $

ADRIANO RAMOS-PINTO Quinta da Ervamoira 10-Year-Old Tawny Porto 19.5% Alcohol

Definitive tawny/medium-amber color, with a golden rim; the spicy, peppery nose is lackluster, considering that it's a 10-year-old tawny—what happened to the meat?; the moderately appealing, semisweet flavors of dried fruit, milk chocolate, and hazelnuts come robed in a smoky background flavor; the chocolatey finish is medium-long and sweeter than the midpalate taste; neither spectacular nor opulent, but a sound, run-of-the-mill tawny nonetheless.

RATING ★ ★ $$

ADRIANO RAMOS-PINTO 1987 Late-Bottled Vintage Porto 19.5% Alcohol

Deep purple/blood-red/crimson tone; the nose has a delicate vanillin/oaky lilt that is comely but unembellished—the later nosings reveal a touch of tobacco smoke; the mouth presence is keenly chocolatey at entry, then it turns smoky/tobacco-like at midpalate, which disappointed me—the deficiency of fruit really puts a beacon on the tannin, which is very dense; whereas any port needs balance between fruit and tannin, this LBV lays bare the weaknesses of this poor-to-fair vintage—it's interesting to note that other 1987s have shown strikingly similar shortcomings—the two-star Niepoort 1987 Vintage Porto and the two-star Delaforce 1987 LBV, to name a couple—only Cockburn's fine (four-star) 1987 Quinta da Tua/Single Quinta has shown genuine complexity and finesse; pass on this Ramos-Pinto.

RATING ★ ★ $$

ADRIANO RAMOS-PINTO 1985 Vintage Porto 20% Alcohol

Pretty medium-to-deep crimson hue; the nose is of citrus, celery, and sage in its early stages—the herbal/vegetal qualities continue through the second pass; in the mouth comes the first hint of fruit, then a black-pepper, gun-powder overlay cancels out the fruit element—it tastes better and richer at the palate entry than down the road toward the medium-length finish; the burst of flavor on the tongue tempts me to give it a nod, but the overall package didn't sufficiently impress me enough to give it a recommendation; not a blockbuster; should peak in the late 1990s.

RATING ★ ★ $$$

ADRIANO RAMOS-PINTO Fine Ruby Porto 20% Alcohol

Prototypical ruby color; the shy, grapy nose requires a lot of coaxing even after 30 minutes of aeration—I resent that—a port nose should not be cas-trated; genteel and polished on the palate as proper but docile flavors of ripe grapes and black pepper envelop the taste buds; barely decent from begin-ning to end—strangely, it doesn't have the sensory scope or intensity of the two white ports from Ramos-Pinto.

RATING ★ $

ADRIANO RAMOS-PINTO 1985 Late-Bottled Vintage / Bottled in 1989; 20% Alcohol

Nearly opaque purple/crimson color; full-bodied, ambrosial, sweet bou-quet of raisins and plums—a calculated, stingy, and stern nose; the stern-ness in the bouquet follows through on the palate; the sweet overture found in the nose settles down in the flavor, going semisweet, almost like bitter-sweet chocolate—it teases you; the forward flavors found at entry are more pleasing than the austere, penurious finish, which is very smoky; the vari-ous parts simply don't fit together properly; lacks harmony.

RATING ★ $

ADRIANO RAMOS-PINTO 1982 Vintage Porto 20% Alcohol

Opaque midnight-purple/black color; the deep, intensely grapy nose shows a touch of the brandy when you deeply inhale—has a kind of fruit-salad nose of moderate appeal; it acts well on the palate, but the lean flavor component leaves me yearning for more fruit and less bitter cocoa taste; somewhere along the line, the grapiness found in the nose escaped detec-tion on the palate; the aftertaste picks up a focused pruniness, which nears richness but doesn't quite make it; a good, but maddeningly inconsistent, port for this average vintage.

RATING ★ $$

ARGELLOS 40-Year-Old Tawny Porto 19% Alcohol

Perfectly clear, very pretty rust/copper/sunset-orange color; loaded in the nose with dazzlingly snappy, off-dry aromas of butterscotch, light English toffee, freshly cracked walnuts—the nose is unbelievably assertive and vig-orous for such an old tawny; the alluring zestiness continues on the palate as the intensely nutty, semisweet flavor romances the taste buds; the after-taste goes a bit sour and flat, but nevertheless this is as good an example of tawny over 30 years old as I've tracked down; even in view of the fact that I'm a graduate of the school that states that 20 years old is the optimum

tawny port category, I recommend this sprightly port with all confidence
... if you can find it.

RATING ★★★   ***Recommended*** $$

BORGES & IRMAO 1983 Vintage Porto 20% Alcohol

Disturbingly murky, dull purple color, laden with clouds of suspended
particles that coat the bowl of the glass; as I have stated previously, I am one
of those old-fashioned people who like to have a bit of sediment floating
about because that usually indicates an unfiltered or lightly filtered wine—
what bothered me about this port was not the sediment, but the port itself,
which was outlandishly turbid; while arresting a portion of the sediment, I
found that decanting did nothing to improve the appearance of the wine it-
self; it possesses a musty, fusty, mildly grapy, and regrettably corky nose; on
palate, the plummy flavor is about the only positive thing going for this port;
a bomb.

RATING ★ $$

BURMESTER 20-Year-Old Tawny Porto 20% Alcohol

Tasted in Oporto; beautiful brick/copper color that dances in the light;
the very complex, yet refined, nose keeps evolving as the port mingles with
the air—it emits appetizing scents of roasted almond, cream, vanilla, pears,
and cocoa; light- to medium-weighted, yet supple; while giving off a lightish appearance, it ends up being an intriguing mosaic of fruit, nut, herb, and
cocoa flavors that all come together in the mesmerizing finish; moderate
sweetness in the extended aftertaste; bravo—a luscious but mannered aged
tawny if there ever was one.

RATING ★★★★   ***Highly Recommended*** $$

CALEM

One of the highlights of my 1990 trip to the Douro Valley was meeting
Joaquim Manuel Calem at his office. I walked in unannounced and was gra-
ciously treated to two hours of conversation with the engagingly candid Mr.
Calem. I learned that he was one of the few port lodges that was still owned
and operated by its founding family (established in 1859). The backbone
of Calem is its property, Quinta do Foz, located at the mouth of the Pinhao
River as it merges with the Douro. Quinta do Foz's 48,000 vines are among
the most coveted in the Cima Corgo district. The terraced, schistose-soil
vineyards face south, southeast, and east, giving them excellent exposure
to the sun. Calem's other big-name property near Pinhao is Quinta do
Sagrado, which has 25,000 vines. While they're not in the same ballpark
as the British lodge monsters, namely Taylor Fladgate, Graham, Dow, and
so forth, I found the Calems to be uniformly fresh, medium-bodied, and af-
fordably priced. What more could anyone desire? This is definitely one of
the port lodges to keep an eye on over the next decade.

CALEM WWW 30-Year-Old Aged Tawny Porto 20% Alcohol

Rich, medium-amber/dark-honey/umber color, the bits of sediment and
mild turbidity are totally inoffensive and actually add to the character of this

fine old tawny; the bouquet is mature, settled, even stately in its opulence—gorgeous off-dry aromas of buttered toast, pine/cedar, and honey-wheat bread treat the olfactory sense to an aged tawny bouquet clinic; on the palate, its full, voluptuous texture serves as the foundation for delectable flavors of mint, overripe grapes, and caramel; the aftertaste is lush, velvety-smooth, sweet, and, most of all, elegant; glom onto this sterling aged tawny to savor all of it through the cool-weather months.

RATING ★ ★ ★ ★　　Highly Recommended　　$$$

CALEM Magnificent 40-Year-Old Aged Tawny Porto 20% Alcohol

Ignore, if you can, the embarrassingly self-serving name; brilliant, pure, medium brown hue, with harvest-gold/rust edges—it's a beauty in terms of appearance; the nose is tangy, zesty, but confident and focused, as vivacious aromas of butter, fennel, old oak, and caramel charm the olfactory sense; on the palate, it's unbelievably lively, fresh, and vibrant for such an old porto—opulent, but not unctuous flavors of leather, raisins, caramel, and wood resin have blended beautifully over time; the tastes crescendo in the fabulous aftertaste, which is luxuriously long, medium-bodied, and mature; one to add to your collection.

RATING ★ ★ ★ ★　　Highly Recommended　　$$$

CALEM 1983 Vintage Porto 20% Alcohol

Pretty, ripe, mature, and deep, but not opaque, ruby/garnet hue; pray tell, by the opulent nose I believe that this may be one of the best Calems I've sampled—a focused, laser-beam type of bouquet that concentrates on the blackberry and cassis scents, neither of which are overblown or overripe—it's a controlled, purposeful port bouquet; in the mouth, the mission launched in the aroma is accomplished in the midpalate arena as firm, but delicate tastes of raisins, dried plums, and blackberry jam bring a serious taste banquet to the palate; solid, off-dry aftertaste; Calem hits the mark dead center on this one; drink now until 2010.

RATING ★ ★ ★ ★　　Highly Recommended　　$$

CALEM 1982 Quinta da Foz Vintage Porto 20% Alcohol

Deep, opaque, sediment-filled, purple/black hue; the viney nose is very closed off from the first nosing through the third pass—by the fourth and final pass, the vinous quality still dominated—it's a less than inviting bouquet; this peculiar port earns all its rating stars in the burly, unruly, even raucous flavor that highlights mellow tannins, rich milk chocolate, and candied cherries—it's a wild mouthful that charms the palate with its wrong-side-of-the-tracks swagger; the finish is anything but sophisticated as barrelfuls of ripe plum and cherry tastes top off this oddball, ruffian port; drink now until 2005.

RATING ★ ★ ★　　Recommended　　$$

CALEM 1980 Quinta da Foz Vintage Porto 20% Alcohol

Mature, blood/crimson color, with a tawny rim—markedly turbid—not to worry—make sure you decant it; the shy, ethereal bouquet clearly requires longer than normal time in the glass to develop fully—even after 30 minutes of aeration, the nose just barely came out to play; the chewy, almost grainy texture is the type of port "grip" that I really relish—it feels good on the tongue—no wimpy port here; the semisweet flavors range from ripe red apples to raspberries to mandarin oranges; in the mouth it has a peculiar, unfocused, almost wild presence that I cautiously liked; the vinous, floral, intense strawberry, herbal finish is long, lean, and very clean; a likable loose cannon.

RATING ★★★   *Recommended* $$

CALEM Fine White Porto 20% Alcohol

Fading-sunlight/pale-straw color; the lovely, round, ripe honeydew melon, sweet-perfume nose has a keenly evident dough-like foundation; on the palate, it's sweet, with supple, forward flavors of vanilla, banana, strawberry, and candied nuts, all gracefully wrapped in a sinewy texture; the medium-length aftertaste showcases the strawberry fruit nicely; one of the best of the sweet and full-bodied style of white port; shines brightest when served slightly chilled either prior to a meal on-the-rocks or with after-dinner sweets.

RATING ★★★   *Recommended* $

CALEM Lagrima White Porto 20% Alcohol

Lovely honey/gold hue, perfect clarity; I tasted this port chilled; the biscuity nose aggressively emits seductive aromas of British butterscotch, light toffee, guava, papaya, jasmine, and even a subtle dash of ginger—it's an endowed, yeasty, sweet, and ripe bouquet that's a total pleasure; the taste is manageably sweet and crammed with intensely fruity flavors of white raisins, bananas, and a backnote of tangerine; the finish veers slightly off line in terms of too much tangy acid, but it's not enough to seriously detract from the splendid nose, texture, and flavor; it's the supple equal of the delicious Lagrima White Porto made by Ramos-Pinto.

RATING ★★★   *Recommended* $

CALEM Old Friends Fine Tawny Porto 20% Alcohol

The attractive reddish/brick-like color tends more to a ruby port than a tawny; even with 15–20 minutes of aeration and various spin cycles of swirling, the floral, musty nose of dried rose petals peaked out of the tasting glass only with great reluctance—but what did emerge was exceedingly inviting; very soft, velvety, pliable, and comfortable on the palate as the lightish structure supports easy, moderately sweet flavors of tart berries, tobacco, and mango; Old Friends finishes well, with a direct flavor of berries; it's little wonder to me why this is Calem's bread-and-butter port.

RATING ★★★   *Recommended* $

CALEM Shipper's Special Reserve Tawny Porto 20% Alcohol

Clean, charming brick/cherry/russet/tawny color; this bountiful, ripe plum nose of marinated fruit (especially strawberries and cranberries) is a fetching cross between customary ruby and tawny bouquets; on palate, its feline bearing is uncomplicated and ready to please; flavorwise, I appreciate its featherweight tastes of blackberries and plums; it finishes deftly and cleanly; anyone expecting a blockbuster should pass on this feminine port; however, those port lovers who appreciate a nimble, balanced, undemanding port for quiet afterdinner sipping will be more than be satisfied with this affordable tawny; not quite as dazzling as the Old Friends Fine Tawny, however.

RATING ★★★   *Recommended* $

CALEM 10-Year-Old Aged Tawny Porto 20% Alcohol

Beguiling medium-brown color, with warm red/vermilion core highlights; the comely nose is soft and delicate in its approach, offering ripe aromas of grape pulp, toasty oak, digestive biscuits, vanilla extract, and dark caramelized sugar, like that which tops crème brulée; in the mouth, the texture is light to medium-bodied, true to the Calem house style; the entry taste is fruity and ripe, then the midpalate goes sweet and candied; the aftertaste is very clean and agile, which is a real plus; overall, for a very light aged tawny, this is a handsome port particularly for anyone who wants to enter the exotic world of aged tawnies gradually and thoughtfully.

RATING ★★★   *Recommended* $$

CALEM 20-Year-Old Tawny Porto 20% Alcohol

Welcoming orange/russet/amber color, whose clarity displays a few tiny specks of sediment—don't bother to decant; the intensely nutty, wheat-toast nose is lively and alluring—while neither forward nor shy, the nose offers caramel, almond, and charred-wood components that are really savory and highly complementary; this lovely port owns a varied melange of dried-fruit and nut flavors, which tail off quietly in the sweet finish; not a thick, jammy aged tawny by any means, this is a solid, well-crafted port with large amounts of finesse and elegance.

RATING ★★★   *Recommended* $$

CALEM 1992 Quinta da Foz Vintage Porto 20% Alcohol

Youthful, sturdy, black/blue/purple tone, cherry rim; the nose is closed for the first two passes, which is not surprising given that it's still a youngster—after 30 minutes of aeration, the third pass reveals a vinous, leafy, earthy, almost hard edge to it, but I attribute this awkwardness to immaturity; the flavor is much more advanced than the aroma, and boasts keen tannins, moderately intense red-berry/red-plum fruit, and a solid backbone of acidity; the finish is somewhat short, but concludes on an appealing wave of plumminess; not destined to be a classic, but a very nice VP all the same; peak drinking from 2000 to 2005.

RATING ★★★   *Recommended* $$

CALEM Fine Ruby Porto 20% Alcohol

Proper crimson/ruby color; subdued nose, with low-gear hints of cinnamon and black-currant jam—the nose reminds me of two or three of California's port-style wines made from Cabernet Sauvignon or Zinfandel; in the mouth, the taste of black cherries dominates and charms the palate; lightish in body; finishes semisweet and a tad on the skimpy, austere side; middle-of-the-pack and serviceable, but it could use more fruit and texture in the aftertaste and, overall, more dimension.

RATING ★ ★ $

Calem Fine Tawny Porto 20% Alcohol

Standard-issue but attractive, burnished-red color, correct clarity; the nose needs some coaxing, but once released it shows some succulent grapy/oaky/pruney character—as a matter of fact, I greatly admired this compelling bouquet by the third nosing; the palate entry offers a flash of grape intensity that all-too-quickly dissipates by midpalate and vanishes completely by the lame-quacker finish; I was mystified and disappointed by the sudden disappearance of the taste impact; I grudgingly give it a second star because of the focused aroma, but it needs something to complement the bouquet further down the line.

RATING ★ ★ $

Calem Vintage Character Porto 20% Alcohol

Standard purple/crimson color; aromatically, this is not a bonecrusher; true to the typically feline Portuguese producer model, it exhibits ripe figs and tobacco in the modest nose; it comes alive on the palate, showing considerably better fruit concentration than in the nose—the pruney flavors are fresh and vivacious; the medium-length aftertaste is sprinkled with black pepper; mission almost accomplished—the aroma is simply too meek for a recommendation.

RATING ★ ★ $

Calem 1986 Late-Bottled Vintage Porto 20% Alcohol

Medium ruby color; the minty, vegetal, herbal nose offers a toasty foundation of ripe prunes and dried fruit, in particular, apricots; medium-weighted, finely textured, and balanced; it has a sound chocolate/pruney entry onto the tongue, then strays off-center slightly into an unimpressive finish that goes a bit flat and flabby; after a better-than-average bouquet and texture, the taste and aftertaste disappointed—give it more focus in these areas and I'd probably recommend it; it needs more acid to balance the fruit.

RATING ★ ★ $

Calem 1985 Vintage Porto 20% Alcohol

Deep ruby/purple color, which plays host to gathering clouds of miniscule sediment—message: Don't worry, but definitely decant; the nose is closed for business in the early going, showing just the barest hints of old leather and citrus—after being coaxed out after 25 minutes of aeration, the aroma blossoms; on palate, this tasty port is quite muscular, concentrated, and fruit-filled in the flavor, then develops an unwelcome metallic taste in the aftertaste; all the way through I enjoyed the cocoa quality, which almost afforded me enough pleasure on its own to overlook the problem in the finish; evaluated twice and downgraded on the second sampling.

RATING ★ ★ $$$

CALEM 1981 Late-Bottled Vintage Porto/Bottled in 1986 20% Alcohol

Light ruby/tawny color; the nose shows only moderate strawberry fruit at the first nosing, then goes rather limp by the third pass; the flavor begins with a bang at palate entry as zesty, agile tastes of mint and strawberry take the lead, but regrettably the lead crumbles by midpalate as an innocuous, flabby/fleshy flavor takes hold—the suddenly neutral, almost tired fruitiness holds sway well into the aftertaste; after a good start, this port completely unraveled way too soon.

RATING ★ $$

CHURCHILL Finest Vintage-Character Porto 20% Alcohol

Superlative blood-red/crimson/deep-purple tone; this beefy, virile, intense beauty is one of the best Vintage Characters in the marketplace—the trouble is finding it; the deep raspberry/cherry bouquet soars from the sampling glass, filling my tasting room; on palate, intense, dense flavors of ripe blackberry, road tar, and cigar box intensify as they mingle with air; it finishes regally and in a concentrated fruit flurry; this baby is loaded, cocked, and ready to cruise.

RATING ★ ★ ★   *Recommended* $

COCKBURN 1983 Vintage Porto 20% Alcohol

Author's note: Cockburn is one of my favorite port lodges, one whose ports are always a joy to consume.

Impenetrable jet-black/India-ink color, with deep purple edge; the mind-bogglingly intense bouquet of raisins, prune juice, and Havana cigar is a textbook vintage-port nose; this heavy-weighted, cellar-stalking, tannic monster is of epic proportions; it has a chewy, chunky feel and pedal-to-the-metal flavors of black cherries, black currant, and licorice; however, these definitely require more time in bottle to come together; on palate, the truckloads of tannin almost make it undrinkable at the present time; this Arnold Schwarzenegger–like port won't peak until 2010–2015 at the earliest; this is the finest vintage port from Cockburn's since their splendid and unforgettable 1927; it displays the kind of unlimited potential that will greatly reward anyone astute enough to stock up on this classic; lay away a case now.

RATING ★ ★ ★ ★ ★   *Highest Recommendation* $$$

COCKBURN 1991 Vintage Porto / Barrel Sample 20% Alcohol

Youthful, inky-purple hue; right from the first nosing I could tell that this one was going to be a plum/blackberry long-distance race—the engaging ripeness is mesmerizing—the bouquet carries not-so-subtle notes of orange rind and vanilla extract, which only add to the immense pleasure of this well-endowed, precocious aroma; in the mouth, it's surprisingly gentle and behaved—I thought it might be briary and rugged, but it's the perfect gentleman, as the plummy, medium-weighted mouth presence dazzles the palate; the aftertaste is rather lean because of the acidity, but delightful nonetheless; not a tannic monstrosity; I expect that its peak drinking time is only 8–12 years down the pike.

RATING ★ ★ ★ ★   *Highly Recommended* $$

COCKBURN 1987 Quinta do Tua Vintage Porto 20% Alcohol

Stunning blood-red rim and purple core, youthful color; the ambrosial, generous, invigorating nose is flush with ripe black cherries, citrus, and raspberry jam; while it no longer exhibits the intensity of youth on palate, its succulent flavors of figs and plums unleash their remaining vitality through to the fruity, medium-length aftertaste; my guess is that the peak years of this gem will be 2002–2008; an admirable effort from a less-than-thrilling vintage.

RATING ★ ★ ★ ★   ***Highly Recommended*** $$

COCKBURN 1970 Vintage Porto 20% Alcohol

Tasted in Paris, not in my tasting facility; the purple/ruby/crimson color is terribly pretty; typical of the lodge style—not overly big, more stylish than brawny; the slight tobacco quality in the somewhat closed nose is fetching, but ethereal; the evolved flavors of ripe plums and tomato show moderate intensity; sound finish of plums and blackberries; should be drunk now until 2000.

RATING ★ ★ ★   ***Recommended*** $$$

COCKBURN Fine Ruby Porto 20% Alcohol

Medium-to-dark ruby; the vivacious, assertive, ripe, intensely plummy nose is a total joy—the chunkiest bouquet among the frontline rubies of the major houses; the flavor is true to the bouquet, as beefy, meaty tastes of chocolate, tar, and ripe red grapes balance well with the noticeable acid level; it finishes clean, long, and ripe as the grapiness comes to the foreground in the throat; very nice job.

RATING ★ ★ ★   ***Recommended*** $

COCKBURN 10-Year-Old Tawny Porto 20% Alcohol

Lovely copper color, with brass-hued edges; steely, metallic, seed-like aromas burst from the glass, then with swirling, a charming nuttiness emerges; after a mediocre nose, the deliciously ripe and grapy flavor hits you between the eyes—the savory, semidry palate doubtless carries this port with developed flavors of cedar, raisins, and a puckery astringency; the aftertaste lasts long and is fruity but lean; no monster, just a classy, solid tawny.

RATING ★ ★ ★   ***Recommended*** $$

COCKBURN Director's Reserve 20-Year-Old Tawny Porto 20% Alcohol

A true connoisseur's delight; a port maker's port; lovely rust amber color, with a sunset-red edge; slightly closed nose at first, then after 10–15 minutes of aeration a heady, raisiny perfume cuts loose in robust waves; on palate, it offers a satiny texture and medium weight; flavorwise, it's a basket of ripe and somewhat dried fruit, pressed flowers, with a faint hint of butterscotch and old, worn leather; the smoky aftertaste is long and ends stylishly in a nutty fashion.

RATING ★ ★ ★   ***Recommended*** $$

COCKBURN 1992 Quinta dos Canais Vintage Porto 20% Alcohol

Opaque, midnight-black/purple; the aroma is intensely ripe, extremely plummy, and even minty—it's a dazzling, racy bouquet that shows good form and density; the palate entry is solid and tart, with a pronounced taste of black fruit—the texture is medium- to full-weighted—by midpalate, the intriguing, atypical flavor leans heavily toward tobacco leaf and black pepper; the aftertaste is fast but solid in a tart, fresh-fruit manner; unspectacular, but the zesty pepperiness kept my attention.

RATING ★★★ *Recommended* $$

COCKBURN Special Reserve Vintage Character Porto 20% Alcohol

Beautiful ruby/crimson color that picks up the light and plays with it in red starbursts; the potent, alcoholic, youthful nose has nuanced hints of pears, apricots, and dried tropical fruit; the rich, ambrosial, rather forward fruit flavors don't have the depth to further the cause begun in the aroma—what a shame; silky texture; decently pleasant, smooth, and simple, but hardly recommendable.

RATING ★★ $

COCKBURN 1990 Late Bottled Vintage Porto 20% Alcohol

Red-brick/light-purple color; the bouquet doesn't have much to offer other than a faint raisiny, slaty aroma—it's weak in the nose; the thin, watery entry is metallic and stemmy, then fortunately by midpalate it exposes some plumpness in the texture and grapiness in the flavor; it finishes cleanly, but with a mild reemergence of the steeliness/stemminess; the midpalate ended up being the best part of this mediocre LBV, an okay port from the undeclared and completely forgettable 1990 vintage; it just crept across the two-star finish line.

RATING ★★ $$

COCKBURN Fine Tawny Porto 20% Alcohol

Lightish brick/cherry-juice color; the closed-in nose is nowhere near as amiable and open as the splendid ruby's—what happened?; this tawny shows better on the palate than in the lame nose, but at the end of the day it's still a lackluster, paper-thin tawny that just simply doesn't stand up well against its competition.

RATING ★ $

CROFT 1970 Vintage Porto 20% Alcohol

Sampled at a Paris tasting, not in my tasting facility; no featherweight here; rich, purple/blood-red color; the nose is jammy, ripe, and dense; on palate, this port displays a very intense, still vigorous, youthful, deeply concentrated plumminess/pruniness that's succulent and round; the long, viscous finish completes the experience with aplomb; anticipated peak: 2004–2010.

RATING ★★★ *Recommended* $$$

DELAFORCE 1991 Quinta da Corte Vintage Porto 20.5% Alcohol

The nearly opaque purple hue heralds a possible tannic, musclebound monster port; the perfumed nose is totally captivating as supple, sweet aromas of black cherry preserves, glycerine, and ripe grapes wash over the olfactory sense—it's a feminine, mannered bouquet of great elegance; but in the end it's on the palate that this sinewy youngster struts its most impressive stuff in round, rich, finely married tastes of black cherries, chocolate, and truffles; the finish is like liquid satin; bravo, Delaforce; drink from 2007 to 2012.

RATING ★ ★ ★ ★   *Highly Recommended* $$

DELAFORCE His Eminence's Choice Reserve Tawny Porto 19.5% Alcohol

Warm, deep rust/blood color; the coy, but very intriguing nose offers atypical aromas of kiwi, watermelon, perfume, and prunes that somehow work nicely together—my weak complaint is that you have to work hard at cajoling the bouquet to come out and play; quite lean on palate with a glorious taste of bittersweet chocolate that dominates until the quick finish, where flavors of pears, peaches, tea, and cocoa dazzle the taste buds; a delectable tawny that is far from the madding crowd.

RATING ★ ★ ★   *Recommended* $

DELAFORCE 1992 Vintage Porto 20% Alcohol

The gloriously rich purple/grape-juice color announces this port's immaturity; the nose remains coy even after vigorous swirling and aeration—by the fourth nosing a ripe juiciness finally peeks out—the aroma is muted, probably because of its youthfulness; in the mouth, this medium-bodied port comes alive as woodsy, cedary, black-plum flavors enchant the taste buds; it's not overly tannic, which leads me to predict that it will peak early, probably anywhere from 2002 to 2008; the finish is direct, uncomplicated, and easy; hardly brilliant, considering the quality of the vintage, but tasty nonetheless.

RATING ★ ★ ★   *Recommended* $$

DELAFORCE 1987 Late-Bottled Vintage Porto / Bottled in 1993 20% Alcohol

Medium-deep ruby/crimson color; the nose is sedate at first, then with some coaxing emerges in gentle waves of soft tannin, grapes, and red plums; the flavor presence is definitely on the light side but shows ample fruit, plus additional flavors of cocoa, vanilla, and red raspberry; the finish is tidy, clean, and medium-long; if this polite port had more flavor impact, it would have gotten recommended; unfortunately, I see no possibility for further development in the bottle; decent, ordinary, but too light, in keeping with this vintage.

RATING ★ ★ $$

DELAFORCE Full Ruby Porto 19.5% Alcohol

Pretty, medium-deep blood/ruby/crimson tone, excellent clarity; the nose is viney, leafy, and grapy, showing neither notable intensity nor complexity—at the third nosing, an intriguing minty quality showed up, adding a touch of roundness to which I responded favorably; while not a block-buster in the mouth, it's decent, as moderately concentrated, off-dry flavors of tobacco leaf, cherry pit, and red grapes make only a minor, and thus un-satisfactory, impact on the taste buds; strangely, there's virtually no aftertaste to address, making the final impression unforgivably lame; the good ap-pearance and attractive bouquet were not matched or enhanced by the mouth presence.

RATING ★★ $

DELAFORCE 1985 Vintage Porto 20.5% Alcohol

Light-to-medium ruby color, a tad lightish for so spectacular a vintage; the genuinely inviting bouquet was mildly fruity, vegetal (grassy), and even a tad smoky in the initial nosing pass, but unfortunately by the third pass it lost most of its charm and impact as a blandness descended to completely dominate the final nosing; in the mouth, it showed some spark and char-acter in the moderately intense and correct red-plum flavor, then curiously that too faded into oblivion by midpalate, leaving a legacy of paper-thin berry in the finish; in comparison to other evaluated 1985 vintage ports, for instance, the Graham (five stars), Quinta do Noval (four stars), Warre (four stars), Fonseca (four stars) and Taylor Fladgate (four stars), this De-laforce is hollow and already well past its prime; avoid.

RATING ★ $$$

DELAFORCE 1970 Vintage Porto 20% Alcohol

Tasted first in Paris in 1990; not one of my favorites from this great vin-tage; the color is brownish/brackish; the dried-out, somewhat flowery bou-quet is dreadfully meek and unexpressive; in the mouth, it's not as sweet and biscuity as other 1970s—the toasty/roasted quality on palate undercuts the nicer hints of tar and fruit; tasted again in the U.S. last year with very similar impressions; avoid.

RATING ★ $$$

Dow 1983 Vintage Porto 20% Alcohol

Author's note: One of the genuine thoroughbred lodges in the Symington family stable, Dow is, in my opinion, vastly neglected in the U.S. market.

Of the 1983s I've sampled, here is my top choice by a nose for "port of the vintage"; the rich purple/Concord-grape-juice color still leaves the clear impression of raw youth, even though it's nearly a decade and a half old; the nose dazzled the daylights out of me, with wave after wave of raspber-ries, ripe pears, violets, juniper, and even an unusual dash of mintiness—the aromas just seem to wash over you; on palate, it's typically Dow, stylish and elegant, brimming with fruit, which is almost as focused as an eau-de-vie; the tannin level nicely supports the fruit and doesn't dominate even at this relatively early stage; heavyweighted and viscous; while the appearance says otherwise, the nose, flavor, and finish are perhaps the most developed of the 1983s I've sampled; I estimate a peak drinking period of 2000 to 2005; along with the Cockburn, find at all cost, it's well worth it.

RATING ★★★★★   *Highest Recommendation* $$$

Dow Vintage Character Porto 20% Alcohol

Author's note: The classiest, best-balanced vintage character of all. The plum/blood-red/purple color is dazzling; it's an exquisite marriage of elegance and authority in the nose, as scents of toasted bread, roasted almonds, ripe plums, and black cherries harmonize perfectly; on palate, the assertive, meaty flavors highlight the fine balance struck by the dense red-fruit taste and the underlying acidity—it's a masterfully produced mouth presence that's more like a 20-year-old tawny than a mere VC; the finish is unbelievably long, unctuous, and elegant; it's the only vintage character I've tasted that's in the "must have" category; superb.

RATING ★ ★ ★ ★   *Highly Recommended* $

Dow 1992 Quinta do Bomfim Vintage Porto 20% Alcohol

Inky purple color; the nose shoots out of the glass in heady waves of extra ripe grapes, paraffin, black Santa Rosa plums, blackberry jam, and even coffee; on the palate, it's buttery rich, immensely tannic, chewy, and chockful of succulent black-raspberry and black-plum flavors that take no prisoners; the aftertaste is potent, satiny, and continues with all the flavor intensity found in the midpalate; the opulence level of this husky 1992 single-quinta VP is much greater than that found in the more nimble 1991 VP—it's the best Dow VP I've sampled since the blockbuster 1983 (five-star winner); seek out and buy.

RATING ★ ★ ★ ★   *Highly Recommended* $ $

Dow 1991 Vintage Porto 20% Alcohol

Very inky, ruby/purple color, nearly opaque; the aroma is herbal, vinous, and vegetal, showing rather scant evidence of grapes or any other fruit for that matter—I can't say that I was wild over this narrowly focused bouquet even after 15 minutes of aeration; this port flashes its true colors in the mouth, where tightly wound flavors of citrus, raspberries, and red fruit come together in a concentrated, almost astringent, but not abundant manner that's really more clean and agile than generous or buxom; the aftertaste is citrusy and lean, with a flash of cocoa flavor in the tail end; to its credit, this port made up lots of ground in the mouth entry and midpalate.

RATING ★ ★ ★   *Recommended* $ $

Dow 1978 Quinta do Bomfim Vintage Porto 20% Alcohol

Deep, dense plum/blood-red color; the concentrated nose reeks of ripe plum, cedar, and nutmeg—it's not a killer bouquet, but it works; the viscous, thick texture (toothpick variety) is awesome—use a spoon to get it out of the bottle; in the mouth, it's handsome, virile, and mature, with flavors of roasted almonds, smoke, road tar, and intense ripe fruit; surprisingly fast finish for such a hunk of port.

RATING ★ ★ ★   *Recommended* $ $ $

Dow 1970 Vintage Porto 20% Alcohol

Tasted in Paris in 1990, then in my office in 1995; both times I was hoping for a little more depth of character from this producer—that is not to say, however, that I didn't appreciate its finer, more sedate virtues—it doesn't pretend to be a blockbuster; black-as-midnight color, with garnet core highlights; in the nose, it's modestly complex, yet gentlemanly, as aromas of ripe cherries, truffles, and dried flowers carry the day; it's correct, silky on palate, but not very expressive; medium-length, sweet finish; classy, elegant—at its peak now.

RATING ★ ★ ★   *Recommended* $$$

Dow 1989 Quinta do Bomfim Vintage Porto 20% Alcohol

Predictably youthful, purple/Concord-grape-juice color; the full-throttle, ferociously green, jammy, grapy aromas have little focus or direction at this stage of development; flavors of mandarine orange, wax, and spice hang limply in the undirected, precocious palate, which is raw and awkward; the mouth-feel is lean, I thought, though tannic; with bottle age, this still ungainly port may fill out—because of its less-than-sterling vintage, however, I doubt that much improvement will take place; pass on it.

RATING ★ ★ $$

FERREIRA Quinta do Seixo 1983 Vintage Porto 20% Alcohol

A producer who is internationally known more for its aged tawnies, Ferreira has hit the vintage jackpot with this stunning 1983 from their flagship vineyards located on picturesque 75-hectare Quinta do Seixo; the deep purple/plum color is flecked with crimson highlights; heady, focused, pruney aromas gently waft up from the glass in gentle waves; on palate, a piquant flavor of strawberry/rhubarb pie is complemented by some tarriness and faint tobacco backnotes; the tannins don't numb your taste buds, but they let you know they're around in the sleek, surprisingly dry aftertaste that doesn't overstay its welcome; bravo; excellent value.

RATING ★ ★ ★ ★   *Highly Recommended* $$$

FERREIRA Duque de Braganca 20-Year-Old Tawny Porto 20% Alcohol

Inviting russet color; the toasty, grapy, pruney, vanilla-like nose is aggressive but very attractive, especially in the first two nosings; in the mouth, the zesty, feisty black-pepper quality is noted on entry—the taste then settles down into serious, deep flavors of cream, raisins, and prunes, all masterfully balanced by an acidic/citrus counterpoint in the opulent, though not heavy, finish, which seemed to last forever; a supple, willowy aged tawny that brims with finesse, elegance, and character.

RATING ★ ★ ★   *Recommended* $$

FERREIRA Quinta do Porto 10-Year-Old Tawny Porto 19.5% Alcohol

Sexy-looking copper/russet color, with bright cherry-red highlights; the sour-candy-like, raisiny nose is flat and virtually nondescript; medium weight; on palate, the taste leans to dryness on palate entry, then flavors of wood and berries open up at the midpalate, ultimately turning semisweet in the fruity finish; understated to the point of being timid; certainly not in the league of the much better 20-year-old Duque de Braganca from the same producer; don't bother with it.

RATING ★ $$

FERREIRA 1970 Vintage Porto 20% Alcohol

Tasted in Paris; the purple/ruby/garnet color is very attractive; the unexciting, obviously mature, neither overly sweet nor complex nose leaves me completely unimpressed—there's nothing to grip onto; in the mouth, it barely has any flavor whatsoever, just a wimpy dried-fruit quality that lasted about five seconds; the finish is lightning fast; I expected much more from this normally outstanding producer; don't waste your money or time.

RATING ★ $$$

FONSECA

This fabled lodge produces some of the most majestic ports on an enviably regular basis. If the label says "Fonseca," it's almost always a safe bet.

FONSECA 1977 Vintage Porto 21% Alcohol

Deep, deep midnight crimson/ruby color that's one step away from being opaque—a wee bit of harmless sediment showing, so I would decant; remarkably focused, laser-beam aromas of black cherries, prunes, grape pomace, spice, juniper, and cream—so finely layered as to be impenetrable; on palate, the satiny cherry/berry flavors take the taste buds on a memorable romp of finesse, intensity, and power; the endlessly rich, raspberry aftertaste is the equal of the 1985 Graham's (five-star quality); a prime example of why vintage port leads the fortified-wine parade by a wide margin in the minds of average consumers—the unabashed succulence and grandeur of this port make it one of the most magnificent ports in the last two decades; peak drinking period will be 2015–2020; buy at least six bottles.

RATING ★ ★ ★ ★ ★   ***Highest Recommendation*** $$$

FONSECA 1970 Vintage Porto 20% Alcohol

Tasted once in Paris and twice in my office; the opaque appearance is as black as your hat; this is a heady, no-nonsense port of classical proportions; the incredibly deep, dazzling, plummy nose is multidimensional—the second mesmerizing pass reveals a spearmint quality that's highly unusual; on palate, it is warm, chewy, fleshy, and intensely pruney, with faint hints of black pepper, mint, and even violets; it's unabashedly sweet and long in the finish; a dashing, devil-may-care beauty that's densely fruity and irresistibly spirity; I'd cellar two or three bottles to pop open at the turn of the century.

RATING ★ ★ ★ ★   ***Highly Recommended*** $$$

FONSECA 1985 Vintage Porto 20.5% Alcohol

Fabulous deep-purple/ruby color that looks like a textbook example of a great vintage port; the nose is layered, clean, and almost tart, giving off hints of grapes, oak, and vanilla wafer right from the first pass; on the palate, the tartness departs and is replaced by sharp, well-defined flavors of perfectly ripe plums, plums that still have plenty of keen acids, but more than ample ripeness; the finish is almost austere at first, then a shot of intense plumminess takes you home in an appealing red-fruit aftertaste; predicted peak is 2004–2010.

RATING ★ ★ ★ ★   ***Highly Recommended*** $$$

FONSECA 1983 Vintage Porto 20.5% Alcohol

Deep ruby/purple/plum hue; the nose is so supple and potent that you almost want to scoop it out with a spoon—the fragrant red-berry-fruit aroma is luscious and well defined; on the palate, the high-gear tannins still pack plenty of punch, yet form the crucial structural underpinning for the sensational fruit components, which impress the taste buds with their firmness; the finish is sweet, succulent, elegant, and simply delicious; while the 1983s from Dow and Cockburn (five-star quality) still rank as my favorites from this underappreciated vintage, this sinewy Fonseca hovers in third place; drink between 2007 and 2012 if you can wait that long.

RATING ★ ★ ★ ★   ***Highly Recommended*** $$$

FONSECA 1988 Late Bottled Vintage Porto / Bottled in 1994; 20% Alcohol

Deep crimson core, youthful purple rim; this tantalizing nose emits seductive scents of pepper, flora, and red fruit, then with aeration the bouquet mysteriously vanishes—I was shocked by the aroma's quick exit; the real story on this port is told by the succulent, medium-bodied taste that delights and excites the palate with high-flying flavors of chocolate-covered cherries, spice, and wood—it's a taste sensation that coddles the taste buds; the aftertaste is short-lived; but it's a good ride of fruit all the same; skip the nose and just drink.

RATING ★ ★ ★   ***Recommended*** $$

FONSECA Bin 27 Vintage Character Porto 20% Alcohol

It's a seriously pretty purple/ruby tone, with blood-red core highlights; the very aromatic nose is swept by powerful waves of ripe fruit—a discernable dash of spiciness really makes the bouquet stand out; on palate, it comes off as being way too sweet as an out-of-control ripeness throttles the taste buds silly; the aftertaste is medium-long and laced with orange peel and nutmeg; tone down the sweetness at midpalate and it might be recommendable, but not like this.

RATING ★ ★ $

FONSECA Tawny Porto 20% Alcohol

Red-brick/tawny color, with pink core highlights; the amply endowed, sweet, forward nose of red raspberry preserves and ripe orange is mildly pleasant—there's a hint of casaba melon in the third and fourth nosings; on palate, this tawny owns a toasty, smoky/wood-fire quality that's quite atypical and very appealing; the fruit component isn't the leading factor in this pleasant tawny at all, though a rich, ripe grapiness emerges in the finish; I responded favorably to the earthy/smoky quality that's present from beginning to end, but the aroma could use some high-octane petrol.

RATING ★ ★ $

FONSECA Siroco White Porto 20% Alcohol

Brilliant, beautiful flaxen/gold hue; the perfumy, grapy nose is soft and has mild foundational aromas of pistachio nuts and banana cream pie; on palate, the dry to off-dry flavor is unfortunately a one-note melody, sporting a bland taste of cardboard—it starts dry at palate entry, then goes off-dry in the midpalate, ending up parchment-dry in the throat; my guess is that the most appropriate application for this uninspiring port is as a mixer with seltzer, ice, and a twist of lemon, served prior to meals; serve well chilled if you happen to get stuck with it.

RATING ★ $

FONSECA **Ruby Porto 20% Alcohol**
Deep ruby/purple color; the hopelessly restrained, reined-in, mildly plummy, fig-like nose barely shows its face even after 25 minutes of aeration and swirling—who needs this?—the satiny smooth texture slinks onto the tongue as the moderately sweet, but understated, taste of plums takes control of the palate; it finishes quietly, as soft echoes of figs and citrus fade on the back of the throat; I had hoped for a better entry-level port from Fonseca than this limp noodle.

RATING ★ $

FONSECA **Guimaraens 1991 Vintage Porto (2nd label of Fonseca) 20.5% Alcohol**
Opaque, midnight-purple/black color; the multilayered nose emits confident aromas of bread dough, blackberries, black currant, plum preserves, pepper, and even a splash of nutmeg—it's a superb, vivacious port nose; medium- to full-bodied, this gorgeous, complex creation lies on the tongue like morning dew on a pasture—it's brimming with ripe plum and blackberry flavors that grow in complexity in the swank, racy aftertaste; drink from 2007 to 2012.

RATING ★ ★ ★ ★   Highly Recommended $$

FONSECA **Guimaraens 1976 Vintage Porto (2nd label of Fonseca) 21% Alcohol**
Impenetrable purple color; the rugged nose is all mint, cedar, tannin, and cassis—it's a massive nose that highlights the cedar/woody element all the way through to the final nosing; on the palate, it's so tannic still that I can almost feel the enamel being stripped off my teeth—but the underlying flavors of ripe black cherry, blackberry, and black currant are complex, delicious, and daunting all at the same time; the finish is as massive as the midpalate; buy a half case and store in the cellar—projected peak 2010–2015.

RATING ★ ★ ★ ★   Highly Recommended $$

FONSECA **Guimaraens 1978 Vintage Porto (2nd label of Fonseca) 21% Alcohol**
Medium ruby/purple tone; this mature, vegetal nose is spiced, stemmy, and altogether delightful—I find the spicy backnote irresistible as it evolves with aeration into a jammy, red-raspberry perfume; the palate presence is medium-bodied in structure and offers a two-tiered flavor impression of black cherry for the surface taste and oak and tannin as the more nuanced underlying taste; the aftertaste is lightish and clean, with a mere hint of cherry fruit; don't wait too long—drink now until 2000.

RATING ★ ★ ★   Recommended $$

GOULD-CAMPBELL 1977 Vintage Porto 20.5% Alcohol

Textbook, deep purple/crimson hue, with medium-heavy sediment—decanting is absolutely necessary; the nose is leafy, vinous, almost vegetal, and peppery upfront, with backnotes of violets, rose petal, and cedar; the heavenly flavor is better and more forward than the nose, as jammy raspberry and plum flavors grip the palate firmly—a viscous, chunky, but totally harmonious 1977 that's the best this oft-neglected port lodge has to offer; if you're searching for a big-boned, fleshy port that just keeps coming at you, stop right here; destined to peak between 2010 and 2015.

RATING ★★★★   ***Highly Recommended*** $$$

GOULD-CAMPBELL 1985 Late-Bottled Vintage Porto 20% Alcohol

Clean, clear, medium-ruby color; the woody, pine-forest nose has layers of paraffin and caraway-seed aromas, which are underscored by an intriguing and highly unusual grassiness/leafiness—it's atypical and singular, but very appealing; this primed LBV presents itself admirably at palate entry with sweet flavors of grapes and plums—not heavyhanded a bit, this is a nimble, medium-weighted port that finishes quietly in a very mannered style—the extra years of wood-aging in oak are clearly evident in the aftertaste; considering the robust nature of the vintage, this savory discovery is an undemanding port that, while hardly classical, shines much brighter than several of the true vintage ports of the same vintage; seek out and drink now.

RATING ★★★   ***Recommended*** $$

GOULD-CAMPBELL 1985 Vintage Porto 20% Alcohol

Very deep purple color, with ruby edges—no sediment to speak of; the exceedingly ripe but fresh nose shows wee bits of tobacco, smoke, and nail polish remover; has a medium-to-full presence that's classy and alluringly graceful; the reserved, finely melded, medium-weighted flavor centers mainly on prunes, but it does have an underlying citrus quality that serves to balance the intense fruitiness; it finishes well but, like the nose and flavor, seems meek for the vintage; I suspect that its sedate posture is more a case of this elegant wine needing more time in bottle than a case of the wimps; as it is, a better-than-average effort that scores admirably for its sheer elegance; drink now until 2004.

RATING ★★★   ***Recommended*** $$$

GOULD-CAMPBELL 1983 Vintage Porto 20% Alcohol

Medium-deep ruby/crimson tone; the initial pass at the nose is disappointing, as it seems shut down, except for minute portions of mint, black pepper, vines, and metal after 15 minutes of aeration and swirling—the aroma simply refuses to emerge—so be it; on the palate, it's medium-weighted and restrained as the modest fruit element bows to the acid—it's a pleasant, middle-of-the-pack port that will never be a bruiser or a charmer; it finishes cleanly, without fanfare; good and correct, but hardly memorable or recommendable; peak is now until 2002.

RATING ★★ $$

GOULD-CAMPBELL 1980 Vintage Porto 20.5% Alcohol

Opaque black, with purple/cherry edges; the strongly vinous, woodsy, and vegetal nose throws out unusual but pleasant aromas of pine, dried leaves, and mushrooms; on palate, it's a shade shy of being downright elegant, as composed, mannered flavors of tannin, overripe grapes, and plums entertain the taste buds in style; the aftertaste falls short and is something of a disappointment after the rousing nose and flavor; although it's decent, I can't get too excited about it, mainly because I felt it held back too much; it may grow more in the bottle, however—it will be interesting to come back to by the turn of the century.

RATING ★★　　$$

GOULD-CAMPBELL 1975 Vintage Porto 20.5% Alcohol

Mature, medium brick/tawny color; the subdued nose is of modest virtue, stingily offering meager hints of black pepper, strawberries, and tired spice; it's most definitely on the lighter side of the character spectrum as the featherweight tannins simply don't have the stuffing to buoy the pleasing berry flavor; the quicksilver finish falls right off the palate like a stone off a cliff; an unexciting port from a fair, but past-its-peak vintage; don't bother with it; requiescat en pace.

RATING ★　　$$

GRAHAM 1985 Vintage Porto 20% Alcohol

Author's note: Perhaps the brightest jewel in the Symington family crown, Graham is responsible for some of my top port experiences.

Miniscule suspended particles pose no problem as long as this viscous port is decanted—impenetrable, midnight-purple/inky black color, with a deep crimson rim; the unbelievably concentrated and focused nose of blackberry jam, black cherries, peppermint and prunes is a classic—a once-in-a-generation bouquet that is simultaneously generous, graceful, potent, yet civil; after the first tasting I'm forced to ask, can vintage port get any suppler or grander than this?—the fourth-gear flavors of cake batter, vanilla, oak, prunes, cocoa, and spearmint explode on the palate; the finish is regal, refined, and decidedly jammy and tannic, but never is it overwhelming; this legend doubtless owns the most stately bearing of the spectacular 1985s; a classic destined to provide many memorable moments for fortunate drinkers for another half century; if you are to buy just one 1985 vintage port, make it this one; do not drink before 2020—why experience it before its prime?

RATING ★★★★★　　*Highest Recommendation*　　$$$

GRAHAM 1983 Vintage Porto 20% Alcohol

Nearly opaque black/purple color; the slightly medicinal, herbal, grapy, vinous, blueberry nose is both compact and closed perhaps because of its youth—afterall, this was a tannic vintage; medium- to heavy-weighted; the wonderful, satiny texture is immensely appealing; in the mouth, it's very tannic, showing as yet unfocused flavors of oranges and spice (primarily black pepper)—an obviously green and unruly youngster yet; this one requires time, probably another 15 years before all the components meld; it's worth noting that at this stage it does not appear to be the succulent blockbuster à la '85 or '77; it is tightly wrapped right now, but what an inviting, savory package of elegance and style to own while it opens gradually with maturity; projected peak 2012–2017.

RATING ★ ★ ★ ★   *Highly Recommended* $$$

GRAHAM 1977 Vintage Porto 20.7% Alcohol

Medium-deep ruby color, with scant evidence of sediment; the subdued, narrowly focused nose of lead pencil, spice, and plums doesn't set the olfactory sense on fire, but it is appealing; the palate immediately shifts into passing gear as lush chocolate flavors detonate on the palate, then quickly subside into a serene, fruity aftertaste that is very long and sweet; not the tannic, chunkmeister style that both Taylor Fladgate and Gould Campbell present for the vintage, but nevertheless a beautifully balanced, composed port of enormous charm that will speak between 2010 and 2015.

RATING ★ ★ ★ ★   *Highly Recommended* $$$

GRAHAM 1970 Vintage Porto 20% Alcohol

Tasted first in Paris, then properly evaluated in my office in 1994; India-ink, black/dense-purple appearance, decant to dispose of the sediment; this 1970 thriller presents the drinker with layer upon luscious layer of ripe but whistle-clean plum/black-cherry/ripe-tomato fruit in both the bouquet and the taste; a slightly spicy, very concentrated, reminiscent-of-vanilla port that will require an additional 15–20 years before reaching its peak in and around 2015–2020; a genuine treasure that will reward port aficionados for decades to come.

RATING ★ ★ ★ ★   *Highly Recommended* $$$

GRAHAM 1991 Vintage Porto 20% Alcohol

Medium dark, ruby/purple hue; thus plump nose has the trademark ripeness of Graham's best efforts—the chewy, chalky, red-fruit, red-grape opulence conquers the nasal cavity on the first nosing pass—unquestionably a lovely as well as elegant bouquet; the palate entry is rich, intensely ripe, and even shows a dash of Belgian dark chocolate—the midpalate textural sensations are truly delightful, as a soft, but firm and directed richness caresses the taste buds; the finish is every bit as deep, layered, and graceful as the midpalate taste; a cellar-worthy port; projected peak is 2015–2020.

RATING ★ ★ ★ ★   *Highly Recommended* $$$

GRAHAM 1988 Malvedos Vintage Porto 20% Alcohol

Now here's a single quinta of a different color—brilliant crimson/purple color; the staggeringly deep, multifaceted nose exhibits showy highlights of spicy freshly ground black pepper, ripe blackberries, and bittersweet chocolate; the velvet-like, sensuous texture makes this thoroughbred slither down the throat; dense, concentrated fruit and chocolate flavors explode on palate; the gorgeous, opulent aftertaste of orange rind, cocoa, and toffee bring an elegant closure to the entire experience; lovely from start to finish; projected peak is 2010–2015.

RATING ★ ★ ★ ★   *Highly Recommended* $$$

GRAHAM 20-Year-Old Tawny Porto 20% Alcohol

Sample bottle showed a mildly cloudy, somewhat turbid tawny/amber color (is it unfiltered?) that I personally would not consider life-threatening but that nonetheless may be viewed by picky consumers as having a problem—a second bottle exhibited the identical cloudiness; the opulent, generous nose emitted scents of vanilla extract, blueberries, and orange rind—a good bouquet, but one that lacked depth and dimension; graceful bearing on palate; light- to medium-bodied; road-tar, cigar-like entry flavors give way to pruney/plummy flavors in dry, candied, and fruity aftertaste; this graceful 20-year-old would have scored higher if not for questionable appearance; excellent nose was a real plus that saved the day.

RATING ★ ★ ★   *Recommended* $$

GRAHAM 30-Year-Old Tawny Porto 20% Alcohol

The best appearance of the Graham aged tawnies—luxurious, tawny/garnet color that flashes blood-red highlights in the core; the solid, remarkably sweet bouquet includes deep-rooted fragrances of dark chocolate/hot cocoa, overripe plums, and hazelnuts—I found this expressive nose to be charming but superficial; in the mouth, the texture coats the tongue like paint as well-developed flavors of dark toffee, nougat, semisweet chocolate, and raisins occupy the taste buds; the aftertaste is sound, but approaches being cloying; not for those people who detest unctuous tawny port.

RATING ★ ★ ★   *Recommended* $$$

GRAHAM 1992 Malvedos Vintage Porto 20% Alcohol

As black as your hat—throws some sediment, therefore decant; the atypical bouquet comes off a bit vegetal and metallic, perhaps even a tad too woody in the first three nosings—this being a cask sample, I would have hoped that the minerally odor had been worked out by the time bottling came around; once in the mouth, however, the unbridled lushness found in the texture and the classically proportioned flavors of berries, grapes, hot cocoa, and gigantic tannins savored in the taste promise enough to redeem the deficiency of the aroma, which may indeed be only a misstep of youth—nevertheless, I'm holding back on a fourth star until I taste the bottled version; this potential charmer should, in time, be larger in scale than the sumptuous Graham 1991 VP.

RATING ★ ★ ★   *Recommended* $$

GRAHAM Six Grapes Vintage Character Porto 20% Alcohol

Black/purple color, nearly opaque; the incredibly rich, jammy nose offers hints of cream and vanilla, which underpin the outlandishly ambrosial cherry/berry bombast; on palate, intense, overripe blackberry flavors mingle with backnotes of coffee bean, tobacco, and ripe pears; viscous, satiny texture and heavy bearing; your basic cornucopia of fruit concentration; the lengthy, almost cloying finish ends on a solid note of blackberry; I think that this port has too much preserve-like, ultrajammy fruit; not everybody's cup of jam; give me more acid for balance.

RATING ★ ★ $

Graham 1984 Late-Bottled Vintage Porto 20% Alcohol

Lovely ruby/cherry-juice color; the restrained nose offers mild aromas of spice and citrus—nothing earth-shattering in the nose; medium-weighted, chunky texture; in the mouth, the ripe, plummy, grapy fruit tastes greet the palate, simply and without fanfare; it's clearly lacking in acid as the fruit dominates the entire mouth experience; unsatisfyingly quick finish; perfect for those who relish viscous, fat, chewy, densely fruited port; to me, it's off-balance.

RATING ★ ★ $$

Graham 1986 Malvedos Vintage Porto 20% Alcohol

This is a Malvedos that I was deeply disappointed in; it owns a bright, blood-red/ruby color; it's floral, spicy, and racy in the nose, which is duly noted and appreciated; on palate, however, it's woefully light, still too youthful, and, strangely, exhibits little vigor in the muted flavors of plums, prunes, and cherries; unenthusiastic and limp in the aftertaste; flabby and wayward, without the expected Graham style that marries power and finesse; while not undrinkable, very poor by Graham standards; the sterling 1988 Malvedos ran it off the table.

RATING ★ $$

Graham 1978 Malvedos Vintage Porto 20% Alcohol

Proper, though mature, plum/ruby color with a slightly orange rim; the lean, clean, and rather simple, straightforward bouquet of prunes and blackberries just fails to impress—there's no other way to put it; lightweight texture; on palate, the chocolate, cocoa, coffee, and road-tar flavors are mildly intriguing, but that's as far as it goes; the fast-forward finish possesses minimal flavor impact and, thus, doesn't end the experience well; forget it, they blew it on this one.

RATING ★ $$

Kopke 1983 Vintage Porto 20% Alcohol

Rich plum core color, with brick/purple edge—it throws off large amounts of infinitesimal sediment—consequently, I strongly recommend first letting this bottle stand upright for a day before decanting; the somewhat restrained, shy nose opens after ten minutes and is measured and modest, offering mild saddle-leather and prune aromas; medium-weighted; in the mouth, it shows a nice, round, fruity presence without being aggressive or unctuous; berry-like flavors emerge in the medium-length finish; an average port—I kept waiting for more character and flavor.

RATING ★ ★ $$$

Niepoort 1992 Vintage Porto 20.5% Alcohol

Royal purple core, with a red-cherry rim; on the nose, it's quietly potent, neither a screamer nor overripe—it's a subdued, polite, gentlemanly bouquet that had me sold by the second nosing—focused and courteous; while the nose is sound, but low key, the mouth presence is anything but, as high-flying, intensely ripe-plum, prune, and raisin flavors devour the palate; the aftertaste is sweet, but nearly as understated as the bouquet; a top-notch beauty with a predicted peak of between 2010 and 2020.

   RATING ★ ★ ★ ★   *Highly Recommended* $$$

NIEPOORT 1983 Vintage Porto 20% Alcohol

Very pretty, brilliant crimson color, with a cherry rim; tasted in Vila Nova de Gaia, Portugal; initially, it's a soft nose, then after 15 minutes ambrosia deluxe breaks loose as all sorts of fruit aromas come to the fore—bananas, apricots, and strawberries mostly; this is a gentlemanly port of medium weight and moderate tannins; on palate, the fruit salad continues, with the lovely addition of a savory creaminess that I found beguiling; extended finish of—you guessed it—ripe fruit; a pleasantly sweet, clean vintage port that you won't have to wait around for; drink now until 2004.

   RATING ★ ★ ★   *Recommended* $$$

NIEPOORT 1987 Vintage Porto 20.5% Alcohol

Plum-like color; the slightly weedy, cherry/plum, piquant nose offers an unwelcome hint of medicine cabinet in the background; the expectedly aggressive, vigorous, fruity, plummy/pruney flavors present a moderately appealing taste experience; mild heat in the extended finish; what it lacks in finesse it makes up for in potency; I estimate a peak period of 1999 to 2002; fair.

   RATING ★ ★ $$$

OFFLEY Boa Vista 1970 Vintage Porto 20% Alcohol

Tasted in Paris only; though I have little experience with them, I'm told that Offley-Forrester consistently produces some of the best values in vintage port; this declared vintage edition is a medium-bodied, nicely fruited, moderately sweet port that provides a pleasant romp in the short term; average at best; take a pass on it in favor of other '70s like Graham, Fonseca, or Quarles Harris.

   RATING ★ ★ $$$

OSBORNE 1992 Vintage Porto 20.5% Alcohol

Rich, ripe, purple tone; this sweet, comely nose is a quantum leap ahead of the pallid nose of the dried-up 1991 edition—pronounced red-fruit aromas come at you in waves; on the palate, the multilayered taste offers glycerin, cassis, blackberry, honey, and plum flavors—the texture is opulent and ropy; the aftertaste is long, tannic, lively, and fresh; the difference between this svelte, stylish, and dense Osborne 1992 and the dismal 1991 is startling; projected peak is from 2005 to 2010; buy and cellar.

   RATING ★ ★ ★ ★   *Highly Recommended* $$$

OSBORNE 1991 Vintage Porto 20.5% Alcohol

Medium-deep purple core, ruby/blood-red rim; during the first two nosings the aroma is fabric-like, mushroomy, dusty, dried-fruit-like and peculiar, then in the third pass it picks up the pace and shows moderate depth of character as the dried-fruit element deepens; in the mouth, the sour plum flavor goes nowhere—the taste is not as bad or offensive as it is lackluster and pedestrian—it severely lacks fruit and, as a result, is way too top-heavy in acid and tannin—at midpalate, there's a flash of chocolate-covered strawberries that saves it from being a one-star loser; not representative of this splendid vintage.

RATING ★ ★ $$$

PRESIDENTIAL 1991 Vintage Porto 20% Alcohol

Inky-purple/crimson color; the deep, voluptuous bouquet is ribboned with layers of chocolate, tobacco, prunes, black raspberry, bread dough, and spice—it's a robust nose that accurately reflects the heartiness of this superb vintage; in the mouth, the ripe, juicy flavors of black fruit (especially black currants and blackberries) envelop the taste buds like a blanket—this is, I believe, the most luscious mouth presence of the Presidential ports that I've sampled; in the finish, a considerable portion of the lushness gets waylaid by too much acid; this entry would have been my first four-star Presidential save for the unexpected and unwelcome note of bitterness in the aftertaste.

RATING ★ ★ ★   *Recommended* $$

PRESIDENTIAL 20-Year-Old Tawny Porto 20% Alcohol

This tawny color shows a lot more redness than the 10-year-old; the aromas of vanilla extract, apples, ripe bananas, nuts, and spice need plenty of aeration and some nasal gymnastics to be fully examined, but once they open up they are harmonious and enjoyable; this is a sleek, galloping thoroughbred on palate, with an opulent, finely balanced nutty/fruitiness; the leisurely aftertaste holds its own with most of the 20-year-olds from the major port lodges; well-structured, ideally balanced, and elegant, this port serves to further my belief that 20-year-old tawnies offer the best combination of age and vigor in the superpremium tawny category.

RATING ★ ★ ★   *Recommended* $$

PRESIDENTIAL 30-Year-Old Tawny Porto 20% Alcohol

Mature brown color; the settled, married aromas of honey-roasted cashews and caramel are solid and enchanting; on palate, the initial flavor impression is rich and quite sweet—after a few seconds the sweetness subsides, allowing the intense, candied, cashew/walnut flavor to shine through; it finishes sweetly and with considerably greater viscosity than the 20-year-old; while this tawny's richness is very alluring, I marginally prefer the overall balance of the Presidential 20-year-old.

RATING ★ ★ ★   *Recommended* $$$

PRESIDENTIAL 10-Year-Old Tawny Porto 20% Alcohol

Lovely chestnut-brown/tawny color, with copper highlights; the subdued, but potent, butter-cream bouquet offers an evergreen/cedar second layer after 15 minutes of aeration; in the mouth, it comes off as being dry initially—then candied, toffee-like, and very clean flavors kick into gear at midpalate; it ends on feminine, tropical-fruit, roasted-almond notes that are moderately attractive in their directness and simplicity; a nice aged tawny that doesn't feign greatness, is agreeable, unpretentious, but average.

RATING ★ ★ $$

PRESIDENTIAL White Porto 20% Alcohol

Deep gold/honey/amber color; distinct butterscotch, one-dimensional nose; on palate entry, a pleasing, nutty, semisweetness greets the taste buds—a tangy, benign, almondy dryness controls the midpalate and follows through to the rather well-focused aftertaste; has too much residual sugar to be a strict aperitif, but it can be served as a chilled cocktail with finger foods; as with virtually all white ports I've evaluated, it doesn't hold a candle to a fino, manzanilla, or amontillado sherry as an appetite stimulant, however.

RATING ★ $

PRESIDENTIAL Ruby Porto 20% Alcohol

Proper ruby/blood-red color; the mild, soft, fruity nose displays a slight cinnamon spiciness; it has an oddly neutral entry, where the acid is easily detected, but any evidence of fruit is left standing at the door—the fruit, which is spare (unusual for a ruby), finally arrives in the throat at the meager, lily-livered finish; so simple and basic as to be invisible and very disappointing; the acid foundation desperately needs more of a fruit counterbalance.

RATING ★ $

PRESIDENTIAL Tawny Porto 20% Alcohol

Very attractive, cherry/brick-red/wine-like color, with a tawny/gold edge; the delicate yet rich aromas are reminiscent of citrus, pineapple, and spice—it's a mildly lively and pleasant aromatic presence; on palate, it has a zesty, peppery, vivacious flavor component that is sweet on entry, then goes dry at the back of the palate; the pepperiness reemerges in the off-dry finish; simple, but offers some fundamental flavor intrigue.

RATING ★ $$

PRESIDENTIAL 40-Year-Old Tawny Porto 21% Alcohol

Medium-brown/cherry-cola color; the shy, fatigued nose, which even after 45 minutes of aeration showed nothing more than a meek oakiness, is so obviously over-the-hill that it's embarrassing; on palate, this senior citizen has unquestionably seen a better day—however, to its defense, I must add that some people greatly relish this type of oxidized, decrepit wine; it presents no challenge and is neither complex nor interesting, but it still offers some evidence of structure via the caramelly finish; no surviving fruit to be had; port producers should know when to bury the dead; with tawny ports 30 years is beginning to push it; a mere shadow of what it used to be.

RATING ★ $$$

PRESIDENTIAL 1985 Vintage Porto 20% Alcohol

The slightly turbid, milky-purple color simply doesn't cut the mustard; insignificant amount of sediment; the dried-fruit-like, austere, and stemmy nose has undertones of leather and lees; off-dry and uninspiring in the mouth; it ends with quite a rush of tartness, then a very pleasant fruitiness, which is extended and elegant; the overall impression is of a mildly complex port that is lean for the vintage and that is struggling for an identity; its lone strong point is the savory aftertaste; a drinkable, but ultimately deficient port whose appearance is troublesome, whose bouquet is too vegetal, whose flavor is mundane, but whose finish tries hard to redeem the whole lot.

RATING ★ $$

PRESIDENTIAL 1977 Vintage Porto 20% Alcohol

Frightfully light in appearance for such a big, tannic vintage; the nose of black pepper and pine needle is mildly pleasant, but lacking in grip, stuffing, and panache; it's too skimpy, brassy, and breezy in the mouth and finish; if this were a port from another, less grand vintage it would be acceptable—but within the context of such a legendary vintage, this slender port is entirely unacceptable; this port lodge mystifies me completely, routinely pumping out thin, watery, below-average ports of little distinction and character.

RATING ★ $$

QUARLES HARRIS 1970 Vintage Porto 20% Alcohol

This is one that surprised me the most at the Paris tasting; it was an absolutely beguiling, full-throttle port with a blood-red/inky-purple color; the downright jammy (blackberries), intense nose is lovely, virile, and muscle-bound; on palate, the generous, hearty, lush flavors and texture fill the mouth with their vivacity and creaminess; outstanding aftertaste is jam-packed with black-fruit richness; the bad news is that it may be difficult to track down in the U.S.

RATING ★ ★ ★ ★   *Highly Recommended* $$$

QUINTA DO CRASTO 1985 Vintage Porto 20% Alcohol

Nearly opaque, deep purple robe, with a brick-colored rim, minor sediment; the intensely grapy, perfumed nose is shy at first pass—20 minutes of aeration helped only minimally with the bouquet's projection; it has a round, chewy, fleshy feel in the mouth; the sweet, jammy flavor is pleasant, but it's also a one-note song—all grapiness and nothing beyond that; the finish is full but goes tart in the tail; I think that the dedicated Quinta do Crasto people (I had the pleasure of visiting them in the Douro in 1990) are doing a good job, but they need to work on complexity of flavor, not just flavor power; this is a barely decent vintage port that displays promise for the small estate-bottling producers who against conventional wisdom age their ports right in the Douro.

RATING ★ $$

QUINTA DO INFANTADO 1983 Vintage Porto 20% Alcohol

Very dark, almost opaque purple, with a ruby edge—throwing off tons of chunky sediment deposits—absolutely must be decanted prior to pouring; viscous, flabby bearing; the sweet, ripe-plum nose exposes a very faint acid/road-tar/almost bitter quality that is a disaster; the rich, unctuous, potent entry leads to midpalate flavors of plums and berries that are nicely melded, but they don't venture past that into any form of complexity; the gentle finish is mildly fruity, then it vanishes altogether just like the 1984 LBV; there is no question that this style represents a serious departure from the established port norm; while I mildly enjoyed the plummy flavor, I failed to find the necessary complexity from nose to aftertaste to make this a better-than-average vintage port.

RATING ★★ $$$

QUINTA DO INFANTADO Late-Bottled Vintage Porto 1983; 20% Alcohol

Reddish/tawny color, with a copper core; the pronounced, though nonaggressive, aromas of raisins and plums fail to take me to the top of the mountain; medium-weighted and moderately viscous; it does own a pleasing bearing on palate; it's nicely structured and balanced between mild fruitness and alcohol—the attractive plummy flavor at entry that gives way to a cream-like taste just before its fast, light finish; not what I'd describe as an opulent, fine, or generous port by any means; more than ready to drink right now; a modest LBV that gives ample, if uninspiring, pleasure.

RATING ★★ $$

QUINTA DO INFANTADO Late-Bottled Vintage Porto 1984; 20% Alcohol

Considerably darker crimson/purple/blood color than the 1983 LBV; aromatically muted at first, then with 15 minutes of aeration the nose opens up, exposing steely, old-saddle-leather, and pruney scents—an unexciting bouquet of little dimension; light-weighted, meandering demeanor; the uncomplicated, fleeting flavors of mild vanilla extract, banana, raspberry, and pear hold promise but virtually no charm; the quicksilver, feathery aftertaste vanished after 60 seconds; "ethereal" is a descriptive term that pops into my head; "simple" is another.

RATING ★ $$

QUINTA DO NOVAL LB Vintage Character Porto 20% Alcohol

Mysteriously, I rarely see this sinewy thoroughbred on any retailer's shelf; tasted both in Portugal and in my office—it blew me away both times; the rich purple/ruby color is dazzling and clean—little sediment; the racy, intense, grapy nose barrels out of the glass like a race horse out of the gate at the Derby; on palate, the lush, pruney, crushed-violets-from-your-yearbook flavors and texture wrap around the taste buds; the floral, dusty, elegant finish lingers for a remarkably long period; this beauty tops many a vintage port in terms of flavor focus and elegance, let alone other vintage characters; superb port making that may well be, along with Dow Vintage Character, the best bargain in all of port; wow.

RATING ★★★★   *Highly Recommended* $

QUINTA DO NOVAL 20-Year-Old Tawny Porto 20% Alcohol

New copper-penny/amber/rust color; the positively smashing nose is sprinkled with fetching fragrances of cream, ripe grapiness, and freshly ground black pepper that blend together in style; medium-weighted, slinky, feline texture—beautifully balanced on palate; the ideal, ambrosial combination of ripe, raisiny fruit, English toffee, roasted hazelnuts, butterscotch, and spice; pleasantly sweet, milk chocolate, elegant finish that coats the throat absolutely knocked me out; this is a high-toned, majestic winner that vintage port lovers should get intimately acquainted with a.s.a.p.

RATING ★★★★   **Highly Recommended** $$

QUINTA DO NOVAL 1991 Vintage Porto 20.5% Alcohol

Black-as-midnight appearance, completely opaque; the nose is vinous and not in the least vivid, flirtatious, or revealing, as slight traces of black cherry, black raspberry, black plum, dough, and clove lurk in the bouquet's background; in the mouth, this complex beauty becomes a serious seductress, as captivating, ropy, round flavors and textures take the willing taste buds prisoner—the layered, substantial mouth presence is decadent, jammy, gigantically tannic, and luscious as wave after wave of black fruit, vanilla, and wood overwhelm the palate; a wall-to-wall mouthful of succulent, tannic port; long, chunky finish; massive, long-lived, and one to have six bottles of in your cellar; projected peak: 2015–2020.

RATING ★★★★   **Highly Recommended** $$

QUINTA DO NOVAL 1985 Vintage Porto 20% Alcohol

Very clean, unremarkable, medium purple color; the generous nose of ripe grapes, black pepper, olives, lead pencil, vanilla, and raisins provides a multilayered, harmonious bouquet of the first rank; it possesses a compelling, luxurious, and satiny feel; on palate, the dark-chocolate, dried-apricot, coffee, off-dry flavors merge in the lush aftertaste in a heavenly, concentrated crescendo of succulent taste; a sinewy, straightforward, no-nonsense port where so many of the '85s are plump and corpulent; bravo, Noval, as always, a superior product; this port lodge continues to be one of the top three or four producers vintage after vintage, port after port. Drink from 2005 to 2010.

RATING ★★★★   **Highly Recommended** $$$

QUINTA DO NOVAL 10-Year-Old Tawny Porto 20% Alcohol

Russet core color, with a tawny rim; the full, bountiful nose is an interesting and pleasing mix of bread dough, oxidation, cardboard, and papaya—it keeps you guessing as to what's coming next; on palate, it exhibits a sensuous silkiness on the tongue, followed by smoky/plummy flavors that go full-throttle into a lusciously sweet, grapy aftertaste that tops off this altogether lovely tawny in grand style; it doesn't feign having the depth of a 20-year-old, but it is one of the more comely, settled, and savory 10-year-old aged tawnies.

RATING ★★★   **Recommended** $$

QUINTA DO NOVAL 1982 Vintage Porto 20.9% Alcohol

Medium crimson/purple, with a mature tawny rim—mildly turbid in the core; it's lean, shy, and closed down in the nose in the first two passes, then after 20 minutes of aeration it offers enticing aromas of mint, citrus, and spice in strictly measured amounts; it's true to the vintage in the flavor department, lacking in tannin, but sweet and fruity; the finish travels nowhere special; overall, probably the worst Noval I've judged; I venture that it's some years past its prime, which probably wasn't that awesome to begin with.

RATING ★ $$$

QUINTA DO NOVAL 1970 Vintage Porto 20% Alcohol

Tasted twice, in Paris and in my office; perhaps port's most cherished lodge produced, to the shock of many experts, an inconsistent and less-than-thrilling 1970, pure and simple; the color has that timeworn look of old saddle leather/mahogany; it's abrupt, medicinal, and alcoholic in the nose; to make matters worse, it's clumsily awkward on the palate in its cloying sweetness—there's too little acidity to counter the overripe fruit; the finish is weary and meek; disappointing and fossilized; can't win them all.

RATING ★ $$$

QUINTA DO VESUVIO 1992 Vintage Porto 20% Alcohol

As opaque as India ink, midnight-purple color; the bouquet is lavish, with a great and memorable concentration of hot paraffin, overripe grapes, cucumber, cane sugar, and sugar beets—it's a classic nose, at once mighty and gentle; in the mouth, the news only gets better as enormous tannin levels greet the taste buds, backed up by even stouter waves of ambrosial fruit flavors of red plums, raspberry jam, honeydew melon, vanilla extract, and sweet oak that engulf the entire palate; this is monster port territory from the compelling start to the velvety finish; grab this decadent thriller while you can—it's a rare superstar and a must-have item; projected peak is 2015–2020.

RATING ★ ★ ★ ★ ★   *Highest Recommendation* $$

QUINTA DO VESUVIO 1991 Vintage Porto 20% Alcohol

Black-as-night core with a deep purple rim; the nose is tightly wrapped and off-dry rather than sweet and open—there are none-too-subtle hints of tobacco, spice, bell pepper, and tar lurking in the background—it's a serious nose; in the mouth, I was surprised at the simple, peasant-like plumpness/roundness of it after enjoying the high-strung, complex nose—it shovels oodles of ripe, easy, red-berry fruit onto the tongue, then fades into a calm, quiet finish that's rich and fruity; it doesn't have the majesty of other '91s, such as Graham, Delaforce Quinta da Corte, or Quinta do Noval, but it's very much its own nimble, vivacious entity; my estimate at its peak drinking time is still 12–15 years down the pike.

RATING ★ ★ ★ ★   *Highly Recommended* $$

SANDEMAN Imperial 20-Year-Old Tawny Porto 20% Alcohol

Sampled once in Paris while in the midst of a crowded tasting that closely resembled a National Hockey League playoff game (I could have been penalized 2 minutes for elbowing several times as I fought my way through the throng of Parisians) and sampled a second time in my office; deep rust/amber color; the amazingly intense, blackberry jam, plummy/raisiny nose can hardly be contained merely by the glass—its seductive perfume fills the room; this special port sings on the palate in zesty, lively flavors of elderberries, cake, and cocoa; the scrumptious aftertaste lulls the taste buds; top-notch; one of the top five of the superb 20-year-old tawny category—considering the competition, that's a great compliment.

RATING ★ ★ ★ ★   *Highly Recommended* $$

SANDEMAN 1988 Quinta do Vau Vintage Porto 20% Alcohol

Displays the crimson/purple robe of youth; the ambrosial nose is vigorous and plummy, with nary a trace of tannin or oak, but it does have barely discernable hints of raisins—with aeration, a nice spiciness develops in the aroma's background; it's rather advanced on the palate (much more so than the still baby-fat-laden 1988 Graham's Malvedos)—flavors of ripe berries take the lead on the explosive taste—it's sweet, but not even close to being cloying or unctuous; the quicksilver finish is disappointing; my guess is that it will peak between 1999 and 2004.

RATING ★ ★ ★   *Recommended* $$

SANDEMAN 1985 Vintage Porto 20% Alcohol

Medium purple/blood-red color—whistle-clean, no sediment whatsoever; the pleasantly minty, cedary, herbal nose is quite different from other 1985 vintage ports, which by and large feature carloads of red and black fruit; zesty, peppery flavors burst forth onto the palate; it finishes cleanly in a bittersweet flourish that is all dark chocolate and mandarin orange; a well-made, atypical, medium-bodied, and vivacious port with more than ample charm and pizzaz; what it lacks in impact and intensity it makes up for in drinkability and verve; not a cellar-worthy port; drink now until 2003.

RATING ★ ★ ★   *Recommended* $$$

SANDEMAN 1982 Vintage Porto 20.5% Alcohol

Light-to-medium ruby/blood-red color; the restrained nose speaks softly of spice, black currant, and mustiness—it's lost its freshness, no doubt—the second pass 15 minutes later reveals a peppery element that wasn't evident in the first nosing; this one really takes flight on the palate entry as ripe berries and plums are nicely balanced by ample acidity—the taste more than redeems the timid, tired nose; the aftertaste is firm to the touch, off-dry, slightly tannic, moderately fruity, and adequately charming; this one got up off the canvas for a middle-round victory; it's ready to drink now.

RATING ★ ★ ★   *Recommended* $$

SANDEMAN 1970 Vintage Porto 20% Alcohol

Tasted first in Paris, then three times in New York; solid, middle-of-the-road 1970 that, while admittedly not at the head of its class, is nevertheless noteworthy; without being flashy or overstated, the aromatic qualities of this port improve dramatically after 20–30 minutes in the glass as well-endowed scents of blackberries and black plums waft up from the glass; it still has plenty of gum-numbing tannin and flavors of ripe prunes and pepper on palate; very pleasant, medium-sweet finish; drink from 2000 to 2005.

RATING ★ ★ ★   *Recommended* $$$

SANDEMAN Founder's Reserve Vintage Character Porto 20% Alcohol

This able-bodied port is not designed to be one of the heavyweights in the class of Quinta do Noval LB or Dow, but nonetheless one very pleasant glass of vintage character; deep ruby/garnet color; it displays a black-pepper bouquet, which is followed by nicely balanced flavors evocative of vanilla, nuts, and pears; not light, not heavy, not youthful, not mature, just right, actually, in every department.

RATING ★ ★ ★   *Recommended* $

SANDEMAN Royal 10-Year-Old Tawny Porto 20% Alcohol

Tawny/orange color, with copper highlights—the appearance is slightly turbid—it's not cloudy enough to be a problem; I wish I could say that I liked the burnt, grapy, doughy nose, but I didn't—has too much of an old foundry smell for my liking; medium- to fully-weighted; on palate, the burnt flavors are lacking in fruit but abundant in earth, smoke, and oak; the texture is delightfully satiny and rich; this is a highly stylistic tawny that fruit mongers will dismiss, but elemental aficionados will applaud; average and nowhere near the stellar quality of the wonderful Sandeman Imperial 20-year-old.

RATING ★ ★ $$

SANDEMAN 1989 Late-Bottled Vintage Porto / Bottled in 1994; 20% Alcohol

Solid, medium purple core with a rose/cherry rim; the succulent nose is all ripe-red plums with a touch of clove as a background aroma—with a few minutes of aeration, the spice note increased—it's a lovely bouquet, period; in the mouth, it shows ample ripe fruit at palate entry and medium weight—the midpalate loses some fruit along the way, which I found disappointing; the short aftertaste shows little fruit; the rapidly diminishing fruit component in the midpalate and the finish forced my hand to reduce this fast-starting LBV from a three-star recommended item to the two-star category.

RATING ★ ★ $$

SANDEMAN 1986 Late-Bottled Vintage Porto / Bottled in 1990; 20% Alcohol

Lightish, but pretty garnet/crimson color; the very understated, slightly vegetal, smoky, road-tar-like nose was on the whole uninspiring and underwhelming; in the mouth, the flavors are notably skintight, smoky, crisp, and oaky, exhibiting scant fruit behind the thick wall of acidity; the rapid-fire aftertaste shows tantalizing flashes of tasty berry fruit, but simply can't deliver them in the face of such high astringency; drinkable, but one expects more fruit evidence from this excellent producer; miserly, lackluster, and cooked.

RATING ★ $$

SMITH-WOODHOUSE 1991 Vintage Porto 20% Alcohol

Dark purple, just about opaque; the nose was reluctant to expose itself in the first two nosing passes—by the third pass, I began to detect unusual aromatic notes of ground red pepper and black pepper—the last nosing introduced a vague fruit element in the background—even though I really had to work at drawing this bouquet out, I ended up liking it very much; in the mouth, the tannins coated my teeth, as lip-smacking tastes of black fruit (primarily, plums and cherries) carry this chunky port forward into the long-lasting, scoop-it-out-with-a-spoon finish; easily one of the two or three best values from the smashing 1991 vintage; the second tasting confirmed all my earlier observations concerning the vigorous tannins, which promise to keep this sturdy number alive well past the year 2010.

RATING ★ ★ ★ ★   *Highly Recommended* $$

SMITH-WOODHOUSE Old Oporto Vintage-Character Porto 20% Alcohol

From one of port's most underappreciated lodges comes this remarkably delicious vintage character, which offers both potency and delicacy in the same glass; sound, purple/ruby color—no sediment; the heady bouquet is loaded with aromas of figs, dates, and road tar; on palate, the lovely, well-mannered flavors of tea leaves, ripe apricot, and honeydew melon are beguiling; the compact finish that doesn't overstay its welcome; very nice wine making.

RATING ★ ★ ★   *Recommended* $

SMITH-WOODHOUSE 1992 Vintage Porto 20% Alcohol

Gorgeous, deep, red-beet-juice/purple tone; this nose is perfumy in the first nosing, then goes curiously meek by the third pass—to clarify, it's not bad, just suddenly shy, which is confounding when one considers the overall depth of the vintage; it shows some manageable tannic astringency at the palate entry, then the medium-deep red-fruit flavors come aboard with something less than a bang; I found that while I definitely liked this port, there wasn't one virtue that turned me on to the point of raves; whereas the delicious 1991 version offers wonderful black-fruit focus and concentration, this 1992 edition presents a pleasant, solid port experience without any potential greatness.

RATING ★ ★ ★   *Recommended* $$

SMITH-WOODHOUSE 1985 Vintage Porto 20% Alcohol

Youthful purple core, with brick edges; the slight, coy nose is stingy at first, then after 30 minutes of aeration it opens up dramatically, revealing woodsy, leafy, herbal aromas that jump from the glass; on palate, it owns a solid, off-dry, tightly knit, exotic flavor base of anise, green pepper, tannin, and citrus; this port could never be accused of being either fruity or fleshy; it finishes almost dry in an astringent, mouth-puckering wave of tannin; a peculiar port, atypical for the vintage; its complexity isn't in its fruit as much as it is in the acid/tannin/intensely herbal flavor components; I really relished the elemental, earthy nose and flavor of this different animal; exhibited good presence and depth; good show; not a cellar animal, drink from 2000 to 2005.

RATING ★ ★ ★   *Recommended* $$$

Smith-Woodhouse 1981 Late-Bottled Vintage Porto / Bottled in 1985; 20% Alcohol

Though it is unfiltered, there is no sediment problem as far as I could detect from the sample bottle—medium-deep plum/royal purple color; the ripe, unabashedly sweet, juicy, and succulent nose reeks of vanilla extract and raisins; it oddly goes semidry on palate, with an interesting melange of orange rind, raisin, and waxy flavors; medium-weighted; the dry aftertaste is fast and lean, with minor dashes of wax and bittersweet chocolate; what intrigued me about this port is how its sweetness level lessened so markedly from nose to tongue to throat, yet it didn't lose charm.

RATING ★ ★ ★   *Recommended* $$

Smith-Woodhouse 1979 Late-Bottled Vintage Porto / Bottled in 1984; 20% Alcohol

Jet-black/midnight-purple, impregnable color—absolutely *must* be decanted—there were large chunks of sediment afloat in every glass I poured; the robust, intensely plummy bouquet shows off subtle hints of cocoa and rich Colombian coffee; the mature, semidry flavors of dried fruit are firm at entry—the flavors eventually fade in midpalate; the fruity finish has a pleasantly biting tail; I wouldn't wait too long to open this handsome LBV despite its formidable color; drink now until 2002.

RATING ★ ★ ★   *Recommended* $$

Smith-Woodhouse 1977 Vintage Porto 20.5% Alcohol

Deep blood-red color—throws tons of minute particles, so definitely decant before serving; the nose is slightly brittle at first, then with aeration it opens nicely into waves of blackberry, autumn leaves, and tropical fruit; it shows a sensuous presence on the palate as tannic flavors of bittersweet chocolate and orange peel vie for leadership; finishes cleanly in a citrusy rush; not a knockout port, but a sound, enjoyable entry just the same; the elevated tannin will keep this port improving for another 10–12 years; I would place the peak drinking period at 2005–2010.

RATING ★ ★ ★   *Recommended* $$$

Smith-Woodhouse 1970 Vintage Porto 20% Alcohol

Tasted once in Paris only; brooding, deep purple/blood-red color; the very pleasant, pruney bouquet is laced with spice and citrus scents and soon gives way to mature, straightforward flavors of overripe black cherries and black plums; rich, jammy finish; doesn't run with the best of the vintage, but is more than serviceable.

RATING ★ ★ ★   *Recommended* $$$

TAYLOR, FLADGATE & YEATMAN

Taylor, Fladgate & Yeatman, founded in 1692, has long been a company of vision, a company of unique first accomplishments in the port trade. These milestones include:

- Taylor was the first producer to offer a dry white port, Chip Dry.
- Taylor is the firm that first developed the Late-Bottled Vintage category. LBVs are ports composed of several wines from one vintage that are kept in wood from four to six years prior to bottling.
- In 1973 Taylor became the Upper Douro's first shipper to offer aged tawny ports at 10, 20, 30, and 40 years old.
- In addition, in the 1950s Taylor initiated the single quinta vintage port category, which takes vintage ports from particular plots of vineyard land in generally undeclared years.
- Perhaps most importantly, Taylor was the first British company to settle in the rugged, inhospitable Upper Douro in 1744. Indeed, a member of the firm, Peter Bearsley, was the first Englishman to set foot in the wild Douro.

TAYLOR FLADGATE 1977 Vintage Porto 21% Alcohol

Gorgeous ruby/purple color, with slight bits of sediment; the nose is very reserved compared to the fruit-basket approach of other 1977s—very peppery, somewhat vegetal in its slant, with subtle undercurrents of cocoa, plums, and even coffee bean; the sublime flavor alone is worth whatever it costs; this tannic, graceful, sinewy elixir offers layer upon layer of juicy, unfathomable, ripe-fruit flavor, but that's just the beginning—well-matched, ideally married tastes of orange, blackberry, cookie batter, plums, and chocolate enchant the taste buds in a peerless symphony of flavor; Taylor '77 is unquestionably the best port I've ever tasted; a perfect fortified wine; the peak drinking period is likely to be anywhere in the 2020–2030 area, perhaps even longer!

RATING ★ ★ ★ ★ ★   *Highest Recommendation* $$$

TAYLOR FLADGATE 1970 Vintage Porto 20% Alcohol

Fasten your seatbelts and prepare for all thrusters going to the max; imposing, chunky, viscous, very tannic, very young, very intense, very very very; brims with slightly overripe plummy fruit, striking sweetness, though not cloying in the least because of the ample acidity; what's in the nose? how about violets, prunes, maraschino cherries, tobacco, a hint of orange rind, and licorice; *the* paramount 1970 experience that won't peak until 2015–2020; hunt down at all cost.

RATING ★ ★ ★ ★ ★   *Highest Recommendation* $$$

TAYLOR FLADGATE 40-Year-Old Tawny Porto 20% Alcohol

Maybe the prettiest of the Taylor aged tawnies—a russet/deep-tawny/old-penny hue, excellent purity; the bouquet is obviously mature as aromas of old wood, worn saddle leather, and dried fruit mingle nicely with a tropical-fruit/pineapple-like scent that I found alluring; toasty, roasted, and nougaty on palate, this port sports an opulence that its younger siblings don't possess and while some might describe it as over-the-hill, I think of it as deliciously mellow and settled; the aftertaste puts a spotlight on the nuttiness, if briefly; an excellent aged tawny by any measure.

RATING ★ ★ ★ ★   *Highly Recommended* $$$

TAYLOR FLADGATE 1991 Quinta de Vargellas Vintage Porto 20.5% Alcohol

Opaque purple/jet-black; the sturdy nose shows a viney, vegetal face in the first nosing, then shifts into an intensely grapy gear in the second pass—by the third nosing, it overflows with concentrated aromas of black plums and dark chocolate; the flavor explodes on the tongue as masses of intense, jammy fruit envelop the palate—it's a sophisticated, surprisingly harmonious flavor considering that it's still a pup; the aftertaste is fine, elegant, and full of latent power, with mellow tannins and oodles of ripe red fruit; don't bother opening until 2012–2017.

RATING ★ ★ ★ ★   ***Highly Recommended*** $ $

TAYLOR FLADGATE 1985 Vintage Porto 20.5% Alcohol

Gorgeous, classic vintage-port ruby/blood-red tone; in the first nosing, the bouquet is found to be mildly spicy, but quite shy—the second pass stands pat—finally, in the third run-through, stately, robust aromas of raspberry preserves, black plums, and caraway seed make the olfactory sense dance; the graceful bearing of the flavor and texture point automatically to Taylor Fladgate's remarkable house style, which routinely pairs strength with finesse without one overshadowing the other; the ideally balanced flavors of plums, dark-grape raisins, oak resin, and cake batter beguile the taste buds as proper tannin holds the structure firmly together; the aftertaste is medium-long and speaks only of plums; predicted peak is 2005–2010.

RATING ★ ★ ★ ★   ***Highly Recommended*** $ $ $

TAYLOR FLADGATE 1983 Vintage Porto 20.5% Alcohol

Sound, medium ruby/purple tone; the nose is closed tighter than my Aunt Mame's mason jars—even after 30 minutes of aeration and wrist-aching swirling, it simply refused to come out and play—so be it; funnily, in the mouth, this port expresses itself in volumes, as very ripe black plum, sweet-oak, and raspberry flavors come together in a tannic, chewy, sweetish, and most of all, harmonious taste; the finish is clean and surprisingly quick; one of the most reticent of the '83s I've evaluated; I look forward to tasting it again in a decade; projected peak is 2008–2012.

RATING ★ ★ ★   ***Recommended*** $ $

TAYLOR FLADGATE 1980 Vintage Porto 21% Alcohol

Classic, dark purple color; the jammy nose bursts forth from the sampling glass in potent, succulent waves of warm, fully matured, black-fruit aromas (especially plums and black currants); on the palate, the texture is full and meaty, and the taste evokes thoughts of black coffee, black-currant Darjeeling tea, and, most telling of all, bittersweet chocolate—it's not a fruity flavor in the least and there's an astringent twang to it particularly in the finish; good showing from this oft-neglected, high-quality vintage; drink now until 2005.

RATING ★ ★ ★   ***Recommended*** $ $

TAYLOR FLADGATE 20-Year-Old Tawny Porto 20% Alcohol

A personal favorite aged tawny of mine since the middle 1980s but, surprisingly, in my last three tastings of it I've felt slightly disappointed;

tawny/brown/red color; the vigorous, swaggering, direct, and dry bouquet of flowers, herbs, citrus, and black tea (Prince of Wales, perhaps) is engaging; the complex flavors are sweet-sour, slightly candied, and floral; medium-weighted, graceful bearing in mouth; the tight, controlled, but nevertheless delicious finish that doesn't seem as lush in 1996 as in years past.

RATING ★ ★ ★　　*Recommended*　　$$

TAYLOR FLADGATE 30-Year-Old Tawny Porto 20% Alcohol

Beautiful, deep tawny/clover-honey/burnished appearance—it's a dazzler; the nose is mustier and more attic-like than I'd like, but it's intriguing nonetheless—official complaint to Taylor: there's not much in the way of fruit in this aroma; in the mouth, things improve significantly as high-toned flavors of red fruit and bittersweet chocolate combine to create a satisfying midpalate experience that redeems the weakness and awkwardness of the nose; the finish mirrors the midpalate, but in a faded way; don't hold onto it, drink it now.

RATING ★ ★ ★　　*Recommended*　　$$$

TAYLOR FLADGATE 1988 Late-Bottled Vintage Porto 20% Alcohol

Exceedingly dark ruby/purple from the core to the edge—a breathtaking, rich-looking black beauty; the pungent nose crackles with black plums, blackberries, paraffin, and black pepper—an opulent bouquet that matches the jammy appearance; while the promise of a massive LBV is not fully realized once it's on the palate, this medium-bodied, chocolatey port is delicious all the same, with a ripe grapiness starting the taste journey—the flavor wavers at midpalate when the high-octane fruit loses some of its profundity; the finish is clean; the great beginning had enough stuffing to last almost all the way to the finish; still recommendable, based on the color, bouquet, and palate entry.

RATING ★ ★ ★　　*Recommended*　　$

TAYLOR FLADGATE Special Tawny Porto 20% Alcohol

Gorgeous, deep blood color, with a brick rim; the compelling, inviting, full, zesty nose of oak, sourdough bread, spice, and cucumber is appealing and even charming; this seductive, sexy tawny has plenty of muscle, but likewise possesses a high degree of finesse as the sweet taste of prunes envelops the entire palate; it finishes classily, as round, full flavors of overripe grapes and plums enchant the taste buds; one of the better rudimentary ports to be found.

RATING ★ ★ ★　　*Recommended*　　$

TAYLOR FLADGATE First Estate Lugar das Lages Vintage-Character Porto 20% Alcohol

Opulent grape/plum color with cherry/garnet edges; the fresh, piquant, spicy, wet-slate nose is zesty in the first nosing, then by the third pass it shuts down; it comes wonderfully alive on palate as the semidry, cinnamony entry expands into an equally semidry midpalate that judiciously brings a succulent blackberry flavor into the picture; it finishes quietly on an elegant note of cola, controlled fruit, and bearable astringency; far from a fruit-basket blockbuster, this direct vintage character is compact, clean, mildly hot, sturdy (as one would expect from this premier producer) and delightful overall; makes an excellent beginner port; drink right away.

RATING ★ ★ ★   ***Recommended*** $

TAYLOR FLADGATE 10-Year-Old Tawny Porto 20% Alcohol

My least favorite of the Taylor aged tawnies; solid, good, appealing appearance of tawny/red honey color; the nose is where I have my biggest problems, as unfulfilling and strangely disjointed aromas of dill, wood smoke, and overripe plums simply don't mesh; in the mouth, it pulls itself together in waves of seriously sweet, toffee, and nougat-like flavors that lavish the taste buds in a creamy, moderately viscous texture; the finish is a bit flat and alcoholic, but okay; average, drinkable, but uninspiring.

RATING ★ ★ $$

TAYLOR FLADGATE Chip Dry White Porto 20% Alcohol

Flat, golden/straw color; the meek nose sends off faint scents of canteloupe and pineapple, but little else; it offers more grace on the palate than most other white ports, with finely woven tastes of baked apple, lemon, and white grapes combining nicely at midpalate; the finish is as timid as the nose and ends up in a lemon meringue style that's low key but hardly charming; wholly unexciting; serve chilled as an aperitif on-the-rocks with a twist of orange or lemon only if you're desperate for white port.

RATING ★ $

TAYLOR FLADGATE Special Ruby Porto 20% Alcohol

Medium ruby/crimson hue; the delicate, acidic, lean nose of strawberries, flowers, earth, and stone holds minor enchantment; it enters the mouth like a brass band, with razor-like, highly acidic flavors of minerals and unripe grapes—please don't misunderstand my perceptions, this isn't an unpleasant sensation at all, it's just sharp, highly stylized, and austere for a ruby port, which is normally round and fruity; the aftertaste is slightly plumper than the initial taste, but still on the wiry side; odd and below par.

RATING ★ $

TAYLOR FLADGATE 1989 Late-Bottled Vintage Porto 20% Alcohol

Medium deep, ruby color with blood-colored core highlights and a cherry-red edge; the bouquet spotlights black pepper, gunpowder, lead pencil, and herbal aromas rather than fruit in the initial nosing, then adds red currant and a touch of vanilla bean by the third pass—certainly not the jammy affair that helped make Taylor Fladgate's 1988 LBV so rewarding a port, but okay nonetheless; on the palate, it's too hard and steely at entry for my taste, though the midpalate finally shows glimpses of ripe grapes— by that time the mere hint of fruit is hardly enough to salvage a recommendation; the finish is slight and undefined; by no means up to Taylor Fladgate's usual brilliance.

RATING ★ $

TAYLOR FLADGATE 1982 Quinta de Vargellas Vintage Porto 20.5% Alcohol

Medium ruby/purple color; the coy nose doesn't reveal much even after 15 minutes of aeration—the closed-off quality is, however, typical for the slow-to-develop Taylor Fladgates, so I didn't think that much about the lack of aroma; as Taylors frequently do, the taste does all the talking—in this case the discourse is tannic and cramped in the fruit department flavorwise, it's not as stingy as the bouquet, showing hints of citrus, cocoa, and red fruit; the astringent aftertaste borders on being metallic; leave this one on the shelf.

RATING ★ $$

WARRE 1991 Vintage Porto 20% Alcohol

Rich, purple/ruby robe; the bouquet is balanced, if slightly closed, but quite lovely in its remoteness—I had hoped for a fruit explosion, but that never materialized; in the mouth, it absolutely sings with major red-currant, plummy ripeness—it's remarkably harmonious, opulent, and elegant—the viscous, medium-bodied texture generously coats the tongue; only moderate tannins indicate a medium-long life expectancy, perhaps 20 years; the finish is graceful and polished; another sterling, juicy example of this superb vintage; projected peak drinking is 2010–2015.

RATING ★ ★ ★ ★   *Highly Recommended* $$

WARRE 1985 Vintage Porto 20% Alcohol

Inky-black/midnight-purple color—genuinely mysterious and beautiful to the eye; the nose emits acetate, nail polish, vines, briary, and vegetal scents—anything but fruit—even some tobacco and anise—I liked it, even though it's atypical for the vintage; the palate is viscous, chewy, and filled with grapy residue that coats the teeth; tastewise it soars with the best of the vintage, as plump, sumptuous flavors of chocolate, plums, and vanilla frosting are balanced by the firm chalkiness; tannic and leathery; anticipated peak drinking time is 2010–2015.

RATING ★ ★ ★ ★   *Highly Recommended* $$

WARRE 1970 Vintage Porto 20% Alcohol

Tasted first in Paris, then twice in my office; while it's not as grand as the Graham or Taylor or Fonseca, it nevertheless is one sturdy, well-made port, consisting of equal parts power and finesse; the fleshy, pruney, peppery aromas ascend from the glass in healthy bursts; on palate, it's well-behaved, tidy, and somewhat closed even now—the nuanced flavor is difficult to analyze, since so little data is presented in the flavor; it finishes with ripe raspberry and plum tastes, then quickly fades; drink from 1998 to 2005.

RATING ★ ★ ★   *Recommended* $$$

WARRE Warrior Vintage-Character Porto 20% Alcohol

A well-balanced vintage character, though it lacks the elegance of Dow and Quinta do Noval LB; cocoa, plums, and red cherries abound in the generous nose, as wave after wave of fierce fruit storms the olfactory sense; on palate, it's medium-weighted, silky-textured; dense flavors of blackberries, strawberries, and plums come to the surface, while underneath there is a soft road-tar quality that appears to be its foundation; nicely made, but if it had more of an acid structure it would be even better.

RATING ★ ★ ★   *Recommended* $

Warre 1979 Quinta do Cavadinha Vintage Porto 20% Alcohol

Deep crimson/ruby color, though not opaque and throws some minor sediment; the dried-fruit nose shows background notes of lemon, rose petals, and black pepper; it's hardly what I'd term sweet in the entry—it's actually more off-dry, then later the sweetness shows up; medium-bodied and rather lithe in texture; the lean, laser-like flavors of dried pears and apricots are supported by an undercurrent of oak and cassis; it finishes nicely and quietly, with low sugar; this average single quinta still carries some punch and elegance, but not enough to push it into three-star territory.

RATING ★ ★ $$

Aromatized Wines, Marsala, Pineau des Charentes, and Vermouths

ome of the most renowned aperitif beverages of all time fall under the subcategory heading of Aromatized Wines. These are wine-based alcoholic beverages of between 16 percent and 20 percent alcohol that have brandy, herbs, honey, quinine, or sometimes everything but the kitchen sink added to them to make them more palatable. Aromatized wines are the fourth level of the wine category after still, sparkling, and fortified, but most closely resemble fortified wines. Aromatized wines are fortified, as are port, marsala, madeira, and sherry, but in a different way from those generally sweet beverages. The bulk of aromatized wines are dry, even astringent and bitter, to the taste. Vermouths are aromatized wines, as are *amaros* (bitters) from Italy, Pineau des Charentes from Cognac, and the so-called aperitif wines from France, Italy, and the U.S., including Lillet, Dubonnet, Cynar, Campari, and Punt e Mes, to name a few.

The process of aromatization dates back to the Greeks and the Romans, who routinely mixed a wide variety of flavorings into their wines to make them easier to quaff. The Romans added some admittedly strange ingredients, including chalk, myrrh, tar, pitch, poppy, boiled seawater, bitumen, and aloe.

Aromatized wines make refreshing warm-weather drinks and are at their best with a twist of orange, lemon, or lime. They should be served well chilled (45–55 degrees Fahrenheit) on their own or on-the-rocks. Please note that once open, aromatized wines rarely last for more than three or four weeks, even if refrigerated.

Aperitifs and Vermouths

CAMPARI Aperitivo 24% Alcohol (Italy)

Pretty cherry-red/brick color, exemplary clarity; the nose is snappy, vivacious, and expectedly bitter, evoking images of fruit pits and botanicals—the woodsy, earthy, quinine-like bouquet is exotic and begs for the complementary slice of citrus, make that orange; while quite candidly I'm not an avid fan of bitters, I didn't find Campari offensively bitter in the taste—in fact, there's a mild touch of sweet-sour fruitiness that exposes itself very briefly at palate entry—the midpalate is sweet, but only moderately bitter; the finish is long, mildly quinine-like, with a dash of sour grapes in the tail end; designed to be served with sweeter citrus fruits, which offset the bitter note—orange is Campari's soulmate; this old drink enjoys enormous popularity in its native Italy, where it's part of daily life for millions.

RATING ★★ $

CARPANO Punt e Mes Amaro Vermouth 16% Alcohol (Italy)

Looks strikingly like a cola, medium-brown color with a reddish core and golden edges, pure; the medicinal, herbal aroma flashes a bit of quinine at the beginning, but fortunately that blows off and what's left behind is a bittersweet, vegetal/herbal smell that's quite subtle and restrained; I liked this vermouth neat—it's bitter for a moment at entry, then it turns pleasantly sweet and guardedly ambrosial at midpalate; the finish is long and is influenced only slightly by the quinine—the icky-sticky, pruney tail end of the aftertaste is nice.

RATING ★★★   *Recommended* $

CINZANO Extra Dry Vermouth 18% Alcohol (Italy)

Pale straw hue; this nose is zesty, vibrant, and brimming with off-dry, slightly candied, and metallic scents of pine tar and damp vegetation; on the palate, it's comely, well-behaved, and keenly off-dry; while it doesn't possess the chic elegance of Noilly Prat, it's roundly delicious in a carefree, whimsical way that's very becoming; more a mixer than a solo flyer.

RATING ★★★   *Recommended* $

CINZANO Rosso Vermouth 16% Alcohol (Italy)

It owns the darkest tawny/brown tone of the high-profile sweet vermouths; the heady perfume speaks decisively of overripe grapes, bitters (quinine), and roots; it's very good, very agile in the mouth and not for an instant does it come off as being clumsy or cloying; the flavor has a quinine twang that folds neatly into the rooty/grapy/citrusy layers; in the aftertaste I pick up considerable amounts of ripe orange and pink grapefruit; good show.

RATING ★★★   *Recommended* $

CYNAR Aperitivo 16.5% Alcohol (Italy)

Looks exactly like cola, deep brown/chestnut hue, very good purity; the bouquet is very reluctant to come out and play from the first nosing to the last—what meager amounts of aroma are there have cooked-vegetable, wet fabric, and steely/metallic qualities that have little or nothing to do with artichoke, the herbaceous plant from which Cynar (pronounced, chee-nahr) is produced; the taste begins off-dry at palate entry, then goes wildly bitter at midpalate, taking on flavors of quinine, road tar, pine needles, and wood resin; the aftertaste is unpleasantly bitter, unappealing, and heavy on the quinine; clearly, Cynar is an acquired taste, one that's better and easier to down in cold, mixed drinks, though I have to say that many other aromatized wines are much tastier on their own; I despised the taste.

RATING ★ $

DuBONNET Rouge Aperitif 19% Alcohol (USA)

The color reminds me of an old Burgundy, a burnished/cranberry/tawny red, excellent clarity; the nose is vinegary, tart, and has subtle hints of pine, fruit kernel, and underripe grapes; the mouth presence is fresh and clean, but thin; the flavor shows moderate, underripe-red-fruit tastes along with a very tart touch of cranberry; it finishes in a sweet-sour flurry that's mildly pleasing; it's not really recommendable neat, but try it with some club soda and a slice of orange—it works that way; it lacks the finesse and overall suppleness of Lillet Red.

RATING ★ ★ $

LILLET White 18% Alcohol (France)

Distinct white-wine appearance, a fetching Vouvray/Chenin Blanc straw/yellow color; the perfumy, gentle nose hints of quinine, minerals, wine, and citrus—it's a decidedly feminine bouquet of delicacy, soft fruitiness, and earth; at entry, the acidy tartness puckers my mouth—by midpalate the clean, fresh, dry, winey flavors caress the taste buds in soft, pillowy blankets of mild citrus and spice; the aftertaste is fast, refreshing, and squeaky-clean; pop in a slice of orange and the worries of the world fade away.

RATING ★ ★ ★   Recommended $

LILLET Red 18% Alcohol (France)

Appearancewise, this aperitif could double for a cherry-red, Grand Cru Beaujolais; the nose is acutely more wine-like and assertive than the Lillet white—the aromas of freshly picked red grapes, black cherries, black raspberries, apricots, and pepper are intoxicating; it behaves in the mouth like a fat, chewy, sun-drenched, off-dry red wine from the Midi in southern France—the elevated alcohol is so skillfully concealed within the layers of fruit salad/grapiness that you never take notice of it; the finish is short, mildly fruity, and clean.

RATING ★ ★ ★   Recommended $

MARTINI & ROSSI Rosso Vermouth 16% Alcohol (Italy)

Cola/tawny hue, with rich gold edges—it seriously resembles a cream sherry; the sexy, sensuous nose highlights sweet ginger, almost like ginger ale and tonic water; it sings on the palate and is absolutely delicious; I would have this supple, sweet, winey, almost sherry-like beauty on-the-rocks and not as a mixer; to the touch, it's velvety, but not in the least thick or syrupy; it's all citrus and grapes on the tongue and in the stately after-taste; really luscious; superb value; bravo.

RATING ★★★★   *Highly Recommended* $

MARTINI & ROSSI Extra-Dry Vermouth 18% Alcohol (Italy)

Pale flaxen/hay color; the aroma is the most curious of the extra-dry ver-mouths in that it's by far the most medicinal and root-like, giving off piquant scents of burnt rubber, compost, bark, and aspirin; what you get in the bouquet you receive in spades in the flavor—fourth-gear medicine-chest/cough syrup; it's not that it's bad-tasting or offensive, I just simply don't care for such intense rootiness; use it as a mixer.

RATING ★★ $

NOILLY PRAT French Dry Vermouth 18% Alcohol (France)

Extremely pale/faint yellow; it's wonderfully alive in the nose, as subtle, delicate, and woodsy hints of juniper, thyme, and laurel waft from the glass; it's dry, clean, and refreshing to the taste—very table-wine-like in its bear-ing and delicacy; the crisp, featherweight finish beautifully brings together the wine/herb influences into a harmonious, light, and refined conclusion; I'd drink it on-the-rocks—it's as lovely an inexpensive aperitif as I could think of; top flight all the way; a major discovery for me.

RATING ★★★★   *Highly Recommended* $

NOILLY PRAT Sweet Vermouth 16% Alcohol (France)

Prune-juice brown/russet/sweet sherry color; the nose is spicy (especially cloves and cinnamon) and pruney, with a backnote of slate, minerals, and a dash of quinine—I'm inclined to add tobacco and molasses to the list of aro-mas, but they are barely discernable—suffice it to say that it's a multilayered bouquet with lots happening simultaneously; quite delicious, though it took me two samplings to get to like it; while not in the rarified air of its cousin from Cognac, Pineau des Charentes, this is a very nice, winey, mod-erately sweet aperitif that could easily be served on its own over ice, though I'd opt for mixing it.

RATING ★★★   *Recommended* $

STOCK Sweet Vermouth 16% Alcohol (Italy)

Attractive mahogany/chestnut-brown hue; restrained, but firm, solid, even stately aromas of roots, herbs, spices, and nuts; moderately viscous tex-ture; restrained even in the sweet-sour flavor, but very appealing nonethe-less—upfront, succulent tastes of tar, tobacco, and resin—not in the least fruity, grapy, or pruney—leans more in the direction of herbs and spice; per-fect on-the-rocks or as a mixer.

RATING ★★★   *Recommended* $

STOCK Extra-Dry Vermouth 18% Alcohol (Italy)

Pale; the fruitiest, seediest fragrance of the extra-dry vermouths, as wave after wave of papaya, guava, aniseed, and licorice fill the nose cavity; it's in-tensely, almost bitterly sour at palate entry, kind of like chomping into an unripe green apple; it settles down in the crisp, tart finish, then promptly falls off the table; so-so, inoffensive; use strictly as a mixer.

RATING ★★ $

Tribuno Extra-Dry Vermouth 18% Alcohol (USA)

Darkest of the extra-dry vermouths—a pale-straw, young Sauvignon Blanc appearance; aromas of Juicy Fruit gum, ripe grapes, pine needles, and spearmint greet the olfactory sense; not unpleasant, but a tad overblown in the nose; the sweetest Extra Dry to the taste—it's also the most overtly grapy; clean, off-dry finish; this is mixer territory.

RATING ★★ $

Tribuno Sweet Vermouth 16% Alcohol (USA)

Medium-deep, almost flat-looking brown color—no incidence of copper or red; the candied nose is way too intense—the ripe peach aroma really comes at you; it's nowhere near as classy or satiny as the imports; tastewise and texturewise, it's pleasant and wholly average; good mixing material, no doubt.

RATING ★★ $

Marsala — Italy

Like port, sherry, and madeira, which it reminds me of the most, marsala is a fortified wine, meaning that brandy is added to it during its production or maturing process. Marsala is born in the steamy vineyards of western Sicily and is made from indigenous white and black grapes, primarily *grillo, cattarratto, perricone, calabrese,* and *nerello mascalese.* The grapes are left on the vine for an extended period so as to provide heavy, unctuous, and very sweet juice for marsala's base wine. Vintage marsalas are rarely seen in the U.S. The types of marsala include *Fine,* which is aged in wood for at least four months and has a strength of 17% alcohol; *Superiore,* which by law must have a minimum of four years in the cask and is 18% alcohol; *Vergine* and *Vergine Stravecchio,* which are dry wines that have been aged for five and ten years in oak, respectively; and *Speciales,* which are flavored marsalas (banana, orange, and others).

Florio Targa 1980 Marsala 19% Alcohol (Italy)

Very attractive, burnished-orange/honey color; aged for eleven years in oak casks and one year in bottle; the nose is nothing short of sensational—ripe, raisin, figs, dates, and walnuts all take turns impressing the hell out of the olfactory sense; on the palate, it's medium-bodied, satiny, and extremely smoky—evidence of the wood is ample as a resiny/oily texture and flavor pop up in midpalate, then bow to the figgy, nimble finish, which is sweetish but anything but cloying and pleasantly long; this marsala should be enjoyed in a small *copita* glass as a slightly chilled aperitif or as a room-temperature *digestif* with fruit and nuts; use the cheaper Florios for the marsala sauce.

RATING ★ ★ ★   ***Recommended*** $

Pineau des Charentes — France

Pineau des Charentes, by definition, is grape juice whose fermentation has been stopped by the addition of cognac to the must, thereby leaving some of the juice's residual sugar behind. The cognac used to halt the fermentation must, by law, be at least a VS-level cognac (outside the U.S., that cognac category is known as Three-Star). This process is known in France as *mutage*.

Regulations state that Pineau des Charentes's alcohol range must fall between 16 and 22 percent. The six that I've sampled have all been 17 percent alcohol. Sweet and fruity to the taste, the best, like Pierre Ferrand's, are irresistible. Pineau des Charentes has its own official *appellation controlée* designation and has been produced in the Cognac region since the sixteenth century. The fact that Pineau des Charentes has been made for four centuries lends perspective as to why it's so prized within France and why the French consume most of what's produced. Almost all cognac producers make a Pineau des Charentes. Unfortunately, Pineau des Charentes does not travel all that well, and, as a result, it is rarely seen in the U.S.

Pineau des Charentes makes an outstanding warm-weather aperitif and should always be served frosty cold (40–45 degrees Fahrenheit). One could even serve it on-the-rocks with a twist of lemon, just like in the bistros of Paris and St. Tropez. Another way of serving it is with a splash of champagne.

On your next trip to France, be sure to hunt some Pineau des Charentes down in Paris wine shops. Or if you're fortunate enough to be close to Cognac, visit any major producer to pick up a bottle or two. Once you get back home and taste it on a warm summer afternoon, you'll be very glad you left some open space in your carry-on bag on the way to France.

Armagnac's version is referred to as *floc de Gascogne*.

A. HARDY et CIE Le Coq d'Or Pineau des Charentes 17% Alcohol

Cherry/brickish/crimson color; the fragrance of ripe cherries flies from the glass, then relaxes as it aerates, taking on a winey posture; the sweet wild-strawberry flavor at palate entry is absolutely luscious, then at midpalate raspberries come into play; the aftertaste is semisweet and lean; the overall package is really wonderful right from the appealing appearance through to the fruity, elegant finish; it's a shame these fantastic and charming beverages are so seldom available in the U.S.

RATING ★ ★ ★ ★   ***Highly Recommended*** $$

PIERRE FERRAND Réserve de Pierre Pineau des Charentes 17% Alcohol

Luminous orange/honey color; in the initial nosing, the aroma is like roasted coffee that's brewing in the morning—subsequent passes discover earthy, smoky backdrop odors of lees and pomace; the toffee flavor explodes on palate entry, then at midpalate deep, round flavors of caramel, candy, and smoke impress the taste buds—by the final in-mouth sampling, there's a very complex interplay between the smoke and fruit; it finishes like liquid silk in the throat, where it exhibits exceptional balance between sugar and acidity; a velvety, grapy winner all the way; aged in cognac casks for 15 years.

RATING ★ ★ ★ ★ ★   *Highest Recommendation* $$

PIERRE FERRAND Sélection Pineau des Charentes 17% Alcohol

Medium amber/gold color; the very delicate, feminine aromas of ripe apricots, mandarin orange, and lees remind me strikingly of Muscat Beaumes-de-Venise, one of my favorite sweet wines of France; it owns a lush, vibrant, dry-sweet posture on palate—the orange, citrusy, acidic flavors start it off in the mouth, then a sublime, spirity, semisweetness takes over and stays well into the finish; it ends on a nutty, white-port-like quality that is charming and ambrosial; a unique, satisfying spirit experience; aged in oak for five years.

RATING ★ ★ ★ ★   *Highly Recommended* $

REMY MARTIN Le Pineau des Charentes 17% Alcohol

Rich, flaxen/gold/Sauternes-like hue; the welcoming fruit-salad bouquet closed down after only a couple of minutes, then reopened for business after nearly ten minutes of aeration—it's a subtle, soft-spoken, butterscotch nose that moves toward the lean end of the aroma scale; on palate, I detect tart, fleshy tropical fruits, especially guava and mango, with a touch of lime—the supple flavor is semisweet and shows hardly any cognac influence; it finishes squeaky-clean and fruity; the ideal spring or summer aperitif; also a savory companion to dessert fruit or tarts.

RATING ★ ★ ★   *Recommended* $

REYNAC Pineau des Charentes 17% Alcohol

Lustrous gold/yellow, the rich color of a Sauternes or Barsac; the sexy bouquet emits solid scents of canteloupe, white raisins, dates, butterscotch, and a bit of key lime pie—it's a friendly, fruity, and inviting aroma that I liked instantly; in the mouth, it's semisweet, with fresh flavors of overripe white grapes, melon, and citrus thrown in for balance; the finish is refreshing, citrusy, and medium-long; begs to be served ice cold with a twist of lemon over ice.

RATING ★ ★ ★   *Recommended* $

REYNAC Pineau des Charentes Rosé 17% Alcohol

See-through crimson/garnet/cranberry-juice hue; the bouquet is soft, fine, and reminds me of kirsch, as the fruit/kernel-like fragrance of red cherry rules the roost—in addition, there's a pleasant herbal/spiciness in the background—it took me three passes to come around to this bouquet, but once I did, I was sold; the entry to the mouth is very tart, clean, and picks up the spice/cherry quality by midpalate; the aftertaste is lovely, fruity, juicy-sweet, and very extended; makes for a satisfying aperitif served chilled on-the-rocks.

RATING ★ ★ ★   _Recommended_ $

FORTIFIED WINES—USA

BONNY DOON VINEYARD Framboise (Raspberry Wine with Grape-Neutral Spirits 17% Alcohol (California)

Sumptuously deep crimson color, really the exact color of blood; the intoxicating nose is fresh, balanced, sweet/tart, piquant, intense, focused, and oozes red raspberry right from the start—a genuinely compelling bouquet of the first rank; on palate, it's clean, more tart than sweet, and medium-bodied for a framboise—that nimble texture, along with the aroma, are its best features; the finish is layered, though not particularly complex, slightly viney/vegetal, but luscious all the way down the throat; a homegrown beauty that's delectable on its own but that is even more outstanding over lemon sorbet.

 RATING ★ ★ ★ ★   ***Highly Recommended*** $

BONNY DOON VINEYARD Cassis (Black-Currant Wine with Grape-Neutral Spirits) 17% Alcohol (California)

Looks strikingly similar to a new vintage port, extreme deep purple in color, very viscous and leggy on the interior wall of the glass; the intense perfume is black-currant in a tart, jammy way rather than being sweet and unctuous—the nose is faithfully vinous, earthy, and leafy, all good indications when black currant is involved—the aroma even sports a curiously appealing backnote of dill; in the mouth, it's tart but not sour, rich but neither cloying nor top-heavy—the black-currant quality is tremendously concentrated at midpalate, dead center on the tongue; the aftertaste is smooth, velvety, mildly tart, and, to describe it in professional terms, incredibly yummy; this would make a superb addition to champagne/sparkling wine to make a splendid Kir Royale.

 RATING ★ ★ ★ ★   ***Highly Recommended*** $

CHRISTIAN BROTHERS Dry Sherry 18% Alcohol (California)

Lovely gold/umber color; the pickled, stale, musty, rotting wood, sauerkraut nose is as inviting as a dirty clothes hamper after the morning aerobics class—a serious letdown after one admires the handsome appearance; the insipid, sour, cardboard-like flavors go nowhere from the limp palate entry to the tart lemonade aftertaste; this offering is a pathetic mess in the nose and the mouth; not to mention, it's hardly what I'd call "dry"; the Brothers aren't being very Christian by selling this swill; a cheap thrill that's big on "cheap" and small on "thrill."

RATING ★ $

CHRISTIAN BROTHERS Golden Sherry 18% Alcohol (California)

Interesting, if odd, saffron color—looks more like a cordial than a fortified wine; the tutti-frutti, one-dimensional nose is candied, then with aeration and swirling in the glass goes as blank as a deer's eyes in your headlights; the bleak, candied, additive-like, sugarwater flavor is a dead end and shows the complexity of a one-celled animal; so it's sweeter than their disastrous Dry Sherry—big deal; one need not be a rocket scientist to immediately discern that this is just the cotton-candied version of the malodorous CB Dry Sherry; do people really buy this horrendous puddle water?

RATING ★ $

CHRISTIAN BROTHERS Meloso Cream Sherry 19% Alcohol (California)

The most sherry-like color and bearing of the inexpensive domestics—rich amber, with dazzling gold highlights; regrettably, it starts to unravel in the nose, which belches out inappropriate fumes of citrus, iodine, medicine-chest, and sulphur aromas; I did like the silky texture and the correct "feel" of it on palate—the flavors at entry are initially awkward, then a thundering sweetness gallops to the rescue by overriding the underlying flowery flavor; has a modestly pleasing finish; my overriding impression was that while this item is mildly enjoyable and drinkable, it's hardly in the league of, say, Spain's Hartley & Gibson Cream Sherry (four-star quality) or Wisdom & Warter Delicate Cream Sherry (four-star quality), which are both roughly in the same price range—so, why bother with this overwrought product?

RATING ★ $

DOMAINE CHARBAY Dessert Chardonnay 17% Alcohol (California)

Pale green color; the nose is painfully shy at first, then after aeration it begins to emerge in a ripe-apple, slightly spicy scent that's mildly charming; on palate, the sweet-sour flavor is fresh and friendly, but not what I'd term profound; the aftertaste is medium-long and a tad sour; the best application for this dessert treat is as its creator, Miles Karakasevic, suggests, serve it ice cold with a slice of orange—it really shines in that arena; this is a lighter, homegrown version of France's sweeter and more viscous Pineau des Charentes, which are made in the Cognac region.

RATING ★ ★ ★   ***Recommended*** $

FICKLIN VINEYARDS Tinta Port 18.5% Alcohol (California)

Handsome, tawny color, with crimson highlights; the luscious, appetizing, mouthwatering, fat nose reeks of overripe grapes, oak, cream, and coconut—perhaps the most enchanting and riveting domestic-fortified-wine bouquet I've encountered; exquisitely balanced, moderately viscous feel in the mouth; it really sings flavorwise on the palate, with multilayered tastes of cocoa, bell pepper, raisins, and paraffin; Tinta Port finishes serenely in a fruity crescendo that encourages another sip; did I ever expect to fall head over heels for a domestic fortified wine? honest answer: no; I guess that's what makes life such an adventure; this stupendous, sumptuous, homegrown beauty is top-drawer all the way; deserved kudos to the Ficklin production staff.

RATING ★★★★   ***Highly Recommended*** $

FICKLIN 10-Year-Old Tawny Port Lot No. 1, 19% Alcohol (California)

Looks like cherry cola—an amazingly pretty chestnut/mahogany color that dazzles the eye; the nose is a concentrated perfume, ripe with walnut, Brazil nut, hard-candy, and nougat aromas that are neither sweet nor dry, but nuttily succulent—the fourth nosing reveals a nuanced, resiny touch of oak; on the palate, the texture is firm and sure while the taste highlights nut meat, candied almonds, caramel corn, and extremely ripe grapes—the taste and bearing remind me more of cream or Pedro Ximenez sherry than aged tawny port—since I'm an ardent fan of sweet sherries, this is meant in the most complimentary way; the finish is long, subdued, and only mildly sweet; one of my two favorite Ficklins; bravo, but change the name.

RATING ★★★★   ***Highly Recommended*** $

FICKLIN VINEYARDS 1957 Vintage Port 20% Alcohol (California)

100% *tinta madeira* grape, bottled in 1960, recorked in 1991; turbid-brown, uncomely appearance, some sediment is thrown; the mature, smoky, rubber-tire, pencil-eraser, musty nose shows only faint hints of grapes—the bouquet grows, but only slightly, in the glass after 30 minutes of aeration; on palate, the concentrated, off-dry fruit finally makes itself known, then at midpalate a lush wave of milk chocolate and honey come to the fore in an impressive manner; the finish is meek, though extended, and offers a quick hit of candy; good, no doubt, but this senior citizen is definitely on the downside of its lifecycle; I would like to have sampled it about a decade ago, when it probably was at its peak; the problematic appearance didn't help in the final scoring; this one's a tough call because, while recommendable, it's clearly living on its résumé; approach it with the understanding that it's past its prime; not much of it left.

RATING ★★★   ***Recommended*** $$$

FICKLIN VINEYARDS 1986 Vintage Port 18.1% Alcohol (California)

Beautiful, classic port appearance—deep ruby color, nearly opaque; even after a full quarter hour of aeration the nose is disappointingly one-dimensional and, at best, restrained—I nosed it a for several minutes, on and off, giving it time to open, but the net result was a predictable aroma of viney/grapiness and nothing else—there's no expansiveness, no layering, no complexity to this stingy nose; on the palate, it's like a different wine, as two layers of flavor enchant the taste buds—the most obvious layer is a choco-latey/pruney top layer, but beneath that is a sturdy, ripe grape (Cabernet

Franc?) taste that's exceedingly pleasant, evolved, and defined; the finish is firm and grapy; the impactful flavor redeemed the limp-noodle nose enough for me to end up recommending it.

RATING ★ ★ ★   *Recommended* $$

Gallo/Livingston Cellars Cream Sherry 18% Alcohol (California)

The very pretty tawny/amber color is a plus; the bracing aromas of steel wool, rust, and wet sand are not—it's as if the lab boys in the Gallo think tank said, "Let's try to make the aroma nutty!" and then proceeded to stink up the nose with heaven knows what; on palate, I have to admit that it at least remotely echoes a cream sherry, albeit one that has its eyes crossed; the aftertaste is smooth, pleasantly sweet, and shockingly extended; by a country mile, the most drinkable of the Gallo sherry line; if not for the land-fill nose, this offering would be a decent fortified wine.

RATING ★ ★ $

Gallo Pale Dry Cocktail Sherry 17% Alcohol (California)

Clear, Muscadet-like appearance—a very pale silver/gray/green color; the ethereal, inoffensive nose evokes mild sweetness, mintiness, and soft egg cream; it is misleadingly described as "dry" on the label because it's any-thing but; its benign, banal character is virtually neutral on palate, exhibit-ing an off-dry flavor in the wispy finish; it's the most neutral-tasting, inert, ghost-like fortified wine I've ever sampled; what little aroma and taste there is is nice, but on the whole it's innocuous and almost totally devoid of sen-sory expression; the cheap vodka of cheap domestic fortified wines.

RATING ★ $

Gallo Sherry 17% Alcohol (California)

Shows a rather dull, dark yellow/gold color; some remote aromatic re-semblance to genuine sherry—the hollow nuttiness at the scent's core is ac-cented by a pungent dill quality, which lurks in the background; it's amaz-ingly sour, bitter, and lemony on palate, to the degree that it's completely unappetizing; the bitterness continues all the way through to the meek af-tertaste; this is really a bad joke that bastardizes the name of genuine "sherry"; this loser is so audaciously terrible that it makes the Cocktail Sherry seem positively smashing; doesn't even deserve the one star.

RATING ★ $

Gallo Cream Sherry 17% Alcohol (California)

Sunshine-yellow/goldenrod hue that's quite appealing to the eye; the medicinal, industrial, petroleum, doctor's-office nose exhibits no evidence whatsoever of sweetness or, for that matter, of wine; an off-balance tidal wave of artificial-tasting sweetness assaults the overmatched taste buds at mid-palate, then disappears in the photoflash finish; doubtless, the worst fortified-wine experience of my professional life; this anemic, foul wine has no redeeming virtue other than its use as a cleaning fluid to scrape the paint off the hull of your Chris Craft—nightmare on Modesto Street; at my kind-est and gentlest, I'll call it vile; the Gallo people should be ashamed for putting this disgusting garbage on the shelves of stores.

RATING ★ $

GALLO Port 18% Alcohol (California)

More a red-wine, ruby/garnet color than the traditional purplish/crimson hue most associated with port; the strawberry-soft-drink nose has a terribly nasty, vinegar-like twang to it—the bouquet, in a word, is revolting; a close second to the Gallo Cream Sherry in the hotly contested race for "worst domestic fortified wine of the century"; so bad that it almost makes one want to become a teetotaler.

RATING ★ $

GLEN ELLEN Imagery Series 1990 Zinfandel Port 20% Alcohol (California)

Youthful, medium purple/ruby color; the round, jammy nose is chockful of blackberry richness, with a briary backnote—the viney/leafy/steely zinfandel quality is unmistakable; rather light to the touch once on the palate; the briary quality discerned in the nose regrettably comes through in the flavor, going frightfully sour in the aftertaste; there's simply not enough heft in the flavor at midpalate to carry this port-like wine along to the next stage, namely, a solid finish, culminating in flavor satisfaction; a decent, honest attempt, however, and I look forward to tasting more fortified wines from the adventurous winemakers of Glen Ellen; I can see potential here.

RATING ★★ $

ORFILA VINEYARDS California Tawny Port 17.8% Alcohol (California)

Opaque, downright muddy, turbid reddish-brown hue, strikingly similar to unrefined prune juice, swirling clouds of very fine sediment capture my attention; the off-dry nose is intensely pruney and raisiny and that's about the extent of it—I didn't find much in the way of depth or scope in this simplistic, juicy nose; the flavor of overripe grapes fills the palate entry, then the nearly cloying raisin quality dominates all through midpalate; the chunky, filmy texture is too over-the-top for me—I feel like I need to floss afterward—mind you, I normally like a tad of sediment, but this is too much even for me; the finish is all raisins and prunes; port, even a domestic effort, should be more than a blast of wrinkled fruit—it should be balanced and elegant as well as substantial; the Orfila staff needs, in my humble opinion, to look at the example set by Ficklin Vineyards with regard to style.

RATING ★ $

ST. GEORGE CELLARS Framboise Royale 16% Alcohol (California)

Has the ruby-red/crimson color of a better red Côte de Beaune Burgundy like a Volnay or a Pommard; the nose is so seductive that it should be rated NC-17—the ripe raspberry perfume entices you into the bowl of the glass, then cuts loose with an incredible burst of ripe raspberry fruit—it's a spectacular bouquet; flavorwise, it's like grabbing a handful of perfectly ripened raspberries and unceremoniously stuffing them into your mouth—that's probably the highest compliment that can be paid to any fruit dessert wine; it's an ideal alcoholic beverage from start to finish; a benchmark for the category; buy by the case; the fruit comes from Oregon and Washington; the wine is fortified with true framboise eau-de-vie.

RATING ★★★★★   ***Highest Recommendation*** $

St. George Cellars Chardonnay Royale 16% Alcohol (California)

Looks the part of a Chardonnay table wine except for the noticeable ropiness of the texture—it clings to to the walls of the glass; the nose is as applelike as it is grapy, giving off assertive sugary notes at first, then with air contact backs off into a crisp, almost tart fruit bouquet that's even a bit like bread dough—an intriguing nose to say the least; on palate, the Chardonnay thumbprint is the foremost flavor element at entry, then a moderately appley sweetness picks up the taste ball and runs like a demon all the way into the subtle aftertaste—this was the one sample that I hated to spit out, so luscious was it; has a passing resemblance to Pineau des Charentes; made from North Coast *chardonnay* grapes.

RATING ★ ★ ★ ★   *Highly Recommended* $

St. George Cellars Poire Royale 16% Alcohol (California)

Lovely, deep harvest-gold/apple-cider hue; the pear perfume is catapulted forward from the sampling glass and rings true to pear from first nosing to the fourth—a one-note bouquet that's as classy and elegant as any domestic *poire* aroma; in the mouth, the flavor impact is more concerned with finesse than with aggressiveness—it's pear nirvana on the tongue as gently sweet and succulent pear flavor puts the taste buds into a pleasurable trance; the aftertaste comes off as soft as a down pillow; I rank this afterdinner dessert wine with the best that America has to offer.

RATING ★ ★ ★ ★   *Highly Recommended* $

St. George Cellars Kirsch Royale 16% Alcohol (California)

The brick-red tone is awfully pretty; though I have a mild aversion to most cherry brandies as well as overly sweet wines (exceptions include the terrific cherry brandies of Bonny Doon and Clear Creek), this sour nose almost makes me a convert—it's direct, tart, and not overly stony/slaty/pit-like or bitter—the fruit element is all there; on palate, the intense, clean cherry fruit completely won me over—there's not a hint of the bitterness that invariably seems to be part-and-parcel of most cherry spirits; the finish is soft, fruity, and immensely pleasurable; made from Montmorency cherries from Washington.

RATING ★ ★ ★ ★   *Highly Recommended* $

St. George Cellars Zinfandel Royale 16% Alcohol (California)

The deep purple color of a new port—an opaque core; the shy nose is loathe to come out and play initially, then with aeration, waves of ripe blackberries and plums emerge, albeit reluctantly—while this is anything but a blockbuster nose, I appreciate its quiet reserve and stateliness; in the mouth, it reminds me of a green, youthful, still astringent vintage port—tart flavors of raspberries, strawberries, and citrus vie for dominance in the midpalate; a good quaff—I'd serve it after dinner with light cheeses or possibly as an aperitif over ice like a sweet vermouth; made from Sonoma County and Napa Valley grapes, this lively dessert wine was aged in French oak.

RATING ★ ★ ★   *Recommended* $

TAYLOR Dry Sherry 18% Alcohol (New York)

Honey-like color; a seriously disturbing airplane-glue aroma mixes grade Z butterscotch in the atrocious nose, which calls to mind a "before" sample from a Hudson River water filtration plant; the unaware producers evidently have never sniffed a true sherry, otherwise they wouldn't have the bald-faced temerity to place the word "Sherry" on the label; a sour, mouth-puckering flavor turns off the palate almost immediately; the finish is harsh and bitter; an irretrievable liquid wasteland, born in the *Vitis lambrusca* vineyards of New York that should be replaced with *Vitis vinifera;* get with the program, Taylor, these are the 1990s.

RATING ★ $

TAYLOR Golden Sherry 18% Alcohol (New York)

Attractive dark-amber/brown color, with russet highlights; in the nose, it betrays the identical airplane-glue (*Vitis lambrusca* grape strain) quality of their Dry Sherry, but this time it's mixed with a kiss of burnt caramel; it actually begins in a decent, toasty manner upon palate entry, then stumbles miserably at midpalate as it descends into an unctuous caramely/butterscotchy concoction fit for neither man nor beast; it's too bad that this sherry got derailed in the taste, because there was some potential here with an appealing appearance and a fleeting hint of flavor quality.

RATING ★ $

TAYLOR Cream Sherry 18% Alcohol (New York)

More a mahogany/tawny port kind of color than an authentic cream sherry—the ruby highlights don't resemble any cream sherry that I'm aware of; predictably, the kernel-like/minerally nose emits the trademark aroma of Taylor sherries, which amounts to the essence of airplane glue; tastes about as much like cream sherry as Claudia Schiffer looks like Ma Kettle; it's frightfully astringent, plus it has no viscosity, sweetness, or ripe fruitiness; it's paper-thin, an awkward shadow; the bitter flavor mirrors a coffee/chocolate liqueur much more than a grape-based fortified wine; the Taylor wine maker must have an uncontrollable hankering for Kahlua; just barely drinkable, but as what, I ask? these poor saps must have gotten their wine-making credentials on the planet Mongo.

RATING ★ $

TAYLOR Port 18% Alcohol (New York)

Pretty color, but way too red to be dubbed a tawny port; the plastic, packing "popcorn" nose is simply nauseating; on palate, this is nothing more than pumped-up, fifth-rate, *Vitis lambrusca* grape juice; a totally inferior product that is brazenly called "port" when it hasn't anything to do with port; this isn't even an honest attempt gone awry.

RATING ★ $

TAYLOR Tawny Port 18% Alcohol (New York)

Concord grape juice look-alike; Concord grape juice smell-alike; Concord grape juice taste-alike, but with pumped-up alcohol; not even worth commenting on other than to say that I'm glad this is the last of Taylor's lethal weapons.

RATING ★ $

WINDSOR VINEYARDS NV Rare Port 19.6% Alcohol (California)

Handsome, advanced, deep ruby/blood-red color; the leafy, woody, vinous nose is only a touch sweet, with delectable, shy hints of spearmint and cinnamon; the pedal-to-the-metal flavors of prunes, chocolate-covered raisins, and chocolate cake frosting are completely arresting—I know, I surrendered; the cake frosting lasts all through the finish; not heavy, chewy, or viscous, this utterly delicious, ideally balanced fortified wine is a discovery of the first order; what I admired most about it is that it clearly isn't trying to emulate the true ports of Portugal—it's California through and through as the Zinfandel and Cabernet Sauvignon show their faces; hats off to wine maker Rick Sayre; mail-order only through Windsor Vineyards.

RATING ★★★★   *Highly Recommended* $

PORT-AUSTRALIA

BROWN BROTHERS Victorian Port 18% Alcohol

Deep mahogany/cola color, with russet highlights; high-octane, extremely sweet, intensely pruney, caramelized nose that reminds me much more of Pedro Ximenez sherry than any true port; the ropy, viscous texture is obviously high in glycerine since it drapes the inside of the glass; tastes of heavy-duty chocolate and toffee headline the flavor marquee from the firm, sweet entry to the gentle mocha-like aftertaste—the sweetness level is pleasant and manageable; I admired the balanced, almost sedate finish; this fortified wine has a lot going for it; comes nicely packaged in a ceramic jug.

RATING ★ ★ ★   *Recommended* $$

BROWN BROTHERS 1987 Vintage Port 20% Alcohol

Pretty, opaque, purple color, with a ruby edge; the nose gives off a vinous, leafy quality that is neither sweet nor dry; in the mouth, it's simple and monotone, offering a one-note flavor component of restrained grapiness that goes waxy in the finish; while agreeable, its innocuousness leaves the drinker looking for more depth, definition, and character than this port can offer; while it has no glaring production flaws, it lacks personality, which ultimately is what brings the consumer back a second time.

RATING ★ $

CHATEAU REYNELLA Old Cave Fine Old Tawny Port 18.5% Alcohol

One of the prettiest non-Portuguese ports I've reviewed—a lustrous, light-catching, blood-red/chestnut/sorrel hue, with russet highlights; the expressive nose leans a touch more to wood, spice, and herb/earth than to fruit, though there is a backnote of dried plums—I wasn't in awe of the bouquet, but I did find it agreeably serviceable; the sweet, concentrated fruitiness at palate entry is quite amplified, then by midpalate a soft overripe red-fruit character dominates all the way through to the surprisingly sedate aftertaste, which offers little in the way of depth or length; other critics have, to my bewilderment, swooned over this very nice but hardly earthshaking port, which offers pleasantly fruited and mildly spicy aromas and flavors in an acceptable package; try it for the experience and comparison to Portugal's tawnies.

RATING ★ ★ ★   ***Recommended*** $

SEPPELT **Trafford Tawny Port 18.5% Alcohol**

Outrageously beautiful rust/burnished-orange/copper color, excellent clarity; the slightly musty bouquet offers a fine range of fruit and nut aromas from pecans to candied apples to raisins—I noted little, if any, wood influence on the nose; in the mouth, it's quite light-bodied but very sweet, as the full-throttle candied fruit and caramel-corn flavors win over the taste buds in a flash; the finish is fast, clean, and over in a minute; this is a port in a hurry, but I genuinely liked it.

RATING ★ ★ ★   ***Recommended*** $

Fortified and Dessert Wines – South Africa

KWV Jerepigo Hanepoot 1975 17.5% Alcohol

Drop-dead gorgeous, medium-amber/rich honey-orange hue, perfect clarity; the nose is a bit musty in the first pass, then that blows off and a sweet, but lean, aroma dominates in the second nosing—the third and fourth passes offer up only a pine-like scent, which neither charms nor impresses; for all that was lacking in the aroma, the flavor makes up for in a sweet, light-bodied mouth presence featuring *muscat*-grape-like flavors of orange peel, white raisins, and spice—but it's the ethereal body that won me over—not cloying, syrupy, or viscous; try it ice cold with a slice of orange in the warm weather months.

    RATING ★ ★ ★   *Recommended* $ $

KWV Red Muscadel Vintage 75 17% Alcohol

Really beautiful, oloroso-sherry/chestnut/mahogany/tawny-brown color, perfect purity; the ambrosial nose is a dazzler—scents of overripe grapes, candied pineapple, baked spiced apples, and caramel highlight this delicate bouquet—by the last pass, it's quite subdued; on palate, the texture is medium-bodied and silky, but not syrupy—the manageably sweet flavors range from citrus to *muscat* grapes to black raisins—it's neither profound nor dense, but it does have a passing resemblance to the sweet sherry type known as Moscatel; the aftertaste is rather short, sweet, and even chocolatey.

    RATING ★ ★ ★   *Recommended* $

KWV 1967 Port Limited Release No Alcohol Designation

This fortified wine has the appearance of an aged tawny port, especially a 20- or 30-year-old variety, medium brown/tawny color with bright golden edges, pure; the nose is decidedly oaky and off-dry, with butterscotch and nuts qualities—it didn't expand or evolve with aeration; it shows a nice sour-fruit component at entry, then goes off-dry to sweet at midpalate—the melded flavors include ripe grapes, brown sugar, sweet oak, and vanilla extract—I wouldn't describe it as complex or port-like, but it does show enough ambrosial, overripe flashes to be compared with cream sherry; worthy of a try.

RATING ★ ★ ★ **Recommended** $$

KWV Full Cream Sherry 19.5% Alcohol

Good-looking, pure, medium amber/tawny tone with copper/russet core highlights; the nose is dull, raisiny, and burnt, with trailing aromas of dried apricots and nuts—the bouquet falls off the table completely in the last nosing; in the mouth, the taste is mildly attractive, sweet in a manufactured sense, and a bit pruney—there's no depth or layering, no nuances or subtleties—it's just a common, blue-collar, sweet, fortified wine that can't compete even with the most mundane true cream sherries from Spain; if it smelled and tasted as terrific as it looks, it would be a winner.

RATING ★ ★ $

KWV Full Tawny Port 19.5% Alcohol

Pure, medium-amber/medium-brown/dark-honey hue; similar to the ruby nose in its total lack of definition and breadth—no fruit in evidence—more of a wood influence than the terrible ruby—the cardboard/oak-cask backnote is its most prominent aromatic feature—things are looking grim; on palate, there's an attempt at respectability as a tart grapiness greets the taste buds at entry—it's moderately pleasant at midpalate as the wood enters the picture and provides an oaky balance to the dried-fruit element; drinkable, simple, and nothing remotely like real tawny port from Portugal.

RATING ★ ★ $

KWV Renasans Medium-Dry Sherry 19.5% Alcohol

Pleasing, golden-yellow/Sauternes-like hue, excellent purity; the soft-pedal nose emits an off-dry, modest, bread-dough aroma that doesn't expand with aeration and swirling—in the final pass, there's a hint of overripe yellow fruit—the nose bears absolutely no resemblance to true sherry from Jérez, Spain—what in the blazes is a company like KWV thinking of when they call this stuff "sherry"? haven't they ever tasted real sherry?—on palate, this loser goes nowhere but down—the sour taste has no charm, tastes like cardboard and very underripe grapes and is unpleasantly resiny; I invite KWV to come back into the world of reality.

RATING ★ $

KWV Full Ruby Port 19.5% Alcohol

Handsome, ruby/blood-red color, very good purity; the nose is monotone, offering a nonfruity, fabric-like aroma in the first two passes—aeration helps little—in the third pass, there's an extremely faint pruniness—a dead-on-arrival bouquet that has nothing to do with port as most of the world knows it; in the mouth, there's, at least, some evidence of dried fruit, but that's about all—a dull, do-nothing, know-nothing fortified wine (I can't even bring myself to refer to this swill as "port") that has the charm of a rock and the depth of rice paper.

RATING ★ $

KWV 1982 Vintage Port 19.5% Alcohol

Silty, sediment-filled, nearly opaque, blood-red color, absolutely requires decanting, the cork was dried out and crumbled miserably; the nose is remotely port-like, as very ripe, vanilla-like aromas gradually evolve with aeration—the third and fourth passes offer a tad more grapiness—hardly a blockbuster bouquet; in the mouth, it's more akin to a berry liqueur than to a true port, as the lack of acidity makes the sweet, grapy/plummy fruit seem chunky and fat—I didn't mind the intense grapiness, but the fruit simply runs amok without the balancing factor of acid; awkward, teaming with dubious-looking sediment, and, on the whole, unacceptable.

RATING ★ $

Montilla – Spain

Montillas are sweet wines that use the identical categorical names as sherry from the Jérez Triangle: *fino, amontillado* (a term derived from Montilla), *oloroso,* and *cream.* While both sherry and montilla wines come from the same southern province of Andalusia, they are born not only in different districts within the region but from different grape types as well. Montilla is the product of the Montilla-Moriles district, which lies inland approximately 100 miles due northeast of Jérez de la Frontera. The primary grape is the *Pedro Ximenez.*

Montilla-Moriles is a very hot, arid district whose soil is white, limey, and chalky. The *Pedro Ximenez* grape type, of which meager amounts are grown in the Sherry Triangle, is named after an infantry soldier from Flanders, one Pedro Ximen, who, legend tells us, introduced the grape to the Montilla-Moriles district. The intense heat during the growing season of Montilla-Moriles encourages sugar levels in *Pedro Ximenez* grapes to soar, which in turn, means that alcohol levels are naturally high. Some of the montillas don't require fortification with brandy, so lofty are their alcohol contents. The commercial center for the Montilla-Moriles area is the beautiful, elevated city of Cordoba.

The following montillas are from the Alvear firm, which was founded in 1729. I found them to be extremely palatable and slightly fatter and less acidic than the majority of sherries from Jérez. Did I like them more than the sherries I've evaluated? Not necessarily. I valued them for what they are—concentrated, voluptuous fortified/dessert wines that deserve to be given a good, leisurely look by anyone who relishes the might and grace of sherry.

ALVEAR Moscatel Montilla 15% Alcohol

Dark brown but not opaque hue, excellent clarity; the nose is my runaway favorite of the Alvears—plump, floral, zesty aromas of violets, roses, ripe pears, apricots, and nectarines are complemented by an unexpected freshness that sets this sweet beauty apart—it's an exhilarating bouquet; on the palate, this moderately viscous montilla has drop-dead wonderful tastes of pears, peaches, kiwi fruit, grapes, vanilla, coconut, and sweetened pineapple; the finish is manageably sweet and very extended in the tropical-fruit element; this is not an unctuous, scoop-out-with-spoon style of sweet fortified wine and that's precisely why it's so uncommon and delicious; an exhilarating experience of the first rank.

RATING ★ ★ ★ ★ ★   ***Highest Recommendation*** $

ALVEAR Cream Montilla 18% Alcohol

Medium brown/pekoe-tea tone, superb purity; the nose is pruney and raisiny, fresh and lively, and not in the least heavy-handed or clunky—there's a ripe-grape backnote that's reined-in for some reason; on the palate, the lightness and silkiness of the texture are fantastically appealing (much like the favorably reviewed Emilio Lustau 1986 Vendemia Cream); at mid-palate, a luscious chocolatey taste meets the red-fruit component, resulting in a genuinely delicious flavor that ushers in the supple, moderately sweet finish, wherein a chocolate-covered-cherry taste brings a delectable closure to the captivating experience; one of the better creams I've evaluated.

RATING ★ ★ ★ ★   ***Highly Recommended*** $

ALVEAR Festival Pale Cream Montilla 13.5% Alcohol

This atypical cream owns the attractive straw hue of a fino or even a California Sauvignon Blanc, absolute clarity; the nose is very soft, with nuanced, barely perceptible aromas of casaba melon, apricot, mild bread dough, musk, and spice—the alluring bouquet is understated to the point of shyness; once in the mouth, however, this feline, low-alcohol, feminine montilla parades its wears, as flavors of melon, peach, pear, apricot, and ripe grapes elegantly charm the palate—being a cream, there's ample sweetness, but the overall agility of the texture make this an easily drinkable cream, one that you're quite happy to have a second glass of; it's supple, yet lean, sweet, but not cloying; I sampled it well chilled.

RATING ★ ★ ★ ★   ***Highly Recommended*** $

ALVEAR Pedro Ximenez Montilla Solera Abuelo Diego 27 15% Alcohol

Medium brown/cola color, excellent purity; the heavyweight, overripe bouquet screams in pruney/raisiny ecstasy—if you have a vigorous sweet tooth, this is right up your tonsils; even though it's supersweet and syrupy it's still only semimassive—it's jammed with grapy, vanilla-wafer flavors, but is sippable; the aftertaste is infinite and lush, but clean; not nearly as colossal as the supersweet sherries such as Argueso (four stars), Emilio Lustau San Emilio (five stars), or Pedro Domecq Venerable (five stars), but a sound, ultrasweet, and properly decadent thoroughbred PX that should be on the shopping list of any megasweet-fortified-wine aficionado.

RATING ★ ★ ★ ★   ***Highly Recommended*** $

Alvear Amontillado Montilla Solera Abuelo Diego 17% Alcohol

Medium amber, good purity; delicate aroma of *flor* (yeast), flowers, and nut meat are attractively complemented by a wood-resin quality—it's an unassuming, understated nose that's off-dry and ethereal; shows a good, crisp presence on the tongue, as tastes of barely ripe apples and grapes, and minerals carry the day; the finish is stone-dry, citrusy, and cleansing; the lack of stuffing was not a problem for me, since I zeroed in on the tart fruit component, which I found quite pleasant; an agile amontillado that's light-footed, inviting, and uncomplicated.

RATING ★ ★ ★   *Recommended* $

Alvear Oloroso Montilla Solera Abuelo Diego 18% Alcohol

Medium-to-dark amber, with copper highlights and ideal purity; the welcoming bouquet emits warm, ripe, but not syrupy aromas of nuts, oak, light caramel, raisins, and cinnamon toast—it's a pleasingly straightforward and easy nose that has a particularly toasty backnote that I liked; in the mouth, the taste is off-dry and has fleeting flavors of grapes *(Pedro Ximenez)*, candied apples, hard candy, and orange peel; the aftertaste is long and off-dry, highlighting the candied-apple taste sensation; with the texture being so spry, the fruit component was free to flash its best stuff; hardly profound, but very good nevertheless.

RATING ★ ★ ★   *Recommended* $

Alvear Fino Montilla (Spain) 16% Alcohol

Tasted moderately chilled; pretty straw color, excellent purity; the animated nose is chockful of sourdough, pineapple, banana, baker's yeast (the *flor*), rose petal, and citrus aromas—it's a full-speed-ahead sour fruit bouquet that's seriously appetizing, compelling, fresh, and friendly; in the mouth, its keen green-apple tartness nearly makes my mouth pucker—the acid/crispness level cleanses the palate immediately, leading to the svelte, light-bodied midpalate, which features unsweetened pineapple and dough primarily, and apple and citrus secondarily; the finish is snappily clean and razor-crisp; this is a slightly more substantial fino style than the ones from Jérez; a superb chilled aperitif.

RATING ★ ★ ★   *Recommended* $

Alvear Amontillado Montilla (Spain) 17% Alcohol

Medium amber color with orange highlights, perfect clarity; this seductive bouquet is off-dry, with subtle notes of nougat, candied pears, and ripe peaches—it's a nimble, lightish bouquet that spotlights the fruit element nicely—on the fourth nosing, I detected late-coming aromas of juniper and wood; the mouth-feel was where I felt disappointed, as suddenly sweet, soda-pop-like flavors unfortunately undercut any complexity or character; mind, I'm not saying that it's bad-tasting, it's just too simplistic and cavalier with reference to my personal experience and understanding of amontillado; the aftertaste goes from off-dry to tart; the tutti-frutti taste and finish unravel all the positives enjoyed in the appearance and bouquet.

RATING ★ $

APPENDIX A

Alphabetical Brandy Summary by Rating Category

COGNAC—FRANCE

Classic—Highest Recommendation
A. DE FUSSIGNY Très Vieille Series Rares Cognac Grande Champagne ★★★★★
A. E. DOR Hors d'Age No. 9 Cognac Grande Champagne ★★★★★
DANIEL BOUJU Très Vieux Brut de Fut Cognac Grande Champagne ★★★★★
DELAMAIN Réserve de la Famille Cognac Grande Champagne ★★★★★
FRAPIN VIP XO Cognac Grande Champagne ★★★★★
FRAPIN Extra Réserve Patrimoniale Cognac Grande Champagne ★★★★★
GABRIEL & ANDREU Borderies Cognac Lot 3 ★★★★★
GABRIEL & ANDREU Petite Champagne Cognac Lot 23 ★★★★★
HINE 1953 Cognac Grande Champagne ★★★★★
MARTELL XO Cordon Suprême Cognac ★★★★★
PIERRE FERRAND Réserve Ancestrale Cognac Grande Champagne ★★★★★
PIERRE FERRAND Abel Cognac Grande Champagne ★★★★★

Superb—Highly Recommended
A. DE FUSSIGNY Vieille Réserve Séries Rares Cognac Fine Champagne ★★★★
A. DE FUSSIGNY XO Cognac ★★★★
A. DE FUSSIGNY Sélection Cognac ★★★★
A. E. DOR XO Cognac Fine Champagne ★★★★
A. E. DOR Hors d'Age No. 8 Cognac Grande Champagne ★★★★
A. HARDY XO Cognac ★★★★
COURVOISIER Succession "J. L." Cognac Grande Champagne ★★★★

COURVOISIER Cour Impériale Cognac Grande Champagne ★★★★
COURVOISIER Chateau Limoges Extra Cognac Fine Champagne ★★★★
COURVOISIER VOC Extra Cognac ★★★★
DANIEL BOUJU VSOP Cognac Grande Champagne ★★★★
DANIEL BOUJU Extra Cognac Grande Champagne ★★★★
DELAMAIN Pale & Dry Très Belle Cognac Grande Champagne ★★★★
DELAMAIN Très Vénérable Cognac Grande Champagne ★★★★
FRAPIN Vieille Cognac Grande Champagne ★★★★
FRAPIN Chateau de Fontpinot Très Vieille Réserve Cognac Grande Champagne ★★★★
GABRIEL & ANDREU Grande Champagne Cognac Lot 18 ★★★★
GIBOIN Napoleon Réserve de Castex Cognac ★★★★
GIBOIN Sélection Borderies de L'Hermitage Cognac ★★★★
GIBOIN XO Royal Cognac Grande Champagne ★★★★
HENNESSY Paradis Cognac ★★★★
HENNESSY Sélection Davidoff Cognac ★★★★
HINE 1952 Cognac Grande Champagne ★★★★
HINE Antique Très Rare Cognac Fine Champagne ★★★★
HINE Triomphe Cognac Grande Champagne ★★★★
HINE Family Réserve Cognac Grande Champagne ★★★★
JEAN DANFLOU Extra Cognac Grande Champagne ★★★★
LEOPOLD GOURMEL L'Age des Fleurs Fins Bois Cognac ★★★★
MARCEL RAGNAUD Grande Réserve Fontvieille Cognac Grande Champagne ★★★★
MARTELL Cordon Bleu Cognac ★★★★
MARTELL Extra Cognac ★★★★
PIERRE CROIZET XO Cognac ★★★★
PIERRE FERRAND Réserve de la Propriété Cognac Grande Champagne ★★★★
PIERRE FERRAND Sélection des Anges Cognac Grande Champagne ★★★★
REMY MARTIN XO Spécial Cognac Fine Champagne ★★★★
REMY MARTIN Extra Perfection Cognac Fine Champagne ★★★★
REMY MARTIN Louis XIII Cognac Grande Champagne ★★★★
SALIGNAC Réserve Cognac Fine Champagne ★★★★

Above Average—Recommended
A. E. DOR VSOP Cognac ★★★
A. HARDY VSOR Cognac ★★★
A. HARDY Napoleon Cognac ★★★
ANSAC VS Cognac ★★★
COURVOISIER Initiale Extra Cognac ★★★
COURVOISIER Napoleon Cognac ★★★
DELAMAIN Vesper Cognac Grande Champagne ★★★
FRAPIN Cuves Rare Cognac Grande Champagne ★★★
GABRIEL & ANDREU Fins Bois Cognac Lot 8 ★★★
GIBOIN VS Cognac ★★★
GIBOIN VSOP Réserve de l'Hermitage Cognac ★★★
HENNESSY XO Cognac ★★★

Jean Danflou Cognac Fine Champagne ★★★
Leopold Gourmel Quintessence Fins Bois Cognac ★★★
Marcel Ragnaud VSER Cognac Grande Champagne ★★★
Marcel Ragnaud Réserve Spéciale Cognac Grande Champagne ★★★
Martell VS Cognac ★★★
Pierre Croizet Napoleon Cognac ★★★
Remy Martin Napoleon Cognac Fine Champagne ★★★
Salignac XO Cognac ★★★

Average—Not Recommended
Courvoisier XO Cognac ★★
Courvoisier VSOP Cognac ★★
Hennessy VSOP "Privilège" Cognac ★★
Hine VSOP Cognac Fine Champagne ★★
Leopold Gourmel L'Age des Epices Fins Bois Cognac ★★
Leyrat Napoleon Cognac ★★
Marcel Ragnaud VE Cognac Grande Champagne ★★
Marnier VSOP Cognac Fine Champagne ★★
Martell VSOP Médaillon Cognac ★★
Nicolas Napoleon VSOP Cognac ★★
Pierre Croizet VSOP Cognac ★★
Staub Napoleon Cognac ★★

Poor—Not Recommended
Chabanneau VS Cognac ★
Courvoisier VS Cognac ★
Hennessy VS Cognac ★
Leopold Gourmel L'Age du Fruit Fins Bois Cognac ★
Leyrat Fine Cognac ★
Leyrat VSOP Cognac ★
Leyrat Brut Absolu Cognac ★
Leyrat Brut de Futs Cognac ★
Louis Royer VSOP Cognac ★
Louis Royer XO Cognac ★
Nicolas Napoleon VS Cognac ★
Remy Martin VS Cognac Fine Champagne ★
Remy Martin VSOP Cognac Fine Champagne ★
Salignac VS Cognac ★
Salignac VSOP Cognac ★
Salignac Napoleon Cognac ★
Staub VS Cognac ★
Staub VSOP Cognac ★

Armagnac—France

Classic—Highest Recommendation
De Montal Réserve Personnelle Armagnac ★★★★★
Sempe Impérial Réserve Baccarat Crown Armagnac ★★★★★

Superb—Highly Recommended

CERBOIS 1985 Bas Armagnac ★★★★
CERBOIS 1962 Bas Armagnac ★★★★
CERBOIS 1955 Bas Armagnac ★★★★
DE MONTAL 1965 Armagnac ★★★★
DE MONTAL 1962 Armagnac ★★★★
DE MONTAL 1939 Armagnac ★★★★
JANNEAU 1966 Armagnac ★★★★
LABERDOLIVE 1982 Bas Armagnac ★★★★
LABERDOLIVE 1976 Bas Armagnac ★★★★
LARRESSINGLE Très Vieil 1934 Armagnac ★★★★
MARCEL TREPOUT 1971 Armagnac ★★★★
MARQUIS DE CAUSSADE Extra S. P. Armagnac ★★★★
MARQUIS DE CAUSSADE 17 Ans Grande Age Armagnac ★★★★
SAMALENS 1966 Vintage Millesime ★★★★
SEMPE Grande Réserve Prism Armagnac ★★★★
SEMPE 1965 Armagnac ★★★★
SEMPE Extra "The Crown of Louis XIV" Blue Limoges Decanter ★★★★

Above Average—Recommended

B. GELAS 12-Year-Old Bas Armagnac ★★★
CERBOIS 1967 Bas Armagnac ★★★
DE MONTAL XO Armagnac ★★★
DE MONTAL 1975 Armagnac ★★★
JANNEAU Réserve de la Maison Grande Fine Armagnac ★★★
LARRESSINGLE XO Grande Réserve Armagnac ★★★
LARRESSINGLE Très Vieil 1960 Armagnac ★★★
MARCEL TREPOUT XO Armagnac ★★★
MARQUIS DE CAUSSADE VSOP Armagnac ★★★
MARQUIS DE CAUSSADE 10 Ans Fine Armagnac ★★★
SAMALENS Relique Ancestrale ★★★
SEMPE Napoleon "The Crown of Napoleon" Green Limoges Decanter
    ★★★
SEMPE X. O. "The Crown of Henry IV" Red Limoges Decanter ★★★
SEMPE 1973 Armagnac ★★★
SEMPE 1924 Armagnac ★★★

Average—Not Recommended

CASTAREDE VSOP Armagnac ★★
CERBOIS 1974 Bas Armagnac ★★
CERBOIS 1965 Bas Armagnac ★★
CERBOIS 1940 Bas Armagnac ★★
DE MONTAL VSOP Armagnac ★★
GERLAND VS Armagnac ★★
JANNEAU VSOP ★★
LARRESSINGLE VSOP Armagnac ★★
SEMPE 1908 Armagnac ★★
SEMPE 15-Year-Old Armagnac ★★

Poor—Not Recommended
DE MONTAL 1961 Armagnac ★
DE MONTAL 1960 Armagnac ★
GERLAND VSOP Armagnac ★
LAPOSTOLLE XO Armagnac ★
NICOLAS NAPOLEON Armagnac VS ★
SAMALENS VSOP Bas-Armagnac ★
SEMPE VSOP Armagnac ★

AMERICAN BRANDY

Classic—Highest Recommendation
CLEAR CREEK DISTILLERY Eau-de-Vie de Pomme Apple Brandy (Oregon)
★★★★★
GERMAIN-ROBIN Pinot Noir Single-Barrel Brandy (California) ★★★★★

Superb—Highly Recommended
BONNY DOON Poire Eau-de-Vie (California) ★★★★
BONNY DOON Cal Del Solo Prunus Eau-de-Vie (California) ★★★★
CARNEROS ALAMBIC QE Alambic Brandy (California) ★★★★
CLEAR CREEK DISTILLERY Williams Pear Brandy (Oregon) ★★★★
CLEAR CREEK DISTILLERY Kirschwasser (Oregon) ★★★★
CREEKSIDE VINEYARDS Grappa (California) ★★★★
DOMAINE CHARBAY Grappa di Marko (California) ★★★★
GERMAIN-ROBIN Shareholder's Blend No. 4 Alambic Brandy (California)
★★★★
GERMAIN-ROBIN Reserve Alambic Brandy (California) ★★★★
GERMAIN-ROBIN XO Select Barrel Reserve Alambic Brandy (California)
★★★★
GERMAIN-ROBIN Zinfandel Grappa (California) ★★★★
GERMAIN-ROBIN Old Vine Zinfandel Grappa (California) ★★★★
GERMAIN-ROBIN V43 Single-Barrel Alambic Brandy (California) ★★★★
GERMAIN-ROBIN V16 Single-Barrel Alambic Brandy (California) ★★★★
GERMAIN-ROBIN Cigar Lover's Blend Alambic Brandy (California) ★★★★
ST. GEORGE SPIRITS Kirsch Eau-de-Vie (California) ★★★★
ST. GEORGE SPIRITS Grappa of Zinfandel (California) ★★★★

Above Average—Recommended
BONNY DOON Cerise Eau-de-Vie (California) ★★★
CARNEROS ALAMBIC XR Alambic Brandy (California) ★★★
CARNEROS ALAMBIC Folle Blanche Brandy (California) ★★★
CLEAR CREEK DISTILLERY Grappa (Oregon) ★★★
CLEAR CREEK DISTILLERY Apple Brandy (Oregon) ★★★
KORBEL Brandy ★★★
ST. GEORGE SPIRITS Grappa of Traminer (California) ★★★

Average—Not Recommended
BONNY DOON 1978 Fine Potstill Brandy (California) ★★
BONNY DOON Nectarine Eau-de-Vie (California) ★★

CARNEROS ALAMBIC Special Reserve Brandy (California) ★★
DOMAINE CHARBAY Calvad'or Apple Brandy (California) ★★
E & J Brandy (California) ★★
GERMAIN-ROBIN Fine Alambic Brandy Lot 12 (California) ★★
PAUL MASSON Grande Amber Brandy ★★
ST. GEORGE SPIRITS Williams Pear Eau-de-Vie (California) ★★
ST. GEORGE SPIRITS Framboise Eau-de-Vie (California) ★★

Poor—Not Recommended
CHRISTIAN BROTHERS Brandy (California) ★
CORONET VSQ Brandy ★
CREEKSIDE VINEYARDS Apple Brandy (California) ★
CREEKSIDE VINEYARDS Grape Brandy (California) ★
E & J VSOP Brandy (California) ★
JACQUIN'S Five-Star Brandy ★

BRANDY AND GRAPPA—ITALY

Classic—Highest Recommendation
AB COLLECTION BACCHE DI Corbezzolo ★★★★★
AB COLLECTION Fiore Di Rosa ★★★★★
AB COLLECTION Grappa Di Moscato d'Asti ★★★★★
GAJA COSTA RUSSI Nebbiolo Grappa ★★★★★
GRAPPA DA VINACCE DI SASSICAIA ★★★★★
JACOPO POLI Sarpa di Grappa ★★★★★

Superb—Highly Recommended
BORTOLO NARDINI Riserva Grappa ★★★★
GRAPPA DI CAPEZZANA Riserva ★★★★
GRAPPA DI ORNELLAIA di Merlot ★★★★
JACOPO POLI Grappa Amorosa di Merlot ★★★★
JACOPO POLI Grappa Amorosa di Torcolato ★★★★
JACOPO POLI Chiara di Moscato Immature-Grape Brandy ★★★★
LUNGAROTTI Grappa di Rubesco ★★★★
MARCHESI DI GRESY 1988 Grappa Martinenga ★★★★
MICHELE CHIARLO Vinacce di Moscato d'Asti Grappa ★★★★
PIAVE Plum-Flavored Grappa ★★★★
TENUTA IL POGGIONE Grappa di Brunello ★★★★

Above Average—Recommended
BANFI Grappa di Moscadello ★★★
BANFI Grappa di Brunello ★★★
BORTOLO NARDINI Rue-Flavored Grappa ★★★
CERETTO Zonchera Nebbiolo ★★★
JACOPO POLI Grappa Amorosa di Vespaiolo ★★★
JACOPO POLI Grappa Amorosa di Pinot ★★★
JACOPO POLI Chiara di Fragnola Immature-Grape Brandy ★★★
MASTROBERARDINO 1987 Grappa Novia Greco di Tufo ★★★

MASTROBERARDINO 1987 Grappa Novia Taurasi ★★★
MICHELE CHIARLO Vinacce di Gavi Grappa ★★★
MICHELE CHIARLO Vinacce di Barolo Grappa ★★★
VECCHIA ROMAGNA Riserva Rara Oltre 15 Anni Brandy ★★★
VECCHIA ROMAGNA Riserva 10 Anni Brandy ★★★

Average—Not Recommended
CANDOLINI Grappa Ruta (Rue Flavored) ★★
CERETTO Brunate Nebbiolo ★★
JACOPO POLI Grappa Amorosa di Cabernet Rating ★★
JACOPO POLI Chiara di Tocai Rossi Immature-Grape Brandy ★★
SARTORI Grappa Delia Valpolicella ★★
VECCHIA ROMAGNA Etichetta Nera Brandy ★★

BRANDY AND BRANDY DE JÉREZ—SPAIN

Classic—Highest Recommendation
GRAN DUQUE D'ALBA Solera Gran Reserva Brandy de Jérez ★★★★★

Superb—Highly Recommended
CARDENAL MENDOZA Solera Gran Reserva Brandy de Jérez ★★★★
CARDENAL MENDOZA Non Plus Ultra Solera Gran Reserva Brandy de Jérez
    ★★★★
CONDE DE OSBORNE Solera Gran Reserva ★★★★
LEPANTO Solera Gran Reserva Brandy de Jérez ★★★★
MASCARO Don Narciso 8- to 10-Year-Old (Catalonia) ★★★★

Above Average—Recommended
MASCARO VO 3-Year-Old (Catalonia) ★★★
MIGUEL TORRES Imperial Brandy Reserva Especial ★★★
ROMATE Solera Reserva Brandy de Jérez ★★★
TERRY PRIMERO Solera Gran Reserva ★★★

Average—Not Recommended
FELIPE II Solera Reserva Brandy de Jérez ★★
MERITO Brandy de Jérez Solera ★★
PEDRO DOMECQ Carlos I Solera Gran Reserva Brandy de Jérez ★★
TERRY 1900 Solera Reserva ★★

Poor—Not Recommended
TERRY Centenario Solera ★
VETERANO Solera Brandy de Jérez ★

EAUX-DE-VIE, FRUIT BRANDIES, AND CRÈMES—EUROPE

Classic—Highest Recommendation
ETTER Poire Williams (Switzerland) ★★★★★
RENE DE MISCAULT Poire William (France) ★★★★★

Retter Himbeer Raspberry Nectar (Austria) ★★★★★
Retter Waldheidelbeer Forest Blueberry Nectar (Austria) ★★★★★
Trimbach Prunelle Sauvage Grande Réserve (France) ★★★★★
Trimbach Kirsch Grande Réserve (France) ★★★★★
Trimbach Mirabelle Grande Réserve (France) ★★★★★
Trimbach Framboise Grande Réserve (France) ★★★★★

Superb—Highly Recommended

Baccate De Peche De Vigne (Peach) (France) ★★★★
Baccate De Mure (Blackberry) (France) ★★★★
Capovilla 1992 Prugne Selvatiche Distillato a Bagnomaria (Italy) ★★★★
Etienne Brana Framboise Raspberry Brandy (France) ★★★★
Etter Kirsch Buger (Switzerland) ★★★★
Etter Pomme Gravine (Switzerland) ★★★★
Etter Pflumli Prune (Switzerland) ★★★★
Etter Framboise Himbeere (Switzerland) ★★★★
Gabriel Boudier Josie Framboise (France) ★★★★
Jacopo Poli Stagione di Lamponi Raspberry Brandy (Italy) ★★★★
Rene De Miscault Framboise Sauvage (France) ★★★★
Retter Gravensteiner Apple Essence (Asutria) ★★★★
Retter Hirschbirne Pear Essence (Austria) ★★★★
Retter Marillen Apricot Essence (Austria) ★★★★
Retter Sour Cherry Nectar (Austria) ★★★★
Trimbach Poire William Grande Réserve (France) ★★★★

Above Average—Recommended

Baccate De Framboise (Raspberry) (France) ★★★
Carton Crème de Cassis de Bourgogne (France) ★★★
Dettling Kirschwasser (France) ★★★
Etienne Brana Poire Williams (France) ★★★
Etter Quitte Coing (Switzerland) ★★★
Jacopo Poli Stagione di Pere Pear Brandy (Italy) ★★★
Jacopo Poli Stagione di Ciliege Cherry Brandy (Italy) ★★★
Rene De Miscault Ginger (France) ★★★
Rene De Miscault Réserve Celeri (France) ★★★
Rene De Miscault Marc de Gewurztraminer (France) ★★★
Rene De Miscault Réserve Kirsch (France) ★★★
Rene De Miscault Vieille Prune (France) ★★★
Retter Williams-Christ Pear Essence (Austria) ★★★
Retter Vogelbeeren Elderberry Nectar (Austria) ★★★
Retter Brombeer Blackberry Nectar (Austria) ★★★
Retter Macintosh Apple Essence (Austria) ★★★

Average—Not Recommended

Rene De Miscault Réserve Quetsch (France) ★★
Retter Original Apple Cuvée Essence (Austria) ★★

Poor—Not Recommended
Baccate De Cerise (Cherry) (France) ★
Baccate De Cassis (Blackcurrant) (France) ★
Gabriel Boudier Cassis (France) ★
Rene De Miscault Myrtille (France) ★
Retter Holunder Rowanberry Nectar (Austria) ★

Appendix B

Alphabetical White Spirits Summary by Rating Category

Gin

Classic—Highest Recommendation
CORNEY & BARROW London Dry Gin (England) ★★★★★
TANQUERAY Special Dry English Gin (England) ★★★★★

Superb—Highly Recommended
BEEFEATER London Dry Gin (England) ★★★★
BOMBAY Sapphire London Dry Gin (England) ★★★★
BRADBURN'S English Gin (England) ★★★★

Above Average—Recommended
BOMBAY Dry Gin (England) ★★★
BOODLES British Gin (England) ★★★
GREENALL'S Original London Dry Gin (England) ★★★
NOTARIS V. O. Genever Moutwijn (Holland) ★★★
SEAGRAM'S Extra Dry Gin (USA) ★★★
SOMERS British Gin with Citrus Flavour (England) ★★★

Average—Not Recommended
GILBEY'S London Dry Gin (USA) ★★
GORDON'S London Dry Gin (USA) ★★
SIR ROBERT BURNETT'S London Dry Gin (USA) ★★

Poor—Not Recommended
FLEISCHMANN'S Distilled Dry Gin (USA) ★

Rum

Classic—Highest Recommendation
Barbancourt Estate Réserve 15-Year-Old Rhum (Haiti) ★★★★★
Clement 1952 (Martinique) ★★★★★

Superb—Highly Recommended
Appleton Dark Rum (Jamaica) ★★★★
Appleton Estate VX 5-Year-Old Rum (Jamaica) ★★★★
Barbancourt Réserve Spéciale 8-Year-Old Rhum (Haiti) ★★★★
Brugal Añejo Gran Reserva Familiar (Dominican Republic) ★★★★
Captain Morgan Private Stock Spiced Rum (Puerto Rico) ★★★★
Clement 1970 (Martinique) ★★★★
Clement 15-Year-Old (Martinique) ★★★★
Flor De Cana Grand Reserve Rum (Nicaragua) ★★★★
Pampero Ron Añejo Deluxe (Venezuela) ★★★★
Pampero Ron Añejo Aniversario (Venezuela) ★★★★
Rhum J. Bally 1982 Agricole (Martinique) ★★★★
Rhum Martinique Vieux 7-Year-Old Agricole (Martinique) ★★★★
Ron Del Barrilito Two-Star Rum (Puerto Rico) ★★★★

Above Average—Recommended
Bacardi Añejo Rum (Puerto Rico) ★★★
Bacardi Gold Reserve Rum (Puerto Rico) ★★★
Barbancourt 4-Year-Old Rhum (Haiti) ★★★
Brugal White Label (Dominican Republic) ★★★
Captain Morgan Coconut Rum (Puerto Rico) ★★★
Captain Morgan Original Spiced Rum (Puerto Rico) ★★★
Clement Blanc (Martinique) ★★★
Clement 10-Year-Old (Martinique) ★★★
Cockspur V.S.O.R. (Barbados) ★★★
Cruzan Premium Diamond Estate 4-Year-Old Rum (US VI) ★★★
Flor De Cana Gold Rum (Nicaragua) ★★★
Flor De Cana Black Label Rum (Nicaragua) ★★★
Gosling's Black Seal Dark Rum (Bermuda) ★★★
Mount Gay Eclipse (Barbados) ★★★
Myers's Platinum White Rum (Jamaica) ★★★
Pampero Ron Premium Gold Rum (Venezuela) ★★★
Rhum Martinique Blanc 3-Year-Old Agricole (Martinique) ★★★
Ron Del Barrilito Three-Star Rum (Puerto Rico) ★★★
Ron Rico Gold Label Rum (Puerto Rico / Bottled in U.S.) ★★★
Ron Rico Spiced Rum & Cola (Puerto Rico / Prepared and Canned in
    U.S.) ★★★
Strummer's Fruited Rum (Jamaica / Bottled in U.S.) ★★★
Toucano Cachaca Rum (Brazil) ★★★

Average—Not Recommended
BACARDI Light Rum (Puerto Rico) ★★
BACARDI Black Rum (Puerto Rico) ★★
BACARDI Limon Rum (USA) ★★
BLUEBEARD'S Authentic Spiced Rum (U.S. Virgin Islands) ★★
BRUGAL Gold Label (Dominican Republic) ★★
CASTILLO Spiced Rum (Puerto Rico) ★★
C. J. WRAY Dry Rum (Jamaica) ★★
CLEMENT 6-Year-Old (Martinique) ★★
CRISTAL Aguardiente (Colombia) ★★
CRUZAN Dark-Dry Rum (U.S. Virgin Islands) ★★
DON Q Cristal Rum 4 (Puerto Rico) ★★
DON Q Gold Rum (Puerto Rico) ★★
FLOR DE CANA Extra Dry Rum (Nicaragua) ★★
JUMBY BAY Proprietor's Rum (Antigua) ★★
MYERS'S Original Dark Rum (Jamaica) ★★
PUSSER'S BRITISH NAVY Admiral's Reserve (British Virgin Islands) ★★
RHUM J. BALLY 1970 Agricole (Martinique) ★★
RON BOTRAN Añejo (Guatamala) ★★
RON LLAVE Oro Supremo Rum (Puerto Rico / Bottled in U.S.) ★★
RON MATUSALEM Golden Label Rum (Puerto Rico) ★★

Poor—Not Recommended
CACIQUE Ron Añejo (Venezuela) ★
COCKSPUR Five-Star (Barbados) ★
CRUZAN Light-Dry Rum (U.S. Virgin Islands) ★
CRUZAN Clipper Spiced Rum (U.S. Virgin Islands) ★
DON Q 151 Rum (Puerto Rico) ★
PIRASSUNUNGA 51 Cachaca (Brazil) ★
PUSSER'S BRITISH NAVY Rum (British Virgin Islands) ★
RHUM J. BALLY 1975 Agricole (Martinique) ★
RON BOTRAN Light Dry (Guatamala) ★
RON BOTRAN Oro (Guatamala) ★
RON LLAVE Blanco Supremo Rum (Puerto Rico / Bottled in U.S.) ★
RON MATUSALEM Carta Plata Rum (Puerto Rico) ★
RON RICO Silver Label Rum (Puerto Rico / Bottled in U.S.) ★
RON RICO Spiced Rum (Puerto Rico / Bottled in U.S.) ★
RON RICO Rum & Cola (Puerto Rico / Prepared and Canned in U.S.) ★
RON RICO Rum & Tonic (Puerto Rico / Prepared and Canned in U.S.) ★
RON VIEJO DE CALDAS (Colombia) ★
ROYAL OAK Select Rum (Trinidad) ★
STUBBS Queensland Dry White Rum (Australia) ★
VENADO Especial Aguardiente (Guatamala) ★

VODKA

Classic—Highest Recommendation
SMIRNOFF Black Vodka (Russian Federation) ★★★★★
STOLICHNAYA Cristall (Russian Federation) ★★★★★

Superb—Highly Recommended

ABSOLUT Kurant Vodka (Sweden) ★★★★
ABSOLUT Citron Lemon Vodka (Sweden) ★★★★
FINLANDIA Vodka 100-proof (Finland) ★★★★
KETEL ONE Vodka (Holland) ★★★★
MOSKOVSKAYA Osobaya Vodka (Russian Federation) ★★★★
STOLICHNAYA Ohranj Orange Vodka (Russian Federation) ★★★★
STOLICHNAYA Limonnaya Lemon Vodka (Russian Federation) ★★★★
STOLICHNAYA Pertsovka Pepper Vodka (Russian Federation) ★★★★

Above Average—Recommended

ABSOLUT Peppar Pepper Vodka (Sweden) ★★★
BURNETT'S Vodka (USA) ★★★
DANZKA Danish Vodka (Denmark) ★★★
DANZKA Citron Lemon-Flavored Vodka (Denmark) ★★★
DENAKA Vodka (Denmark) ★★★
FINLANDIA Vodka 80-proof (Finland) ★★★
GORDON'S Citrus Vodka (USA) ★★★
LASKA Vodka (Czech Republic) ★★★
MAJORSKA Vodka (USA) ★★★
NIKOLAI Gold Vodka (USA) ★★★
PRIVIET Vodka (Russian Federation) ★★★
ROYALTY Vodka (Holland) ★★★
SKYY Vodka (USA) ★★★
SMIRNOFF Citrus Twist Vodka (USA) ★★★
STOLICHNAYA Vodka (Russian Federation) ★★★
STROVIA Vodka (Russian Federation) ★★★
TAAKA Platinum Vodka (USA) ★★★
TANQUERAY Sterling Vodka (England) ★★★
TARKHUNA (Georgian Republic) ★★★
WODKA WYBOROWA Vodka (Poland) ★★★

Average—Not Recommended

ABSOLUT Vodka (Sweden) ★★
ATTAKISKA Vodka (Alaska-USA) ★★
DANZKA Danish Vodka (Denmark) ★★
FINLANDIA Cranberry Vodka (Finland) ★★
GORDON'S Pepper-Flavored Vodka (USA) ★★
LUKSUSOWA Vodka (Poland) ★★
TANQUERAY Sterling Citrus Vodka (England) ★★

Poor—Not Recommended

CELSIUS Scandinavian Vodka (Denmark) ★
FINLANDIA Pineapple-Flavored Vodka (Finland) ★
GORDON'S Wildberry Vodka (USA) ★
SMIRNOFF Vodka (USA) ★

TEQUILA AND MEZCAL—MEXICO

Classic—Highest Recommendation
HERRADURA Añejo Estate-Bottled 100% Blue Agave Tequila ★★★★★
HERRADURA Special Old Añejo Estate-Bottled 100% Blue Agave Tequila
   ★★★★★
EL TESORO DE DON FELIPE Añejo Tequila ★★★★★

Superb—Highly Recommended
CHINACO Añejo Tequila 100% Blue Agave ★★★★
JOSE CUERVO 1800 Tequila ★★★★
JOSE CUERVO Tradicional Reposado 100% Blue Agave Tequila ★★★★
HERRADURA Silver Estate-Bottled 100% Blue Agave Tequila ★★★★
HERRADURA Gold Estate-Bottled 100% Blue Agave Tequila ★★★★
PATRON Añejo 100% Blue Agave Tequila ★★★★
PORFIDIO Añejo 100% Blue Agave Tequila ★★★★
SAUZA Hornitos Reposado 100% Blue Agave Tequila ★★★★
SAUZA Conmemorativo Añejo Tequila ★★★★
SAUZA Tres Generaciones Añejo Tequila ★★★★
EL TESORO DE DON FELIPE Silver Tequila ★★★★

Above Average—Recommended
CHINACO Blanco Tequila 100% Blue Agave ★★★
CHINACO Reposado Tequila 100% Blue Agave ★★★
JOSE CUERVO Especial Gold Tequila ★★★
PATRON Silver 100% Blue Agave Tequila ★★★
TORADA Reposado Tequila ★★★
TORADA Añejo Tequila ★★★
EL VIEJITO Reposado Tequila ★★★
EL VIEJITO Añejo Tequila ★★★

Average—Not Recommended
CAMINO REAL Gold Tequila ★★
JOSE CUERVO White Tequila ★★
DOS REALES Añejo Tequila ★★
MONTE ALBAN Mezcal with Agave Worm ★★
PORFIDIO Añejo Single-Barrel 100% Blue Agave Tequila ★★
TORADA White Tequila ★★
EL TORO Gold Tequila ★★

Poor—Not Recommended
CASTENADA Gold Tequila ★
DOS REALES Plata Tequila ★
ENCANTADO Mezcal de Oaxaca Lot 1 ★
FONDA BLANCA Gold Tequila ★
GAVILAN Gold Tequila ★
GUSANO ROJO Mezcal with Agave Worm ★
MONTEZUMA Gold Tequila ★
OLÉ White Tequila ★
EL TORO White Tequila ★

Appendix C

Alphabetical Whiskey Summary by Rating Category

Scotch Whisky

Blended Scotch Whiskies

Classic—Highest Recommendation
Royal Salute 21-Year-Old Blended Scotch Whisky ★★★★★

Superb—Highly Recommended
Chivas Regal 12-Year-Old Blended Scotch Whisky ★★★★
Cutty Sark Imperial Kingdom Blended Scots Whisky ★★★★
Duggan's 12-Year-Old Blended Scotch Whisky ★★★★
J & B J.E.T. 12-Year-Old Blended Scotch Whisky ★★★★
J & B Ultima Blended Scotch Whisky ★★★★
Johnnie Walker Gold Label 18-Year-Old Blended Scotch Whisky
★★★★
Pinch The Dimple 15-Year-Old Blended Scotch Whisky ★★★★
Speyside 21-Year-Old Blended Scotch Whisky ★★★★
Usquaebach Deluxe 8-Year-Old Blended Scotch Whisky ★★★★
Usquaebach Reserve Blended Scotch Whisky ★★★★
Usquaebach Original Blended—Stonecrock Flagon ★★★★
White Horse Blended Scotch Whisky ★★★★

Above Average—Recommended
Ballantine's Gold Seal 12-Year-Old Blended Scotch Whisky ★★★
Buchanan's Deluxe 12-Year-Old Blended Scotch Whisky ★★★
Cutty Sark 12-Year-Old Blended Scots Whisky ★★★
Cutty Sark 18-Year-Old Blended Scots Whisky ★★★
Dewar's 12-Year-Old Blended Scotch Whisky ★★★

DUGGAN'S DEW Blended Scotch Whisky ★★★
FAMOUS GROUSE 12-Year-Old Blended Scotch Whisky ★★★
J & B Select Blended Scotch Whisky ★★★
JOHNNIE WALKER Black Label 12-Year-Old Blended Scotch Whisky ★★★
JOHNNIE WALKER Blue Label Blended Scotch Whisky ★★★
OLD SMUGGLER Blended Scotch Whisky ★★★
ORIGINAL MACKINLEY Blended Scotch Whisky ★★★
STEWART'S Cream of the Barley Blended Scotch Whisky ★★★
WILLIAM GRANT'S Family Reserve Blended Scotch Whisky ★★★

Average—Not Recommended

BALLANTINE'S Finest Blended Scotch Whisky ★★
DESMOND & DUFF 12-Year-Old Blended Scotch Whisky ★★
FAMOUS GROUSE Blended Scotch Whisky ★★
GRAND MACNISH Blended Scotch Whisky ★★
PIG'S NOSE Blended Scotch Whisky ★★
SCORESBY Rare Blended Scotch Whisky ★★
SOMETHING SPECIAL 12-Year-Old Blended Scotch Whisky ★★
USQUAEBACH Special 12-Year-Old Blended Scotch Whisky ★★

Poor—Not Recommended

100 PIPERS Blended Scotch Whisky (Bottled in U.S.) ★
CLUNY Blended Scotch Whisky (Bottled in U.S.) ★
CLUNY 12-Year-Old Blended Scotch Whisky ★
CUTTY SARK Blended Scots Whisky ★
DEWAR'S White Label Blended Scotch Whisky ★
GLENDROSTAN Blended Scotch Whisky ★
HAMASHKEH Blended Scotch Whisky (Kosher) ★
INVER HOUSE Rare Blended Scotch Whisky ★
J&B RARE Blended Scotch Whisky ★
JOHNNIE WALKER Red Label Blended Scotch Whisky ★
MARTIN'S VVO Blended Scotch Whisky ★
MUIRHEAD'S Blended Scotch Whisky ★
PASSPORT Blended Scotch Whisky ★
QUEEN ANNE Blended Scotch Whisky (Bottled in U.S.) ★
SPEY CAST Deluxe 12-Year-Old Blended Scotch Whisky ★

SINGLE-MALT, PURE-MALT, SINGLE-GRAIN, AND SPECIALLY BOTTLED GRAIN SCOTCH WHISKIES

Classic—Highest Recommendation

BOWMORE 30-Year-Old Islay Single Malt ★★★★★
BOWMORE 25-Year-Old (Distilled 1968) Islay Single Malt ★★★★★
BLACK BOWMORE 1964 Islay Single Malt ★★★★★
CLYNELISH 1965 Northern Highlands Single Malt—Whyte & Whyte Label
★★★★★
CLYNELISH 22-Year-Old Northern Highlands Single Malt / Cask Strength
(Rare Malt Selection) ★★★★★

GLENFARCLAS 1959 Speyside Single Malt—Whyte & Whyte Label ★★★★★

GLENLIVET 21-Year-Old Speyside Single Malt ★★★★★

GLENROTHES 1966 Speyside Single Malt—Whyte & Whyte Label ★★★★★

HIGHLAND PARK 12-Year-Old Orkney Islands Single Malt ★★★★★

HIGHLAND PARK 1985 Orkney Islands Single-Malt, Cask Sample—Whyte & Whyte Label ★★★★★

LONGMORN 15-Year-Old Speyside Single Malt ★★★★★

MACALLAN 18-Year-Old Speyside Single Malt ★★★★★

MACALLAN 25-Year-Old Speyside Single Malt ★★★★★

SPRINGBANK 1975 Campbeltown Single Malt—Whyte & Whyte Label ★★★★★

SPRINGBANK 1989 Campbeltown Single Malt—Whyte & Whyte Label ★★★★★

Superb—Highly Recommended

ABERFELDY 1978 Central Highlands Single Malt—Whyte & Whyte Label ★★★★

ABERLOUR 25-Year-Old Speyside Single Malt ★★★★

ABERLOUR Antique Very Fine Aged Speyside Single Malt ★★★★

AUCHENTOSHAN 18-Year-Old Lowland Single Malt ★★★★

AUCHENTOSHAN 21-Year-Old Lowland Single Malt ★★★★

BALBLAIR 10-Year-Old Northern Highlands Single Malt—The Gordon & MacPhail Series ★★★★

BALVENIE 10-Year-Old "Founder's Reserve" Speyside Single Malt ★★★★

BALVENIE 12-Year-Old "Doublewood" Speyside Single Malt ★★★★

BENRIACH 1976 Speyside Single Malt—The Spirit of Scotland Series ★★★★

BLADNOCH 1980 Lowlands Single Malt—Whyte & Whyte Label ★★★★

BOWMORE 17-Year-Old Islay Single Malt ★★★★

BOWMORE 21-Year-Old Islay Single Malt ★★★★

BOWMORE 22-Year-Old Islay Single Malt ★★★★

BOWMORE 1988 Islay Single Malt—Whyte & Whyte Label ★★★★

BRAES OF GLENLIVET 1979 15-Year-Old Speyside Single Malt Single-Barrel (Sherry) / Cask Strength—Whyte & Whyte Label ★★★★

BRORA 1972 Northern Highland Single Malt—The Spirit of Scotland Series ★★★★

CAOL ILA 1974 Islay Single Malt—The Signatory Series ★★★★

CAOL ILA 1979 Islay Single Malt—Whyte & Whyte Label ★★★★

CLYNELISH 1980 Northern Highlands Single Malt, Cask Sample—Whyte & Whyte Label ★★★★

CRAGGANMORE 12-Year-Old Speyside Single Malt ★★★★

DALMORE 12-Year-Old Northern Highlands Single Malt ★★★★

GLENFARCLAS 105 8-Year-Old Speyside Single Malt ★★★★

GLENFARCLAS 12-Year-Old Speyside Single Malt ★★★★

GLENFARCLAS 15-Year-Old Speyside Single Malt ★★★★

GLENFIDDICH 15-Year-Old Speyside Single-Malt Scotch / Cask Strength
★★★★

GLENFIDDICH 30-Year-Old Speyside Single Malt, Silver Stag's Head Edition ★★★★

GLENGOYNE 1969 Vintage Reserve Unfiltered Central Highlands Single Malt ★★★★

GLENLIVET 12-Year-Old Speyside Single Malt ★★★★

GLENLIVET 18-Year-Old Speyside Single Malt ★★★★

GLENMORANGIE 18-Year-Old Northern Highlands Single Malt ★★★★

GLENMORANGIE 1971 Northern Highlands Single Malt, 150th Anniversary Limited-Bottling Edition ★★★★

GLENMORANGIE 12-Year-Old Sherry Wood Finish Northern Highlands Single Malt ★★★★

GLENROTHES 1979 16-Year-Old Speyside Single Malt ★★★★

HIGHLAND PARK 1986 Orkney Islands Single Malt—Whyte & Whyte Label ★★★★

KNOCKANDO 1980 Distilled / 1994 Bottled Speyside Single Malt ★★★★

KNOCKANDO 21-Year-Old Speyside Single Malt ★★★★

KNOCKANDO 18-Year-Old Speyside Single Malt ★★★★

LAGAVULIN 16-Year-Old Islay Single Malt ★★★★

LAPHROAIG 1977 Islay Single Malt ★★★★

LINKWOOD 15-Year-Old Speyside Single Malt ★★★★

LONGMORN 1981 Speyside Single Malt, Cask Sample—Whyte & Whyte Label ★★★★

MACALLAN 12-Year-Old Speyside Single Malt ★★★★

MORTLACH 22-Year-Old Speyside Single Malt, Cask Strength (Rare Malt Selection) ★★★★

MORTLACH 1983 Speyside Single Malt, Cask Strength—Whyte & Whyte Label ★★★★

PORT ELLEN 1974 Islay Single Malt—Whyte & Whyte Label ★★★★

ROYAL BRACKLA 1978 Speyside Single Malt—Whyte & Whyte Label ★★★★

SCOTCH MALT WHISKY SOCIETY Cask 6.16 Glen Deveron Speyside Single Malt ★★★★

SCOTCH MALT WHISKY SOCIETY Cask 99.2 Glenugie Eastern Highlands Single Malt ★★★★

SCOTCH MALT WHISKY SOCIETY 99.5 Glenugie Eastern Highlands Single Malt ★★★★

SCOTCH MALT WHISKY SOCIETY 17.6 Scapa Orkney Islands Single Malt ★★★★

SINGLETON OF AUCHROISK 1983 Speyside Single Malt ★★★★

SINGLETON OF AUCHROISK 1981 Speyside Single Malt ★★★★

SINGLETON OF AUCHROISK 1976 Speyside Single Malt ★★★★

SINGLETON OF AUCHROISK 1975 Speyside Single Malt ★★★★

SPRINGBANK 12-Year-Old Campbeltown Single Malt—The James MacArthur Series ★★★★

SPRINGBANK 23-Year-Old Campbeltown Single Malt—The James MacArthur Series ★★★★

STRATHISLA 12-Year-Old Speyside Single Malt ★★★★

STRATHISLA 25-Year-Old Speyside Single Malt—The Gordon & MacPhail
Series ★★★★

USQUAEBACH 15-Year-Old Highland Pure Malt ★★★★

Above Average—Recommended

ABERLOUR 10-Year-Old Speyside Single Malt ★★★

ARDBEG 1974 Islay Single Malt—The Signatory Series ★★★

AUCHENTOSHAN 10-Year-Old Lowland Single Malt ★★★

BALVENIE 15-Year-Old Single-Barrel Speyside Single Malt ★★★

BENRIACH 10-Year-Old Speyside Single Malt ★★★

BOWMORE 10-Year-Old Islay Single Malt ★★★

BRUICHLADDICH 1969 Islay Single Malt—The Signatory Series ★★★

BRUICHLADDICH 15-Year-Old Islay Single Malt ★★★

BUNNAHABHAIN 1964 Islay Single Malt—The Signatory Series ★★★

CAOL ILA 1980 Islay Single Malt—Whyte & Whyte Label ★★★

CAOL ILA 12-Year-Old Islay Single Malt—The James MacArthur Series
★★★

DAILUIANE 1971 Speyside Single Malt—The Spirit of Scotland Series
★★★

DALWHINNIE 15-Year-Old Highlands Single Malt ★★★

DEERSTALKER 12-Year-Old Speyside Single Malt ★★★

GLEN ALBYN 1980 Northern Highlands Single Malt—Whyte & Whyte
Label ★★★

GLEN DEVERON 5-Year-Old Speyside Single Malt ★★★

GLENFIDDICH 21-Year-Old Speyside Single Malt, Wedgwood Decanter
Edition ★★★

GLEN GARIOCH 15-Year-Old Eastern Highlands Single Malt ★★★

GLEN GARIOCH 21-Year-Old Eastern Highlands Single Malt ★★★

GLENGOYNE 17-Year-Old Southern Highlands Single Malt ★★★

GLEN GRANT Speyside Single Malt ★★★

GLENMORANGIE 10-Year-Old Northern Highlands Single Malt ★★★

GLENMORANGIE 12-Year-Old Port Wood Finish Northern Highlands Single Malt ★★★

GLENMORANGIE 12-Year-Old Madeira Wood Finish Northern Highlands
Single Malt ★★★

GLEN MORAY 12-Year-Old Speyside Single Malt ★★★

GLEN ORD 12-Year-Old Northern Highlands Single Malt ★★★

GLENROTHES 1975 Speyside Single Malt—Whyte & Whyte Label ★★★

GLENROTHES 12-Year-Old Speyside Single Malt ★★★

GLENTROMIE 12-Year-Old Highland Malt ★★★

GLENTURRET 15-Year-Old Eastern Highlands Single Malt ★★★

GLENTURRET 1979 Eastern Highlands Single Malt—Whyte & Whyte Label
★★★

INCHGOWER 12-Year-Old Speyside Single Malt—The James MacArthur Series ★★★

INVERGORDON 10-Year-Old Single-Grain Whisky ★★★

ISLE OF JURA 10-Year-Old Isle of Jura Single Malt ★★★

KNOCKANDO 12-Year-Old Speyside Single Malt ★★★
LAPHROAIG 15-Year-Old Islay Single Malt ★★★
LITTLEMILL 8-Year-Old Lowlands Single Malt ★★★
OBAN 14-Year-Old Western Highlands Single Malt ★★★
ROSEBANK 8-Year-Old Lowlands Single Malt ★★★
ROSEBANK 1974 Lowlands Single Malt—The Signatory Series ★★★
ROYAL BRACKLA 1972 Speyside Single Malt—The Spirit of Scotland Series ★★★
ROYAL LOCHNAGAR Selected Reserve Eastern Highlands Single Malt ★★★
SCOTCH MALT WHISKY SOCIETY Cask 86.5 Glen Esk Eastern Highlands Single Malt ★★★
SCOTCH MALT WHISKY SOCIETY 77.2 Glen Ord Northern Highlands Single Malt ★★★
TAMDHU 10-Year-Old Speyside Single Malt ★★★
WOLFE'S GLEN 10-Year-Old Highland Single-Grain Whisky ★★★

Average—Not Recommended
AUCHENTOSHAN Select Lowland Single Malt ★★
BRUICHLADDICH 10-Year-Old Islay Single Malt ★★
BUNNAHABHAIN 12-Year-Old Islay Single Malt ★★
CARDHU 12-Year-Old Speyside Single Malt ★★
CARSEBRIDGE 28-Year-Old Grain Whisky—The James MacArthur Series ★★
DUMBARTON 1961 Grain Whisky—The Signatory Series ★★
EDRADOUR 10-Year-Old Central Highland Single Malt ★★
GLENDRONACH 12-Year-Old Speyside Single Malt (Sherry Cask) ★★
GLENDULLAN 1983 Speyside Single Malt—Whyte & Whyte Label ★★
GLENFIDDICH Special Old Reserve Speyside Single Malt ★★
GLEN GARIOCH 12-Year-Old Eastern Highlands Single Malt ★★
GLENGOYNE 12-Year-Old Central Highlands Single Malt ★★
GLEN KEITH 1983 Speyside Single Malt ★★
GLEN MOHR 1978 Northern Highlands Single Malt—Whyte & Whyte Label ★★
INVERGORDON 7-Year-Old Single-Grain Whisky ★★
LOCH DHU 10-Year-Old Speyside Single Malt (Mannochmore Distillery) ★★
OLD FETTERCAIRN 10-Year-Old Eastern Highlands Single Malt ★★
ROYAL LOCHNAGAR 12-Year-Old Eastern Highlands Single Malt ★★
SCOTCH MALT WHISKY SOCIETY Cask 53.5 Caol Ila Islay Single Malt ★★
SCOTCH MALT WHISKY SOCIETY 99.4 Glenugie Eastern Highlands Single Malt ★★
SCOTCH MALT WHISKY SOCIETY 49.4 St. Magdalene Lowland Single Malt ★★
TALISKER 10-Year-Old Isle of Skye Single Malt ★★
TULLIBARDINE 10-Year-Old Southern Highlands Single Malt ★★

Poor—Not Recommended
ARDMORE 12-Year-Old Speyside Single Malt—The James MacArthur Series ★

BEN NEVIS 27-Year-Old Western Highlands Single Malt—The James
   MacArthur Series ★
BOWMORE Legend Islay Single Malt ★
BRUICHLADDICH 21-Year-Old Islay Single Malt ★
DALLAS DHU 1974 Speyside Single Malt—The Signatory Series ★
GLEN GARIOCH 1984 Eastern Highlands Single Malt ★
GLENKINCHIE 10-Year-Old Lowland Single Malt ★
GLENLOCHY 25-Year-Old Western Highlands Single Malt / Cask Strength
   (Rare Malt Selection) ★
GLEN MHOR 1965 Northern Highlands Single Malt—The Signatory Series
   ★
GLEN MORAY 15-Year-Old Speyside Single Malt ★
LAPHROAIG 10-Year-Old Islay Single Malt ★
NORTH BRITISH 1964 Grain Whisky—The Signatory Series ★
ORIGINAL OLDBURY SHEEP DIP 8-Year-Old Pure Malt ★
TOBERMORY Island of Mull Single Malt ★
TOMATIN 10-Year-Old Speyside Single Malt ★
TOMATIN Speyside Single Malt 1966—The Signatory Series ★

AMERICAN WHISKEY

Classic—Highest Recommendation
A.H. HIRSCH 16-Year-Old Pot Still Straight Bourbon ★★★★★
A.H. HIRSCH 20-Year-Old Pot Still Straight Bourbon ★★★★★
MAKER'S MARK Limited-Edition Kentucky Straight Bourbon ★★★★★
W. L. WELLER Centennial 10-Year-Old Kentucky Straight Bourbon
   ★★★★★
WILD TURKEY Kentucky Spirit Single-Barrel Kentucky Straight Bourbon
   Barrel No. 10, Rick No. 9, Warehouse D ★★★★★

Superb—Highly Recommended
ANCIENT AGE 100 Bottled-in-Bond Kentucky Straight Bourbon ★★★★
ANCIENT AGE Barrel 107 Special Edition 10-Year-Old Kentucky Straight
   Bourbon ★★★★
BAKER'S 7-Year-Old Kentucky Straight Bourbon / Small Batch ★★★★
BLANTON'S Single-Barrel Kentucky Straight Bourbon 46.5% Alcohol Bar-
   rel No. 444, Rick No. 9, Warehouse H—Bottled in Oct. 1993 ★★★★
BOOKER'S BOURBON Kentucky Straight Bourbon / Small Batch ★★★★
EAGLE RARE 10-Year-Old Kentucky Straight Bourbon ★★★★
EAGLE RARE 15-Year-Old Kentucky Straight Bourbon ★★★★
ELIJAH CRAIG 18-Year-Old Single-Barrel Kentucky Straight Bourbon, Bar-
   rel No. 007 ★★★★
EVAN WILLIAMS 1987 Single-Barrel Kentucky Straight Bourbon Barrel No.
   051 ★★★★
GENTLEMAN JACK Rare Tennessee Whiskey ★★★★
HANCOCK'S RESERVE Single-Barrel Kentucky Straight Bourbon ★★★★
KNOB CREEK 9-Year-Old Kentucky Straight Bourbon / Small Batch
   ★★★★

MAKER'S MARK Kentucky Straight Bourbon ★★★★

OLD CHARTER Proprietor's Reserve 13-Year-Old Kentucky Straight Bourbon ★★★★

OLD FITZGERALD Very Special 12-Year-Old Kentucky Straight Bourbon ★★★★

OLD FITZGERALD 1849 8-Year-Old Kentucky Straight Bourbon ★★★★

OLD RIP VAN WINKLE Kentucky Bourbon 15 Years Old ★★★★

ROCK HILL FARMS Single-Barrel Kentucky Straight Bourbon, Barrel No. 60 ★★★★

VAN WINKLE Special Reserve Kentucky Bourbon, Lot B, 12 Years Old ★★★★

WILD TURKEY Straight Rye ★★★★

WILD TURKEY Rare Breed Straight Kentucky Bourbon Barrel Proof ★★★★

Above Average—Recommended

ANCIENT AGE Preferred Blended Whiskey ★★★

ANCIENT AGE 90 Kentucky Straight Bourbon ★★★

ANCIENT ANCIENT AGE Kentucky Straight Bourbon ★★★

BENCHMARK Single-Barrel Kentucky Straight Bourbon ★★★

BLANTON'S Single-Barrel Kentucky Straight Bourbon, Barrel No. 74, Rick No. 25, Warehouse H—Bottled in Dec. 1994 ★★★

ELIJAH CRAIG Kentucky Straight Bourbon ★★★

ELMER T. LEE Single-Barrel Kentucky Straight Bourbon ★★★

EVAN WILLIAMS Single-Barrel Vintage 1986 Kentucky Straight Bourbon ★★★

EVAN WILLIAMS 7-Year-Old Kentucky Straight Bourbon ★★★

GEORGE DICKEL Special Barrel Reserve 10-Year-Old Tennessee Whisky ★★★

HENRY MCKENNA 10-Year-Old Single-Barrel Kentucky Straight Bourbon, Barrel No. 9 ★★★

I.W. HARPER Gold Medal 15-Year-Old Kentucky Straight Bourbon ★★★

JIM BEAM 4-Year-Old Kentucky Straight Bourbon ★★★

OLD FORESTER Bottled in Bond Kentucky Straight Bourbon ★★★

OLD GRAND DAD Kentucky Straight Bourbon ★★★

OLD GRAND DAD 114 Barrel-Proof Kentucky Straight Bourbon ★★★

OLD OVERHOLT 4-Year-Old Straight Rye Whiskey ★★★

OLD RIP VAN WINKLE Kentucky Straight Bourbon 10 Years Old ★★★

PAPPY VAN WINKLE'S Family Reserve 20-Year-Old Kentucky Straight Bourbon ★★★

REBEL YELL Kentucky Straight Bourbon ★★★

WILD TURKEY 8-Year-Old 101 Kentucky Straight Bourbon ★★★

WOODFORD RESERVE Distiller's Select Kentucky Straight Bourbon Labrot & Graham Distillery ★★★

Average—Not Recommended

BASIL HAYDEN'S 8-Year-Old Kentucky Straight Bourbon / Small Batch ★★

HENRY MCKENNA Kentucky Straight Bourbon ★★

Jack Daniels Old Time No. 7 (Black) Tennessee Whiskey ★★
Old Forester Kentucky Straight Bourbon ★★
Old Rip Van Winkle Kentucky Straight Bourbon 10 Years Old ★★
Old Williamsburg No. 20 Kentucky Straight Bourbon ★★
Seagram's Seven Crown American Blended Whiskey ★★

Poor—Not Recommended

Ancient Age Kentucky Straight Bourbon ★
Carstairs White Seal Blended Whiskey ★
Old Williamsburg Kentucky Straight Bourbon ★
Old Williamsburg No. 20 Kentucky Straight Bourbon, Barrel-Proof ★
Wild Turkey Straight Kentucky Bourbon ★
Wilson American Blended Whiskey ★

APPENDIX D

Alphabetical Liqueur Summary by Rating Category

Classic—*Highest Recommendation*
BENEDICTINE D.O.M. Liqueur (France) ★★★★★
CHARTREUSE Green (France) ★★★★★
DOMAINE CHARBAY "Nostalgie" Black Walnut Liqueur (USA) ★★★★★
DOMAINE CHARBAY "Lara" Persimmon Liqueur (USA) ★★★★★
DRAMBUIE Liqueur (Scotland) ★★★★★
GIOVANNI BUTON Sambuca (Italy) ★★★★★
GRAND MARNIER Cuvée du Centenaire 1827–1927 (France) ★★★★★
GRAND MARNIER Cuvée Spéciale 1827–1977 Cent cinquantenaire Liqueur (France) ★★★★★
MARCEL TREPOUT Liqueur d'Amour des Mousquetaires (France) ★★★★★
RETTER Pfirsich Peach Liqueur (Austria) ★★★★★

Superb—*Highly Recommended*
ARTIC Vodka & Peach Liqueur (Italy) ★★★★
BAILEY's Original Irish Cream (Ireland) ★★★★
BAUCHANT Napoleon Liqueur (France) ★★★★
CAPRINATURA Lemon Liqueur (Italy) ★★★★
CARNEROS ALAMBIC Pear de Pear Liqueur (USA) ★★★★
CAROLANS Finest Irish Cream (Ireland) ★★★★
CAROLANS Irish Coffee Cream (Ireland) ★★★★
COINTREAU (France) ★★★★
DI SARONNO Amaretto (Italy) ★★★★
DR. MCGILLICUDDY's Vanilla Schnapps (Canada) ★★★★
FRANGELICO Liqueur (Italy) ★★★★
GIOVANNI BUTON Amaretto (Italy) ★★★★
GIOVANNI BUTON Gran Caffè Espresso (Italy) ★★★★

GODET Belgian White Chocolate Liqueur (Belgium) ★★★★
GODIVA Chocolate Liqueur (USA) ★★★★
GRAND MARNIER Cordon Rouge Liqueur (France) ★★★★
IRISH MIST Liqueur (Ireland) ★★★★
JOHNNIE WALKER Liqueur (Scotland) ★★★★
KAHLUA Royale Cream Liqueur (Holland) ★★★★
KAMORA Coffee Liqueur (Mexico) ★★★★
KAMORA French Vanilla Coffee Liqueur (Mexico) ★★★★
LA GRANDE PASSION Liqueur (France) ★★★★
LAZZARONI Amaretto (Italy) ★★★★
LILLEHAMMER Scandinavian Berry Liqueur (Denmark) ★★★★
LIQUORE STREGA (Italy) ★★★★
MANDARINE NAPOLEON Grande Liqueur Impériale (Belgium) ★★★★
OBLIO Sambuca (Italy) ★★★★
O'CASEY'S Irish Country Cream Liqueur (Ireland) ★★★★
OPAL NERA Black Sambuca (Italy) ★★★★
OUZO No. 12 (Greece) ★★★★
RETTER Cassis Johannisbeer Liqueur (Austria) ★★★★
ROMANA Della Notte Black Sambuca (Italy) ★★★★
RUMPLE MINZE Peppermint Schnapps (Germany) ★★★★
SHERIDAN'S Original Double Liqueur (Ireland) ★★★★
STREGA Sambuca (Italy) ★★★★
TAAM PREE Cherry Kosher Liqueur (USA) ★★★★
TIRAMISU (Italy) ★★★★
TRIMBACH Liqueur de Framboise (France) ★★★★
VILLA MASSA Liquore di Limoni (Italy) ★★★★

Above Average—Recommended
AMARETTO DI LORETO (Italy) ★★★
ARTIC Vodka & Melon Liqueur (Italy) ★★★
B & B Liqueur (France) ★★★
BARTENURA Sambuca Kosher (Italy) ★★★
BISMARK Goldwasser Cinnamon Schnapps (USA) ★★★
BUCKSHOT Original Wild West Liqueur (USA) ★★★
CHERRY HERRING Liqueur (Denmark) ★★★
CAROLANS Light Irish Cream (Ireland) ★★★
CAYMANA Banana Cream Liqueur (Ireland) ★★★
CHINCHON Dulce Anis Liqueur (Spain) ★★★
CLEMENT Creole Shrubb Rum Liqueur (Martinique) ★★★
COCOBAY Chocolate & Coconut Schnapps (USA) ★★★
COCO RHUM Coconut & Puerto Rican Rum Liqueur (USA) ★★★
CRYSTAL COMFORT Liqueur (USA) ★★★
DEKUYPER Original Peachtree Schnapps (USA) ★★★
DEKUYPER Amaretto (USA) ★★★
DEVONSHIRE Royal Cream Liqueur (England) ★★★
ECHTE KROATZBEERE Wild Blackberry Liqueur (Germany) ★★★
FRAGONARD Liqueur de Cognac X.O. (France) ★★★
GIOVANNI BUTON Crema Cacao (Italy) ★★★

GOLDSCHLAGER Cinnamon Schnapps Liqueur (Switzerland) ★★★
GREENY Apple Schnapps (Germany) ★★★
HENRI BARDOUIN Pastis (France) ★★★
JAGERMEISTER Liqueur (Germany) ★★★
KAHLUA Licor de Café (Mexico) ★★★
KAHLUA Almond Moo Moo (USA) ★★★
KALDI 100% Columbian Coffee Liqueur (Columbia) ★★★
KAMORA Hazelnut Coffee Liqueur (Mexico) ★★★
KMV VAN DER HUM Liqueur (South Africa) ★★★
MALIBU Liqueur (Canada) ★★★
METAXA Grande Fine Liqueur (Greece) ★★★
MONTENEGRO Amaro (Italy) ★★★
OBLIO Caffé Sambuca (Italy) ★★★
OUZO BY METAXA (Greece) ★★★
PATRON XO Café Coffee Liqueur with Tequila (Mexico) ★★★
PEARLE DE BRILLET Liqueur (France) ★★★
ROMANA Sambuca Classico (Italy) ★★★
SAFARI Exotic Liqueur (Holland) ★★★
SAMBUCA DI ANGELA (Italy) ★★★
SOUTHERN COMFORT Liqueur (USA) ★★★
ST. BRENEDAN'S Superior Irish Cream (Ireland) ★★★
TAAM PREE Banana Kosher Liqueur (USA) ★★★
TAAM PREE Blackberry Kosher Liqueur (USA) ★★★
TAAM PREE Kummel Kosher (USA) ★★★
TIA MARIA Blue Mountain Coffee Liqueur (Jamaica) ★★★
TORRES Gran Torres Orange Liqueur (Spain) ★★★
TRIMBACH Liqueur de Poire (France) ★★★
YUKON JACK Canadian Liqueur (Canada) ★★★

Average—Not Recommended
AFTER SHOCK Cinnamon Liqueur (Canada) ★★
ALIZE DE FRANCE (France) ★★
ANCIENT AGE Mint Julep Liqueur (USA) ★★
ARTIC Vodka & Lemon Liqueur (Italy) ★★
BAILEY'S Original Light Irish Cream (Ireland) ★★
BARTENURA Amaretto Kosher (Italy) ★★
CAPUCELLO Cappucino Liqueur (Holland) ★★
DER SAURE FRITZ Citrus & Lime Schnapps (Germany) ★★
DRACULA'S POTION Blackcurrant & Cherry Schnapps (Germany) ★★
DR. MCGILLICUDDY's Mentholmint Schnapps (Canada) ★★
KAHLUA Mudslide (USA) ★★
KAHLUA Milkquake (USA) ★★
LIQUORE GALLIANO (Italy) ★★
METAXA Seven-Star Amphora Liqueur (Greece) ★★
METAXA Classic Liqueur (Greece) ★★
MOLINARI Sambuca Extra (Italy) ★★
O'DARBY Irish Cream (Ireland) ★★
ORIGINAL CANTON Delicate Ginger Liqueur (China) ★★

PERNOD Spiritueux Anise (France) ★★
ROYALE CHAMBORD Liqueur de France (France) ★★
TAAM PREE Pear Kosher Liqueur (USA) ★★
TUACA Liqueur (Italy) ★★
VANDERMINT Chocolate Liqueur (Holland) ★★
YUKON JACK Snakebite with Lime (Canada) ★★
YUKON JACK Black Jack Liqueur (Canada) ★★

Poor—Not Recommended

BORGHETTI Café Sport Espresso Liqueur (Italy) ★
COPA DE ORO Licor de Café (Mexico) ★
CREME DE GRAND MARNIER Liqueur (France) ★
EARL GREY English Liqueur (England) ★
EMMETS Ireland Cream (Ireland) ★
FERNET BRANCA Bitters Liqueur (Italy) ★
GAETANO Amaretto (USA) ★
GIOVANNI BUTON Amaro Felsina (Italy) ★
GIOVANNI BUTON Coca (Italy) ★
HIRAM WALKER Sambuca (Italy) ★
JACQUIN'S Amaretto (USA) ★
LEROUX Irish Cream (USA) ★
LICOR 43 Liqueur (Spain) ★
MIDORI Melon Liqueur (Japan) ★
MOZART Chocolate Liqueur (Austria) ★
O'MARA'S Irish Country Cream (Ireland) ★
ORAN MOR Malt Whisky Liqueur (Scotland) ★
PRALINE Pecan Liqueur (USA) ★
SABRA Chocolate Orange Kosher Liqueur (Israel) ★
SAZERAC Cocktail (USA) H★
SERRANA Licor de Café (Mexico) ★
TAAM PREE Chocolate Truffle Kosher Liqueur (USA) ★
TAAM PREE Anisette Kosher (USA) ★
WILD TURKEY Liqueur with Honey (USA) ★

APPENDIX E

Alphabetical Fortified-Wine Summary by Rating Category

SHERRY—SPAIN

Classic—Highest Recommendation
DOMECQ Venerable Pedro Ximenez Sherry ★★★★★
LUSTAU "Emilin" Moscatel Superior Sherry ★★★★★
LUSTAU "San Emilio" Pedro Ximenez Sherry ★★★★★
LUSTAU Old East India Sherry ★★★★★
SANDEMAN Royal Corregidor Rare Oloroso Sherry ★★★★★

Superb—Highly Recommended
ARGUESO Pedro Ximenez Sherry ★★★★
DOMECQ Amontillado 51-1a Sherry ★★★★
DOMECQ Sibarita Palo Cortado Sherry ★★★★
DON ZOILO Solera Reservada Cream Sherry ★★★★
HARTLEY & GIBSON Cream Sherry ★★★★
HARVEY'S Rare Oloroso Sherry ★★★★
HIDALGO Jérez Cortado Estate-Bottled Sherry ★★★★
HIDALGO Amontillado Napoleon Estate-Bottled Sherry ★★★★
HIDALGO Cream Napoleon Estate-Bottled Sherry ★★★★
LUSTAU "Capatez Andres" Deluxe Cream Sherry ★★★★
LUSTAU "Escuadrilla" Rare Amontillado Sherry ★★★★
LUSTAU 1986 Vendimia Cream Sherry ★★★★
LUSTAU "Superior" Rare Cream Solera Sherry ★★★★
FINO DEL PUERTO 1/143, José Luis Gonzalez Obregon, Sherry (Lustau) ★★★★
MANZANILLA AMONTILLADA 1/21, Manuel Cuevas Jurado, Sherry (Lustau) ★★★★
OLOROSO "Pata de Gallina" 1/38, Juan Garcia Jarana, Sherry (Lustau) ★★★★

SANDEMAN Imperial Corregidor Rarest VVO Oloroso Sherry ★★★★
SANDEMAN Royal Ambrosante Rare Palo Cortado Sherry ★★★★
VALDESPINO Inocente Fino Sherry (Spain) ★★★★
VALDESPINO Amontillado Sherry (Spain) ★★★★
WISDOM & WARTER Delicate Cream Solera 1902 Sherry ★★★★

Above Average—Recommended
DELGATO ZULETA Cream Sherry ★★★
DOMECQ La Ina Fino Sherry ★★★
DOMECQ Celebration Cream Sherry ★★★
HARTLEY & GIBSON Amontillado Sherry ★★★
HIDALGO La Gitana Manzanilla Estate-Bottled Sherry ★★★
LUSTAU "Papirusa" Light Manzanilla Sherry ★★★
LUSTAU "Jarana" Light Fino Sherry ★★★
LUSTAU "Los Arcos" Dry Amontillado Sherry ★★★
LUSTAU "Peninsula" Palo Cortado Sherry ★★★
LUSTAU "Emperatriz Eugenia" Very Rare Dry Oloroso Sherry ★★★
AMONTILLADO DEL PUERTO 1/10, José Luis Gonzalez Obregon, Sherry
    (Lustau) ★★★
PALO CORTADO 1/50, Vides, Sherry (Lustau) ★★★
SANCHEZ ROMATE Manzanilla Sherry ★★★
SANCHEZ ROMATE Fino Sherry ★★★
SANCHEZ ROMATE Amontillado Sherry ★★★
SANCHEZ ROMATE Cream Sherry ★★★
SANDEMAN Royal Esmeralda Rare Amontillado Sherry ★★★
SANDEMAN Don Fino Light Dry Sherry ★★★
WISDOM & WARTER Pale Fino Solera 1908 Sherry ★★★
WISDOM & WARTER Extra Amontillado Solera 1912 Sherry ★★★

Average—Not Recommended
DELGATO ZULETA Amontillado Sherry ★★
DELGATO ZULETA Oloroso Sherry ★★
DELGATO ZULETA East India Cream Sherry ★★
DOMECQ Rio Viejo Oloroso Sherry ★★
DRY FLY Medium-Dry Sherry ★★
GONZALEZ BYASS Tio Pépé Fino Sherry ★★
GONZALEZ BYASS La Concha Amontillado Sherry ★★
GONZALEX BYASS Nectar Cream Sherry ★★
HARTLEY & GIBSON Manzanilla Sherry ★★
HARTLEY & GIBSON Fino Sherry ★★
HARVEY'S Dry Cocktail Sherry ★★
HARVEY'S Shooting Sherry / Oloroso ★★
HARVEY'S Bristol Cream Sherry ★★
AMONTILLADO FINO 1/75, Alberto Lorente Piaget, Sherry (Lustau) ★★
SANDEMAN Armada Cream Oloroso Sherry ★★

Poor—Not Recommended
DELGATO ZULETA Fino Sherry ★
DOMECQ Primero Amontillado Sherry ★

DON ZOILO Manzanilla Sherry ★
DON ZOILO Fino Sherry ★
DON ZOILO Amontillado Sherry ★
GONZALEZ BYASS Amontillado del Duque Viejo Sherry ★
GONZALEZ BYASS Apostoles Oloroso Abocado Sherry ★
HARTLEY & GIBSON Oloroso Sherry ★
HARVEY'S Amontillado Sherry ★
SANDEMAN Character Medium-Dry Sherry ★
SANDEMAN Dry Don Amontillado Sherry ★

MADEIRA

Superb—Highly Recommended
BLANDY'S Malmsey 10-Year-Old Madeira ★★★★
COSSARTS Duo Centenary Celebration Bual Madeira ★★★★
COSSARTS Verdelho 1934 Madeira ★★★★
LEACOCK'S Bual 10-Year-Old Madeira ★★★★

Above Average—Recommended
BLANDY'S Bual Medium-Rich Madeira ★★★
BLANDY'S Malmsey Rich Madeira ★★★
COSSARTS Rainwater Madeira ★★★
COSSARTS No. 22 Malmsey Madeira ★★★
COSSARTS Special Reserve Malmsey Madeira ★★★
JUSTINO HENRIQUES Malmsey 1964 Madeira ★★★
JUSTINO HENRIQUES Verdelho 1934 Madeira ★★★
LEACOCK'S Superlative Rich 15-Year-Old Madeira ★★★

Average—Not Recommended
COSSARTS Viva Madeira ★★
COSSARTS No. 92 Bual Madeira ★★
JUSTINO HENRIQUES Bual 1964 Madeira ★★
JUSTINO HENRIQUES Malmsey 1933 Madeira ★★

Poor—Not Recommended
BLANDY'S Sercial Dry Madeira ★
BLANDY'S Verdelho Half-Dry Madeira ★
BLANDY'S Rainwater Medium-Dry Madeira ★
COSSARTS Malvasia 1933 Madeira ★
JUSTINO HENRIQUES Sercial 1940 Madeira ★
JUSTINO HENRIQUES Verdelho 1954 Madeira ★

PORT—PORTUGAL

Classic—Highest Recommendation
COCKBURN 1983 Vintage Porto ★★★★★
DOW 1983 Vintage Porto ★★★★★
FONSECA 1977 Vintage Porto ★★★★★
GRAHAM 1985 Vintage Porto ★★★★★

QUINTA DO VESUVIO 1992 Vintage Porto ★★★★★
TAYLOR FLADGATE 1977 Vintage Porto ★★★★★
TAYLOR FLADGATE 1970 Vintage Porto ★★★★★

Superb—Highly Recommended
ADRIANO RAMOS-PINTO Quinta do Bom Retiro 20-Year-Old Tawny Porto
    ★★★★
ADRIANO RAMOS-PINTO 30-Year-Old Tawny Porto ★★★★
BURMESTER 20-Year-Old Tawny Porto ★★★★
CALEM WWW 30-Year-Old Aged Tawny Porto ★★★★
CALEM Magnificent 40-Year-Old Aged Tawny Porto ★★★★
CALEM 1983 Vintage Porto ★★★★
COCKBURN 1991 Vintage Porto / Barrel Sample ★★★★
COCKBURN 1987 Quinta do Tua Vintage Porto ★★★★
DELAFORCE 1991 Quinta da Corte Vintage Porto ★★★★
DOW Vintage-Character Porto ★★★★
DOW 1992 Quinta do Bomfim Vintage Porto ★★★★
FERREIRA Quinta do Seixo 1983 Vintage Porto ★★★★
FONSECA 1970 Vintage Porto ★★★★
FONSECA 1985 Vintage Porto ★★★★
FONSECA 1983 Vintage Porto ★★★★
FONSECA GUIMARAENS 1991 Vintage Porto ★★★★
FONSECA GUIMARAENS 1976 Vintage Porto ★★★★
GOULD-CAMPBELL 1977 Vintage Porto ★★★★
GRAHAM 1983 Vintage Porto ★★★★
GRAHAM 1977 Vintage Porto ★★★★
GRAHAM 1970 Vintage Porto ★★★★
GRAHAM 1991 Vintage Porto ★★★★
GRAHAM 1988 Malvedos Vintage Porto ★★★★
NIEPOORT 1992 Vintage Porto ★★★★
OSBORNE 1992 Vintage Porto ★★★★
QUARLES HARRIS 1970 Vintage Porto ★★★★
QUINTA DO NOVAL LB Vintage Character Porto ★★★★
QUINTA DO NOVAL 20-Year-Old Tawny Porto ★★★★
QUINTA DO NOVAL 1991 Vintage Porto ★★★★
QUINTA DO NOVAL 1985 Vintage Porto ★★★★
QUINTA DO VESUVIO 1991 Vintage Porto ★★★★
SANDEMAN Imperial 20-Year-Old Tawny Porto ★★★★
SMITH-WOODHOUSE 1991 Vintage Porto ★★★★
TAYLOR FLADGATE 40-Year-Old Tawny Porto ★★★★
TAYLOR FLADGATE 1991 Quinta de Vargellas Vintage Porto ★★★★
TAYLOR FLADGATE 1985 Vintage Porto ★★★★
WARRE 1991 Vintage Porto ★★★★
WARRE 1985 Vintage Porto ★★★★

Above Average—Recommended
ADRIANO RAMOS-PINTO Quinta da Urtiga Single Quinta Porto ★★★
ADRIANO RAMOS-PINTO 1991 Vintage Porto ★★★

Adriano Ramos-Pinto 1983 Vintage Porto ★★★
Adriano Ramos-Pinto Fine White Porto ★★★
Adriano Ramos-Pinto Lagrima White Porto ★★★
Argellos 40-Year-Old Tawny Porto ★★★
Calem 1982 Quinta da Foz Vintage Porto ★★★
Calem 1980 Quinta da Foz Vintage Porto ★★★
Calem Fine White Porto ★★★
Calem Lagrima White Porto ★★★
Calem Old Friends Fine Tawny Porto ★★★
Calem Shipper's Special Reserve Tawny Porto ★★★
Calem 10-Year-Old Aged Tawny Porto ★★★
Calem 20-Year-Old Tawny Porto ★★★
Calem 1992 Quinta da Foz Vintage Porto ★★★
Churchill Finest Vintage-Character Porto ★★★
Cockburn 1970 Vintage Porto ★★★
Cockburn 1990 Late-Bottled Vintage Porto ★★★
Cockburn Fine Ruby Porto ★★★
Cockburn 10-Year-Old Tawny Porto ★★★
Cockburn Director's Reserve 20-Year-Old Tawny Porto ★★★
Cockburn 1992 Quinta dos Canais Vintage Porto ★★★
Croft 1970 Vintage Porto ★★★
Delaforce His Eminence's Choice Reserve Tawny Porto ★★★
Delaforce 1992 Vintage Porto ★★★
Dow 1991 Vintage Porto ★★★
Dow 1978 Quinta do Bomfim Vintage Porto ★★★
Dow 1970 Vintage Porto ★★★
Ferreira Duque de Braganca 20-Year-Old Tawny Porto ★★★
Fonseca 1988 Late-Bottled Vintage Porto / Bottled in 1994 ★★★
Fonseca Guimaraens 1978 Vintage Porto ★★★
Gould-Campbell 1985 Late-Bottled Vintage Porto ★★★
Gould-Campbell 1985 Vintage Porto ★★★
Graham 20-Year-Old Tawny Porto ★★★
Graham 30-Year-Old Tawny Porto ★★★
Graham 1992 Malvedos Vintage Porto ★★★
Niepoort 1983 Vintage Porto ★★★
Presidential 1991 Vintage Porto ★★★
Presidential 20-Year-Old Tawny Porto ★★★
Presidential 30-Year-Old Tawny Porto ★★★
Quinta Do Noval 10-Year-Old Tawny Porto ★★★
Sandeman 1988 Quinta do Vau Vintage Porto ★★★
Sandeman 1985 Vintage Porto ★★★
Sandeman 1982 Vintage Porto ★★★
Sandeman 1970 Vintage Porto ★★★
Sandeman Founder's Reserve Vintage-Character Porto ★★★
Smith-Woodhouse Old Oporto Vintage-Character Porto ★★★
Smith-Woodhouse 1992 Vintage Porto ★★★
Smith-Woodhouse 1985 Vintage Porto ★★★

SMITH-WOODHOUSE 1981 Late-Bottled Vintage Porto / Bottled in 1985
★★★

SMITH-WOODHOUSE 1979 Late-Bottled Vintage Porto / Bottled in 1984
★★★

SMITH-WOODHOUSE 1977 Vintage Porto ★★★

SMITH-WOODHOUSE 1970 Vintage Porto ★★★

TAYLOR FLADGATE 1983 Vintage Porto ★★★

TAYLOR FLADGATE 1980 Vintage Porto ★★★

TAYLOR FLADGATE 20-Year-Old Tawny Porto ★★★

TAYLOR FLADGATE 30-Year-Old Tawny Porto ★★★

TAYLOR FLADGATE 1988 Late-Bottled Vintage Porto ★★★

TAYLOR FLADGATE Special Tawny Porto ★★★

TAYLOR-FLADGATE First Estate Lugar das Lages Vintage-Character Porto
★★★

WARRE 1970 Vintage Porto ★★★

WARRE Warrior Vintage-Character Porto ★★★

Average—Not Recommended

ADRIANO RAMOS-PINTO Quinta da Ervamoira 10-Year-Old Tawny Porto
★★

ADRIANO RAMOS-PINTO 1987 Late-Bottled Vintage Porto ★★

ADRIANO RAMOS-PINTO 1985 Vintage Porto ★★

CALEM Fine Ruby Porto ★★

CALEM Fine Tawny Porto ★★

CALEM Vintage Character Porto ★★

CALEM 1986 Late-Bottled Vintage Porto ★★

CALEM 1985 Vintage Porto ★★

COCKBURN Special Reserve Vintage-Character Porto ★★

DELAFORCE 1987 Late-Bottled Vintage Porto / Bottled in 1993 ★★

DELAFORCE Full Ruby Porto ★★

DOW 1989 Quinta do Bomfim Vintage Porto ★★

FONSECA Bin 27 Vintage-Character Porto ★★

FONSECA Tawny Porto ★★

GOULD CAMPBELL 1983 Vintage Porto ★★

GOULD-CAMPBELL 1980 Vintage Porto ★★

GRAHAM Six Grapes Vintage-Character Porto ★★

GRAHAM 1984 Late-Bottled Vintage Porto ★★

KOPKE 1983 Vintage Porto ★★

NIEPOORT 1987 Vintage Porto ★★

OFFLEY Boa Vista 1970 Vintage Porto ★★

OSBORNE 1991 Vintage Porto ★★

PRESIDENTIAL 10-Year-Old Tawny Porto ★★

QUINTA DO INFANTADO 1983 Vintage Porto ★★

QUINTA DO INFANTADO 1983 Late-Bottled Vintage Porto ★★

SANDEMAN Royal 10-Year-Old Tawny Porto ★★

SANDEMAN 1989 Late-Bottled Vintage Porto / Bottled in 1994 ★★

TAYLOR FLADGATE 10-Year-Old Tawny Porto ★★

WARRE 1979 Quinta do Cavadinha Vintage Porto ★★

Poor—Not Recommended
ADRIANO RAMOS-PINTO Fine Ruby Porto ★
ADRIANO RAMOS-PINTO 1985 Late-Bottled Vintage / Bottled in 1989 ★
ADRIANO RAMOS-PINTO 1982 Vintage Porto ★
BORGES & IRMAO 1983 Vintage Porto ★
CALEM 1981 Late-Bottled Vintage Porto / Bottled in 1986 ★
COCKBURN Fine Tawny Porto ★
DELAFORCE 1985 Vintage Porto ★
DELAFORCE 1970 Vintage Porto ★
FERREIRA Quinta do Porto 10-Year-Old Tawny Porto ★
FERREIRA 1970 Vintage Porto ★
FONSECA Siroco White Porto ★
FONSECA Ruby Porto ★
GOULD-CAMPBELL 1975 Vintage Porto ★
GRAHAM 1986 Malvedos Vintage Porto ★
GRAHAM 1978 Malvedos Vintage Porto ★
PRESIDENTIAL White Porto ★
PRESIDENTIAL Ruby Porto ★
PRESIDENTIAL Tawny Porto ★
PRESIDENTIAL 40-Year-Old Tawny Porto ★
PRESIDENTIAL 1985 Vintage Porto ★
PRESIDENTIAL 1977 Vintage Porto ★
QUINTA DO CRASTO 1985 Vintage Porto ★
QUINTA DO INFANTADO 1984 Late-Bottled Vintage Porto ★
QUINTA DO NOVAL 1982 Vintage Porto ★
QUINTA DO NOVAL 1970 Vintage Porto ★
SANDEMAN 1986 Late-Bottled Vintage Porto / Bottled in 1990 ★
TAYLOR FLADGATE Chip Dry White Porto ★
TAYLOR FLADGATE Special Ruby Porto ★
TAYLOR FLADGATE 1989 Late-Bottled Vintage Porto ★
TAYLOR FLADGATE 1982 Quinta de Vargellas Vintage Porto ★

AROMATIZED WINES, MARSALA, PINEAU DES CHARENTES, AND VERMOUTHS

Classic—Highest Recommendation
PIERRE FERRAND Réserve de Pierre Pineau des Charentes (France)
★★★★★

Superb—Highly Recommended
MARTINI & ROSSI Rosso Vermouth (Italy) ★★★★
NOILLY PRAT French Dry Vermouth (France) ★★★★
A. HARDY ET CIE Le Coq d'Or Pineau des Charentes (France) ★★★★
PIERRE FERRAND Sélection Pineau des Charentes (France) ★★★★

Above Average—Recommended
CARPANO Punt e Mes Amaro Vermouth (Italy) ★★★
CINZANO Extra Dry Vermouth (Italy) ★★★

CINZANO Rosso Vermouth (Italy) ★★★
LILLET White (France) ★★★
LILLET Red (France) ★★★
NOILLY PRAT Sweet Vermouth (France) ★★★
STOCK Sweet Vermouth (Italy) ★★★
FLORIO Targa 1980 Marsala (Italy) ★★★
REMY MARTIN Le Pineau des Charentes (France) ★★★
REYNAC Pineau des Charentes (France) ★★★
REYNAC Pineau des Charentes Rosé (France) ★★★

Average—Not Recommended
CAMPARI Aperitivo (Italy) ★★
DUBONNET Rouge Aperitif (USA) ★★
MARTINI & ROSSI Extra-Dry Vermouth (Italy) ★★
STOCK Extra-Dry Vermouth (Italy) ★★
TRIBUNO Extra-Dry Vermouth (USA) ★★
TRIBUNO Sweet Vermouth (USA) ★★

Poor—Not Recommended
CYNAR Aperitivo (Italy) ★

FORTIFIED WINES—USA

Classic—Highest Recommendation
ST. GEORGE CELLARS Framboise Royale (California) ★★★★★

Superb—Highly Recommended
BONNY DOON VINEYARD Framboise (Raspberry Wine with Grape Neutral
   Spirits (California) ★★★★
BONNY DOON VINEYARD Cassis (Black-Currant Wine with Grape-Neutral
   Spirits) (California) ★★★★
FICKLIN VINEYARDS Tinta Port (California) ★★★★
FICKLIN 10-Year-Old Tawny Port Lot No. 1 (California) ★★★★
ST. GEORGE CELLARS Chardonnay Royale (California) ★★★★
ST. GEORGE CELLARS Poire Royale (California) ★★★★
ST. GEORGE CELLARS Kirsch Royale (California) ★★★★
WINDSOR VINEYARDS NV Rare Port (California) ★★★★

Above Average—Recommended
DOMAINE CHARBAY Dessert Chardonnay ★★★
FICKLIN VINEYARDS 1957 Vintage Port (California) ★★★
FICKLIN VINEYARDS 1986 Vintage Port (California) ★★★
ST. GEORGE CELLARS Zinfandel Royale (California) ★★★

Average—Not Recommended
GALLO/LIVINGSTON CELLARS Cream Sherry (California) ★★
GLEN ELLEN Imagery Series 1990 Zinfandel Port ★★

Poor—Not Recommended

CHRISTIAN BROTHERS Dry Sherry (California) ★
CHRISTIAN BROTHERS Golden Sherry (California) ★
CHRISTIAN BROTHERS Meloso Cream Sherry (California) ★
GALLO Pale Dry Cocktail Sherry (California) ★
GALLO Sherry (California) ★
GALLO Cream Sherry (California) ★
GALLO Port (California) ★
ORFILA VINEYARDS California Tawny Port (California) ★
TAYLOR Dry Sherry (New York) ★
TAYLOR Golden Sherry (New York) ★
TAYLOR Cream Sherry (New York) ★
TAYLOR Port (New York) ★
TAYLOR Tawny Port (New York) ★

BIBLIOGRAPHY

DISTILLED SPIRITS

Alcohol Distiller's Handbook. Desert Publications/Cornville, Arizona. 1980.

Les Alcools du Monde, by Gilbert Delos. Editions Hatier/Paris, France. 1993.

The Book of Bourbon and Other Fine American Whiskeys, by Gary Regan and Mardee Haidin Regan. Chapters Publishing Ltd/Shelburne, Vermont. 1995.

Brandy de Jerez, by Vicente Fernández de Bobadilla. Consejo Regulador de la Denominacio Específica "Brandy de Jerez"/Madrid, Spain. 1990.

Cognac, by Nicholas Faith. David R. Godine Publisher/Boston, Massachusetts. 1987.

Cognac: The Treowe Knaulage, by Jean-Marc Soyez. Bureau National Interprofessionnel du Cognac/Cognac, France.

The Genesis of Cognac. Dupuy Compton Publishing/France.

Grossman's Guide to Wines, Beers, and Spirits, by Harriet Lembeck. Scribners/New York, New York. 1983.

Handbook of Fine Brandies, by Gordon Brown. Macmillan/New York, New York. 1990.

The Science and Technology of Whiskies, edited by J. R. Piggott, R. Sharp, and R. E. B. Duncan. John Wiley/New York, New York. 1989.

Scotch: The Whisky of Scotland in Fact and Story, by Sir Robert Bruce Lockhart. Putnam/London, U.K. 1951.

The Scotch Whisky Industry Record, by H. Charles Craig. Index Publishing/Dumbarton, Scotland. 1994.

Scots on Scotch, edited by Philip Hills. Mainstream
Publishing/Edinburgh, Scotland. 1991.

The Social History of Bourbon, by Gerald Carson. University Press of
Kentucky/Lexington, Kentucky. 1963.

The Spirit of Puerto Rican Rum, by Blanche Gelabert. Discovery
Press/Puerto Rico. 1992.

Spirit of the Age, by Alf McCreary. Old Bushmills Distillery/County
Antrim, Ireland. 1983.

The Spirit of Whisky, by Richard Grindal. Warner Books/London, U.K.
1992.

Spirits & Liqueurs, by Peter Hallgarten. Faber & Faber/London, U.K.
1983.

Whisky and Scotland, by Neil M. Gunn. Souvenir Press/London, U.K.
1977.

FORTIFIED WINES

Barco Rabelo Um Retrato de Família, by Octávio Lixa Filgueiras. A. A.
Calem and Filho/Oporto, Portugal. 1987.

A Celebration of Taylor Fladgate Port 1992, edited by Christopher
Foulkes. Mitchell Beazley Publishers/London, U.K. 1992.

Confraria do Vinho do Porto. Instituto do Vinho do Porto/Oporto,
Portugal. 1988.

The Factory House at Oporto: Its Historic Role in the Port Wine Trade, by
John Delaforce. Christie's Wine Publications/Bromley, Kent, U.K.
1990.

*The House of Sandeman: The Story of Sherry, Capa Negra Brandy and
Port,* George G. Sandeman/London, U.K. 1955.

Madeira: The Island Vineyard, by Noel Cossart. Christie's Wine
Publications/London, U.K. 1984.

Port: An Essential Guide to the Classic Drink, by Andrew Jefford. Exeter
Books/New York, New York. 1988.

Port Wine: Notes on Its History, Production & Technology, by A. Moreira
da Fonseca, A. Galhano, E. Serpa Pimentel, and J. R-P Rosas. Instituto
do Vinho do Porto/Portugal. 1991.

Sherry: The Noble Wine, by Manuel González Gordon. Quiller
Press/London, U.K. 1990.

The Simon & Schuster Pocket Guide to Fortified And Dessert Wine, by
Roger Voss. Mitchell Beazley Publishers/London, U.K. 1989.

The Story of Port, by Sarah Bradford. Christie's Wine
Publications/London, U.K. 1983.

Los Vinos de Jerez. Consejo Regulador de las Denominaciones de
Origen/Jerez de la Frontera, Spain. 1987.

*Vintage Port: The Wine Spectator's Ultimate Guide for Consumers,
Collectors and Investors,* by James Suckling. Wine Spectator Press/San
Francisco, California. 1990.